MICHIGAN

LAURA MARTONE

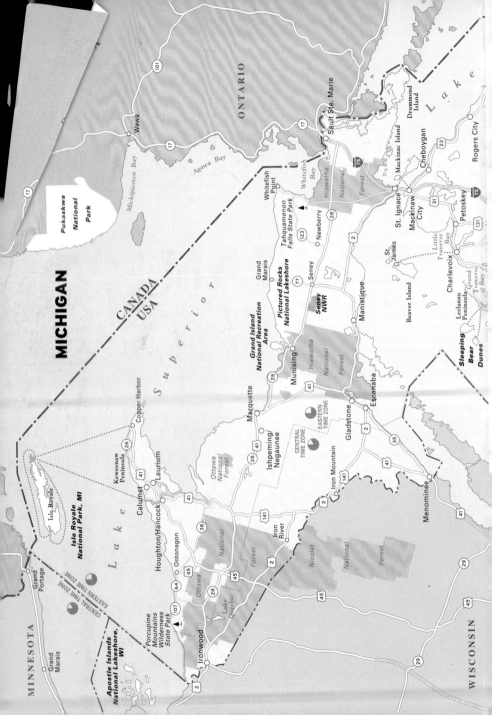

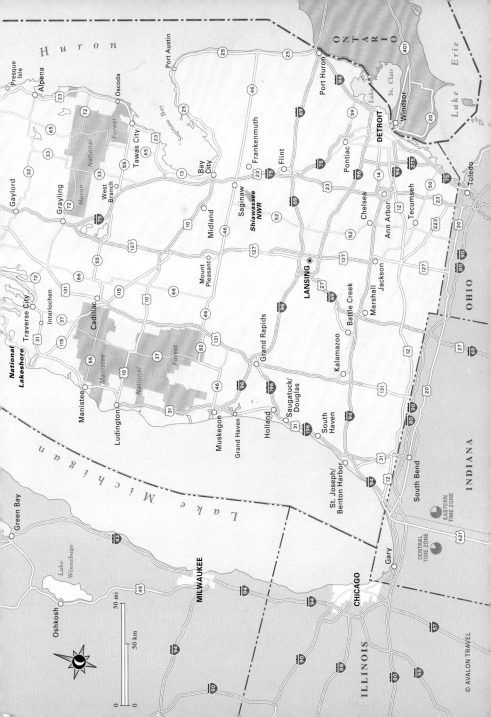

Contents

DISCOVER
Michigan

Michigan, a state known mainly for motors and Motown, possesses much diversity; its offerings are varied and often unexpected. Boasting more than 11,000 inland lakes, this multifaceted place also contains countless art galleries, award-winning wineries, and championship golf courses, and the length of its lighthouse-studded coastline is second only to Alaska.

Out-of-towners who consider it a typical Midwestern state, with frigid winters and flat cornfields, will be surprised. Though winters are indeed cold, the topography is amazingly manifold: a dramatically changing landscape of windswept beaches, rushing rivers, pine forests, remote islands, rugged mountains, impressive waterfalls, enormous sand dunes, and surrounding lakes so massive they resemble never-ending seas.

Unlike the urban metropolis of Detroit, most of Michigan has a small-town vibe, especially in the north. On a typical summer day, you could spend the morning on the shores of Lake Michigan, watching sailboats drift on the vibrant blue waters; then explore quaint coastal communities like Petoskey or Charlevoix; and finish the afternoon by picking wild blueberries amid the shady pines of northeastern Michigan.

While most tourists visit in spring and summer, winters have grown popular, too. Despite bitter cold and heavy snowfalls, adventurers enjoy skating across frozen lakes, riding snowmobiles through glistening forests, or braving the isolated hinterlands of the Upper Peninsula. Of course, little compares to traveling along serpentine country roads in autumn, flanked by apple orchards and crimson maple trees.

Divided into two extremely distinct peninsulas – the mitten-shaped Lower Peninsula and the breathtaking Upper Peninsula – Michigan is the only U.S. state that is surrounded by four of the five Great Lakes. How apt that its name is derived from the Native American word *michigama*, meaning "large lake" – and that it's long been known as the Great Lakes State.

The Lower Peninsula boasts a wealth of rural areas, nostalgic villages, college campuses, resort towns, and the urban centers of Detroit and Flint. Places like Traverse City are also favored by tourists, and yet the Upper Peninsula – a vast tract of forests, beaches, and mountains – has remained elusive to many. In fact, the Upper Peninsula is often overlooked by Michiganders as much as the rest of the nation.

The key to appreciating Michigan is to embrace its diversity. Given so much to see and experience, your love affair with this remarkable state will forever evolve.

Planning Your Trip

Where to Go

Detroit and Southeast Michigan

When considering Detroit, many think of both its musical and automotive heritage as well as its reputation for crime and corruption. Visitors are often surprised by the cultural attractions that abound in southeastern Michigan, from ethnic enclaves like Hamtramck to impressive museums like The Henry Ford. Detroit is also ideal for those seeking an active nightlife; the city boasts three major casino resorts, in addition to one in nearby Windsor, Canada.

The Thumb

This region sees fewer crowds than the towns along Lake Michigan. Travelers who appreciate

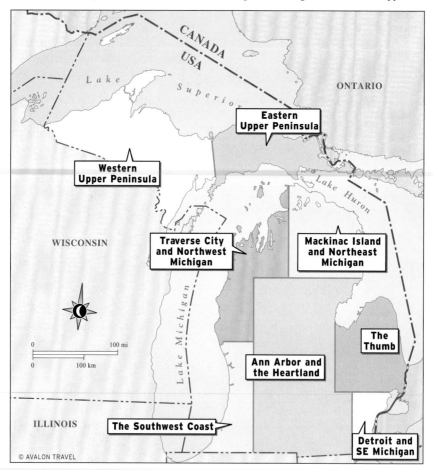

Sleeping Bear Dunes

a slower pace and more old-fashioned vibe will enjoy fishing in Lake Huron, touring ancient petroglyphs, strolling through small coastal villages, exploring Frankenmuth (a Bavarian-style village known for its year-round Christmas store), observing birds in the Shiawassee National Wildlife Refuge, and visiting historic sites within the region.

Ann Arbor and the Heartland

This is the only part of Michigan not bordered by at least one of the Great Lakes. Still, this vast region contains college sports teams, scenic lakes, unique cultural attractions like Kalamazoo's Air Zoo, and some of the state's largest cities. The Heartland could keep you busy for weeks, especially once you've discovered the enormous casino in Mount Pleasant.

The Southwest Coast

Michigan's most compact region, this shoreline is certainly the easiest to visit. Traveling from Harbor Country to the White Lake area requires less than a three-hour drive—but oh, what a drive! Along the way, you'll spy sand dunes, lighthouses, resort towns, art galleries, coastal state parks, and the state's only major amusement park. This region also constitutes one of two key wine-producing areas in the state.

Traverse City and Northwest Michigan

Every summer, tourists flock to Traverse City, the self-proclaimed "Cherry Capital of the World." The surrounding area is popular among visitors due to the wondrous Sleeping Bear Dunes, the wild rivers of Manistee National Forest, the wineries of the Leelanau Peninsula, and the lovely bays, lakes, and beaches. Northwest Michigan is also known for its superb golf courses and ski resorts.

Mackinac Island and Northeast Michigan

With its pine forests, canoeing rivers, inland lakes, and championship golf courses, Northeast Michigan is an outdoor enthusiast's paradise. The area's biggest attraction, the auto-free Mackinac Island, is definitely a step back in time, luring visitors with its quaint shops, carriage rides, and historic hotels.

Eastern Upper Peninsula

Most travelers reach the U.P. by crossing the Mackinac Bridge into St. Ignace. From here, you can explore many cultural attractions, including lighthouses, a shipwreck museum, and the Soo Locks near Sault Ste. Marie. You'll find terrific fishing spots like the Manistique Lakes, excellent canoeing rivers like the Two Hearted, incredible views at Pictured Rocks National Lakeshore, and acres of forest land.

Western Upper Peninsula

For seekers of solitude, this region promises all that and more. Although the Keweenaw Peninsula boasts a wealth of historic mining sites, and the Ironwood area has a number of popular ski resorts, much of this region consists of vast wilderness areas, including some of the highest mountains in the Midwest. Here, backpackers can lose themselves within expansive forests, kayakers can explore the frigid waters of Lake Superior, and the truly daring can venture to isolated Isle Royale.

Keweenaw Peninsula

When to Go

Summer is the most popular time to visit Michigan—people flock here for the beaches, inland lakes, and major events like the National Cherry Festival. July is typically the warmest month. In northern Michigan, it's also the buggiest. Time a camping trip in mid-June or after mid-August, when the mosquitoes and black flies are less bothersome.

Autumn may be the best time to visit. Days are cool, night skies are clear, bugs are gone, and fall colors are outstanding. For peak color, the second week of September in the U.P. and the second week of October for the Lower Peninsula are usually the best times.

Winter usually descends in December in the U.P., in January in the L.P., and can stick around through March. For snow sports, February is your safest bet to ensure good cover.

Spring emerges in southern Michigan in early May, working its way northward. With moderate temperatures and blossoming trees, this season is ideal for foliage lovers.

Before You Go

Reservations may be necessary, especially for popular B&Bs during the summer. Michigan is a seasonal place—some attractions and accommodations are only open late spring-early fall. If you come during the off-season, make sure to call ahead.

Your best bet for navigating this sprawling state is to bring your own vehicle or rent a car. All major airports have rental car services.

Foreign travelers will need passports, adapter plugs, and current converters; anyone planning to travel to and from Canada should have proper identification as well. All visitors should be prepared for a variety of weather conditions—even in summer, jackets and umbrellas may be necessary. Attire is casual, though nicer restaurants and churches appreciate business casual. If your plans include golfing and bird-watching, you might want to bring your favorite clubs and binoculars. Fishing gear, canoes, bikes, and other such equipment are easy enough to rent once you get here.

The Best of Michigan

Whether you're a longtime resident or a first-time visitor to the Great Lakes State, Michigan's top cultural and natural attractions are worth a trip.

Detroit to Kalamazoo

If you've started your adventure in the Motor City, head about eight miles southwest to Dearborn, where you'll encounter The Henry Ford, a fascinating complex of interactive historic exhibits. From Dearborn, head west along the I-94 corridor, through cities like Ann Arbor and Battle Creek. Two notable sights are the Marshall Historic District, an area about 100 miles west of Dearborn that encompasses hundreds of 19th-century homes and businesses, and Kalamazoo's Air Zoo, an enormous complex devoted to the history of aviation that's situated 36 miles west of Marshall.

the Mackinac Bridge

Saugatuck to Traverse City

From the Kalamazoo area, head north on US-131 for about 18 miles and continue on M-89 for roughly 33 miles, toward the Art Coast, a cluster of art galleries in and around the towns of Saugatuck and Douglas. After spending some time amid the area's shops, restaurants, and inns, drive north on US-31 to the incredible Sleeping Bear Dunes National Lakeshore, a marvelous 35-mile stretch of beaches, dunes, and lakes that lies alongside Lake Michigan and about 174 miles north of Saugatuck. From the lakeshore headquarters in Empire, head east on M-72 for 24 miles to Traverse City, an ideal base from which to explore gorgeous Grand Traverse Bay, popular with boaters and surrounded by several scenic resort towns, golf resorts, and award-winning wineries.

Mackinac Bridge to Munising

Expect a 100-mile drive on US-31 from Traverse City, through the towns of Charlevoix and Petoskey, to the amazing five-mile-long Mackinac Bridge, one of the world's longest suspension bridges. After crossing the bridge and passing through St. Ignace, head north for about 50 miles on I-75 to Sault Ste. Marie, Michigan's oldest city. Here, you'll glimpse another engineering marvel, the Soo Locks, through which massive freighters pass between Lakes Huron and Superior. For an up-close view, take a Soo Locks Boat Tour.

Head west for about 76 miles through the Hiawatha National Forest to Tahquamenon Falls, one of the largest waterfall systems east of the Mississippi. Afterward, drive about 25 miles north to Whitefish Point, where you'll find the Great Lakes Shipwreck Museum, the only museum dedicated to the perils of maritime transportation on the Great Lakes. Roughly 115 miles farther west lies Pictured Rocks National Lakeshore, a fabulous stretch of sand dunes, desolate beaches, sandstone cliffs, and shady forests beside Lake Superior.

wintertime in the Keweenaw National Historical Park

The Keweenaw Peninsula

If you're willing to venture farther into the wilds of the U.P., head west from Munising on M-28/US-41 for about 145 miles to the heart of the Keweenaw Peninsula. Here, history buffs will enjoy the Keweenaw National Historical Park. From nearby Houghton, adventurous hikers, backpackers, kayakers, and wildlife enthusiasts can take a ferry ride to Isle Royale National Park, a wild, isolated archipelago in the northern reaches of Lake Superior.

Straits of Mackinac to the Thumb

Once you're done exploring the Upper Peninsula, head south to Mackinaw City, which lies about 266 miles from Houghton, and board a ferry for Mackinac Island, a charming vacation spot that has long banned automobiles in favor of bikes and horse-drawn carriages. Rife with Victorian mansions, this nostalgic island offers a true step back in time. Back on the mainland, drive south for about 58 miles through the Gaylord golf mecca, a large concentration of top-notch golf courses, and continue south for roughly 27 miles to Hartwick Pines State Park, home to the largest stand of virgin white pines in the Lower Peninsula. End your tour of Michigan on a festive note by heading south on I-75 for about 125 miles, toward the Bavarian-style town of Frankenmuth, site of German shops and festivals, all-you-can-eat chicken dinners, and a year-round Christmas store.

An Art Coast Getaway

The adjacent towns of Saugatuck and Douglas lie at the heart of Michigan's "Art Coast," a stretch of art galleries and artist studios in the southwestern part of the state, along the eastern shore of Lake Michigan. If you appreciate visual arts of all kinds, then you may relish a three-day tour of the region, which is easy to reach via train, plane, boat, bus, or car.

Day 1

Before your trip, reserve a room at one of the area's charming bed-and-breakfasts, such

Top 10 Beaches

THE SOUTHWEST COAST

- **Warren Dunes State Park:** Situated north of Sawyer, this park offers three miles of sandy beaches, with incredibly high dunes. Beachcombers and swimmers crowd the southern end every summer. Farther inland, hikers and bird-watchers will find a bit more solitude.

- **Oval Beach:** Families flock to this popular Saugatuck-area beach, where swimmers can enjoy relatively warm waters in summer and adventurers can explore the nearby dunes.

- **Holland State Park:** One of Michigan's loveliest and most accessible beaches lures hundreds of swimmers and sunbathers on summer weekends. The park offers campgrounds, volleyball courts, amazing sunsets, a nearby boating lake, and terrific lighthouse views.

- **Grand Haven State Park:** Easy to reach from downtown Grand Haven, this sandy swimming beach is usually crowded with sun-seekers and metal-detecting enthusiasts in summer. Others come for the fishing pier, campground, picnic area, and photo-worthy lighthouses.

- **Muskegon State Park:** Part of a diverse 1,233-acre park, this two-mile stretch of sand attracts tons of swimmers, beachcombers, surfers, and picnickers every year. Head inland for hiking, fishing, and other recreational opportunities.

NORTHWEST MICHIGAN AND THE UPPER PENINSULA

- **Silver Lake State Park:** Perhaps the highlight of Oceana County, this stretch of sand is favored among off-road enthusiasts—it's the only place in the state where off-road dune driving is allowed.

- **Sleeping Bear Dunes National Lakeshore:** It's a must that you visit this natural wonder during your trip to Michigan. Here, you'll find a curvy stretch of Lake Michigan shoreline, with some of the tallest dunes in the state, and ideal places to canoe, fish, hike, and, in winter, ski.

- **Pictured Rocks National Lakeshore:** Although the U.P.'s Lake Superior coast isn't ideal for swimmers—given the lake's frigid temperatures year-round—the beaches here are perfect for beachcombers, bird-watchers, hikers, and sea kayakers with wetsuits. For relative solitude, venture toward Grand Sable Dunes.

NORTHEAST MICHIGAN AND THE THUMB

- **Tawas Point State Park:** East of Tawas City, this park is noted for its pure-white sandy beach, its warm waters, its well-preserved lighthouse, and its incredible view of the sunrise over Lake Huron.

- **Port Crescent State Park:** Near the tip of the Thumb, this locale offers three miles of sandy beaches and dunes. Less popular than spots along Lake Michigan, it ensures you a better chance of finding peace and quiet amid the great outdoors.

Pictured Rocks National Lakeshore

as the Victorian-style Twin Oaks Inn, the antiques-filled Maplewood Hotel, or of which lie gic Wickwood Country Inn, all of which lie within easy walking distance of Saugatuck's thriving downtown area. After checking into your hotel, stroll amid the shops and art galleries that line streets like Water, Butler, Griffith, and Mason. Notable places here include the Singapore Bank Bookstore, Mother Moon, and Good Goods. While shopping, be sure to stop by the Saugatuck Drug Store, where you can savor homemade shakes and sodas at the old-fashioned soda fountain. Another tasty stop is American Spoon, which sells a wide assortment of delicious preserves and other regionally produced condiments. If you're not too full after sampling their wares, head to Chequers of Saugatuck for dinner. Here, at this pub-like restaurant, you'll encounter British staples like shepherd's pie, fish and chips, bangers and mash, and Guinness stew.

Day 2

If you've chosen to stay at one of Saugatuck's B&Bs, then you can begin the day with a scrumptious, on-site breakfast before continuing your tour of the downtown area. Art lovers can stop by all the galleries that they might have missed, including the Saugatuck Center for the Arts, which, in addition to presenting various visual art exhibits, also hosts an array of plays, concerts, film screenings, and lecture series. If you haven't yet tired of art, hop on the Blue Star Highway and head south to Douglas, home to such well-respected respositories as the Button-Petter Gallery, the convergence of two longstanding fine art galleries.

From May to October, you might prefer a ride on the Star of Saugatuck II, a two-level sternwheeler that offers narrated trips along the Kalamazoo River. If it's a sunny day, be sure to board the gingerbread-style Chain Ferry, which shuttles visitors across the river to the family-friendly Oval Beach,

a sandy, ever-popular stretch of beach beside Lake Michigan. For a less-crowded alternative, pick up a salad or an overstuffed sandwich, a few pastries, and some other portable snacks at Pumpernickel's Eatery, and then head north to Saugatuck Dunes State Park, a 1,000-acre preserve that offers a 2.5-mile stretch of undeveloped beach alongside Lake Michigan, 200-foot-high coastal dunes, 13 miles of well-marked hiking trails, and, normally, plenty of solitude.

Upon your return to Saugatuck, freshen up at your hotel, and then head to the Restaurant Toulouse for dinner. This Provençal-inspired bistro offers tableside fireplaces, live jazz on Saturday nights, and French country cuisine.

Day 3

Wake up with a stroll to Ida Red's Cottage, a popular eatery that serves breakfast all day long. After checking out of your hotel, consider extending your area tour for a few more hours. Outdoor enthusiasts, for instance, might enjoy an 18-hole round of golf at the Ravines Golf Club, which features an Arnold Palmer-designed course, or a pleasant horseback ride at the Wild West Ranch near the town of Allegan.

If you're not tired of sampling local foods, drive instead to Crane Orchards in nearby Fennville. Here, depending on the season, you can pluck cherries, peaches, and apples in the delightful U-pick orchard. During September and October, you can also stroll through the impressive, 20-acre corn maze, which changes every year. Be sure, too, to sample one of the homemade sandwiches, soups, or fruit pies on offer at the adjacent Crane's Pie Pantry Restaurant & Bakery. Then, before heading home, consider driving south on the Blue Star Highway, where, between Saugatuck and South Haven, you'll encounter the Blue Coast Artists, a collective of 12 artists who provide a behind-the-scenes look into their studios and galleries every spring, summer, and fall.

Music and Motor Cars

Detroit's nicknames—Motown and the Motor City—underscore its rich musical and automotive heritage. Visitors will find an array of sites, activities, and annual festivals that celebrate the city's contributions to American music and industry.

MUSEUMS AND HISTORIC HOMES

In the Detroit area, tour the region's vintage car collections, musical heritage exhibits, and former auto baron homes. Begin in downtown Detroit, where the GM Renaissance Center presents the **GM Showroom,** a 40,000-square-foot, year-round display of vintage vehicles, concept cars, and new models.

Afterward, head to the Cultural Center and view an authentic auto assembly line at the **Detroit Historical Museum.** At the nearby **Charles H. Wright Museum of African American History,** music lovers can learn about performers such as John Lee Hooker and Aretha Franklin. Just a bit north, the **Motown Museum** is a small repository of costumes, records, photographs, and other memorabilia that celebrate the likes of Marvin Gaye, Diana Ross, Stevie Wonder, and The Temptations.

Head southwest to Dearborn, where you'll find **The Henry Ford,** a museum complex that explores American history, industry, and innovation. Tour Ford's childhood home, a collection of presidential limousines and other vintage cars, and a Ford truck assembly line. History buffs may also enjoy visiting **Fair Lane,** Henry Ford's former Dearborn estate, and the **Edsel & Eleanor Ford House,** a Cotswold-style mansion in Grosse Pointe Shores.

DETROIT'S MUSICAL NIGHTLIFE

Detroit has been a favored city among musicians as varied as Smokey Robinson, Bob Seger, and Eminem. In the Theater District, the **Music Hall Center for the Performing Arts** has, for more than 85 years, hosted legendary musical acts. Detroit's lively nightclubs, including **Baker's Keyboard Lounge** and **Flood's Bar & Grille,** offer live jazz music and delicious soul food.

YEARLY CELEBRATIONS

In January, auto lovers can attend the **North American International Auto Show,** which promises a first look at the latest innovative vehicle designs. Two other car-related celebrations include the **Chevrolet Detroit Belle Isle Grand Prix,** a challenging race that usually takes place in the spring, and the **Woodward Dream Cruise,** a mid-August event that highlights vintage cars. On Labor Day weekend, meanwhile, the **Detroit Jazz Festival** presents open-air jazz concerts alongside the Detroit River.

the North American International Auto Show

A Romantic Weekend on Mackinac Island

Situated between Michigan's Upper and Lower Peninsulas, Mackinac Island is an ideal spot for a romantic getaway, especially during the summer. Whether you reach this nostalgic place via ferry or plane, you and your sweetheart will surely have a memorable weekend.

Friday

Prior to your getaway, reserve a room at one of the island's more unique hotels, such as the Chippewa Hotel Waterfront, the Hotel Iroquois, or the Mission Point Resort, all of which feature luxurious suites and spectacular views. If cost is no issue, you might prefer the exquisite Grand Hotel, where the 1980 romance *Somewhere in Time* was filmed.

After checking into your hotel, take a narrated horse-drawn carriage tour of the island, which will introduce you to some of its best landmarks and attractions. For a romantic dinner, consider the Yankee Rebel Tavern, which offers fireplace seating, an ample wine and beer selection, and a variety of winning selections, from slow-roasted ribs to pistachio-crusted whitefish.

Saturday

Start the day with breakfast at or near your hotel, then head to the Mackinac Island Bike Shop. Here, you'll find a wide selection of rental bikes, ideal for exploring this 2,200-acre paradise. Pick up a free island map and explore as much as your desire and stamina will allow. Begin with the bustling downtown area, along Main and Market Streets, where you can browse shops, sample fudge, and visit historic homes, such as the Biddle House and the Benjamin Blacksmith Shop, both of which are included with admission to Fort Mackinac.

For lunch, head up to the Fort Mackinac Tea Room, where you can enjoy delicious

a bicycle built for two on Mackinac Island

Top 5 Hikes

The Great Lakes State is, perhaps not surprisingly, a haven for outdoor enthusiasts of all skill levels. The Upper and Lower Peninsulas offer hundreds of miles of hiking trails, from easy paths to advanced backpacking routes.

THE UPPER PENINSULA

- **Escarpment Trail:** This 4.3-mile well-maintained trail in Porcupine Mountains Wilderness State Park winds east along a sheer escarpment, crossing Cloud Peak and Cuyahoga Peak and offering a stunning view of the Lake of the Clouds. During the winter, this trail is also popular among cross-country skiers.

- **Tahquamenon River Trail:** Day hikers favor this four-mile, family friendly path in the 50,000-acre Tahquamenon Falls State Park. Passing through an old-growth forest, this scenic trail leads from the Lower Falls to the Upper Falls. Along the way, you can access several overlooks of the stunning waterfalls.

THE LOWER PENINSULA

- **Dunes Trail:** Encompassing more than 71,000 acres, Sleeping Bear Dunes National Lakeshore provides lots of options for hikers. Of the more than 100 miles of designated trails on offer, the most popular choice is this strenuous 3.5-mile hike, which stretches across steep, rugged dunes. Along the way, enjoy a spectacular view of Glen Lake.

- **Kal-Haven Trail:** For a longer trek, consider this 34-mile route, which extends from Kalamazoo to South Haven. Tracing an abandoned railroad, this trail crosses various bridges and passes through several small towns. It's also popular among bikers, bird-watchers, cross-country skiers, and snowmobilers.

- **Highbanks Trail:** This 7-mile, ungroomed trail about 14 miles west of Oscoda follows the Au Sable River Valley, offering picturesque views of this popular canoeing river from the bluffs on the south shore, not to mention terrific opportunities for wildlife lovers. You'll encounter photogenic sites like the Lumberman's Monument and the Canoer's Memorial. Cross-country skiers also favor this trail, which is free to use year-round.

soups, salads, and sandwiches from a picturesque terrace. Afterward, stroll amid the former barracks and other buildings that comprise the whitewashed fort, which overlooks the marina. Observe the musket firings and cannon salutes reenacted by costumed guides, then ride to the Grand Hotel and take a leisurely stroll through the landscaped grounds.

If you still have energy, venture across Mackinac Island State Park, which encompasses much of the island. Along the way, you'll see vibrant forests, limestone bluffs, lake vistas, and curious rock formations, such as Skull Cave and Arch Rock. When you're ready, head toward the marina, return your bikes, and opt for a casual dinner at the Seabiscuit Café, which stays open late and serves several delectable entrées, from steak burgers to curry chicken to French Creole jambalaya.

Sunday

Head to the Chippewa Hotel Waterfront—if you're not already staying here—and have breakfast at the Pink Pony Dining Room, which offers omelets, pancakes, and fresh berry parfaits amid stunning marina views. Then, take one last stroll through the downtown area, and if there's time, visit the Original Mackinac Island Butterfly House & Insect World, where you'll spy hundreds of vibrant butterflies amid a tropical garden. Afterward, check out of your hotel and return to the mainland via ferry or plane.

Historic Lighthouses

During the 19th and early 20th centuries, the Great Lakes served as the principal transportation routes for the industries in this region. More than 100 lighthouses were erected along Michigan's coastline. Most remain intact and many are still operational. Some have become inns, museums, or private homes. Others are closed to the public, but nearly all can be viewed—and photographed.

Detroit to the Thumb

Detroit contains several curious structures, such as the 80-foot-tall marble Livingstone Memorial Lighthouse on Belle Isle. From here, head north on I-94 to Port Huron, where you can tour the *Huron* Lightship, which retired in 1970 as the last lightship in service on the Great Lakes and is now a National Historic Landmark. Visitors are welcome to explore this vessel, which is docked on the St. Clair River, as well as the nearby Fort Gratiot Lighthouse, an 86-foot-tall brick structure established in 1829 and still active today.

Next, drive north on M-25, skirting the Thumb's coast. Near Port Hope, the operational 89-foot-tall Pointe aux Barques Lighthouse, lit in 1857, is now a museum featuring lighthouse equipment and shipwreck artifacts. After touring the Thumb's lighthouses, stay the night in the Port Austin area, where you'll find several affordable motels and campgrounds, plus The Bank 1884 Food & Spirits, which offers fine dining in a casual setting.

Northeast Michigan

On the second day of your lighthouse trip, venture west on M-25 to Bay City, hop onto I-75, and continue along US-23, which traces the Lake Huron shore. There are several historic lighthouses in this region, some of which are inactive and can only be viewed by boat. In Tawas Point State Park, about three hours from Port Austin, you'll spy the operational Tawas Point Lighthouse, one of the state's most well-kept lights. Farther along US-23,

Tawas Point Lighthouse

Pointe aux Barques Lighthouse

Point Light Station, the oldest operating lighthouse on Lake Superior and now part of a complex that includes the Great Lakes Shipwreck Museum. Afterward, join a guided tour of the 1874 Au Sable Light Station on the eastern end of Pictured Rocks National Lakeshore. Then, head farther west along the Lake Superior shore and spend the afternoon in the historic port of Marquette, where the Marquette Maritime Museum offers informative tours of the 1866 Marquette Harbor Lighthouse. After dinner, consider staying at the lovely 1896 Big Bay Point Lighthouse Bed and Breakfast, one of the nation's few lighthouse inns; reserve a room well in advance.

Take a leisurely four-hour drive via CR-550 and US-41 to the tip of the Keweenaw Peninsula. Here, you can join a narrated round-trip cruise through Copper Harbor's formerly bustling port, to the 1866 Copper Harbor Lighthouse, where a host will guide visitors through the historic complex, which includes shipwreck artifacts, a small maritime museum, and incredible lake views. From Copper Harbor, head west to Eagle Harbor, where the fog signal building beside the 1871 Eagle Harbor Light now serves as a maritime history museum. Stop for dinner and head south to Ahmeek, where you can stay overnight in the romantic Sand Hills Lighthouse Inn, constructed in 1917 and now serving as a Victorian-style bed-and-breakfast. Reservations might be necessary here, too.

Northwest Michigan and the Southwest Coast

Die-hard history buffs might want to linger in the U.P. and take a morning boat ride to remote Isle Royale for a look at the 1855 Rock Harbor Lighthouse, but as an alternative, you can simply drive back toward the Lower Peninsula, cross the Mackinac Bridge, and, from Mackinaw City, head south on I-75 and US-31, toward Charlevoix. From here, you can take a ferry to Beaver Island, home to the 1858 Beaver Head Lighthouse and the 1870 St. James Harbor Light. Back on the mainland, head toward Traverse City, where you'll find the 1870 Old Mission Point Lighthouse

you'll find the Sturgeon Point Lighthouse, built in 1869 and still active today—as both a lighthouse and a maritime museum. Continue along the Lake Huron shore, where you'll spy the 1840 Old Presque Isle Lighthouse, now a museum; the 1870 New Presque Isle Lighthouse, also open to the public; and the 1897 40 Mile Point Lighthouse, a 52-foot-tall lighthouse with attached keeper's quarters. En route to the Mackinac Bridge, you'll encounter the castle-like Old Mackinac Point Lighthouse, erected in 1892 and now a fascinating museum. After touring the Lake Huron shore, stay the night in Mackinaw City, which boasts several hotels and restaurants.

The Upper Peninsula

Drive across the Mackinac Bridge and head toward the shore of Whitefish Bay. Stop in Brimley, where the 1870 Point Iroquois Light Station, now a maritime museum, invites visitors to tour a restored light keeper's home and climb the tower for views of the river and bay. Next, visit the 1849 Whitefish

Top 10 Golf Resorts

Michigan is known as "America's summer golf mecca," the Gaylord area alone boasts nearly 20 courses, and the U.P. offers a number of seasonal choices, too. While the state has several private clubs—such as Oakland Hills Country Club, which hosted the 2008 PGA Championship—there's also a wide array of public courses and resorts. Here are 10 of the best options in the northern half of the Lower Peninsula, indeed the state's most popular region for golfers.

- **Tullymore Golf Resort:** On the road from Grand Rapids to Cadillac, you'll find this popular locale, celebrated for its pair of spectacular 18-hole courses: Tullymore and St. Ives.

- **Arcadia Bluffs Golf Club:** Located along a gorgeous stretch of Lake Michigan shoreline, this world-class resort offers an 18-hole golf course that's long been considered the best public course in the state, by golfers and golfing magazines alike.

- **Grand Traverse Resort and Spa:** With comfortable accommodations, excellent dining, a top-notch spa, an indoor water park, a 24-hour dog care facility, and three on-site golf courses (The Bear, The Wolverine, and Spruce Run), this 900-acre resort in Acme has easily become one of Michigan's finest golfing destinations.

- **A-Ga-Ming Golf Resort:** Overlooking lovely Torch Lake, not far north of Traverse City, this longstanding resort presents three 18-hole courses: Torch, Antrim Dells, and Sundance.

- **Shanty Creek Resorts:** Divided into three villages—Cedar River, Schuss, and Summit—this enormous Bellaire resort features several dining, lodging, and spa options, numerous downhill skiing runs, and four championship golf courses: Cedar River, Schuss Mountain, Summit G.C., and Arnold Palmer's The Legend.

- **Boyne Highlands Resort:** Just north of Petoskey, this year-round resort offers superb lodging, four spectacular golf courses (The Heather, Arthur Hills, Donald Ross Memorial, and The Moor), a lighted par-3 course, and access to a wealth of seasonal activities, from fishing to dogsledding.

- **Hidden River Golf & Casting Club:** Between Petoskey and Mackinaw City, you'll find this handsome resort, which appeals to golfers as well as fly-fishing enthusiasts.

- **Black Lake Golf Club:** Operated by the UAW, this magnificent golf course is part of the union's 1,000-acre family center, which sits astride picturesque Black Lake near the town of Onaway.

- **Treetops Resort:** This year-round resort near Gaylord keeps visitors busy with downhill skiing in winter, horseback riding in summer, a full-service spa, and, of course, five stunning golf courses: Masterpiece, Premier, Signature, Tradition, and Treetops.

- **Garland Lodge & Resort:** Considered one of the state's most beautiful resorts, this rustic destination presents four magnificent golf courses (Fountains, Reflections, Swampfire, and Monarch) amid the woods of northeastern Michigan.

and the 1858 Grand Traverse Lighthouse, a well-preserved structure in Leelanau State Park. Here, visitors can climb the lighthouse tower, stroll through the museum, and enjoy sandwiches and pastries in the gift shop. Stay overnight in Traverse City.

Spend the last day of your lighthouse tour exploring the Lake Michigan coastline, an area rife with museums, hotels, campgrounds, restaurants, and, of course, lighthouses. Take M-22 south to the operational 1858 Point Betsie Lighthouse, a lovely brick structure with attached keeper's quarters. Via US-31, visit the 112-foot-tall 1867 Big Sable Point Lighthouse in Ludington State Park and the 1874 Little Sable Point Light in Silver Lake State Park. Continuing south on US-31, you'll spy the 1875 White River Light Station, now a maritime museum; climb the spiral staircase for an incredible view of Lake Michigan. Farther south, you'll encounter several crimson-hued, operational structures, including the Grand Haven South Pier Lighthouses, a range-light system linked by a catwalk, and the 1907 Holland Harbor Light, nicknamed "Big Red."

A Taste of Wine Country

In recent years, Michigan is gaining a reputation for crafting award-winning wines. Although wineries are dispersed throughout the state, Michigan has two main winemaking areas in the Lower Peninsula—along the Southwest Coast and around Grand Traverse Bay. Both regions, which together contain nearly 50 wineries, benefit from a lake-effect climate that protects the vines with snow cover in winter and extends the growing season for up to a month.

Wine connoisseurs should take at least a week, preferably during summer or fall, to sample the state's finest wineries.

Lake Michigan Shore Wine Country

There are 15 wineries and several tasting rooms along this stretch of the Southwest Coast, from New Buffalo to Grand Haven. Take a couple of days to experience the best of them.

Begin with the southern half of the wine trail, just east of Harbor Country. To reach these inland vineyards, take Red Arrow Highway to Lemon Creek Road. At the 150-acre Lemon Creek Winery & Fruit Farm, visitors can sample wines in the tasting room, take an informal tour of the vineyard, and pick whatever fruit is in season.

Afterward, drive south on Burgoyne Road, turn right onto Mount Tabor Road, and stop at the Tabor Hill Winery & Restaurant, known for its mid-priced, award-winning wines. Following a tour or tasting, have lunch in the first-rate restaurant.

Your last stop of the day should be the Round Barn Winery, which lies northwest of Tabor Hill. This family-owned winery, distillery, and brewery invites visitors to tour the vineyard, sample wines in the unique farmhouse, and take a winemaking class. Afterward, drive north to St. Joseph, where you can stay the night in The Boulevard Inn & Bistro, a terrific spot to enjoy dinner (or

the Ciccone Vineyard & Winery, Leelanau Peninsula

the vineyard at Chateau Grand Traverse

breakfast) on an outdoor terrace overlooking Lake Michigan.

The following day, head east on I-94 to M-40, where you'll find two longstanding wineries in Paw Paw. The first, the family-owned St. Julian Winery, is actually the oldest and largest winery in the state; it provides year-round tours and tastings. Just up the road lies Warner Vineyards, the state's second-oldest winery, offering self-guided tours and a wonderful deck on which to sip champagne. Before heading north to the Leelanau Peninsula, veer toward the coast, where towns like Saugatuck offer diversions of their own. In South Haven, stay at The Last Resort B&B Inn and have a casual meal at fun-loving Clementine's.

Leelanau Peninsula

Following breakfast, head north on US-31 to Traverse City, just over a three-hour trip.

From here, wineries and tasting rooms stretch north along either shore of the West Arm of Grand Traverse Bay. After dining in one of Traverse City's downtown eateries, drive west on M-72, toward the Leelanau Peninsula, which nurtures more than two dozen wineries. Take CR-651 north to Cedar, follow Schomberg Road to French Road, and spend the afternoon sampling merlot and other vintages at Chateau Fontaine, a long-ago potato farm and cow pasture now transformed into 30 acres of grapevines. Head east to Suttons Bay, where you'll find Black Star Farms, a fascinating winery and distillery, with a tasting room and a luxurious bed-and-breakfast—an ideal, if pricey, place to spend the next four nights.

Over the following three days, feel free to explore some of the other wineries that line this picturesque peninsula. Take special note of several locales in Suttons Bay, including Raftshol Vineyards, a former dairy enterprise and cherry orchard that now produces over 1,000 cases of bordeaux varietal red wines annually; Chateau de Leelanau, which presents a tasting room not far from Grand Traverse Bay; Ciccone Vineyard & Winery, a Tuscan-inspired winery and tasting room owned by Madonna's parents; and L. Mawby Vineyards, specializing in sparkling wines and offering a year-round tasting room. You should also stop by Leelanau Cellars, which is situated north of Suttons Bay and provides a fine tasting room for sampling everything from riesling to baco noir.

Old Mission Peninsula

If your taste buds haven't yet wearied of reds and whites, you should spend the last day of your weeklong wine tour amid the eight wineries of the Old Mission Peninsula, accessible via Traverse City. Make sure to explore two wineries in particular: Chateau Grand Traverse and Chateau Chantal, both of which offer free or inexpensive tastings, winery tours, and luxurious accommodations with incredible views.

DETROIT AND SOUTHEAST MICHIGAN

Although Detroit's official motto—*Speramus meliora; resurget cineribus*—resulted from a catastrophic fire that nearly destroyed the fledgling town in 1805, its meaning could just as easily refer to modern times: "We hope for better things. It will rise from the ashes." This is a city, after all, that has witnessed its share of soaring highs and crushing lows, and yet has always managed to come back swinging.

Detroit truly hit the map when Henry Ford's assembly line transformed the town—and the world—forever. With the assistance of the "Big Three" (Ford, General Motors, and Chrysler), the Motor City thrived during the first half of the 20th century. Reliance on a single industry, however, inevitably led to downswings that mimicked those of the auto industry, plunging the racially divided metropolis into years of crime and unemployment—modern problems that have, at times, been exaggerated by the national media.

But the Motor City is defined less by its adversity and more by its innovation and fortitude. Crime is not the crippling issue it once was, and development has helped to revitalize the downtown area. Unofficially nicknamed the Renaissance City in the 1970s, Detroit has finally begun to shed its troubled past. Although it's still a work-in-progress, this tenacious town—also known for its Motown music, rock 'n' roll vibe, and legendary sports figures—has improved its tarnished image since the turn of the new millennium, and nowhere is that more apparent than along the waterfront.

Dominating the Detroit skyline, the

© 123RF.COM

HIGHLIGHTS

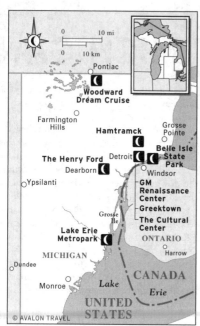

LOOK FOR ◖ TO FIND RECOMMENDED SIGHTS, ACTIVITIES, DINING, AND LODGING.

◖ **GM Renaissance Center:** Towering above the Detroit River since the late 1970s, the 73-story Ren Cen is home to GM's world headquarters, a 1,300-room hotel, a fitness center, a movie theater, and numerous shops and restaurants. Visitors can take a free, one-hour tour of the enormous complex, which also includes a vintage auto collection, a tropical atrium overlooking the river, and incredible views of the Detroit and Windsor skylines (page 32).

◖ **Belle Isle State Park:** Situated in the Detroit River, Belle Isle has long been a treasured spot for visitors and area residents alike. Highlights include designated biking paths, a zoo, a swimming beach, a conservatory, golf facilities, the Dossin Great Lakes Museum, two fishing piers, and numerous historic edifices (page 33).

◖ **Greektown:** One of several ethnic enclaves in the Detroit metropolitan area, this historic neighborhood invites visitors to experience Greek culture at its best. Here, you'll find the longstanding Pegasus Taverna, the annual Detroit Greek Independence Day Parade, and a flashy casino (page 38).

◖ **The Cultural Center:** Art and culture lovers flock to this part of Midtown, which boasts two art museums, three history museums, a science center, an anthropology museum, a children's museum, and several well-preserved Victorian structures, plus nearby theaters and art galleries (page 38).

◖ **Hamtramck:** Founded in the early 20th century, this village has long lured Polish immigrants and other Europeans. While the neighborhood is more culturally diverse these days, visitors can still come here for Polish sausages, European baked goods, and traditional artwork (page 57).

◖ **The Henry Ford:** At this curious complex, visitors can view Henry Ford's childhood home, Thomas Edison's Menlo Park laboratory, President Kennedy's limousine, Rosa Parks's bus, and a working 19th-century farm. You can also hitch a ride to the Ford truck assembly plant for an informative walking tour (page 59).

◖ **Lake Erie Metropark:** South of Detroit lies this well-preserved, 1,607-acre recreation area, popular among hikers, bird-watchers, anglers, golfers, cross-country skiers, and those who appreciate stunning views of the Detroit River, Lake Erie, and North America's first international wildlife refuge (page 68).

◖ **Woodward Dream Cruise:** This annual mid-August parade down Woodward Avenue, from Ferndale to Pontiac, has become the world's largest one-day automotive event, luring 1.5 million people and more than 40,000 classic cars from around the globe (page 70).

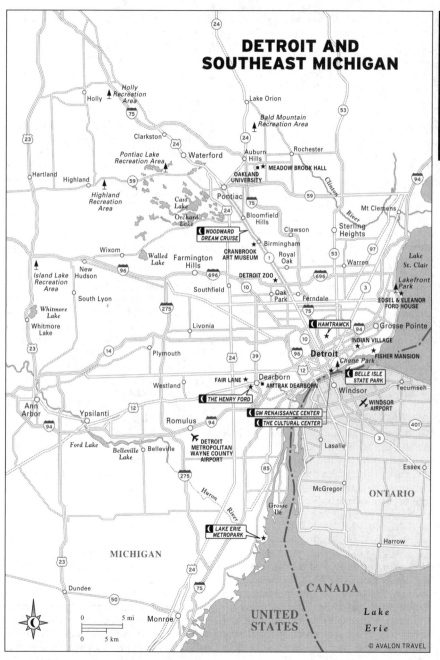

DETROIT AND SOUTHEAST MICHIGAN

Holly
Holly Recreation Area
Lake Orion
Bald Mountain Recreation Area
Clarkston
Rochester
Waterford
Auburn Hills
Hartland
Highland
OAKLAND UNIVERSITY
MEADOW BROOK HALL
Pontiac Lake Recreation Area
Highland Recreation Area
Cass Lake
Pontiac
Bloomfield Hills
Mt Clemens
Orchard Lake
Sterling Heights
WOODWARD DREAM CRUISE
Clawson
Wixom
Birmingham
Walled Lake
CRANBROOK ART MUSEUM
Royal Oak
Warren
Island Lake Recreation Area
New Hudson
Farmington Hills
DETROIT ZOO
Lake St. Clair
South Lyon
Southfield
Oak Park
Ferndale
Lakefront Park
Whitmore Lake
EDSEL & ELEANOR FORD HOUSE
Whitmore Lake
Livonia
HAMTRAMCK
Grosse Pointe
INDIAN VILLAGE
Plymouth
Detroit
FISHER MANSION
Chene Park
Westland
FAIR LANE
Dearborn
BELLE ISLE STATE PARK
THE HENRY FORD
AMTRAK DEARBORN
Windsor
Tecumseh
Ann Arbor
Ypsilanti
GM RENAISSANCE CENTER
WINDSOR AIRPORT
Romulus
THE CULTURAL CENTER
Ford Lake
Belleville Lake
Belleville
DETROIT METROPOLITAN WAYNE COUNTY AIRPORT
Lasalle
Essex
Grosse Ile
McGregor
ONTARIO
Huron River
LAKE ERIE METROPARK
Harrow
MICHIGAN
Dundee
CANADA
Monroe
UNITED STATES
Lake Erie

0   5 mi
0   5 km

© AVALON TRAVEL

once-controversial Renaissance Center has undergone an extensive renovation, transforming the distinctive office, hotel, and retail complex into the world headquarters of General Motors. In addition, the city has embarked upon an ambitious development project along the Detroit River, which it shares with Windsor, Canada. When completed, the Detroit Riverfront will comprise a new harbor, the expanded William G. Milliken State Park, and a network of biking and jogging trails. Other recent downtown enhancements include a new ballpark for the Detroit Tigers, an adjacent football stadium for the Detroit Lions, and three casino resorts.

Detroit's many suburbs have also experienced a revival, marked by the opening of such attractions as the Holocaust Memorial Center in Farmington Hills and the Arab American National Museum in Dearborn, both of which celebrate the rich diversity of Detroit's people. Beyond the greater Detroit metropolitan area, visitors will discover a wealth of activities in Southeast Michigan, from skiing on Mt. Holly to watching the Woodward Dream Cruise. Despite decades of struggle, it seems that Detroit and its surrounding towns are finally on the upswing, once again affirming the city's two-century-old motto.

ORIENTATION

Almost prophetically, early Detroit was laid out like the spokes of a wheel. The plan—laid down by Judge Augustus Woodward, the first chief justice of the new Michigan territory—foreshadowed the city's major industry by more than a century. Woodward arrived in 1805 to find no more than a burned-out trading post on the narrow straits of the river—*détroit*, incidentally, means "straits." While little else remains of Woodward's grandiose plans to make Detroit the "Paris of the Midwest," the city's main streets—Jefferson Avenue, Gratiot Avenue, Woodward Avenue, Grand River Avenue, Michigan Avenue, and Fort Street—still echo that early hexagonal grid, shooting off at diagonal angles from a central axis. Woodward serves as the city's main dividing

line, splitting the landmass and its residents into east and west.

Compared to most U.S. urban areas, Detroit isn't too difficult to navigate. Though the city, its suburbs, and the rest of Southeast Michigan constitute a sprawling tapestry of distinct neighborhoods and communities, several bisecting highways and interstates make it easy to get around. For instance, I-75 snakes through downtown Detroit, linking southern towns like Monroe to northern destinations like Royal Oak, Pontiac, and Holly. Other major routes include I-96 from Lansing; I-696, which passes through Farmington Hills, Southfield, and Ferndale; and I-94, which cuts across the southern part of the Heartland, passes north of Detroit's Cultural Center and west of the Grosse Pointe suburbs, and heads north toward Port Huron.

PLANNING YOUR TIME

Southeast Michigan is a relatively small area, easy to traverse with a car. Several major routes link Detroit and its suburbs to other parts of the state, including I-75 from Flint, I-96 from Lansing, or I-94 from Battle Creek. Getting here via other forms of transportation is also a snap. The Detroit Metro Airport (DTW) serves as a hub for Delta Air Lines. In addition, Amtrak serves Dearborn, Detroit, Royal Oak, Birmingham, and Pontiac. Greyhound also offers regular bus services to three stations in the area: Detroit, Southfield, and Pontiac.

Unlike other parts of Michigan, Detroit and its suburbs aren't terribly dependent on the shifting seasons. Most museums, shops, and restaurants are open in winter as well as summer. No matter when you visit, however, you'll need at least three days to explore the region's key attractions, such as downtown Detroit and the Henry Ford complex in Dearborn. Five days is preferable, especially if you plan to make a trip across the border to Windsor, Ontario, in Canada.

Just remember that Detroit is a big, unpredictable city, and crime can definitely be a concern here. Tourist areas, such as the waterfront and the Cultural Center, are well patrolled, but it's important to stay vigilant even in relatively safe areas. For added protection, always travel with someone else, hide your money and identification beneath your clothing, and leave valuable jewelry back at home. It's also helpful to know the location of a few different police stations, just in case.

For more information about Detroit and its suburbs, consult the **Detroit Metro Convention & Visitors Bureau** (211 W. Fort St., Ste. 1000, Detroit, 313/202-1800, www.visitdetroit.com, 9am-5pm Mon.-Fri.) or **Travel Michigan** (Michigan Economic Development Corporation, 300 N. Washington Sq., Lansing, 888/784-7328, www.michigan.org).

HISTORY

Few think of Detroit as an old city. But it is, in fact, one of the Midwest's oldest, founded in 1701 by Antoine de la Mothe Cadillac (born Antoine Laumet) for King Louis XIV of France.

Early Detroit was alternately ruled by the British and the French. In 1763, Pontiac, the Ottawa war chief, ordered an attack on British posts all over Michigan. Tired of the abuse suffered by the British army, Pontiac united the many Indian nations living around Detroit in a determined effort to capture the fort and restore French rule. Chiefs of the Ottawa, Huron, Potawatomi, and Chippewa tribes attended a secret war council. According to legend, however, a squaw tipped off the British, and Pontiac's men were met by a waiting British army. Rebuffed and defeated, Pontiac was later assassinated in 1769. Today, Pontiac's Rebellion is still regarded as one of the most formidable Native American uprisings in American history.

In 1783, Britain yielded the area to the United States in the Treaty of Paris. Local tribes, however, disputed the U.S. claim, so it wasn't until 1796 that Detroit finally unfurled the stars and stripes. The city fell again during the War of 1812 but was recaptured by the Americans a year later. Despite discouraging reports from initial settlers, people continued to pour in from the east. Between 1830 and 1860,

the population doubled with every decade, and the city became best known as a nucleus of beer brewing and stove making.

By the turn of the 20th century, the auto industry had changed everything, making Detroit the fifth-largest U.S. city. The state's first self-propelled vehicle was likely a steam-powered car built by John and Thomas Clegg of Memphis, Michigan, in 1884. Later, Ransom Olds of Lansing developed a gasoline-powered auto and founded the Olds Motor Vehicle Company. In 1896, Charles C. King, an engineer and auto designer, drove the first car through the streets of Detroit; in the same year, Henry Ford tested his Quadricycle, which chugged along fairly well, despite no brakes and no reverse gear.

It was Ford and his later perfection of the assembly line that changed the face of the city—and America—seemingly overnight. Between 1905 and 1924, thousands of immigrants poured in from all over the world, attracted by Henry Ford's then-unheard-of wage of $5 per day. By 1917, 23 companies in Detroit and its suburbs were busy assembling vehicles for an ever-eager public. The Motor City had arrived.

By the 1930s and 1940s, Detroit was the place to be. Lively and full of energy, it was home to after-hours bars known as "blind pigs" (that is, police—"pigs"—turned a "blind eye" to Prohibition-era hideouts that served liquor) and "black and tan" clubs where people of all races mingled. But things began to sour after World War II. As in other U.S. cities, the middle class began to head for the suburbs. Bigger and better freeways took people farther and farther away from the heart of the city, leaving behind vacant storefronts, vacant houses, empty streets, and empty lives too soon filled by poverty and crime.

The 1960s were difficult years. One bright spot was the birth of the Motown Sound, which began in the tiny basement studio of Berry Gordy Jr. Like the city, Motown had a hard-driving beat, and it quickly took over airwaves across the country. Detroit became known for producing more than cars, with

HAUNTED DETROIT

America's major cities all have their share of tragic histories, ranging from notorious murders to massive flu epidemics to calamitous fires. Such incidents have often inspired the belief that some buildings, cemeteries, and other historic places are haunted by the spirits of long-ago victims. Detroit is no exception. Founded well over three centuries ago, the Motor City has certainly witnessed a plethora of terrible incidents, from violent crimes to deadly race riots, so it may come as no surprise that it, too, has its share of haunted locales. If you enjoy visiting such places, here are nine of the most popular in and around the city:

· **Fair Lane:** Completed in 1914, Henry Ford's grand estate Fair Lane (1 Fair Lane Dr., Dearborn, 313/884-4222, www.henryfordestate.org) encompasses more than 1,300 acres, at the center of which lies an impressive mansion that served as the home of Henry and Clara Ford from 1915 until 1950. Although most visitors come to stroll amid the well-landscaped grounds and tour the well-appointed rooms of the main house, others are hoping to catch a glimpse of the former butler, whose spirit supposedly continues to clean, fix, and straighten the rooms as he once did in life.

· **Fort Shelby Hotel:** In 1927, famed architect Albert Kahn erected a 21-story tower beside the 10-story structure that had been built on the corner of Lafayette Boulevard and 1st Street in 1916. Together, the two buildings comprised the Fort Shelby Hotel, whose fortunes rose and fell with those of Detroit. Following an extensive renovation mid-2007-late 2008, the buildings reopened as a DoubleTree Suites by Hilton Hotel (525 W. Lafayette Blvd., 313/963-5600, http://doubletree3.hilton.com) and the Fort Shelby Tower Apartments (527 W. Lafayette Blvd., 313/962-1010, www.fortshelby.com), but no matter how fancy it might look these days, the former Fort Shelby Hotel hasn't quite escaped its rocky history. Some visitors, after all, still claim to have seen the loitering ghost of a drunken homeless man who allegedly drowned in the once-flooded basement.

· **Historic Elmwood Cemetery:** Established in 1846, the 86-acre Historic Elmwood Cemetery (1200 Elmwood Ave., 313/567-3453, www.elmwoodhistoriccemetery.org) is the oldest continuously operating, nondenominational cemetery in Michigan. It's also the site of the Battle of Bloody Run, an ambush by Chief Pontiac's army on British soldiers, supposedly making it one of the city's best ghost-hunting locations.

· **Historic Fort Wayne:** While Historic Fort Wayne (6325 W. Jefferson Ave., 313/833-1805 or 810/853-8573, www.hauntedfortwaynedetroit.com), which was constructed in 1845 on the banks of the Detroit River, never actually endured a battle, the crumbling structure certainly still has a curious history. After all, it served as a major staging area for American soldiers during the Civil War and both World Wars, and it also housed

"Hitsville U.S.A." churning out rhythmic top-10 tunes by artists such as Marvin Gaye, Stevie Wonder, the Supremes, and Smokey Robinson and the Miracles.

The late 1960s brought massive unrest to the country and the worst race riot in Detroit's history. In 1967, Detroit was the site of one of 59 racial "disturbances" around the country, a tragedy in which more than 43 people were killed. The nightly news in cities throughout the world showed a Detroit in flames, leaving a lasting impression on the country and a deep scar on the city's psyche.

The riots touched off an even greater exodus, the infamous "white flight" that left Detroit with a black majority in less than five years. By the 1970s, downtown had become a virtual desert after business hours. Controversial mayor Coleman Young, who ruled the city for two decades, once said you could shoot a displaced people during both the Great Depression and the 12th Street race riots of 1967. Over the years, visitors have reported ghostly sightings and other unfathomable occurrences on the fort's grounds.

· **The Majestic:** One of Detroit's finest entertainment centers, The Majestic (4140 Woodward Ave., 313/833-9700, www.majesticdetroit.com) consists of The Majestic Theatre, a spacious concert hall opened in 1915; The Majestic Stick, a smaller but equally well-respected live music venue; the Majestic Café, a well-regarded restaurant; and The Garden Bowl, a 16-lane bowling alley that's been active for a century. Supposedly, the complex is haunted by the ghost of Harry Houdini, who gave one of his final performances at The Majestic in 1926.

· **Masonic Temple:** Constructed in 1912 by George D. Mason, Detroit's grand Masonic Temple (500 Temple Ave., 313/832-7100, www.themasonic.com) is the largest in the world, boasting more than 1,000 rooms, not to mention a variety of secret staircases and hidden passages. Sadly, Mason spent so much money on the building's construction that he eventually went bankrupt, lost his wife, and subsequently jumped to his death from the roof of the temple. Since then, security guards and visitors alike have experienced cold spots, bizarre shadows, and inexplicable pranks, heard slamming doors that can't be explained, and even spotted the ghost of Mason himself.

· **Saint Andrew's Hall:** Once home to the St. Andrew's Society of Detroit, a group of upper-class Scottish Americans, Saint Andrew's Hall (431 E. Congress St., 313/961-6358 or 313/961-8961, www.saintandrewsdetroit.com) is now one of Detroit's most popular live music venues. Curiously, rapper Eminem got his start in the basement of Saint Andrew's, known as The Shelter. Supposedly, the basement is also home to a ghost who enjoys chasing visitors from the hall; some say that it might be one of the former tenants, who, given his Scottish roots, might prefer bagpipes to rap music.

· **2 Way Inn:** Founded in 1876, the 2 Way Inn (17897 Mt. Elliott St., 313/891-4925, www.2wayinn.com) is considered the oldest bar in Detroit. Both past and present owners of the property claim to have seen the cowboy-like ghost of Philetus Norris, a Union spy, archaeologist, and Yellowstone National Park superintendent that once lived and worked here.

· **The Whitney:** Built in 1894 by lumber baron David Whitney, The Whitney (4421 Woodward Ave., 313/832-5700, www.thewhitney.com) is now one of the city's fanciest fine-dining restaurants. Apparently, it's also haunted by the tuxedo-clad ghost of Whitney himself. According to witnesses, he tends to operate the elevator on his own and can often be heard washing and stacking dishes in the kitchen.

cannon down Woodward in those years without hitting a soul.

Today, some 3.9 million people call Detroit and its suburbs home. They comprise myriad ethnic groups, with more than 880,000 African Americans in the metropolitan area and the country's largest population of Bulgarians, Chaldeans, Belgians, and Arabs (the most outside the Middle East).

While the city has courted big business almost since the first horseless carriage jounced awkwardly off the assembly line, Detroit has never been a major tourist destination. An active tourism bureau has attempted to change that, with frequent events for national and international media and an aggressive campaign to attract visitors from other parts of the country as well as Europe and Japan.

In 1996, the much-celebrated anniversary of the "birth" of the car turned an international spotlight on the city, with favorable reports in both the *New York Times* and *USA Today.* Detroit responded with a centennial bash and invited the entire world. In 2001, the city celebrated its third century with exhibitions, events, and a month-long riverfront party with visits that included both tall ships and the Temptations. Stevie Wonder led the homecoming concert, which attracted approximately one million people (ironically, more than the city's current population).

While city boosters don't expect flashy events such as these to erase the memories of Detroit in flames during the 1967 riots, they hope that they'll help to heal the wounds that have too long plagued the city—and perhaps ameliorate more recent troubles, such as Mayor Kwame Kilpatrick's 2008 resignation and subsequent felony conviction for obstruction of justice or, for that matter, the Michigan governor's 2013 declaration of a financial emergency for the city of Detroit.

Sights

ON THE WATERFRONT

Motown's earliest history was made on its waterfront, so a tour is a fitting start to any exploration of the city.

Hart Plaza

If it's a sunny day (regardless of the season), stroll the boardwalk near Hart Plaza and watch for one of the thousands of hulking freighters that traverse the Detroit River annually. Once, the waterfront, with its active port, was the city's livelihood. During the 20th century, however, Detroit turned its back on its former front door, choosing to erect faceless factories and anonymous office towers along its riverbanks instead of the more gracious green spaces popular during the previous century. Luckily, recent efforts have strived to correct the mistake: When completed, the **Detroit Riverfront** (www.detroitriverfront.org) will comprise a new harbor, a network of biking and jogging trails, and over five miles of public parks and plazas, linked by a continuous riverwalk.

For now, strollers can enjoy a three-mile stretch of the riverwalk and places like the expanded William G. Milliken State Park and the 14-acre Hart Plaza, a popular venue for summertime festivals and concerts. Opened in 1975 and named after the late U.S. Senator Philip Hart, Hart Plaza is the site of the breathtaking **Horace E. Dodge Fountain,** which was designed in 1978 by Isamu Noguchi. This impressive fountain propels more than one million gallons of water per hour into the air via more than 300 streaming nozzles and jets. Another key landmark in Hart Plaza is the **Gateway to Freedom International Memorial to the Underground Railroad,** which was sculpted by Ed Dwight and dedicated in October 2001—in honor of both Detroit's tricentennial and its pivotal role as a 19th-century gateway for thousands of African American slaves seeking freedom in nearby Canada.

◖ GM Renaissance Center

Next to Hart Plaza is the gleaming **GM Renaissance Center** (100 Renaissance Center, 313/567-3126, www.gmrencen.com), known to Detroiters as Ren Cen. Soaring high into the sky, this fortress-like, 73-story hotel/office/retail complex dominates the Detroit skyline, with seven steel towers containing more than 5.5 million square feet of space, including a 1,300-room Marriott hotel, two foreign consulates, a fitness center, a four-screen movie theater, and dozens of restaurants and stores.

Of course, the road to the Ren Cen's present incarnation was rather rocky at best. The project was originally proposed by Henry Ford II, partially as a response to the 1967 riots. Ford—always a powerful name in Detroit—used his considerable influence to convince friends and foes alike to invest in the riverside

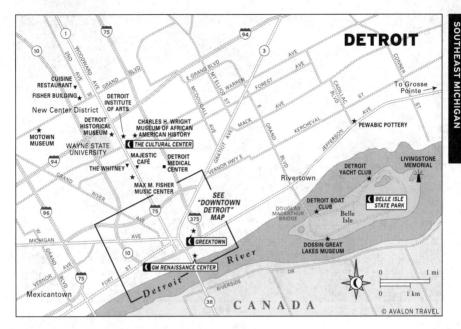

complex. With big-name retailers such as Gucci and Cartier, it was intended to draw suburbanites back to downtown Detroit. But it didn't work. The Ren Cen was a huge white elephant from the moment it opened in 1977. Designed by John Portman, best known for building hotel atriums, it was a confusing maze of circles and elevators that ultimately led nowhere. By 1983, many of the original retailers had pulled out and most of the investors had defaulted on their loans.

The center received a much-needed facelift and helpful new directional signs in the mid-1980s, but it never became the city's much-heralded savior. Through the 1980s and much of the 1990s, the Ren Cen was supported by various companies—including Ford, ANR Pipeline, and others—some of which have kept offices here. In 1996, however, it received a huge shot in the arm with General Motors' announcement that it had purchased the landmark to use as its new world headquarters. In a major boost for the city, GM moved the majority of its workers into the Ren Cen in 1999. A

major internal reorganization followed, leaving the space a bit less confusing.

The Ren Cen is still one of the largest privately financed developments in U.S. history, with more than $380 million contributed by private investors. Representing a huge investment in the city's future, it is worth seeing on that basis alone. Once inside, you'll need a map to navigate. Otherwise, you can take a free one-hour tour (313/568-5624, noon and 2pm Mon.-Fri.) through this Detroit landmark. Tours, which are offered on a first-come, first-served basis, depart from the Pure Detroit store, situated on Level 1 of Tower 400, and feature sights like a world map carved in granite, a vintage auto collection, the world's tallest vertical glass sculpture, a tropical atrium overlooking the Detroit River, and breathtaking views of the Detroit and Windsor skylines.

◖ Belle Isle State Park

At one time, 30 million tons of cargo were transported along the Detroit River, linking the city with more than 200 overseas ports.

© SNEHIT/123RF.COM

Anna Scripps Whitcomb Conservatory, Belle Isle State Park

Nowadays, you can still feel the water's tug on Belle Isle, accessible via the Douglas MacArthur Bridge at East Jefferson Avenue and East Grand Boulevard. This 982-acre, 2.5-mile-long urban sanctuary, stranded a half mile out in the river, between Detroit and Windsor, Ontario, has been a public park since 1879, when the city purchased it for a now paltry $200,000 from the heirs of a wealthy local family.

Named after the then-governor's daughter, Isabelle Cass, it was designed in 1883 by Frederick Law Olmsted, the famous landscape architect known for his work on New York's Central Park. One of the city's most underrated (and often neglected) jewels, Belle Isle gets a little rowdy on summer weekends, when teenagers from surrounding neighborhoods cruise the narrow streets and pathways looking for action. Although patrolled by both mounted police and squad cars, it's not a safe place to be at night.

On weekdays, however, it's peaceful, especially off-season. Belle Isle is a haven for bird-watchers and for families who flock here to fish from the north and south piers, relax on Detroit's only swimming beach, and tour the vintage glass **Anna Scripps Whitcomb Conservatory** (313/821-5428, 10am-5pm Wed.-Sun., free), which features collections of ferns, orchids, cacti, and other plants. Kids will especially appreciate the small playground, the giant slide ($1 pp), the **Belle Isle Nature Zoo** (313/852-4056, 10am-5pm Wed.-Sun. May-Nov., 10am-4pm Wed.-Sun. Dec.-Apr., free), which oversees a one-acre deer enclosure, and the intriguing **Dossin Great Lakes Museum** (100 Strand Dr., 313/833-5538, www.detroithistorical.org, 11am-4pm Sat.-Sun., free), which traces the development of Great Lakes-area shipping from sailing vessels to modern freighters, many of which can still be seen from the riverfront.

Other visitors to Belle Isle come to jog, circle the island by bike, practice golf on the driving range and various greens, or just set up a picnic lunch under one of the gazebos and watch passing freighters. Boating enthusiasts, meanwhile, can wander around the

80-foot-tall marble **Livingstone Memorial Lighthouse,** which operated from 1882 to 1930, or check out the pleasure craft docked at the 1922 **Detroit Yacht Club.** Other curious historic structures include the 1908 **Belle Isle Casino,** the 1923 **James Scott Memorial Fountain,** the 1941 **International Peace Memorial,** and numerous other monuments. Admission to the island is free, though there has been an ongoing debate about charging a nominal admission to help defray maintenance costs.

It isn't the island's first controversy. Native Americans called Belle Isle "Rattlesnake Island" because of the number of snakes. Later, hogs were brought in by 18th-century settlers to destroy the rattlers, giving rise to the name Isle au Cochon ("Hog Island" in French) until 1845, when it was rechristened Belle Isle. Throughout its long history, the island has been used both as a dueling ground and as a place of quarantine for troops, most recently during the cholera epidemic of 1932. Since the early 1970s, four different groups—the Friends of Belle Isle, the Belle Isle Botanical Society, the Belle Isle Women's Committee, and the Friends of the Belle Isle Aquarium—have strived to protect the island, and in 2009, they joined forces to form the **Belle Isle Conservancy** (8109 E. Jefferson Ave., 313/331-7760, www. belleisleconservancy.org). In late 2013, its advocates went a step further by making it an official state park.

Pewabic Pottery

On Jefferson Avenue, not far from Belle Isle, is another oasis, **Pewabic Pottery** (10125 E. Jefferson Ave., 313/626-2000, www.pewabic.org, 10am-4pm Mon.-Fri.). Founded by Mary Chase Perry Stratton in 1903, this arts-and-crafts pottery is housed within a picturesque Tudor Revival building, now a National Historic Landmark. Best known for their innovative and iridescent glazes, shown to great advantage in the tiles commissioned for many of the city's civic and residential structures, Pewabic tiles can be found in the stunning 1929 art deco Guardian Building, several

downtown People Mover stations, and the Shedd Aquarium in Chicago.

Now a nonprofit ceramic arts center and a living museum, Pewabic continues to produce the handcrafted vessels and architectural tiles that brought it initial fame. Visitors peer into huge, fiery kilns on a self-guided tour during business hours. A landmark of Detroit's arts community, the pottery is a pilgrimage for potters and ceramic artists from around the country as well as the site of popular classes, workshops, and lectures for all ages. But don't look for the secret to the pottery's lustrous glaze—Stratton took it to the grave, leaving her successors to carry on with only an approximation of the original formula.

Riverboat Tours

For a terrific view of Detroit's skyline, consider taking a ride on the Detroit River, the world's busiest international waterway. **Diamond Jack's River Tours** (313/843-9376, www. diamondjack.com, tours 1pm and 3:30pm Thurs.-Sun., $17 adults, $15 seniors over 60, $13 children 6-16, children under 6 free) offers two-hour narrated riverboat cruises June-August. There are two departure points for these informative tours: Detroit's Rivard Plaza and Wyandotte's Bishop Park. Be advised, however, that tours are available on a first-come, first-served basis; in other words, individual reservations are not accepted, so it's prudent to arrive at least 30 minutes, if not an hour, before departure time.

DOWNTOWN DETROIT

Woodward Avenue marks the entrance to the city's official downtown business district. This area may be quiet after business hours, but during the day, it hops with office workers who toil in the banks, insurance companies, and other corporations.

The first stop on any architectural tour is the **Wayne County Building** (600 Randolph St.) on the east end of Cadillac Square, an early example of the Roman Baroque Revival style in Michigan. Built from 1897 to 1902, it's one of the oldest buildings in the city. Look up to see its ornamental cornices—they depict General "Mad" Anthony Wayne conferring with the Indians. (General Wayne, incidentally, served during the Revolutionary War and negotiated a treaty that claimed all the lands between the Ohio and Mississippi Rivers for the United States.) Not surprisingly, it was listed on the National Register of Historic Places in 1975.

History buffs may also appreciate the art deco **Guardian Building** (500 Griswold St., www.guardianbuilding.com), a 40-story, Aztec-inspired structure that has been designated a National Historic Landmark. Friendly guards in the 1929 superstructure are usually pleased to share tidbits about the breathtaking building or point you in the right direction for a self-guided tour of its Pewabic-accented interior.

Meanwhile, the buildings of Woodward Avenue cast a long shadow over **Harmonie Park** (www.harmoniepark.com), the center of an area once known as Paradise Valley, an impoverished African American neighborhood that was also a hotbed of jazz and other artistic activity from the 1920s to the 1950s. If Woodward's desolation threatens to overwhelm you, this elegant enclave—nestled between Grand Circus Park, Randolph Street, and Gratiot Avenue—will restore your hope in the city's future. New energy has transformed a formerly deserted area into the city's hottest nightspot. Much of the credit goes to local architectural firm Schervish Vogel Merz, who believed in the area long before anyone else saw a future in its warehouse-style buildings and vintage storefronts. Today, Harmonie Park is surrounded by pubs, galleries, and airy artists' lofts.

Theater District

Not far from Harmonie Park lies the official entrance to Detroit's Theater District. Once the city's most exclusive address, the neighborhood known as Brush Park had deteriorated almost to the point of no return before local boy Mike Ilitch—owner of the nationwide Little Caesars Pizza chain as well as the Detroit Tigers baseball and Detroit Red Wings hockey teams—stepped in and bought the aging **Fox Theatre** (2211 Woodward Ave., 313/471-3200 or 313/471-6611, www.olympiaentertainment.com) in 1988.

What followed was a painstaking and often slow $8 million restoration that eventually returned the gaudy yet glamorous structure to its original glory. The 5,048-seat Fox is truly a marvel of 1920s architecture. Built in 1928 by William Fox, it was designed in the style of an Arabian tent. The exotic Thai-Byzantine style borrows motifs from a range of cultures, including Persian, Burmese, Indian, Thai, and Chinese. There are gold-leafed, hand-stenciled walls, marble-finish pillars, gold-tusked elephants, winged lions, a sunburst ceiling, and dreamlike decorative figures throughout. The lobby is six stories high, with 300,000 sparkling glass jewels, loads of brass, and a 13-foot, two-ton stained-glass chandelier. No wonder it was listed on the National Register of Historic Places in 1985 and, following the successful restoration, designated a National Historic Landmark in 1989.

Today, the Fox is one of the nation's most successful theater operations, with almost nightly presentations, including touring Broadway musicals, big-name concerts, restored film epics, and other special events. You can't miss the 125-foot multicolored neon marquee, which stretches to the 10th floor of the Fox office building. And here's a bit of trivia: During the 1920s, the Fox was the first theater in the United States to sell candy on-site.

Spurred by the resounding success of the Fox, other theaters soon followed. One contrast to the cavernous Fox is the intimate **Gem & Century Theatres** (333 Madison Ave., 313/963-9800, www.gemtheatre.com), a joint cabaret-style venue with 450 seats. Founded in 1903 by a women's group hoping to have an "uplifting influence on the community," the Gem degenerated into a burlesque and adult movie theater before ultimately closing in 1978. Soon afterward, foresighted businessman Chuck Forbes, owner of most of the city's vintage theaters, restored it as a complement to the Fox and a stop for national comedy acts, small plays, and musical revues. It reopened in

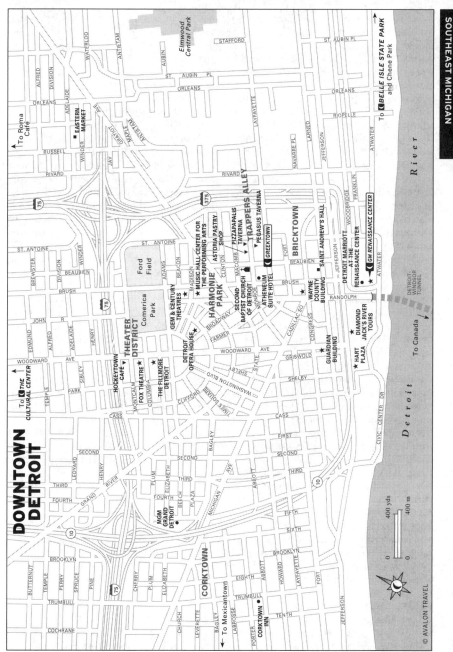

DOWNTOWN DETROIT

Elmwood Central Park

◄ BELLE ISLE STATE PARK and Chene Park

Detroit River

To Roma Café →

■ EASTERN MARKET

◄ To Canada

To THE CULTURAL CENTER ◄

Ford Field

Comerica Park

★ MUSIC HALL CENTER FOR THE PERFORMING ARTS

ASTORIA PASTRY SHOP

PIZZAPAPALIS TAVERNA

PEGASUS TAVERNA

TRAPPERS ALLEY

◄ GREEKTOWN

BRICKTOWN

SAINT ANDREW'S HALL ■

Detroit Marriott at the Renaissance Center

◄ GM RENAISSANCE CENTER

HARMONIE PARK

SECOND BAPTIST CHURCH OF DETROIT

ATHENEUM SUITE HOTEL

WAYNE COUNTY BUILDING

THEATER DISTRICT

GEM & CENTURY THEATRES ★

HOCKEYTOWN CAFÉ ▼

MONTCALM

FOX THEATRE ★

THE FILLMORE DETROIT ★

DETROIT OPERA HOUSE ★

DIAMOND JACK'S RIVER TOURS ★

GUARDIAN BUILDING

★ HART PLAZA

DETROIT WINDSOR TUNNEL

To Canada →

MGM GRAND DETROIT

CORKTOWN

To Mexicantown →

CORKTOWN INN ●

0   400 yds
0   400 m

© AVALON TRAVEL

1991. Threatened by the new Comerica Park ballpark—home to the Detroit Tigers—it was moved to its present location in 1997. As the world's heaviest building ever to be moved on wheels, it even made the pages of *Guinness World Records.*

Luciano Pavarotti and Dame Joan Sutherland were just a few of the big names who jetted into Motown in 1996 to attend the opening of the restored **Detroit Opera House** (1526 Broadway St., 313/237-7464, www.michiganopera.org). Designed in 1922 by C. Howard Crane as a vaudeville stage, the 7,000-square-foot theater served as a parking garage for most of the 1970s. David Di Chiera, the former university professor who founded the Michigan Opera Theatre in 1971 as a way to bring opera to kids, did the seemingly impossible when he raised $36 million for the opera's new 2,700-seat home. Today, it acts as an important cultural resource, luring Broadway musicals as well as opera and ballet productions.

Other area theaters include **The Fillmore Detroit** (2115 Woodward Ave., 313/961-5451, www.thefillmoredetroit.com), a live music venue built in 1925 as the State Theatre, and the **Music Hall Center for the Performing Arts** (350 Madison St., 313/887-8500, www.musichall.org), built in 1928 by the widow of auto baron John Dodge for the production of "legitimate" theatrical productions. Its stage has been graced by luminaries such as Lucille Ball, W. C. Fields, Martha Graham, Ella Fitzgerald, Lillian Hellman, and others. Music lovers, meanwhile, flock to the **Max M. Fisher Music Center** (3711 Woodward Ave., 313/576-5100 or 313/576-5111, www.dso.org), which, since 2003, has housed The Music Box, a 450-seat performance hall, as well as the acoustically perfect Orchestra Hall, which was built in 1919 and has long been home to the acclaimed Detroit Symphony Orchestra.

◖ Greektown

Once a pioneer farm and now the city's best-known ethnic area, **Greektown** (www.greektowndetroit.org) has long been a bright spot

downtown and one of the few districts that jump after midnight. Despite the unfortunate failure of the Trappers Alley shopping and entertainment complex that once thrived here, this restored stretch of Monroe Street still attracts both natives and visitors. (It also attracts parking enforcement officers, so if you park at one of the plentiful metered spots around Monroe, be sure to bring plenty of change.)

At the core of it all is a Greek neighborhood that dates back to 1915. Although most of the original residents have moved to the suburbs and the majority of restaurants and bakeries have gone upscale, you'll still find a few coffeehouses where old-timers gather to drink strong coffee or sip sweet retsina and play cards. One original grocery remains: Open the rusty screen door of the **Athens Grocery & Bakery Co.** (527 Monroe St., 313/961-1149, 9:30am-midnight Mon.-Thurs. and Sun., 9:30am-2am Fri., 10am-2am Sat.), and you'll walk past windows full of neatly arranged loaves of bread, sinfully sweet Greek pastries, and shiny tins of pungent imported olives.

Other highlights include two of Detroit's most notable churches. **Old St. Mary's Church** (646 Monroe St., 313/961-8711, www.oldstmarysdetroit.com), one of the city's most beautiful Roman Catholic structures, dates to 1841, serves as Detroit's third-oldest Catholic parish, and is, curiously, the city's first German church. Meanwhile, the **Second Baptist Church of Detroit** (441 Monroe St., 313/961-0920, www.secondbaptistdetroit.org, free) was established in 1836 by several former slaves who had left the First Baptist Church due to discrimination against African Americans. Once a stop on the Underground Railroad, Second Baptist also established the first school for black children, and its congregation has included the country's first black schoolteacher, several presidents of the Detroit NAACP, and the first African American to receive the Nobel Peace Prize.

◖ The Cultural Center

Head north along Woodward Avenue from downtown, and you'll run right into the

Cultural Center, part of **Midtown Detroit** (www.detroitmidtown.com). Bordered by bustling **Wayne State University** to the west and the **Detroit Medical Center** to the east, this is where you'll find a plethora of art galleries, performance venues, shops, and restaurants, plus most of the city's art and civic museums. It's also home to the **International Institute of Metropolitan Detroit** (111 E. Kirby St., 313/871-8600, www.iimd.org), which, besides offering citizenship classes and other educational programs, presents the inexpensive International Cafe, the longstanding International Festival in early October, and the Ethel Averbach International Doll Collection, supposedly the world's largest collection of dolls dressed in native costumes. Roughly a block away from the International Institute, you'll also encounter the main branch of the **Detroit Public Library** (5201 Woodward Ave., 313/481-1300, www.detroit.lib.mi.us, noon-8pm Tues.-Wed., 10am-6pm Thurs.-Sat.), which opened in 1921 and now features a variety of engrossing collections, such as the Burton Historical Collection, which contains thousands of volumes, pamphlets, and papers that shed some light on the histories of Detroit and Michigan from the 1600s to the present, and the equally comprehensive E. Azalia Hackley Collection of African Americans in the Performing Arts, which encompasses rare books, manuscripts, photographs, recordings, and sheet music that explore everything from early 19th-century plantation life in the American South to the Motown Recording Company.

Here, in the Cultural Center, you can also wander the "Streets of Old Detroit" (or at least an idealized version of them) in the basement of the **Detroit Historical Museum** (5401 Woodward Ave., 313/833-1805, www.detroithistorical.org, 9:30am-4pm Tues.-Fri., 10am-5pm Sat.-Sun., free). You'll trudge along irregular cobblestones that once lined city streets past re-creations of barber shops, grocery stores, and other vintage businesses. The display, which opened in 1951 and has since been updated, traces several periods of Detroit history.

The permanent exhibit "Frontiers to Factories" traces the city's history from a trading post to an industrial giant, with a walk-in diorama from the 1750s, a railway station, and a mock turn-of-the-20th-century exposition. Other highlights of the collection include the Glancy Train display, one of the world's largest; special exhibits about Detroit's leaders, symbols, and entertainment venues; and an exhibition simply named "America's Motor City," which traces the history of the car, the city, and the people who changed the world when they came to work here. The exhibit's highlight is the "body drop," a segment of a 1953 assembly line in which the outer shell of a later-model Cadillac is lowered from the ceiling onto an engine body set up on an eye-level platform. It was taken from the assembly line at the now-demolished Clark Street Cadillac plant. Following an extensive renovation and the 2012 reopening, visitors can also experience an expanded "Doorway to Freedom: Detroit and the Underground Railroad" exhibit as well as five new permanent exhibitions: the "Gallery of Innovation," the "Allesee Gallery of Culture," the "Kid Rock Music Lab," "Legends Plaza," and "Detroit: The Arsenal of Democracy."

Detroit has always been a blue-collar town, yet city founders amassed enough green during the heyday of the auto industry to fund what eventually became one of the country's finest art museums. The **Detroit Institute of Arts** (DIA, 5200 Woodward Ave., 313/833-7900, www.dia.org, 9am-4pm Tues.-Thurs., 9am-10pm Fri., 10am-5pm Sat.-Sun., $8 adults, $6 seniors, $5 college students, $4 children 6-17, children under 6 and area residents free) attracts more than 500,000 visitors each year. The sometimes-confusing 100-plus galleries contain some of the greatest art treasures of the world, including works by Van Gogh, Rodin, Rembrandt, Bruegel, and other masters.

The museum strives to present an encyclopedic collection, with a multicultural scope that traces creativity in all of its forms, from prehistory through the present. Important collections include the French Impressionist, Italian (the largest outside Italy), German Expressionist, African, Asian, Native American, and 20th-century. It's worth hunting for the museum's generally accepted best works, including Rodin's pensive masterpiece, *The Thinker;* Bruegel's *The Wedding Dance* (look closely and you may see some remnants of paint on the bulging codpieces; they were once painted over); Van Eyck's tiny treasure, *Saint Jerome in His Study;* and Rembrandt's enlightened *The Visitation.*

While the building may seem to be full of art made by and for the ruling class, the city's workers have the last laugh in the breathtaking *Detroit Industry* frescoes. Mexican muralist Diego Rivera captured the droning monotony of the assembly line in 27 huge panels surrounding the museum's central courtyard. Rivera spent nine months in Detroit from 1932 to 1933 before unveiling the series to great controversy. A visionary Edsel Ford stood up to virulent criticism of the Mexican socialist's frescoes, which were damning in their innate criticism of capitalism. Many city leaders wanted the walls whitewashed as soon as the scaffolding came down, but Ford stood firm, defending the murals, which, unlike another series in New York's Rockefeller Center, were saved.

Relax and rest your feet with a cup of java or something stronger in the **Kresge Court** (11am-3pm Tues.-Thurs., 11am-9pm Fri., 11am-4pm Sat.-Sun.), a soaring green and light-filled space modeled after Florence's Bargello Palace, or enjoy soups, salads, sandwiches, and other treats in **CaféDIA** (11:30am-2:30pm Tues.-Thurs., 11:30am-2:30pm and 4pm-9pm Fri., 11:30am-3pm Sat.-Sun.). If you're visiting on a weekend, stick around long enough to take in a movie at the museum's acclaimed 1,150-seat **Detroit Film Theatre** (313/833-3237 or 313/833-4005), which offers important premieres by new and established directors and is one of the few venues in the city to show restored, rarely seen classics in their correct aspect ratios. *Variety* called it "the best buy for cineastes in America."

Art lovers will also enjoy the **Museum of**

Contemporary Art Detroit (MOCAD, 4454 Woodward Ave., 313/832-6622, www.moca-detroit.org, 11am-5pm Wed. and Sat.-Sun., 11am-8pm Thurs.-Fri., $5 adults, students and children under 12 free), a cavernous museum that, in addition to presenting fascinating exhibitions, offers a unique gift shop, a small café, and assorted lectures, concerts, films, and literary readings. Another highlight of the city's Cultural Center is the **Michigan Science Center** (5020 John R St., 313/577-8400, www.mi-sci.org, 9am-3pm Wed.-Fri., 10am-6pm Sat., noon-6pm Sun., $13-24 adults, $10-20 children 2-12, children under 2 free), which reopened to the public in July 2001. The center now includes a digital planetarium, two theaters, one science stage, the state's only IMAX dome theater, and areas devoted to motion, life sciences, matter, energy, waves, and vibration.

History buffs, meanwhile, may relish a chance to visit the **Charles H. Wright Museum of African American History** (315 E. Warren Ave., 313/494-5800, www.thewright.org, 9am-5pm Tues.-Sat., 1pm-5pm Sun., $8 adults, $5 seniors 62 and over and children 3-12, children under 3 free), which hosts the annual African World Festival and serves as the world's largest institution devoted to exploring the African American experience. Meanwhile, Wayne State University's recently renamed **Gordon L. Grosscup Museum of Anthropology** (4841 Cass Ave., Old Main, 1st Fl., 313/577-2598, http://clasweb.clas.wayne.edu/anthromuseum, 10am-4pm Mon.-Thurs., 10am-2pm Fri., free), which was established in 1958, houses both permanent and temporary exhibits, many of which feature artifacts from various sites throughout Detroit, from Fort Wayne to Belle Isle to the GM Renaissance Center.

Another intriguing site is the **First Congregational Living Museum** (33 E. Forest Ave., 313/831-4080, www.friendsoffirst.com, 9am-5pm daily, free), which is housed within the First Congregational Church of Detroit and its Albert Kahn-designed Angels' Wing Community House. Visitors to the church may appreciate strolling among the ornate religious paintings that line the walls of the 120-year-old sanctuary; just be advised that this is an active church, which means that it's best to visit on weekday afternoons (2pm-4pm Tues.-Fri.). While here, you may also be able to experience the "Underground Railroad Flight to Freedom Tour" (hours vary Tues.-Sat., $12 adults, $10 children 3-17, $8 seniors 62 and over, children under 3 free), a reenactment during which participants are shackled and led to liberation by a "conductor." Because this experience involves volunteer actors, however, the church staff requires a minimum of 20 participants for each tour.

For a different aspect of Detroit's history, head to the **Hellenic Museum of Michigan** (67 E. Kirby St., 313/871-4100, www.hellenicmi.org, noon-4pm Sat., donation suggested), which opened in 2010 in the hopes of becoming a modern-day version of the "Mouseion" (House of the Muses) of ancient Alexandria. Although still in its early stages, the museum will eventually, through the use of artifacts, photographs, oral histories, and personal documents, present the numerous artistic and intellectual achievements of Hellenic culture from ancient times to the present. It also aims to chronicle the considerable struggles, triumphs, and contributions of the Greek immigrants that settled throughout Michigan, including Detroit. During the summer months, the museum presents traditional Greek music, dancing, and cuisine during their weekly Kefi Nights, which usually take place on Thursday (6pm-10pm).

Even children will appreciate the Cultural Center, which, besides the fascinating Michigan Science Center, is home to the **Detroit Children's Museum** (6134 2nd Ave., 313/873-8100), the country's third-oldest children's museum. Founded in 1917, this kid-friendly attraction is temporarily closed to the public due to lack of funding, and only open to Detroit-area public schools.

New Center

Situated about a mile north of the Cultural Center, the commercial district known as **New Center** (www.newcenterplace.com), which was named in part as an optimistic effort to replace the city's ailing downtown, was once best known for its most famous resident, General Motors. The twin towers of GM's corporate headquarters housed thousands of workers; for decades, its lavish 1st-floor showrooms were filled year-round with the latest models, hot off the drawing boards located in the upstairs offices.

Much to the chagrin of GM's employees and executives, the corporate headquarters were surrounded by a once-fine neighborhood that had become seedy and derelict. With the clout and bankroll to pull off what few other companies in the world could at the time, GM spent millions upon millions buying, rehabbing, and reselling the old homes in the surrounding neighborhood—renamed New Center. The idea was to spruce up the company's surroundings, draw its employees and other middle- and upper-income families back downtown, and, hopefully, spur more area redevelopment.

While the New Center neighborhood slowly began to improve, GM ended up leaving the

Detroit's New Center area

area anyway and moving downtown to the Ren Cen in 1999. Since then, the GM building, which has since been renamed Cadillac Place, has struggled to attract tenants. Among those who have moved in are local health care offices as well as various government agencies of Michigan.

Of the New Center's two main attractions, the **Fisher Building** (3011 W. Grand Blvd.) is perhaps the most interesting. Even if you're not an architecture fan, it's worth seeing for the dazzling ceiling mosaics alone. The Architectural League of New York recognized the Fisher Building as the world's most beautiful commercial structure shortly after it was built in 1928. Albert Kahn, one of the city's best-known architects, made lavish use of expensive materials, including 420 tons of bronze, marble, Minnesota granite, and 24-karat gold. Today, the building's 30-story central tower and two 11-story wings house the Fisher Theatre, shops, restaurants, and office space.

Dwarfed by the Fisher Building and Cadillac Place is the diminutive **Motown Museum** (2648 W. Grand Blvd., 313/875-2264, www.motown-museum.org, 10am-6pm Tues.-Sat. Sept.-June, 10am-6pm Mon.-Fri., 10am-8pm Sat. July-Aug., $10 adults, $8 seniors 62 or older and children 5-12, children under 5 free). Known to many across the country as "Hitsville U.S.A.," this is where the Motown Sound exploded from the now-legendary Studio A and soon had teenagers around the country "Dancin' in the Streets."

Berry Gordy Jr. bought the unremarkable two-story house in 1959 as a fledgling songwriter with a dream of managing singers. Today, the state historic site looks much as it would have in the early 1960s, with an office and tape library filled with reel-to-reel tape machines, company manuals, and newspaper clippings. The 2nd floor re-creates Gordy's 1959-1960 apartment, where he and his staff would spend nights packing records to ship to radio stations around the country. The museum's most prized display, however, is the original Studio A, where top tunes such as "Stop

in the Name of Love" and "My Girl" were recorded. Diana Ross and the Supremes, Smokey Robinson and the Miracles, Martha Reeves and the Vandellas, Gladys Knight and the Pips, Lionel Ritchie and the Commodores, The Temptations, the Four Tops, the Marvelettes, Marvin Gaye, Stevie Wonder, and the Jackson Five all recorded in this studio during their early careers. Other artifacts on display in the two museum buildings (at its zenith, the company owned seven buildings along West Grand Boulevard) include rare photos, gold records, flashy costumes, and similar memorabilia. Just be advised that the museum is closed on major holidays and that cameras and cell phones are not allowed inside.

Mexicantown

The smell of fresh tortillas baking at the **La Jalisciense Tortilla Factory** (2650 Bagley St., 313/237-0008, www.tortillamundo.com) leads hungry diners and curious visitors to Bagley Street, the main thoroughfare of the city's Mexican district. Located about five miles from downtown on the city's southwest side, the neighborhood is divided by I-75, so there's an eastern and western side, with shops, restaurants, and homes on both. Here's where you'll find colorful Mexican *mercados* and see elderly Mexican women, heads covered with an old-fashioned lace mantilla, praying with their rosaries in one of the historic churches, including **Ste. Anne de Detroit Catholic Church** (1000 Ste. Anne St., 313/496-1701, www.ste-anne.org, free), the city's oldest, founded in 1701. During the summer, the area hosts a popular outdoor market on Sunday where you can pick up fresh chili peppers and other spicy souvenirs.

The Mexican restaurants grouped along the streets around Bagley provide the area's main income and job base. Here, you'll find authentic Mexican cuisine, such as salt-rimmed margaritas, soft-shell tacos full of spicy meat and onions, and soft, flaky *sopaipillas* that rival the best south of the border. Queen of them all is the **Xochimilco Restaurant** (3409 Bagley St., 313/843-0179, 11am-2am daily, $4-14), where Mexican art and the eyes of God cover the walls, and where weekend waits can stretch to over an hour. Many flock to Xochimilco for the inexpensive lunch specials, though other fans of Mexican fare may prefer less-crowded competitors, such as the **Mexican Village Restaurant** (2600 Bagley St., 313/237-0333, www.mexicanvillagefood.com, 11am-10pm Sun.-Thurs., 11am-midnight Fri.-Sat., $5-21).

Entertainment and Events

NIGHTLIFE

When the sun goes down, the lights come on around the city. No matter what your style is, Detroit offers plenty of places where you can party and, more importantly, listen to good music, from alternative sounds at **Saint Andrew's Hall** (431 E. Congress St., 313/961-6358 or 313/961-8961, www.saintandrews-detroit.com, show times and ticket prices vary) to smooth jazz at the longstanding **Baker's Keyboard Lounge** (20510 Livernois Ave., 313/345-6300, www.theofficialbakerskeyboardlounge.com, 11am-midnight Tues.-Thurs., 11am-2am Fri., 4pm-2am Sat., 1pm-midnight Sun.), which claims to be the world's oldest jazz club. Another popular hangout is **Flood's Bar & Grille** (731 St. Antoine St., 313/963-1090, www.floodsdetroit.com, 4pm-midnight Mon., 3pm-2am Tues.-Fri., 7pm-2am Sat.-Sun., $5-10 cover), which features jazz, R&B, sweet soul, or karaoke nightly.

CASINOS

In late 1996, city voters approved a controversial referendum permitting casino gambling within city limits. More than 15 years later, three casinos are now open—and remain controversial. Whether gambling is the struggling inner city's angel or devil is still being decided, not only at the craps tables but also in the hearts of residents.

For those who enjoy rolling the dice, options include **MGM Grand Detroit** (1777 3rd St., 877/888-2121, www.mgmgranddetroit.com), a flashy, art deco palace that draws its inspiration from the Hollywood of yesteryear and offers nearly 4,000 slot and video poker machines, roughly 100 table games, and a nonsmoking poker room. Beyond gaming activities, MGM Grand also features a full-service hotel, a sports pub, two Wolfgang Puck restaurants, a luxurious spa, four unique bars, a pulsating nightclub, and plenty of live entertainment. Motown in all its glory provides the theme for the locally owned **MotorCity Casino Hotel** (2901 Grand River Ave., 866/752-9622, www.motorcitycasino.com), housed in a former Wonder Bread warehouse and connected by skywalks to downtown restaurants and parking. In addition

MORE THAN MOTOWN

Detroit has always been a complex town. Its many facets have spawned many monikers – not the least of which honors its status as the birthplace of a groundbreaking musical style. But Motown legends like Martha Reeves, Diana Ross, Smokey Robinson, Mary Wells, Gladys Knight, and Stevie Wonder aren't the only musically oriented folks to have spent their formative years in and around Detroit. Southeastern Michigan has also nurtured a brood of well-known rock 'n' rollers and hip-hop stars, including:

- Sonny Bono
- Alice Cooper
- Eminem
- Glenn Frey
- Bill Haley
- Madonna
- Ted Nugent
- Iggy Pop
- Kid Rock
- Bob Seger

to a smoke-free poker room, 59 table games, and more than 2,900 slot and video poker machines, the MotorCity Casino encompasses a comfortable hotel, a relaxing spa, a roomy concert hall, and several dining options, from award-winning Iridescence to a delectable buffet. The **Greektown Casino-Hotel** (1200 St. Antoine St., 313/223-2999, www.greektown-casino.com), meanwhile, is the city's most spacious, with Las Vegas-style gaming and easy access to the city's liveliest neighborhood. As with its competitors, it, too, provides a stylish hotel, live entertainment, and various dining and nightlife options.

THE ARTS

Productions at the 5,048-seat **Fox Theatre** (2211 Woodward Ave., 313/471-3200 or 313/471-6611, www.olympiaentertainment. com, show times and ticket prices vary) include touring Broadway musicals, big-name concerts, restored film epics, and other special events. The tiny and jewel-like **Gem & Century Theatres** (333 Madison Ave., 313/963-9800, www.gemtheatre.com, show times and ticket prices vary) is a cabaret-style venue that has, since being relocated in the late 1990s, featured national comedy acts, small plays, and musical revues; today, it's a popular spot for weddings and other special events. The restored **Detroit Opera House** (1526 Broadway St., 313/237-7464, www.michiganopera.org, show times and ticket prices vary), home of the Michigan Opera Theatre, attracts full-scale productions of opera, ballet, and Broadway musicals.

Other area theaters include **The Fillmore Detroit** (2115 Woodward Ave., 313/961-5451, www.thefillmoredetroit.com, show times and ticket prices vary), a live music venue built in 1925 as the State Theatre; the **Music Hall Center for the Performing Arts** (350 Madison St., 313/887-8500, www.musichall.org, show times and ticket prices vary), which features contemporary ballet, live concerts, music festivals, and more; and the **Fisher Theatre** (3011 W. Grand Blvd., 313/879-5433 or 313/872-1000, www.broadwayindetroit.com), which opened as a movie and vaudeville house in

1928 and now features both modern and classic Broadway shows. For classical music, consider the **Max M. Fisher Music Center** (3711 Woodward Ave., 313/576-5100 or 313/576-5111, www.dso.org, show times and ticket prices vary), home to the acclaimed Detroit Symphony Orchestra.

FESTIVALS AND EVENTS

Detroit hosts numerous events and celebrations throughout the year, including January's **North American International Auto Show** (COBO Center, 1 Washington Blvd., 248/643-0250 or 313/877-8777, www.naias.com, $13 adults, $7 seniors 65 and over and children 7-12, children under 7 free), which still offers the world a first-hand look of what cars will look like in the near and distant future. In early April, Greektown comes alive with the annual **Detroit Greek Independence Day Parade** (http://detroit-greekparade.blogspot.com, free), which is typically held on Monroe Street, the main thoroughfare of this historic enclave.

In 2009, the longstanding Detroit Belle Isle Grand Prix, which, much to the chagrin of naturalists, used to take over the beloved island every Labor Day weekend, was indefinitely suspended, due to lack of funding. To the delight of many, however, this popular event returned to Belle Isle in the spring of 2013. Now, the weekend-long **Chevrolet Detroit Belle Isle Grand Prix** (313/748-1800 or 866/464-7749, www.detroitgp.com) occurs in late May or early June and features various races on Belle Isle's 2.3-mile road course, considered one of the most challenging in the world.

In late June, the St. Nicholas Greek Orthodox Church holds the annual **Opa! Fest** (760 W. Wattles Rd., Troy, 248/362-9575, www.opafest.com, $2 pp, children under 12 free), a weekend filled with Greek music, traditional Greek folk dancing, Greek arts and crafts, cooking demonstrations, and, of course, Greek cuisine, from kabobs and gyros to pastries and wine. Another popular summertime event is the **African World Festival** (313/494-5824, free), which has been hosted by the **Charles H. Wright Museum of African**

ELMORE LEONARD'S MOTOR CITY

Born in New Orleans, Elmore John Leonard Jr. (1925-2013), the son of a General Motors employee, spent the bulk of his adolescent and teenage years in Detroit. Following high school, he served in the U.S. Navy for three years. After graduating from the University of Detroit with an English and philosophy degree, he began to write ad copy for clients like Chevrolet. Eventually, however, his love of fiction proved to be too great an urge to resist.

While maintaining his advertising job, he began to pen Western stories, popular in the 1950s. When the Western market shrank a decade later, Leonard decided to focus on a full-time writing career. Soon, he'd crafted his first crime novel, *The Big Bounce* (1969). Over the ensuing years, he continued to write crime novels (often set in his hometown), gradually gaining a loyal cult following. Adapting several of his stories into screenplays helped to fund his fiction career – until the publication of two bestsellers propelled *Time* to christen him the "Dickens from Detroit" in 1984.

For the next three decades, Leonard, who lived in a Detroit suburb until his death, continued to write best-selling crime novels and short stories, some of which have become popular films and television shows, including *Get Shorty* (1995), *Jackie Brown* (1997), *Out of Sight* (1998), *Killshot* (2008), *Justified* (2010-present), and *Freaky Deaky* (2012). Even his Western tales have made a resurgence: In 2007, Russell Crowe and Christian Bale starred in *3:10 to Yuma*, the second adaptation of his eponymous short story.

If you're curious about Leonard's sharp-tongued take on gritty Detroit, visit the author's official website (www.elmoreleonard.com) or consider perusing the following titles:

UNKNOWN MAN NO. 89 (1977)

When a skillful Detroit process server is hired to search for a missing stockholder, he becomes the unwitting target of a lethal triple-cross.

THE SWITCH (1978)

Hoping to make some easy ransom money, two ex-cons kidnap the wife of a Detroit developer who, unfortunately for them, has no desire to get her back.

CITY PRIMEVAL (1980)

A dedicated homicide detective strives to stop a psychopathic murderer in the Motor City.

TOUCH (1987)

A former Franciscan monk with faith-healing powers finds it difficult to be a saint in the city.

FREAKY DEAKY (1988)

After his fishy suspension from the Detroit police force, a determined sergeant must uncover a web of scams, perpetrated by an ex-con, a former Black Panther, a movie dynamite expert, and an alcoholic auto industry heir.

OUT OF SIGHT (1996)

A career thief forms an unlikely relationship with a sexy U.S. marshal, which leads them both from sunny Florida to the gritty streets and posh suburbs of Detroit.

MR. PARADISE (2004)

When two roommates – a lingerie model and an escort – get involved with a retired Detroit-based lawyer, murder, greed, and pandemonium ensue.

UP IN HONEY'S ROOM (2007)

In World War II-era Detroit, a young U.S. marshal befriends a free-spirited American woman in the hopes that she'll lead him to her husband – a German-born butcher who's giving shelter to German prisoners of war, perhaps even the marshal's latest target.

American History (315 E. Warren Ave., 313/494-5800, www.thewright.org, 9am-5pm Tues.-Sat., 1pm-5pm Sun., $8 adults, $5 seniors 62 and over and children 3-12, children under 3 free) for the past three decades. Usually taking place in mid-August, this beloved festival features world music, jazz and blues, a folk village, an international marketplace, ethnic cuisine, traditional dances, and other tantalizing diversions.

Over Labor Day weekend, there's at least one event worth attending. From Hart Plaza to Cadillac Square, the **Detroit Jazz Festival** (313/447-1248, www.detroitjazzfest.com, free) presents a wide array of open-air concerts and a world-class selection of music masters—the largest free jam in the world. Festival attendees can also experience lively interviews, panel discussions, and presentations by musicians, journalists, and jazz radio hosts. Throughout the year, festival organizers and the Detroit public school system offer a "Jazz Infusion Program," designed to teach students improvisation and other jazz-related skills in an effort to support the city's vital jazz community and ensure its survival.

Shopping

GM RENAISSANCE CENTER

Downtown shoppers can spend at least a couple of hours browsing the boutiques inside the Ren Cen (100 Renaissance Center, 313/567-3126, www.gmrencen.com). Options run the gamut, from **The Runway** (313/568-7977, 10am-6pm Mon.-Fri., 11am-4pm Sat.-Sun.), which sells high-end men's and women's apparel, to the charming **Renaissance 500 Shoppe** (313/259-6510, 7am-5:30pm Mon.-Fri.), where the friendly staff provides fine tobacco products and other specialty items.

EASTERN MARKET

There is one place in the city where old and young, Eastsider and Westsider, black and white meet. Bring your wagon or grocery bag to the historic **Eastern Market** (2934 Russell St., 313/833-9300, www.detroiteasternmarket. com), between Mack and Gratiot Avenues, on a Saturday morning, and you'll find a fragment of old Detroit, a colorful cornucopia of smells, sights, and sounds. In a city that's known great cycles of boom and bust, Eastern Market is as perennial as the fruit and flowers it sells.

Built on the site of an early hay and wood market, this bustling, six-block area near Greektown has lured Detroiters since 1891. Shoppers come to buy meat, cheese, produce, fruit, and flowers from large, open-air stalls and wholesale/retail specialty shops. Many wholesalers are the descendants of the Belgian, German, and Polish farmers who frequented the market generations ago, or the Italian and Lebanese merchants who began catering to the booming city in the 1920s.

Saturdays are busiest, when the farmers market runs 6am-4pm and thousands of shoppers pour into the area to browse, bargain, and buy among goods that range from fresh chitlins to fresh cilantro. Highlights include the flower stalls (the market is the largest bedding center in the world) and the aromas at **Germack's,** the oldest pistachio importer in the United States.

Sports and Recreation

SPECTATOR SPORTS

The Motor City boasts more professional sports teams than most major U.S. cities, and Detroiters are among the country's most loyal fans, with thousands cheering on the home teams at Lions football, Pistons and Shock basketball, Tigers baseball, and Red Wings hockey games. Most are played at sparkling modern suburban stadiums, much like their counterparts across the country.

Historic Tiger Stadium, which once stood at Michigan Avenue and Trumbull Street, was demolished in 2009. Legendary and longtime home to the **Detroit Tigers** (http://detroit.tigers.mlb.com), it was replaced in April 2000 by the glitzy **Comerica Park** (2100 Woodward Ave., 313/962-4000 or 866/668-4437), where baseball games usually take place April-October. While it will never be Tiger Stadium, Comerica Park certainly has its fans. With a

family-friendly philosophy that includes a Ferris wheel and a pedestrian museum, it has attracted city and national attention as one of the best of the new breed of ballparks. The location in the heart of the vintage Theater District is also prime.

Just east of Comerica Park is the relatively new **Ford Field** (2000 Brush St., 313/262-2013), which is home to the **Detroit Lions** (www.detroitlions.com) and typically features football games September-December. Basketball lovers, meanwhile, can seek out the NBA's **Detroit Pistons** (www.nba.com/pistons) or the WNBA's **Detroit Shock** (www.wnba.com/shock) at **The Palace** (6 Championship Dr., Auburn Hills, 248/377-0100, www.palacenet.com) November-April, and, of course, hockey fans can cheer on the **Detroit Red Wings** (http://redwings.nhl.com) at **Joe Louis Arena** (19 Steve Yzerman Dr., 313/396-7000

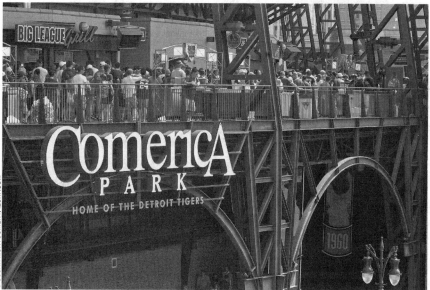

Comerica Park

or 313/471-6606, www.olympiaentertainment.com) October-April.

BIKING

If you're looking for a leisurely bike ride, head to **William G. Milliken State Park and Harbor** (1900 Atwater St., 313/396-0217, free), which was formerly known as Tri-Centennial Park and now offers a bike path not far from the Detroit River. Experienced bikers, on the other hand, should head beyond the city limits, where the **Highland Recreation Area** (5200 E. Highland Rd., White Lake, 248/889-3750, www.michigan.gov/dnr, 8am-10pm daily) offers 16 miles of trails that make up some of the area's most challenging mountain biking routes. Another option is **Pinckney State Recreation Area** (8555 Silver Hill Rd., Pinckney, 734/426-4913, www.michigan.gov/dnr), home to the 17-mile Potawatomi Trail, which has been ranked in the nation's top 10 routes and also caters to hikers and, in winter, cross-country skiers. To enter the two recreation areas, an annual Recreation Passport is required for both residents ($11 vehicles, $5 motorcycles) and nonresidents ($30.50 vehicles or motorcycles); luckily, though, these passports will allow you access to all of the Michigan state parks and recreation areas that charge a fee.

BOATING AND FISHING

Given Detroit's proximity to the Detroit River, Lake Erie, and Lake St. Clair, it might come as no surprise that boating and fishing are popular activities here. If you don't have a boat of your own, simply contact the **Michigan Charter Boat Association** (MCBA, 800/622-2971, www.michigancharterboats.com), which can help you locate and join sailing excursions and fishing charters. Of course, if don't want to stray too far, head to **William G. Milliken State Park and Harbor** (1900 Atwater St., 313/396-0217, free), which offers easy access to shore fishing alongside the Detroit River.

WINTER ACTIVITIES

As with the rest of Michigan, Detroit certainly gets its share of snow and ice during the winter months. So, if you enjoy cold-weather diversions, you're in luck. Ice skating, ice fishing, sledding, tobogganing, cross-country skiing, and downhill skiing are all popular in and around the city. Ice skaters, for example, can head to **Campus Martius Park** (800 Woodward Ave., www.campusmartius-park.org, 7am-10pm), a 2.5-acre public square and year-round entertainment venue that also features a world-class rink during the winter. Apparently, even national and Olympic ice-skating champions have performed here. Another option for wintertime recreationists is **Lake Erie Metropark** (32481 W. Jefferson, Brownstown, 734/379-5020, www.metroparks.com, 6am-10pm daily, $7/vehicle daily, $20-30/vehicle annually), a 1,607-acre recreation area that lies about 27 miles south of downtown Detroit. Here, cross-country skiers can embrace 4.25 miles of marked, groomed trails; ice-fishing enthusiasts can search for perch, bass, and other species on Lake Erie; and sledders can plummet down a large hill near the wave pool complex.

Accommodations

Detroit offers hotels, motels, and inns to suit all budgets. Although most downtown accommodations are of the business-class, hotel-chain variety, you'll even find a few Victorian-style inns and casino resorts.

UNDER $150

Close to downtown attractions, the **Hotel St. Regis** (3071 W. Grand Blvd., 313/873-3000 or 855/408-7738, www.hotelstregisdetroit.com, $94-144 d) provides 124 renovated rooms and suites, free wireless Internet access, valet parking ($20 daily), a 24-hour business center, and an on-site restaurant, La Musique (6am-10pm Mon.-Thurs., 8am-11pm Fri.-Sat., 8am-10pm Sun.). West of Detroit's stadiums and theaters, the 150-room **Corktown Inn** (1331 Trumbull St., 313/496-1400, www.corktowninn.com, $70-100 d) is a solid option for budget-conscious travelers who need little more than clean beds, laundry services, free parking, wireless Internet access, and proximity to Detroit's main attractions.

$150-300

If you don't mind paying a bit more, then consider the ◖ **Atheneum Suite Hotel** (1000 Brush Ave., 313/962-2323 or 800/772-2323, www.atheneumsuites.com, $199-259 d), downtown's best all-suite hotel. Located in the heart of Greektown, it borrows classical motifs from the surrounding neighborhood in its 174 luxury suites, all with separate living rooms, marble bathrooms, free wireless Internet access, and other convenient amenities. Wheelchair-accessible suites are also available here.

Another solid option is the **Detroit Marriott at the Renaissance Center** (GM Renaissance Center, 400 Renaissance Dr., 313/568-8000 or 888/236-2427, www.marriott.com, $179-299 d), which provides terrific views of the Detroit River as well as easy access to the Ren Cen's shops and restaurants, Detroit's three casinos, and the tunnel to Windsor, Canada. Here, you

can also enjoy high-speed Internet access, a fitness center, a business center, and an on-site restaurant.

For traditional chain lodgings, consider the **Hilton Garden Inn Detroit Downtown** (351 Gratiot Ave., 313/967-0900, www.hiltongardeninn.com, $159-229 d), set within the Harmonie Park neighborhood, only a block from Comerica Park and Ford Field. Housing 198 rooms and suites, the Hilton also offers free wireless Internet access, a business center, two on-site restaurants, a fitness center, an indoor pool, and plenty of wheelchair-accessible features. Another mid-range option is the **Holiday Inn Express Hotel & Suites Detroit Downtown** (1020 Washington Blvd., 313/887-7000 or 888/233-0353, www.ihg.com, $150-180 d), which lies halfway between the MGM Grand Detroit and Greektown Casino-Hotel, and within walking distance of Campus Martius Park. Besides affordable guest rooms, the Holiday Inn also features suites with fully equipped kitchens, plus a fitness center, an indoor heated pool, a 24-hour business center, valet parking ($20 daily), free high-speed Internet access, and a complimentary breakfast bar. You might also try **Courtyard Detroit Downtown** (333 E. Jefferson Ave., 313/222-7700 or 888/236-2427, www.marriott.com, $159-219 d), with 260 oversized rooms, free wireless Internet access, an extensive health club, an enormous indoor pool, and an outdoor aboveground tennis court/running track that offers terrific views of the city's surrounding vintage architecture.

CASINO RESORTS

For even more amenities, consider staying at one of Detroit's three downtown casino resorts. The shimmering ◖ **MGM Grand Detroit** (1777 3rd St., 888/646-3387 or 877/888-2121, www.mgmgranddetroit.com, $249-499 d) houses an enormous gaming space, a full-service spa, pampering hotel rooms, live entertainment, four unique bars, a lively nightclub, and several dining options, including the Wolfgang Puck Pizzeria & Cucina as well as Wolfgang Puck Steak. The **MotorCity Casino Hotel** (2901 Grand River Ave., 866/752-9622, www.motorcitycasino.com, $223-332 d) also promises more than Las Vegas-style games, including a 24-hour fitness center, a luxurious spa, live concerts, varied dining options, and 400

stylish, state-of-the-art rooms and suites. Even Greektown has its own resort, the **Greektown Casino-Hotel** (1200 St. Antoine St., 313/223-2999 or 877/424-5554, www.greektowncasino.com, $99-249 d), which offers several restaurants, a video poker lounge, a wide range of gaming tables and slot machines, and amenities like ergonomic desks, plush bedding, and free parking.

Food

GREEKTOWN

Greektown is a delightful place come mealtime, and most Detroiters have their favorite Greektown restaurant. Top choices include the **New Parthenon** (547 Monroe St., 313/963-8888, www.newparthenon.com, 11am-3am daily, $9-24), which serves various salads, sandwiches, kabobs, gyro platters, and seafood dishes, and the upscale **(Pegasus Taverna** (558 Monroe St., 313/964-6800, www.pegasustavernas.com, 11am-1am Mon.-Thurs., 11am-3am Fri.-Sat., 11am-midnight Sun., $7-32), which offers specialties like a tart *avgolemono* (chicken lemon soup), flaky spinach pie, *pastitsio* (Greek macaroni), and flaming *saganaki* cheese, lit with a flourish and a cry of "Opa!" from the waiter. Afterward, many diners wander over to the popular **(Astoria Pastry Shop** (541 Monroe St., 313/963-9603, www.astoriapastryshop.com, 8am-midnight Sun.-Thurs., 8am-1am Fri.-Sat., $2-11) for baklava and other Greek and European pastries laid out neatly behind gleaming glass counters. Incidentally, the Pegasus Taverna has a second location in St. Claire Shores, while the Astoria Pastry Shop also offers its treats to the residents of Royal Oak, so even in the suburbs, you can sample the flavors of Greektown.

Of course, not everything worth seeing in Greektown is Greek. **PizzaPapalis Taverna** (553 Monroe St., 313/961-8020, www.pizzapapalis.com, 11am-1am daily, $5-24) is where Motown meets the Windy City. Only the

name is Greek: Deep-dish pies are the specialty. Meanwhile, **(Fishbone's** (400 Monroe St., 313/965-4600, www.fishbonesusa.com, 6:30am-midnight Sun.-Thurs., 6:30am-1am Fri.-Sat., $9-65) is a New Orleans-inspired eatery that opened in the mid-1980s and has been jammed ever since. It serves up surprisingly authentic gumbo and jambalaya, in addition to ribs, steaks, seafood, and sushi, and you can usually expect live music on Friday and Saturday nights. Given its popularity, it's no wonder that there are also locations in Southfield and St. Claire Shores.

THEATER DISTRICT

Detroit's impressive Theater District is home to more than just gorgeously restored entertainment venues; it also boasts a decent array of restaurants, which, depending on the hours, might be ideal for a post-game or pre-show meal. Located behind the Comerica Park scoreboard, the **Elwood Bar & Grill** (300 Adams Ave., 313/962-2337, www.elwoodgrill.com, 11am-2pm Mon.-Tues., 11am-8pm Wed.-Sat., $6-9) might just be Detroit's most recognizable art deco-style diner. Built in 1936 by local architect Charles Noble, relocated in 1997, and subsequently renovated, the Elwood is, not surprisingly, a popular spot for sports fans, particularly given its menu items, which range from chicken wings and Coney-style hot dogs to patty melts and club sandwiches. Another equally casual option is the **(Hockeytown**

CONEY CUISINE

Philly may have the cheese steak and Chicago its deep-dish pie, but Detroit has *the* Coney Island. No, not the amusement park – the hot dog. Detroiters take their coneys very seriously, downing thousands of these hot dogs annually. Curiously, the name Coney Island serves simultaneously as both a destination and a dish.

Family-owned and operated since 1917, **American Coney Island** (114 W. Lafayette, 586/219-0995, www.americanconeyisland. com) is the place where a wiener with skin, beanless chili, onions, and mustard was first called "one with everything." Although this beloved 24-hour eatery now also serves soups, salads, desserts, and spinach pie, it's the dogs that lure a clientele ranging from cops on the beat to fur-clad suburbanites grabbing a bite after a show at the Fox Theatre. American Coney Island has garnered the respect of a long list of celebrities, too, including Michigan governors, famous musicians and athletes, and well-known actors like Bill Cosby, Tim Allen, and Jeff Daniels.

Cafe (2301 Woodward Ave., 313/471-3400, www.hockeytowncafe.com, 11am-close Mon.-Sat., Sunday hours vary, $8-19). Though not far from the Fox Theatre, this bustling sports bar is, as the name implies, more popular among sports fans headed to or from the nearby Comerica Park and Ford Field. During hockey season, patrons can even hop the restaurant's free shuttles to the Joe Louis Arena. Diners here can anticipate frequent drink specials; vittles like chicken wings, salads, pizza, ribs, and burgers; and a host of high-definition TVs broadcasting a variety of sporting events. Curiously, there are also gluten-free options on the menu, from nachos to breadless sandwiches.

EASTERN MARKET

After shopping in the Eastern Market, head over to the **Roma Café** (3401 Riopelle St., 313/831-5940, www.romacafe.com, 11am-10pm Mon.-Fri., 11am-11pm Sat., $14-29), Detroit's oldest Italian restaurant, established in 1890. While classic dishes such as gnocchi, lasagna, eggplant parmigiana, and tiramisu abound here, you'll also find treats like breaded frog legs, filet mignon, and broiled whitefish.

WOODWARD AVENUE

If you get hungry while exploring the Cultural Center, stop by the **((Majestic Café** (4140 Woodward Ave., 313/833-9700, www.majesticdetroit.com, 11am-10pm Wed.-Thurs., 11am-midnight Fri.-Sat., 10am-10pm Sun., $8-22), an eclectic eatery offering hummus, fish tacos, baked ziti, soft-shell crab poboys, and more. It packs in the Wayne State University and Detroit Medical Center crowds at lunch. For a decidedly fancier experience, make a reservation at ((**The Whitney** (4421 Woodward Ave., 313/832-5700, www.thewhitney.com, 8am-10pm Mon.-Fri., 5pm-10pm Sat., 11am-2:30pm and 4pm-8pm Sun., $28-79), Detroit's grandest restaurant, housed in an ornate 120-year-old mansion and offering live entertainment on weekends, plus exquisite dishes such as beef Wellington, stuffed lobster, roasted lamb rack, and bourbon-glazed salmon. A prix-fixe theater menu is also available. In addition, with a 48-hour advance reservation, you can enjoy high afternoon tea on weekdays, and the trendy **Ghostbar** is open 5pm-close Monday-Saturday.

NEW CENTER DISTRICT

Even the New Center district has its own gem: the ((**Cuisine Restaurant** (670 Lothrop Rd., 313/872-5110, www.cuisinerestaurant.com, 5pm-close Tues.-Sun., $22-32), situated behind the Fisher Building. If you're willing to spend a fair amount, treat yourself to one of

Chef Paul Grosz's progression menus ($50-80 pp), which might include dishes like white and green asparagus, creamed Maine lobster with leeks and tapioca, almond-crusted soft-shell crabs, roasted Alaskan halibut, wild sturgeon with potato gnocchi, and strawberry Charlotte. The restaurant also offers vegetarian options and a superb wine list.

Information and Services

INFORMATION

For free information about Detroit, consult the **Detroit Metro Convention & Visitors Bureau** (211 W. Fort St., Ste. 1000, 313/202-1800 or 800/338-7648, www.visitdetroit.com, 9am-5pm Mon.-Fri.). The two daily newspapers, the **Detroit News** (www.detnews.com) and the **Detroit Free Press** (www.freep.com) are supplemented by a wide variety of suburban dailies and weeklies, as well as the weekly **Detroit Metro Times** (www.metrotimes.com). The *Metro Times* is the city's first—and most successful—alternative rag, with thoughtful reporting on a variety of civic and social issues, extensive entertainment listings (a great place to check out your options on any given night), and consciousness-raising (if not eyebrow-raising) classifieds and want ads. It's distributed freely at bins throughout the city and suburbs. Another good read is **Hour Detroit** (www.hourdetroit.com), a tabloid-size, full-color magazine that's full of thought-provoking and entertaining editorials.

Local radio and television stations, such as Detroit's ABC affiliate **WXYZ** (www.wxyz.com), are also excellent sources for regional information. Pick up a copy of the *Detroit News* or check the website (www.detnews.com) for a list of channels.

SERVICES

As a major urban center, Detroit has no shortage of necessary services, from banks to mailing centers to grocery stores. The metropolitan area boasts several post offices, including one inside the Ren Cen. For locations and hours, contact the **United States Postal Service** (USPS, 800/275-8777, www.usps.com).

Dial **911** for emergency police, fire, or ambulance assistance. In nonemergency situations, contact the **Detroit Police Department** (1301 3rd St., 313/596-2200 or 313/596-1300, www.detroitmi.gov); you can also dial 311 within the city limits. Remember, too, that the area code for Detroit and Dearborn telephone numbers is 313, while the area codes for Oakland County (including Birmingham, Royal Oak, Pontiac, and most of the northern suburbs) are 248 and 947.

For medical assistance, you'll find several hospitals in the metropolitan area. One option is the **Detroit Medical Center** (DMC, 888/362-2500, www.dmc.org), which has a number of facilities in the vicinity.

Getting There and Around

Most international travelers arrive by air, while American tourists tend to come via train, bus, or car.

GETTING THERE
By Plane

The **Detroit Metropolitan-Wayne County Airport** (DTW, 1 Detroit Metropolitan Airport Tram, 734/247-7678, www.metroairport.com), also known as the Detroit Metro Airport, spreads out over some 7,000 acres, 21 miles southwest of the city in Romulus, just off I-94 and Merriman Road. With 12 airlines, including 4 foreign, Detroit Metro offers service to more than 160 nonstop destinations. Consult the website for current carriers, which range from Air Canada to United.

Sedan or limo service from the airport to downtown hotels and area suburbs (and vice versa) is available by reservation. Typically, a one-way ride costs $31-98, depending on the destination. For more information, contact **Metro Airport Taxi** (800/745-5191, www.metroairporttaxi.org), **Metro Airport Limo** (734/322-0240 or 800/654-1215, www.dtwmetrotaxi.com), **Metroride** (248/666-0222 or 800/320-1683, www.detroitmetroairport.com), or **Rendezvous Limousine** (800/875-4667, www.rendezvous-limo.com).

Detroit Metro also has many car rental services: some on-site, others off-site but accessible via a dedicated shuttle service. For details, consult **Avis** (800/331-1212, www.avis.com), **Budget** (800/527-0700, www.budget.com), and **Enterprise** (800/325-8007, www.enterprise.com), or peruse the listings on the DTW website.

By Train

Via the Michigan Services route, **Amtrak** (800/872-7245, www.amtrak.com) offers convenient daily service to five metro area stops: Dearborn, Detroit, Royal Oak, Birmingham, and Pontiac. The downtown station is located at 11 West Baltimore Avenue in the New Center, while the suburban Dearborn stop is situated at 16121 Michigan Avenue.

By Bus

Greyhound (800/231-2222, www.greyhound.com) serves downtown Detroit (1001 Howard St., 313/961-8011, 5:30am-1:30am daily). Be extra careful at this station—it's not located in the best part of town. Daytime arrivals and departures are always a good idea.

By Car

Many travelers arrive in the Detroit area via car. While several federal and state highways make it easy to navigate the Motor City, most motorists rely on interstates to reach Detroit. If you're headed from Flint, for instance, take I-75 South to downtown Detroit; without traffic, the 69-mile trip usually takes about an hour. From Toledo, on the other hand, head north on I-75 for about 61 miles; without traffic, you should arrive in downtown Detroit in roughly an hour. From Lansing, meanwhile, take I-96 East, which passes through Farmington Hills and Southfield en route to Detroit's Mexicantown; this particular route covers about 90 miles and normally requires about 80-90 minutes of driving. I-94 is another handy route into the city; from Ann Arbor to the west, it's roughly 45 miles (or 45 minutes, without traffic) via I-94 East to Detroit, while from Port Huron to the northeast, it's approximately 63 miles (or an hour, without traffic) via I-94 West to Detroit. If you're headed from Chicago, you can also utilize I-94 East to reach Detroit; without traffic, the 283-mile trip normally takes about four hours. Just be advised that, en route from the Windy City, you'll encounter the Indiana Toll Road.

GETTING AROUND
By Car

Detroit, not surprisingly, is full of freeways. I-75 is the major north-south thoroughfare, with I-96, I-696, and I-94 heading east-west. Avoid traveling any of these routes during rush hours (generally 6am-10am and 3pm-7pm) or allow plenty of extra time. It's wise to seek out alternate routes such as I-275, which splits off from I-696, and to pick up a map of the area to ensure that you don't get lost (which is an easy thing to do).

Of course, if you've arrived in Detroit via plane, train, bus, boat, or some other means, and you don't have a car of your own, there's no need to worry. Rental car companies—including Avis, Budget, and more—can be found at the Detroit Metro Airport. Likewise, you can also rely on taxis to navigate the city. **Checker Cab** (313/963-7000, www.checkercab-det. com, $2.50/pickup, $1.60/mile), for instance, has been driving passengers around the greater Detroit area since 1921. From the airport to downtown hotels, it typically costs about $40 per trip, while it's roughly $10 from downtown Detroit to the New Center district. Typically, a waiting charge will run you about $15 per hour or more.

Whether you rely on your own or someone else's vehicle, just remember that seat belts are required by Michigan law; in other words, all drivers, front-seat passengers, and children 8-15 years old must wear seat belts while in a moving vehicle. Otherwise, law enforcement officials can (and often do) stop and ticket motorists solely for not being buckled up.

Mass Transit

Most would agree that mass transit in Detroit is a joke. (This is the city that invented the car, after all.) The **Detroit Department of Transportation (DDOT)** is the state's largest transit system; it serves Detroit and 25 suburban communities. DDOT buses and bus stops are recognizable by their trademark green and yellow colors.

Detroit People Mover

Buses operate on 50 routes during the day and evenings from 6am until approximately 1am; 14 of the most popular routes operate 24 hours daily. Consult **DDOT** (313/933-1300 or 888/336-8287, www.ci.detroit.mi.us/ddot, one-way $1.50 adults, $0.75 students, $0.50 seniors) for routes and schedules.

While downtown, you can also take advantage of the **Detroit People Mover** (313/224-2160 or 800/541-7245, www.thepeoplemover.com, 6:30am-midnight Mon.-Thurs., 6:30am-2am Fri., 9am-2am Sat., noon-midnight Sun.), which admittedly never quite lived up to the high expectations. Still, it's a handy way to travel, with a bird's-eye view of the city from its elevated track. For 75 cents, you'll get a 15-minute ride along a three-mile track that circles the heart of the business district. Even if you don't ride, it's worth a visit to check out the 13 People Mover stations, which boast works by local artists. The Detroit People Mover operates through the city's notable areas, including the Civic Center, Greektown, and the Theater District, with easy access to major attractions, such as the GM Renaissance Center and the Joe Louis Arena.

Windsor, Ontario

A city of 211,000, Windsor sits along the southern banks of the Detroit River, just across from the Motor City. "Civilized" is the word that comes to mind when Detroiters talk about Windsor. Although separated only by a river, this Canadian city has a virtually nonexistent crime rate, a full plate of excellent restaurants, and a friendly and civic-minded populace who are happy to welcome Yanks. Detroiters have long shuttled back and forth to enjoy Windsor's restaurants, casinos, European-style shops, terrific riverfront views, and, yes, strip clubs.

SIGHTS
The **Windsor Wood Carving Museum** (850 Ouellette Ave., 519/977-0823, www.windsorwoodcarvingmuseum.ca, 10am-5pm Tues.-Fri., 10am-4pm Sat., donation suggested) offers a glimpse into historical carvings as well as contemporary work by some of Canada's finest craftspeople. The expansive one-room museum allows for close-up viewing of most of the pieces. **The Park House Museum** (King's Navy Yard Park, 214 Dalhousie St., Amherstburg, 519/736-2511, www.parkhousemuseum.com, 11am-4pm daily June-Aug., 11am-4pm Mon.-Fri. Sept.-May, $2 adults, $1.50 seniors, $1 children), meanwhile, has the unique distinction of being the oldest house in the Windsor area and the oldest house from Detroit. The house was built near the mouth of the Rouge River in Detroit in the 1790s, but when the city was turned over to the Americans with the signing of the Jay Treaty, Alexander MacKintosh, a loyalist to the crown, moved the house to Amherstburg in 1796.

SHOPPING
Wander Ouellette Avenue, the main drag, and the narrow streets surrounding it. Shops are full of imported clothing and books (both new and used, many with British publishers), and the T-shirt stands are ubiquitous. One standout is **Shanfields-Meyers** (188 Ouellette Ave., 519/253-6098, www.shanfields.com, 10am-5pm daily), a family-owned business that opened in 1946 and now houses a sparkling array of crystal, including a whole room devoted to Waterford, and a wide selection of discounted china and gifts.

ACCOMMODATIONS AND FOOD
Accommodations
Windsor is full of nice hotels, including the **Windsor Riverside Inn** (333 W. Riverside Dr., 519/977-9777 or 800/267-9777, www.windsorriversideinn.com, $105-159 d), which is

© HELGIDINSON/123RF.COM

a view of the Ambassador Bridge

conveniently located near downtown Windsor and the Detroit River and offers spectacular views of the Detroit skyline. It also features pet-friendly rooms, a fitness center, an indoor pool and sauna, a 24-hour business center, complimentary Internet access, and free parking. For an equally affordable stay, try the pet-friendly **Travelodge Hotel Downtown Windsor** (33 E. Riverside Dr., 519/258-7774, www.travelodge.com, $95-150 d), which offers free wireless Internet access, a fitness center, a heated indoor pool, an on-site restaurant, and proximity to Caesars Windsor.

Of course, if you're looking for a bit more luxury, consider staying at **Caesars Windsor** (377 E. Riverside Dr., 800/991-7777, www.caesarswindsor.com, $110-233 d) itself, the city's premier gambling resort. Boasting 758 luxurious rooms and suites in two towers that overlook the Detroit River, Caesars also provides amenities like full concierge service and complimentary valet parking. It doesn't hurt that you'll also have easy access to various table

games and slot machines, a world-class poker room, live concerts and comedy shows, several stylish bars, upscale shops, a soothing spa, an indoor pool, a fully equipped gym with incredible views, and several restaurants, from Taza, a Mediterranean grill, to Neros, a superb steakhouse.

Food

While the shopping is good in Windsor, it doesn't compare to the eating. Top restaurants include **The Cook's Shop Restaurant** (683 Ouellette Ave., 519/254-3377, http://cooksshoprestaurant.wordpress.com, 5pm-10pm Tues.-Thurs. and Sun., 5pm-11pm Fri.-Sat., $15-24), a tiny basement eatery where everything is homemade, including the melt-in-your-mouth gnocchi, tortellini, and other pastas prepared tableside on a rolling cart. Another option, **The Mini** (475 W. University Ave., 519/254-2221, 11:30am-10pm Tues.-Fri., 5pm-10pm Sat., 4pm-8pm Sun., $7-14) started out with one tiny room (hence the name) and then expanded as the restaurant's Vietnamese cuisine and fruit slushes caught on with diners from Windsor and across the way.

INFORMATION

For more information about Windsor, consult **Tourism Windsor, Essex, Pelee Island** (333 W. Riverside Dr., Ste. 103, Windsor, Ontario, 519/255-6530 or 800/265-3633, www.tourismwindsoressex.com, 8:30am-4:30pm Mon.-Fri.).

GETTING THERE AND AROUND

While Windsor has its own airport—the **Windsor International Airport** (YQG, 3200 CR-42, 519/969-2430, www.yqg.ca)—most visitors will probably be making a day trip from Detroit via car. Two routes connect Detroit and Windsor: the **Ambassador Bridge** (www.ambassadorbridge.com, one-way $5 passenger vehicles and motorcycles, $10 buses) and the **Detroit-Windsor Tunnel** (www.dwtunnel.com, one-way to Windsor $4.75 passenger and commercial vehicles, $8.50 buses, one-way to Detroit $4.50 passenger and commercial vehicles, $8.50 buses). Claustrophobes tend to opt for the bridge, though the tunnel is faster and more direct.

If you don't have your own car, you can always rent a vehicle or hire a taxi or sedan at the Detroit Metro Airport. **Checker Cab** (313/963-7000, www.checkercab-det.com, $2.50 per pickup, $1.60 per mile), for instance, charges about $46 for a one-way trip from the airport to downtown Windsor, while, for the same trip, **Metro Airport Taxi** (800/745-5191, www.metroairporttaxi.org) usually charges passengers around $75, which includes airport fees and toll charges.

Just remember that this is an international border, and nowadays, U.S. citizens must confirm both proof of identity and proof of citizenship (by using, for instance, a driver's license and a birth certificate) in order to enter Canada. Unfortunately, returning to the United States will require a valid U.S. passport.

The Suburbs

Ironically, the same fast cars that made the Motor City what it was in its heyday are also what crippled it. Bigger and better cars, and more and more efficient freeways only served to take Detroiters farther and farther away from the core city. Most suburbs are bedroom communities that bear little interest for the visitor. Some exceptions include Hamtramck, a Polish neighborhood north of downtown Detroit; Dearborn, where Henry Ford was born and eventually inspired what has become one of the state's largest tourist attractions; Royal Oak, home to the Detroit Zoo; Birmingham, an enclave of chic boutiques and fine art galleries; and Grosse Pointe, where Lake Shore Drive still boasts some of the area's finest homes.

◖ HAMTRAMCK

"A Touch of Europe in America," reads the sign approaching **Hamtramck** (www.hamtramck.com), a Polish stronghold since World War I. Given that its residents have stubbornly withstood annexation, this curious community has survived as a "city within a city," 2.5 square miles completely within Detroit city limits.

Named for a German-French Canadian colonel who served during the post-Revolutionary Indian Wars, the strange-sounding hamlet was settled as a village of mostly German farms in 1901, but a new Dodge auto factory and its promise of jobs swelled the population from 3,589 to 45,615 between 1910 and 1920—the largest increase anywhere in the United States. Many were Polish immigrants, earning

Hamtramck the nickname "Little Poland." Today, the auto plant is closed and the Polish population has dropped from 90 percent to about 40 percent (the slack is taken up by Albanians and African Americans), but the nickname and culture remain.

Sights and Shopping

Drive along Joseph Campau Street, Hamtramck's main drag, and you'll find Polish bakeries, Polish bookstores, Polish clubs, and shops hawking Polish sausage. There's even a tribute at the corner of Belmont and Joseph Campau Streets to the Polish pope, John Paul II, who visited this ethnic enclave in the mid-1980s. Stop at the **Polish Art Center** (9539 Joseph Campau St., 313/874-2242 or 888/619-9771, www.polartcenter.com, 9:30am-6pm Mon.-Sat., 11am-3pm Sun.) for unusual goods such as folk art rugs, leaded glass, Ukrainian-decorated eggs, and *szopkas,* intricate Nativity scenes made of tinfoil. Afterward, take a tour of the **Saint Florian Roman Catholic Church** (2626 Poland St., 313/871-2778, www.stflorianparish.org), one of the last of the old Polish churches. Founded in 1907 and completed in 1926, this stately church now serves hundreds of faithful parishioners, including Polish, Albanian, and Asian residents, among others.

Detroiters have long known about the old-world charms of Hamtramck. Joseph Campau's glass storefronts have a vintage 1930s feel, full of Polish imports, discount clothing, and baked goods and meats. Hamtramck's quirky 1930s flair and cheap rents have attracted artists such as potter/jeweler Marcia Hovland and filmmakers Chuck Cirgenski and Janine Menlove. Hollywood-backed *Polish Wedding* (1998), a movie starring Claire Danes, Lena Olin, and Gabriel Byrne, was filmed here in late 1996. With the new wave of artists and filmmakers have come urbane coffeehouses, late-night alternative-music cafés, and colorful studios and shops that add a new hipness to this old-world enclave.

Food

Many Polish suburbanites return to Hamtramck with their families on weekends to sip *czarnina* (duck's blood soup), linger over *nalesniki* (crepes), and consume pierogies (filled dumplings) before heading home with loaves of fresh pumpernickel or rye and a few Polish pastries, such as *paczki* (plump jelly doughnuts), to enjoy later. Highlights of Polish Hamtramck include the **New Palace Bakery** (9833 Joseph Campau St., 313/875-1334, www.newpalace-bakery.com, 6am-6pm Mon.-Sat.), the most popular of the many bakeries, and the **Polonia Restaurant** (2934 Yemans St., 313/873-8432, www.polonia-restaurant.net, 11am-8pm Mon.-Thurs., 11am-9pm Fri.-Sat., 1pm-7pm Sun., $5-9), housed in a former 1930s food co-op.

Getting There

Well known locally, Hamtramck can be hard to find for the visitor. To get here from downtown Detroit, follow I-375 North to I-75 North, take the Holbrook Street exit, turn right onto Holbrook, and then turn left onto Joseph Campau Street. Without traffic, this six-mile trip usually takes about 15 minutes.

DEARBORN

Home to Ford's international headquarters and the largest collection of Arabic-speaking peoples in the United States, Dearborn is rightly known as "the town that Ford built." After all, there was little here but farmland when Henry Ford was born in a small white farmhouse at the corner of Ford Road and Mercury Drive—a house that you can now see at The Henry Ford's acclaimed Greenfield Village.

Sights

ARAB AMERICAN NATIONAL MUSEUM

While in Dearborn, make time for at least a taste of its Arabian culture. Most of Dearborn's Arab citizens live in the neighborhoods that line Warren and Dix. (The Dix neighborhood lies in the shadow of the Ford Rouge Plant, one of the largest factories in the world.) Its working-class residents are more than 90 percent Arab, primarily from Yemen. The south end boasts signs that are in both English and Arabic, headscarves are common on women, and many men wear traditional skullcaps. The restaurants and shops along Dix offer sights and sounds heard in the Arabian peninsula, including a call to prayer broadcast five times daily from a local mosque. So, while here, take some time to visit the fascinating **Arab American National Museum** (13624 Michigan Ave., 313/582-2266, www.arabamericanmuseum. org, 10am-6pm Wed.-Sat., noon-5pm Sun., $8 adults, $4 seniors, students, and children 6-12, children under 6 free), the first and only museum in the United States devoted to Arab American history and culture. Here, through the use of art, artifacts, documents, and photographs, you'll see several permanent exhibits that explore Arabian culture, the experiences of Arabian immigrants coming to and living in America, and the influence of Arab Americans and their organizations on the American way of life. In addition, you'll encounter rotating exhibits, which can range from student art displays to immersive multimedia exhibitions that illustrate the anger, frustration, ebullience, and hope associated with the Arab Spring uprisings.

◖ THE HENRY FORD

Today, Dearborn is best known to tourists as the location of **The Henry Ford** (20900 Oakwood Blvd., 313/982-6001 or 800/835-5237, www.hfmgv.org), a favorite field trip for local schoolchildren and one of the state's biggest tourism draws. In the adjacent **Greenfield Village** (9:30am-5pm daily mid-Apr.-Oct., 9:30am-5pm Fri.-Sun. Nov., $24 adults, $22 seniors 62 and over, $17.50 children 5-12, children under 5 free), Henry gathered buildings and other structures in an attempt to show how America grew from an agrarian to an industrial society. It's a charming—if disconcerting—time machine, a patchwork quilt of unrelated people and places, where a 16th-century English Cotswold cottage sits a few hundred yards from an 18th-century New England saltbox. Other features include Ford's childhood home, Thomas Edison's Menlo Park laboratory, and a working 19th-century farm.

Ford sent his pickers across the Midwest and New England to assemble enough artifacts to fill the 12-acre **Henry Ford Museum** (9:30am-5pm daily, $17 adults, $15 seniors 62 and over, $12.50 children 5-12, children under 5 free) next to the village. Inside is one vast collection after another, including several presidential limousines (including President Kennedy's and Ronald Reagan's), the world's greatest holdings of 19th-century farm and kitchen tools (the old washing machines are a stitch), a fine grouping of American furniture, and many artifacts that trace the evolution of the electric lightbulb (Edison was a great friend of Ford's; the complex was originally called the Edison Institute).

Worth the price of admission alone is the excellent exhibit known as "The Automobile in American Life," which nostalgically shows the car's effect on the American landscape. There's a 1950s McDonald's sign, complete with oversized golden arches; a 1946 diner from Marlboro, Massachusetts, where an egg salad sandwich cost 15 cents; a VW camper van, complete with a handy awning; and a Holiday Inn guest room, circa 1960. The evolution of the auto industry is explained using TV monitors and restored automobiles from each period.

Also worth a peek is the permanent "Made in America" exhibit, which traces the evolution of American manufacturing. Far from dull, it explains technology in an entertaining manner, accented by film clips, including one from the *I Love Lucy* show in which Lucy joins a candy-making assembly line with disastrous results. One exhibit, "With Liberty & Justice for All," presents the highlights of four revolutions in America—the American Revolution, the Civil War, the women's suffragist movement, and the Civil Rights era—and features such iconic artifacts as Abraham Lincoln's chair and the bus that Rosa Parks famously rode.

With thousands of items and the adjacent village, the entire complex is more than a bit overwhelming, especially since the museum has an admittedly confusing layout. A good idea is to split a visit into two days, with one day earmarked to explore each half. You might need even more time if you plan to visit other on-site features like the **IMAX Theatre** (show times vary daily, $10-13.75 adults, $9-12.75 seniors

HOMES OF THE AUTO BARONS

As Detroit grew to become the "Motor Capital of the World," opportunities to amass great fortunes grew with it. The automobile "royalty" that emerged took on a pampered lifestyle befitting their status and built great estates full of art and intricate workmanship. Today, these four estates offer visitors the chance to see firsthand how the auto pioneers lived during the heyday of the auto industry.

FISHER MANSION

The only estate within the city limits, the **Fisher Mansion** (383 Lenox Ave., 313/331-6740, www.detroitiskconlive.com), inspired by William Randolph Hearst's San Simeon, was built by Lawrence P. Fisher of the Fisher Body Company, a talented playboy who once courted actress Jean Harlow and who spent millions of his huge fortune constructing this magnificent riverfront estate. It has been described as "glitz bordering on garish." Completed in 1928, it's most noted for its ornate stone and marble work, exquisite European handcrafted stained-glass windows, doors and arches carved from woods imported from India and Africa, and rare black walnut and rosewood parquet floors. More than 200 ounces of gold and silver leaf highlight the decorative ceilings and moldings.

The mansion was neglected after Fisher's death and was jointly purchased for just $80,000 in 1975 by Alfred Brush Ford, great-grandson of Henry Ford, and Elisabeth Reuther Dickmeyer, daughter of legendary United Auto Workers chief Walter Reuther. Together, they restored the mansion and donated it to the International Society for Krishna Consciousness, of which they are members. Today, the mansion serves as the Bhaktivedanta Cultural Center, which welcomes the public to daily worship services and special cultural events. Although there are no official tours, visitors to the Fisher Mansion will encounter a fine art gallery and an exhibit about India's colorful heritage.

EDSEL & ELEANOR FORD HOUSE

Where Jefferson Avenue becomes Lake Shore Road stands the **Edsel & Eleanor Ford House** (1100 Lake Shore Rd., Grosse Pointe Shores, 313/884-4222, www.fordhouse.org, house tours 10am-4pm Tues.-Sat., noon-4pm Sun. Apr.-Dec., noon-1:30pm Tues.-Fri., noon-4pm Sat.-Sun. Jan.-Mar., closed on major holidays and for two weeks in winter, $12 adults, $11 seniors, $8 children 6-12, children under 6 free). The Cotswold-style mansion, designed by noted local architect Albert Kahn, was built in 1929 for Henry Ford's only son, who raised his four children in this house. Much of the interior paneling and furniture was lifted from distinguished old English manors; even the roof is of imported English stones expertly laid by imported Cotswold roofers.

What makes the house especially interesting is that it remains much as it did when the Fords lived here. Edsel died in 1943, but his wife, Eleanor Clay Ford, left the estate virtually untouched after that, meaning that it represents a style of living and quality of craftsmanship that is rapidly vanishing, if not completely gone. Throughout is evidence of the Fords' love of art, with copies of masterpieces now replacing the originals that were donated to the downtown Detroit Institute of Arts.

Visitors can experience a 13-minute video about the Fords, an hour-long guided tour that leads them through the distinctive dwelling, and a self-guided tour of the grounds and outer buildings (9:30am-6pm Tues.-Sat., 11:30am-6pm Sun. Apr.-Dec., 11:30am-4pm Tues.-Sun. Jan.-Mar.). Highlights include a stylish art deco recreation room by famed industrial designer Walter Dorwin Teague; Edsel's personal study, lined with framed family photos and images of luminaries like Thomas Edison; and the Tudor-style playhouse created in 1930 for daughter Josephine's seventh birthday. Note that behind-the-scenes tours ($15 pp, children under 6 free), which include a guided house tour and access to the grounds, are also available. Of course, those who decide not to tour the house can simply meander amid the grounds ($5 pp, children under 6 free).

FAIR LANE

Of the four auto baron estates, Henry Ford's **Fair Lane** (1 Fair Lane Dr., Dearborn, 313/884-4222, www.henryfordestate.org, tours 10:30am-2:30pm Tues.-Sun. Apr.-Dec., 1:30pm Tues.-Sun. Jan.-Mar., $12 adults, $11 seniors and students, $8 children 6-12, children under 6 free) is, surprisingly, the least baronial. By the time it was completed in 1914, Ford had become active in World War I politics and spent a lot of time helping the war effort in Europe. Nonetheless, it is justly listed as a National Historic Landmark.

Fair Lane encompasses more than 1,300 acres. For some, the natural landscape by Jens Jensen is the highlight of a visit; for others, it's the estate's many technical feats, including the extensive six-level hydroelectric power plant created by Ford and his good buddy Thomas Edison. In this house, Ford entertained some of the world's most influential people, including Charles Lindbergh (also a Detroit native), President Herbert Hoover, and the Duke of Windsor. It's an unusual combination of a Scottish baronial structure and the Prairie style developed by Frank Lloyd Wright. Two-hour tours uncover quirky details such as Henry's basement bowling alley and his penchant for birds (he once had 500 birdhouses on the premises) as well as Clara's passion for roses. A small but choice gift shop stocks a wide selection of books on related subjects.

During the summer of 2013, ownership of the historic estate passed to a nonprofit organization that will oversee an extensive restoration. Unfortunately, the property will remain closed to the public during this time.

MEADOW BROOK HALL

Last but not least is Rochester's **Meadow Brook Hall** (480 S. Adams Rd., 248/364-6200, www.oakland.edu/mbh, tours 11:30am-2:30pm daily June-Aug., 1:30pm Mon.-Fri., 11:30am-2:30pm Sat.-Sun. Jan.-May and Sept.-Nov., $15 adults, $10 seniors 62 and over, children under 13 free). John Dodge and his brother Horace were among the car makers responsible for Detroit's sudden catapult into big business. John died suddenly in 1920, leaving behind a vast fortune and a widow, Matilda (his former secretary), who remarried a wealthy lumberman, Alfred Wilson, in 1925. Together, Alfred and Matilda toured Europe and dreamed of a grand estate north of the city. They built the 110-room Tudor-style Meadow Brook Hall in the late 1920s for the then-astonishing sum of $4 million. Interiors were copied from drawings of English estates.

More than 85 years later, Meadow Brook is still largely intact, in part because Mrs. Wilson left the estate to Oakland University, which still administers the property. Rooms – including a two-story ballroom, game rooms copied from old English pubs, and Matilda's bathroom accented with locally made Pewabic tile – still house original family collections and furnishings. A walk in the surrounding woods reveals a six-room playhouse known as Knole Cottage, built for Frances Wilson, Matilda's daughter; typically, the playhouse is open noon-5pm daily during the Holiday Walk (house tours 11am-5pm daily, $20 adults, $5 children 3-17, children under 3 free), an annual celebration that usually takes place late November-December 23. Throughout the year, a behind-the-scenes tour ($15 adults, $10 seniors, children under 13 free), which offers a glimpse at rarely seen parts of the mansion, may also be available.

© LAURA MARTONE

The Henry Ford

62 and over, $8.50-9.75 children under 13) and the **Benson Ford Research Center** (9:30am-5pm Tues.-Fri.). In addition, tour buses regularly leave for the **Ford Rouge Factory Tour** (9:30am-5pm Mon.-Sat., $15 adults, $14 seniors 62 and over, $11 children 3-12, children under 3 free), a five-part excursion that culminates with a stroll through the Ford F-150 truck assembly plant.

Accommodations

For those who'd prefer not to stay overnight in downtown Detroit, the city's suburbs offer a number of lodging options, and Dearborn is no exception. **The Dearborn Inn** (20301 Oakwood Blvd., 313/271-2700, www.marriott.com, $139-229 d), for instance, has a terrific location on 23 lush acres. The 229 refined guest rooms and the five Colonial-style guest homes make this a unique hotel experience. Amenities at this smoke-free Marriott property include plush bedding, flat-screen HDTVs, high-speed Internet access, a fitness center, a

business center, an on-site restaurant, and an outdoor swimming pool.

Another stylish option is the pet-friendly **Adoba Hotel** (600 Town Center Dr., 313/592-3622, www.adobadearborn.com, $159-199 d), an enormous, postmodern steel-and-glass monolith designed by architect Charles Luckman and housing more than 770 rooms and suites. Not surprisingly, it's one of the largest hotels in the Hyatt chain. The on-site restaurant, Giulio & Sons, serves well-prepared steaks, seafood, and northern Italian specialties. Not far away, **The Henry** (300 Town Center Dr., 313/441-2000, www.behenry.com, $149-259 d), which was built with Ford money, attracts power brokers from across the country as well as a few understated rock stars and visiting celebrities. The award-winning TRIA is known for its excellent, if pricey, continental cuisine, and the elegant rooms feature contemporary artwork, custom furnishings, and free high-speed Internet access. Other on-site amenities include a fitness center, an indoor swimming pool, and massage treatment rooms.

Food

Dearborn offers its share of vittles, too. **(Big Fish** (700 Town Center Dr., 313/336-6350, www.muer.com, 11am-10pm Mon.-Thurs., 11am-11pm Fri., 11:30am-11pm Sat., 1pm-9pm Sun., $10-40), part of the Muer seafood restaurant family, is a popular lunch spot that can also get pretty crowded during dinner. Some say the unusual name is a reference to the Big Three execs who power lunch at the original location in Dearborn (there's also one in Trenton, New Jersey). Others say it's a reference to the menu, which mainly features seafood. The atmosphere is dark and clubby, accented with fishing and nautical motifs. Specialties include the seafood jambalaya, seared diver scallops, steamed Dungeness crab, and any of the excellent daily specials.

Information

For more information about Dearborn, consult the **Dearborn Area Chamber of Commerce** (22100 Michigan Ave., Dearborn, 313/584-6100, www.dearbornchamber.org, 9am-5pm Mon.-Fri.) or the **Detroit Metro Convention & Visitors Bureau** (211 W. Fort St., Ste. 1000, Detroit, 313/202-1800 or 800/338-7648, www.visitdetroit.com, 9am-5pm Mon.-Fri.).

Getting There

Many travelers choose to access Dearborn via train; **Amtrak** (800/872-7245, www.amtrak.com), after all, offers regular service to the town's station at 16121 Michigan Avenue. If, on the other hand, you're driving from downtown Detroit, you can simply take M-10 North and I-94 West to reach Dearborn. Without traffic, this 10-mile trip should take about 15 minutes.

FARMINGTON HILLS
Holocaust Memorial Center

America's first freestanding **Holocaust Memorial Center** (28123 Orchard Lake Rd., 248/553-2400, www.holocaustcenter.org,

9:30am-5pm Sun.-Thurs., 9:30am-3pm Fri., $8 adults, $6 seniors 55 and over, $5-6 students) provides a vivid portrayal of the Holocaust. Features include extensive material and state-of-the-art display techniques that enhance this visceral experience.

Information

For more information about Farmington Hills, consult the **Greater Farmington Area Chamber of Commerce** (33425 Grand River Ave., Ste. 101, Farmington, 248/919-6917, www.gfachamber.com, 9am-5pm Mon.-Fri.) or the **Detroit Metro Convention & Visitors Bureau** (211 W. Fort St., Ste. 1000, Detroit, 313/202-1800 or 800/338-7648, www.visitdetroit.com, 9am-5pm Mon.-Fri.).

Getting There

If you're driving from downtown Detroit, simply take M-10 North, merge onto I-696 West, and follow M-5 East to reach Farmington Hills. Without traffic, this 29-mile trip should take roughly 32 minutes.

ROYAL OAK
Sights and Shopping

Heading north on Woodward from downtown Detroit, Royal Oak is one of the first suburbs you'll encounter after you cross 8 Mile Road. It's the only suburb in the Detroit area where you'll find green hair, unusual pierced body parts, and whips and chains in the window of **Noir Leather** (124 W. 4th St., 248/541-3979, www.noirleather.com, 11am-9pm Mon.-Thurs., 11am-10pm Fri.-Sat., noon-7pm Sun.), a fetish fashion boutique founded in 1983. Nowhere else in Michigan will you find a store sign that reads "Absolutely no return on bondage items for sanitary reasons."

Royal Oak was a sleepy (some said "dying") suburb in the 1970s, known only by its nickname—Royal Joke—and as the site of the respected 125-acre **Detroit Zoo** (8450 W. 10 Mile Rd., 248/541-5717, www.detroitzoo.org, 9am-5pm daily Apr.-Labor Day, 10am-5pm daily Sept.-Oct., 10am-4pm daily Nov.-Mar., $14

© L. DIGGS OF PICTURE THIS...

fountain in Royal Oak's Detroit Zoo

adults, $12 seniors 62 and over, $9 children 2-15, children under 2 free). The zoo, long a popular city attraction, is home to more than 1,300 animals, from flamingos and trumpeter swans to wolverines and gorillas. Three of the most favored exhibits are the Wildlife Interpretive Gallery, site of a popular hummingbird/butterfly garden; the Arctic Ring of Fire, which features polar bears and Arctic species; and the Holden Museum of Living Reptiles.

In the mid-1980s, the city's gay population was concentrated in Royal Oak, filling the two main commercial streets with vintage clothing and record shops, antiques emporiums, and funky coffeehouses. While a few of the original boutiques remain, others have been replaced by high-rent glitzy home furnishings shops and restaurants, which now characterize much of the area. Despite this, Royal Oak is still a lively place, where the streets are filled with a pleasing variety of families and punks, gays and straights. Main Street and Washington Avenue, the two main drags, are great spots for window-shopping and people-watching. And it seems as if a new eatery opens almost every day here, giving it one of the best and most extensive restaurant scenes in metro Detroit.

Worthwhile stops include the sinful **Gayle's Chocolates** (417 S. Washington Ave., 248/398-0001, www.gayleschocolates.com, 10am-6pm Mon.-Wed., 10am-8pm Thurs.-Sat., noon-7pm Sun. fall-spring, 10am-6pm Mon.-Tues., 10am-8pm Wed.-Thurs., 10am-10pm Fri.-Sat., noon-7pm Sun. summer), the first in the city to offer cappuccino and espresso (now found on just about every corner). Another feature is the popular juice bar (try the carrot-apple-ginger), but Gayle's heart remains in the chocolate-making facility located upstairs, which churns out some of the best truffles in the country. Also worth a peek are **Vertu** (514 S. Washington Ave., 248/545-6050, www.vertumodern.com, noon-6pm Tues.-Sat.), known for its 20th-century designs, including furniture by Charles and Ray Eames, George Nelson, and Eero Saarinen, and **Dos Manos** (210 W. 6th St., 248/542-5856 or 800/572-4957, www.dosmanos.com, 10am-6pm daily), where you'll find Latin American handicrafts.

Food

When it's time to eat in Royal Oak, you'll be hard-pressed to choose. In the mood for seafood? If so, head to **Tom's Oyster Bar** (318 S. Main St., 248/541-1186, www.tomsoysterbar.com, 11am-10pm Mon.-Tues., 11am-11pm Wed.-Thurs., 11am-midnight Fri., noon-1am Sat., noon-10pm Sun., $8-40), which features the area's most extensive selection of—surprise!—oysters, as well as tasty steaks and innovative fresh seafood. **BD's Mongolian Barbecue** (430 S. Main St., 248/398-7755, www.gomongo.com, 11am-10pm Sun.-Fri., 11am-11pm Sat., $6-21), meanwhile, lets you watch as chefs whip up your stir-fry creation on a huge, central grill. Since its opening in 1992, it's become so popular that it has established outposts in other metro Detroit suburbs, not to mention various U.S. states, from Illinois to Florida.

Information

For more information about Royal Oak, consult the **Royal Oak Downtown Development Authority** (211 Williams St., Royal Oak, 248/246-3280, www.downtownroyaloak.org) or the **Detroit Metro Convention & Visitors Bureau** (211 W. Fort St., Ste. 1000, Detroit, 313/202-1800 or 800/338-7648, www.visitdetroit.com, 9am-5pm Mon.-Fri.).

Getting There

Some travelers may choose to access Royal Oak via **Amtrak** (800/872-7245, www.amtrak.com), which offers train service to the sheltered platform at 202 South Sherman Drive. If, on the other hand, you opt to drive from downtown Detroit, simply take I-75 North and Woodward Avenue to reach Royal Oak. Without traffic, this 14-mile trip should take less than 30 minutes.

BIRMINGHAM

Naysayers were concerned that downtown Birmingham—a chic enclave of expensive shops and galleries—would shrivel and die when the even more chic Somerset Collection, a gleaming shopping complex, opened on nearby West Big Beaver Road late in 1996. Birmingham has proven remarkably resilient, however, and remains a tony 'burb with one of the few thriving downtown areas in surrounding Oakland County. Shoppers from all over the metro area come here to see and be seen, to linger in cafés and restaurants, and to exercise their credit cards in the unusual boutiques.

Shopping

Even if you're not a shopper, Birmingham is worth a trip for its art galleries, one of the most impressive concentrations in the Midwest. Here, you'll even find cutting-edge contemporary art at places like the **Robert Kidd Gallery** (107 Townsend St., 248/642-3909, www.robertkiddgallery.com, 11am-5:30pm Tues.-Sat.), which has been in existence since 1976. More than a dozen influential art outlets are grouped along a section of Woodward north of downtown known as "Gallery Row."

Accommodations

In Birmingham, ◖ **The Townsend Hotel** (100 Townsend St., 248/642-7900, www.townsendhotel.com, $250-300 d) is the posh—if relatively unpretentious—European-style hostelry where Paul McCartney stayed when he performed in Detroit in 2005. Nothing but the best is good enough here—Belgian linens, pillows of the fluffiest down, yards of marble in the baths, and a restaurant staffed with world-class chefs who cater to the guests' every whim. You'll feel as if you've stepped into a Ralph Lauren ad. Located near Birmingham's fashionable shops and galleries, it's also a favorite stop for afternoon tea, served every afternoon.

Information

For more information about Birmingham, consult the **Birmingham Principal Shopping District** (151 Martin St., Birmingham, 248/530-1200, www.enjoybirmingham.com) or the **Detroit Metro Convention & Visitors Bureau** (211 W. Fort St., Ste. 1000, Detroit, 313/202-1800 or 800/338-7648, www.visitdetroit.com, 9am-5pm Mon.-Fri.).

Getting There

Some travelers may choose to access Birmingham via **Amtrak** (800/872-7245, www.amtrak.com), which offers train service to the sheltered platform at Villa Road and Lewis Street. If, on the other hand, you opt to drive from downtown Detroit, simply take I-75 North and Woodward Avenue to reach Birmingham. Without traffic, this 20-mile trip should take about 30 minutes.

BLOOMFIELD HILLS

For a look at how the other half (actually, the other 1 percent) lives, turn the wheel north to Bloomfield Hills. Long the suburb of choice for CEOs, Big Three bigwigs, and other members of the city's power brokers, it ranks as the state's richest town as well as the second-wealthiest in the country. Past and present residents have included Detroit Pistons captain Isaiah Thomas and the queen of soul, Aretha Franklin. Unlike Grosse Pointe, which still struggles with the remains of its WASPish heritage, it doesn't matter if you're black or white in Bloomfield Hills. Money is the great equalizer.

If Grosse Pointe epitomizes "old money," Bloomfield Hills attracts its newer, shinier counterpart. Huge houses are spread throughout its rolling hills—a geographic anomaly in southeastern Michigan. Most are late 20th century, although older models can be found clustered around Cranbrook, former home of newspaper magnate George Booth, who founded the *Detroit News*. Drive the winding lanes and you'll find Old Tudor, Georgian, and other 1920s-era mansions. One notable exception is the "Smith House" at 5045 Pon Valley Road, which was designed by Frank Lloyd Wright in 1946.

Cranbrook

Despite its celebrities, Bloomfield Hills remains best known as home to **Cranbrook** (39221 N. Woodward Ave., 877/462-7262, www.cranbrook.edu), a renowned, 315-acre arts and educational complex. Here, famed Finnish architect Eliel Saarinen created a lush and lovely refuge for artists and students.

Cranbrook is known throughout the world for the integrated aesthetics of its environment. All buildings, gardens, sculpture, and interiors are treated as an integral and important part of a whole. This creative cohesion is the result of two men, patron newspaper magnate George Booth and artist Eliel Saarinen. Booth, one of the early city expatriates, bought a rundown farm in Bloomfield Hills in 1904 and commissioned noted Detroit architect Albert Kahn to build him a large, Tudor-style mansion there. Grandson of an English coppersmith, Booth was a noted proponent of the arts-and-crafts movement, which preached a reunification of life and art. After a 1922 trip to Rome, where he visited the American Academy, he decided to create a school of architecture and design.

While the school is still known throughout the world, equal acclaim is drawn by the **Cranbrook Art Museum** (248/645-3323, www.cranbrookartmuseum.org, 11am-5pm

Cranbrook Art Museum

Wed.-Sun. June-Aug., 10am-5pm Tues.-Fri., 11am-5pm Sat.-Sun. Sept.-May, $8 adults, $6 seniors 65 and over, $4 students, children under 13 free), which is operated by the **Cranbrook Academy of Art** (248/645-3300, www.cranbrookart.edu) and serves as the largest museum in southeastern Michigan devoted to modern and contemporary art, architecture, and design. It presents exhibits by both students as well as prominent faculty members. Another popular attraction here is the **Cranbrook Institute of Science** (248/645-3200 or 877/462-7262, http://science.cranbrook.edu, 10am-5pm Tues.-Thurs., 10am-10pm Fri.-Sat., noon-4pm Sun., $13 adults, $9.50 seniors 65 and over and children 2-12, children under 2 free), a family-friendly science and natural history museum with a collection of more than 200,000 objects and artifacts. In addition to galleries devoted to geology, anthropology, astronomy, Native Americans, and other riveting subjects, popular diversions here include a planetarium ($5 pp, $1 children under 2), a live bat program ($5 pp, $1 children under 2), and an observatory that's open (and free) to the public on Friday and Saturday evenings, weather permitting.

Accommodations

If you're hoping to stay overnight in Bloomfield Hills, head to the **Radisson Hotel Detroit-Bloomfield Hills** (39475 Woodward Ave., 248/644-1400, www.radisson.com, $110-160 d), a comfortable property in a prime location. In addition to more than 150 rooms and suites, the Radisson offers a fitness center, an indoor heated pool, a business center, three on-site dining options, free high-speed Internet access, and shuttle service within a 10-mile radius.

Information

For more information about Bloomfield Hills, consult the **City of Bloomfield Hills** (45 E. Long Lake Rd., Bloomfield Hills, 248/644-1520, www.bloomfieldhillsmi.net) or the **Detroit Metro Convention & Visitors Bureau** (211 W. Fort St., Ste. 1000, Detroit, 313/202-1800 or 800/338-7648, www.visitdetroit.com, 9am-5pm Mon.-Fri.).

Getting There

If you're driving from downtown Detroit, take M-10 North and US-24 North to reach Bloomfield Hills. Without traffic, this 26-mile trip should take roughly 30 minutes.

GROSSE POINTE

Five cities actually make up the area collectively known as Grosse Pointe on Detroit's far east side. Taken as a whole, Grosse Pointe Shores, Grosse Pointe Farms, Grosse Pointe Woods, the city of Grosse Pointe, and Grosse Pointe Park make up one of the metro area's wealthiest suburbs, a land of landscaped estates, big trees, big homes, and even bigger money.

A summer community in the 1840s, Grosse Pointe began to change about 1910, when wealthy Detroiters sought to separate themselves from the immigrants who crowded the growing city. The wealthiest built mansions that imitated the elegant country houses of England, France, and Italy, importing stone fireplaces and entire rooms that were later incorporated into new construction.

This is where the city's prominent old families settled; many descendants of this founding aristocracy still live here. For years (through roughly the 1950s), prospective home buyers were screened by a Grosse Pointe real estate broker's infamous point system designed to perpetuate WASP homogeneity. Today, you'll find a much more diverse population, although, like most of Detroit's suburbs, it's still predominantly white. Grosse Pointe Park is the most liberal and Democratic, with a number of smaller homes and modest, middle-class 1920s housing. One area, now known as the Cabbage Patch because its early Belgian residents grew the vegetable in their yards, was developed to house servants from the nearby estates.

Sights

Many of the largest mansions have been razed, although a few remain along Lake Shore Drive. It's a beautiful drive in any season, with the Detroit River attracting joggers, freighter-watchers, and others who come just to ogle the architecture. To get a peek at the inside of one of the area's original estates, stop at the former **Alger House,** now known as the **Grosse Pointe War Memorial** (32 Lake Shore Dr., Grosse Pointe Farms, 313/881-7511, www.warmemorial.org, 9am-9pm Mon.-Sat., free). Built in 1910, this roomy Italian Renaissance-style mansion was originally the home of a founder of the Packard Motor Company and now serves as a community center.

Information

For more information about Grosse Pointe, consult the **Grosse Pointe Chamber of Commerce** (63 Kercheval Ave., Ste. 16, Grosse Pointe, 313/881-4722, www.grossepointechamber.com, 9am-5pm Mon.-Fri.) or the **Detroit Metro Convention & Visitors Bureau** (211 W. Fort St., Ste. 1000, Detroit, 313/202-1800 or 800/338-7648, www.visitdetroit.com, 9am-5pm Mon.-Fri.).

Getting There

If you're driving from downtown Detroit, take East Jefferson Avenue to reach Grosse Pointe. Without traffic, this eight-mile trip should take about 20 minutes.

Southeast Michigan

In the towns surrounding the Detroit metropolitan area, visitors will find nostalgic downtown districts, historic museums, inland lakes, and recreation areas galore—all a relatively quick drive from Detroit via interstates and major highways.

GROSSE ILE

Not far from the Detroit River International Wildlife Refuge, Grosse Ile is a lengthy, bottle-shaped island in the Detroit River, just north of the entrance to Lake Erie.

Sights

LIGHTHOUSES

While Grosse Ile isn't a huge tourist destination, there are two nearby lighthouses worth a look: the **Grosse Ile North Channel Range Front Light,** a white, 50-foot-tall octagonal tower lit in 1906 and deactivated in 1963, and the **Detroit River Light** in Lake Erie, only accessible via boat. Although the **Grosse Ile Historical Society** (P.O. Box 131, Grosse Ile, MI 48138, 734/675-1250, www.gihistory.org) offers an annual one-day tour of the Grosse Ile lighthouse, the Detroit River Light, which was built in 1885 and is still an active navigational aid operated by the U.S. Coast Guard, can only be viewed from the outside. Curiously, the Detroit River Light has also been known as the Bar Point Shoal Light.

◀ LAKE ERIE METROPARK

Perhaps surprising to some, southeastern Michigan boasts several parks and natural areas, ideal for outdoor enthusiasts weary of Detroit's downtown bustle. Perhaps even more surprising, the Detroit area is the site of North America's first international wildlife refuge. Established in 2001, the **Detroit River International Wildlife Refuge** (Brownstown Charter Township, 734/365-0219, www.fws.gov/midwest/detroitriver) comprises islands, marshes, coastal wetlands, and waterfront terrain along the lower Detroit River and western shoreline of Lake Erie. Though public access is limited, you can appreciate at least part of the refuge by visiting the **Lake Erie Metropark** (32481 W. Jefferson, Brownstown, 734/379-5020, www.metroparks.com, 6am-10pm daily in summer, 7am-8pm daily in winter, $7/vehicle daily, $20-30/vehicle annually), a well-preserved, 1,607-acre recreation area situated south of Grosse Ile and offering stunning views of the nearby river, lake, and islands. Popular among outdoor enthusiasts, the metropark features three miles of shoreline, an 18-hole golf course (734/379-0048), hiking and biking trails, a swimming pool, a marina and boat launches (7am-9pm daily Memorial Day-Labor Day, $7 daily, $20-35 annually), and the **Marshlands Museum and Nature Center** (9am-5pm daily in summer, 1pm-5pm Mon.-Fri., 9am-5pm Sat.-Sun. in winter, free with admission to the park). While anglers, kayakers, and bird-watchers enjoy this peaceful place in the spring, summer, and fall, the Lake Erie Metropark is also favored during the winter months, when cross-country skiers can enjoy 4.25 miles of flat, groomed trails.

Food

If you're hungry after visiting Grosse Ile, return to the mainland and grab a bite to eat. One tasty option is the **Speedboat Bar & Grill** (749 Biddle Ave., Wyandotte, 734/282-5750, www.speedboatbar-grill.com, 11am-10pm Tues.-Thurs., 10am-2am Fri., 11am-2am Sat., $4-17), home of the masterpiece swine burger, maybe the perfect bar burger. It's thick and juicy and served with spicy rings of jalapeño, pepper cheese, chili, and fried onions. Or you can opt for a brimming bowl of the spicy red chili, a consistent award-winner. This joint is definitely worth a special trip downriver.

Information

For more information about Grosse Ile, consult the **Township of Grosse Ile** (9601 Groh Rd., Grosse Ile, 734/676-4422, www.grosseile.com, 8am-5pm Mon.-Fri.).

Getting There

To reach Grosse Ile Township from downtown Detroit, take M-10 North and I-75 South to West Road East, turn right onto Allen Road, turn left onto Van Horn Road, take another left onto West Jefferson Avenue, and then take an immediate right onto Grosse Ile Parkway, which connects the mainland to Grosse Ile. Without traffic, this 27-mile trip should take about 40 minutes.

MONROE

On the banks of the River Raisin, in Michigan's southeastern corner, lies the city of Monroe, Michigan's third-oldest community. Its location made it the natural crossroads for the Native Americans, the French missionaries, and the fur trappers who settled in the area. Caught between the British Army and the U.S. forces during the War of 1812, Monroe is also the site of the deadliest battle during the war, when after having been pushed back into Canada, the British counterattacked, killing 300 Americans in the Battle of the River Raisin. "Remember the Raisin" became America's rally cry after the Indian allies of the British killed another hundred injured soldiers who were unable to retreat after the battle. In the 19th century, Monroe also became home to General George A. Custer and his wife, Elizabeth.

Sights and Shopping

History buffs might enjoy a visit to the **Monroe County Historical Museum** (126 S. Monroe St., 734/240-7780, www.co.monroe.mi.us/museum, by appt. Mon.-Tues., 10am-5pm Wed.-Sat., noon-5pm Sun., $4 adults, $2 children 5-17, children under 5 free), a Georgian-style public building that houses one of the largest collections of 18th- and 19th-century artifacts relating to southeastern Michigan. Of course, with shopping and dining possibilities galore, this quaint town offers more than just history. Check out the year-round **Monroe Farmers Market** (17 E. Willow St., www.farmersmarketmonroe.com, 6am-noon Tues. and Sat. June-Oct., 7am-1pm Sat. Nov.-May) for some locally produced treats.

To better enjoy the riverfront, you can purchase an inexpensive bike from **Jack's Bicycles** (206 S. Monroe St., 734/242-1400, www.jacksbike.com, 10am-6pm Mon.-Fri., 10am-4pm Sat.), a fantastic shop with a huge variety of bikes, plus sporty apparel. If you want to splurge on yourself or someone else, check out **Frenchie's** (15 E. Front St., 734/242-5840, www.frenchiesjewelry.com, 10am-5pm Mon.-Fri., 10am-3pm Sat.), where you can browse through their extensive coin, stamp, and fine jewelry collections.

Information

For more information about Monroe, contact the **Monroe County Convention and Tourism Bureau** (103 W. Front St., 734/457-1030, www.monroeinfo.com, 10am-6pm Tues.-Fri., 9am-4pm Sat.) or the **Monroe County Chamber of Commerce** (P.O. Box 626, Monroe, MI 48161, 734/384-3366, www.monroecountychamber.com, 8:30am-5pm Mon.-Fri.).

Getting There

From downtown Detroit via car, take I-75 South to Monroe. Without traffic, this 40-mile trip should take about 40 minutes.

PONTIAC

In its heyday, Pontiac was a booming General Motors town. While still the home of several manufacturing plants, it's clear that Pontiac has seen better days. Nevertheless, the town still has a lot to offer for visitors and residents alike.

Sights

Perched on 4.5 acres of well-groomed land and home to the Oakland County Pioneer and Historical Society, the **Pine Grove Historical Museum** (405 Cesar Chavez Ave., 248/338-6732, www.ocphs.org, 11am-4pm Tues.-Thurs., $5 adults, $3 children under 13) comprises what was once known as Pine Grove, the former estate of Moses Wisner, one of Michigan's pre-Civil War governors. Today, it encompasses the Wisner Mansion and several outbuildings, including a summer kitchen, an outhouse, a smokehouse, and a root cellar. On the premises, you'll also encounter the Drayton Plains one-room schoolhouse and a carriage house that's home to a research library as well as the Pioneer Museum. The collections here include classic automobiles, 19th-century tools and farming implements, and vintage clothing from the 19th and early 20th centuries, including military uniforms from the Civil War, the Spanish-American War, World War I, and World War II.

Entertainment and Events
NIGHTLIFE

Surprisingly, Pontiac has a thriving club scene, boasting some of southeastern Michigan's hippest joints. **Clutch Cargo's** (65 E. Huron, 248/333-2362 or 248/333-0649, www.clutchcargos.com, show times and ticket prices vary) is a nightclub and music venue that regularly books big-name talent. The **Tonic Night Club** (29 S. Saginaw St., 248/334-7411, www.tonicdetroit.com, 10pm-2am Thurs., 9pm-2am Fri.-Sun., cover varies), meanwhile, offers multiple dance floors and some of Detroit's hottest DJs; over the years, it's welcomed a plethora of celebrities, from Prince to Justin Timberlake.

WOODWARD DREAM CRUISE

Begun in 1995 as a small fundraiser for the Ferndale community, this annual mid-August parade down Woodward Avenue has become the world's largest one-day automotive event, luring 1.5 million people and more than 40,000 classic cars from around the globe. The **Woodward Dream Cruise** (www.woodwarddreamcruise.com) stretches 16 miles though Ferndale, Pleasant Ridge, Huntington Woods, Berkley, Royal Oak, Birmingham, Bloomfield Hills, Bloomfield Township, and Pontiac, taking over Woodward Avenue through each of these towns—truly a spectacle to behold. Luckily, it's free to watch, but find your spot early, as it gets very crowded all along the route.

Sports and Recreation
GOLF

While golfers will find the largest concentration of well-regarded golf courses in the northern half of the Lower Peninsula, southeastern Michigan has a few notable spots as well. One such option is **Shepherd's Hollow Golf Club** (9085 Big Lake Rd., Clarkston, 248/922-0300, www.shepherdshollow.com, daily Apr.-Oct., $40-75 pp w/cart). Situated northwest of Pontiac and Waterford, this scenic championship course offers 27 holes amid 350 acres of rolling, wooded terrain.

Information

For more information about Pontiac, consult the **City of Pontiac** (47450 Woodward Ave., 248/758-3000, www.pontiac.mi.us).

Getting There

Some travelers reach Pontiac via **Amtrak** (800/872-7245, www.amtrak.com) or **Greyhound** (248/333-2499 or 800/231-2222, www.greyhound.com), which offer regular train and bus service, respectively, to the station building at 51000 Woodward Avenue. If, on the other hand, you're driving from downtown Detroit, take I-375 North, merge onto I-75 North, and follow the I-75 Business Loop to Woodward Avenue, which will lead you to Pontiac. Without traffic, this 31-mile trip should take about 35 minutes.

AUBURN HILLS
Shopping

In recent years, the Detroit area has seen an influx of outlet malls. One of the biggest and best is located in Auburn Hills.

The **Great Lakes Crossing Outlets** (4000 Baldwin Rd., 877/746-7452, www.shopgreatlakescrossingoutlets.com, 10am-9pm Mon.-Sat., 11am-6pm Sun., holiday hours vary) has almost 200 stores and restaurants. With everything from Brooks Brothers to Nike, the mall is sure to satisfy your shopping fix. Even movie lovers will be happy here; there's an enormous AMC multiplex on-site. If you're visiting during the holiday season, plan for huge crowds and long walks from your parking spot.

Information

For more information about Auburn Hills, contact the **Auburn Hills Chamber of Commerce** (3395A Auburn Rd., 248/853-7862, www.auburnhillschamber.com, 9am-4pm Mon.-Thurs., 9am-1pm Fri.).

Getting There

From downtown Detroit via car, take I-375 North, I-75 North, and Lapeer Road to reach Auburn Hills. Without traffic, this 33-mile trip should take about 35 minutes.

THE THUMB

Michigan's Lower Peninsula is hard to miss on any U.S. map. Shaped by three of the Great Lakes, it unmistakably resembles a mitten, a hackneyed image for some but nonetheless apt for a state that endures such long, cold winters. As with any normal mitten, there's a thumb-like protrusion—here, the large, rural peninsula along Michigan's southeastern shore, sandwiched between Lake Huron and Saginaw Bay. Called "the Thumb" by locals and tourists alike, this flat, isolated region offers a quiet alternative to bustling Detroit.

Save for peripheral destinations like Port Huron, Frankenmuth, and the cities along I-75, much of this fertile area has been overlooked by contemporary travelers, just as many of Michigan's 19th-century settlers bypassed it in favor of seemingly better farmland elsewhere.

The European immigrants who did establish the Thumb's earliest communities embraced the region's bounty by initiating some of Michigan's most critical industries, such as logging, fishing, shipbuilding, and automobile manufacturing.

Today, those who venture off the interstate—rather than zip by, en route to the dunes, hills, and orchards of the north—are treated to a unique place, filled with ample farms, nostalgic towns, and tranquil beaches that boast fewer crowds than those along Lake Michigan. While most tourists aim for the Bavarian-style attractions of Frankenmuth or the cultural diversions of Saginaw and Bay City, the Thumb offers a wealth of other curiosities, many of which relate to the region's diverse history.

Along the Lake Huron shore lie a variety of

© PORT AUSTIN KAYAK & BIKE RENTAL

HIGHLIGHTS

LOOK FOR **◖** TO FIND RECOMMENDED SIGHTS, ACTIVITIES, DINING, AND LODGING.

◖ Flint Cultural Center: Some visitors might be surprised to discover such a wealth of art and culture so close to the grittiness of downtown Flint, but this impressive collection of museums and theaters presents enough options, from auto exhibits to comedy shows, to fill several days (page 76).

◖ Crossroads Village & Huckleberry Railroad: In the midst of Flint's modern indus-

trial vibe lies this authentic 19th-century community, which offers a snapshot of long-ago rural life (page 79).

◖ Bronner's CHRISTmas Wonderland: It doesn't matter if it's the height of summer, or if you have enough Bibles and Christmas ornaments to last a lifetime; this enormous, eye-popping repository of holiday goodies, open all year-round, should be a stop (page 86).

◖ Bird-Watching near Saginaw: The Saginaw River area abounds with excellent bird-watching sites, from the 9,700-acre Shiawassee National Wildlife Refuge to the less well known Crow Island State Game Area. Diehards will delight in the plethora of bird species (page 94).

◖ Sanilac Petroglyphs Historic State Park: During the summer months, those interested in Michigan's earliest inhabitants can hike amid the petroglyphs near the Cass River, several miles south of Bad Axe. Still a mystery after years of study, these ancient drawings are the Lower Peninsula's only known prehistoric rock carvings attributed to Native Americans (page 104).

◖ Diving in Lake Huron's Underwater Preserves: Scuba divers will find over 30 major shipwrecks within the Thumb Area Bottomland Preserve and Sanilac Shores Underwater Preserve (page 110).

◖ Port Huron Museum: With exhibits that relate to Port Huron's arts, history, and marine heritage, the museum encompasses four separate sites, including the *Huron* Lightship, the Thomas Edison Depot Museum, the Fort Gratiot Lighthouse, and the town's former library (page 111).

nautical sights, including the quaint fishing port of Caseville; Port Huron's stunning Fort Gratiot Lighthouse, Michigan's oldest lighthouse; and numerous shipwrecks that make up the Thumb Area Bottomland Preserve.

Also intriguing is Flint's Crossroads Village, a community of restored 19th-century buildings that transport visitors to a simpler time, when hoop skirts and hard work prevailed. The Thumb's rarely visited interior offers its own

THE THUMB

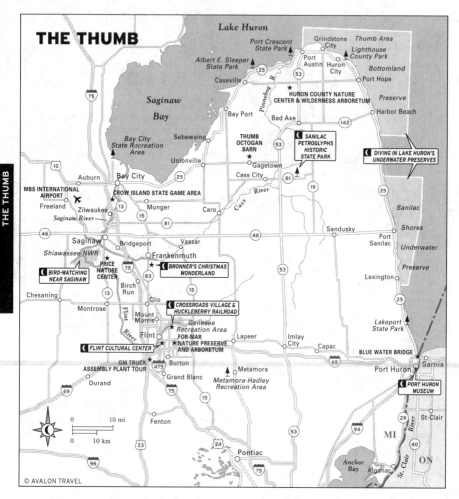

THE THUMB

Lake Huron

Grindstone City

Thumb Area

Port Crescent State Park

Lighthouse County Park

Albert E. Sleeper State Park

Port Austin

Huron City

Bottomland

Port Hope

Caseville

Preserve

Saginaw Bay

HURON COUNTY NATURE CENTER & WILDERNESS ARBORETUM

Bay Port

Harbor Beach

Bay City State Recreation Area

Sebewaing

Bad Axe

THUMB OCTAGON BARN

SANILAC PETROGLYPHS HISTORIC STATE PARK

Unionville

DIVING IN LAKE HURON'S UNDERWATER PRESERVES

Gagetown

Auburn

Bay City

Cass City

Sanilac

MBS INTERNATIONAL AIRPORT

CROW ISLAND STATE GAME AREA

Cass River

Shores

Freeland

Zilwaukee

Munger

Caro

Sandusky

Port Sanilac

Underwater

Saginaw River

Saginaw

Bridgeport

Vassar

Preserve

Shiawassee NWR

Frankenmuth

Lexington

BIRD-WATCHING NEAR SAGINAW

PRICE NATURE CENTER

BRONNER'S CHRISTMAS WONDERLAND

Chesaning

Birch Run

Montrose

Clio

CROSSROADS VILLAGE & HUCKLEBERRY RAILROAD

Mount Morris

Genesee Recreation Area

Lakeport State Park

Flint

FOR-MAR NATURE PRESERVE AND ARBORETUM

Lapeer

Imlay City

Capac

BLUE WATER BRIDGE

FLINT CULTURAL CENTER

GM TRUCK ASSEMBLY PLANT TOUR

Burton

Metamora

Port Huron

Sarnia

Durand

Grand Blanc

Metamora-Hadley Recreation Area

PORT HURON MUSEUM

St-Clair

MI

Fenton

ON

Pontiac

Anchor Bay

Algonac

© AVALON TRAVEL

0   10 mi
0   10 km

share of historic sites—namely the mysterious Native American petroglyphs south of Bad Axe; Gagetown's preserved Thumb Octagon Barn, built in the fashion of 1920s-era agricultural structures; and Lapeer's Greek Revival-style homes, part of the National Register of Historic Places.

Outdoor enthusiasts may especially appreciate this laid-back region, where bicyclists can explore the Genesee Recreation Area, bird-watchers can view ducks and eagles at the Shiawassee National Wildlife Refuge, and deep-sea anglers can board fishing charters in Port Austin. Various annual events—from car shows to county fairs—make the Thumb an even more enticing stopover before exploring the rest of the Great Lakes State.

PLANNING YOUR TIME

Except for the towns along the I-75 corridor, the Thumb is probably one of the least visited regions in Michigan's Lower Peninsula. For some residents and seasonal visitors, the potential for fewer crowds, even in summer, is perhaps the area's biggest asset. So, whether you're headed south to Detroit, west to Lake Michigan, or north to the Upper Peninsula, you should take some time to visit the villages, beaches, state parks, and cultural attractions that the Thumb comprises.

At minimum, you should reserve three days, though two weeks will allow you more time to experience the urban hot spots, interior sites, and Lake Huron coastline. Realistically, you could spend at least two days in each of the destinations along I-75, particularly if you plan to visit museums as well as nearby nature preserves and golf courses. Frankenmuth alone could fill a solid day with its quaint shops, historic structures, Bavarian cuisine, and year-round Christmas store.

Depending on your interests, the coastal towns and interior villages can each be explored in half a day's time. Cultural sites are usually concentrated along the shore or within historic downtown districts, and most towns only offer one main recreation area. In fact, the only two coastal locales that might require multiple days are Port Austin and Port Huron.

Bear in mind that only the major cities, such as Saginaw, have public transit, so reaching the rest of the Thumb will require a vehicle—either your own or a rental car from one of several agencies in the cities along I-75. Since the bulk of the Thumb's attractions lie around its perimeter, it's relatively easy to reach them via car. From Flint, I-75 leads to Bay City, from which M-25 traces the coast to Port Huron, where I-69 returns to Flint, roughly forming a 270-mile loop. Of course, this circuitous route makes it difficult to have one home base while visiting the Thumb.

When preparing your trip, remember that the Thumb is a seasonal place. While a wintertime visit can be fun in a year-round town like Frankenmuth, many of the region's more isolated inns, restaurants, and attractions are only open during the summer. In addition, although most of the Thumb's towns and rural areas are relatively safe to visit, you need to use caution when visiting cities like Flint. As in other urban areas, you should secure your belongings, avoid walking alone at night, and consult residents about other safety concerns.

For more information about the Thumb area, consult the **Thumb Area Tourism Council, Inc.** (TATC, Millington, 810/569-6856, www.thumbtourism.org); **ThumbTravels.com** (P.O. Box 340, Port Austin, MI 48467, www.thumbtravels.com); **Visit Michigan's Thumb** (Harbor Beach, http://michigan-thumb.com); the **Tip of The Thumb Heritage Water Trail** (P.O. Box 92, Caseville, MI 48725, www.thumbtrails.com); and the **Huron County Economic Development Corporation** (250 E. Huron Ave., Rm. 303, Bad Axe, 989/269-6431 or 800/358-4862, www.huroncounty.com).

HISTORY

As in the rest of Michigan, the Thumb's original inhabitants were a variety of Native American tribes, some of whom left their remnants behind in the form of ancient rock carvings in Sanilac County. By the early 1800s, many European settlers had bypassed this region in favor of seemingly better farmland in the center of the Lower Peninsula. Some pioneers, however, recognized the Thumb's many benefits, including its timber, fisheries, and fertile land, and began establishing towns like Flint, today the Thumb's largest city. Once an important river crossing on the Pontiac Trail—a link to several Indian routes that crossed the wilderness—Flint owes its existence to Jacob Smith, a Detroit fur trader, who in 1819 persuaded the Ojibwa and Potawatomi Indians to surrender the lands of Saginaw County. Not long after Smith settled on the present site of modern-day Flint, other colonists followed, establishing a post office, a bank, a factory, and other necessary establishments; by 1855, it was an incorporated city.

The Thumb's sleepy personality belies its past as one of the most important lumber centers in the United States. During the mid-1800s, millions of logs were sent down the Saginaw River, to be processed by the waiting mills of Saginaw and Bay City. The explosion of the logging business created the need for log-hauling carts and wagons—all of which were produced in Flint. The thriving timber industry generated great fortunes, many of which were later used to fund the establishment of the auto industry.

Saginaw Bay, meanwhile, witnessed the development of the state's largest commercial fishing industry as well as some of the biggest shipyards ever established on the Great Lakes. But, like many of the industries that helped to fortify the United States, some of these enterprises faded to make room for more modern pursuits.

Travel by ship and by rail eventually gave way to the age of the automobile, igniting southeastern Michigan's most significant industry during the 20th century. By the 1890s, Flint became known for producing road carts, followed by carriage manufacturers and the birth of the Buick Motor Company in 1904. Likewise, when the Thumb's timber was virtually depleted, residents turned to agriculture for a new way of life. Today, the region's commodities include fish, sugar beets, navy beans, grains, corn, various fruits, and, of course, automobiles.

Flint and Vicinity

Gritty Flint is now, and seems like it always has been, a worker's town. The city's economy has long been yoked to General Motors' plants. As long as the plants were booming, the city did well. By the mid-1980s, however, skyrocketing unemployment, corporate downsizing, and increased global competition had challenged the city's financial way of life forever. The city tried to launch an indoor theme park based on car culture, but AutoWorld, expected to boost the local economy and fuel tourism, was an embarrassing failure. Independent filmmaker and native son Michael Moore documented the city and its relationship with General Motors in the biting satire *Roger and Me,* filling Americans with images that are likely to haunt this weary town forever.

Despite its blue-collar image, Flint hides a rich cultural life. The abrasive Moore is just one of a long line of artists and activists native to the Flint area. Others include assembly line author Ben Hamper, whose book, *Rivethead,* topped the *New York Times* best-seller list for several weeks in 1991; writer Edmund G. Love, author of *Subways Are for Sleeping;* comedienne Sandra Bernhard, perhaps best known for her stint on the sitcom *Roseanne;* actor Seamus Dever, whose most famous role has been that

of Detective Kevin Ryan on *Castle;* and 1960s activist and White Panther Party founder John Sinclair. The Flint Cultural Center, meanwhile, offers an impressive array of exhibits and live performances, and in recent years, dedicated locals have revitalized the downtown area, even resurrecting Flint's once-celebrated arches along Saginaw Street.

While most of Flint's attractions get little recognition outside the local area, many are well worth visiting, especially for those interested in labor relations or the evolution of the automobile. Surrounding communities, such as Burton and Genesee, also offer a plethora of recreational opportunities, from nature preserves to golf courses.

SIGHTS
◖ Flint Cultural Center
Not far from downtown Flint, the **Flint Cultural Center** (810/237-7333, www.flint-culturalcenter.com) houses several of the city's more notable museums and performance venues, including the Sloan Museum, the Longway Planetarium, The Whiting, the Flint Institute of Arts, the Flint Institute of Music, and the Flint Youth Theatre.

Flint's labor and manufacturing history is told with surprising candor in a

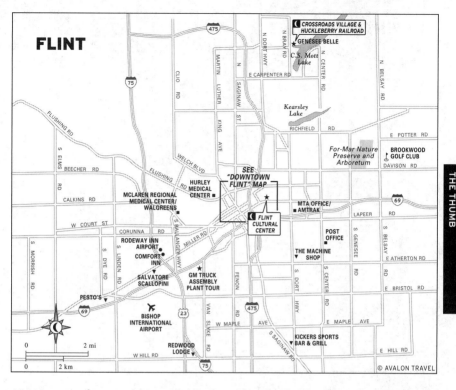

FLINT

CROSSROADS VILLAGE &
HUCKLEBERRY RAILROAD

GENESEE BELLE

C.S. Mott
Lake

Kearsley
Lake

For-Mar Nature
Preserve and
Arboretum

BROOKWOOD
GOLF CLUB

HURLEY
MEDICAL
CENTER

SEE
"DOWNTOWN
FLINT" MAP

FLINT
CULTURAL
CENTER

MTA OFFICE/
AMTRAK

MCLAREN REGIONAL
MEDICAL CENTER/
WALGREENS

POST
OFFICE

THE MACHINE
SHOP

RODEWAY INN
AIRPORT

COMFORT
INN

SALVATORE
SCALLOPINI

GM TRUCK
ASSEMBLY
PLANT TOUR

PESTO'S

BISHOP
INTERNATIONAL
AIRPORT

KICKERS SPORTS
BAR & GRILL

REDWOOD
LODGE

0   2 mi

0   2 km

© AVALON TRAVEL

10,000-square-foot permanent exhibit on "Flint and the American Dream" at the city's **Sloan Museum** (1221 E. Kearsley St., 810/237-3450, www.sloanlongway.org, 10am-5pm Mon.-Fri., noon-5pm Sat.-Sun., $9 adults, $8 seniors 60 and over, $6 children 3-11, children under 3 free). The museum, which focuses on local history and culture, has an impressive collection of neon signs, period clothing, classic motorcycles, and antique automobiles, including the oldest production-model Chevrolet in existence. This particular model is worth a look even if you're not a car buff. Exhibits trace the city from Native American hunting and gathering (check out the life-size tepee), through commercial fur trapping and logging, and finally to its identity as an auto manufacturing center. (A 1912 pennant promotes Good Roads Day with the slogan "No More Mud!")

Another highlight is the nearby **Buick Automotive Gallery** (303 Walnut St., 810/237-3440, www.sloanlongway.org, included w/ Sloan Museum admission), home to the largest collection of vintage, one-of-a-kind, and experimental Buick vehicles, including an M18 Hellcat tank destroyer and a recently restored 1954 Wildcat II.

The **Longway Planetarium** (1310 E. Kearsley St., 810/237-3400, www.sloanlongway.org, shows 12:30pm-3:30pm daily, $5 adults, $4 seniors and children 3-11, children under 3 free) claims the state's largest sky screen. The huge, 60-foot domed screen used to reproduce the night sky is as large as those in New York and Chicago. Changing multimedia shows explore the skies, constellations, science fiction, and space travel. Laser shows are offered on Saturday evenings. Call for a current schedule of programs.

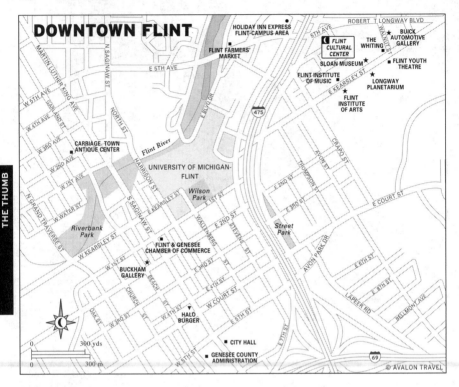

Flint Institute of Arts

Like Detroit, Flint benefited from the velvet-lined pockets of a number of wealthy auto industrialists. Generous donations from local citizens built the **Flint Institute of Arts** (FIA, 1120 E. Kearsley St. in the Cultural Center, 810/234-1695, www.flintarts.org, 10am-5pm Tues.-Sat., 1pm-5pm Sun., free, temporary exhibits $7 adults), now the state's second-largest museum of the arts. Dedicated to "making art available, accessible and approachable," the permanent collection of more than 7,500 pieces is strong in areas that include contemporary paintings and sculpture, Asian art, African artifacts, glass paperweights, and 19th-century French paintings (predominantly landscapes), including ever-popular works by the French Impressionists. The Bray Gallery houses a fine array of European paintings, furniture, and tapestries that range from the 15th to the 18th centuries.

Buckham Gallery

In downtown Flint, the alternative, artist-run **Buckham Gallery** (134½ W. 2nd St., 810/239-6233, www.buckhamgallery.org, noon-5pm Wed.-Fri., 10am-3pm Sat., free, special event prices vary) is dedicated to showing "contemporary cutting-edge art, with no censorship or interference," making for some interesting shows. Established in 1984, the space is also often used for performance art and poetry readings.

GM Truck Assembly Plant Tour

Perhaps Flint's most interesting attraction—and a good way to better understand the city's psyche—is the **GM Truck Assembly Plant** (G-3100 Van Slyke Rd.), which offers free tours by appointment Monday-Thursday. The workhorse plant was built in 1947 to make Chevrolets; it was the birthplace of the first Corvairs as well as generations of military

© FLINT INSTITUTE OF ARTS

Flint Institute of Arts

vehicles from World War II to the Gulf War. More recently, it has churned out GMC and Chevy vans and full-size pickups. This is the plant where Ben Hamper, a.k.a. the Rivethead, worked from 1977 to 1987, but the infamous rivet line has since been replaced by robots. Automation and market forces have slashed the plant's employment from a high of 8,500 to about 2,500 workers today.

Veteran auto workers give 90-minute tours, which include a look at "gatekeeping," the dramatic part of assembly when the car's side panel is joined to the vehicle's floor; a visit to the ladder line, where the frame is riveted together; and the finishing line, where the final result is road-tested. Reservations are a must, and remember that only GM vehicles are allowed in the main parking lot. Non-GM vehicles must be parked in the bus lot, which is situated about 500 feet north of the GM lot. For more information, contact the **Flint & Genesee Chamber of Commerce** (519 S. Saginaw St., Ste. 200, 810/600-1404, www.flintandgenesee.org, 8am-5pm Mon.-Fri.).

Crossroads Village & Huckleberry Railroad

After touring the city's modern factories, you'll gain a renewed appreciation for the hardships of the early Industrial Age. The often-hazardous working habits of the pre-industrial 19th century are the focus at the charming but truthful **Crossroads Village & Huckleberry Railroad** (6140 Bray Rd., 810/736-7100, www.geneseecountyparks.org, 10am-5pm Wed.-Sun., for village $10 adults, $8 children 2-12, for village, train, and boat $16 adults, $12.50 children). This restored village has 35 vintage buildings that show a variety of industries, complete with the era's authentic grit, noise, and pervasive smoke. An 1836 gristmill, a sawmill, a cider mill, a print and blacksmith shop, and more give visitors an idea of Genesee County in the mid-1800s. Numerous special weekend events are held throughout the year, especially during holidays.

The 40-minute ride on the Huckleberry Railroad is also a treat; the narrow-gauge train, a collection of vintage wooden coaches

THE SECOND MOTOR CITY: ORIGIN OF THE LABOR MOVEMENT

While Detroit is considered the birthplace of automobile manufacturing, Flint is credited with the start of the American labor movement. As the auto industry grew during the early 20th century, workers from all across the country flocked to factories in Detroit and its surrounding cities, including Flint, Saginaw, and Bay City.

By the 1920s, the industry was booming – until the Great Depression descended upon the nation, causing massive unemployment. In order to save money, car companies began demanding higher productivity for lower wages. Soon, autoworkers were disgusted with the poor working conditions, high-speed assembly lines, and lack of job security. Using solidarity to garner more control, they began to form unions.

In 1935, autoworkers organized the United Automobile Workers of America (UAW), also known as the International Union, United Automobile, Aerospace and Agricultural Implement Workers of America, which General Motors (GM) refused to recognize as the bargaining agent for their workforce. When Flint-area workers heard about GM's plan to move work to factories where the UAW had a weaker hold, they initiated Michigan's first large-scale, sit-down strike on December 30, 1936.

Continuing into the new year, the sit-down was an effective way of protest: As long as workers remained in the plant, management could not replace them with others. Unfortunately, Flint's infamous strike resulted in severe riots that ultimately injured 16 workers and 11 police officers.

On March 12, 1937, the sit-down strike finally ended with an agreement under which GM recognized the UAW as their workers' bargaining representative. The success of the UAW inspired the birth of unions across America, jump-starting the modern labor movement and ushering in an age of good wages and extensive benefits for thousands of autoworkers throughout Michigan and the rest of the country.

Of course, some may argue that unions have now grown as powerful, if not more so, than the car companies themselves. Today, this fragile balance of power has led to new financial problems, such as the controversial government bailout of GM and Chrysler in January 2009. For many, this bailout was only necessary because car companies were forced, despite falling profits, to maintain high union wages. Granted, other issues were also to blame, including the slow development of alternative energy vehicles, an unsustainable number of brands and dealerships, and the launch of no-interest financing plans to lure buyers.

---

and steam locomotives, leads guests through scenic woods and alongside lovely Mott Lake. Also nearby is the *Genesee Belle,* a paddlewheel riverboat that takes visitors on scenic 45-minute cruises on Mott Lake during the summer.

ENTERTAINMENT AND EVENTS
Nightlife
Though Flint isn't known for its nightlife scene, those seeking respite will find a few bars and music clubs in town. If you're looking for a casual hangout, **Kickers Sports Bar & Grill** (5577 S. Saginaw Rd., 810/695-2060, www.kickerssportsbar.com, 11am-2am Mon.-Sat., no cover) can keep you busy all night. Besides watching football, basketball, and countless other televised sports, you can play pool, darts, or video games and choose from a wide selection of draft and bottled beers, wines, and cocktails. The grub's not bad either; the extensive menu includes bar favorites like fried pickles, loaded potato skins, and battered mushrooms as well as an assortment of salads, sandwiches, burgers, pastas, pizzas, even ribs and fajitas. The joint also offers plenty of specials, from 25-cent chicken wings on Monday to

all-you-can-eat crab legs on Friday, and happy-hour specials are available 11am-9pm every day.

If your musical tastes run a bit more hard-core, never fear. Since 2002, **The Machine Shop** (3539 S. Dort Hwy., 810/715-2650, www.themachineshop.info, show times and ticket prices vary) has hosted a variety of rock performers, from Blind Melon to Kid Rock.

The Arts

The **Flint Cultural Center,** an unassuming art mecca at the heart of an industrial town, houses several winning performance venues. For concerts, operas, dance shows, and Broadway musicals, reserve your seat at **The Whiting** (1241 E. Kearsley St., 810/237-7337, www.thewhiting. com, show times and ticket prices vary), where recent programs have included *The Wizard of Oz* and an evening with comedian Bill Cosby. Other plays and musicals are featured at the **Flint Youth Theatre** (1220 E. Kearsley St., 810/237-1530, www.flintyouththeatre.com, show times and ticket prices vary), and the nearby **Flint Institute of Music** (FIM, 1025 E. Kearsley St., 810/238-1350, www.thefim. com, show times and ticket prices vary) presents concerts by the Flint Symphony Orchestra.

Fairs and Festivals

Flint-area residents don't need much of an excuse to hold an annual event, especially during the pleasant summer season. In mid-June, the Flint Institute of Arts hosts the **Flint Art Fair** (810/234-1695, www.flintartfair.org, free), which presents the work of over 150 contemporary artists and craftsmen from the United States, Canada, and places as far away as Bermuda. Art lovers will appreciate the chance to peruse sculpture, glasswork, photography, textiles, and fine jewelry, among other impressive treasures.

In mid-August, the four-day **Back to the Bricks Cruise Weekend** (810/232-8903, www. backtothebricks.org, free) celebrates the region's industrial roots with a parade of classic vehicles, hot rods, sports cars, vintage trucks, and customized motorcycles through downtown Flint.

© FLINT AREA CVB

THE THUMB

vintage cars at the annual Back to the Bricks Cruise Weekend

Also in mid-August, the **Genesee County Fair** (Everett A. Cummings Center, G-6130 E. Mount Morris Rd., Mount Morris, 810/687-0953, www.gcf.org, free, special event prices vary) offers a countrified change of pace to Flint's auto-related attractions and events. For a solid week, you'll be treated to livestock shows, agricultural exhibits, pig races, pie-eating contests, and, if you find yourself missing engines, demolition derbies.

One of the area's most eagerly anticipated events is the annual **Michigan Renaissance Festival** (12600 Dixie Hwy., Holly, 800/601-4848, www.michrenfest.com, 10am-7pm Sat.-Sun. late Aug.-early Oct., $20 adults, $18 seniors and students, $11 children), which has brought revelry and pageantry to southeastern Michigan since 1979. Over the course of seven weekends, this popular, family-friendly event typically lures more than 220,000 yearly visitors to its permanent home, a 312-acre property just 12 miles south of Flint. Here, you'll encounter a slew of authentic costumes, roving minstrels, live performances, staged jousts, and other activities, from archery competitions to human chess matches. Many attendees also appreciate the property's centerpiece: an 18-acre replica of a 16th-century village, a collection of authentic, open-air cottages featuring a variety of old-fashioned vittles, from sugary mead to smoked turkey legs, as well as handcrafted, Renaissance-style wares, from pewter dishes and musical instruments to elegant capes and menacing swords.

SHOPPING

While the Flint area is, by no means, a shoppers' mecca, there are a few stops worth a look. One such place is the **Carriage Town Antique Center** (503 Garland St., 810/238-1444, www. randolphhouse1872.com, 11am-5pm Tues.-Sun.), a large, recently renovated repository of antique furniture, vintage clothing, and old-fashioned jewelry.

In a region that's well known for its bountiful farms and orchards, it's hard to pass up a produce market. Luckily, the **Flint Farmers' Market** (420 E. Boulevard Dr., 810/232-1399, www.flintfarmersmarket.com, 8am-5pm Tues., Thurs., and Sat.) is open three days a week; in addition to produce vendors, you'll find a bakery, an art gallery, and a popular eatery known as Steady Eddy's, which offers a surprising number of vegetarian dishes. For more fresh fruit and veggies, you should take a side trip to **Montrose Orchards** (12473 Seymour Rd., Montrose, 810/639-6971, www.montroseorchards.com, 9am-5pm Mon.-Sat., noon-5pm Sun.), a family-owned farm open mid-May-December. Besides seasonal blueberry fields, pumpkin patches, a bakery, and other market goodies, the farm offers several family-friendly activities, including hayrides.

SPORTS AND RECREATION
Parks and Preserves

The **Genesee Recreation Area** (7004 N. Irish Rd., 810/736-7100, www.geneseecountyparks.org, 8am-sunset daily, seasons vary throughout park, free) offers a pleasant contrast to Flint's urbanity. It covers more than 4,500 acres along the Flint River off I-475, with beaches, biking paths, a boat launch, a campground, fishing sites, and hiking and horse trails.

Southeast of Flint, the 380-acre **For-Mar Nature Preserve and Arboretum** (2142 N. Genesee Rd., Burton, 810/789-8567, www. geneseecountyparks.org, 8am-sunset Wed.-Sun., buildings close at 5pm, free) includes a patchwork of woodlands, restored prairies, open fields, meadows, ponds, and Kearsley Creek, as well as an arboretum planted with specimen trees, shrubs, and vines. Seven miles of up-and-down hiking trails weave through a diverse habitat. Two trails are wheelchair-accessible. An interpretive center has a live bird-viewing area and several animal and reptile displays, including the Foote Bird Museum, which contains more than 600 stuffed and mounted specimens.

Golf

Every summer, golfers flock to Michigan for its numerous, well-groomed courses, and the Flint area, host of the annual Buick Open, is no exception. Just a short drive from the city lie three public 18-hole golf courses: **Brookwood Golf Club** (6045 Davison Rd., Burton, 810/742-4930, www.imarecreation.org/brookwood-golf-club, daily Apr.-mid-Nov., $20-40 pp w/cart); **Captain's Club at Woodfield** (10200 Woodfield Dr., Grand Blanc, 810/695-4653, www.captainsclubatwoodfield.com, daily Apr.-Oct., $18-49 pp w/cart); and **Fenton Farms Golf Club** (12312 Torrey Rd., Fenton, 810/629-1212, www.fentonfarms.com, daily Apr.-Oct., $15-27 pp w/cart).

ACCOMMODATIONS

Although most travelers tend to make day trips to the Flint area, it's certainly possible to stay overnight. For the most part, though, you'll encounter a number of chain hotels, including the **Comfort Inn** (2361 Austin Pkwy., 810/232-4222, www.comfortinn.com, $100-120 d), and **Holiday Inn Express Flint-Campus Area** (1150 Robert T. Longway Blvd., 810/238-7744, www.hiexpress.com, $90-160 d), and

Roadway Inn Airport (2325 Austin Pkwy., 810/232-7777, www.roadwayinn.com, $80-100 d).

Camping

Within the Genesee Recreation Area, Genesee County operates the **Wolverine Campground.** Located in the 2,000-acre Holloway Reservoir Regional Park, this summer-only spot has a nice setting in a pine forest, with 195 tent sites, several shower and restroom buildings, a boat launch, and a guarded swimming beach. Reservations are recommended. Contact the **Genesee County Parks and Recreation Commission** (5045 Stanley Rd., 810/736-7100 or 800/648-7275, www.geneseecountyparks. org, $12-22 daily).

FOOD

According to the *Flint Journal,* **Halo Burger** (810/238-4607, www.haloburger.com, hours vary, $5-10) serves up the best burgers in town, with 11 locations in the Flint area. For a more lively atmosphere, head to the ● **Redwood Lodge** (5304 Gateway Center Dr., 810/233-8000, www.theredwoodlodge.com, 11am-11pm Mon.-Thurs., 11am-midnight Fri., noon-midnight Sat., noon-10pm Sun., $11-27), a rustic eatery that offers a fine wine selection, excellent cuisine (from seafood pasta to signature steaks), and a lounge featuring live music.

Just off I-75 at the Miller Road exit, **Salvatore Scallopini** (G-3227 Miller Rd., 810/732-1070, www.salvatorescallopini.com, 11am-10pm Mon.-Thurs., 11am-11pm Fri.-Sat., noon-10pm Sun., $12-18) is part of a statewide chain known for its authentic Italian cuisine and seafood. An even better choice for Italian dishes is **Pesto's** (G-5275 Miller Rd., 810/732-4390, www.pestos.com, 10:30am-10pm Mon.-Sat., noon-8pm Sun., $8-20), where you'll find homemade dressings, scrumptious specials, and desserts big enough for two.

INFORMATION AND SERVICES

Flint offers all the services that a traveler might need or want, from tourism bureaus to pharmacies. For more information about the Flint area, contact the **Flint & Genesee Chamber of Commerce** (519 S. Saginaw St., Ste. 200, 810/600-1404, www.flintandgenesee. org, 8am-5pm Mon.-Fri.) or visit www.genesee-fun.com. For government issues, contact **City Hall** (1101 S. Saginaw St., www.cityofflint. com) or the **Genesee County Administration** (1101 Beach St., www.co.genesee.mi.us). For local news and events, pick up a daily copy of the *Flint Journal* (www.flintjournal.com or www.mlive.com).

Flint and its surrounding communities have several **U.S. post offices** (USPS, 800/275-8777, www.usps.com), including a **downtown location** (601 S. Saginaw St., 810/257-1526, 10am-4pm Mon.-Fri.). For late-night drop-offs, try one of the **Burton-area offices** (2333 S. Center Rd., 7am-11pm Mon.-Sun.).

In case of an emergency, you can contact the **Hurley Medical Center** (1 Hurley Plaza, 810/257-9000, www.hurleymc.com) or the **McLaren Regional Medical Center** (401 S. Ballenger Hwy., 810/342-2000, www.mclaren-regional.org). In addition, there are several area pharmacies, including a 24-hour **Walgreens** (502 S. Ballenger Hwy., 810/424-9270, www. walgreens.com).

Whether you're the victim of an auto accident, a medical emergency, or a crime, it may be necessary to contact the police. If so, you can dial **911** from any mobile or public phone.

While in town, you might need to replenish your travel fund. If so, rest assured that there are plenty of banks in the area, including ones with round-the-clock access. Chase, for instance, has a 24-hour ATM at the **Hurley Medical Center,** the **McLaren Regional Medical Center,** and the **Genesee Towers** (210 W. 1st St., www.chase.com).

GETTING THERE AND AROUND
Getting There

Visitors can reach Flint via air, train, bus, or car. For information about flights into and out of Flint, contact the **Bishop International Airport** (FNT, G-3425 W. Bristol Rd.,

810/235-6560, www.bishopairport.org). Although this regional airport has limited flights, major carriers like Delta and American Airlines offer daily trips to and from Atlanta, Chicago, Dallas, and other major cities. From here, you can get a ride to your hotel or another destination via services like **Flint Bishop Shuttle and Taxi** (810/214-0186, www.flint-bishopshuttle.herobo.com).

It's also possible to travel into Flint via train. **Amtrak** (800/872-7245, www.amtrak.com) offers a route from Chicago, with stops across Michigan, including Kalamazoo, Battle Creek, East Lansing, Flint, and Detroit. For information about schedules, visit the Flint station (1407 S. Dort Hwy.), where **Greyhound** (810/232-1114 or 800/231-2222, www.greyhound.com) and **Indian Trails** (800/292-3831, www.indiantrails.com) also provide regular bus service.

Given Genesee County's well-designed expressway system, traveling into and around Flint via car is also easy. From Detroit, you can drive northwest on I-75 North and connect to I-475 North, which crosses I-69 and runs directly through downtown Flint; without traffic, this 68-mile trip should take you a little over an hour. From Saginaw, head southeast on I-75 South/US-23 South and take I-475 South to downtown Flint; without traffic, this 37-mile trip should take roughly 38 minutes.

Flint is also accessible from Port Huron or Lansing via I-69, an east-west interstate; from Port Huron, the 67-mile trip will take about an hour, while the 56-mile trip from Lansing will require at least 55 minutes. If you're headed from Chicago, take I-90 East, I-94 East, and I-69 North to reach Flint; without traffic, the 274-mile trip will take about four hours. Just be advised that, en route from the Windy City, parts of I-90 East and I-94 East serve as the Indiana Toll Road.

Getting Around

If you arrive in Flint via air or train, you can easily rent a vehicle from various rental agencies, such as **Alamo** (810/239-4341 or 800/462-5266), **Avis** (810/234-7847 or 800/331-1212), **Budget** (810/238-8300 or 800/527-0700), **Enterprise** (810/235-1101 or 800/261-7331), **Hertz** (810/234-2041 or 800/654-3131), or **National** (810/239-4341 or 800/227-7368). If you'd rather not drive, consider using Flint's public bus system to get around town. For information on routes and schedules, contact the **Mass Transportation Authority** (MTA, 1401 S. Dort Hwy., 810/767-0100, www.mtaflint.org, one-way $1.50-2.50 pp). You might also consider joining a bus tour of the area; for more information, contact **Blue Lakes Charters & Tours** (12154 N. Saginaw Rd., Clio, 800/282-4287, www.bluelakes.com).

Frankenmuth

It would be easy to dismiss Frankenmuth as overcommercialized kitsch. "Michigan's Little Bavaria" once was a quiet and undistinguished German farm town of just more than 4,000, but has since grown to become the state's top tourist attraction, with an estimated three million visitors each year.

Frankenmuth houses the world's largest Christmas store, a two-mile-long street of pseudo-Bavarian shops, and three restaurants that serve all-you-can-eat, family-style chicken dinners. Buoyed by the seemingly endless flow

of visitors, the area has expanded over the years to include an 18-hole public golf course and the Midwest's largest outlet mall.

Despite the Bavarian image it relentlessly pushes today, much of Frankenmuth's history echoes that of other Saginaw Valley towns. A group of 15 young Lutherans from an area near Nuremberg founded the city in 1845 (Frankenmuth means "courage of the Franconians"). This optimistic group followed the call to become missionaries in America, with hopes of tending to the growing Saginaw

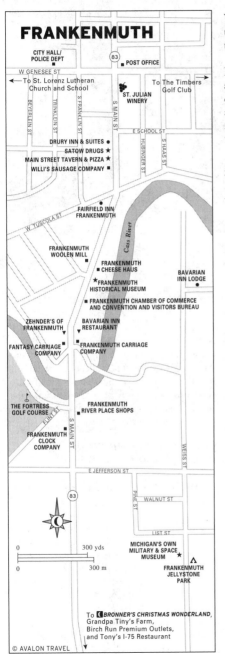

FRANKENMUTH

CITY HALL/
POLICE DEPT
83
POST OFFICE
W GENESEE ST
← To St. Lorenz Lutheran
Church and School
To The Timbers
Golf Club
ST. JULIAN
WINERY
E SCHOOL ST
DRURY INN & SUITES ●
SATOW DRUGS ★
MAIN STREET TAVERN & PIZZA ★
WILLI'S SAUSAGE COMPANY ■
FAIRFIELD INN
FRANKENMUTH
W TUSCOLA ST
Cass River
FRANKENMUTH
WOOLEN MILL
FRANKENMUTH
■ CHEESE HAUS
★FRANKENMUTH
HISTORICAL MUSEUM
BAVARIAN
INN LODGE
■ FRANKENMUTH CHAMBER OF COMMERCE
AND CONVENTION AND VISITORS BUREAU
ZEHNDER'S OF
FRANKENMUTH
BAVARIAN INN
RESTAURANT
FANTASY CARRIAGE ■
COMPANY
■FRANKENMUTH CARRIAGE
COMPANY
THE FORTRESS
GOLF COURSE
FRANKENMUTH
■ RIVER PLACE SHOPS
FRANKENMUTH
CLOCK
COMPANY
S MAIN ST
E JEFFERSON ST
PINE ST
WALNUT ST
WEISS ST
83
LIST ST
0   300 yds
0   300 m
MICHIGAN'S OWN
MILITARY & SPACE
MUSEUM
Λ
FRANKENMUTH
JELLYSTONE
PARK
To ☾BRONNER'S CHRISTMAS WONDERLAND,
Grandpa Tiny's Farm,
Birch Run Premium Outlets,
and Tony's I-75 Restaurant
© AVALON TRAVEL

Valley German community and converting the local Ojibwa Indians to Christianity along the way.

The Indians stood steadfast, and the Franconians' mission soon failed. Still, more and more Germans immigrated to the area, drawn by abundant opportunities for logging and a growing community. German, in fact, remained the community's principal language until well into the 1920s.

Once the forests were stripped by the logging business, settlers turned to farming. The chicken-dinner craze Frankenmuth enjoys today started as an attraction for traveling salesmen, but later became a staple of the Detroit Sunday drive set in the 1920s and 1930s. They had more reason to steer toward Frankenmuth in the 1950s, when signmaker Wally Bronner, who sadly passed away in early 2008, opened a Christmas decorating shop as a sideline to his regular business. By the 1970s, the city had been expanded into the Bavarian nerve center it is today.

SIGHTS
Old Frankenmuth

Beneath the commercialism, however, is a genuine German community, where people are old-world friendly and everyone knows everyone else. Old Frankenmuth can still be found in a number of places in town, which are, not surprisingly, the places most tourists skip.

Satow's Drugs (308 S. Main St., 989/652-8001, www.satowdrugs.com, 7:30am-9pm Mon.-Sat., 8am-4pm Sun., $3-6) has a coffee shop where locals hang out, soups are made from scratch, and prices are reminiscent of the 1950s. The **Main Street Tavern & Pizza** (310 S. Main St., 989/652-2222, 10am-2:30am Mon.-Sat., noon-2:30am Sun., $4-11) is owned by a former baker from Zehnder's, who makes all the fragrant bread and buns on the premises. His cheeseburger is made from local beef and cheese; a house specialty is the pizza made with Italian sausage from Willi's Sausage Company next door. Wash it down with a once-locally made Carling's or a Frankenmuth Pilsner for

THE THUMB

© LAURA MARTONE

Bronner's CHRISTmas Wonderland

a delicious meal filled with old-world flair at a reasonable price.

The 1880 **St. Lorenz Lutheran Church** (W. Tuscola and Mayer Rd., 989/652-6141, www.stlorenz.org, 9am-noon Mon.-Sat. June-Sept., free) houses the largest congregation, east of the Mississippi, of the conservative Missouri Synod of the Lutheran Church. Self-guided tours reveal scenes of Lutheran and Frankenmuth history, an early cemetery, a small museum, and a reconstruction of the first settlers' original log church and parsonage.

Frankenmuth Historical Museum

The **Frankenmuth Historical Museum** (613 S. Main St., 989/652-9701, www.frankenmuth-museum.org, 10:30am-5pm Mon.-Thurs., 10:30am-8pm Fri., 10am-8pm Sat., 11am-7pm Sun., $2 adults, $1 children) traces the city's rich past through possessions and letters from the original settlers. Displays explore the city's connections to logging, Prohibition, the rise of the chicken-dinner phenomenon, and the Frankenmuth brewery. The museum shop

is a pleasant surprise among all the cookie-cutter shops along Main Street, with vintage-style toys, sophisticated crafts, and an excellent selection of books regarding the city and surrounding area. Note that the museum has shorter hours in winter, and bilingual tours are available.

Bronner's CHRISTmas Wonderland

Check any cynicism at the door when visiting **Bronner's CHRISTmas Wonderland** (25 Christmas Ln., 989/652-9931 or 800/255-9327, www.bronners.com, 9am-9pm Mon.-Sat., noon-7pm Sun., free), truly a phenomenon. Prepare yourself for a building that encompasses almost 100,000 square feet—that's nearly two football fields—filled with more than 350 decorated Christmas trees, 800 animated figures, 500 styles of Nativity scenes from 75 countries, 6,000 kinds of glass ornaments, Bibles in more than 30 languages, Advent calendars, lighted villages, and nutcrackers. Many of the offerings are from Eastern Europe, but the staff has worked hard in recent years to add diversity to the store's offerings. These days, you can find books on Hanukkah and Kwanzaa, as well as non-Caucasian Santas and Nativity characters. The complex, which encompasses 27 acres, also contains the Silent Night Memorial Chapel, a replica of the Austrian church that was built where "Silent Night" was first sung in 1818. Note that hours are shorter January-May; the store is closed on New Year's Day, Easter, Thanksgiving, and Christmas.

Grandpa Tiny's Farm

A historical 45-acre working farm founded by William "Tiny" Zehnder, **Grandpa Tiny's Farm** (7775 Weiss St., 989/652-5437 Apr.-Oct. or 989/871-2937 Nov.-Mar., www.grandpatinysfarm.com, 10am-5pm Mon.-Sat., noon-5pm Sun. Apr.-Oct., $5 pp) invites visitors, especially children, to interact with bunnies, lambs, goats, and other farm animals. Guides give personal tours through the farm, where plowing and wool-spinning demonstrations, narrated horse-drawn wagon rides, and other activities highlight the importance of the area's agricultural history.

Other Attractions

St. Julian Winery (127 S. Main St., 989/652-3281, www.stjulian.com, 9am-6pm Mon.-Sat., noon-6pm Sun., free tours), the state's largest wine company (based in Paw Paw), has a free tasting room here that showcases the company's many wines and sparkling juices. There's also a small winery on-site, where solera cream sherry is aged.

Michigan's Own Military and Space Museum (1250 Weiss St., 989/652-8005, www.michigansmilitarymuseum.com, 10am-5pm Mon.-Sat., 11am-5pm Sun. Mar.-Dec., $7 adults, $3 children 6-18) features exhibits about Michigan governors, astronauts, and veterans of several foreign wars.

FESTIVALS

As one of Michigan's top tourist destinations, Frankenmuth hosts its share of annual events, including a music festival in August and a holiday celebration in November. Every January, **Zehnder's Snowfest** (800/863-7999, www.zehnders.com, outdoor events free) honors winter with fireworks, live entertainment, ice-carving competitions, and cozy treats.

In May, the **World Expo of Beer** ($5 adults, children under 16 free), Michigan's largest beer sampling event, brings together over 150 beers from breweries around the world; during the two-day event, visitors can enjoy live bands, watch brewing demonstrations, and vote for their favorite beer. The following month, the four-day **Frankenmuth Bavarian Festival** ($7 adults, children under 16 free) highlights German culture with traditional music and food. Of course, what German town would be complete without its very own Oktoberfest? The **Frankenmuth Oktoberfest** ($8 adults, children under 16 free), which takes place in late September, showcases all things German, including music and dance performers brought directly from the mother country. For more information about these and other events, call 800/386-3378 or visit www.frankenmuthfestivals.com.

SHOPPING
Main Street

Unlike Flint, Frankenmuth is definitely a popular spot for shopaholics. Main Street alone offers a plethora of quaint emporiums, including toy stores, fudge shops, and German-inspired boutiques like the **Frankenmuth Clock Company** (966 S. Main St., 989/652-2933, www.frankenmuthclock.com, 9am-6:30pm daily), an importer of genuine, ornately crafted Black Forest cuckoo clocks. Also along this stretch, you'll find specialty food shops such as **Willi's Sausage Company** (316 S. Main St., 989/652-9041, www.willissausages.com, 9am-5pm Sun.-Wed., 9am-6pm Thurs.-Sat.) and the **Frankenmuth Cheese Haus** (561 S. Main St., 989/652-6727, www.frankenmuthcheesehaus.com, 9:30am-6pm daily).

For a unique experience, stop by Michigan's oldest woolen mill. Established in 1894, **Frankenmuth Woolen Mill** (570 S. Main St.,

© LAURA MARTONE

Frankenmuth River Place Shops

989/652-6555, www.thewoolenmill.com, 10am-8pm Sun.-Thurs., 10am-9pm Fri.-Sat.) invites visitors to watch the working mill in action; afterward, feel free to peruse the merchandise, a variety of warm sweaters and comforters.

Resembling a European village—albeit newer-looking than most—**Frankenmuth River Place Shops** (925 S. Main St., 989/652-9043, www.frankenmuthriverplace.com, 10am-6pm Sun. Thurs. and 10 am-8pm Fri.-Sat. Jan.-May, 10am-8pm Sun.-Thurs. and 10am-9pm Fri.-Sat. June, 10am-9pm daily July-Aug., 10am-7pm Sun.-Thurs. and 10am-9pm Fri.-Sat. Sept.-Dec.) is Frankenmuth's only mall. Among its more than 30 shops and attractions, you'll find a quilt store, a glass art gallery, an incredible mirror maze, and Michigan's largest bead store. May-October, River Place is also the launching point for one-hour narrated tours on the *Bavarian Belle Riverboat* (866/808-2628, www.bavarianbelle.com, departure times posted daily, $9 adults, $4 children 5-12, children under 5 free).

Birch Run

Once just an obscure village eight miles southwest of Frankenmuth, Birch Run is now the state's discount shopping capital, with more than 140 stores within its famed **outlet mall** (12240 S. Beyer Rd., 989/624-6226, www.premiumoutlets.com, 10am-9pm Mon.-Sat., 11am-7pm Sun., closed Easter, Thanksgiving, and Christmas), the second largest in the world. Plunder the offerings of Nike, Ann Taylor, Columbia Sportswear, Polo/Ralph Lauren, Liz Claiborne, J. Crew, Eddie Bauer, Easy Spirit, American Eagle, Pottery Barn, and more. Situated at the second-busiest exit on I-75 (the first being Orlando, Florida), Birch Run now contains a movie palace and a motor speedway—improvements designed to make the town a true weekend destination for the shopping set.

GOLF

For golfers, there are three options near Frankenmuth. Zehnder's, probably the town's most famous restaurant and hotel, offers **The Fortress Golf Course** (950 Flint St., 800/863-7999, www.zehnders.com, daily May-Oct., $30-45 pp w/cart), an 18-hole championship course not far from Main Street. If you find yourself overwhelmed by Frankenmuth's Bavarian vibe, head five miles west of town to the **Green Acres Golf Course** (7323 Dixie Hwy., Bridgeport, 989/777-3510, www.green-acresgc.net, daily Apr.-Oct., $28-30 pp w/cart). As an alternative, you can also visit **The Timbers Golf Club** (7300 Bray Rd., Vassar, 989/871-4884, www.timbersgolfclub.com, daily Apr.-Oct., $28-34 pp w/cart), a wooded course about five miles east of Frankenmuth.

ACCOMMODATIONS

Frankenmuth has several bed-and-breakfast inns, such as the **Bender Haus Bed and Breakfast** (337 Trinklein St., 989/652-8897, $95-115 d). In addition, there's no shortage of chain hotels in the area, including **Drury Inn & Suites** (260 S. Main St., 989/652-2800, www.druryhotels.com, $100-140 d) and **Fairfield**

the *Bavarian Belle* Riverboat, docked beside Frankenmuth's River Place

© FRANKENMUTH CHAMBER OF COMMERCE/CVB

Inn Frankenmuth (430 S. Main St., 989/652-5000, www.marriott.com, $84-160 d).

In downtown Frankenmuth, you can also opt for the 🎔**Bavarian Inn Lodge** (1 Covered Bridge Ln., 888/775-6343, www.bavarianinn.com, $105-255 d), set back behind the restaurant and shops along the Cass River. The 360 rooms are clean and bright, with balconies and Bavarian touches. Each is named in honor of one of the town's early inhabitants, complete with family pictures. The lodge is especially popular with kids, who flock here to hang out at the indoor water park, mini-golf course, and Family Fun Center, which includes video games and more.

Families may also appreciate **Zehnder's Splash Village Hotel and Waterpark** (1365 S. Main St., 800/863-7999, www.zehnders.com, $149-299 d, $179-469 suites). Situated near the southern edge of Frankenmuth, beside Bronner's CHRISTmas Wonderland, Zehnder's features 146 nonsmoking rooms and suites, a video arcade, a 30,000-square-foot indoor water park, and complimentary shuttle service to the Zehnder's restaurant and The Fortress Golf Course.

Camping

Despite the plethora of tourist-oriented hotels and inns in Frankenmuth, there is an option for those who enjoy sleeping amid the great outdoors. Not far from Bronner's Christmas store, the year-round **Frankenmuth Jellystone Park** (1339 Weiss St., 989/652-6668, www.frankenmuthjellystone.com, $58-178 daily) offers tent sites, full RV hookups, a laundry, heated restrooms, an indoor pool, a playground and mini-golf course, and free wireless Internet access.

FOOD

No visit to Frankenmuth would be complete without a meal at 🎔 **Zehnder's of Frankenmuth** (730 S. Main St., 800/863-7999, www.zehnders.com, 11am-9:30pm daily, $15-22), a historic complex that comprises a marketplace and America's largest family restaurant. With nine dining rooms, the restaurant can seat more than 1,500 guests at any given time.

© LAURA MARTONE

Zehnder's of Frankenmuth

The full-service menu includes seafood, steaks, European desserts, and all-you-can-eat, family-style chicken dinners. South of the downtown area, Zehnder's also offers a whimsical hotel and water park and an 18-hole golf course.

Thousands of chicken dinners are also sold annually at the vast **Bavarian Inn Restaurant** (713 S. Main St., 989/652-9941 or 800/228-2742, www.bavarianinn.com, 11am-9pm Sun.-Thurs., 11am-9:30pm Fri.-Sat., $20-23), which seats 1,200. If you'd rather skip the poultry, the Bavarian Inn Restaurant also offers German specialties such as sauerbraten and strudel. Skip the restaurant itself if you like your food spicy, however; Frankenmuth caters to a largely senior citizen crowd, and many diners find the food a bit bland.

Like any good tourist mecca, Frankenmuth and Birch Run have plenty of restaurants, including the usual rash of fast-food places and chains. Across from Birch Run's discount mall, **Tony's I-75** (8781 Main St., 989/624-5860, 6am-10pm Sun.-Thurs., 6am-11pm Fri.-Sat., $8-12) is a longstanding local eatery that started in downtown Saginaw and is still known for its huge, overstuffed sandwiches and thick shakes. Lines can be long, so plan on a wait or visit during off-hours.

INFORMATION AND SERVICES

For more information about Frankenmuth, contact the **Frankenmuth Chamber of Commerce and Convention & Visitors Bureau** (635 S. Main St., 800/386-8696, www.frankenmuth.org, 8am-6pm Mon.-Wed., 8am-8pm Thurs.-Fri., 10am-8pm Sat., and noon-6pm Sun. June-Aug, 8am-5pm Mon-Fri., 10am-5pm Sat., and noon-5pm Sun. Sept.-May). For city-related issues, contact **City Hall** (240 W. Genesee St., www.frankenmuthcity.com). For local news, pick up a copy of *Frankenmuth News* (www.frankenmuthnews.com).

As a tourist town, Frankenmuth offers a variety of necessary services. For mailing needs, visit the area **post office** (119 N. Main St., 989/652-6751, www.usps.com, 8:30am-5pm Mon.-Fri., 9am-noon Sat.). In case of an emergency, contact the **Frankenmuth Police Department** (240 W. Genesee St., 989/652-8371). For medical emergencies, dial **911** or contact the **Mobile Medical Response** (989/758-2900, www.mobilemedical.org).

GETTING THERE AND AROUND

While you won't be able to take a plane, train, or bus to Frankenmuth, getting there by car is a relative snap. From Detroit, for instance, you simply need to take northbound I-75 to exit 136 (Frankenmuth/Birch Run), drive two miles east on Birch Run Road, and head north on M-83 for 5.7 miles, where the route becomes Main Street; the total 93-mile trip will take you about 90 minutes. From Saginaw, take southbound I-75/US-23 to exit 144 (Frankenmuth/Bridgeport), drive two miles southeast on Dixie Highway, head east on Junction Road for four miles (where the route becomes Genesee Street), and continue on Genesee for about a mile to Main Street; without traffic, this 15-mile trip will take you about 25 minutes. Once within the city limits, you can drive to most places, walk through the downtown area, or board a carriage ride by contacting the **Fantasy Carriage Company** (780 S. Mill St., 989/777-4757, noon-9pm Mon.-Fri., 11am-10pm Sat., 11am-9pm Sun.) or the **Frankenmuth Carriage Company** (4520 S. Gera Rd., 989/652-3101, noon-9pm daily).

Saginaw

Saginaw, the industrial heart of east-central Michigan, stretches for four miles along both banks of the Saginaw River. It was formerly a logging and agricultural center, and the only remnants of the city's logging era are scores of old wooden houses built with money gained from the felling of the city's forests.

Saginaw Bay appears variously on 17th- and 18th-century French maps as "Sikonam," "Sakonam," "Saaguinam," and "Saquinam." Southeastern Michigan was generally described as "Saquinam Country" as early as 1688. Later, when lumber camp raconteurs told of Paul Bunyan's legendary feat of "logging off the Saginaw Country," the reference included the entire Lower Peninsula.

Native Americans lived peacefully on these lands for centuries. The earliest whites to penetrate the Saginaw Valley were Canadians. In 1816, Louis Campau built a fur-trading post near downtown. Two years later, at the request of Governor Lewis Cass, he built a council house and helped Cass negotiate the Treaty of 1819 with the Ojibwa. Sensing growing friction, the white settlers stationed troops at Fort Saginaw in 1822. The following year, a harsh winter, disastrous floods, and a summer fever epidemic prompted the garrison's commander to inform the War Department that "nothing but Indians, muskrats, and bullfrogs could possibly exist here." To the delight of the area's Native Americans, the post was abandoned in 1823.

Although that early pessimism stalled the development of Saginaw, the white settlers didn't stay away long. By the 1850s, the lumberjacks moved in, bringing with them 14 busy, buzzing sawmills by 1857. Their prey: the heavily forested land around the city. That lasted until about the late 1880s, when timber was replaced by coal as the city's principal industry.

Remnants of those years can still be seen. One example is the stunning Montague Inn, which houses an elegant inn and restaurant in the Georgian-style mansion of a former sugar beet magnate.

SIGHTS
Museums and Cultural Sights

Easily dismissed as an aging industrial center, Saginaw is a city of surprises. One of the most delightful is the **Japanese Cultural Center, Tea House, and Gardens of Saginaw** (527 Ezra Rust Dr., 989/759-1648,

THE THUMB

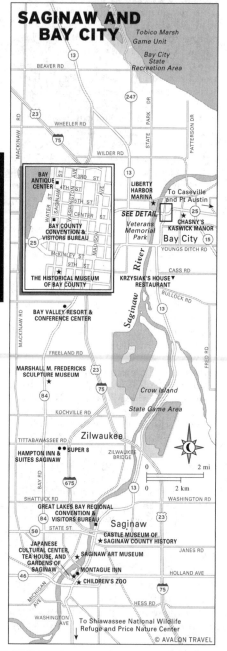

www.japaneseculturalcenter.org, noon-4pm Tues.-Sat. Apr.-Oct., free, $3 pp for tour and tea ceremony), an authentic Japanese teahouse and garden. The traditional 16th-century-style teahouse was built in 1985, designed to resemble a Zen monastery. It is one of the few places in the United States where visitors can see a formal Japanese tea ceremony performed in an authentic setting. Behind the teahouse, the Friendship Garden is a variation of a traditional Japanese garden, with delicate plantings and an arched footbridge over a stream. Many of the garden's trees, bridges, and stones came directly from Japan. Saginaw was chosen as the center's unlikely site because of its relationship with the city of Tokushima, Japan, Saginaw's sister city.

The serene formal tea ceremony, designed to promote inner tranquility, is performed at 2pm on the second Saturday of each month year-round. At other times, visitors can tour the teahouse and garden, learn more about the ancient Zen ritual of tea, and contemplate its importance in Japanese architecture, politics, and religion. Admission to the ceremony includes a cup of tea and a traditional Japanese sweet.

Another surprise is the **Marshall M. Fredericks Sculpture Museum** at Saginaw Valley State University (SVSU, 7400 Bay Rd., 989/964-7125, www.marshallfredericks.org, noon-5pm Mon.-Sat., free). The Scandinavian American artist who became one of the state's most renowned sculptors studied under famous Swedish artist Carl Milles and is best known for his elegant bronze gazelles in Detroit's Belle Isle conservatory and for the Coleman A. Young Municipal Center's symbolic *Spirit of Detroit*. The gallery features original works, more than 200 original plaster models, photos of pieces installed around the world, a collection of bronze casts in the nearby sculpture garden, and original sketches. The Sculptor's Studio, a space created in 2003 to showcase the casting process, contains over 300 of Fredericks's clay models, molds, tools, and sculptures.

The **Saginaw Art Museum** (1126 N. Michigan Ave., 989/754-2491, www.saginawartmuseum.org, 10am-5pm Tues.-Sat., 1pm-5pm Sun., $5 adults, children under 16

Japanese Cultural Center, Tea House, and Gardens of Saginaw

free) features local and international artists displaying their works in a 1904 Georgian Revival mansion. Highlights include a research library, fine collections of 19th- and 20th-century American art, and a garden restored to reflect the home's original plantings.

The **Castle Museum of Saginaw County History** (500 Federal Ave., 989/752-2861, www.castlemuseum.org, 10am-4:30pm Tues.-Sat., 1pm-4:30pm Sun., $1 adults, $0.50 children) is one of the city's most recognizable landmarks. Constructed in 1898 by architect William Aiken, the limestone building, originally a U.S. post office, was intended to replicate a French chateau. Today, the museum chronicles the region's rich heritage, with artifacts and dioramas that explore the area's former fur trading, logging, farming, and manufacturing industries.

Saginaw Children's Zoo

The **Children's Zoo** at Celebration Square (1730 S. Washington Ave., 989/759-1408, www.saginawzoo.com, 10am-5pm Mon.-Sat., 11am-6pm Sun., $7 pp) is a bargain-priced zoo at a manageable size. It features more than 130 animals, most native to the region. The timber wolves and bald eagles are especially popular with kids.

ENTERTAINMENT AND EVENTS
The Arts

The Dow Event Center (303 Johnson St., 989/759-1330, www.doweventcenter.com, show times and ticket prices vary), home to the Saginaw Spirit Hockey Club, hosts various concerts and Broadway musicals year-round. In addition to classic films, the **Temple Theatre** (203 N. Washington Ave., 989/754-7469, www.templetheatre.com, show times and ticket prices vary), a grand 1927 performance venue, presents performances by the **Saginaw Choral Society** (www.saginawchoralsociety.com) and **Saginaw Bay Symphony Orchestra** (www.saginawbayorchestra.com).

Festivals

Saginaw is home to a large Hispanic community,

LOUIS CAMPAU: FATHER OF TWO MICHIGAN TOWNS

Born in Detroit in 1791, Louis Campau, a French explorer and the nephew of trader Joseph Campau, was a key figure in the settlement of two modern Michigan cities. In 1815, after fighting in the War of 1812, he established a fur-trading post near what would eventually become downtown Saginaw.

Soon afterward, at the request of Governor Lewis Cass, he built a council house, where he helped Cass negotiate the Treaty of Saginaw in 1819 with the Native American tribes of the Great Lakes region, including the Ojibwa, Ottawa, Potawatomi, and Chippewa. In effect, the Native Americans ceded more than six million acres in the central portion of the Lower Peninsula to the white settlers, who benefited from the region's bountiful timber, salt, and fisheries.

In 1822, troops were stationed at Fort Saginaw to monitor the growing tension between the settlers and the Native Americans. The following year, Campau plotted the town.

In 1826, Campau moved southwest and established a trading post at the convergence of several important Ottawa Indian trails in what is now Grand Rapids. Although other permanent white settlers, including Rix Robinson and Baptist minister Isaac McCoy, had arrived before him, Campau is credited as the "father" of Grand Rapids, a distinction solidified by his 1831 purchase of the entire downtown business district from the U.S. government. For the rest of his life, he helped to build and promote Grand Rapids, where he died in 1871 at the age of 79.

many of whom initially settled here to work on the construction of the state's railroads. Many of their descendants stayed on to work at area sugar beet refineries. Saginaw and Bay City's sugar beet industry makes Michigan the fifth-largest sugar beet producer in the country. In May, the Saginaw area is home to the state's largest **Cinco de Mayo** festival and parade, held on Ojibway Island behind the teahouse in Rust Park.

Southwest of Saginaw, the community of Chesaning hosts the annual **Saginaw County Fair** (989/845-2143, www.saginawcountyfair. org). Usually held in late July, this family-friendly event stages everything from rodeos to scavenger hunts.

SHOPPING

While not a shoppers' paradise like Frankenmuth and Birch Run, Saginaw is an ideal place to look for antiques. Situated within the historic district, you'll find **Adomaitis Antiques & Theatrics** (412 Court St., 989/790-7469, www.adomaitis.com, 10:30am-5pm Mon.-Sat.), a repository of vintage clothing and costumes. Watch for their occasional estate sales, too. If you can't find what you need

at Adomaitis, head to **The Antique Warehouse** (1122 Tittabawassee, 989/755-4343, www.theantiquewarehouse.net, 10am-6pm Mon.-Sat., noon-6pm Sun.), one of Michigan's largest antiques malls, housing 70 antiques dealers, 12 specialty shops, and a café. You could conceivably spend an entire day perusing its inventory, including toys, jewelry, furniture, and more.

The Saginaw area also boasts Michigan's largest village of country "shoppes," the **Pride and Country Village** (5965 Holland Rd., 989/754-5807, www.prideandcountry. com, 10am-6pm Mon.-Sat., 11am-5pm Sun.). Consisting of several renovated historic structures, with over 40,000 square feet of shopping possibilities, this unique complex offers a variety of country-style treasures, from candles in the 1899 schoolhouse to handcrafted furnishings in the five-level 1904 farmhouse.

RECREATION

Bird-Watching

SHIAWASSEE NATIONAL WILDLIFE REFUGE

Nature takes center stage at the **Shiawassee National Wildlife Refuge** (6975 Mower Rd.,

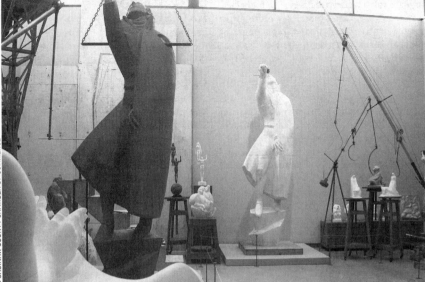

the studio space in the Marshall M. Fredericks Sculpture Museum

989/777-5930, www.fws.gov/midwest/shiawassee, 7:30am-4pm Mon.-Fri.), just southwest of Saginaw. The refuge and the nearby **Green Point Environmental Learning Center** (3010 Maple St., 989/759-1669) share a location near the union of four rivers—the Flint, the Tittabawassee, the Cass, and the Shiawassee—all of which converge to form the Saginaw River.

Covering more than 9,700 acres, the refuge was established in 1953 as a wetland for migrating waterfowl, and is now widely regarded as one of the top 25 birding sites in the United States. A checklist available at the headquarters lists more than 270 species that frequent the refuge. In October, some 30,000 ducks and 25,000 geese converge on the area, as well as songbirds, wading birds, owls, hawks, and even bald eagles. About 500 tundra swans migrate through annually.

An observation deck and a wheelchair-accessible blind are strategically placed for prime viewing. The refuge has more than 13 miles of hiking trails, open sunrise to sunset, including a 4.5-mile Woodland Trail that loops through bottomland hardwoods and skirts the Tittabawassee River. The adjacent Green Point is operated under a co-op agreement with the U.S. Fish and Wildlife Service, with 76 acres of diverse habitat and an interpretive center. Because it lies in the floodplain of the Tittabawassee River, the Green Point trail system is often under water. It can be a magnet for mosquitoes, so be sure to bring repellent.

CROW ISLAND STATE GAME AREA

Each year, thousands drive over one of the state's best bird-watching areas without realizing it's there. The Crow Island State Game Area stretches along the Saginaw River from the foot of the Zilwaukee Bridge to Bay City and covers more than 1,000 acres. The area serves as a giant overflow basin for Michigan's largest watershed. M-13 runs along the Saginaw River's east bank and splits the preserve into east and west. It, too, is an excellent bird-watching area for waterfowl, ospreys, bald eagles, night herons, great egrets, and more. For more information, contact the **Michigan Department of Natural Resources's Saginaw Bay District Office** (503 N. Euclid Ave., 989/684-9141, www.michigan.gov/dnr).

Hiking

The Saginaw County Parks and Recreation Commission manages the secluded 186-acre **Price Nature Center** (6685 Sheridan Rd., 989/790-5280, www.saginawcounty.com/parks, 8am-sunset daily), located five miles south of Saginaw, near the Bridgeport exit on I-75. A good spot for day hikes, the center features a 200-year-old beech and maple forest, three miles of hiking and cross-country skiing trails, a picnic pavilion, and a rustic campground.

ACCOMMODATIONS AND FOOD

Plenty of chain hotels can be found along the I-75 corridor and beside I-675, including the **Super 8** (4848 Towne Centre Rd., 989/791-3003, www.super8.com, $48-60 d). Saginaw's most distinctive lodging choice is the **◖ Montague Inn** (1581 S. Washington Ave., 989/752-3939, www.montagueinn. com, $85-160 d), an elegantly restored three-story brick Georgian mansion with a library, sitting rooms, and a gracious dining room that is open to the public. All of the 17 guest rooms have private baths, and all are furnished with period pieces, including four-poster beds, wing chairs, and other antiques. Rates include a lavish breakfast.

If you're not in the mood for escargot, chicken Florentine, or other equally tempting dishes at the Montague Inn, there are indeed more casual options in the Saginaw area. For just a quick bite, try **Crumbs Gourmet Cookie Café** (4882 Gratiot Rd., 989/498-4010, www.crumbscaters.com, 6:30am-9pm Mon.-Thurs., 6:30am-10pm Fri., 7am-5pm Sat.-Sun., $2-9), where you'll find coffee, smoothies, soups, salads, wraps, and, of course, chocolate chip cookies on the menu.

INFORMATION AND SERVICES

For more information about Saginaw, contact the **Saginaw County Chamber of Commerce** (515 N. Washington Ave., 2nd Fl., 989/752-7161, www.saginawchamber.org, 8am-4:30pm Mon.-Fri.) or the **Great Lakes Bay Regional Convention & Visitors Bureau** (515 N. Washington Ave., 3rd Fl., 989/752-7164 or 800/444-9979, www.visitgreatlakesbay.org, 8am-4:30pm Mon.-Fri.). For city-related issues, contact **City Hall** (www.saginaw-mi. com). For local news, pick up a copy of the *Saginaw News* (www.saginaw-news.com or www.mlive.com).

Saginaw offers the kind of services necessary for any mid-sized town. For mailing needs, visit one of several area **post offices** (1300 Cumberland St., 989/771-5738, www.usps.com, 8:30am-5pm Mon.-Fri., 9am-noon Sat.). In case of medical, safety, or fire emergencies, you can dial **911** at any time; for non-emergencies, contact the **Police Department** (612 Federal St., 989/759-1229) or the **Fire Department** (801 Federal St., 989/759-1376). For medical treatment, contact **St. Mary's of Michigan** (800 S. Washington Ave., 989/907-8000, www.stmarysofmichigan.org). Prescriptions can be filled at any one of several pharmacies, including a 24-hour **Walgreens** (4989 State St., 989/791-3088, www.walgreens.com).

GETTING THERE AND AROUND

The closest airport to Saginaw is the **MBS International Airport** (MBS, 8500 Garfield Rd., Freeland, 989/695-5555, www.mbsairport.org), which also serves Bay City and Midland. You can also access Saginaw via **Greyhound** (989/753-5454 or 800/231-2222, www.greyhound.com) or **Indian Trails** (800/292-3831, www.indiantrails.com), both of which provide bus service to the station at 511 Johnson Street.

Most travelers, however, reach Saginaw via I-75. If you're headed north from Flint, for instance, you can either take exit 149-AB to

M-46 West or exit 150 to I-675; either way, it will usually take you 40 minutes to cover the 38-mile distance. From Bay City, meanwhile, you can take M-25 West, followed by I-75 South/US-23 South to exit 155, where the I-675 bypass will guide you to the northern edge of Saginaw; the 17-mile trip will take you about 24 minutes.

Once you reach Saginaw, you can opt to drive through town or hop a bus. For information about routes and schedules, contact the **Saginaw Transit Authority Regional Services** (STARS, 615 Johnson St., 989/907-4000, www.saginaw-stars.com, one-way $1.25 adults, $0.60 seniors 62 and over and children shorter than fare box).

Bay City

Lying three miles upstream from the point where the Saginaw River enters Saginaw Bay, Bay City today bears no resemblance to the rip-roaring mill town it was at the end of the 19th century. Little remains of the color and flavor of the days when bawdy Bay City attracted thousands of lumberjacks who came in with the spring log drives to work in the mills after months of toiling in the surrounding woods.

The first white settlers came here to trade with the Indians, founding Bay City in 1831. After 1860, however, the once-quiet community became the center of the area's logging industry. By 1872, there were 36 mills buzzing along the banks of the river, some of which were among the largest in the country. The whine of saws biting into logs could be heard 10 hours each day, and the smell of fresh lumber was said to be strong enough to flavor food.

Logs waiting to be milled lined the banks of the river. With the logs came the lumberjacks who patronized the saloons along the city's Water Street, looking for liquor and women. Around 1890, Bay City reached the height of its boom and the peak of its population—then declined about as quickly as it grew. The city's logging industry abruptly ceased after the stands of timber in Saginaw Valley were depleted and a Canadian export duty caused the abandonment of many mills. Bay City narrowly missed becoming one of the state's ghost towns by smartly developing industries revolving around soft-coal mining, commercial fishing, and beet sugar.

The last of the sawmills that once lined both banks of the Saginaw River were leveled in the late 1930s. Today, large freighters navigate the channel that was once filled with logs driven down from the river's upper reaches. The logging period of what is now the state's second-largest port is still reflected in the city's many wood-framed houses, as well as the opulent mansions built by the lumber barons.

In recent decades, Bay City gained notoriety as the birthplace of Madonna. The native daughter is persona non grata these days, though, after a few less-than-flattering comments about her hometown (referring to it as the "armpit" of the United States) that made their way into the national media. Today, Bay City is a vibrant place, with terrific bird-watching spots, historic architecture, maritime attractions, and a host of other recreational and cultural diversions.

SIGHTS
Maritime Legacy
Bay City has other claims to fame besides the Material Girl. With roughly 35,000 residents, it's the state's second-largest port. Many of those residents can be found enjoying the city's well-maintained parks system, including the five-mile **Riverwalk,** which follows the west bank of the Saginaw River, accessing an 820-foot pier and passing through **Veterans Memorial Park** and the **Liberty Harbor Marina.** Walkers, cyclists, inline skaters, and passing freighters from all over the world make for a colorful scene.

THE THUMB

HARRY DEFOE: FROM PRINCIPAL TO SHIPBUILDER

Given that his father, Joseph, was a Great Lakes sailor and his uncle, John, was a local boat builder, it's no surprise that Harry J. Defoe, born in 1875, had shipbuilding in his blood. As a child, the Bay City native enjoyed whittling toy boats and watching them float down the Saginaw River. Eventually, he used wood and scrap metal to build working steamboats. Although Defoe became a teacher and later a school principal, the river stayed on his mind.

So, in 1905, with the assistance of his brother Frederic, a New York-based attorney, and his brother-in-law George Whitehouse, a fish merchant, he established the Defoe Boat & Motor Works. By 1917, the company had begun producing torpedo chasers and steam-powered vessels for the U.S. Navy. After World War I, Defoe built self-starting speedboats and pleasure yachts, one of which was later owned by Presidents Eisenhower, Kennedy, and Nixon.

Following the Great Depression, the U.S. government tried to help the entire shipping industry, including Defoe's company; World War II resulted in even more government contracts. Defoe's unique timesaving method – whereby workers started the vessel in an upside-down position and then righted it for completion –

allowed him to craft numerous sub-chasers, infantry landing craft, destroyer escorts, freight carriers, troop transports, and rescue tugs for the U.S. Navy, making his company, then known as the Defoe Shipbuilding Company and overseeing more than 4,000 workers, one of Bay City's largest employers.

Even after the war, Defoe's company prospered, building pleasure yachts and harbor tugs. The crew of one Defoe ship, the RV *Knorr*, even discovered the wreck of the RMS *Titanic*. Despite Defoe's death in 1957, during a business trip to Washington DC, his company continued under the supervision of his sons Thomas and William. The Bay City yard saw the creation of enormous warships and guided missile destroyers, and the company was incorporated in 1956.

By the mid-1960s, however, the firm was beginning to suffer. Shipyards on the East and West Coasts had fewer delivery dilemmas; aging equipment and federal cutbacks in domestic shipbuilding didn't help matters either. In 1976, with fewer than 100 workers, Defoe's company finally closed its doors, but many of its well-crafted vessels continue to sail the open seas.

Historic Sites

On the east side of town, lumber magnates built grand homes along Center Avenue and the surrounding streets. Center Avenue is the heart of the historic district, with more than 250 structures listed on the national and state historic registers. A few, including **Chesny's Keswick Manor** (1800 Center Ave., 989/893-6598, www.keswickmanor.com), have been opened to the public as bed-and-breakfasts.

Even more impressive than the grand homes is Bay City's **City Hall** (301 Washington Ave., 989/894-8147, 8am-5pm Mon.-Fri., free), completed in 1897 and listed on the National Register of Historic Places. A $3.1 million restoration in 1980

earned it mention by the Smithsonian Institution as one of the 10 most outstanding historic restorations in the United States. The Romanesque-style stone building dominates the city skyline with a 125-foot clock tower. Visitors are welcome to take a self-guided tour and climb the 68 steps in the clock tower, which affords impressive views of Bay City, the Saginaw River, and the surrounding countryside. The Bay County Historical Museum also offers guided tours.

The Historical Museum of Bay County

The Historical Museum of Bay County (321 Washington Ave., 989/893-5733, www.

bchsmuseum.org, 10am-5pm Mon.-Fri., noon-4pm Sat.-Sun., free, donations welcome) traces the development of the county from pre-Columbian times through the 20th century. Displays include period rooms, Native American artifacts, and exhibits on the fur trade, logging, and shipbuilding.

ENTERTAINMENT AND EVENTS
The Arts
Bay City is home to the state's oldest continuously operating community theater, **Bay City Players** (1214 Columbus Ave., 989/893-5555, www.baycityplayers.com, show times and ticket prices vary), which presents several plays, musicals, and youth programs annually. Recent shows have included *Twelve Angry Men* and *Chicago*.

Festivals
Every July, the **Munger Potato Festival** (www.mungerpotatofest.com, $10 pp) lures visitors to the town of Munger, southeast of Bay City, for figure-eight auto derbies, potato giveaways, and more.

SHOPPING
Not surprising, given Bay City's rich history, the city's downtown district can be a fruitful spot for antiquing, with **Bay Antique Center** (1020 N. Water St., 989/893-1116, www.antiquecenteronline.com, 10am-5pm Mon.-Thurs. and Sat., 10am-8pm Fri., noon-5pm Sun.) claiming the better part of a city block. In 1999, it was named the state's best antiques mall by readers of *AAA Michigan Living* magazine, and it's even bigger today. A large showroom includes more than 400 booths overflowing with furniture, kitchen items, and more.

For a change of pace, head five miles west of Bay City to **Warmbier Farms** (5300 Garfield Rd., Auburn, 989/662-7002, www.warmbierfarms.com, 9am-6pm Mon.-Thurs., 9am-5pm Fri.-Sat., 11am-3pm Sun.), which specializes in home and garden decor, from wreaths to pond floats, and presents a variety of seasonal activities, including wreath-making classes.

RECREATION
The 2,800-acre **Bay City State Recreation Area** (3582 State Park Dr., 989/667-0717, www.michigan.gov/dnr, 8am-10pm daily, annual $11 Recreation Passport for Michigan residents or $8.40 day-use fee/$30.50 yearly Recreation Passport for nonresidents required) connects the Frank N. Andersen Trail, the Bay City State Park, and the Tobico Marsh. Together, they offer a sandy beach along Saginaw Bay, two 32-foot observation towers, a fishing pier, a variety of hiking, biking, and cross-country skiing trails, and a boardwalk with fixed spotting scopes for watching waterfowl and shorebirds like herons, gulls, and egrets.

The paved 1.6-mile Frank N. Andersen Trail follows an abandoned rail grade to Tobico Marsh, an 1,800-acre refuge that is one of the largest coastal marshes on the Great Lakes. The **Saginaw Bay Visitor Center** (10am-6pm Mon.-Sat., noon-6pm Sun. Memorial Day-Labor Day, noon-4pm Tues.-Sun. Sept.-May) contains permanent and changing exhibits depicting life in the wetlands, a 15-minute multimedia presentation on wetlands development, and a bird observation room and wet lab. Although the recreation area is open all year, bird-watching is especially enjoyable during the spring and fall migratory seasons.

ACCOMMODATIONS
The **Bay Valley Resort & Conference Center** (2470 Old Bridge Rd., 989/686-3500, www.bayvalley.com, $81-189 d) comprises nice grounds, a lobby full of antiques, and an 18-hole championship Jack Nicklaus/Desmond Muirhead golf course. Opened in 1973, the resort offers nearly 150 spacious rooms and suites, plus live entertainment and weekly drink specials in the Players Lounge.

Perhaps more intriguing, a 19th-century lumber baron's mansion is now the **Keswick Manor** (1800 Center Ave., 989/893-6598, www.keswickmanor.com, $75-200 d). It's been updated with plenty of modern comforts, even whirlpool tubs. Amenities include lush breakfasts, exquisite linens and towels, landscaped grounds, and 24-hour tea and coffee service.

Camping

Depending on the weather, the Bay City State Recreation Area can be a delightful place to camp during spring, summer, and fall, especially if you're interested in hiking, biking, fishing, or bird-watching. The on-site campground offers nearly 200 sites at $16 per night. For reservations, contact the **Saginaw Bay Visitor Center** (989/667-0717).

FOOD

While in Bay City, try **Krzysiak's House Restaurant** (1605 Michigan Ave., 989/894-5531, www.krzysiaks.com, 6:30am-9pm Mon.-Thurs., 6:30am-10pm Fri.-Sat., 6:30am-8pm Sun., $6-26) for Polish dishes and a popular weekend seafood buffet.

INFORMATION AND SERVICES

For more information about Bay City, contact the **Bay County Convention & Visitors Bureau** (100 Center St., 989/893-1222 or 800/444-9979, www.visitgreatlakesbay.org, 8:30am-5pm Mon.-Fri.) or the **Bay Area Chamber of Commerce** (901 Saginaw St., 989/893-4567, www.baycityarea.com, 8:30am-5pm Mon.-Fri.). For city-related issues, contact **City Hall** (301 Washington Ave., www.baycitymi.org). For local news, pick up a copy of the *Bay City Times* (www.mlive.com).

In addition, Bay City offers a variety of services that travelers might require. To mail a package or postcard, visit one of several area **post offices** (1000 Washington Ave., 989/895-5555, www.usps.com, 8:30am-5:45pm

Mon.-Fri). In case of medical, safety, or fire emergencies, you can dial **911** at any time; for non-emergencies, contact the **Bay City Police Department** (501 3rd St., 989/892-8571). For medical treatment, contact the **Bay Regional Medical Center** (1900 Columbus Ave., 989/894-3000, www.bayregional.org).

GETTING THERE AND AROUND

The closest airport to Bay City is the **MBS International Airport** (MBS, 8500 Garfield Rd., Freeland, 989/695-5555, www.mbsairport.org), which also serves Saginaw and Midland. In addition, you can access Bay City via **Greyhound** (989/893-6589 or 800/231-2222, www.greyhound.com) and **Indian Trails** (800/292-3831, www.indiantrails.com), both of which provide bus service to the station at 1124 Washington Avenue.

Most travelers, however, reach Bay City via I-75, US-10, or M-25. If you're headed north from Flint, for instance, simply take I-475 North to I-75 North/US-23 North to M-25 East, a 50-mile route that, without traffic, will take about 50 minutes. From Midland, take US-10 East to M-25 East, a 19-mile route that, without traffic, will take roughly 20 minutes. From Port Austin, meanwhile, follow M-25 West for approximately 66 miles along the coast, a trip that will require at least 90 minutes.

Once you reach Bay City, you can opt to drive through town or tour the area via bus. For information about routes and schedules, contact the **Bay Metropolitan Transit Authority** (1510 N. Johnson St., 989/894-2900, www.baymetro.com, one-way $1 adults, $0.75 students, $0.50 seniors, children under 6 free).

Sebewaing to Port Austin

From Bay City, M-25 meanders east along Saginaw Bay and Lake Huron. Along the way is a chain of small fishing ports, including Sebewaing, Bay Port, and Caseville, popular places for cottages but with little to stop most passing travelers. Caseville, originally known as Port Elizabeth, was once an important terminal for lake and rail shipping, with a prosperous salt well and ironworks. Today, most find the area remarkable only for its small, quiet towns; large, prosperous farms; and tabletop flat landscape punctuated by long stretches of blue water.

Still, these coastal towns offer a few diversions en route to Port Austin and the rest of the Lake Huron shore. Most notable are their annual summertime events, including the curiously named Cheeseburger in Caseville.

Port Austin, meanwhile, is known as the "tip of the Thumb." Bob Talbert, a columnist for the *Detroit Free Press,* calls it "the best spot in Michigan to view the sunrise and sunset." Downtown Port Austin is a comfortable, simple place, full of old-fashioned dime stores, soda fountains, collectible shops, and halls run by local legions, and the surrounding waters are popular among deep-sea anglers.

The city was first visited in 1837 by a fugitive of the Canadian Patriotic War, who found an excellent hiding place on this stretch of shore. Others soon followed, with a permanent settlement established not long after. Port Austin later became well known for Pointe aux Barques, a point extending north into Lake Huron that became a wealthy resort enclave of prominent Detroiters. The point is named for the large rocks offshore, many of which resemble the prows of ships.

SIGHTS

In Sebewaing, regional artists are showcased at the **Burns Gallery** (27 N. Center St., 1pm-4pm Sat.-Sun.). Recent exhibits have featured colorful quilts, watercolor paintings, and local photography. For information about upcoming events, contact the Lake Huron Community Arts Council (989/883-2450).

Halfway between Caseville and Port Austin, south of M-25, lies the **Huron County Nature Center & Wilderness Arboretum** (800/358-4862, www.huronnaturecenter.org, 24 hours daily, free). This 280-acre nature center has rolling sand ridges and shallow, wet depressions known as swales that are traversed by an interpretive trail system, including one suitable for wheelchairs. Trees, plants, vines, and wildflowers are protected here for educational and scientific purposes.

Three miles of sugary sand beach and banks of dunes (unusual in this part of the state) are the highlights of the 565-acre **Port Crescent State Park** (1775 Port Austin Rd., 989/738-8663, www.michigan.gov/dnr, 24 hours daily, annual $11 Recreation Passport for Michigan residents or $8.40 day-use fee/$30.50 yearly Recreation Passport for nonresidents required). A three-mile trail winds through wooded dunes and above the banks of the Pinnebog River, climbing up to provide some great views of Saginaw Bay, not to mention birds and other wildlife. The park's east side has a modern RV and tent campground near what was the village of Port Crescent, which disappeared in the 1930s. The stack from a sawmill is all that remains of this old industrial town; an interpretive display at the site chronicles its rise and fall.

FESTIVALS

While not as active as other Thumb-area towns, Sebewaing and Caseville each celebrate their culture with a handful of annual events. In June, Sebewaing's **Michigan Sugar Festival** offers standard festival fare, including sidewalk sales, tractor pulls, a petting zoo, midway games, and fireworks. Caseville, meanwhile, hosts two curious events: **Shanty Days,** which celebrates February's winter chill with polar bear dips and ice-fishing contests, and **Cheeseburger in Caseville,** a 10-day festival in August inspired by Jimmy Buffet's laid-back vibe and featuring sand sculptures, cheeseburger-eating contests, steel drum performances, and Caribbean jewelry making, among other tropical-themed activities. For more information, contact the Caseville Chamber of Commerce (www.casevillechamber.com).

SHOPPING

Port Austin's limited shopping options are clustered along a two-block stretch of Lake Street in the downtown area. Here, and on surrounding streets, you can expect to find an assortment of antiques and collectibles. Housed in a historic 19th-century brick building, **Heins Hardware** (8735 Lake St., 989/738-7311, www.heinshardware.com, 8:30am-5:30pm Mon.-Sat.) satisfies a wide array of everyday needs; above the shop is **Lisa's Loft,** the place to go for cards and gifts.

RECREATION
Hiking and Biking

Near Caseville, **Albert E. Sleeper State Park** (6573 State Park Rd., 989/856-4411, www.michigan.gov/dnr, 24 hours daily, annual $11 Recreation Passport for Michigan residents or $8.40 day-use fee/$30.50 yearly Recreation Passport for nonresidents required) draws most of its visitors because of its half-mile arc of wide sand beach on Saginaw Bay. Sleeper (once called Huron State Park and renamed in 1944 for the governor who created the state park system) is popular with suburbanites looking for that "up north" escape without the long drive. The 723-acre park is quite heavily wooded, mostly with oak and other hardwoods. Nearly five miles of hiking/biking trails wind through the lightly developed park. Pick up a self-guiding brochure at the park office to identify native trees, shrubs, and wildflowers, and learn how Native Americans used them. Trails are groomed for cross-country skiing in winter.

Canoeing and Kayaking

Quiet-water paddlers can spend an entire day exploring the Pinnebog, a river that seems to tie itself in knots as it searches for an outlet to Saginaw Bay. Nearly four miles of river run through the Port Crescent State Park and attract anglers for trout, walleye, salmon, and perch. A private livery, **Tip-A-Thumb Canoe Rental** (2471 Port Austin Rd., 989/738-7656, May-Oct., $20 pp), rents canoes and kayaks for leisurely paddles down the winding river. To explore the Lake Huron shore, rent a kayak from **Port Austin Kayak & Bike Rental** (95 W. Spring St., 989/550-6651, www.portaustinkayak.com, May-Sept., $15 hourly, $37 daily). Guided tours take you to intriguing rock formations and secluded beaches. Bike rentals and yoga classes are also available.

Fishing

"Deep-sea" fishing is popular throughout the Great Lakes, and the waters around the tip of the Thumb are considered some of the best. Charter boats operate out of many Thumb communities; the **Thumb Area Charter Boat Association** (www.thumbareacharterboats.com) is a good clearinghouse of information about fishing opportunities in the area. Just remember that a valid state fishing license is required for anyone over 17. Visit www.mdnr-elicense.com for more information about obtaining a license from the Michigan Department of Natural Resources.

ACCOMMODATIONS AND FOOD

The area around Sebewaing and Caseville offers only a handful of overnight options. One such place is the **Fish Point Lodge** (4130 Miller Ave., Unionville, 989/674-2631, www.fishpointlodge.com, $70-100 d), a century-old inn located near the marshes of Saginaw Bay, making it an ideal locale for waterfowl hunting and, in winter, ice fishing. Besides the main lodge, there are cabins and RV sites for rent. A boat launch as well as guided hunting and fishing tours are also available.

Another option is the **Bella Vista Inn & Sunset Bay Resort** (6024 Port Austin Rd.,

Caseville, 989/856-2500, www.bella-caseville. com, $69-94 d, $159-199 for cabins and cottages). If you get hungry, the waterfront resort offers **Hersel's on the Bay Grill & Lounge** (2pm-2am Tues.-Fri., 9am-2am Sat.-Sun. July-Aug., 2pm-2am Fri.-Sat. Sept.-June, $6-18), an ideal spot to watch the sunset over a steak dinner.

C The Bank 1884 Food & Spirits (8646 Lake St., Port Austin, 989/738-5353, www. thebank1884.com, 8am-3pm and 5pm-9pm daily May-Oct., 5pm-9pm Sat.-Sun. Nov.-Dec., $5-27), also a national historic site, is considered by many to offer the finest dining in the Thumb. The 1884 red-washed brick building, formerly a bank, opened as a restaurant in 1982, decorated with the original 1st-floor teller's cage, stained glass, and oversized historical photographs of Huron County. It has attracted a loyal crowd and high praise ever since, including a review from the *New York Times* speculating that The Bank "would give big city restaurants a run for the gold card." The menu changes regularly; two long-standing specialties have been the lake perch fillets and the broiled walleye. Reservations are recommended.

Camping

Albert E. Sleeper State Park includes a 226-site campground that's quite popular on summer weekends. It's located on the south side of M-25, but there's a pedestrian bridge over the highway that safely links it to the beach. The campsites are equipped with electrical service; modern restrooms and rental cabins are also available. For campground reservations, contact the **Michigan Department of Natural Resources** (800/447-2757, www.michigan. gov/dnr, $25-80 daily).

In addition, **Port Crescent State Park,** closer to Port Austin, has a modern 137-unit RV and tent campground. It's very popular in summer—especially the sites right next to the beach. Make reservations by contacting the **Michigan Department of Natural Resources** (800/447-2757, www.michigan.gov/dnr, $27 daily).

INFORMATION AND SERVICES

For more information about Sebewaing and Caseville, contact the **Sebewaing Chamber of Commerce** (222 N. Center St., www.sebe-waingchamber.com) or the **Caseville Chamber of Commerce** (6632 Main St., 989/856-3818, www.casevillechamber.com, 10am-4pm Mon.-Sat.). Also, if you need a **post office** while visiting the area, you're in luck; there's one in each town (49 N. Center St., Sebewaing, 989/883-3550, or 7060 Main St., Caseville, 989/856-2273).

For more information about the Port Austin area, contact the **Greater Port Austin Area Chamber of Commerce** (2 W. Spring St., 989/738-7600, www.portaustinarea.com, 9am-1pm Mon., Wed., Fri., and Sat.). For local news, pick up a copy of the **Huron Daily Tribune** (www.michigansthumb.com) or the **Lakeshore Guardian** (www.lakeshoreguardian. com), a monthly publication.

Although not an enormous town, Port Austin does have its share of necessary services. For banking needs, visit the **Port Austin State Bank** (62 E. State St., 989/738-5235). To mail a letter, head to the town's only **post office** (8710 North St., 989/738-5264, www.usps. com, 8am-4:30pm Mon.-Fri., 8am-11:30am Sat.). For medical services, contact the **Huron Medical Center** (1100 S. Van Dyke Rd., Bad Axe, 989/269-9521, www.huron-medical-center.org). To report a crime or emergency, contact the **Police Department** (17 W. State St., 989/738-5180).

GETTING THERE AND AROUND

While Sebewaing and Caseville can both be reached via boat, the easiest way for most travelers to visit these two fishing ports is via car. If not driving your own, you'll have to rent a vehicle in a larger town like Flint or Saginaw. Either way, you can follow M-25 East from Bay City to Sebewaing, a 29-mile trip that typically takes about 40 minutes. From Port Austin, you can take M-25 West to Caseville, an 18-mile

THE THUMB

distance that usually requires around 23 minutes to cover.

Like all the towns along the Thumb's Lake Huron shore, Port Austin is easy to reach via car. From Bay City (to the southwest) or Port Huron (to the southeast), you can follow M-25 along the shore to Port Austin, at the tip of the Thumb; from Bay City, the 66-mile trip usually takes about 90 minutes, while the 88-mile route from Port Huron requires almost two hours of driving time. From Flint, you can take I-69 East to exit 168 and head north on M-53; without traffic, the 109-mile route will take at least two hours. Once in Port Austin, you can then drive, walk, or hop a bus. For route information, contact the **Thumb Area Transit** (TAT, 1513 Bad Axe Rd., Bad Axe, 989/269-2121 or 800/322-1125, www.tatbus.com).

Bad Axe and Interior

Definitely the least visited part of the Thumb, the interior towns and counties promise an even more laid-back experience than some of the coastal areas. Family-owned farms, 19th-century homes, quaint shopping districts, and slow-moving villages like Caro and Lapeer transport visitors back to a simpler time. Ancient petroglyphs south of Bad Axe can take you back even further.

SIGHTS
◖ Sanilac Petroglyphs Historic State Park
One of the state's great mysteries is at **Sanilac Petroglyphs Historic State Park** (2501 Germania Rd., Cass City, www.michigan. gov/dnr, 10am-5pm Wed.-Sun. Memorial Day-Labor Day, annual $11 Recreation Passport for Michigan residents or $8.40 day-use fee/$30.50 yearly Recreation Passport for nonresidents required), a historic site about 13 miles south of Bad Axe via M-53 and Germania Road. The Michigan Archaeological Society raised private funds to purchase the 240-acre site and eventually transferred the land to the State of Michigan, which now maintains it.

The park holds the only known prehistoric rock carvings attributed to Native Americans in the Lower Peninsula. The petroglyphs are aboriginal rock carvings that were chipped into exposed sandstone up to 1,000 years ago. Fires that swept through the area in the late 1800s cleared the vegetation that once protected sandstone slabs near the Cass River. Once the fires burned out, astonished locals were surprised to discover newly exposed carvings of animals and hunters. Some claim that they were created as recordings of dreams, visions, or significant events during hunting or religious rituals. Far off the beaten tourist path, they receive few visitors, which has undoubtedly helped protect these fragile treasures.

A 1.5-mile interpretive trail weaves through the park and educates visitors about its many historical facets, including the petroglyphs, Indian villages, and remains of Holbrook, a logging town that vanished nearly a century ago. This pleasant trail also cuts across the Cass River twice, weaving through woods and open meadows. The rest of the park is undeveloped with no staff or services, including restrooms. For information, contact **Albert E. Sleeper State Park** (989/856-4411, www.michigan. gov/dnr).

Thumb Octagon Barn
In the midst of rural Tuscola County lies an impressive, eight-sided structure, called the "round barn" by local residents. Designed by James Purdy, former owner of the surrounding acreage, and completed in 1924, the oddly shaped **Thumb Octagon Barn** (989/665-0081, www. thumboctagonbarn.org, 9am-sunset daily, free) resembled a structure that Purdy had once seen on a trip to Iowa. At the time, it was believed that such a barn would increase productivity, combining livestock pens, granaries, and other agricultural buildings in one spot; ultimately,

PETROGLYPHS SHROUDED IN CONTROVERSY

Situated within the center of Michigan's Thumb area, the ancient sandstone carvings that now comprise **Sanilac Petroglyphs Historic State Park** have been the subject of controversy ever since their discovery in the late 19th century. Although most paleontologists, cryptozoologists, and evolutionists agree that the petroglyphs provide a glimpse into the lives of early Native American artists who dwelled in what is now Michigan's Lower Peninsula, they cannot concur on the meaning behind the images, even after years of intense study.

For instance, one of the faded etchings depicts the legendary "underwater panther," a spiny, horned mountain lion that supposedly inhabited area lakes and was, according to Native Americans, the cause of storms. Some scientists insist that this creature resembles the long-extinct stegosaurus, lending credence to their belief that dinosaurs might have lived long enough to interact with ancient peoples.

Equally strange are the religious symbols that appear amid these ancient carvings, such as Christian crosses and Jewish menorahs. These, along with the presence of Roman numerals and letters, provide possible proof that Christopher Columbus was not the first representative of the Old World to encounter the Americas and make a lasting impression.

While creationists have embraced the validity of such interpretations, evolutionists could just as easily attribute the petroglyphs to less mysterious sources, including Indian mythology or human imagination, the kind that could transform an elk into a dinosaur-like creature. No matter what you believe about the petroglyphs of Sanilac County, however, one thing is certain: Although scientists and explorers will probably never fully understand the origin of these ancient carvings, the wonder indeed lies in the possibilities.

THE THUMB

---

however, farmers recognized the expense and ineffectiveness of such eight-sided barns.

After Purdy sold the farm in 1942, the 520-acre property swapped hands many times before Michigan's Department of Natural Resources (DNR) purchased the barn, house, and 80 remaining acres in 1991. Unfortunately, the DNR had no intention of preserving the buildings; only the land was of interest. So, in 1993, a group of locals campaigned to preserve the Thumb Octagon Barn as a key landmark. Today, as restoration efforts continue, visitors can learn more about America's agricultural heritage in the early 20th century by touring the farm May-October or attending Fall Family Days just after Labor Day. Donations are appreciated.

To reach the barn, take M-53 south of Bad Axe and head west on Bay City-Forestville Road; the barn is situated just one mile east of Gagetown.

Lapeer County Courthouse and Vicinity

Built in 1946, the **Lapeer County Courthouse** (287 W. Nepessing St., www.ci.lapeer.mi.us) is Michigan's oldest active courthouse. With its four fluted Doric columns and three-tiered rear tower, it's also a terrific example of Greek Revival-style architecture, which justifies its inclusion on the National Register of Historic Places.

Lapeer, in fact, boasts several entries on the National Register, including many within the **Piety Hill Historic District,** an irregularly shaped area west of the downtown business district. These restored houses represent an array of architectural styles, from Romanesque and Italianate to Gothic Revival and Queen Anne. Take a moment to stroll through this well-preserved neighborhood, roughly bordered by Cramton, Calhoun, Park, and Main Streets.

FESTIVALS

The Thumb's interior plays host to numerous annual events, including the three-day **Bad Axe Hatchet Festival** (989/269-6936, www.badaxehatchetfestival.com, free), a mid-June event that presents a variety of family-friendly activities, from pony wagon rides to chainsaw carving. Every August, the **Huron County Fair** (Huron County Fairgrounds, 501 Fair St., Bad Axe, 989/883-3997, $3 pp) offers livestock shows, harness racing, and demolition derbies, among other rustic diversions, while Imlay City's **Blueberry Festival** (810/724-1361, www.imlaycitymich.com, free) celebrates the berry season with car shows and, of course, pie-eating contests. Imlay City, "gateway to the Thumb," is also home to the **Eastern Michigan Fair** (Eastern Michigan Fairgrounds, 810/724-4145, www. easternmichiganstatefair.com, $12-15 pp), another August event that offers midway games, amusement rides, and tractor pulls.

While most events take place during the summer, a few honor cold-weather holidays. Each October, Caro hosts the **Tuscola County Pumpkin Festival** (989/673-2511, www.tuscolapumpkinfest.com, free), a four-day event that celebrates autumn with pumpkin pie sales, pumpkin decorating contests, and a grand parade.

RECREATION

South of Lapeer, the 723-acre **Metamora-Hadley Recreation Area** (3871 Herd Rd., Metamora, 810/797-4439 or 800/447-2757, www.michigan.gov/dnr, 8am-10pm daily, annual $11 Recreation Passport for Michigan residents or $8.40 day-use fee/$30.50 yearly Recreation Passport for nonresidents required) lures a variety of outdoor enthusiasts. Hikers and cross-country skiers appreciate the six miles of groomed trails, while boaters, canoeists, and anglers flock to the 80-acre Lake Minnewanna in the park's center. The property also includes a swimming beach, fishing pier, picnic area, and 214-site campground with a camp store and modern restrooms.

ACCOMMODATIONS AND FOOD

Although the Thumb presents better overnight options along the shore, there are in fact possibilities if you decide to stay within the interior. In Sandusky, the **Thumb Heritage Inn** (405 W. Sanilac Ave., 810/648-4811, www.thumbheritageinn.com, $50-85 d) provides clean, comfortable rooms, including suites with hot tubs. For slightly nicer accommodations, try the **Days Inn** in Imlay City (6692 Newark Rd., 810/724-8005, www.daysinn.com, $55-107 d); here, you'll find free high-speed Internet access and a heated indoor pool. Of course, if you get hungry during your trek through the Thumb's interior, feel free to grab some home-style comfort food at **Apple Tree Family Dining** (845 S. Main St., Lapeer, 810/664-5200, 7am-10pm daily, $5-14).

INFORMATION AND SERVICES

For more information about the Thumb's interior, contact the **Bad Axe Chamber of Commerce** (989/269-6936, www.badaxemich.com), the **Village of Caro** (317 S. State St., 989/673-2226, www.carovillage.net, 8am-5pm Mon.-Fri.), the **Sandusky Chamber of Commerce** (105 E. Sanilac Ave., Ste. 4, 810/648-4445, www.sanduskychamber.us), the **Sanilac Economic Alliance** (810/648-7000, www.sanilaccounty.org), the **Imlay City Area Chamber of Commerce** (150 N. Main St., 810/724-1361, www.imlaycitymich.com), and the **Lapeer Area Chamber of Commerce** (108 W. Park St., 810/664-6641, http://lapeerareachamber.org, 9am-5pm Mon.-Fri.).

For county-related issues, contact the **Huron County Building** (250 E. Huron Ave., Bad Axe, www.co.huron.mi.us), **Tuscola County** (www.tuscolacounty.org), **Sanilac County** (www.sanilaccounty.net), and **Lapeer County** (www.lapeercountyweb.org). For area news, pick up a copy of the *County Press* (www.countypress.com).

Although the interior towns are fairly small, you'll definitely find a few services here and there. For medical issues, contact the **Huron**

Medical Center (1100 S. Van Dyke Rd., Bad Axe, 989/269-9521, www.huron-medical-center.org) or the **Lapeer Regional Medical Center** (1375 N. Main, Lapeer, 810/667-5500, www.lapeerregional.org). For mailing needs, there are **post offices** (www.usps.com) in Bad Axe, Sandusky, Imlay City, and Lapeer.

GETTING THERE AND AROUND

If you have a vehicle, the towns within the Thumb's interior are easy to reach and, given their relatively small size, easy to navigate. From Port Austin, you can drive south on M-53 for 17 miles to Bad Axe and then an additional 58 miles to Imlay City; all told, it will take you about 90 minutes to get from Port Austin to Imlay City. Along the way, you can drive west on M-81 to Caro or head east on M-46 to Sandusky. From Imlay City, you can then reach Lapeer by driving south to I-69 West

and taking the interstate to exit 155, a 17-mile route that will normally take about 20 minutes. Incidentally, you can also reach Imlay City by following I-69 East from Flint and turning left onto M-53 North, a 35-mile trip that will take about 36 minutes, or by taking I-69 West from Port Huron to M-53 North, a 36-mile trip that will take about 37 minutes.

It's also possible to reach Lapeer via train. **Amtrak** (800/872-7245, www.amtrak.com) offers a route from Chicago, with stops across Michigan, including Kalamazoo, Battle Creek, East Lansing, and Flint. For schedule information, visit the Lapeer station at 73 Howard Street.

Although most people travel through the Thumb's interior via car, Huron County also has a bus service. For route information, contact **Thumb Area Transit** (TAT, 1513 Bad Axe Rd., Bad Axe, 989/269-2121 or 800/322-1125, www.tatbus.com).

THE THUMB

Grindstone City to Lakeport

Along the Lake Huron shore lies a string of coastal villages, including Harbor Beach and Port Sanilac. While some are little more than ghost towns, all are rich in history, culture, and natural delights, including several well-preserved 19th-century buildings and two underwater preserves.

GRINDSTONE CITY

For more than a century, this village took advantage of its plentiful supply of abrasive rock and produced some of the finest grindstones in the world, exporting them to England and other markets around the globe. Two factories operated until World War I, when the development of carborundum quickly made grindstone quarrying unprofitable. Almost overnight, the town's greatest asset went from being highly prized to virtually worthless. Huge stones, many up to six feet in diameter, were left behind to litter the beach. Also left behind were old docks, stores, houses, mills, and office

buildings. Many a grindstone can still be spotted as local lawn art.

HURON CITY

Just four miles south of Grindstone City lies the ghost of Huron City. Though not quite a ghost town, it certainly is a faded image of its past. Langdon Hubbard had big plans for Huron City when he arrived here from Connecticut in the 1870s, buying up thousands of acres of woodland and building sawmills that churned out thousands of feet of lumber a day. But his grand plans were dashed in 1881, when a huge fire—not uncommon in logging regions where dry clear-cut land easily ignited—roared across the Thumb and destroyed his young empire.

Huron City was partially rebuilt—Hubbard even contributed a public roller rink. But the area's water had been contaminated by salt-making, a secondary industry in the area. By 1884, the population had dwindled from 1,500 to about 15.

THE THUMB

© THUMB AREA TOURISM COUNCIL

the House of Seven Gables in Huron City

Huron City's quick demise makes its most dominant building all the more fascinating. The Italianate **House of Seven Gables** (989/428-4123, www.huroncitymuseums. com, 10am-6pm Mon. and Sat., 11am-6pm Sun. May-June and Sept., 10am-6pm Thurs.-Mon. July-Aug., $10 adults, including mansion and village, $5 children 10-15) was rebuilt by Langdon Hubbard after the 1881 fire. It later became the summer residence of Hubbard's son-in-law, William Lyon Phelps, a wildly popular Yale English teacher dubbed "America's favorite college professor" by *Life* magazine during the 1930s. The Hubbard family lived in the house from 1881 until 1987, when it was turned into an informal house museum.

As a result, the house offers an almost unparalleled glimpse into a past era, not someone's interpretation of what life must have been like. The family's books lie piled on tables, the ornate 1886 pool table looks ready for a match, the walls are lined with campy portraits of the beloved Hubbard dogs and cats, and the "state-of-the-art" 1915 kitchen even shows off its fancy and strange-looking dishwasher. Along with the House of Seven Gables, the public can visit the other remaining buildings of Historic Huron City, including the general store, inn, church, and barns.

Port Hope

From Huron City, M-25 curves south along Lake Huron. About seven miles south lies the lakeshore town of Port Hope. The 1857 Pointe aux Barques Lighthouse guards the coastline here. It's surrounded by the pleasant **Lighthouse County Park** (7320 Lighthouse Rd., 888/265-2583, www.huroncountyparks. com, May-Oct., free), which is located between Huron City and Port Hope. The park includes a 110-site campground, picnic area, beach, and small lighthouse museum.

HARBOR BEACH

From Port Hope, M-25 continues south toward Harbor Beach, home to the largest man-made freshwater harbor in the world. The need to improve on the natural harbor was prompted by

Michigan's busy logging industry in the 1870s. More and more ships were plying the waters up and down the Lake Huron shore and across Saginaw Bay; in stormy weather, they needed a safe refuge from strong currents and heavy seas. The federal government began work on a harbor in 1873, and worked on the gargantuan project for more than two decades. When completed, the breakwall stretched 8,000 feet! It continues to do duty today, along with the 1881 Coast Guard Station and 1885 lighthouse.

Originally named Sand Beach, Harbor Beach was once notorious as the site of an illegal money factory. In the mid-19th century, counterfeit U.S. currency and Mexican dollars were made here and distributed throughout the Americas.

Frank Murphy ranks as Harbor Beach's most famous son—the Michigan governor who is best known for collective bargaining during the 1937 Flint sit-down strike, paving the way for the rise of the United Auto Workers (UAW). He went on to become U.S. Attorney General and U.S. Supreme Court Justice. The 1910 **Frank Murphy Birthplace** (142 S. Huron Ave., 989/479-3363, noon-4pm Tues.-Fri., by appointment Sat.-Sun. Memorial Day-Labor Day, $2 adults, $1 children) serves as a repository for Murphy's personal memorabilia. While the contents prove interesting, the house itself is plain in comparison with the Hubbards' mansion in Huron City.

PORT SANILAC

Until the mid-1850s, the Port Sanilac area was known as Bark Shanty Point, a name that was heatedly defended in an issue of the village's alternative newspaper, the *Bark Shanty Times*. The *Times* was produced by placing a sheet of newsprint on the counter of the town's general store; townsfolk simply wrote news or commentary on the sheet of paper until it was filled up.

Port Sanilac's past is preserved at the **Sanilac County Historical Museum** (228 S. Ridge St., 810/622-9946, www.sanilaccountymuseum. org, 11am-4pm Wed.-Fri., noon-4pm Sat.-Sun. May-Dec., $6 adults, $5 children 5-12). Housed in a nicely restored Victorian mansion,

the 1872 Loop-Harrison House, the museum contains most of its original furnishings, as well as old-fashioned medical instruments, antique glassware, military and American Indian artifacts, and an original Bark Shanty post office stamp. The grounds also include a dairy museum, a restored late 19th-century cabin, a general store, and a barn with exhibits relating to the fishing, logging, and blacksmithing trades.

LAKEPORT STATE PARK

About 20 miles south of Port Sanilac on M-25, **Lakeport State Park** (7605 Lakeshore Rd., 810/327-6224, 8am-10pm daily, annual $11 Recreation Passport for Michigan residents or $8.40 day-use fee/$30.50 yearly Recreation Passport for nonresidents required) preserves more than a mile of fine sand beach on southern Lake Huron. The 556-acre park was established in 1936, making it one of Michigan's oldest state parks. A couple of miles to the north, in a separate unit of the park, a popular campground offers 315 modern sites that are just a short walk from another beach and some lakeside bluffs. From the park's low bluffs, you can see distant views of freighter traffic heading in and out of the gateway to the upper Great Lakes. Other park amenities include a picnic shelter, beach house, and playground. For campground reservations, contact the **Michigan Department of Natural Resources** (800/447-2757, www.michigan.gov/dnr).

FESTIVALS

The towns alongside Lake Huron celebrate with a variety of annual events. In mid-July, the **Maritime Festival** (www.harborbeach-chamber.com) presents activities throughout Harbor Beach, including historical tours and fireworks displays. Also in July, the **Bark Shanty Days Festival** (www.portsanilac. net) lights up Port Sanilac with an array of competitions, from horseshoe tournaments to sandcastle contests. In mid-September, Lexington offers its own dose of culture with the **Bach and Friends Festival** (www.lexarts. com, ticket prices vary), a four-day musical extravaganza.

SHOPPING

While the Lake Huron shore isn't a hotbed of shopping potential, there's at least one noteworthy stop. **Angel's Garden** (7260 Huron Ave., Lexington, 810/359-2496, www.angelsgardengifts.com, daily Apr.-Dec.), a former harness shop built in the 1840s, now houses a massive collection of angel sculptures, garden accessories, and other unique gifts.

RECREATION
Boating and Fishing

Lake Huron is a wonderful place to explore via boat, whether you're a pleasure cruiser or a die-hard angler. Grindstone City has an artificially constructed harbor and a state-owned boat launch, ideal for private boaters and anglers who want to experience this quiet coast on their own.

If you don't have a boat, however, never fear. Charter boats operate out of many Thumb communities; just contact the **Thumb Area Charter Boat Association** (www.thumbareacharterboats.com) for a list of accredited boat captains and fishing guides. Before heading out, remember to purchase a valid state fishing license for anyone over 17; visit www.mdnr-elicense.com for more information.

C Diving

Two of Michigan's excellent underwater preserves lie off this stretch of Lake Huron shoreline. Situated between Port Austin and Harbor Beach, 19 major shipwrecks lie within the 276-square-mile **Thumb Area Bottomland Preserve.** Most sites are 100 feet deep or more, accessible only to advanced divers. An exception is the popular *Chickamauga,* a 322-foot turn-of-the-20th-century schooner—it was built in the late 1890s, only to founder in 1919. Resting in just 35 feet of water, it's in a relatively protected area about a half mile east of Harbor Beach.

Farther south, the **Sanilac Shores Underwater Preserve** between Port Sanilac and Lexington contains some recent shipwreck finds, including the 250-foot *Regina,* a freighter that sank in 1913 but wasn't discovered until 1986. Sanilac Shores shipwrecks tend to be in a little shallower water, and many are in excellent condition. For information on both preserves and a listing of dive shops and charters, contact the **Huron County Economic Development Corporation** (989/269-6431, www.huron-county.com) or the **Michigan Underwater Preserve Council** (MUPC, 800/970-8717, www.michiganpreserves.org).

ACCOMMODATIONS

Perched just 500 feet from Lake Huron in Port Sanilac, the **Raymond House Inn** (111 S. Ridge St., 810/622-8800, www.theraymondhouseinn.com, $75-110 d) is an impressive 1871 home that's been converted to an inn. The inn has seven bedrooms on the 2nd floor, an on-site art gallery and gift shop, and free wireless Internet access.

INFORMATION AND SERVICES

For more information about Grindstone City and Huron City, contact the **Greater Port Austin Area Chamber of Commerce** (2 W. Spring St., 989/738-7600, www.portaustin-area.com, 9am-1pm Mon., Wed., Fri., and Sat.). For more information about the Lake Huron shore, contact the **Harbor Beach Chamber of Commerce** (www.harborbeachchamber.com), the **Village of Port Sanilac** (56 N. Ridge St., 810/622-9963, www.portsanilac.net), and the **Lexington Business Association** (810/359-7774, www.lexingtonmichigan.org).

For local and regional news, consult the *Huron Daily Tribune* (www.michigansthumb.com), the *Lakeshore Guardian* (www.lakeshoreguardian.com), or the *Sanilac County News* (www.sanilaccountynews.com).

Despite the small size of these coastal towns, travelers will find many of the services they require. For mailing needs, there are at least three nearby **post offices** (110 School St., Harbor Beach, 989/479-3429; 34 N. Ridge St., Port Sanilac, 810/622-8295; and 5204 Main St., Lexington, 810/359-8591). If you run into any trouble along the coast, dial **911** or contact the **police** in Port Sanilac (810/622-9131).

GETTING THERE AND AROUND

As with all of the Thumb's coastal towns, Grindstone City, Huron City, Harbor Beach, Port Sanilac, and Lakeport are easy to reach via car. Whether you're coming from Bay City or Port Huron, you can simply follow M-25 along the shore to each of these destinations; the route from Grindstone City to Lakeport is roughly 73 miles in length and will take at least 90 minutes to traverse. Given the relatively small size of these coastal towns, you can drive or walk within each locale. For bus route information, contact the **Thumb Area Transit** (TAT, 1513 Bad Axe Rd., Bad Axe, 989/269-2121 or 800/322-1125, www.tatbus.com).

Port Huron

At the southern end of M-25, Port Huron sits at the juncture of Lake Huron and the St. Clair River, which is part of a vital shipping route that links Lake Huron and Lake Erie. Port Huron stretches some eight miles along the lake and this international river boundary, opposite Sarnia, Ontario.

On any given day, visitors can watch as a steady procession of pleasure craft, oil tankers, and bulk freighters file past the city. The most dramatic vantage point is from the crest of the **Blue Water Bridge,** which rises 152 feet over the water and looks down to where Lake Huron meets the St. Clair River. Walk across for the best views.

Due to its strategic geographical position, Port Huron is one of the oldest settlements in Michigan and, in fact, one of the earliest outposts in the American interior. The French built Fort St. Joseph here in 1686, mainly to seal off the entranceway to the upper Great Lakes from the rival English. The first permanent settlement was established in 1790. In 1814, the Americans built Fort Gratiot on the Fort Joseph site, also an attempt to repel the British. The fort was occupied off and on after the Civil War, when it served as a recruiting station.

In the late 1800s, four local villages—Peru, Desmond, Huron, and Gratiot—united to form Port Huron and helped develop the area into a lumber center. When the big trees ran out, Port Huron weathered the industry's demise better than most Michigan cities, since it had already diversified into shipbuilding, railroading, and oil and natural gas distribution. Despite these early industries, the city rejected the bids of chemical companies to build plants here, fearing environmental and safety problems. The plants instead found a home on the Sarnia side of the river, and today make up the 20-mile-long "chemical valley"—Canada's greatest concentration of chemical companies and the creator of most of the pollution in the lower St. Clair River.

SIGHTS
〔 Port Huron Museum

You can experience a slew of nautical history at the **Port Huron Museum** (1115 6th St., 810/982-0891, www.porthuronmuseum.org, 11am-5pm daily, all four sites $15 pp, children under 5 free). Housed in a former library that dates to 1904, the two-story museum includes a restored freighter pilothouse (you can even work the wheel, signal the alarm horn, and ring the engine bell), marine-related items, and objects recovered from Lake Huron shipwrecks. The museum has something for everyone, from Indian artifacts to contemporary paintings by local artists. One of the most interesting exhibits displays objects recovered from digs on the site of Edison's boyhood home, which include evidence of an early laboratory. Currently, the museum oversees three other sites as well: the Thomas Edison Depot Museum, the Fort Gratiot Lighthouse, and the *Huron* Lightship. Until recently, the museum also operated the U.S. Coast Guard Cutter *Bramble,* a World War II

the *Huron* Lightship, docked on the St. Clair River

vessel formerly used as an icebreaker until it was decommissioned in 2003; today, it's privately owned.

THOMAS EDISON DEPOT MUSEUM

Port Huron's most famous resident was no doubt native son Thomas Alva Edison (1847-1931), who was born here and stayed until adulthood. He is honored at **Thomas Edison Park,** located under the enormous Blue Water Bridge. In the bridge's shadow is the restored **1858 Grand Trunk Depot,** where Edison boarded the Detroit-bound train daily to sell fruits, nuts, magazines, and newspapers. He used much of his earnings to buy chemicals for the small laboratory he had set up in the train's baggage car. The depot now houses a museum dedicated to Edison; it contains historical photos and displays, including artifacts excavated from the site of Edison's boyhood home. For more information, contact the **Port Huron Museum** (810/982-0891, www.phmuseum.org, included w/museum admission), which oversees the Thomas Edison Depot Museum.

LIGHTHOUSES

Just north of the Blue Water Bridge, Michigan's oldest lighthouse, the **Fort Gratiot Lighthouse** (800/852-4242, 11am-5pm Fri.-Mon. May-Oct.), stands 86 feet tall over **Lighthouse Park.** The original tower was poorly constructed in 1825 and crumbled just four years later. It was replaced in 1829 by the much sturdier brick structure that stands today. That still makes it the state's oldest light and older than even Michigan itself, which wasn't admitted to the Union until 1837. The lighthouse was automated in 1933, and it continues to flash a warning to mariners coming south from Lake Huron. Call for tour information.

At nearby Pine Grove Park, you can take a self-guided tour of the 1921 *Huron* **Lightship** (810/982-0891, www.phmuseum.org, daily June-Aug., Thurs.-Mon. Sept.-Dec and Apr.-May, included w/museum admission), operated by the Port Huron Museum. This 97-foot vessel served as a floating lighthouse visible from 14 miles away. Retired in 1970, the *Huron* Lightship was the last to operate on the Great

EDISON'S EARLY YEARS

Port Huron's Edison statue, near the Blue Water Bridge

Although Thomas Alva Edison (1847-1931) was technically born in Milan, Ohio, it's no surprise that the town of Port Huron, Michigan, has long claimed him as a native son. After all, he spent much of his childhood in this bustling port city.

Born on February 11, 1847, Edison was the last of the seven children of Samuel and Nancy Edison – an exiled Canadian activist and an accomplished schoolteacher, respectively. In 1854, the Edison family moved to Port Huron, where young Edison attended public school for less than three months. A hyperactive child, who had suffered partial hearing loss from an early bout with scarlet fever, he was deemed "difficult" by his teacher. Consequently, his mother pulled him from the school and began to teach him at home.

By the age of 11, Edison had demonstrated an insatiable appetite for knowledge, reading books on an assortment of topics and developing a process for self-education that would influence the rest of his life. At the age of 12,

he persuaded his parents to let him sell newspapers to passengers along the Grand Trunk Railroad line. Utilizing his access to the news bulletins teletyped to the station office, he decided to publish his own small newspaper, the *Grand Trunk Herald,* which became an immediate success and served as the first in a long line of Edison's entrepreneurial ventures.

Meanwhile, he exploited his railroad access to conduct chemical experiments in a small laboratory that he'd established in a train baggage car, but an unfortunate chemical fire resulted in his expulsion from the train, after which he was forced to sell his newspapers at various stations along the route. Another accident, however, would favorably alter the course of Edison's life and career. While working for the railroad, he saved a child from being killed by an errant train, and as a reward, the child's grateful father instructed him on how to operate a telegraph.

By the age of 15, Edison had learned enough to be employed as a telegraph operator, and for the next few years, he traversed the Midwest as an itinerant telegrapher, while finding to time to read, study electrical science, and experiment with telegraph technology. Around the age of 19, he decided to make a permanent move from his family's home in Port Huron, and over the next few years, he worked as a telegraph operator for the *Associated Press* in Louisville, Kentucky, and the Western Union Company in Boston, before moving to New York City and developing his first invention: the Universal Stock Printer, which synchronized several stock tickers' transactions and was sold to the Gold and Stock Telegraph Company for $40,000.

At the age of 22, this now-successful inventor quit his work as a telegrapher to devote himself full-time to inventing. In 1870, he set up his first laboratory and manufacturing facility in Newark, New Jersey, where he employed several machinists. After several more inventions and much financial success, Edison relocated his expanding operations to Menlo Park, New Jersey – a place that has become synonymous with some of Edison's greatest inventions, from the phonograph to the incandescent electric lightbulb.

THE THUMB

© 123RF.COM

Fort Gratiot Lighthouse at Lighthouse Park in Port Huron

Lakes. The park also offers a view of the bridge and passing boat traffic on the St. Clair River, and is an interesting place to watch anglers scoop up walleye and steelhead.

Tours

For a closer look at the St. Clair River, sign on for a two-hour trip on the *Huron Lady II* (810/984-1500, www.huronlady.com, $20 adults, $10 children 5-12), a 65-foot excursion boat that cruises under the Blue Water Bridge and heads out onto Lake Huron, where it treats passengers to views of giant freighters as they load and unload their cargo. Call for reservations.

EVENTS

Port Huron and its surrounding communities hold a variety of events throughout the year, from fishing tournaments to arts and crafts shows. One intriguing option is the **St. Clair Flats Historical Encampment** (Algonac State Park, Algonac, 810/765-5605) in mid-September. During the two-day event,

historical interpreters demonstrate the crafts, skills, and games of the different peoples, both Europeans and Native Americans, that inhabited the Great Lakes region during the mid-1700s.

Of course, the Blue Water Area hosts its biggest annual event in mid-July, the **Port Huron to Mackinac Race.** The race attracts some 300 sailboats for the trip up the Huron shore to Mackinac Island; in preceding days, sailors and spectators pack the area's restaurants and hotels. Don't plan to show up without reservations. Contact the **Bayview Yacht Club** (www.byc.com) for more information.

SHOPPING

For crafters, a visit to **Mary Maxim** (2001 Holland Ave., 810/987-2000, www.marymaxim. com, 10am-6pm Mon.-Sat., 11am-5pm Sun.), an enormous emporium of needlework and home decor, is a must. Others will relish Port Huron's downtown district, where you'll find jewelry boutiques, furniture stores, and more.

GOLF

The Port Huron area boasts a dozen golf courses, including the **Holly Meadows Golf Course** (4855 Capac Rd., Capac, 810/395-4653, www.hollymeadows.com, daily Mar.-Nov., $16-23 pp w/cart), **Rattle Run Golf Course** (7163 St. Clair Hwy., St. Clair, 810/329-2070, www.rattlerun.com, daily Mar.-Nov., $25-49 pp w/cart), and **Black River Country Club** (3300 Country Club Dr., Port Huron, 810/982-9595, www.blackriver-golfclub.com, daily Apr.-Oct., $25-48 pp), an 18-hole championship course founded in 1926 that offers stunning views of the Black River.

ACCOMMODATIONS AND FOOD

Located just south of the Grand Trunk Depot and near the former Fort Gratiot site, the ◖ **DoubleTree by Hilton Hotel Port Huron** (500 Thomas Edison Pkwy., 810/984-8000, www.doubletree.hilton.com, $90-125 d, $165-395 suites) is the city's nicest and largest hotel. It has some wonderful bridge and water views, which anyone can enjoy from the hotel's elegant dining room.

A more laid-back dining option along the waterfront is the **Quay Street Brewing Company** (330 Quay St., 810/982-4100, www.quaybrewing.com, 11:30am-9pm Mon.-Thurs., 11:30am-10pm Fri.-Sat., noon-8pm Sun., $7-17), a spacious, multilevel restaurant, bar, and brewery that serves up salads, sandwiches, steak, seafood, and handcrafted beers in a family-friendly atmosphere.

INFORMATION AND SERVICES

For more information about the Port Huron area, contact the **Blue Water Area Convention & Visitors Bureau** (520 Thomas Edison Pkwy., 800/852-4242, www.bluewater.org, 8am-5pm Mon.-Fri., 10am-3pm Sat.) and the **Blue Water Area Chamber of Commerce** (920 Pine Grove Ave., 810/985-7101, www.bluewaterchamber.com, 8:30am-4:30pm Mon.-Fri.). If you're interested in Port Huron's maritime heritage, visit www.maritimecapitalgl.com.

For city-related issues, contact the **Municipal Office Center** (100 McMorran Blvd., www.porthuron.org). For county-related issues, visit the official St. Clair County website: www.st-claircounty.org. For local news, pick up a daily copy of the *Times Herald* (www.thetimesherald.com).

As one of the largest cities in the Thumb, Port Huron provides travelers with everything they might need during their trip. For mailing issues, visit the **post office** (1300 Military St., 810/989-7900, www.usps.com). In case of a medical emergency, you can contact the **Port Huron Hospital** (1221 Pine Grove Ave., 810/987-5000, www.porthuronhospital.org). A 24-hour pharmacy is available for all your prescription needs: **Rite Aid** (2910 Pine Grove Ave., 810/987-3663, www.riteaid.com). For all other emergencies, dial **911** at any time. In a non-emergency situation, you can also contact the **Port Huron Police Department** (810/984-8415).

GETTING THERE AND AROUND

Although the closest airport is in the Detroit area, a few hours southwest of town, travelers can easily reach Port Huron via train. **Amtrak** (800/872-7245, www.amtrak.com) offers a route from Chicago, with stops across Michigan, including East Lansing and Flint. For schedule information, visit the Port Huron station at 2223 16th Street.

Still, the most likely access is via car; there are three major routes to and from Port Huron. From Detroit, you can take I-94 East and the I-69 Business Loop to Port Huron, a 64-mile route that usually takes about an hour. From Flint, follow I-69 East to the I-69 Business Loop, a 67-mile trip that requires a little over an hour. If you have ample time, you can instead opt for the 154-mile scenic route along the Thumb's coastline; this drive, via M-25, will take you from Bay City to Port Austin to Port Huron in about 3.25 hours. Of course, the town can also be reached from Ontario, Canada, across the **Blue Water Bridge** (www.michigan.gov/mdot, $3 passenger vehicles,

© EHRLIF/123RF.COM

The Blue Water Bridge connects Port Huron, Michigan, and Sarnia, Ontario.

$3.25 per truck/bus axle); just remember that motorists often experience a delay when traversing the international border crossing. Also keep in mind that U.S. citizens must confirm both proof of identity and proof of citizenship (by using, for instance, a driver's license and a birth certificate) in order to enter Canada. Unfortunately, returning to the United States will require a valid U.S. passport.

ANN ARBOR AND THE HEARTLAND

From any point in the Great Lakes State, at least one of the five Great Lakes (all but Lake Ontario) is never more than 90 miles away. That's auspicious news for Michigan's Heartland—also known as Central Michigan—the only region that doesn't sit astride the coast. Stretching from the southern state line to the middle of the Lower Peninsula, this wide swath of rolling prairies, scenic lakes, weathered barns, and abundant farmland contains some of the state's finest educational institutions and largest cities, including Grand Rapids, Kalamazoo, Midland, and Lansing, the state capital since 1847.

As with the Thumb, travelers often overlook Michigan's Heartland. Early settlers of the 19th century, however, recognized the appeal of this centralized region. A surge of eager, frontier-bound settlers resulted in the creation of some of Michigan's most picturesque towns, including Marshall, which has been designated a National Historic Landmark District for its varied 19th-century architecture. Migrating Easterners were also responsible for the establishment of many of the Heartland's private colleges, in towns such as Hillsdale, Albion, Alma, and Olivet. A hotbed of academia, the Heartland also has its share of major universities—most notably, the University of Michigan in Ann Arbor, with other standouts nearby, including Western Michigan University in Kalamazoo, Michigan State University in East Lansing, and Central Michigan University in Mount Pleasant.

Besides strolling through the well-groomed campuses and well-preserved villages that

HIGHLIGHTS

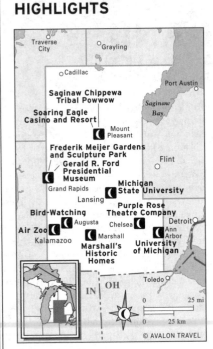

◖ Bird-Watching Near Augusta: The W. K. Kellogg Bird Sanctuary is one of America's pioneer wildlife conservation centers. Hike amid 180 acres of diverse habitats, which nurture hundreds of bird species (page 140).

◖ Air Zoo: Devoted to aviation and space exploration, this enormous complex invites visitors to explore an incredible assortment of interactive exhibits and historic displays, including flight simulators, World War II-era bombers, astronaut artifacts, and a pseudo-paratrooper jump (page 146).

◖ Gerald R. Ford Presidential Museum: In addition to celebrating the lives of President Ford and his wife, the museum offers temporary exhibits from the Smithsonian Institution and the National Archives (page 149).

◖ Frederik Meijer Gardens and Sculpture Park: This impressive collection of gardens also boasts a tropical conservatory as well as sculptures by Auguste Rodin, Claes Oldenburg, and Henry Moore (page 151).

◖ Michigan State University: Stroll through several lovely gardens, attend Big 10 football games, view an assortment of art and science exhibits, and catch a wide array of live performances at the Wharton Center (page 155).

◖ Soaring Eagle Casino and Resort: One of the Midwest's largest casinos offers thousands of slot machines and table games, several restaurants, over 500 luxurious rooms, a soothing spa, and live entertainment (page 162).

◖ Saginaw Chippewa Tribal Powwow: In early August, the Saginaw Chippewa Indian Tribe hosts a gathering of the clans that showcases traditional dancing, drumming, chanting, and cuisine (page 162).

◖ University of Michigan: Even if you're not a U of M student, you can still appreciate the school's wide array of diversions, including museums, art galleries, gardens, live theaters, and, of course, football (page 122).

◖ Purple Rose Theatre Company: Founded by award-winning actor Jeff Daniels, this Chelsea-based playhouse was named in honor of the Woody Allen film *The Purple Rose of Cairo* (1985). Audiences travel far and wide to catch the latest play at this renowned theater (page 130).

◖ Marshall's Historic Homes: Picturesque Marshall contains over 850 19th-century homes and businesses, in a variety of architectural styles. In 1991, the town was designated a National Historic Landmark District (page 136).

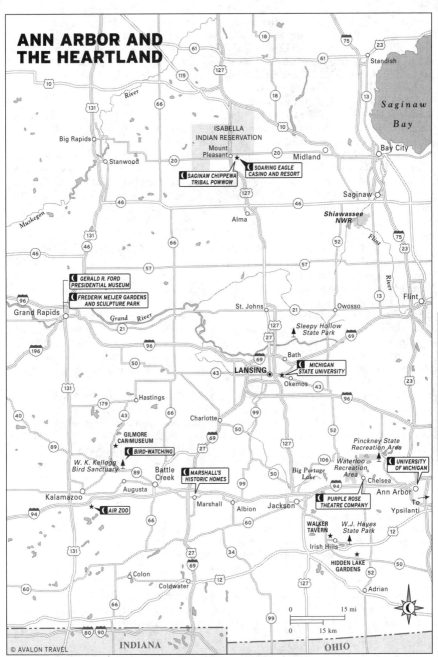

© AVALON TRAVEL

comprise Michigan's Heartland, travelers will find a myriad of other outdoor and cultural pursuits here as well. Whether exploring the Gerald R. Ford Presidential Museum, marveling at Kalamazoo's Air Zoo, hiking through the W. K. Kellogg Bird Sanctuary, or watching a show at the Purple Rose Theatre Company (established by Chelsea native and Hollywood actor Jeff Daniels), coast-conscious visitors will be grateful for the inland detour.

PLANNING YOUR TIME

Michigan's Heartland is an enormous place, extending from the Indiana border to M-20, near the center of the Lower Peninsula; it's bordered on the eastern side by Ann Arbor and Midland, and on the western side by Kalamazoo and Grand Rapids. Given its size, what you're able to see depends on your schedule; likewise, your interests will determine how long you plan to linger in the Heartland. If you only intend to visit the area's major cities, like Lansing and Battle Creek, you should put aside about 5 days. You'll need at least 10 days, however, if you also want to explore the region's outdoor attractions and smaller towns like Chelsea, Marshall, and Mount Pleasant.

Reaching the Heartland is easy. Given the presence of several major towns and cities, it's possible to get here by plane, train, or bus. The region has several commercial airports, in or near places like Kalamazoo, Grand Rapids, Lansing, Midland, and nearby Flint and Detroit. Amtrak and Greyhound both offer routes to Kalamazoo, Battle Creek, East Lansing, Jackson, Ann Arbor, and Grand Rapids. Needless to say, though, the Heartland is not a compact region, so, despite the presence of several public transit systems, having a car is a must—whether you bring your own or rent one in an airport. Major highways and interstates—such as US-23, US-127, US-131, I-69, I-75, I-94, and I-96—make it a snap to get from one end of the Heartland to the other— if you have the time.

The good news is that, save for the

Heartland's major museums, annual festivals, and college football games, this centralized region isn't as much of a draw for tourists as coastal locales like Saugatuck, Holland, and Traverse City. So, crowds are often less of a problem here—unless, of course, you simply hate big cities in general.

For more information about Michigan's Heartland, consult **Travel Michigan** (Michigan Economic Development Corporation, 300 N. Washington Sq., Lansing, 888/784-7328, www.michigan.org) or the **West Michigan Tourist Association** (WMTA, 741 Kenmoor Ave., Ste. E, Grand Rapids, 616/245-2217, www.wmta.org).

HISTORY

By the 1830s, Michigan fever had become an epidemic. Pioneer families from all over the East Coast headed west via the newly completed Erie Canal, passed through Detroit, and continued along the new Detroit-Chicago Road, which cut across the southern half of the state's Lower Peninsula. Their final destination: Michigan's rolling prairies, with rich soil and fertile land that the federal government was selling for the bargain-basement price of $1.25 an acre.

Many of the early settlers were Easterners, leaving already-overwhelming cities to seek better opportunities for themselves and their families. The onrush between 1825 and 1855 spurred the settlement of some of Michigan's largest towns, including Battle Creek and Jackson. That early growth was soon augmented by the railroad; by 1849, Michigan Central began making regular state crossings, disgorging thousands of optimistic settlers along the way.

In the region known as Michigan's Heartland, the most visible evidence of these early settlers can be found in the Greek Revival homes and clean-lined architecture of the cities and villages they built. They also founded a number of Eastern-style private colleges, a concentration unmatched elsewhere in the state.

Ann Arbor and Vicinity

Few would dispute the claim that Ann Arbor, with its population of roughly 116,100, is one of the most interesting cities in the state—if not the country. Home to the well-reputed University of Michigan, part of the Big Ten Conference, it transcends the typical college-town atmosphere with its unique blend of large-city verve and small-town friendliness. Located about 40 miles west of Detroit, Ann Arbor is now a regional research center as well as the suburb of choice for Detroit intelligentsia. Popular with all demographic groups, the city has been awarded the title "Quintessentially Cool College Town" by *Seventeen,* rated the second most "Woman Friendly City in America" by *Ladies Home Journal,* and ranked #46 on *Money* magazine's 2010 list of the "Best Places to Live" in America.

The media continues to heap accolades on the city, in part because of its appealing blend

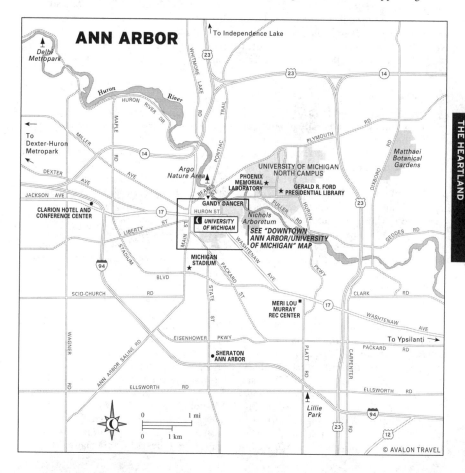

© AVALON TRAVEL

of big-city vitality and small-town Midwestern friendliness. This is Michigan, after all. While there's plenty of typical college-town angst, folks are genuinely helpful when you ask for directions and are always ready to recommend a favorite restaurant.

The city is dominated by the well-known university, which occupies most of the area just east of downtown. Historic U of M, founded in 1817, is one of the nation's great public institutions, with a long reputation for excellence in academics and athletics. The university is proud of its statistics, including having the largest pre-law and pre-med programs in the country; graduates that include eight NASA astronauts, one president, numerous actors and filmmakers, and several Pulitzer Prize and Nobel Prize winners; and a diverse student body that represents all 50 states and more than 100 foreign countries.

SIGHTS
◖ University of Michigan

A campus tour of the **University of Michigan** (www.umich.edu) reveals the expected and the less expected—both backpacked and Birkenstocked students and a quirky collection of 2,500 rare musical instruments. The heart of it all is the **"Diag,"** the diagonal walkway crossing the original 40-acre campus between State Street, North University, and South University. Many of the buildings house classrooms, and on many days this is the site of student protest demonstrations and outdoor concerts. Ann Arbor, while still politically aware these days, is not the hotbed of activism it was in the 1960s, when an ongoing campaign began here to legalize marijuana.

For a terrific view, climb the eight floors to the map room in the **Harlan Hatcher Graduate Library.** Afterward, cross State Street, where you'll find the venerable **Michigan Union** (530 S. State St., 734/763-5750, 7am-2am Mon.-Sat., 9am-2am Sun. fall/winter, 7am-midnight Mon.-Thurs., 7am-2am Fri.-Sat., 9am-midnight Sun. spring/summer), built in the 1920s and site of President Kennedy's announcement to form the Peace Corps. Just

north of the Diag, you'll find another historic student union, the **Michigan League** (911 N. University Ave., 734/764-0446, 7am-11pm daily), opened in 1929 as a center for women's social and cultural activities on campus; today, it houses a gift shop, an information center, a 640-seat theater, and a small inn for visitors.

Across from the League is the **Burton Memorial Tower,** a campus landmark that's capped by one of the world's heaviest carillons, containing 43 tons of bells. Another campus favorite is the **Law Quadrangle,** home of U of M's respected law school. Built 1923-1933, the picturesque quad was modeled after Britain's Cambridge University. The level of workmanship in the Gothic building was rare even in the arts-and-crafts inspired 1920s. Rest your feet in the library's hushed reading room, where maize and blue plaster medallions decorate the ceiling.

No visit to Wolverine territory would be complete without a stop at **Michigan Stadium** on Stadium Street and Main. The largest collegiate stadium in the United States, it draws more than 105,000 screaming fans for home games and post-game tailgating marathons. Constructed in 1927, this historic stadium has remained open and active ever since, even through a massive, much-needed renovation that was completed in 2010.

Campus Museums

Established in 1817, U of M has long been a leading research institution; over the years, it's developed extensive collections. Most are housed in the university's exceptional museums. The **University of Michigan Museum of Natural History** (1109 Geddes Ave., 734/764-0480, www.lsa.umich.edu/ummnh, 9am-5pm Mon.-Sat., noon-5pm Sun., donation suggested) is one of the best natural science museums in the country, with displays on prehistoric life, dinosaurs, anthropology, Native Americans, Michigan wildlife, and geology. Most of the highlights—especially the dinosaur dioramas—are on the 2nd floor.

Among the top 10 U.S. university art museums, the **University of Michigan Museum**

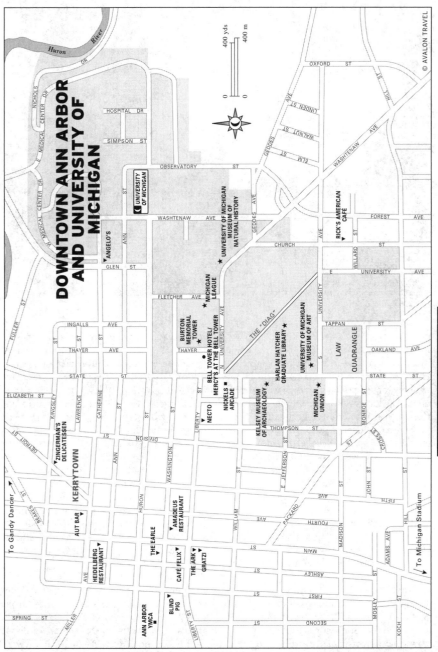

THE HEARTLAND

© AVALON TRAVEL

DOWNTOWN ANN ARBOR AND UNIVERSITY OF MICHIGAN

0   400 yds
0   400 m

UNIVERSITY OF MICHIGAN

Huron River

NICHOLS DR

E MEDICAL CENTER DR

N MEDICAL CENTER DR

FULLER ST

HOSPITAL DR

SIMPSON ST

OBSERVATORY ST

WASHTENAW AVE

ANGELO'S

ANN ST

GLEN ST

FLETCHER AVE

INGALLS ST

THAYER ST

STATE ST

MICHIGAN LEAGUE ★

BURTON MEMORIAL TOWER

UNIVERSITY OF MICHIGAN MUSEUM OF NATURAL HISTORY ★

GEDDES AVE

N UNIVERSITY AVE

THE "DIAG"

HARLAN HATCHER GRADUATE LIBRARY ★

UNIVERSITY OF MICHIGAN MUSEUM OF ART ★

OXFORD ST

HILL ST

LINDEN ST

WALNUT ST

ELM ST

GEDDES

WASHTENAW AVE

RICK'S AMERICAN CAFÉ ▼

FOREST AVE

CHURCH ST

WILLARD ST

E UNIVERSITY AVE

TAPPAN ST

OAKLAND AVE

LAW QUADRANGLE

STATE ST

MONROE ST

CROSS ST

JOHN ST

FIFTH

ELIZABETH ST

KINGSLEY

LAWRENCE

CATHERINE ST

ANN ST

DIVISION ST

WASHINGTON

ZINGERMAN'S DELICATESSEN ▼

KERRYTOWN

AUT BAR ▼

BELL TOWER HOTEL/ MERCY'S AT THE BELL TOWER ●

NECTO ■

NICKELS ARCADE ■

LIBERTY ST

KELSEY MUSEUM OF ARCHAEOLOGY ★

THOMPSON ST

E JEFFERSON AVE

MICHIGAN UNION ★

WILLIAM ST

PACKARD

FOURTH AVE

MADISON ST

ADAMS AVE

To Michigan Stadium →

To Gandy Dancer ↖

DETROIT ST

BEAKES ST

SPRING ST

MILLER AVE

HEIDELBERG RESTAURANT ▼

THE EARLE ▼

CAFÉ FELIX ▼

THE ARK ▼

GRATZI ▼

AMADEUS RESTAURANT ▼

HURON ST

ANN ARBOR YMCA ■

BLIND PIG ▼

FIRST ST

SECOND ST

MAIN ST

ASHLEY ST

MOSLEY ST

KOCH

© 123RF.COM

University of Michigan

of Art (525 S. State St., 734/764-0395, www. umma.umich.edu, 10am-5pm Tues.-Sat., noon-5pm Sun., free though $5 donation suggested) has a permanent collection of more than 15,000 regularly rotated pieces, including works by big names like Picasso, Miró, Cézanne, and more. Masterpieces include Max Beckmann's *Begin the Beguine,* Monet's *The Break-up of the Ice,* and the especially strong collection of Whistler prints. The knowledgeable staff works hard to make art more accessible and relevant to the general public, with a high-caliber museum shop, enthusiastic docents, and a weekly series of gallery talks, art videos, and slide lectures. In March 2009, the museum completed a massive renovation of its historic home, Alumni Memorial Hall, and unveiled a 53,000-square-foot expansion dedicated to its lead benefactors, Maxine and Stuart Frankel.

Other intriguing museums include the **Gerald R. Ford Presidential Library** (1000 Beal Ave., 734/205-0555, www.ford.utexas. edu, 8:45am-4:45pm Mon.-Fri., free), an enormous collection of letters, reports, photographs, televised campaign commercials, audiotapes of speeches, and other archival materials, and the **Sindecuse Museum of Dentistry** (Kellogg Building, 1011 N. University Ave., www.dent. umich.edu, 8am-6pm Mon.-Fri., free), a rare collection of over 10,000 objects focused on the history of dentistry from the 18th century to the present. In addition, the **Stearns Collection of Musical Instruments** (1100 Baits Dr., 734/764-0583, www.music.umich. edu, 10am-5pm Mon.-Fri., free) is a fascinatingly quirky repository of over 2,500 musical instruments collected by drug manufacturer Fred Stearns. The collection features permanent and occasional displays throughout the Earl V. Moore Building of the School of Music, Theatre & Dance in the North Campus area.

University Gardens

If you enjoy perusing collections of a more natural kind, then take some time to stroll through the University of Michigan's lovely gardens. The **Matthaei Botanical Gardens** (1800 N. Dixboro Rd., 734/647-7600, www.

lsa.umich.edu/mbg, grounds 8am-sunset daily, conservatory 10am-4:30pm Tues. and Thurs.-Sun., 10am-8pm Wed., $5 adults, $2 students, grounds free) is an ideal place for a nature walk. In addition to an expansive conservatory of tropical, warm-temperate, and desert plants, you'll find picturesque gardens, several nature trails, and a re-created prairie.

The **Nichols Arboretum** (1610 Washington Heights Rd., 734/647-7600, www.lsa.umich.edu/mbg, 8am-sunset daily, free) offers some of the area's best hiking trails and a natural area that serves as an education and research facility for the university. It's located next to the central campus and offers more than 400 identified tree species, a variety of plant collections, as well as a lush peony garden, which blooms in early summer.

ENTERTAINMENT AND EVENTS
Nightlife

Like many college towns, Ann Arbor offers up some eclectic nightlife. The **Blind Pig** (208 S. 1st St., 734/996-8555, www.blindpigmusic.com, Wed.-Mon., show times and ticket prices vary) was one of the first clubs outside of Seattle to give Nirvana a boost; besides rock 'n' roll, the hip space features reggae and blues artists. The city's gay community convenes Friday night at the New York-style **Necto** (516 E. Liberty, 734/994-5436, www.necto.com, 9pm-2am Mon. and Thurs.-Sat., cover charges vary), a dance club that features a different theme each night, including industrial, top 40, and gay.

One of the best known of Ann Arbor's clubs is **The Ark** (316 S. Main St., 734/761-1451, www.a2ark.org, show times and ticket prices vary), a 400-seat venue that has been hosting local, national, and international acoustic performers since 1965. The club moved to larger digs on South Main in the former Kline's Department Store several years ago, but the philosophy is the same: Book the best of folk and roots musicians. Period.

The Arts

The University of Michigan is a hotbed of live music and other performing arts. If you're interested in such cultural pursuits, contact the **University Musical Society** (UMS, 734/764-2538, www.ums.org, show times and ticket prices vary), which oversees a wide assortment of choral and chamber concerts, dance and theatrical performances, jazz and piano series, even family-friendly shows. Performance venues are situated throughout the campus, including the **Lydia Mendelssohn Theatre** (911 N. University Ave.), the **Hill Auditorium** (825 N. University Ave.), and the **Power Center for the Performing Arts** (121 Fletcher St.), among others.

Ann Arbor Summer Festival

For three weeks each summer (usually mid-June-early July), the **Ann Arbor Summer Festival** (734/994-5999, www.annarborsummerfestival.com) presents a dizzying array of concerts, dance performances, films, exhibitions, parties, and other activities throughout Ann Arbor. The festival, a beloved community event for over 25 years, features an eclectic mix of performers, which, in recent years, has

Ann Arbor Street Art Fair

© DANIEL MARTONE

THE HEARTLAND

included Mandy Patinkin, Garrison Keillor, Willie Nelson, and the Funk Brothers.

Another beloved summertime event is the **Ann Arbor Street Art Fair** (734/994-5260, www.artfair.org), which usually takes place during a four-day weekend in mid-July. Founded in 1960, this is the oldest of the four art fairs that now take place in Ann Arbor. For many residents and out-of-towners, it's also the best, luring an impressive collective of painters, photographers, sculptors, woodworkers, jewelry makers, and other artists from around the world to the streets of downtown Ann Arbor.

SHOPPING

The area along State Street remains the main campus commercial strip, with a funky mix of coffeehouses, bookstores, and urbane boutiques. A standout is the historic 1915 **Nickels Arcade**, a small, European-style arcade filled with ever-changing boutiques and galleries between State and Maynard. One longtime favorite is **Bivouac** (336 S. State St., 734/761-6207, www.bivouacannarbor.com, hours vary), the resource for Ann Arbor-area campers, hikers, climbers, and skiers.

More shopping is concentrated on and around **Main Street** (www.mainstreetannarbor.org) in the city's vintage downtown. Once a mainstay of longtime German businesses, it has since become a stylish place for browsing, people-watching, and noshing. The **Selo/Shevel Gallery** (301 S. Main St., 734/761-4620, www.seloshevelgallery.com, 11am-7pm Mon.-Thurs. and Sat., 11am-10pm Fri., noon-6pm Sun.) has one of the state's best collections of handmade contemporary jewelry as well as a nice selection of art glass. Try **Falling Water Books & Collectables** (213 S. Main St., 734/747-9810, www.fallingwatermi.com, 10am-9pm Mon.-Thurs., 10am-10pm Fri.-Sat., 11am-7pm Sun.) for arty gifts, journals, jewelry, candles, and other New Age goodies.

Kerrytown District

Once forlorn and forgotten, this old commercial strip north of downtown is enjoying its second go-round as a retail district, boasting

the impressive **Peoples Food Co-op** (216 N. 4th Ave., 734/994-9174, www.peoplesfood.coop, 8am-10pm Mon.-Sat., 9am-10pm Sun.), Ann Arbor's only community-owned grocery store. Two other popular shopping options are the colorful (if pricey) open-air **Ann Arbor Farmers Market** (315 Detroit St., 734/994-3276, www.a2gov.org/market, 7am-3pm Wed. and Sat.), where early risers will find the finest flowers and produce, and the **Ann Arbor Artisan Market** (317 S. Division St., 734/913-9622, www.artisanmarket.org, 11am-4pm Sun.), a find for arts-and-crafts lovers.

Top restaurants and interesting indoor shops also lure visitors into the **Kerrytown Market & Shops** (415 N. 5th Ave., 734/662-5008, www.kerrytown.com, shop hours vary), where you can browse through boutiques such as **Mudpuddles**, a kids' store featuring puppets, wildlife mobiles, award-winning games, and other delights; the gourmet-inspired **Everyday Cook;** the 5,000-square-foot **Hollander's,** the premier place for decorative paper and bookbinding supplies; and **Mathilde's Imports,** offering a unique selection of women's apparel from Latin America, Europe, and Southeast Asia. For more information about this one-of-a-kind shopping district, contact the **Kerrytown District Association** (www.kerrytown.org).

COLLEGE SPORTS

If you're a sports fan visiting Ann Arbor during the fall football season, you might consider catching a U of M Wolverines game, which can be a rousing all-day affair. For information about tickets and schedules—or for details about any university sporting event, from baseball to ice hockey—contact the **University of Michigan Athletics Ticket Office** (1000 S. State St., 734/764-0247, www.mgoblue.com, 8:30am-5pm Mon.-Fri., ticket prices vary).

ACCOMMODATIONS
Under $150

Lodgings in Ann Arbor aren't as varied as the entertainment or dining options. Most are chain hotels that can't be missed on your way into town. The 223-room **Holiday Inn** (3600

Plymouth Rd., 734/769-9800, www.ichotels-group.com, $106-180 d), for instance, has an indoor pool, a fitness center, a beauty salon, laundry facilities, and high-speed Internet access, plus convenient in-room coffeemakers and irons. A more affordable option is the pet-friendly **Comfort Inn & Suites** (2376 Carpenter Rd., 734/477-9977, www.comfortinn.com, $80-157 d), which offers 50 comfortable rooms, an indoor pool and exercise room, free wireless Internet access, and other basic amenities.

On the eastern edge of town, the **Clarion Hotel and Conference Center** (2900 Jackson Rd., 734/665-4444, www.clarionhotel.com, $80-130 d), a full-service, pet-friendly hotel, provides an indoor/outdoor pool, a sauna, a fitness center, a restaurant and lounge, cable television, complimentary Internet access, and abundant free parking. To the south lies the elegant **(Sheraton Ann Arbor** (3200 Boardwalk, 734/996-0600, www.sheratonannarbor.com, $114-185 d), with its fitness center, sauna, heated pool, gift shop, excellent steakhouse, and 197 tasteful guest rooms.

Budget-conscious travelers will appreciate the **Lamp Post Inn** (2424 E. Stadium Blvd., 734/971-8000 or 877/971-8001, www.lamppostinn.com, $49-79 d), which offers a free continental breakfast, comfortable rooms with complimentary wireless Internet access, and convenient shopping at the adjacent Lamp Post Plaza. For history buffs, the restored **(Vitosha Guest Haus** (1917 Washtenaw Ave., 734/741-4969, $75-149 d) promises more than just 11 old-fashioned rooms, Internet access, a deluxe breakfast, afternoon tea, English-style gardens, and a pet-friendly policy; the stone chalet was built by Dr. Dean Meyer in 1917 and occupied by Unitarians before becoming a sophisticated cultural retreat, a favorite among artists and scholars.

$150-250

For a unique option, consider the intimate **(Bell Tower Hotel** (300 S. Thayer, 734/769-3010, www.belltowerhotel.com, $169-210 d), which offers 66 rooms and suites, right in the middle of campus. It's a surprisingly elegant place, with accommodations decorated in a crisp, traditional English style, as well as the on-site Mercy's at the Bell Tower, one of the city's finest French restaurants.

If you prefer the coziness of a bed-and-breakfast, the **Ann Arbor Bed & Breakfast** (921 E. Huron St., 734/994-9100, www.annarborbedandbreakfast.com, $159-229 d) might suit your needs. Just steps from some of the university's finest performance venues, the inn features hearty breakfasts, wireless Internet access, and free covered parking. Two of the guest studios even come with kitchenettes.

FOOD

Ann Arbor, along with surrounding Washtenaw County, is home to more than 275 restaurants, a number seldom found in comparably sized cities.

Downtown

Reliable choices in downtown Ann Arbor include **Afternoon Delight** (251 E. Liberty, 734/665-7513, www.afternoondelightcafe.com, 8am-3pm Mon.-Sat., 8:30am-3pm Sun., $4-9), an ideal spot for homemade soups, deli sandwiches, and scrumptious desserts, and **Amadeus Restaurant** (122 E. Washington, 734/665-8767, www.amadeusrestaurant.com, 11:30am-2:30pm and 5pm-10pm Tues.-Thurs., 11:30am-2:30pm and 5pm-11pm Fri., 11:30am-11pm Sat., 11am-3pm Sun., $15-24), a cozy European-inspired café and patisserie that features hearty Polish, central European, and vegetarian entrées.

Another nearby favorite is **(Gratzi** (326 S. Main St., 734/663-6387, www.gratzirestaurant.com, 11:30am-10pm Mon.-Thurs., 11:30am-11pm Fri.-Sat., 4pm-9pm Sun., $9-30), serving up Northern Italian fare in a vintage 1920s theater. For the best view of the large, Bacchanalian murals, sit in the balcony. If you'd prefer lighter fare, such as terrific coffee, pastries, and gourmet sandwiches, head for **Café Felix** (204 S. Main St., 734/662-8650, www.cafefelix.com, 11am-midnight Mon.-Thurs., 11am-1am Fri., 9am-1am Sat.,

© DANIEL MARTONE

the Heidelberg Restaurant

THE HEARTLAND

9am-10pm Sun., $7-18), a pleasant European-style bistro and Ann Arbor's first full-menu tapas bar.

North of Downtown

To the north, you'll find the three-story **Heidelberg Restaurant** (215 N. Main St., 734/663-7758, www.heidelbergannarbor.com, 11am-10pm Mon.-Thurs., 11am-midnight Fri.-Sat., 3pm-2am Sun., $9-18), an integral part of Ann Arbor's fine dining tradition since the early 1960s. The basement level, the Rathskeller, serves as a traditional German bar; the main dining room presents German specialties like sauerbrauten and Wiener schnitzel; and the top floor, The Club Above, offers live entertainment seven nights a week.

Kerrytown District

Head a few blocks into the Kerrytown District, where you shouldn't miss **Zingerman's Delicatessen** (422 Detroit St., 734/663-3354, www.zingermansdeli.com, 7am-10pm daily,

$5-19), a story in itself. Gastronomes and food critics alike consider this New York-style deli the best deli in the Midwest—maybe the nation. Most head for the deli counter, offering more than 100 sandwiches, side salads, and fragrant imported cheeses. The grocery side of the store has homemade breads and surrounding shelves stocked with the best of everything, from jams to olive oils. The grocery counter is busiest on weekday mornings, after work, and all day on weekends; the sandwich area is mobbed for lunch and dinner. Consider calling ahead, to have your order waiting, and plan on eating at the relaxed Zingerman's Next Door, where you can linger as long as you want over a meal.

Around the University of Michigan

If you're looking for a decent breakfast spot near campus, consider **Angelo's** (1100 E. Catherine, 734/761-8996, www.angelosa2.com, 6am-3pm Mon.-Sat., 7am-2pm Sun., $5-10), the hands-down favorite for their famous deep-fried French toast, made with homemade raisin bread and loaded with fresh berries. For a more sophisticated dining experience, reserve a table at the **Gandy Dancer** (401 Depot St., 734/769-0592, www.muer.com, 11am-10pm Mon.-Thurs., 11am-11pm Fri., 4:30pm-11pm Sat., 10am-9pm Sun., $22-50), part of the Muer seafood restaurant chain. Housed inside the restored 1886 Michigan Central Depot, this elegant restaurant showcases creative seafood dishes like wasabi pea-encrusted tuna and pan-seared jumbo sea scallops with smoked bacon and asparagus. The delectable Sunday brunch features live jazz.

INFORMATION AND SERVICES

For more information about Ann Arbor, contact the **Ann Arbor Area Convention & Visitors Bureau** (120 W. Huron St., 734/995-7281, www.annarbor.org, 8:30am-5pm Mon.-Fri.) or the **Ann Arbor Area Chamber of Commerce** (115 W. Huron St., 3rd Fl.,

734/665-4433, www.annarborchamber.org, 9am-5pm Mon.-Fri.). For information about Washtenaw County, visit www.ewashtenaw. org. For local news and entertainment, consult **Ann Arbor.com** (www.annarbor.com) or **WCBN** (88.3 FM, www.wcbn.org), the University of Michigan's student-run radio station.

Sizable Ann Arbor offers all the services required by travelers, from grocery stores to banks to pharmacies. For mailing needs, stop by one of Ann Arbor's many **post offices** (200 E. Liberty St., 734/662-2009, www.usps. com). As a college town, Ann Arbor is also a terrific place to snag free wireless Internet access, so find a coffee shop, such as **Café Verde** (734/994-9174, www.peoplesfood.coop, daily), and start surfing.

In case of an emergency that requires police, fire, or ambulance services, dial **911** from any cell or public phone. For medical assistance, consult the **University of Michigan Health System** (1500 E. Medical Center Dr., 734/936-4000, www.med.umich.edu).

GETTING THERE AND AROUND

Reaching Ann Arbor is a snap. Both **Amtrak** (325 Depot St., 800/872-7245, www.amtrak.com) and **Greyhound** (116 W. Huron St., 734/662-5511 or 800/231-2222, www. greyhound.com) serve the city. In addition, you can fly into the **Detroit Metropolitan-Wayne County Airport** (DTW, 1 Detroit Metropolitan Airport Tram, Detroit, 734/247-7678, www.metroairport.com), rent a vehicle from one of eight national car rental agencies, and head west on I-94 to Ann Arbor, a 26-mile trip that, without traffic, will take about a half hour. Of course, you can also hitch a ride from **Metro Airport Taxi** (800/745-5191, www.metroairporttaxi.org), which costs about $42-49 for a trip between the Detroit airport and Ann Arbor.

Not surprisingly, motorists can reach Ann Arbor from a variety of directions. From Flint, for instance, you can take I-69 West to I-75 South, continue onto US-23 South, merge

onto M-14 West, and follow the US-23 South Business Route into Ann Arbor, a 55-mile trip that, without traffic, will take about 53 minutes. From Chicago, meanwhile, you can take I-90 East and I-94 East to reach Ann Arbor, passing through towns like Kalamazoo, Battle Creek, Marshall, and Jackson; without traffic, this 240-mile trip will require just over 3.5 hours. Just be advised that, en route from the Windy City, parts of I-90 East and I-94 East serve as the Indiana Toll Road.

Once you arrive in Ann Arbor, though, you'll discover that it's a walking town. Residents who don't have cars (as well as the majority of students at the University of Michigan) use foot power or zip around town on bikes or in-line skates. There's also a reliable public bus system, the **Ann Arbor Transportation Authority** (734/996-0400 or 734/973-6500, www.theride.org, one-way $1.50 adults, $0.75 students 6-18, children under 6 and seniors free), which delivers passengers around the main campus as well as farther afield. In addition, you can also depend on **Ann Arbor Taxi** (734/883-6921, www.annarbortaxi.com), which offers service to and from the Detroit airport as well as transportation around the Ann Arbor area and other parts of southeastern Michigan.

Naturally, you can also drive around the Ann Arbor area. Whether you've brought your own car or a rental, watch for the easy-access parking garages spread throughout the city. There's also plenty of street parking available, but be aware that the city has very thorough parking enforcement officers. In other words, bring plenty of change for the parking meters and make note of any instructive signs.

YPSILANTI

Not far from Ann Arbor, you'll encounter the town of Ypsilanti. Besides being the home of **Eastern Michigan University** (EMU, 734/487-1849, www.emich.edu), Ypsilanti features two unique museums. The **Michigan Firehouse Museum** (110 W. Cross St., 734/547-0663, www.michiganfirehousemuseum.org, 10am-4pm Tues.-Sat., noon-4pm Sun., $5 adults, $3

© LYNDA HUMMEL

cruise nights in Ypsilanti

children 2-16, children under 2 free) offers a look at Michigan's firefighting history, while also promoting fire safety and prevention. The **Ypsilanti Historical Museum** (220 N. Huron St., 734/484-0080 or 734/482-4990, www.ypsilantihistoricalsociety.org, 2pm-5pm Tues.-Sun., free) provides a glimpse of Ypsilanti's history since its founding in 1860.

Also in Ypsilanti, you'll find the **Riverside Arts Center** (76 N. Huron St., 734/480-2787, www.riversidearts.org), which presents exhibits and performances in the theater space. For a bite to eat, visit **Aubree's Pizzeria & Tavern** (39 E. Cross St., 734/483-1870, www.aubrees.com, 11am-2am Mon.-Sat., noon-2am Sun., $7-17), which offers a variety of comfort foods and pizza selections.

For more information about the Ypsilanti area, consult the **Ypsilanti Area Convention & Visitors Bureau** (106 W. Michigan Ave., 734/483-4444, www.visitypsinow.com). To reach the town itself, simply take Washtenaw Avenue from Ann Arbor; without traffic, the eight-mile trip should take about 18 minutes.

CHELSEA

Considered by many to be little more than a trendy suburb of neighboring Ann Arbor, Chelsea has begun to make a name for itself, thanks to a big-name Hollywood star who still resides in this picturesque little town, and a big swath of public land just west of town.

◖ Purple Rose Theatre Company

When he's not off making movies, actor Jeff Daniels eschews the Tinseltown glitz for his hometown of Chelsea. Despite a crammed film schedule, Daniels keeps busy running the **Purple Rose Theatre Company** (137 Park St., 734/433-7673, www.purplerosetheatre.org, box office 10am-6pm Mon.-Fri., show days noon-10pm Sat., noon-4pm Sun., $20-40 pp), which he founded in 1991, naming it after the Woody Allen film *The Purple Rose of Cairo,* in which he'd starred six years prior. This critically acclaimed regional playhouse features classic plays such as *A Streetcar Named Desire* as well as modern works, even plays written by Daniels himself.

JEFF DANIELS: MICHIGAN'S TOP PROMOTER

Certainly one of the more recognizable faces in Michigan, actor Jeff Daniels has been gracing movie screens for more than three decades. In 2008, he also appeared in a television commercial for the Michigan Economic Development Corporation, part of a national campaign to promote Michigan's tourism and business opportunities.

Born in Athens, Georgia, in 1955, Jeffrey Warren Daniels grew up in Chelsea, Michigan, where his family has owned a lumber company since the 1920s. After marrying his high school sweetheart in 1979, he began to pursue an acting career. Some of his early films included *Terms of Endearment* (1983), *The Purple Rose of Cairo* (1985), and *Arachnophobia* (1990).

In 1991, he founded the Purple Rose Theatre Company in his hometown of Chelsea. Although he, his wife, and his three grown children still consider Michigan home, Daniels has continued to work in Hollywood, turning in memorable performances in films like *Gettysburg* (1993), *Speed* (1994), *Pleasantville* (1998), *Blood Work* (2002), *Imaginary Heroes* (2004), *The Lookout* (2007), *Howl* (2009), and *Looper* (2012), not to mention the TV series *The Newsroom* (2012-present).

Even with such success, Daniels has never forgotten his Midwestern roots. In 2001, he wrote, directed, and starred in *Escanaba in da Moonlight*, a quirky comedy about deer-hunting season in the Upper Peninsula. Despite an incredibly busy film schedule, he's also lent his voice to radio spots that promote Michigan tourism and used his well-known persona to lure businesses here. While some residents find it hard to be hopeful in times of downsizing auto factories and an uncertain economy, many have appreciated his sincerity and commitment. It's admirable, after all, that a movie star as famous as Jeff Daniels would eschew the Hollywood scene and use his celebrity status to support the people of his home state.

After catching a show at this landmark theater, head to the town's other big-name attraction: **The Common Grill** (112 S. Main St., 734/475-0470, www.commongrill.com, 11am-10pm Tues.-Thurs., 11am-11pm Fri.-Sat., 11am-9pm Sun., $10-30), a superb restaurant founded in 1991 by former employees of Detroit's Chuck Muer restaurant chain. The Grill helped put sleepy Chelsea on the map, and waits easily reach two hours on weekends. Folks come for the signature fish dishes and the chic yet comfortable atmosphere, which includes painted Hopperesque scenes of old Chelsea (including the Jiffy Baking Company's tower) on the exposed brick walls.

Waterloo Recreation Area

Sprawling across two counties and some 20,000 acres, the Waterloo Recreation Area (16345 McClure Rd., 734/475-8307, www. michigan.gov/dnr, hours vary daily, annual $11 Recreation Passport for Michigan residents or $8.40 day-use fee/$30.50 yearly Recreation Passport for nonresidents required) counts as the largest park in the Lower Peninsula. The park's landscape clearly shows evidence of the glaciers that once blanketed this part of the state. Waterloo is located at the intersection of the Kalamazoo and the Missaukee moraine systems, where two glaciers collided thousands of years ago. The ice sheets ripped apart massive mountains of rock from the Canadian shield to the north, carrying fragments with them as the ice moved across this part of the state—a journey one park interpreter has described as "the movement of pancake batter on a hot griddle."

The area is a pleasing patchwork of field, forest, and lake. Pick up a map at park headquarters to help you navigate around this expansive place, which contains 11 fishing lakes, several beaches and picnic areas, and miles of hiking, biking, equestrian, and cross-country skiing trails. Here, you'll also find the year-round

THE HEARTLAND

Gerald E. Eddy Discovery Center, which offers engaging exhibits about Michigan's geologic features, and the 1,000-acre **Haehnle Audubon Sanctuary,** a favorite fall hangout of sandhill cranes.

Waterloo maintains four campgrounds in all ($12-24 daily). Equestrian (for campers with horses) and Green Lake are rustic areas, with nice wooded sites. Portage Lake and Sugarloaf are large, modern campgrounds, with sites near (but not on) their namesake lakes.

Information

For more information about Chelsea, consult the **Chelsea Area Chamber of Commerce** (310 N. Main St., Ste. 120, 734/475-1145, www.chelseamichamber.org, 10am-4pm Mon.-Fri.).

Getting There and Around

Chelsea is situated about halfway between Ann Arbor and Jackson, so it's easily accessible via car, motorcycle, or RV. From downtown Ann Arbor, for instance, head north on the I-94 Business Route, take I-94 West to exit 159, and follow M-52 North to Chelsea; without traffic, the 17-mile trip should take about 23 minutes. From Jackson, take I-94 East to M-52 North, which will take you directly to Chelsea; without traffic, this 24-mile trip usually takes about 29 minutes. Once here, you can park the car and take a stroll (or ride a bike) through the downtown area.

Jackson and Vicinity

If you're looking for Michigan's liberal stronghold, don't look in Jackson. The Republican Party was founded in this small city of 33,400 back in 1854. More than a thousand Free Soilers, Whigs, and Democrats gathered here, where they adopted the Republican name, issued a platform, and nominated candidates for state office. A tablet still marks the site at the corner of Franklin and 2nd Streets. The Jackson area has also been home to several astronauts. Moreover, it has often claimed fame as "Nuge Country," a nod to Ted Nugent, rocker and bow hunter extraordinaire, who lives nearby. As if that isn't enough, Jackson holds the Midwest's largest and oldest Civil War muster each August, attracting more than 1,200 costumed reenactors from across the country who gather here for battle, balls, and ballistics.

Like many once-booming industrial cities in mid-Michigan, downtown Jackson was hit hard by unemployment and the "malling" of America. Few shops still occupy the city's stately Victorian and art deco storefronts. Even Jacobson's—the posh department store chain founded in Jackson, with stores that once stretched to Florida—closed its downtown store here and eventually filed for bankruptcy in 2002.

But even a flat economy can't affect the wealth of wonderful lakes in surrounding Jackson County. Hundreds of natural lakes dot the countryside, keeping the Jackson area near the top of the list for those in southern Michigan and northern Indiana looking for an easy weekend getaway. Area golf courses, museums, antiques shops, and vineyards only sweeten the deal for many vacationers.

SIGHTS
Ella Sharp Museum of Art and History

Trace the development of the Jackson area at the **Ella Sharp Museum of Art and History** (3225 4th St., 517/787-2320, www.ellasharp. org, 10am-5pm Tues.-Wed. and Fri.-Sat., 10am-7pm Thurs., galleries $5 adults, $3 children 5-12, children under 5 free, house tours $3 adults, $3 children 5-12, children under 5 free). Sharp's mother was a rich expatriate who had invested in western Michigan land in the 1800s and later came to live on it—a rarity, since most investors were absentee landlords. Ella, born in Jackson, grew into a successful reformer who worked to improve rural life through good government, women's associations, and conservation. She also was a pack rat, so plenty of 19th-century artifacts and memorabilia fill this museum complex, which includes Ella Sharp's 1857 farmhouse, an 1840 log cabin, a one-room schoolhouse, and the Midwest's finest wildlife art collection.

The Cascades

Perhaps in response to the awe-inspiring waterfalls of the Upper Peninsula, Jackson has one of the largest man-made waterfalls in North America. Better known as **The Cascades** (1992 Warren Ave., 517/788-4320, 11am-11pm daily May-Sept., $3 pp, children under 6 free), they were a creation of "Captain" William Sparks, a well-known area industrialist, philanthropist, and former mayor. This is truly an amazing slice of Americana: 18 separate falls up to 500 feet high, six fountains of various heights and patterns, 1,200 colored lights, and choreographed show tunes. Kids especially love it. The falls and surrounding 465-acre Sparks County Park date back to the early 1930s, when Sparks, a three-time mayor and chamber of commerce president, developed the whole shebang and presented it as a gift to his beloved city. You can make a day of it here, since the falls are augmented by a golf course, a picnic area, fishing ponds, tennis courts, and paddleboat rentals.

Southeast Michigan Pioneer Wine Trail

While the winemaking region of southeastern Michigan is no match for the wineries that line the Southwest Coast and surround Grand Traverse Bay, connoisseurs will still appreciate the selections that constitute the **Southeast Michigan Pioneer Wine Trail** (www.pioneerwinetrail.com). In Jackson, you'll find **Sandhill Crane Vineyards** (4724 Walz Rd., 517/764-0679, www.sandhillcranevineyards.com, 11am-6pm Mon.-Sat., noon-6pm Sun.), an award-winning, family-owned winery with a year-round tasting room. Other area wineries include the **Lone Oak Vineyard Estate** (8400 Ann Arbor Rd., Grass Lake, 517/522-8167,

www.loneoakvineyards.com, noon-7pm daily), established in 1997 and offering complimentary tastings, and the **Pentamere Winery** (131 E. Chicago Blvd., Tecumseh, 517/423-9000, www.pentamerewinery.com, 11am-7pm Tues.-Fri., 10am-7pm Sat., noon-5pm Sun.), where you can even take classes on the techniques of tasting and evaluating wines.

FESTIVALS AND EVENTS

The **Ella Sharp Museum of Art and History** (3225 4th St., 517/787-2320, www.ellasharp.org) holds three interesting annual events: the **Sugar & Shearing Festival,** a late March event that celebrates the arrival of springtime with sheep-shearing and maple sugar demonstrations; the **Art & Wine Festival,** which invites visitors to the museum grounds in early June for the chance to sample area wines and peruse regional artwork; and the **Fall Harvest Festival,** an October event that celebrates autumn with pumpkin painting, a farmers market, and an antique tractor trade.

For something completely different, plan a trip around the annual **Hot Air Jubilee** (Jackson County Airport, 3606 Wildwood Ave., 517/782-1515, www.hotairjubilee.com, $10 adults, children 6-12 free) in mid-July. Watching nearly 70 colorful hot air balloons take to the sky at once is quite a dazzling sight. Besides the balloons, the weekend features an arts-and-crafts show, stunt kite demonstrations, carnival rides, aircraft and antique military displays, and live entertainment. Stick around until sunset for the Balloon Night Glow, a spectacular light show of tethered balloons.

SPORTS AND RECREATION
Michigan International Speedway

The **Michigan International Speedway** (12626 US-12, Brooklyn, 517/592-6666, www.mispeedway.com, racing times and ticket prices vary), which opened in 1968, offers one of the country's premier auto racing facilities. Featuring over 80,000 seats and a large RV campground, the track presents NASCAR races (for the Truck, Sprint Cup, and Nationwide series) mid-June- mid-August. In addition, the speedway often presents official driving schools during the warmer months, so if you have a lead foot, perhaps you should try some legal speeding instead.

Golf

The Jackson area is nuts for golf and hides a number of high-quality public courses. Two good choices are the **Arbor Hills Golf Club** (1426 Arbor Hills Rd., 517/750-2290, www.arborhillsgolf.com, daily Apr.-Oct., $22-28 pp w/ cart), formerly a private club for over 80 years, and the **Cascades Golf Course** (1992 Warren Ave., 517/788-4323, www.cascadesgolfcourse. com, daily Apr.-Oct., $27-35 pp w/cart), established in 1929 and voted Jackson's best golf course in 2007.

ACCOMMODATIONS AND FOOD

You'll find a range of reasonably priced chain hotels clustered near the I-94 interchange in Jackson. Three include the **Hampton Inn** (2225 Shirley Dr., 517/789-5151, www.hamptoninn. com, $119-139 d), the **Fairfield Inn** (2395 Shirley Dr., 517/784-7877, www.marriott.com, $94-149 d), and the **Country Hearth Inn** (1111 Boardman Rd., 517/783-6404, www.country-hearth.com, $63-83 d).

This is meat-and-potatoes country, and you're going to have a tough time beating it. If you're happy to join in, try **Steve's Ranch** (311 Louis Glick Hwy., 517/787-4367, www.steves-ranch.com, 6am-10pm Mon.-Sat., 6am-8pm Sun., $10-30), a longtime favorite for omelets, burgers, and, of course, steaks.

INFORMATION AND SERVICES

For more information about Jackson, contact the **Jackson County Convention & Visitors Bureau** (141 S. Jackson St., 517/764-4440, www.visitjacksonmi.com, 8am-5pm Mon.-Fri.) or the **Greater Jackson Chamber of Commerce** (141 S. Jackson St., 517/782-8221, www.gjcc.org, 8am-5pm Mon.-Fri.). For local news and events, consult the *Jackson Citizen Patriot* (www.mlive.com/citpat).

For groceries and prescriptions, stop by **Meijer** (3333 E. Michigan Ave., 517/787-8722, www.meijer.com), part of an enormous regional chain. For mailing needs, visit one of Jackson's many **post offices** (113 W. Michigan Ave., 517/768-0611, www.usps.com), and for banking assistance, consult **Flagstar** (www. flagstar.com), which has several branches in town.

In case of an emergency, dial **911** from any cell or public phone. For medical services, consult **Allegiance Health** (205 N. East Ave., 517/788-4800, www.allegiancehealth.org).

GETTING THERE AND AROUND

Both **Amtrak** (501 E. Michigan Ave., 800/872-7245, www.amtrak.com) and **Greyhound** (127 W. Cortland, 517/789-6148 or 800/231-2222, www.greyhound.com) serve Jackson. In addition, the town is situated halfway between the **Detroit Metropolitan-Wayne County Airport** (DTW, 1 Detroit Metropolitan Airport Tram, Detroit, 734/247-7678, www.metroairport. com) and the **Kalamazoo/Battle Creek International Airport** (AZO, 5235 Portage Rd., 269/388-3668, www.azoairport.com), from which you can easily rent a vehicle and head to Jackson via I-94. From the Detroit airport, for instance, you can simply take I-94 West to exit 139, turn left onto M-106 South, and head 2 miles south to downtown Jackson; without traffic, this 61-mile trip will take you about an hour. From the Kalamazoo airport, meanwhile, you can just take I-94 East to exit 138, turn right onto M-50 East/US-127 South Business Route, and head a couple of miles into downtown Jackson; without traffic, this 64-mile trip will take you about an hour.

Of course, if you've driven to Michigan, there are a number of other ways to reach Jackson. From Lansing, for example, you can follow I-496 East for 5 miles, and then head to Jackson via M-50 East/US-127 South Business Route; without traffic, the 39-mile trip will take about 40 minutes. Once you reach Jackson, you can drive, bike, or even walk around town. It's also possible to rely on the **Jackson Area Transportation Authority** (JATA, 517/787-8363, www.jacksontransit. com, one-way $1.50 adults, $1 students, $0.75 seniors and children), which offers bus service around the Jackson area.

THE IRISH HILLS AND LENAWEE COUNTY

Southeast of Jackson via US-127 South and US-12 East, the lovely Irish Hills have long been a popular family getaway, dotted with summer cottages owned by residents of Michigan, Indiana, and Ohio. The area was formed during the last ice age, when huge ice chunks swept across the land, leaving behind a varied landscape of round kettle-hole lakes, steep valleys, and picturesque sweeping meadows. It got its name from Irish settlers who thought the region resembled their homeland.

You can enjoy the area's natural state at **W. J. Hayes State Park** (1220 Wamplers Lake Rd., Onsted, 517/467-7401, www.michigan.gov/ dnr, hours vary daily, annual $11 Recreation Passport for Michigan residents or $8.40 day-use fee/$30.50 yearly Recreation Passport for nonresidents required). The 654-acre park, which lies 23 miles southeast of Jackson and isn't far from the Michigan International Speedway, features two popular fishing lakes tucked amid gentle rolling hills. Facilities include a sandy swimming beach, a boat launch, a picnic area, and 185 modern campsites.

Nearby, the **Cambridge Junction Historic State Park** (13220 M-50, Brooklyn, 517/467-4414, hours vary, free) features the 1832 **Walker Tavern,** which tells the story of the spine-crunching Chicago Road, the chief route of settlement during the 1830s pioneer boom. Now a fine small state historical museum, it illustrates how travelers once piled into the tavern's few sleeping rooms, shared beds, and passed much of their time in the 1st-floor bar and dining room. Daniel Webster and James Fenimore Cooper stayed here on expeditions west.

Information

For more information about the Irish Hills, contact the **Lenawee County Conference & Visitors Bureau** (209 N. Main St., Adrian, 517/263-7747, www.visitlenawee.com).

Marshall

When Lansing was chosen as the seat of the state government in 1847, no city was more surprised and more disappointed than Marshall, located 31 miles west of Jackson. The State Senate originally passed a bill designating Marshall the capital, a measure defeated by just one vote in the House. Marshall was so sure of its upcoming role as the capital city that it set aside a site known as Capitol Hill. It even built a governor's mansion, which still exists today.

Being spurned by the legislature, though, gave Marshall a reprieve from rampant development, and today it ranks as one of the country's best-preserved 19th-century towns, with just under 7,100 residents. Lined by large shade trees and an outstanding collection of 1840s and 1850s Greek and Gothic Revival-style homes, house-proud Marshall has become a poster child for historic preservation, an example of what can be done when businesses and homeowners work together. The town has been featured in dozens of travel articles and architectural magazines. "Marshall's small-town pride is a genteel descendant of the boosterism that Sinclair Lewis savaged in *Main Street* and *Babbitt*," once declared the *New York Times*.

Before Marshall was old enough to turn heads for its architecture, it was carving out a niche as a center of the patent medicine boom in the early 1900s, producer of such classic tonics as Lydia Pinkham's Pink Pills for Pale People. It wasn't until the 1920s that a savvy mayor, Harold Brooks, first recognized the city's fine architecture and led a crusade to maintain it. The first home tour was held in 1964 and remains a large and popular annual event half a century later. Marshall's designated National Historic Landmark District includes over 850 homes and businesses, the country's largest district in the "small urban" category. One National Park Service manager called Marshall "a textbook of 19th-century small-town architecture."

There's a rich and controversial history hiding behind those pretty 19th-century facades, too. Marshall drew nationwide attention in 1846 when Adam Crosswhite, a slave who had escaped from Kentucky and lived in Marshall for two years, was seized by slave hunters. The whole town rose up in his support. Local abolitionists helped Crosswhite and his family escape to Canada, arrested the slave hunters, and tried them in Federal District Court. Although the Marshall abolitionists lost in court, the Crosswhite case was instrumental in the creation of the 1850 Fugitive Slave Act, which in turn contributed to the tensions that later caused the Civil War.

SIGHTS
◖ Historic Homes

The best way to see the area's historic homes is on the annual home tour held the weekend after Labor Day. At other times, you can still enjoy the city's architecture with the help of an excellent (and free) walking-tour brochure available at the chamber of commerce and a number of local shops and inns.

One of the first stops should be the lavishly quirky **Honolulu House** (107 N. Kalamazoo Ave., 269/781-8544, www.marshallhistoricalsociety.org, 11am-5pm daily May-Sept., noon-5pm Thurs.-Sun. Oct., $5 pp), home to the Marshall Historical Society and described by the *New York Times* as "the architectural equivalent of a four-rum cocktail served in a coconut." Featuring a pagoda-shaped tower and decorative pineapple trim, the Polynesian-style home was built in 1860 by Michigan Supreme Court judge Abner Pratt, who served as U.S. consul to the Sandwich Islands (now Hawaii) 1857-1859. His wife's poor health forced the couple to return to Marshall, where they brought back their love of the tropics. Pratt's

wife died shortly upon their return, and Pratt himself succumbed to pneumonia soon afterward—perhaps because of his stubborn habit of wearing tropical-weight clothing during the long and cold Midwestern winters.

Inside, the house features 1880s replicas of Pratt's original tropical murals, a riot of purples, pinks, and dozens of other rich colors, and several exquisite fireplaces. Many of the other furnishings did not belong to the Pratts, but represent Marshall history, such as the Marshall Folding Bathtub in the basement. Disguised as a cabinet, it's a rare reminder of the city's patent medicine boom.

Other fine examples of early Marshall architecture can be found two blocks north of the Honolulu House on Kalamazoo Street. They include the home of Mayor Harold Brooks, who spurred the city's revival; the 1857 Italianate Adams-Schuyler-Umphrey House, built on land once owned by James Fenimore Cooper; the 1907 Sears-Osborne House, ordered from the Sears catalog at the turn of the 20th century for just $1,995; the 1886 Queen Anne-style Cronin-Lapietra House, one of the city's most ornate, designed by the Detroit firm best known for the city's Michigan Central Railroad Terminal; and the 1843 Greek Revival Camp-Vernor-Riser House, once home to the founder of Vernor's Ginger Ale.

American Museum of Magic

Renowned magician David Copperfield has called the **American Museum of Magic** (107 E. Michigan Ave., 269/781-7570, www.americanmuseumofmagic.org, by appointment 2nd weekend of each month, $5 adults, $3.50 seniors and children, children under 5 free) one of his "favorite places on earth" and, if you believe the local rumor mill, wants to purchase the museum and move it to Las Vegas. For now, anyway, this fascinating attraction remains in Marshall, housed in a historic 1868 building.

The late Robert Lund, a retired automotive writer, and his wife, Elaine, opened the American Museum of Magic in 1978, after spending years collecting "notional whimsies, cabalistic surprises, phantasmagorical bewilderments, and unparalleled splendors." Roughly translated, that means anything and everything remotely related to the practice of magic. Spanning six continents and over four centuries, this extensive collection of more than 87,000 artifacts and memorabilia includes showbills, programs, books, magazines, photographs, and antique props (even the milk can used by Harry Houdini for a popular escape stunt).

FESTIVALS AND EVENTS

Marshall's must-see event is, of course, the **Annual Historic Home Tour** (269/781-8544, www.marshallhistoricalsociety.org, $15-20 pp), which usually occurs the weekend after Labor Day and is a wonderful way to view hundreds of historic buildings. While strolling along the shady streets of Marshall, visitors can listen to choirs, quartets, and brass bands, the nostalgic sounds of the 19th century.

If you happen to be in town in mid-October, you may be able to check out one of the most unique festivals, **Marshall Scarecrow Days** (800/877-5163). As the name suggests, this weeklong event focuses on scarecrows, scarecrows, and more scarecrows. You'll see a variety of scarecrows in gardens and yards throughout Marshall. There's even a parade that features costumed children and "live" scarecrows.

Southwest of Marshall, Colon's **Magic Get Together** is worth a look, even if you're not a magician. Begun in 1934 as a sales incentive, this annual August gathering of magicians has lured some of the best names in the business, from Harry Blackstone to Lance Burton. For more information, contact **Abbott's Magic Company** (124 St. Joseph St., Colon, 269/432-3235, www.magicgettogether.com, 9am-5pm Mon.-Fri., 9am-4pm Sat.), with its enormous inventory of magic books and supplies.

ANTIQUE SHOPPING

Modern Marshall, with a downtown full of lacy Victorian homes and storefronts, has become an immensely popular weekend getaway for Detroit- and Chicago-area residents. They come to ogle the architecture, shop at a number of well-stocked (if somewhat expensive) antiques stores and malls, and stay in one of the town's historic bed-and-breakfast inns.

You'll find most of the best shops along several blocks of Michigan Avenue and its cross streets. For antiques, try the **Marshall Antique Center** (119 W. Michigan Ave., 269/789-0077, 11am-5pm Tues.-Sat., noon-4pm Sun.), which houses quality dealers in a historic home, or **Keystone Architectural and General Antiques** (110 E. Michigan Ave., 269/789-1355, www.keystoneantiques.com, 1pm-5pm Wed.-Fri. and Sun., 10am-5pm Sat.), with an outstanding collection of vintage furniture, leaded glass, old light fixtures, hand-knotted Persian rugs, and other antique furnishings.

ACCOMMODATIONS AND FOOD

Established in 1835, **◖ The National House Inn** (102 Parkview, 269/781-7374, www.nationalhouseinn.com, $110-170 d) is the oldest operating inn in the state. This former stagecoach stop along the Chicago Road once served as a station on the Underground Railroad. Guest rooms range from the elegant Victorian-style Ketchum Suite to smaller, pleasant country-style rooms with folk art portraits on the walls. A tip: The old road in front of the inn is now a busy intersection. Ask for a room overlooking the garden if you desire peace and quiet.

Your best budget bet is the **Arbor Inn** (15435 W. Michigan Ave., 269/781-7772, www.arborinnmarshall.com, $45-69 d), a comfortable hotel with an outdoor pool, situated along a strip of fast-food restaurants beyond the historic downtown.

For cheap eats, head to **Louie's Bakery** (144 W. Michigan Ave., 269/781-3542, 5:30am-5pm Mon.-Fri., 5:30am-3:30pm Sat.), the kind of old-fashioned bakery you might remember from childhood, with gooey cakes, pies, and sweet rolls galore.

Wayne and Marjorie Cornwell introduced their first turkey sandwich at a county fair over 40 years ago. Today, their campy, country-style restaurant and turkey farm just north of Marshall is known as **◖ Cornwell's**

Turkeyville U.S.A. (18935 15½ Mile Rd., 269/781-4293, www.turkeyville.com, 11am-8pm daily, $4-9). The menu includes everything from a classic buttered turkey sandwich to a piled-high turkey Reuben to a turkey stir-fry. An adjacent 170-seat dinner theater presents afternoon and evening performances of family favorites.

INFORMATION AND SERVICES

For more information about Marshall, contact the **Marshall Area Chamber of Commerce** (323 W. Michigan Ave., 269/781-5163 or 800/877-5163, www.marshallmi.org, 8:30am-7pm Mon.-Fri., 10am-4pm Sat.-Sun.). If you require more than just information, you'll find everything you need in surrounding towns like Battle Creek and Jackson, including groceries, pharmacies, gas stations, laundries, and banks. Marshall, too, has its share of businesses, including two **post offices;** consult www.usps.com for locations and hours. In case of an emergency, dial **911** from any cell or public phone. For medical services, visit **Oaklawn Hospital** (200 N. Madison Ave., 269/781-4271, www.oaklawnhospital.org).

GETTING THERE AND AROUND

Marshall is surrounded by several larger towns, such as Battle Creek, Kalamazoo, East Lansing, Ann Arbor, and Jackson—all of which have bus and train stations, serviced by **Greyhound** (800/231-2222, www.greyhound.com) and **Amtrak** (800/872-7245, www.amtrak.com), respectively. In addition, it's not far from the **Kalamazoo/Battle Creek International Airport** (AZO, 5235 Portage Rd., Kalamazoo, 269/388-3668, www.azoairport.com) and the **Capital Region International Airport** (LAN, 4100 Capital City Blvd., Lansing, 517/321-6121, www.flylansing.com), from which you can easily rent a vehicle and head to Marshall via I-94 East and I-69 South, respectively. From the Kalamazoo airport, for instance, you can simply take I-94 East and Old US-27 North to Marshall; the 34-mile trip usually takes about a half hour. From the Lansing airport, meanwhile, you can just take the I-96 West Business Route and I-96 East, continue onto I-69 South, merge onto I-94 East, and follow Old US-27 North to Marshall; without traffic, the 50-mile trip should take you roughly 50 minutes.

Of course, if you've driven to Michigan, there are a number of other ways to reach Marshall, such as taking I-94 West from Ann Arbor, a 65-mile trip that usually requires about an hour, or following I-69 North from Fort Wayne, Indiana, an 89-mile trip that, without traffic, takes about 90 minutes. Once you reach Jackson, you can then drive, bike, or even walk around town.

Battle Creek

To generations of American youngsters, Battle Creek was the home of Tony the Tiger, that g-r-r-r-e-a-t and magical place where they sent their cereal box tops in exchange for free gifts and toys. For decades before that, however, Battle Creek was known as the home of the Church of Seventh-Day Adventists and for the work done at the church's sanitarium, the Western Health Reform Institute, which opened in 1866. John Harvey Kellogg joined the founders in 1876 and spent the next 25 years developing the sanitarium into an institution recognized around the world for its regimen of hydrotherapy, exercise, and vegetarian diet.

Part of that regimen was a new, healthy, grain-based flaked breakfast that Kellogg cooked up in 1894. An alternative to traditional breakfast foods such as grits, bacon, and eggs, Kellogg's creation went on to revolutionize the breakfast-foods industry and to fuel the economy of this former settlement. From 1901 to 1905, more than 1,500 new homes cropped up

SOJOURNER TRUTH

Described by one biographer as a "riveting preacher and spellbinding singer who dazzled listeners with her wit and originality," Sojourner Truth was born around 1797 as Isabella Baumfree. She spent her childhood and early adulthood as a slave, suffering abuse at the hands of her masters and giving birth to several children. Towering more than six feet, she gained her freedom in New York State in the late 1820s, dropped her given name, and moved west on a "sojourn to preach truth." Her antislavery crusade took her into both small rural churches and the office of President Abraham Lincoln.

She settled in Battle Creek, an abolitionist stronghold, in 1857 and continued to help her people along the Underground Railroad to Canada. While revisionist history has claimed that she never physically assisted runaway slaves, she no doubt inspired many of them with her fiery oratories, which preached economic competence, self-improvement, and social tolerance. A few days before she died in 1883, she said, "I isn't goin' to die, honey, I'se goin' home like a shootin' star." Her funeral was described as the biggest that Battle Creek had ever seen. She is buried in Oak Hill Cemetery by a simple old-fashioned square monument – still a popular pilgrimage spot – just steps away from the ornate marble mausoleum of cereal pioneer C. W. Post.

to house the workers and others who converged on Battle Creek, hoping to capitalize on its renown as the "Health City." (This bizarre tale was the basis for *The Road to Wellville*, a 1994 Hollywood film starring Anthony Hopkins, which painted a not-too-positive portrait of the Kellogg family and phenomenon.)

Today, Battle Creek is still home to the Kellogg Company as well as Post Cereals (recently transferred from Kraft Foods to Ralcorp). It's also home to the "World's Longest Breakfast Table," a downtown event held as part of the annual Battle Creek Cereal Festival in June.

SIGHTS
Museums and Historic Sites
If you're curious about the Kelloggs, you can visit the sanitarium, now the **Battle Creek Federal Center** (74 N. Washington Ave., 269/961-7015, www.dlis.dla.mil). Recognized on the National Register of Historic Places, the building now houses governmental and military offices, though there are still artifacts and other items on display about the Kellogg era.

If you're looking for an engaging place to take the kids, try the newly renovated **Kingman Museum** (175 Limit St., 269/965-5117, www.

kingmanmuseum.org, 9am-5pm Tues.-Fri., 1pm-5pm Sat., $7 adults, $6 seniors 65 and over, $5 children 3-18). The museum offers a wide array of paleontological and anthropological artifacts, from fossils and skulls to Native American war shields. Visitors can also catch a star show in the new planetarium.

Binder Park Zoo
More modern species can be found at the **Binder Park Zoo** (7400 Division Dr., 269/979-1351, www.binderparkzoo.org, 9am-5pm Mon.-Fri., 9am-6pm Sat., 11am-6pm Sun. late Apr.-mid-Oct., $6 pp Mon.-Fri., $8 pp Sat.-Sun.), a small but choice zoo that houses exotic and domestic animals in natural settings. Highlights include the **Swamp Adventure,** a boardwalk that takes you over bird-filled bogs, marshes, and swamps, and **Wild Africa,** a pseudo-savannah with giraffes, zebras, ostriches, antelope, and other animals of the region.

Parks and Gardens
The Kelloggs preached plenty of fresh air as part of their health regimen. Battle Creek, therefore, excels in its number of parks and recreational opportunities. Among the most

unusual is the **Battle Creek Linear Park** (269/966-3431, www.bcparks.org, sunrise-sunset daily), a 17-mile system that links wooded areas, open fields, and parks with a continuous paved pathway. It's a favorite of local cyclists, skaters, and joggers. Walkers and other nature lovers, in particular, head to the **Leila Arboretum** (928 W. Michigan Ave., 269/969-0270, www.leilaarboretumsociety.org, sunrise-sunset daily, free), part of Linear Park. This excellent 72-acre botanical garden is one of the best reasons to visit Battle Creek. The gift of Mrs. Leila Post Montgomery, it contains more than 3,000 species of trees and shrubs (many dating back to the 1920s), laid out in the manner of famous European gardens. Highlights include a rhododendron garden, a breathtaking flowering tree collection, and a children's garden.

FESTIVALS AND EVENTS

Battle Creek hosts several celebrations throughout the year. For over five decades, the **Battle Creek Cereal Festival** has celebrated the city's most famous industry in mid-June with a parade, live entertainment, and the world's longest breakfast table, offering complimentary cereals, fruit juice, and other Kellogg's breakfast foods. Started in 1956 as part of the Kellogg Company's Golden Jubilee, it has become a beloved annual tradition in downtown Battle Creek. Another popular event is the **International Festival of Lights,** during which Linear Park is decorated with lighted holiday displays late November-New Year's Eve. For more information about both events, visit www.bcfestivals.com.

SPORTS AND RECREATION
Golf

If you're visiting Battle Creek during the warmer months and are game for a round of golf, take a drive out to **Gull Lake View Golf Club & Resort** (7417 N. 38th St., Augusta, 269/731-4149 or 800/432-7971, www.gulllakeview.com, daily Apr.-Oct., $39-57 pp), the oldest and largest golf resort in southwestern Michigan. En route from Battle Creek

to Kalamazoo, this longstanding, family-operated resort offers top-notch lodging and dining, plus five championship golf courses: Gull Lake View East, Gull Lake View West, Stonehedge North, Stonehedge South, and Bedford Valley.

Hiking and Skiing

Naturalists will appreciate the **Kellogg Forest** (7060 N. 42nd St., Augusta, 269/731-4597, 8am-8pm in summer, 8am-sunset in winter, free), begun by cereal king W. K. Kellogg as a demonstration project for reforesting abandoned farms. Michigan State University maintains the 716-acre property as an experimental forest, which includes more than 200 species of trees, 2.5 miles of road, and 35 miles of hiking and cross-country skiing trails. Hikers and skiers also use the forest's 25 miles of ungroomed firebreaks separating experimental stands of trees, and picnickers favor the forest, too.

🄲 Bird-Watching

Ornithologists and other bird lovers flock to the experimental **W. K. Kellogg Bird Sanctuary** (12685 E. C Ave., Augusta, 269/671-2510, www.kbs.msu.edu, 9am-7pm daily May-Oct., 9am-5pm daily Nov.-Apr., $4 adults, $2 seniors, $1 children 2-12), one of North America's pioneer wildlife conservation centers. W. K. Kellogg started the sanctuary in 1928 as a refuge for Canada geese, which were then threatened by a loss of habitat to agriculture and urbanization. Today, Canada geese thrive at the 180-acre sanctuary, now part of MSU's W. K. Kellogg Biological Station, along with other native waterfowl, including ducks and swans that stay year-round. Also present are several species of raptors and game birds, from red-tailed hawks to pheasants, which you can view from several observation areas on the grounds. Many other species migrate through the region in spring and fall.

Situated along the waterfront of Wintergreen Lake, the grounds can be explored year-round on self-guided trails. A bookstore on-site includes information on how to transform your backyard into a bird sanctuary following the

RETURN OF THE TRUMPETER SWAN

The trumpeter swan, the world's largest waterfowl, can weigh up to 35 pounds when fully grown, with a wingspan of nearly eight feet. Similar in appearance to other white swans, its distinguishing characteristic is its all-black bill. Trumpeter swans typically create large nests in marshy areas, among cattails and other aquatic plants.

Centuries ago, trumpeter swans were abundant throughout the Great Lakes region, even in southern Michigan. In fact, Antoine de la Mothe Cadillac, founder of Detroit, noted their presence along the Detroit River in 1701. As European settlers spread throughout the state, however, the swan population plummeted. During the late 19th century, hunters captured swans for their fine down, while settlers drained crucial marsh habitat. By 1933, only 66 trumpeter swans remained in the continental United States, mainly in remote parts of Alaska and the Rocky Mountains.

During the mid-1980s, Michigan initiated a reintroduction program, intended to establish three self-sustaining populations of at least 200 swans by the year 2000. Despite early failures, biologists were able to incubate eggs collected from zoos and rear the cygnets for two years before releasing them into prime wetland habitat. In 1989, biologists from the Michigan Department of Natural Resources and the W.K. Kellogg Bird Sanctuary traveled to Alaska to collect eggs from wild populations as well.

By 2000, the program was considered a success. At the time, more than 400 trumpeter swans dwelled in Michigan: in the southwestern and northeastern parts of the Lower Peninsula, and in the U.P.'s Seney National Wildlife Refuge.

In recent years, the W.K. Kellogg Bird Sanctuary, which today nurtures over 20 year-round trumpeter swans, has continued reintroduction efforts. Since 2003, the sanctuary has released 28 swans in order to establish breeding populations elsewhere, including 6 that were transported to Sleeping Bear Dunes in 2007. In 2004, Michigan State University conducted a population survey throughout the state; the findings revealed that 655 trumpeter swans were then living in Michigan: roughly 45 percent in the U.P., 26 percent in the Lower Peninsula's northwestern region, and 29 percent in the L.P.'s southern portion.

For more information about conservation efforts, consult the **Michigan Department of Natural Resources** (www.michigan.gov/dnr) or the **W.K. Kellogg Bird Sanctuary** (www. kbs.msu.edu).

same principles and planting guidelines used in the refuge.

ACCOMMODATIONS AND FOOD

Situated amid rolling meadows, **◖Greencrest Manor** (6174 Halbert Rd., 269/962-8633, www.greencrestmanor.com, $135-275 d) is an unlikely find—a French chateau in the middle of the Midwestern prairie. Eight rooms, including six suites, are decorated with lots of chintz and antiques. For something less expensive, try the **Baymont Inn & Suites** (4725 Beckley Rd., 269/979-5400, www.baymontinns.com, $80-129 d), which includes free breakfast, high-speed Internet access, and access to a pool.

Battle Creek offers plenty of dining options, from fast-food establishments to fancier fare. One solid choice is the **Arcadia Brewing Company** (103 W. Michigan Ave., 269/963-9690, www.arcadiaales.com, 11am-9pm Mon.-Thurs., 11am-10pm Fri., noon-10pm Sat., $7-18), a microbrewery that specializes in British-style ales and offers an adjacent restaurant and tavern called TC's Wood-Fired Fare. For hearty all-American cuisine, consider **Finley's American Grill** (140 E. Columbia, 269/968-3938, www.finleys-rcfc.com, 11am-10pm Sun.-Thurs., 11am-11pm Fri.-Sat., $6-17), part of a popular southern Michigan chain, with locations in Jackson, Kalamazoo, and Lansing. If you're in the mood for Italian dishes, stop by **Fazoli's** (5445 Beckley Rd., 269/979-8662, www.fazolis.com, 11am-9pm daily, $6-14), part of a nationwide chain that offers pasta bowls, panini sandwiches, pizzas, and tasty favorites like fettuccine alfredo and meat lasagna.

INFORMATION AND SERVICES

For more information about Battle Creek, contact the **Battle Creek/Calhoun County Convention & Visitors Bureau** (77 E. Michigan Ave., Ste. 100, 269/962-2240, www.battlecreekvisitors.org, 8:30am-5pm Mon.-Fri.). For local news, entertainment, and sports, consult the *Battle Creek Enquirer* (www.battlecreekenquirer.com) or watch **WWMT** (www.wwmt.com), the CBS television affiliate that serves Battle Creek, Kalamazoo, and Grand Rapids.

Battle Creek offers all the services necessary for travelers, including groceries, pharmacies, gas stations, laundries, banks, and post offices. In case of an emergency, dial **911** from any cell or public phone. For medical assistance, consult the **Battle Creek Health System** (300 North Ave., 269/966-8000, www.bchealth.com).

GETTING THERE AND AROUND

Battle Creek is accessible via plane, train, bus, and, naturally, car. The **Kalamazoo/Battle Creek International Airport** (AZO, 5235 Portage Rd., Kalamazoo, 269/388-3668, www.azoairport.com) is situated about 25 miles to the southwest, while the **Capital Region International Airport** (LAN, 4100 Capital City Blvd., Lansing, 517/321-6121, www.flylansing.com) lies roughly 59 miles to the northeast. You can rent a vehicle at both locations, from which it'll take you about 24 minutes from Kalamazoo and an hour from Lansing to reach Battle Creek. In addition, **Amtrak** (800/872-7245, www.amtrak.com), **Greyhound** (269/964-1768 or 800/231-2222, www.greyhound.com), and **Indian Trails** (800/292-3831, www.indiantrails.com) all serve the same station (119 S. McCamly St.) in town.

If you have a car, you can reach Battle Creek via I-94, I-69, and several state highways and county roads. From downtown Detroit, for instance, you can take M-10 North and I-75 South, merge onto I-96 West, continue onto M-14 West and I-94 West, and follow M-66 North to downtown Battle Creek. Once here, you can stick with your car, opt for your feet or a bike, or use **Battle Creek Transit** (269/966-3474, one-way $1.25 adults, $0.60 seniors, free for children shorter than fare box), which offers bus service in and around town.

Kalamazoo and Vicinity

Yes, there really is a city named Kalamazoo. In reference to the area's bubbling natural springs, the name is derived from an Indian word meaning "place where the water boils." Its notoriety came later, when it inspired the Big Band-era song, "I Gotta Gal in Kalamazoo," as well as Carl Sandburg's poem.

From Grand Rapids, Kalamazoo is a straight shot south on US-131. Produce from the nearby vegetable-growing region, pharmaceutical industries, and several papermaking plants form the foundation of the city's diverse economy. Academia provides steady employment, too:

Kalamazoo is home to Western Michigan University and a number of respected private schools, including the academically renowned Kalamazoo College, site of a popular annual Bach festival and internationally known for its K-Plan, which includes international study and required internships.

Kalamazoo's population of approximately 75,100 comprises a sizable gay community, a substantial African American community, a burgeoning alternative music scene, a number of big-city refugees, and an almost even split between liberals and conservatives.

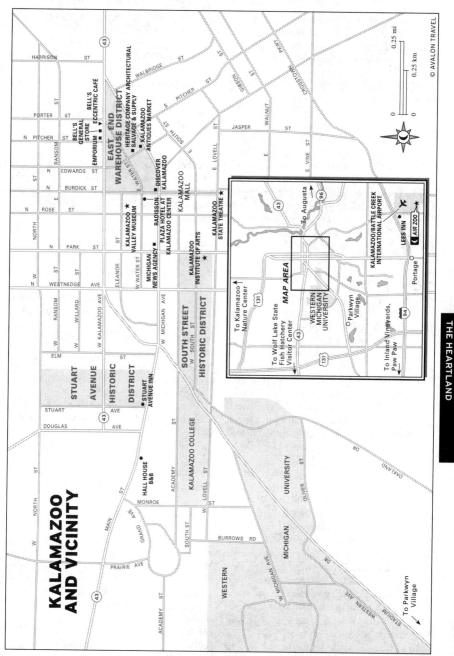

KALAMAZOO AND VICINITY

THE HEARTLAND

0.25 mi
0.25 km

MAP AREA

To Augusta
To Kalamazoo Nature Center
To Wolf Lake State Fish Hatchery Visitor Center
WESTERN MICHIGAN UNIVERSITY
Parkwyn Village
KALAMAZOO/BATTLE CREEK INTERNATIONAL AIRPORT
AIR ZOO
LEES INN
Portage
To Inland Vineyards, Paw Paw

EAST END WAREHOUSE DISTRICT
HERITAGE COMPANY ARCHITECTURAL SALVAGE & SUPPLY
KALAMAZOO ANTIQUES MARKET
BELL'S CAFÉ
ECCENTRIC CAFÉ
BELL'S GENERAL STORE
EMPORIUM

DISCOVER KALAMAZOO
RADISSON PLAZA HOTEL AT KALAMAZOO CENTER
KALAMAZOO MALL
KALAMAZOO STATE THEATRE
KALAMAZOO VALLEY MUSEUM
MICHIGAN NEWS AGENCY
KALAMAZOO INSTITUTE OF ARTS

SOUTH STREET HISTORIC DISTRICT

STUART AVENUE HISTORIC DISTRICT
STUART AVENUE INN

HALL HOUSE B&B

KALAMAZOO COLLEGE

WESTERN MICHIGAN UNIVERSITY

To Parkwyn Village

Kalamazoo's balanced economy and population represent such a slice of the American pie that the *Wall Street Journal* featured the city as a focus group during the 1992 presidential election.

While the poet Carl Sandburg didn't think much of Kalamazoo, its downtown streets reveal many of the vanishing pleasures of small-town life: quaint paths perfect for walking, a gracious downtown park, vintage architecture, interesting shops (including a number of antiques outlets), and several top-of-the-line bed-and-breakfasts. There's a great sense of civic pride and an active population that truly gets involved in city affairs. While not really a final destination, Kalamazoo makes a great stop en route to Harbor Country to the south or Lake Michigan's well-known resort communities in the north.

SIGHTS

Built in 1927, the opulent Spanish-style **Kalamazoo State Theatre** (404 S. Burdick St., 269/345-6500, www.kazoostate.com, show times and ticket prices vary) now showcases rock, blues, country, and folk concerts. The interior is a rare example of the work of famed architect John Eberson, who re-created an exotic Mediterranean town with a working cloud machine and stars that really twinkle.

Unlike many other Michigan towns, Kalamazoo experienced few boom-and-bust cycles in the last century, thanks to its plentiful and diversified industry. Houses were well maintained, and many stayed in families for generations. You can see the results of that care in the **South Street Historic District.** Impressive houses went up here between 1847 and World War I, in architectural styles ranging from Greek and Gothic Revival to Georgian and Tudor. Just north of Kalamazoo College, along Stuart and Woodward between West Michigan and North, business owners built large suburban homes in what is now known as the **Stuart Avenue Historic District** to display the wealth they amassed after the Civil War. You'll find a variety of elaborate Queen Anne, Italianate, and Eastlake homes here, including the meticulously restored **Stuart Avenue Inn** bed-and-breakfast.

If you appreciate Frank Lloyd Wright's architecture, the city's **Parkwyn Village,** at Taliesin and Parkwyn Drives in southwest Kalamazoo, was designed as a cooperative neighborhood by the famed architect in the late 1940s and includes examples of his Usonian style. You can view more Wright homes in the 11000 block of Hawthorne, south of the city of Galesburg.

SHOPPING

Downtown Kalamazoo, which is known as "Central City," offers six distinct shopping districts: Kalamazoo Mall, East End, South Town, Haymarket, Arcadia, and Bronson Park. The streets around the Kalamazoo State Theatre constitute **Kalamazoo Mall** (www.downtownkalamazoo.org), home to coffeehouses, galleries, restaurants, bakeries, and a diverse selection of resale and vintage clothing shops. Stretching from Lovell to Eleanor Streets, it was the first open-air downtown pedestrian mall created by blocking a city street to car traffic. Like many downtown shopping districts, it's suffered from the encroachment of suburban malls, but still offers popular cafés, funky stores that cater to the college crowd, and a gourmet market, among other delights.

If you haven't tired of shopping for antiques in Michigan, head for the **Kalamazoo Antiques Market** (130 N. Edwards St., 269/226-9788), which represents more than 30 quality dealers selling vintage clothing, unique jewelry, vinyl records, pottery, and lots of household stuff. You might also consider the **Emporium** (313 E. Kalamazoo Ave., 269/381-0998, 7pm-9pm Mon.-Fri., 2pm-6pm Sat.-Sun.), worth seeking out for its vintage furniture, despite its unusual hours.

To explore a vintage newsstand, visit the **Michigan News Agency** (308 W. Michigan Ave., 269/343-5958, www.michigannews.biz, 7am-8pm daily), which dates to the 1940s. Inside, you'll find everything from the everyday to the truly eclectic: the usual maps, tobaccos, comics, and newspapers, as well as more than 6,000 magazine titles and 15,000 paperbacks.

The friendly and knowledgeable owners don't seem to mind if you spend the better half of the day perusing their publications. There's also a small selection of books by local writers.

SPORTS AND RECREATION
Spectator Sports
While Kalamazoo might not boast the professional teams of, say, Detroit, sports fans will still find several seasonal options here. If you'd like to catch an IHL hockey game, consider visiting the city October-April, when the **Kalamazoo Wings** (3600 Vanrick Dr., 269/345-1125, www.wingsstadium.com, game times and ticket prices vary) thrash across the ice of Wings Stadium. Of course, if that's not enough, consider the full roster of men's and women's sports at Western Michigan University, where the **WMU Broncos** (1903 W. Michigan Ave., 269/387-8092, www.wmubroncos.com, game times and ticket prices vary) play everything from basketball to soccer to football.

Hiking and Bird-Watching
Nature lovers won't find a much better spot than the **Kalamazoo Nature Center** (7000 N. Westnedge Ave., 269/381-1574, www.naturecenter.org, 9am-5pm Mon.-Sat., 1pm-5pm Sun., $6 adults, $5 seniors 55 and over, $4 children 4-13). At 1,100 acres, it ranks as one of the largest nature centers in the Midwest, with over 11 miles of trails, an arboretum, an herb garden, a restored 1858 homestead housing crafts and local artifacts, and a peaceful glen that was the favorite stomping ground of author James Fenimore Cooper. Other exhibits include a free-flying butterfly zone, an indoor bird-watching area that looks out over the trees and grounds, and a re-created 1830s settlers' farm.

ACCOMMODATIONS
Lee's Inn (2615 Fairfield Rd., 269/382-6100, www.leesinn.com, $77-125 d) is one of the more affordable lodgings in town, with an indoor pool, high-speed wireless Internet access, and a bright, airy breakfast room. For other reasonable deals, Kalamazoo offers a wide assortment of chain hotels and motels, including **Comfort Inn** (739 W. Michigan Ave., 269/384-2800, www.comfortinn.com, $100-145 d), an ideal location for exploring the downtown area.

For a more distinctive experience, consider the **(** **Stuart Avenue Inn** (229 Stuart Ave., 269/342-0230, www.stuartavenueinn.com, $75-100 d), widely regarded as the city's best B&B. It comprises three adjacent 19th-century homes (including the Bartlett-Upjohn House of pharmaceutical fame) and lovely perennial gardens. The present owners furnished the inn's well-appointed rooms with many of their own antiques as well as goodies collected on shopping sprees around the state. The **Hall House Bed and Breakfast** (106 Thompson St., 269/343-2500, www.hallhouse.com, $109-199 d) offers six rooms in a restored 1923 home. Just steps away from private Kalamazoo College, it's popular with families of students and visiting professors.

FOOD
You can't leave Kalamazoo without stopping by the highly touted **(** **Bell's Eccentric Café** (355 E. Kalamazoo Ave., 269/382-2332, www.bellsbeer.com, 11am-midnight Mon.-Wed., 11am-1am Thurs.-Sat., noon-midnight Sun., $3-7), part of Bell's Brewery, formerly known as the Kalamazoo Brewing Company, a forerunner of the brewpub craze. Owner Larry Bell's more than 20 acclaimed brews, including Amber Ale, Kalamazoo Stout, and Cherry Stout, have won a loyal following in Chicago, where much of his output is sold. While you're downing a few pints, nibble on some munchies in the smoke-free eatery. This appealing spot has board games scattered around the tables, table tennis, and live acoustic music on Friday and Saturday nights. In warm weather, casual crowds congregate on the outdoor "beer garden" patio.

INFORMATION AND SERVICES
For more information about the Kalamazoo area, contact the **Discover Kalamazoo** (141

E. Michigan Ave., Ste. 100, 269/488-9000, www.discoverkalamazoo.com, 8am-5pm Mon.-Fri.). For local news, entertainment, and sports, consult the **Kalamazoo Gazette** (www.mlive.com/kzgazette) or watch **WWMT** (www.wwmt.com), the CBS television affiliate that serves Battle Creek, Kalamazoo, and Grand Rapids.

With its assortment of groceries, pharmacies, gas stations, laundries, banks, and other helpful establishments, Kalamazoo can fulfill most travelers' needs. For mailing issues, you'll find over a dozen **post offices** in and around Kalamazoo; visit www.usps.com for locations and hours.

In case of an emergency, dial **911** from any cell or public phone. For medical assistance, consult **Borgess Health** (1521 Gull Rd., 269/226-7000, www.borgess.com).

GETTING THERE AND AROUND

Kalamazoo is accessible via plane, train, bus, and, of course, car. The **Kalamazoo/Battle Creek International Airport** (AZO, 5235 Portage Rd., 269/388-3668, www.azoairport.com), for example, is just south of town; from there, you can hail a taxi or hire a rental car. In addition, **Amtrak** (800/872-7245, www.amtrak.com), **Greyhound** (269/337-8201 or 800/231-2222, www.greyhound.com), and **Indian Trails** (800/292-3831, www.indiantrails.com) all serve the same station (459 N. Burdick St.).

If, however, you've chosen to drive around the state of Michigan, you can easily reach Kalamazoo via I-94, US-131, and several state highways or county roads. From downtown Detroit, for instance, you can take M-10 North and I-75 South, merge onto I-96 West, continue onto M-14 West, and follow I-94 West to Kalamazoo; without traffic, the 143-mile trip should take less than 2.25 hours. From Chicago, meanwhile, you can take I-90 East, merge onto I-94 East, and follow the I-94 East Business Route/US-131 Business Route to Kalamazoo, a 147-mile trip that usually requires about 2.25 hours. Just be advised that,

en route from the Windy City, parts of I-90 East and I-94 East serve as the Indiana Toll Road.

Of course, you can also reach Kalamazoo from Grand Rapids via US-131 South and the US-131 South Business Route; without traffic, this 51-mile journey should take about 49 minutes. Once here, you can simply stick with your car, opt for walking or biking when convenient, or use **Kalamazoo Metro Transit** (269/337-8222, www.kmetro.com, one-way $1.50 adults, $0.75 seniors and children less than 48 inches tall), which provides bus service in and around town.

GREATER KALAMAZOO
C Air Zoo

Just south of the Kalamazoo/Battle Creek International Airport, you'll spy the excellent **Air Zoo** (6151 Portage Rd., 269/382-6555, www.airzoo.org, 9am-5pm Mon.-Sat., noon-5pm Sun., $10 pp). Considered the nation's premier museum of military aircraft, the three-campus Air Zoo stands out because of its emphasis on education. Not only can visitors examine vintage planes, like the Curtiss P-40 Warhawk or Grumman F-14A Tomcat, they can also sit at the controls of state-of-the-art flight simulators and get a small taste of what fighter pilots experience.

This enormous museum also features educational flight-related displays, such as a 2,000-square-foot exhibit chronicling the history of aircraft carriers (complete with over 400 archival photographs and three large models). In addition, the Air Zoo's original facility (now its East Campus) houses the Michigan Space Science Center, a 17,000-square-foot repository of space artifacts, from a Gemini crew-training simulator to a full-size replica of a Mercury space capsule. This impressive facility, much of which was once located near Jackson, offers an interactive exhibit as well. The International Space Station Exhibit uses hands-on demonstrations, simulations, models, theaters, and other experiences to illustrate the history and everyday operations of the largest international peacetime project in the world.

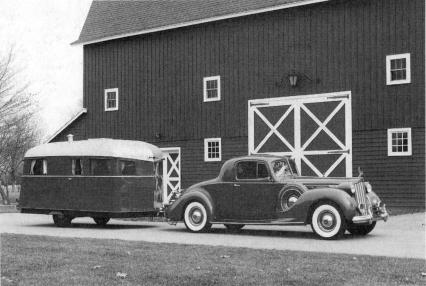
Gilmore Car Museum, near Kalamazoo

Gilmore Car Museum

While in the Kalamazoo area, you simply must put aside a few hours for the **Gilmore Car Museum** (6865 Hickory Rd., Hickory Corners, 269/671-5089, www.gilmorecarmuseum.org, 9am-5pm Mon.-Fri., 9am-6pm Sat.-Sun. May-Oct., $12 adults, $11 seniors 62 and over, $9 children 7-15), considered one of the top five car museums in the United States. Situated on 90 landscaped acres northeast of Kalamazoo, not far from Gull Lake, the Gilmore Car Museum houses nearly 200 vintage automobiles in several restored historic barns. Exhibits range from an 1899 locomotive to the infamous 1948 Tucker to muscle cars of the 1970s. Other treats include a new miniature museum and an authentic 1941 diner, a great place for an afternoon snack. All buildings are wheelchair-accessible.

Grand Rapids

Grand Rapids—the state's second-largest city, with a population of 190,400—owes its development and name to the rapids of the free-flowing Grand River, a place of gathering and exchange since Louis Campau established a trading post here in 1826. The power and transportation afforded by the river, coupled with the abundance of wood from the neighboring forests, made the growth of the city's furniture industry a natural.

By 1854, logging had become an important industry, and Grand Rapids entered the most vigorous phase of its development. Huge quantities of logs were floated down the Grand to Grand Rapids' mills. Upstream mill owners, seeing the valuable timber floating unattended

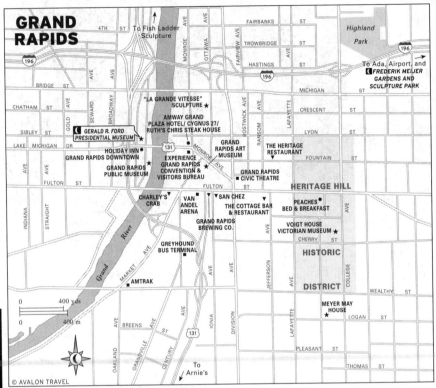

THE HEARTLAND

past their mills, often stole the logs and cut them into lumber. This practice, known as "hogging," precipitated fierce brawls along the Flat, Rogue, Grand, and other area rivers and caused the birth of the "river driver," a colorful character who rode the logs downstream to ensure they reached their final destination safely.

Grand Rapids was not always the Calvinist stronghold it is today. During the 1860s, Campau Square was notorious for its brothels, gambling houses, and basement bars. It became better known for its furniture making in 1876, when the city's wares were displayed at America's centennial celebration in Philadelphia. In 1880, the incorporation of the Wolverine Chair and Furniture Company helped solidify that reputation; by 1900, Grand Rapids was nicknamed "Furniture City." The moniker still sticks today, since the area

serves as headquarters for Herman Miller and Steelcase, two of the largest office furniture companies in the country.

Grand Rapids went through a decline in the early 1980s, but somehow managed to reinvent itself as a thriving showcase for the arts, local history, and business. Today, the downtown sparkles with busy hotels, shopping areas, pedestrian malls, and public artworks. One of the most striking downtown sights is Alexander Calder's dramatic sculpture, *La Grande Vitesse*, a 42-ton strawberry-red sculpture that pays homage to the rapids that built the city. Controversial at first, it has since become a symbol of Grand Rapids. More recent city improvements include a new ecofriendly Grand Rapids Public Museum and the addition of one of the nation's largest lion exhibits at the John Ball Zoo.

Much of the redevelopment can be attributed to the area's loyal and exceedingly generous business community, a group that includes the headquarters for the Meijer Corporation (pioneers of the dual grocery/discount store phenomenon) and Amway, that genius of direct marketing, which racks up annual sales in the billions. The names DeVos and Van Andel—the founding families of Amway—seem to top the list of every charitable cause in town. Most of the business and civic leaders are alumni of nearby Holland's Hope College (part of the Reformed Church in America) or of Grand Rapids' Calvin College, run by the Christian Reformed Church. Grand Rapids, by the way, is the epicenter of religious publishing in the United States.

Hardworking Grand Rapids may be known for its Protestant work ethic, but a surprising amount of diversity hides beneath the city's Calvinist veneer. Yes, it's a Republican stronghold, but Grand Rapids is also home to an active alternative press and one of the state's largest Native American populations. The city's older neighborhoods celebrate a mix of cultures, comprising Asian, Latino, African American, Lithuanian, Ukrainian, German, and Polish communities.

SIGHTS
Heritage Hill Historic District

As a manufacturing city with many locally owned businesses, Grand Rapids housed early residents who earned considerable riches and weren't shy about displaying them. Prominent families, including those who owned the city's famed furniture factories, built their mansions on the city's hillside where they could overlook their domain, from far above the smoke and soot their factories generated. **Heritage Hill** (616/459-8950, www.heritagehillweb.org) was their neighborhood of choice from roughly 1840 through 1920. Located just east of downtown, it displays the wealth of Grand Rapids' lumber boom, with more than 60 architectural styles reflected in its 1,300 residences. Considered the city's first neighborhood, Heritage Hill is now one of the largest urban historic districts in the country.

As in most of America's urban areas, today's Heritage Hill residents are more economically and racially diverse. The neighborhood is overseen by the Heritage Hill Association, an active group of organizers who work hard at maintaining both their property and the area's sense of community. Among the most spectacular homes are those built by the city's one-time lumber barons, plus a few others designed or inspired by Frank Lloyd Wright.

The highlight has to be the **Meyer May House** (450 Madison Ave., 616/246-4821, www.meyermayhouse.steelcase.com, 10am-1pm Tues. and Thurs., 1pm-4pm Sun., free), an anomaly in this predominantly Victorian neighborhood. It was designed in 1906 by Frank Lloyd Wright for a prominent local clothier, founder of the May's clothing store chain. Vincent Scully, an architectural historian, has called the Meyer May House the most beautifully and completely restored of Wright's Prairie houses. "To come suddenly into that interior . . . is to be wholly caught up and carried along by something rarely experienced: absolute peace, integral order, deep quiet grandeur and calm—all of it achieved in a house of no more than moderate size," he has said. Through the generous funding of Steelcase, the nationally famous Grand Rapids office furniture maker, the house has since been restored to reflect Wright's original organic building concept, with custom-made furniture, art glass, carpets, light fixtures, even linens.

◖ Gerald R. Ford Presidential Museum

The **Gerald R. Ford Presidential Museum** (303 Pearl St. NW, 616/254-0400, www.ford.utexas.edu, 9am-5pm daily, closed on major holidays, $7 adults, $6 seniors, $3 children 6-18) honors Michigan's only native-born president in this triangular building on the west bank of the Grand River. The nation's 38th president—named to the post on August 9, 1974, after the infamous resignation of Richard Nixon—Ford grew up in Grand Rapids and represented the

THE HEARTLAND

© DANIEL MARTONE

Gerald R. Ford Presidential Museum

Fifth Congressional District in Michigan from 1948 to 1973, when he became the nation's vice president.

Renovated in 1997, the museum portrays both the private life and public challenges of Ford, president for just two years. The most popular attraction is the full-size replica of the Oval Office as it looked while Ford was president and the holographic tour of the White House. Other exhibits include a surprisingly moving section on Nixon's resignation and Ford's subsequent pardon, the events surrounding the fall of Saigon, and a multimedia re-creation of 1970s pop culture. Visitors can also see President Ford's burial site.

Other Museums

In 2007, the longstanding **Grand Rapids Art Museum** (GRAM, 101 Monroe Center, 616/831-1000, www.artmuseumgr.org, 10am-5pm Tues.-Thurs. and Sat., 10am-9pm Fri., noon-5pm Sun., $8 adults, $7 seniors and students, $5 children 6-17) was moved from its original spot and reborn within an environmentally friendly building that has been hailed by architectural critics throughout the world. Inside, extensive collections include fine 19th- and 20th-century prints, paintings, photographs, sculptures, and decorative arts with an emphasis on furniture.

The art museum's major competition for the dollars and time of museum-goers is the **Grand Rapids Public Museum** (272 Pearl St. NW, 616/456-3977, www.grmuseum.org, 9am-5pm Mon.-Sat., noon-5pm Sun., closed on major holidays, $8 adults, $3 children 3-17). Arguably the city's best museum, the Public is housed in a spectacular structure and ranks as the largest general museum in the state. It cost $35 million to build in 1995, much of it a gift from Amway cofounder Jay Van Andel.

The Grand Rapids Public Museum holds an outstanding permanent collection of incredible size and scope. Here, you can witness the massive flywheel of a 1905 Corliss-type steam engine that once powered the city's furniture factories in "The Furniture City" exhibit, walk through a re-creation of 1890s Grand Rapids,

© DANIEL MARTONE

Grand Rapids Public Museum

take a turn aboard a restored 1928 Spillman carousel, or see stars at the Roger B. Chaffee Planetarium. The groundbreaking exhibit "Anishinabek: The People of This Place" sensitively explores the culture and artifacts of the Anishinabe people, western Michigan's Native Americans. An illuminating explanation of the state's indigenous Ottawa, Chippewa, and Potawatomi peoples, it includes video interviews that trace the modern challenges of Native Americans and the stereotypes that continue to haunt them.

◖ Frederik Meijer Gardens and Sculpture Park

Another local benefactor—Fred Meijer, owner and founder of the Meijer grocery/discount stores—has given back to his hometown with the spectacular **Frederik Meijer Gardens and Sculpture Park** (1000 E. Beltline Ave. NE, 616/957-1580, www.meijergardens.org, 9am-5pm Mon. and Wed.-Sat., 9am-9pm Tues., noon-5pm Sun., $12 adults, $9 seniors and students, $6 children 5-13, $4 children 3-4), which

opened its doors in 1995. Its 125 acres encompass a 15,000-square-foot tropical conservatory (the state's largest), an outdoor area of colorful flower gardens complemented by ponds, woods, and wetlands, and an extensive collection of sculpture—including works by Auguste Rodin, Henry Moore, Claes Oldenburg, and Coosje van Bruggen. Quotations throughout the gardens by Michigan poets, such as Theodore Roethke and Jim Harrison, connect people to the plants.

THE ARTS

Grand Rapids' performing arts scene is rich and diverse, offering everything from Michigan's only professional ballet company to summertime concerts at the outdoor amphitheater in Frederik Meijer Gardens. One must-see is the **Grand Rapids Civic Theatre** (30 Division Ave., 616/222-6650, www.grct.org, show times and ticket prices vary), which represents a grand piece of the city's architecture. The largest community theater in Grand Rapids and one of the largest in the United States, this impressive

THE MAKING OF A PRESIDENT

Born in Omaha, Nebraska, as Leslie Lynch King Jr., the man who would eventually be known as Gerald R. Ford Jr. (1913-2006), actually spent the first few years of his life, along with his mother, Dorothy Ayer Gardner, at the home of his maternal grandparents in Grand Rapids, Michigan. Before he'd reached the age of three, Ford's mother, who had previously divorced his abusive father in 1913, married a paint salesman named Gerald Rudolff Ford. Never formally adopted, the future president didn't legally change his name to Gerald Rudolph Ford Jr. until 1935.

Raised in Grand Rapids with three half-brothers from his mother's second marriage, Ford seemed to enjoy a solid relationship with both his mother and his stepfather. As a child, he was involved in the Boy Scouts of America, earning the highest rank of Eagle Scout. In fact, he was the only U.S. president to have earned such an honor.

While in Grand Rapids, Ford attended Grand Rapids South High School, where he became a star athlete and the captain of his football team. Attracting the attention of college recruiters, he eventually enrolled as an undergraduate in the University of Michigan, where, as center and linebacker, he helped the Wolverines achieve undefeated seasons and national titles in both 1932 and 1933. Following his graduation in 1935 with a Bachelor of Arts in economics, he accepted an assistant coaching job for the football and boxing teams at Yale University, after which he attended and graduated from Yale Law School.

Over the ensuing decades, he opened a law practice with a friend, enlisted in the U.S. Navy during World War II, married a department store fashion consultant, with whom he had four children, and spent 25 years as a member of the U.S. House of Representatives. Eventually, he replaced Spiro Agnew as vice president in the Nixon presidential administration and, following Nixon's Watergate scandal and subsequent resignation, became the nation's 38th president. During his one presidential term,

landmark offers six main-stage and two children's productions annually in a restored 1903 theater once known as The Majestic.

ACCOMMODATIONS AND FOOD

For one of the best downtown values, consider the **Holiday Inn Grand Rapids Downtown** (310 Pearl St. NW, 616/235-7611, www.holidayinn. com, $102-174 d), centrally located near the Gerald Ford and other public museums, with high-speed Internet access, a pool, a fitness center, a restaurant, and clean, attractive rooms. Pets are allowed.

At the other end of the spectrum, the ◖ **Amway Grand Plaza Hotel** (187 Monroe NW, 616/774-2000, www.amwaygrand.com, $170-275 d) ranks as the finest lodging in Grand Rapids and one of Michigan's top hotels. Two hotels actually make up the complex: the original 1913 Pantlind, and the newer Glass

Tower, completed in 1981. Depending on your mood, you can choose from a lush traditional or cool contemporary room. In all, the two house more than 680 rooms, nine restaurants and coffee shops, several elegant boutiques, and a state-of-the-art fitness center.

The city's oldest operating bar and restaurant, **The Cottage Bar & Restaurant** (18 LaGrave Ave., 616/454-9088, www.cottagebar.biz, 11am-midnight Mon.-Thurs., 11am-12:30am Fri.-Sat., $4-8), concocts Grand Rapids' best burgers and three different styles of chili. The outside café is a popular meeting place in good weather.

Tapas, paella, and other specialties of the Iberian peninsula draw crowds tired of the all-too-common prime rib and pasta to sunny ◖ **San Chez** (38 W. Fulton, 616/774-8272, www.sanchezbistro.com, 11:30am-10pm Mon.-Thurs., 11:30am-11pm Fri., noon-11pm Sat., 4pm-10pm Sun., $4-20). Lively and fun, it he made the controversial decision to pardon Richard Nixon for any crimes that he might have committed against the country during his presidency. In addition, he tried to battle rising inflation, confronted a potential swine flu epidemic, supported the Equal Rights Amendment, officially ended American involvement in the Vietnam War, faced two assassination attempts, and ultimately lost his bid for reelection to Jimmy Carter.

In the years following his presidency, Ford kept fairly busy. He moved with his wife to Denver, Colorado, and, in 1977, established the Gerald R. Ford Institute of Public Policy at Michigan's Albion College. In 1981, he opened the Gerald R. Ford Presidential Library on the North Campus of his alma mater, Ann Arbor's University of Michigan, and established the Gerald R. Ford Presidential Museum in Grand Rapids. By 1988, he was a member of several corporate boards, and in 2001, he received the John F. Kennedy Profiles in Courage Award for his controversial decision to pardon Richard Nixon in order to heal the nation following the Watergate scandal. That was the same year that he broke from the Republican Party by supporting equal treatment of gay and lesbian couples.

Five years later, at the age of 93, President Ford died at his home in Rancho Mirage, California, having become the longest-lived U.S. President, being 45 days older than Ronald Reagan was when he passed away. He also had the distinction of being the only person ever to hold the presidential office without being elected as president or vice president. Of course, despite his rocky road as president, he was considered by many to be an honest, kind-hearted, likable "everyman," no doubt a hallmark of his Midwestern roots. It's no wonder, then, that Grand Rapids citizens are generally proud of their native son – and perhaps it explains why several sites in and around Grand Rapids bear his name, including the Gerald R. Ford Middle School, the Gerald R. Ford International Airport, and the Gerald R. Ford Freeway, the stretch of I-196 that passes through Allegan, Ottawa, and Kent Counties.

draws an eclectic crowd with entrées such as spiced Moroccan meatballs and lamb ribs with raspberry chili sauce.

Charley's Crab (63 Market Ave. SW, 616/459-2500, www.muer.com, 11:30am-4pm and 4:30pm-10pm Mon.-Thurs., 11:30am-4pm and 4:30pm-11pm Fri., 4:30pm-11pm Sat., 10am-9pm Sun., $12-35) is part of Chuck Muer's well-loved, nationwide chain of seafood restaurants. Try one of the fresh catches or one of the always-tasty pastas, or load up on carbs at the Sunday brunch. The signature rolls have been copied by a number of restaurants across the state. In good weather, ask for an outside table overlooking the Grand River.

INFORMATION AND SERVICES

For more information about the Grand Rapids area, contact the **Experience Grand Rapids Convention & Visitors Bureau** (171 Monroe Ave. NW, Ste. 700, 616/459-8287, www.visitgrandrapids.org, 9am-5pm Mon.-Fri.) or the **Grand Rapids Area Chamber of Commerce** (111 Pearl St. NW, 616/771-0300, www.grandrapids.org, 8:30am-5pm Mon.-Fri.). For official city-related information, visit www.grand-rapids.mi.us. For local news, entertainment, and sports, consult the **Grand Rapids Press** (www.mlive.com/grpress) or watch **WOOD** (www.woodtv.com), the NBC television affiliate.

Grand Rapids offers all the services you might require, including gas stations, laundries, and banks. For groceries, prescriptions, and other supplies, stop by a **Meijer** superstore (www.meijer.com); there are several in the area. For mailing needs, you'll find over a dozen **post offices** in and around Grand Rapids; visit www.usps.com for locations and hours.

In case of an emergency, dial **911** from any cell or public phone. For medical assistance, consult **Spectrum Health** (866/989-7999, www.spectrum-health.org), which oversees several hospitals and medical centers in the region.

GETTING THERE AND AROUND

As with several other towns in the Heartland, Grand Rapids is accessible via plane, train, bus, and, naturally, car. **Gerald R. Ford International Airport** (GRR, 5500 44th St. SE, 616/233-6000, www.grr.org), for instance, lies southeast of town; from there, you can hire a rental car via Avis, Budget, and other national chains or opt for a luxury sedan from **Metro Cars** (616/827-6700 or 800/456-1701, www.metrocars.com), which offers 24-hour dispatch service from the airports in both Detroit and Grand Rapids. Typically, a ride from the Ford airport to downtown Grand Rapids will cost about $40. Meanwhile, **Amtrak** (431 Wealthy St. SW, 800/872-7245, www.amtrak.com) also serves the city. In addition, it's also possible to reach Grand Rapids by bus; **Greyhound** (616/456-1700 or 800/231-2222, www.greyhound.com) and **Indian Trails** (800/292-3831, www.indiantrails.com) both provide service to the same station (250 Grandville Ave. SW).

Of course, if you've chosen to drive around the state of Michigan, you can also reach Grand Rapids via I-96, I-196, US-131, and several state highways and county roads. From downtown Detroit, for instance, you can take M-10 North, merge onto I-696 West, continue onto I-96 West, and follow I-196 West to Grand Rapids; without traffic, the 158-mile trip should take around 2.25 hours. From Chicago, meanwhile, you can take I-90 East, merge onto I-94 East, and follow I-196 North and I-196 East, a 178-mile trip that usually requires about 2.75 hours. Just be advised that, en route from the Windy City, parts of I-90 East and I-94 East serve as the Indiana Toll Road.

Once in Grand Rapids, Michigan's second-largest city, you'll probably want to stick with your car to get around. If you're tired of driving, though, you can almost always hop aboard **The Rapid** (616/776-1100, www.ridetherapid.org, one-way $1.50 adults, $0.75 seniors, children under 42 inches free), an outstanding public transit system that even links Grand Rapids to surrounding towns, from Wyoming to Grandville.

Lansing and East Lansing

In the 1940s, the WPA *Guide to Michigan* described Lansing as a place where "the political activity of a state capital, the rumbling tempo of an industrial city, and the even temper of a farming community are curiously blended." Over 70 years later, it's still an apt description.

Curiously, Lansing was developed by a legislative prank. Until 1847, Detroit was the state's capital, as mandated in a provision in the 1835 constitution. When the provision expired, legislators (two of whom had been burned in effigy by Detroit rowdies) decided that the Detroit border was in constant danger of invasion and voted to move the capital. Where to put it, however, posed a problem. After months of wrangling and debating just

about every settlement in lower Michigan, someone jokingly suggested Lansing, a wide spot in the road that consisted of one log house and a sawmill. Amid laughs and for want of a better solution, it won the vote. The state's seat of government was moved in 1847.

Even the name was a lark. The original settlement was named after Lansing, New York, and a New York chancellor. When it became the new capital, many wanted to rename the tiny town Michigan or Michigamme. But the legislature once again became bogged down in political infighting. Lansing it remained.

Once the decision was made and the place had a name, it began to grow. By the time the

© 123RF.COM

the state capitol building in Lansing

city was incorporated in 1859, it had 4,000 residents, a number of small businesses, a new capitol building, and two newspapers to cover it all. The city received another economic boost in the early 1900s, when R. E. Olds began making his "merry Oldsmobile" here.

Today, Lansing is the state's governmental seat, headquarters for many trade and professional associations, and home to heavy industry. East Lansing, a neighboring community that is part of the capital city in all respects except government, is the home of Michigan State University, part of the Big Ten conference. Ironically, the powers-that-be also selected the university site by default.

Urban decay and rampant freeway construction have bruised downtown Lansing, and the city is often all but empty after five o'clock. While it has been described as a city in search of a center, it has a surprising amount to offer once you find it: good museums, a full plate of MSU events, some of the state's loveliest and most accessible gardens, and even a minor league baseball team, the Lansing Lugnuts.

SIGHTS
◖ Michigan State University

Dubbed "Moo U," Michigan State University was established in 1855 as the country's first agricultural college and the forerunner of the nationwide land-grant university system. Despite its nicknames and rather well-known reputation as a party school, the campus has a long, rich history and an excellent reputation in many fields of study—especially agricultural ones, of course. Credit for its founding goes to a group of enlightened Michigan farmers who began lobbying in 1849 for a state college to promote modern agriculture. They chose the 677 acres of forest five miles east of the new state capital, in part because they wanted the school to be autonomous and not tied to an existing university.

Today, the MSU campus has grown to more than 5,000 beautifully landscaped acres, home to more than 7,000 different species and varieties of trees, shrubs, and vines. In the older part of the campus, curving drives and Gothic buildings create a park-like setting, shaded by

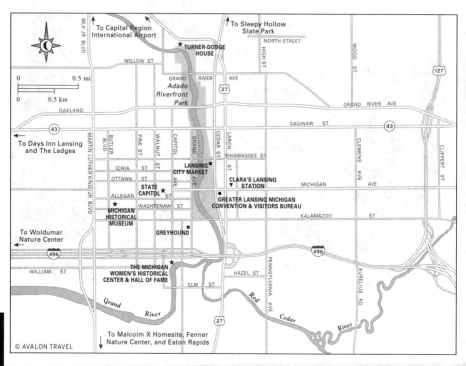

© AVALON TRAVEL

huge beeches and some gnarled white oaks that date back more than 200 years. Students walk to class through what has become a true arboretum with the passing of time, home to more than 5,000 varieties of woodsy plants and trees.

The campus has long been regarded as one giant outdoor laboratory. Very few planted environments in the Midwest have enjoyed such sustained commitment for more than 150 years. At one point, a school policy expected three hours per day of manual labor from all students, part of the hands-on laboratory approach that helped the university maintain the campus and also enabled poor students to afford a college education. Today, both students and professional landscapers maintain the university's impressive collection of gardens.

Campus Gardens

Among MSU's extensive plantings are the **Horticulture Gardens** (B-110 Plant and Soil Sciences Building, 517/353-3770, www.hrt. msu.edu/our-gardens, sunrise-sunset daily, free). The gardens are responsible for transforming a bleak-looking, post-1960 section of campus into a dramatic environment. Once as flat and bare as the newest subdivision, the 14-acre area is now full of pergolas, gazebos, arbors, and topiary. The entrance is off Bogue Street, south of Wilson Road, not far from the Wharton Center. Before venturing into the gardens, pick up a map at the Plant and Soil Sciences Building.

South of the Horticulture Gardens is the year-round **Clarence E. Lewis Landscape Arboretum** (517/355-5191, www.hrt.msu.edu, sunrise-sunset daily, free), dedicated in 1984 as an instructional arboretum for students interested in landscape development. The ever-growing collection of demonstration gardens experiment with vegetables, fruit, herbs, conifers, and native plants. You'll also be able

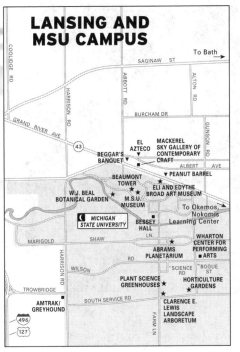

LANSING AND MSU CAMPUS

has been called one of the Midwest's best-kept secrets. In 2001, Michigan's leading public natural and cultural history museum also became the state's first museum to receive Smithsonian affiliate status. Three floors of exhibits concentrate on the history of the Great Lakes region; on display are numerous tools, quilts, folk art pieces, and other archaeological artifacts. Popular stops include the fur-trader's cabin and the life-size dinosaur dioramas.

Also on campus, at the intersection of Auditorium and Physics Roads, the relatively new **Eli and Edythe Broad Art Museum** (547 E. Circle Dr., 517/884-3900, www.broadmuseum.msu.edu, 10am-5pm Tues.-Thurs. and Sat.-Sun., noon-9pm Fri., closed on major holidays, free), which has inherited an impressive array of artwork from Kresge Art Museum, which closed in 2012, now houses a permanent collection that spans numerous centuries from the ancient Greek and Roman periods to the contemporary era. Designed by award-winning architect Zaha Hadid, the dynamic glass-and-steel edifice contains thousands of works of art, from Greek and Roman antiquities to Renaissance illuminations to 20th-century sculptures from artists like Alexander Calder and Jenny Holzer. Wide-ranging highlights include a dramatic *Vision of St. Anthony of Padua* by Francisco Zurburán, Andy Warhol's *Marilyn,* and a solid collection of art from the 1960s and 1970s, an era often overlooked by other museums. In keeping with the mission of the museum, future acquisitions will likely focus on other modern and contemporary works from 1945-present.

Other Museums

Part of the huge Michigan Library and Historical Center, the **Michigan Historical Museum** (702 W. Kalamazoo St., 517/373-3559, www.michigan.gov/museum, 9am-4:30pm Mon.-Fri., 10am-4pm Sat., 1pm-5pm Sun., free) has become a pilgrimage for many history buffs. With three floors and more than 30 permanent galleries, it tells a detailed story of Michigan's rise from wilderness to industrial powerhouse. Unlike at

to walk through a water garden, a sculpture garden, a Japanese garden, and a topiary garden, among other displays. Another campus area worth a special stop is the **W. J. Beal Botanical Garden** (www.cpa.msu.edu/beal), founded in 1873 and believed to be the oldest continuously operated garden of its type in the country. Situated between the Red Cedar River and West Circle Drive, this outdoor museum of living plants includes more than 2,000 species arranged by family and economic use, as well as exotic flowering landscape specimens and an enlightening section on endangered plants.

Campus Museums

With a collection of more than one million items, the 150-year-old **Michigan State University Museum** (W. Circle Dr., 517/355-7474, www.museum.msu.edu, 9am-5pm Mon.-Fri., 10am-5pm Sat., 1pm-5pm Sun., donation suggested), situated east of Beaumont Tower,

THE HEARTLAND

© GREATER LANSING CVB

a packed Spartan football game at MSU

many self-serving state museums, however, the narrative here is frank and intelligent. Placards explain how within a few generations of contact with European settlers, the state's Native American cultures transformed from self-sufficient lifestyles to those with a dependence on manufactured goods. The museum also contains an excellent and detailed copper-mining exhibit that's probably better than any found in the U.P. today. It features a walk-through copper mine and videos on life in the mining camps.

The 3rd floor chronicles more recent history, including the dawn of the automobile age and the Great Depression. On the lower level, a small but choice museum store offers lighthouse prints, jewelry crafted from Petoskey stones, and one of the state's best selections of books relating to the history of African Americans. The Michigan Library and Historical Center complex also houses the state archives and state library, a popular pilgrimage spot for genealogists from around the country. The building itself is of interest, too, designed by prominent

Detroit architect William Kessler, who relied largely on native building materials.

Not far from downtown Lansing, **The Michigan Women's Historical Center & Hall of Fame** (213 W. Main St., 517/484-1880, www.michiganwomenshalloffame.org, noon-5pm Wed.-Fri., noon-4pm Sat., 2pm-4pm Sun., $2.50 adults, $2 seniors, $1 children 5-18) honors the mostly unsung achievements of the state's native daughters through changing and permanent exhibitions. It celebrates the lives and contributions of Michigan women such as Sojourner Truth, a former slave and crusader for human rights; Laura Smith Haviland, an organizer of one of the state's first Underground Railroad stations; Anne Howard Shaw, a minister and physician whose dynamic leadership resulted in the passage of the 19th Amendment; and Gilda Radner, a courageous Detroit-born actress and comedienne.

Adado Riverfront Park
Lansing's Louis F. Adado Riverfront Park and Trail System ranks as one of the finest

urban green spaces in the state. This green-belt stretches on both sides of the Grand River from Kalamazoo Avenue just north of I-496 to North Street, three miles downstream. A riverwalk, popular with joggers and in-line skaters, runs along the entire east side of the river.

FAMOUS SPARTANS AND WOLVERINES

Established during the 19th century, both Michigan State University (MSU) and the University of Michigan (UM) have long, rich histories, with an even longer list of attendees and graduates. Here are just some of their more notable alumni:

FORMER MSU SPARTANS

- James Caan, actor
- Jim Cash, screenwriter
- John Engler, Michigan governor
- Jim Harrison, poet/novelist/essayist
- Earvin "Magic" Johnson, NBA player
- Sam Raimi, screenwriter/director/producer
- Robert Urich, actor
- Timothy Zahn, science fiction writer

FORMER UM WOLVERINES

- Selma Blair, actress
- Tom Brady, NFL quarterback
- Gerald R. Ford, U.S. president
- David Alan Grier, actor/comedian
- James Earl Jones, actor
- Lawrence Kasdan, screenwriter/director/producer
- Christine Lahti, actress
- Lucy Liu, actress
- Madonna, singer/actress
- Arthur Miller, playwright/essayist
- Susan Orlean, journalist
- David Paymer, actor/director
- Gilda Radner, actress/comedienne
- Mike Wallace, journalist/media personality

ENTERTAINMENT
Nightlife

East Lansing's best club is arguably **Rick's American Café** (224 Abbot Rd., 517/351-2288, www.ricksamericancafe.com, 6:30pm-close Mon.-Sat., 8pm-close Sun., cover charges vary), with great live acts, top-notch DJs, and drink specials every night. Things tend to get loud, so be prepared. **The Green Door Blues Bar & Grill** (2005 E. Michigan Ave., 517/482-6376, www.greendoorlive.com, 3pm-2am Mon.-Sat., 7pm-2am Sun., no cover) features some top-notch jazz and blues acts and dynamite drink specials, while offering the kind of moody lounge atmosphere you might find in a bigger city.

The Arts

BoarsHead Theater (425 S. Grand Ave., 517/484-7805, www.boarshead.org, show times and ticket prices vary), central Michigan's oldest professional theater, offers a season of dynamic productions at the city's Center for the Arts. This talented troupe performs October-May, and tries especially hard to make theater accessible to everyone.

Lovers of Broadway musicals, dance, comedy routines, and other special events can get their fill at the **Wharton Center for Performing Arts** (517/353-1982, www.whartoncenter.com, show times and ticket prices vary) on the MSU campus. This renowned venue boasts four unique stages—the Pasant Theatre, the MSU Concert Auditorium, the Fairchild Theatre, and Cobb Great Hall, where the Lansing Symphony Orchestra regularly performs.

SHOPPING

Not far from Adado Riverfront Park is the **Lansing City Market** (333 N. Cedar St., 517/483-7460, www.lansingcitymarket.com, 9am-6pm Tues. and Thurs.-Fri., 8am-5pm Sat.). Established in 1909 and relocated to its current spot in 1938, this year-round market attracts plenty of vendors offering fruit,

THE HEARTLAND

© GREATER LANSING CVB

Lansing's Michigan Historical Museum

vegetables, sandwiches, baked goods, and more. After making your purchases, eat at a picnic area near the river.

SPORTS AND RECREATION
Spectator Sports

MSU has a spectator sport for everyone, from football to basketball, hockey to baseball. For scheduling and ticket information on Spartan sporting events, contact the **MSU Athletic Ticket Office** (Jenison Field House, 517/355-1610, www.msuspartans.com, 10am-6pm Mon.-Fri. Aug.-Apr., 10am-5pm Mon.-Fri. May-July).

Golf

Although northern Michigan boasts even more award-winning golf courses, the Heartland has its share of eye-catchers. **Eagle Eye Golf Club** (15500 Chandler Rd., Bath, 517/641-4570, www.hawkhollow.com, daily Apr.-Oct., $40-65 pp) is one such place, located about 10 miles northeast of Lansing on I-69. Even better, this exceptional course is part of a spread that includes three others: the 9-hole Falcon, the 27-hole Hawk Hollow, and the Little Hawk putting course.

ACCOMMODATIONS AND FOOD

There's no lack of lodgings in the Lansing area, thanks to Big Ten fans and business travelers. You'll find a long list of reliable franchise options, including the **Hampton Inn** (525 N. Canal Rd., 517/627-8381, www.hamptoninn. com, $69-129 d), with well-maintained rooms and a free breakfast bar—an affordable spot for your football-weekend accommodations. For a bit more luxury, try the **Kellogg Hotel & Conference Center** (55 S. Harrison Rd., East Lansing, 517/432-4000, www.kelloggcenter. com, $114-369 d), the only four-star hotel on MSU's campus.

Housed in a restored Victorian-style train station, **Clara's Lansing Station** (637 E. Michigan Ave., 517/372-7120, www.claras.com, 11am-10pm Mon.-Thurs., 11am-midnight Fri.-Sat., 10am-10pm Sun., $9-24) is chock-full of vintage memorabilia, from old train schedules to antique sheet music. The enormous menu is equally eclectic, with a full range of salads, sandwiches, pizzas, pastas, hefty entrées, and ice cream drinks. If you're in the mood for seafood, check out **Mitchell's Fish Market** (2975 Preyde Blvd., 517/482-3474, www.mitchells-fishmarket.com, 11:30am-10pm Mon.-Thurs., 11:30am-11pm Fri.-Sat., 11:30am-9pm Sun., $15-32), where you'll find everything from exotic seafood to local catches.

You can't beat the combination of good burgers, friendly service, inexpensive prices, and cold beer at **Ⓒ Peanut Barrel** (521 E. Grand River, East Lansing, 517/351-0608, www.peanutbarrel.com, 10am-midnight daily, $4-6). The olive burger is simply to die for. For some good ol' Mexican cuisine, stop by **El Azteco** (225 Ann St., East Lansing, 517/351-9111, www.elazteco.me, 11am-midnight Tues.-Sat., 11am-11pm Sun.-Mon., $5-12), where the atmosphere isn't as dank as it once was, but the food still screams of fine dive cuisine.

INFORMATION AND SERVICES

For more information about Lansing and East Lansing, contact the **Greater Lansing Michigan Convention & Visitors Bureau** (1223 Turner St., Ste. 200, 888/252-6746, www.lansing.org, 8:30am-5pm Mon.-Fri.). For official city-related information, visit www.lansingmi.gov. For local news, entertainment, and sports, consult the **Lansing State Journal** (www.lansingstatejournal.com) or watch **WLNS** (www.wlns.com), the CBS television affiliate that serves Lansing and Jackson.

Between Lansing and East Lansing, you'll surely find everything you need during your trip, from gas stations to banks. For groceries, prescriptions, and other supplies, stop by a **Meijer** superstore (www.meijer.com); there are several in the area. For mailing needs, you'll find over a dozen **post offices** in the Lansing/East Lansing area; visit www.usps.com for locations and hours.

In case of an emergency, dial **911** from any cell or public phone. For medical services, stop by **Sparrow Hospital** (1215 E. Michigan Ave., 517/364-1000, www.sparrow.org).

GETTING THERE AND AROUND

To reach Lansing, travelers can fly into the **Capital Region International Airport** (LAN, 4100 Capital City Blvd., 517/321-6121, www.flylansing.com), where it's possible to hire a taxi or rent a car from one of four different rental agencies. You can also access the Lansing area by taking an **Amtrak** train (800/872-7245, www.amtrak.com) or **Greyhound** bus (517/332-2595 or 800/231-2222, www.greyhound.com) to the East Lansing station (1240 S. Harrison Rd.). There's an additional Greyhound station in Lansing (420 S. Grand Ave., 517/482-4246), which also serves as a regular stop for **Indian Trails** (800/292-3831, www.indiantrails.com).

Of course, if you're headed to Lansing and East Lansing via car, you'll be delighted to know that, given its centralized location in the Lower Peninsula's southern half, you can easily access the capital via I-69, I-96, US-127, and several state highways and county roads. From downtown Detroit, for instance, you can take M-10 North, merge onto I-696 West, continue onto I-96 West, and follow I-496 West to downtown Lansing; without traffic, the 91-mile trip should take around 80 minutes. From Chicago, meanwhile, you can take I-90 East, merge onto I-94 East, continue onto I-69 North, and follow I-496 East, a 218-mile trip that usually requires about 3.25 hours. Just be advised that, en route from the Windy City, parts of I-90 East and I-94 East serve as the Indiana Toll Road.

Once in Lansing, Michigan's capital city and one of the state's largest towns, you'll probably want to navigate the area via car. If you're tired of driving, though, simply hop aboard a bus operated by the well-regarded **Capital Area Transportation Authority** (CATA, 517/394-1000, www.cata.org, one-way $1.25-2.50 adults, children under 42 inches free). As with most capital cities and college towns, however, Lansing and East Lansing also have several reliable cab companies. One such option is **Spartan Cab/Yellow Cab** (517/482-1444, www.capitoltransport.com), which offers 24-hour service every day of the year.

Mount Pleasant

As exemplified by the city seal, Mount Pleasant's history was indelibly shaped by four elements—its Native American heritage as well as agriculture, education, and the discovery of oil. Native Americans, who had been promised lands in an 1855 treaty, began settling within Isabella County the following year. When a timber scout named David Ward purchased the land on the southern side of the Chippewa River, directly opposite what is today the Isabella Indian Reservation, he decided to call the fledgling village Mount Pleasant. Soon, merchants, artisans, and farmers flocked to the area.

The town gradually expanded, and by 1892, there was even a community college, the Central Michigan Normal School and Business Institute, which would eventually become today's Central Michigan University. The discovery of oil in 1928 changed the fortunes of the burgeoning town, which soon boasted hotels, restaurants, oil companies, and plenty of new residents. During the oil boom, many other industries left the area, but oil production kept Mount Pleasant from becoming a ghost town.

Today, Mount Pleasant (with a population of 26,180) is a more laid-back town, celebrated for its rich Chippewa heritage. Its two biggest attractions are, in fact, an Indian-owned casino and an annual powwow. Of course, the area's numerous golf courses, military memorials, recreational parks, and CMU football games also entice visitors.

ZIIBIWING CENTER

The Midwest's premier Native American museum, the **Ziibiwing Center of Anishinabe Culture & Lifeways** (6650 E. Broadway, 989/775-4750, www.sagchip.org/ziibiwing, 10am-6pm Mon.-Sat., $6.50 adults, $3.75 seniors 60 and over and children 5-17) demonstrates the rich culture and history of the Great Lakes' Anishinabe tribe. The permanent "Diba Jimooyung" exhibit illustrates the amazing history of the original inhabitants of the Great Lakes, including their prophecies and their struggle to preserve their land, language, and culture. At different times during the year, the museum often hosts traveling exhibits about tribes from other parts of Michigan and elsewhere in the United States.

ENTERTAINMENT AND EVENTS

◖ Soaring Eagle Casino and Resort

You might not think that one of the Midwest's largest casinos would be situated in the Mount Pleasant area—instead of in a more tourist-centric place along the coast—but it might make more sense when you consider that the Indian-owned **Soaring Eagle Casino and Resort** (6800 Soaring Eagle Blvd., 888/732-4537, www.soaringeaglecasino.com, 24 hours daily, prices vary) is located next to the state's largest Native American reservation, the Isabella Indian Reservation, home to the Saginaw Chippewa tribe. With its enormous gaming area, six restaurants, and more than 500 well-appointed rooms, the resort can pack in a ton of partygoers at any given moment. Even if you don't like gaming, you can still relax in one of the on-site pools or spend the day at the spa. After dining in one of the resort's eateries or fine restaurants, catch a show at the concert hall, where big-name entertainment often takes to the stage.

◖ Saginaw Chippewa Tribal Powwow

For over 20 years, the annual **Saginaw Chippewa Tribal Powwow** (7070 E. Broadway, 989/775-4000, www.sagchip.org, free) has offered visitors the opportunity to observe and experience traditional Native American dress, dancing, drumming, chanting, cuisine, and crafts. The competition, held in early August, attracts performers from all over the United

an exhibit at the Ziibiwing Center of Anishinabe Culture & Lifeways

THE HEARTLAND

States, making it one of the biggest events in the Indian Nation—and a terrific place for outsiders to learn about Native American culture.

SPORTS AND RECREATION
College Sports
Throughout the year, the Central Michigan University Chippewas stage a wide range of sporting events, from football to women's basketball. If you're interested in catching a game while you're in Mount Pleasant, contact the **CMU Athletics Ticket Office** (989/774-3045, www.cmuchippewas.com).

Golf
The Mount Pleasant area offers several decent golf courses. Two options include **Bucks Run Golf Club** (1559 S. Chippewa Rd., 989/773-6830, www.bucksrun.com, daily Apr.-Nov., $30-85 pp w/cart), situated on 290 gorgeous acres that include wetlands, three lakes, and the Chippewa River, and **Riverwood Resort** (1313 E. Broomfield Rd., 989/772-5726, www.riverwoodresort.com, daily Apr.-Oct., $12-48

pp), which offers 27 classic holes, a spacious clubhouse, several deluxe villas, and two dozen bowling lanes.

ACCOMMODATIONS AND FOOD
If you're looking for lodgings beyond the casino, check out **The Green Suites** (5665 E. Pickard Rd., 989/772-2905, www.greensuites. co, $140-200 d), Mount Pleasant's only all-suite hotel. With its proximity to the Soaring Eagle Resort and several nearby golf courses, it's an ideal spot for those visiting the Mount Pleasant area. Suites range in size, from 995-square-foot one-bedroom suites to spacious 1,687-square-foot chambers, but all contain a living room, a dining area, and a kitchen.

The Soaring Eagle Casino isn't the only game in town for food either. **The Brass Cafe and Saloon** (128 S. Main St., 989/772-0864, www.thebrasscafe.com, 11am-10pm Tues.-Sat., $8-16) offers a wide range of menu choices, featuring innovative American and global cuisine. Set within two turn-of-the-20th-century shopfronts, this popular eatery offers an intimate setting for relaxing after a hard day of golf or gambling.

INFORMATION AND SERVICES

For more information about Mount Pleasant, consult the **Mount Pleasant Area Convention & Visitors Bureau** (114 E. Broadway, 989/772-4433, www.mountpleasantwow.com, 8am-5pm Mon.-Fri.). For local and regional news, consult the **Morning Sun** (www.themorningsun.com).

Mount Pleasant might not be as large as other Heartland cities, but it still has its share of groceries, banks, gas stations, and the like. In fact, there's a **Meijer** superstore (www.meijer.com) and a **post office** (www.usps.com) at the same location (1015 E. Pickard St., 989/772-4700).

In case of an emergency, dial **911** from any phone. For medical services, head to **Central Michigan Community Hospital** (1221 South Dr., 989/772-6700, www.cmch.org).

GETTING THERE AND AROUND

To reach Mount Pleasant, which is conveniently situated in the middle of the Lower Peninsula, visitors can fly into **MBS International Airport** (MBS, 8500 Garfield Rd., Freeland, 989/695-5555, www.mbsairport.org), where it's possible to rent a car from one of five national rental agencies. From there, you can then take US-10 West and continue onto M-20 West, toward Mount Pleasant; the 39-mile trip will take about 50 minutes. **Greyhound** (989/772-4246 or 800/231-2222, www.greyhound.com) and **Indian Trails** (800/292-3831, www.indiantrails.com), meanwhile, also offer bus service to the area (300 W. Broomfield St.).

Of course, most folks will likely be driving from elsewhere in Michigan. Luckily, M-20 and US-127 pass directly through the Mount Pleasant area. So, it's a relative snap to reach Mount Pleasant from a variety of destinations. From Lansing, for instance, you can simply take I-496 East, merge onto US-127 North, and take the US-127 Business Route to Mount Pleasant, a 70-mile trip that normally takes a little over an hour. From downtown Detroit, meanwhile, you can take I-375 North, continue onto I-75 North, merge onto US-10 West, and follow M-20 West to Mount Pleasant; without traffic, this 155-mile trip should require less than 2.5 hours. If you're headed from northern Michigan, it's also easy to access Mount Pleasant. From Traverse City, for example, just take South Garfield Avenue, Voice Road, and Clark Road to M-113 East, turn right onto US-131 South and continue toward M-115 East, merge onto US-10 East, and follow US-127 South to Mount Pleasant; without traffic, the 112-mile trip will take roughly two hours. Once here, you can either drive around town or hop aboard one of the buses provided by the **Isabella County Transportation Commission** (ICTC, 2100 E. Transportation Dr., 989/772-9441 or 989/773-2913, one-way $2 adults, $1.50 children under 18, $1 seniors 60 and over), on which the students and faculty members of Central Michigan University greatly depend.

Midland

When the lumbermen withdrew from Midland to follow the green frontier north, the city might have become just another ghost town if it weren't for Herbert H. Dow. In 1890, Dow began a series of experiments to extract chemicals from the common salt brine that was below the surface of most of central Michigan, eventually founding Dow Chemical Company.

Although the 24-year-old was called "Crazy Dow" by the locals when he arrived in town with little but a good idea, he was a surprisingly farsighted inventor and humanitarian who founded a well-planned city of neat streets and good architecture. Today, this city of 42,000 continues to benefit from Dow's influence, and many of the city's attractions—from sports to cultural activities—bear his fingerprints.

SIGHTS

If your schedule's tight, and you have time for only one attraction in Midland, make it the **Dow Gardens** (1809 Eastman Ave., 800/362-4874, www.dowgardens.org, 9am-8:30pm daily mid-Apr.-Labor Day, 9am-6:30pm daily Labor Day-Oct., 9am-4:15pm daily Nov.-mid-Apr., $7 adults, $1 children 6-17) and the buildings designed by Alden B. Dow, Herbert's son. Alden Dow was one of Frank Lloyd Wright's original Taliesin fellows, and

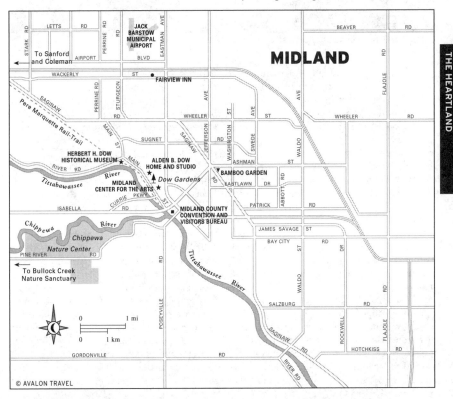

THE HEARTLAND

Alden Dow's home and studio, nestled beside the Dow Gardens

he had a long and distinguished architectural career. Like Wright, he tried to merge architecture and nature, insisting that "gardens never end and buildings never begin."

Developed by Herbert and Alden Dow over the course of more than 70 years, the garden's lovely landscape began as Herbert Dow's extended 10-acre backyard. When he arrived in Midland, the town was a barren landscape of sad stumps left behind by the lumber industry. In 1899, Dow began to landscape the space around his house to show his fellow townsfolk what they could do with their yards. He took his hobby seriously, and corresponded with Luther Burbank and other leading horticulturists of his era. During his lifetime, Dow planted 5,000 fruit trees, including 40 varieties of plums.

Unlike other historic American gardens, which owe a design debt to the formal gardens of Europe, the Dow Gardens are original, an unusual place of unfolding environments often likened to Japanese or Oriental styles. Always an enthusiastic traveler, Dow traveled to Japan frequently and became friends with a noted designer of Tokyo parks.

Texture, form, and contrast are as important here as more obvious displays of blooms. The gardens were renovated in the 1970s by Alden Dow as a retirement project, and more than a thousand trees and shrubs were added. Fantasy environments, including a jungle walk and a yew maze, reveal Dow's gentle, playful spirit. Don't miss the wheelchair-accessible sensory trail, the herb garden, and the extensive garden of perennials.

The **Midland Center for the Arts** (MCFTA, 1801 W. St. Andrews Rd., 989/631-5930, www. mcfta.org, hours and prices vary daily depending on venue and event) is another Alden Dow building. Inside the anthropomorphic, Guggenheim-style structure are two museums, two performance venues, several art studios and lecture halls, and the Saints & Sinners Lounge, a popular hangout before and after concerts and plays. Although there's a lot to see and do at the MCFTA, families favor the **Alden B. Dow Museum of Science and Art**

(10am-4pm Tues.-Wed. and Fri.-Sat., 10am-8pm Thurs. June-Aug., 10am-4pm Wed., Fri., and Sat., 10am-8pm Thurs., 1pm-5pm Sun. Sept.-May, $9 adults, $6 children 4-14, children under 4 free), which features rotating art and science exhibits, a hands-on Hall of Ideas, and a ferocious-looking mastodon that's especially popular with kids.

RECREATION

In Midland, cyclists favor the **Pere Marquette Rail-Trail** (989/832-6870), a 30-mile-long asphalt trail that's also a hit for those on foot, with in-line skates, or with wheelchairs or strollers. It begins in downtown Midland near the **Tridge,** a three-way pedestrian footbridge spanning the confluence of the Tittabawassee and Chippewa Rivers. The Tridge is a local landmark, and a gathering spot for picnics, concerts, festivals, and more. From there, the rail-trail follows Saginaw Road to Coleman, passing by the Dow Historical Museum and Bradley Home before reaching the towns of Averill and Sanford.

Hikers have another option in Midland. After a visit in the 1970s, the vice president of the National Audubon Society called the **Chippewa Nature Center** (400 S. Badour Rd., 989/631-0830, www.chippewanaturecenter. com, visitors center 8am-5pm Mon.-Fri., 9am-5pm Sat., 1pm-5pm Sun., free) "one of the finest—if not *the* finest—private nature centers in the world." More recently, the National Park Service cited the center for its outstanding educational accomplishments and designated it a National Environmental Study Area. The 1,200-acre center sits along the Pine River and was designed (not surprisingly) by Alden Dow to merge with the living world around it. Its most striking feature is the River Overlook, a 60-foot-long, glass-walled room cantilevered over the Pine River, with great views of the center's birdlife and wildlife.

The center offers an unusually rich mix of things to see, including an authentic log homestead, items discovered from on-site archaeological digs, and a display that's a good all-around introduction to the area's natural

THE HEARTLAND

the Tridge, a unique footbridge in Midland

the Chippewa Nature Center

© MIDLAND COUNTY CVB

© MIDLAND COUNTY CVB

history. Other highlights include well-executed dioramas that show Michigan geology and scenes from the Saginaw Valley Indian culture. Despite the wide range of attractions, the center's hallmark is the seclusion, peace, and beauty of its surroundings. A map available at the visitors center guides visitors through the 13-mile trail system that parallels the Chippewa River. Popular with hikers and cross-country skiers, the trails include artificially created wetlands, begun in 1990 to compensate for a wetlands destroyed to build a nearby shopping mall.

ACCOMMODATIONS AND FOOD

Although Midland is no mecca of lodging and dining options, you'll find a variety of dependable chain motels clustered near the intersection of Wackerly and Eastman. Try the 90-room **Fairview Inn** (2200 W. Wackerly St., 989/631-0070, www.fairviewinnmidland.com, $79-109 d).

Not far from the hotel is **Bamboo Garden** (721 S. Saginaw Rd., 989/832-7967, 11am-10pm Mon.-Sat., 1pm-7pm Sun., $9-16), a classy Chinese restaurant with a relaxing atmosphere and reliably good food, including sizzling steak, Buddha duck, and moo shu pork with Mandarin pancakes.

Camping

For campers, **Black Creek State Forest Campground** (220 W. Ellsworth, 989/275-5151, daily mid-Apr.-Nov., $20 daily) offers 23 semi-modern sites (as in no electricity or showers), which can accommodate tents or RVs. Sites are available on a first-come, first-served basis. Campers can enjoy nearby hiking trails, bird-watching opportunities, a boat launch, and access to several lakes and rivers ideal for anglers.

INFORMATION AND SERVICES

For more information about the Midland area, contact the **Midland County Convention & Visitors Bureau** (300 Rodd St., 989/839-9522, www.midlandcvb.org). For other services, you'll have no trouble finding groceries, banks, post offices, and the like. If you need help in an emergency situation, dial **911** from any cell or public phone. For medical assistance, head to the **MidMichigan Medical Center** (4005 Orchard Dr., 989/839-3000, www.midmichigan.org).

GETTING THERE AND AROUND

Travelers can fly directly into the **MBS International Airport** (MBS, 8500 Garfield Rd., Freeland, 989/695-5555, www.mbsairport.org), where it's possible to rent a car from one of five major rental agencies. From there, head to Midland via Garfield Road, US-10 West, and M-20 West; without traffic, the 13-mile trip should take about 20 minutes.

Of course, most folks will likely be driving from elsewhere in Michigan. From Mount Pleasant, for instance, you can simply take M-20 East to downtown Midland, a 27-mile trip that usually takes about 33 minutes. From downtown Bay City, meanwhile, you can just take M-25 West, continue onto US-10 West, and follow M-20 West to downtown Midland; without traffic, the 19-mile trip takes roughly 23 minutes. Once you've arrived, you can then drive, bike, or walk around town.

THE SOUTHWEST COAST

Celebrated for its dramatic sand dunes and glorious sunsets, Michigan's Southwest Coast attracts thousands of tourists annually. The westerly winds that blow across Lake Michigan are responsible for pushing sun-warmed, surface waters closer to shore, making the beaches here perfect for swimming during the summer months. Over the last century, wealthy tourists from Detroit, Grand Rapids, and Chicago flocked to the sunny shores of southwestern Michigan and helped to transform a string of coastal villages into the posh resort towns of today. This 130-mile stretch of picturesque coastline, extending from the Indiana border to just north of Muskegon, offers a wide array of diversions, including golf courses, bike paths, Saugatuck's art galleries, fishing and boating charters, several state parks, and annual events like Holland's Tulip Time Festival.

The same temperate climate that lures beach-loving visitors to this part of Michigan is also responsible for the inland abundance of agriculture: ever-flourishing fields, orchards, and vineyards. Popular mild-weather pastimes in this area include touring one of the Midwest's finest wine-growing regions and plucking bushels of fresh produce at several U-pick farms. At such seasonal establishments, visitors are also welcome to sample other gourmet delicacies, including homemade jams, honey, maple syrup, salsa, and baked goods.

Such diversity has earned the Southwest Coast a variety of monikers over the years, including "Michigan's Gold Coast," "The Art Coast of Michigan," and "The Riviera of the Midwest." But, no matter what it's called, the Southwest Coast is an understandably popular

© SARA SIMMONS

HIGHLIGHTS

Michigan's Adventure
Muskegon
Grand Haven
Lake Michigan
Tulip Time Festival
Holland
Saugatuck-Area Art Galleries
Saugatuck/Douglas
Fennville
Lake Michigan Shore Wine Trail
South Haven
St. Joseph/Benton Harbor
Blossomtime Festival
Warren Dunes State Park
New Buffalo
INDIANA
Gary
0   25 mi
0   25 km   © AVALON TRAVEL

(Lake Michigan Shore Wine Country: Wineries and tasting rooms lure wine connoisseurs to the southwestern corner of Michigan's Lower Peninsula. Award-winners include the Tabor Hill Winery, the Round Barn Winery, and Warner Vineyards (page 182).

(Blossomtime Festival: This annual celebration of blossoming fruit trees spotlights the agricultural splendor of southwestern Michigan (page 186).

(Saugatuck-Area Art Galleries: Together, the adjacent coastal villages of Saugatuck and Douglas are known as the "Art Coast of Michigan," boasting roughly 20 fine art, studio, craft, and specialty galleries (page 194).

(Tulip Time Festival: Holland honors its Dutch heritage with this annual springtime event, which, in addition to colorful tulip displays, features trolley tours, live concerts, variety shows, several parades, fireworks extravaganzas, carnival rides, local artwork, and traditional dancing (page 204).

(Michigan's Adventure: Children and teenagers (not to mention their parents) are especially fond of this Muskegon-area amusement and water park, where you'll find over 60 rides and attractions, including one of the nation's highest and longest wooden roller coasters (page 213).

(Warren Dunes State Park: This impressive, year-round park offers a three-mile stretch of beaches, several hiking and cross-country skiing trails, numerous modern and rustic campsites, and stupendous views from atop rugged 260-foot-high sand dunes (page 174).

destination for vacationers, especially in the summertime, when the vibrant blue waters of Lake Michigan, formed by enormous glaciers during the last great ice age, entice weary travelers and residents to put aside day-to-day worries for a while and simply contemplate the magnificence of nature.

PLANNING YOUR TIME

Practically the entire western coast of Michigan's Lower Peninsula—including the resort towns and incredible beaches that dot

the southern half—is a major tourist draw, especially during the state's traditionally mild summers. So, if you're not fond of crowds, you might want to avoid places like Saugatuck and Warren Dunes State Park during the popular months of July and August. Even during the off-season, however, the area will appeal to art lovers, golfing enthusiasts, beachcombers, wine connoisseurs, cross-country skiers, and many other fun-seekers.

Unlike many of the state's other regions, the Southwest Coast is fairly easy to explore. Save

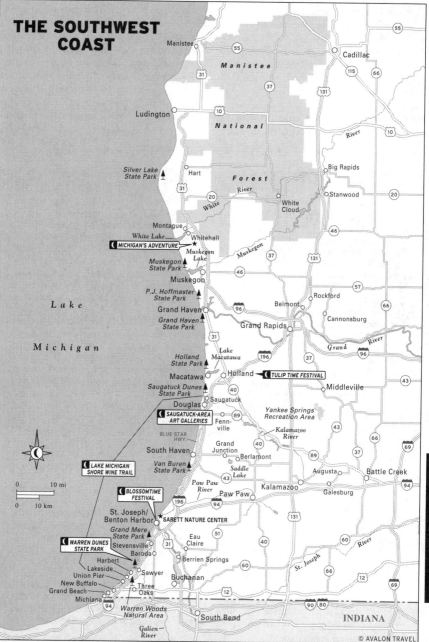

THE SOUTHWEST COAST

Manistee

Cadillac

Manistee

Ludington

National

Silver Lake
State Park

Hart

Forest

River

Big Rapids

Stanwood

White Cloud

Montague

Whitehall

White Lake

MICHIGAN'S ADVENTURE

*Muskegon
Lake*

Muskegon
State Park

Muskegon

P.J. Hoffmaster
State Park

Belmont

Rockford

Cannonsburg

*Lake
Michigan*

Grand Haven

Grand Haven
State Park

Grand Rapids

Grand River

Holland
State Park

*Lake
Macatawa*

Macatawa

Holland

TULIP TIME FESTIVAL

Middleville

Saugatuck Dunes
State Park

Douglas

Saugatuck

SAUGATUCK-AREA
ART GALLERIES

Fenn-
ville

*Yankee Springs
Recreation Area*

*Kalamazoo
River*

BLUE STAR
HWY.

South Haven

Grand
Junction

Berlamont

LAKE MICHIGAN
SHORE WINE TRAIL

Van Buren
State Park

*Saddle
Lake*

Augusta

Battle Creek

*Paw Paw
River*

Paw Paw

Kalamazoo

Galesburg

BLOSSOMTIME
FESTIVAL

St. Joseph/
Benton Harbor

SARETT NATURE CENTER

Grand Mere
State Park

Stevensville

Baroda

Eau
Claire

Berrien Springs

*St. Joseph
River*

WARREN DUNES
STATE PARK

Harbert

Lakeside

Union Pier

Sawyer

Buchanan

New Buffalo

Three
Oaks

Grand Beach

Michiana

*Warren Woods
Natural Area*

South Bend

INDIANA

*Galien
River*

0   10 mi

0   10 km

© AVALON TRAVEL

for a few inland vineyards and villages, most of the area's most popular destinations lie close to the coast, accessible via I-94, I-196, and US-31. It's literally a snap to drive from Michiana to Montague, a journey that usually requires less than three hours. Of course, to really enjoy this coastal trip, you should allow yourself at least five days, making sure to see South Haven, Saugatuck, Holland, Grand Haven, and Muskegon along the way. Double the time, and

you'll be able to linger in Saugatuck's art galleries, catch a few annual events, play a few rounds of award-winning golf, take a bike ride on the Kal-Haven Trail, and explore some of the vineyards and U-pick farms in the region's interior.

Despite the presence of a commercial airport and a superb public transit system in Muskegon (arguably the largest town on the Southwest Coast) as well as Amtrak train services to towns like New Buffalo, Niles, Dowagiac, St. Joseph,

CITIZEN POTAWATOMI NATION

Michigan's earliest inhabitants were, of course, Native Americans, and while some of their descendants still dwell here, many others have long since departed the Great Lakes State. One such tribe was the Potawatomi, one of several Algonquian-speaking peoples who occupied the Great Lakes region from prehistoric times through the early 19th century. Once part of a larger group that included the Chippewa and Ottawa, the autonomous Potawatomi lived in southwestern Michigan over 500 years ago.

Following the Beaver Wars of the mid-1600s, many Potawatomi moved to Wisconsin, where they became trappers for French fur traders. Soon, the Potawatomi began hiring other local tribesmen to collect and trap furs, which they would sell or trade to the French, thus expanding their tribal control over a five-million-acre estate that comprised Wisconsin, Illinois, Michigan, Indiana, and part of Ohio.

For most of the 1700s, the Potawatomi thrived. Adapting well to their environs, they traveled by canoe, fished in area lakes and streams, hunted waterfowl and larger game, harvested wild rice and berries, and cultivated an assortment of crops. The Potawatomi wore distinctive clothing, dwelled in birch-bark wigwams, and embraced communal events like the springtime tapping of sugar maple trees.

Unfortunately, the Potawatomi did not escape the fate of many other Native Americans; by 1800, white settlements had begun to displace tribal villages. In the fall of 1838, one group of the Potawatomi, the Mission Band, was forced to leave Indiana and march over

660 miles to a reserve in Kansas. Several members died along the way, inspiring the event's name: the Potawatomi Trail of Death.

For over 20 years, the Mission Potawatomi remained in Kansas, eventually settling small farms, many of which were later taken by white settlers and traders. In 1867, Mission Potawatomi members signed a treaty that allowed them to sell their Kansas lands and purchase new lands in present-day Oklahoma. After adopting U.S. citizenship, the Mission Band became known as the Citizen Potawatomi.

By the 1870s, the Citizen Potawatomi had formed several communities near present-day Shawnee. The Dawes Act of 1887, however, forced them to accept individual allotments again, and half of their reservation was lost during the 1891 government-sanctioned land run. Although many tribal members left for places like California and Texas, many stayed in Oklahoma. Now the ninth-largest tribe in America, the Citizen Potawatomi Nation (www.potawatomi.org) owns several grocery stores and banks, not to mention a casino resort.

Luckily, though, that's not the end of the Potawatomi story in Michigan. In 1994, President Clinton restored tribal recognition to the **Pokagon Band of Potawatomi Indians** (www.pokagon.com), which currently services over 4,500 citizens in a 10-county area, including four counties in southwestern Michigan. In fact, the Pokagon Band has three casinos of its own: the **Four Winds Casinos** (866/494-6371, www.fourwindscasino.com) in New Buffalo (11111 Wilson Rd.), Hartford (68600 Red Arrow Hwy.), and Dowagiac (58700 M-51 S.).

Bangor, and Holland, you'll probably be better off with a vehicle of your own—whether it's a motorcycle, an RV, or a rental car. You'll benefit, too, from smart packing. As with the rest of Michigan, the Southwest Coast is a seasonal place. Bring warm clothes in winter, bathing suits in summer, and always be prepared for surprises—even in August, rain and cool temperatures are indeed possible. In addition, you should pack according to your interests; although you can procure most goods (from batteries to toiletries) in all the coastal towns, you'll usually need to bring specialty items, such as your own golf clubs, along for the ride. So, it's important to consider your plans before embarking on your trip.

For more information about the Southwest Coast, consult the **Michigan Beachtowns Association** (www.beachtowns.org), the **Southwestern Michigan Tourist Council** (2300 Pipestone Rd., Benton Harbor, 269/925-6301, www.swmichigan.org), or the **West Michigan Tourist Association** (WMTA, 741 Kenmoor Ave., Ste. E, Grand Rapids, 616/245-2217, www.wmta.org).

HISTORY

The history of the Southwest Coast is steeped in stories of Indians, French explorers, lumber, and agriculture. Many area towns still bear Indian names, like Paw Paw and Muskegon. Several rivers, such as the Grand near what is today Grand Haven, empty into Lake Michigan, creating the perfect transportation system for logs; consequently, southwestern Michigan prospered during the logging era. After the Civil War, a growing number of sawmills buzzed along its shoreline, helping to make it one of the leading lumber-producing regions in the country. Most of the lumber used to rebuild Chicago after the Great Fire in 1871 was felled in the forests of southwestern Michigan.

Once the forests were plucked nearly bare, the region became better known for its shipping ports and bountiful produce, luring settlers from places as far afield as America's East Coast and the Netherlands. By the late 19th century, the main mode of transportation shifted from rivers to railroads, and then to roads built for automobiles. With the car came the tourists and one of southwestern Michigan's nicknames, "Michigan's Gold Coast." Today, a string of resort towns stretch north from the Indiana border, serving as base camps for exploring the region's wealth of hiking trails, antiques shops, wineries, U-pick farms, and remnants of the Southwest Coast's prosperous agricultural and shipping history, such as the Morton House, built by one of the founding families of Benton Harbor.

Harbor Country

Eight lakefront resort communities cluster north of the Indiana border: Michiana, Grand Beach, New Buffalo, Union Pier, Lakeside, Harbert, Sawyer, and, just a few miles inland, Three Oaks. Known collectively as Harbor Country, they've also been dubbed the "Riviera on Lake Michigan" and the "Hamptons of the Midwest." Perhaps that's an exaggeration, but with a kernel of truth. Just an hour from Chicago's Loop, Harbor Country has indeed become the summer escape of choice for well-heeled Windy City expatriates—including film critic Roger Ebert, novelist Andrew Greeley,

architect Stanley Tigerman, and scores of others. The well-to-do weekend at a chorus line of glass-fronted luxury homes and condos lining Lake Michigan, shopping, dining, and driving from town to town. (A few words to the wise: Skip the area in summer if you loathe crowds and hate to shop.)

Behind the area's silver-spoon facade, however, are vestiges of its original sleepy charm. Tony shops and art galleries may line the main streets, but the legendary sand, surf, and sunsets are still famous, and, for the most part, still free. Hotels, inns, and restaurants exist in all price ranges. While travelers can easily drop $200 for a steak dinner for two at the Four Winds Casino Resort, they can just as easily chow down on a huge breakfast of eggs, bacon, and thick French toast at Rosie's in downtown New Buffalo for less than $10.

SIGHTS

◖ Warren Dunes State Park

Raised in nearby Three Oaks, E. K. Warren was a well-known inventor, entrepreneur, philanthropist, conservationist, and community leader, but perhaps the most celebrated legacy of his fortitude and foresight is **Warren Dunes State Park** (12032 Red Arrow Hwy., Sawyer, 269/426-4013, daily, annual $11 Recreation Passport for Michigan residents or $8.40 day-use fee/$30.50 yearly Recreation Passport for nonresidents required). On hot summer weekends, an exodus from Chicago descends on the southern end of the park, jamming a stretch of beach and crunching up the 240-foot Tower Hill dune, with views all the way to the Chicago skyline. It's also a favorite of weekend hang gliders. To get away from the crowds, explore the back dunes farther from the water (but stay off fragile dune grasses!) or head for the northern two-thirds of the park—largely ignored by the weekend crowds and undeveloped save for six miles of hiking and skiing trails. The Yellow Birch nature trail includes a wheelchair-accessible, bird-watching boardwalk at its north end, frequented by more than 100 bird species.

The ecology of the dunes is a fascinating study in biodiversity. Because of the way dunes form, plant communities can change drastically as you move inland. Closest to the water are the newest "active" dunes, still ever-changing piles of windswept sand. Farther inland, vegetation like marram grass takes hold and begins to stabilize the dunes. Even farther back from the water, older dunes have established larger plant communities that include jack pine, black oak, and a variety of shrubs. In between the dunes, swales filled with bogs and fens harbor water-loving plants like leatherleaf and carnivorous pitcher plants. The result is a staggering array of plants, including many not often seen in northern climates.

Grand Mere State Park

For years, **Grand Mere State Park** near Stevensville (269/426-4013, daily, annual $11 Recreation Passport for Michigan residents or $8.40 day-use fee/$30.50 yearly Recreation Passport for nonresidents required) was the well-kept secret of locals and summer residents. Although the area has since been discovered by out-of-towners, it remains remarkably natural (though still within earshot of the interstate). The 985-acre park preserves a valuable habitat of three interdunal lakes, scooped out by glaciers and once part of a larger bay. Shoreline currents carrying sediments have built sandbars and spits across the bay mouth, creating the small inland lakes. Two more lakes once existed south of the current three, now filled in as wooded swamps and remnant bogs. The diverse ecological community supports a distinctive array of birds, including yellow-throated warblers, mockingbirds, summer tanagers, and Bell's vireos. Grand Mere is one of only a dozen Michigan areas listed as national natural landmarks. Several trails wind among the open sand dunes, and it's a half-mile walk to reach the park's one mile of Lake Michigan shoreline—happily, a far enough distance to deter many beachgoers.

Museums and Gardens

Established in 1989, the **New Buffalo Railroad Museum** (530 S. Whittaker St., 269/469-5409, www.newbuffalo.com/museums.shtml) celebrates the area's history with an interesting collection of artifacts, documents, and photographs. The museum—which is housed inside a replica of the original Pere Marquette Railroad Depot, alongside the railroad tracks just one mile north of I-94—even has a working miniature train display that depicts the 1920s-era Pere Marquette Railroad Yards.

Situated in downtown Three Oaks, roughly 10 miles east of Lake Michigan, is the delightful **Three Oaks Spokes Bicycle Museum and Information Center** (1 Oak St., 269/756-3361, 9am-5pm daily, free, donation welcome).

Housed inside the historic 1898 Michigan Central Railroad Depot, the museum offers a collection of bicycles from the 1860s through the present, including a spine-crunching 1870s model known as the Boneshaker and an unusual chainless bike from the 1890s. The museum also provides information about the history of cycling and the town of Three Oaks, plus area maps and brochures.

In 1941, a Chicago schoolteacher, Kay Boydston, and her husband, Walter, bought 12.5 acres between Berrien Springs and Buchanan to serve as their country home. There, Kay began experimenting with horticulture and, over the next 20 years, created perennial and lilac gardens, a boxwood garden, a fern trail, and an enchanting rock garden. With the help of philanthropists Lawrence and Mary Plym, the property gradually became the 105-acre **Fernwood Botanical Garden & Nature Preserve** (13988 Range Line Rd., Niles, 269/695-6491, www.fernwoodbotanical.org, 10am-6pm Tues.-Sat., noon-6pm Sun. May-Oct., 10am-5pm Tues.-Sat., noon-5pm Sun. Nov.-Apr., $7 adults, $5 seniors 65 and over, $4 children 13-18, $3 children 6-12).

Today, highlights include the arboretum, which was added in the 1970s, a reconstructed tallgrass prairie (in bloom May-Aug.), a fern conservatory, an art gallery, and a nature center, which comprises an outdoor bird-feeding station and evolving nature exhibits. Near the visitors center, which contains a gift shop and a library, is a charming herb and sensory garden grouped by use, including culinary, medicinal, and pest-repellent qualities. Music lovers will also appreciate these lovely environs; outdoor music festivals and chamber concerts occur throughout the year.

ENTERTAINMENT AND EVENTS
Four Winds Casino Resort
Opened in 2007 by the Pokagon Band of Potawatomi Indians, the **Four Winds Casino Resort** (11111 Wilson Rd., New Buffalo, 866/494-6371, www.fourwindscasino.com, 24 hours daily) is the only land-based casino in southwestern Michigan. In addition to the 130,000-square-foot casino, which offers over 3,000 slot machines and gaming tables, the Four Winds houses a luxurious hotel, six restaurants, four bars, and live entertainment.

Festivals and Events
In the fall, many of the communities in Harbor Country celebrate **Harvest Days** (269/469-5409, www.harborcountry.org/harvestdays), a four-day event in mid-October that honors the autumn harvest with hayrides, pumpkin patches, a scarecrow contest, and a farmers market. In addition, many of the shops, galleries, and restaurants in New Buffalo, Union Pier, Lakeside, and other nearby villages host events like open houses, artist receptions, culinary demonstrations, and family activities.

Inland from the coast, the town of Three Oaks has fewer than 1,700 residents most of the year, but in late September, three times that number converge on the area for the **Apple Cider Century** (888/877-2068, www.applecidercentury.com, fees vary), a one-day cycling event that winds amid orchards, forests, vineyards, and a handful of area towns. Since it began in 1974, the event has grown into the Midwest's largest one-day, 100-mile ride. It's sponsored by the Three Oaks Spokes Bicycle Club, and all proceeds help to finance organizations like the Rails-to-Trails Conservancy as well as the Backroads Bikeway, a lovely system of 12 self-guided biking trails.

Farther east, the town of Niles hosts three annual events worth attending. In early June, the **Niles Bluegrass Festival** (www.nilesbluegrass.com, free) presents four days of food, crafts, and traditional bluegrass performances at the town's Riverfront Park, which is also host to free Sunday concerts throughout the summer. In late July, the **Niles Riverfest** (www.nilesriverfest.net, free) invites people of all ages to celebrate the St. Joseph River with raft races, live entertainment, car shows, and more. In early fall, the four-day **Four Flags Area Apple Festival** (269/683-8870, www.fourflagsapplefestival.org, prices vary) promotes the apple harvest with plenty of food, crafts, carnival rides, parades, contests, and free entertainment.

WOODPECKER WATCH

Bird-watchers regularly flock to **Warren Woods Natural Area,** situated between the towns of Sawyer, Union Pier, and Three Oaks in the southwestern corner of Michigan's Lower Peninsula. After all, this 311-acre preserve, which contains the last known stand of virgin beech-maple forest in southern Michigan, is home to a variety of migratory and native birds, including warblers and other songbirds. Of course, many bird-watchers specifically come for the chance to spot pileated woodpeckers.

For those who have never before observed a pileated woodpecker (*Dryocopus pileatus*) in the wild, here are a few curious facts about this prevalent, nonmigratory, and incredibly adaptable bird:

- The pileated woodpecker is a large, crow-sized North American woodpecker, with a primarily black body, white stripes along the neck, a slender, chisel-like bill, and a flaming-red, triangular crest.

- Adults are typically 16 to 19 inches in length, span 26 to 30 inches across the wings, and weigh 9 to 12 ounces.

- The flight pattern of a pileated woodpecker is strong but undulating, unlike the straight path of a crow.

- The largest nonextinct woodpecker in the United States, the pileated inhabits deciduous forests in New England, cypress swamps in the American Southeast, the Great Lakes region, boreal forests throughout Canada, and parts of the Pacific Northwest. Overall, it prefers mature forests and heavily wooded parks, though it's been known to frequent suburban areas.

- It's closely related to the white-bellied woodpecker and the black woodpecker, and it's similar in size and plumage to the extremely rare, if not extinct, ivory-billed and imperial species.

- The call of a pileated woodpecker is a loud, far-carrying whinny, often described as a wild "jungle bird" call, and its drumming can also be very loud, often sounding like the amplified striking of a hammer on a tree.

- Although the pileated woodpecker will for-

SHOPPING

In Harbor Country, there are as many clothing boutiques, furniture stores, and other shops as you and your credit card can handle. For something unique, bypass the tony downtown emporiums and head out on the highway. The offbeat galleries and antiques shops that have sprouted up along the **Red Arrow Highway,** from Union Pier to Sawyer, are one of the area's chief charms. Everything from "serious" art to campy Popsicle stick lamps can be found here, and it's easy to spend the day wandering, stopping to rest and refuel along the way. In between shops, the highway passes old cottage compounds, ramshackle resorts, and elegant lakefront estates that grew like weeds in the 1910s and 1920s.

Galleries seem to dominate at the southern end of Harbor Country. **Courtyard Gallery** (813 E. Buffalo St., New Buffalo, 269/469-4110 or 800/291-9287, www.courtyardfineart.com, 11am-5pm Wed.-Mon., by appointment Tues.) showcases a broad array of oils, watercolors, bronzes, and sculptured glass. Local artists dominate at **Local Color Gallery** (16187 Red Arrow Hwy., Union Pier, 269/469-5332, www.localcolorartgallery.com, noon-5pm daily). In Lakeside, visitors can purchase rustic furniture, accents, and outdoor structures made of discarded tree trunks, branches, twigs, and reclaimed wood from barns and old buildings at **Hearthwoods Custom Furnishings** (15310 Red Arrow Hwy., 269/469-5551, www.hearthwoods.com, 10am-6pm daily summer, 11am-6pm Mon.-Sat. and noon-5pm Sun. winter).

Farther north, roadside antiquing haunts fill former cottages, old brick storefronts, and cavernous warehouses. In Harbert, hunt away at **Dunes Antique Center** (13560 Red Arrow Hwy., 269/449-4103, www.dunesantiques.

age for food on vines, small branches, and the ground, especially around fallen trees, it prefers to feed from the vertical surfaces of large trees, and its diet of choice consists of berries, nuts, seeds, and insects, such as carpenter ants, termites, flies, caterpillars, grasshoppers, cockroaches, and wood-boring beetles.

- Typically, pileated woodpeckers create large holes in the cavities of dead or fallen trees to accommodate their nests. Following a mating, the pair of pileated woodpeckers will incubate three to five eggs for about two weeks, followed by a monthlong nesting period. While raising their young in the tree hole, the male and female will defend their territory in all seasons, mainly by drumming trees and chasing, calling, striking, and jabbing any interlopers.

- Possible predators of the pileated woodpecker include American martens, red-tailed hawks, great horned owls, weasels, squirrels, rat snakes, and gray foxes.

- Once abandoned, the nests of pileated wood-peckers can make good homes for other animals, including songbirds, owls, tree-nesting ducks, other woodpeckers, bats, and raccoons.

- While many people dislike pileated wood-peckers due to the considerable damage that they can inflict on trees, they can actually be quite beneficial. After all, they control many insect populations, such as tree beetles, and provide nurturing, insect-filled holes for other bird species.

Not surprisingly, Warren Woods Natural Area, which became a national natural landmark in 1967 and is alternatively known as Warren Woods State Park, is also popular among hikers and wildflower enthusiasts. For more information about the preserve, contact **Warren Dunes State Park** (12032 Red Arrow Hwy., Sawyer, 269/426-4013), which oversees management of the preserve. Just remember that a day-use fee or annual Recreation Passport is required to enter Warren Woods.

com, 10am-5pm daily July-Aug., 10am-5pm Wed.-Mon. Sept.-June), or try **Harbert Antique Mall** (13887 Red Arrow Hwy., 269/469-0977, www.harbertantiquemall.com, 10am-6pm daily).

While in a shopping mood, don't forget that you're in one of Michigan's leading agricultural regions. During summer and fall, you'll find many produce stands and farmers markets in and around Harbor Country. So, take a quick trip to **Shelton Farms** (1832 S. 11th St., Niles, 269/684-3230, www.sheltonfarms.com, 8:30am-7pm Mon.-Thurs. and Sat., 8:30am-8pm Fri., 9am-6pm Sun.), where you'll find grapes, strawberries, apples, flowers, even Christmas trees.

SPORTS AND RECREATION
Golf
Although Harbor Country isn't known for its amazing golf, you'll find several courses open to the public. The **Whittaker Woods Golf Community** (12578 Wilson Rd., New Buffalo, 269/469-3400, www.golfwhittaker.com, daily Mar.-Nov., $40-89 pp w/cart), for instance, presents an 18-hole championship golf course amid 400 acres of woods and wetlands. The clubhouse, a renovated 1920s-era farmhouse, contains a pro shop, full locker rooms, and a restaurant that overlooks the course and offers weekend entertainment.

Hiking and Bird-Watching
If all this conspicuous consumption wears you out, you can find plenty of simpler pleasures in Harbor Country, too. Situated three miles north of Three Oaks, the **Warren Woods Natural Area** (269/426-4013, daily, annual $11 Recreation Passport for Michigan residents or $8.40 day-use fee/$30.50 yearly Recreation

its required) protects e state's last remaining est. Along the banks of River, beeches, maples, so large that two people around them. A 3.5-mile trail the woods and along the Galien. Warren Woods is known far and wide among bird-watchers, due partly to its location on the Lake Michigan shoreline and to the forest's abundant deadwood, perfect for nesting. Warbler sightings can be particularly good here.

E. K. Warren, a Three Oaks shopkeeper who made his fortune by inventing an affordable corset crafted from turkey feathers, bought the property in 1879, determined to preserve the land at a time when other businessmen were looking only to exploit it. Today, the area is designated a national natural landmark. The only concessions to human visitors are pit toilets, a wooden footbridge spanning the Galien River, a small parking lot, and one picnic table. In spring, you may notice an abundance of wildflowers and morel mushrooms, but keep in mind that all plants are protected in this area. To reach Warren Woods, take the Red Arrow Highway to Union Pier, turn east on Elm Valley, and follow it five miles.

Biking

Harbor Country is an incredibly scenic place for a bike ride, especially during September and October, when the changing leaves are particularly vibrant. The **Backroads Bikeway** is a picturesque system that includes a dozen self-guided trails on paved roads, varying 5-60 miles in length. The routes cross gurgling streams and rolling hills, traverse meadows and farmland, and provide access to Warren Dunes and Warren Woods. For trail brochures, regional bike touring information, and bike rentals, consult the **Three Oaks Spokes Bicycle Museum and Information Center** (1 Oak St., 269/756-3361).

ACCOMMODATIONS

The eight communities of Harbor Country offer as many lodging choices as a mid-sized city, with prices to match. Though you won't find many bargains among the bunch, it would be a shame to visit Harbor Country and not stay at one of its distinctive small inns. For budget accommodations, your best bet is to stick with franchises along I-94.

In New Buffalo, you'll find at least two unique options. **The Harbor Grand** (111 W. Water St., 888/605-6800, www.harbor-grand.com, $189-219 d) is a waterfront inn featuring an indoor pool, a massage therapy center, complimentary high-speed Internet access, and luxurious rooms with fireplaces, spa showers, and harbor views. It's also just a short walk from downtown New Buffalo and a Lake Michigan beach. Meanwhile, 50 acres of spring-fed lakes, wildflower meadows, and whispering pines stretch behind the gates of **Sans Souci Euro Inn & Cottages** (19265 S. Lakeside Rd., 269/756-3141, www.sans-souci.com, $165-180 d), the perfect retreat for a romantic getaway. Choose from two luxury suites, two vacation homes, or two lakeside cottages, all featuring European-style decor and wireless Internet access.

A little farther north, Union Pier offers a wealth of lodging choices. *Chicago* magazine voted ❨ **The Inn at Union Pier** (9708 Berrien St., 269/469-4700, www.in-natunionpier.com, $165-250 d) one of the region's "best small inns." With a primo location just 200 steps from Lake Michigan, this inn features an outdoor hot tub, gourmet breakfasts, and 16 spacious rooms, many decorated with antique Swedish ceramic fireplaces—according to the owners, the largest private collection in the country. The **Pine Garth Inn** (15790 Lakeshore Rd., 269/469-1642, www.pinegarth.com, $160-210 d) was built in 1905 as a private summer home. It opened its doors to guests in 1989 and has been a favorite ever since. The unique building is constructed so that the lake and its often-magnificent sunsets can be seen from every room. A more retro option is the ❨ **Fire Fly Resort** (15657 Lakeshore Rd., 269/469-0245, www.fireflyresort.com, $130-220 d), a complex of private cottages built in the 1930s as an escape for city dwellers. Guests will enjoy comfortable furnishings, outdoor grills, picnic nooks, perennial gardens, and proximity to the beach.

Nature lovers should opt for the ◖**Lakeside Inn** (15251 Lakeshore Rd., Lakeside, 269/469-0600, www.lakesideinns.com, $90-185 d), a historic resort built in the late 19th century, completed in 1915, and designated a state historic landmark in 2004. Today, the inn offers over 30 rooms, a cozy lobby, an exercise room, and picturesque surroundings, including a garden, a shady grove, and a nearby beach, the ideal spot to watch the sunset.

Camping

Camping may be your best bet if you're looking to travel cheaply through pricey Harbor Country. **Warren Dunes State Park** (12032 Red Arrow Hwy., Sawyer, 269/426-4013, daily Mar.-Oct., annual $11 Recreation Passport for Michigan residents or $8.40 day-use fee/$30.50 yearly Recreation Passport for nonresidents required) offers 182 modern and 36 semi-modern (no electricity or showers) sites for $16-27 per night, as well as three mini-cabins with woodstoves and bunks for $45 per night. For reservations—which are recommended May-September, especially on weekends—contact the **Michigan Department of Natural Resources** (800/447-2757, www.michigan.gov/dnr).

To the north, the town of Bridgman maintains the **Weko Beach Campground** (5239 Lake St., 269/465-3406 Apr.-mid-Oct., 269/465-5407 mid-Oct.-Mar., www.bridgman.org), which offers developed (water and electricity) and semi-developed sites for $25-30 per night, as well as cabins for $45 per night. Situated along the sunny shores of Lake Michigan, this campground welcomes tents and RVs; amenities include hot showers, outdoor grills, picnic areas, a playground, a concession stand, and a dump station.

FOOD

In New Buffalo, you'll find **Redamak's** (616 E. Buffalo St., 269/469-4522, www.

redamaks.com, noon-10:30pm Mon.-Sat. and noon-10pm Sun. summer., noon-9:30pm Mon.-Thurs., noon-10:30pm Fri.-Sat., and noon-10pm Sun. spring and fall, closed Nov.-Feb., $4.50-12), known for the hamburger that made New Buffalo famous, as well as its casual, friendly dining. Another popular eatery in New Buffalo is **Rosie's** (128 N. Whittaker St., 269/469-4382, 7am-2pm daily, $2-8), which serves a slew of breakfast favorites, from buttermilk pancakes to Spanish omelets, as well as a limited lunch menu featuring burgers and hot dogs.

New Buffalo is also home to the Four Winds Casino Resort, which offers several dining options, including the **Copper Rock Steakhouse** (11111 Wilson Rd., 866/494-6371, www.fourwindscasino.com, 5pm-10pm Sun.-Thurs., 5pm-11pm Fri.-Sat., $28-85). Besides a mouthwatering selection of dry-aged steaks, you'll also find several tempting seafood dishes here, from crab-stuffed shrimp to whole Maine lobsters, not to mention over 400 wines.

Meanwhile, Union Pier is home to the **Red Arrow Roadhouse** (15710 Red Arrow Hwy., 269/469-3939, www.redarrowroadhouse. com, 5pm-10pm Mon.-Thurs., 5pm-11pm Fri., noon-10pm Sat.-Sun., $8-21), which serves inexpensive, home-style fare in a casual, lodge-style atmosphere. Features include an enclosed patio and weeknight discounts September-May. Up in Harbert, the delectable, old-fashioned **Harbert Swedish Bakery** (13698 Red Arrow Hwy., 269/469-1777, www.harberts-wedishbakery.com, 7am-3pm Fri.-Mon. May-Labor Day) has been here since poet Carl Sandburg ran a goat farm nearby. Open seasonally, it still specializes in traditional Swedish breads and cakes.

INFORMATION AND SERVICES

For more information about Harbor Country and the surrounding area, contact the **Harbor Country Chamber of Commerce** (530 S. Whittaker St., Ste. F, New Buffalo, 269/469-5409, www.harborcountry.org, 9am-5pm

Mon.-Fri.) or the **Four Flags Area Council on Tourism** (321 E. Main St., Niles, 269/684-7444, www.fourflagsarea.org, 10am-3pm Tues. and Thurs.). For local news, consult the *Harbor Country News* (www.harborcountry-news.com).

If you have any mailing needs, you'll find post offices in New Buffalo, Union Pier, Lakeside, Harbert, Sawyer, and Three Oaks. Refer to www.usps.com for **post office** locations and hours. Despite the small size of these lakeside communities, many have necessary services like auto shops, groceries, and banks, including several branches of **Fifth Third Bank** (www.53.com) and **Horizon Bank** (www.accesshorizon.com).

In case of an emergency that requires police, fire, or ambulance services, dial **911** from any cell or public phone. For medical services, visit the **Lakeland Regional Medical Center** (1234 Napier Ave., St. Joseph, 269/983-8300, www.lakelandhealth.org) or the **Lakeland Community Hospital** (31 N. St. Joseph Ave., Niles, 269/683-5510, www.lakelandhealth.org).

GETTING THERE AND AROUND

Although **Amtrak** (800/872-7245, www.amtrak.com) has a sheltered platform in New Buffalo (226 N. Whittaker St.) as well as train stations in both Niles (598 Dey St.) and Dowagiac (200 Depot Dr.), reaching Harbor Country and subsequently navigating across this region is much easier if you have a rental car or a vehicle of your own. From Muskegon, for instance, you can simply head south on US-31, merge onto I-94 West, and take exit 6 toward Union Pier, a 114-mile trip that usually takes less than two hours. From Indiana, meanwhile, you can simply drive north along the coast of Lake Michigan, either on US-12 or I-94. US-12 also gives you easy access to the Four Flags Area, where you'll find the festivals of Niles and the wineries of Buchanan and Berrien Springs. If, on the other hand, you're headed from Chicago, just follow I-90 East and I-94 East through Indiana, take exit 1 for M-239/La Porte Road, and continue into downtown New Buffalo; without traffic, the 70-mile trip will take about 70 minutes. Just be advised that, en route from the Windy City, parts of I-90 East and I-94 East serve as the Indiana Toll Road.

St. Joseph and Benton Harbor

Once called Newberryport, the area now known as St. Joseph grew as a rest stop for travelers between Detroit and Chicago. Set on a bluff overlooking Lake Michigan, "St. Joe" is a pleasant city of 8,300 people with attractive historic buildings and a vibrant downtown shopping district, lined with art galleries, trendy boutiques, and charming coffeehouses. Ship captains and lumber barons built many of the town's 19th-century Victorians; today, vacationers and second-home owners enjoy the bluff-top views of the area's lovely beaches and parks.

Home to the Whirlpool world headquarters and one of the country's oldest Christian communities, Benton Harbor, St. Joseph's slightly larger northern neighbor, has a burgeoning arts community of its own. Together, the two towns present the well-attended Blossomtime Festival, the state's oldest multi-community festival, every spring, and not far away lies a string of wineries that make up the Lake Michigan Shore Wine Trail.

SIGHTS
Beaches
Many visitors need no more entertainment than the **Silver Beach County Park,** the lovely municipal beach that skirts downtown St. Joseph, a favorite spot for anglers and anyone wishing for a front-row seat to watch the sunset. From here—and from **Tiscornia Beach,** situated near

THE SOUTHWEST COAST

the northern bank of the St. Joseph River—you'll spy the North Pier, a long cement breakwater jutting 1,000 feet into the lake, leading to twin lighthouses that guard the harbor. The farther light is cylindrical, while the other is perched atop an octagonal, red-roofed structure, a replica of the 1859 lighthouse that once stood on the bluff. The well-photographed **North Pierhead Lighthouse** was once featured on a U.S. postal stamp commemorating Great Lakes-area lighthouses. When lined up, these two lights guide mariners to St. Joseph's harbor. They remain as one of only two range-light systems in the Great Lakes region; the other is in Grand Haven, farther north.

Of course, the lighthouses aren't the only worthy attractions here. Just steps from family-friendly Silver Beach, kids will relish a ride on the **Silver Beach Carousel** (333 Broad St., 269/982-8500, www.silverbeachcarousel.com, 4pm-8:30pm Thurs., 11am-5pm Fri.-Sat., and noon-5pm Sun. Jan.-Mar., 10am-5pm Thurs.-Sat. and noon-5pm Sun. Apr.-May, 10am-10pm daily June-Aug., 4pm-8:30pm Thurs., 11am-9pm Fri.-Sat., and noon-5pm Sun. Sept.-Dec., $2/ride), which contains 48 unique, hand-carved carousel figures, from horses and tigers to clown fish, and two chariots, including one that's wheelchair-accessible. Open year-round, the lighted, music-enhanced carousel also features historical photographs chronicling St. Joseph's past. In addition, Silver Beach boasts **Michigan's tallest kaleidoscope,** the **Whirlpool Compass Fountain** (5pm-9pm daily May, 11am-10pm daily Memorial Day weekend-Labor Day weekend, noon-2pm and 5pm-9pm daily Sept., noon-2pm and 5pm-9pm Sat.-Sun. Oct., free), where kids can cool off in the summer, and the **Curious Kids' Discovery Zone** (333 Broad St., 269/982-8500, www.curiouskidsmuseum.org, 10am-5pm Mon.-Thurs., 10am-6pm Fri.-Sat., noon-5pm Sun. June-Labor Day, 4pm-8:30pm Thurs., 11am-5pm Fri.-Sat., noon-5pm Sun. Sept.-May, $6 pp, children under 3 free), which presents water-related exhibits as well as a climbing wall.

Museums and Historic Sites

Housed in an old brick four-square house above Lake Michigan, St. Joseph's clever **Curious Kids' Museum** (415 Lake Blvd., 269/983-2543, www.curiouskidsmuseum.org, 10am-5pm Mon.-Sat. and noon-5pm Sun. June-Aug., 10am-5pm Wed.-Sat. and noon-5pm Sun. Sept.-May, $4-6 pp) ranks as one of the best museums of its kind in the state. From the minute they walk in the door, kids (and adults) are treated to bright, colorful displays—including the lobby murals by eccentric Niles cartoonist/artist Nancy Drew—that are both engaging and playful. Excellent exhibits teach but don't preach: Kids can explore a rainforest, navigate a ship through the Great Lakes, experience what it's like to be handicapped, or follow an apple crop through autumn processing and sell the results at a farm stand.

Down the street at the **Krasl Art Center** (707 Lake Blvd., 269/983-0271, www.krasl.org, 10am-4pm Mon.-Wed. and Fri.-Sat., 10am-9pm Thurs., 1pm-4pm Sun., donation suggested), visitors find both energetic volunteers and a schedule of well-chosen changing exhibits. Four galleries display fine art, contemporary works, folk arts and crafts, creations by regional artists, and occasional traveling exhibitions. A gallery shop offers art-related gifts and other goodies, and the center encourages patrons to take a SculpTour, a self-guided tour of outdoor sculptures in St. Joseph and Benton Harbor.

The **Heritage Museum and Cultural Center** (601 Main St., St. Joseph, 269/983-1191, www.theheritagemcc.org, 10am-4pm Tues.-Sat. and noon-4pm Sun. Memorial Day-Labor Day, 10am-4pm Tues.-Sat. Sept.-May, $5 adults, $1 children 6-17, children under 6 free) explores the area's culture and history with exhibits, lectures, walking tours, and extensive archives. Recent exhibits have explored St. Joseph's lighthouses and southwestern Michigan's fruit belt.

While St. Joseph's history harkens back to the 1670s, Benton Harbor's origins began in 1835, when Eleazar Morton and his family became the first white settlers on the northern side of the St. Joseph River. By 1849, they owned 500 acres of farmland, including a peach orchard and a hilltop house overlooking what would become Benton Harbor, founded in part by Eleazar's son Henry. Today, the **Morton House Museum** (501 Territorial Rd., 269/925-7011, www.mortonhousemuseum.org, tours 10am-4pm Mon.-Wed., noon-5pm Sun. May-Sept., $5 adults, $3 seniors 62 and over, $3 children 6-15), the oldest standing home in Benton Harbor, educates visitors about life in the 19th century.

Box Factory for the Arts

Until 1989, the Williams Brothers Box Factory, built near the turn of the 20th century, served as a manufacturing plant for various decorative and specialty boxes. Since 1995, the historic building has been used as an arts facility for local artists and residents. Today, the **Box Factory for the Arts** (1101 Broad St., St. Joseph, 269/983-3688, www.boxfactoryforthearts.org, 10am-4pm Mon.-Sat., 1pm-4pm Sun., free) houses a gift shop, a café, three art galleries, and 37 artists' studios. The center also offers art classes and workshops, presents films on Friday nights, and holds concerts every Saturday evening.

◖ Lake Michigan Shore Wine Country

Thanks to the moderating effects of nearby Lake Michigan, a pocket of southwestern Michigan from Buchanan to Fennville basks in a microclimate surprisingly good for growing grapes. With its sandy soils, gently rolling terrain, and dependable snow cover needed to protect the fragile vines, it has been compared to the wine-producing areas of northern Europe, including France's renowned Champagne region.

While that may be wishful thinking, the state is indeed becoming more and more recognized for its winemaking. (Southwest Michigan is one of two recognized wine regions in the state; the other is farther north, in the Traverse City area.) Early on, wineries experimented with hardy but overly sweet grapes such as Concord and Catawba. As tastes grew more sophisticated and drier wines became the vogue, French hybrids were introduced, including vidal blanc, from white grapes, and chancellor and chambourcin, from red.

In recent years, Michigan's award-winning wines have become genuine competition for California's crop. Now, Michigan winemakers are building on their growing success by developing their marketing sense along with their grapes. Like California, Michigan works aggressively to promote the picturesque vineyards as a tourist attraction. On weekends, busloads of tourists pour into the St. Julian Winery in Paw Paw for tours. Tabor Hill has a restaurant overlooking its gorgeous vineyards. Warner Vineyards has an elegant tasting room and a charming patio.

Each of the wineries, vineyards, and tasting rooms in this part of the state indeed makes a pleasant warm-weather pilgrimage. You may wish to plan your visit for the weekend after Labor Day, when the three-day Paw Paw Wine & Harvest Festival features free wine-tastings. For more information about Michigan wines, contact the **Lake Michigan Shore Wine Trail** (www.lakemichiganshorewinetrail.com) or the **Michigan Grape and Wine Industry Council** (517/284-5733, www.michiganwines.com).

DOMAINE BERRIEN CELLARS AND WINERY

Established in 2001 on part of a family-owned 80-acre fruit farm six miles east of Lake Michigan, **Domaine Berrien Cellars and Winery** (398 E. Lemon Creek Rd., Berrien Springs, 269/473-9463, www.domaineberrien.com, noon-5pm Wed.-Mon. May-Dec., noon-5pm Fri.-Sun. Jan.-Apr.) is one of the first vineyards you'll encounter on the road from St. Joseph. Although relatively new to the scene, Domaine Berrien has already garnered a reputation for excellent handcrafted wines, including their award-winning selections like pinot noir, cabernet franc, syrah, pinot grigio, and traminette. Visitors can tour the winemaking area and enjoy a glass of wine with locally made cheeses and sausages on an outside patio overlooking the scenic vineyards.

LEMON CREEK WINERY& FRUIT FARM

Just down the road from Domaine Berrien lies the **Lemon Creek Winery & Fruit Farm** (533 E. Lemon Creek Rd., Berrien Springs, 269/471-1321, www.lemoncreekwinery.com, 10am-6pm Mon.-Sat., noon-6pm Sun.). The vineyards are part of a 150-acre fruit farm that has been in the Lemon family for roughly 160 years. The farm began growing grapes in the early 1980s as a way of diversifying crops. The winery opened in 1984, eventually drawing more than 100 awards. Well-known varietals include ruby rose and the full-bodied meritage.

Visitors are welcome to wander among the neatly labeled vines outside the tasting room and picnic at the nearby tables. Afterward, sign on for one of the informal tours that give an overview of wine production, from grape growing through bottling. If the tour inspires you to try your hand at winemaking at home, you can purchase pre-picked grapes or head out to the fields to pluck your own. U-pick options also include raspberries, sweet cherries, nectarines, plums, peaches, and a variety of apples.

FREE RUN CELLARS

Chris and Matt Moersch, the current general manager and winemaker/distiller, respectively, of the family-run Round Barn Winery, opened a sister winery, **Free Run Cellars** (10062 Burgoyne Rd., Berrien Springs, 269/471-1737, www.freeruncellars.com, noon-6pm Sat. and noon-5pm Sun. Feb.-Mar., noon-6pm Fri.-Sat. and noon-5pm Sun. Apr.-May and Nov.-Dec., noon-5pm Sun.-Thurs. and noon-6pm Fri.-Sat. June-Labor Day, noon-5pm Sun.-Mon. and Thurs., noon-6pm Fri.-Sat. Sept.-Oct., closed Jan.). Hailing from a family with over 25 years of grape-growing and wine-producing experience, the brothers claim they're using this new venture to enhance their family's legacy, "with a reverence to tradition, the desire to explore

new ideas, and the free run to find our own style of winemaking." Although no tours are offered, wine connoisseurs can sample wines in the on-site tasting room or visit the year-round tasting room in Union Pier.

TABOR HILL WINERY & RESTAURANT

Today's **Tabor Hill** (185 Mount Tabor Rd., Buchanan, 269/422-1161 or 800/283-3363, www.taborhill.com, 10am-5pm Mon.-Tues., 10am-9pm Wed.-Sat., noon-6pm Sun., tours noon-4:30pm daily May-Oct. and noon-4:30pm Sat.-Sun. Nov.-Apr.) is a far cry from the winery's early commune-like days under visionary founder and salesman Len Olson. David Upton, an heir to the Whirlpool fortune, rescued the ailing operation in the late 1970s, eventually turning it into one of the state's largest producing wineries, best known for its mid-priced wines made from French hybrid grapes, including the classic demi-sec (known as the "President's Wine" because it has been served

© JEFF GREENBERG

the Tabor Hill winery in Buchanan

© ROUND BARN WINERY

the Round Barn Winery in Baroda

at the White House), the dry riesling, and the grand mark—all award-winners.

If you're lucky, you'll catch winemaker Michael Merchant giving a tour. After a tour or tasting, consider a stop at Tabor Hill's glass-walled, year-round restaurant, where you can watch workers tending the vines and songbirds crowding the feeders. Views sometimes stretch to the distant Lake Michigan dunes. Entrées such as New Zealand elk chop and macadamia nut-crusted tilapia are always first-rate and feature homemade breads and fresh-from-the-field ingredients. Tabor Hill also has tasting rooms in Bridgman, Benton Harbor, and Saugatuck.

ROUND BARN WINERY

Nestled in the rolling hills of the Southwest Coast's countryside, the **Round Barn Winery** (10983 Hills Rd., Baroda, 800/716-9463, www.roundbarnwinery.com, noon-6pm Fri., 11am-6pm Sat., noon-5pm Sun. Jan.-Mar., noon-5pm Sun.-Thurs., noon-6pm Fri., 11am-6pm Sat. Apr.-May and Nov.-Dec., 11am-6pm Mon.-Fri., 11am-7pm Sat., noon-6pm Sun. June-Oct.) is a family-owned winery, distillery, and brewery. Once known as the Heart of the Vineyard, it was opened in 1992 by Rick Moersch, formerly a winemaker at Tabor Hill, and specializes in handcrafted wines, fruit brandies, vodka, and microbrews.

An 1880s post-and-beam farmhouse serves as the tasting room, where you can learn about the winery's unique winemaking style, which incorporates techniques pioneered at Michigan State University. A former science teacher, Moersch is more than willing to explain the winery's unique characteristics, including its choice of the French-influenced Alsatian style of winemaking, the unusual vine-trellising system introduced by Michigan State University, and the necessity of yeast in making complex wines. The winery hosts winemaking classes and holiday events throughout the year; there's an additional tasting room in Union Pier.

HICKORY CREEK WINERY

The southernmost winery in the Lake Michigan Shore Wine Country, **Hickory Creek** (750 Browntown Rd., Buchanan, 269/422-1100, www.hickorycreekwinery. com, 11am-6pm Fri.-Sat., noon-6pm Sun., by appointment Mon.-Thurs.) is the product of three distinct perspectives; the winery's trio of owners, all of whom share a lifelong passion for winemaking, hail from three premier wine-growing nations: America, Australia, and Germany. Hickory Creek specializes in crafting world-class wines from grapes grown exclusively along Lake Michigan's eastern shore. Current selections include riesling, chardonnay, pinot noir, gewürztraminer, and apple wine.

CONTESSA WINE CELLARS

Between Benton Harbor and Paw Paw, you'll find **Contessa Wine Cellars** (3235 Friday Rd., Coloma, 269/468-5534, www.contessawine-cellars.com, noon-5pm daily), the brainchild of third-generation winemaker Tony Peterson, who longed to blend traditional winemaking practices with old-world ambience. Here, visitors are treated to an enormous selection of wines, from a full-bodied merlot to a dry white divino, served in an elegant tasting room that's reminiscent of an Italian villa. The view's not bad either; from the winery's European-style terrace, you can look across acres of stunning orchards, nestled in the verdant Coloma Valley.

KARMA VISTA VINEYARDS AND WINERY

Just a little farther east, on the road to Paw Paw, you'll encounter **Karma Vista** (6991 Ryno Rd., Coloma, 269/468-9463, www.karmavista. com, 11am-5pm Mon. and Wed.-Sat., noon-5pm Sun.), which prides itself on being "one of Michigan's newest wineries from one of the state's oldest farm families." Situated on a serene

hillside above the town of Coloma, Karma Vista promises a relaxing experience for wine connoisseurs. Those with a sense of humor will also appreciate this quirky winery, where the colorful wine labels will elicit a chuckle. Who, after all, can resist sampling selections like Cha Cha Chardonnay, Watusi Red, Stone Temple Pinot, and Moondance Merlot?

ST. JULIAN WINERY

Family-owned **St. Julian** (716 S. Kalamazoo St., Paw Paw, 269/657-5568, www.stjulian. com, 9am-6pm Mon.-Sat., noon-6pm Sun.) has always prided itself on making good wines that are accessible to a wide variety of tastes and budgets. The winery is located on a busy commercial strip and is heavily marketed to tour buses and groups, so it isn't exactly on par with the personalized attention given by smaller boutique wineries. What the oldest and largest winery in the state does well is wine education and wine-related tourism: Its year-round tours include an informative audiovisual show and a visit to the bottling line and fermenting room. Visitors in late August and September can watch grapes being delivered and crushed. The winery and its Union Pier, Dundee, and Frankenmuth tasting rooms are open year-round.

WARNER VINEYARDS

Next to St. Julian's, **Warner Vineyards** (706 S. Kalamazoo St., Paw Paw, 269/657-3165 or 800/756-5357, www.warnerwines.com, 10am-5pm Mon.-Sat., noon-5pm Sun.), the state's second-oldest winery, operates out of an appealing 1898 waterworks building. Founded in 1938, Warner boasts one of the Midwest's few champagne cellars, which realistically simulates the chalk storage vaults of the Champagne region of France. Visitors can take a short, self-guided tour, then relax afterward over a glass of bubbly (or any of the other Warner wines) on the charming wine deck. Warner's specialties include their award-winning dry champagne and the popular

THE SOUTHWEST COAST

Fenn Valley Vineyards and Wine Cellar in Fennville

© DANIEL MARTONE

liebestrauben and holiberry. Warner also offers a tasting room in South Haven.

FENN VALLEY VINEYARDS AND WINE CELLAR

The northernmost winery in Lake Michigan Shore Wine Country, **Fenn Valley** (6130 122nd Ave., Fennville, 269/561-2396, www.fennvalley.com, 11am-5pm Mon.-Sat., 1pm-5pm Sun.) isn't far from the art galleries of Saugatuck and Douglas. Since 1973, this family-operated winery has been producing award-winning handcrafted wines that benefit from the combination of a favorable climate, traditional winemaking techniques, and modern technology. Vineyard tours are offered on weekends August-October; tastings are included for a nominal fee. Cellar tours and special events are offered year-round. Fenn Valley also has a tasting room in nearby Saugatuck.

FESTIVALS AND EVENTS
◖ Blossomtime Festival

Among southwestern Michigan's many warm-weather events, one highlight is the Blossomtime Festival, usually held in early May in the neighboring communities of St. Joseph and Benton Harbor. Begun in 1923 to promote the area's agricultural industry, the **Blossomtime Festival** (269/926-7397, www.blossomtimefestival.org) celebrates the coming of spring with a Grand Floral Parade featuring more than 125 floats, tractors, antique cars, bands, and costumed performers from several surrounding communities. As the oldest and largest multi-community festival in Michigan, Blossomtime also fills the weeklong celebration with children's events, food tents, pageants, and more.

Other Area Festivals

Given the Southwest Coast's notoriety as a significant wine-producing region, it's no surprise that the **Paw Paw Wine & Harvest Festival** (269/655-1111, www.wineandharvestfestival.com) takes place every September, the weekend after Labor Day. During the three-day event, festival-goers can enjoy live music, carnival rides, car shows, turtle derbies, and grape-stomping contests. Meanwhile, wine connoisseurs are treated to free winery tours and wine-tastings at St. Julian Winery and Warner Vineyards, all weekend long.

To the southeast, in nearby Cass County, you'll find at least two other fun-filled events. In late July or early August, the six-day **Cass County Fair** (Cassopolis, 269/445-8265, www. casscountymifair.com, $6 adults, $1 children 6-12) invites revelers to watch or participate in dog shows, livestock competitions, demolition derbies, tractor pulls, parades, and other farm-related activities. In mid-May, the **Dogwood Fine Arts Festival** (Dowagiac, 269/782-1115, http://dogwoodfinearts.org) entices lovers of art, music, dance, and literature with a week of lectures, concerts, performances, and readings from regional artists.

SHOPPING

While St. Joseph's State Street shopping district contains myriad bookstores, gift shops, clothing boutiques, and jewelry emporiums, perhaps the highlight of this region is its bountiful produce. Nature's fruits can be enjoyed at two of the area's largest growers: **Fruit Acres Farm Market & U-Pick** (3390 Friday Rd., Coloma, 269/208-3591, www.fruitacresfarms.com, 9am-7pm daily June-Oct.) and **Tree-Mendus Fruit Farm** (9351 E. Eureka Rd., Eau Claire, 269/782-7101, www.treemendus-fruit.com, 10am-6pm Wed.-Mon. June-Aug., 10am-6pm Fri.-Mon. Sept.-Oct.).

Since 1964, the family-operated Fruit Acres has provided area communities with a wide range of fresh produce and products. Today, the 230-acre orchard boasts seasonal crops of plums, peaches, black cherries, tree-ripened apricots, and crisp apples. The market also sells apple cider; flowers, fruit, and vegetables from other area farmers; and locally made jams, jellies, salsas, and other condiments. During the season, visitors can pick their own fruit every Saturday and Sunday. Leashed dogs are welcome.

Tree-Mendus is one of the area's best U-pick farms, with acres upon acres of apples, pears, cherries, nectarines, peaches, plums, and more. Don't miss the chance to bite into one of the special heritage apples, a hobby of Tree-Mendus's curator. Besides the full fields, there's also a full roster of special events such as pony rides, harvest-time activities, and the International Cherry Pit-Spitting Championship.

Meanwhile, if you fancy a drive, head northeast on I-94 to the town of Coloma. Here, surrounded by peach orchards and not far from Contessa Wine Cellars, you'll find **The Chocolate Garden** (2691 Friday Rd., Coloma, 269/468-9866, www.chocolategarden.com, 9am-8pm daily late May-Oct., 10am-6pm daily Nov.-late May), which has long been known for its delicious, handmade chocolate truffles. At present, there are roughly two dozen flavors, ranging from lemon drop (made with white chocolate) to black licorice (made with milk chocolate) to cayenne kick (made with dark chocolate).

SPORTS AND RECREATION
Golf

Near the intersection of I-94 and I-196, **Lake Michigan Hills Golf Club** (2520 Kerlikowske Rd., Benton Harbor, 269/849-4653, www.lakemichiganhills.com, daily Apr.-Oct., $40-55 pp w/cart) has been voted one of the best public golf courses in southwestern Michigan by *Michigan Golfer* magazine. Farther inland, you'll find several other well-favored courses, including **Paw Paw Lake Golf Course** (4548 Forest Beach Rd., Watervliet, 269/463-3831, www.pawpawlakegolfcourse.com, daily Apr.-Oct., $42-57 pp w/cart) and **Indian Lake Hills Golf Course** (55321 Brush Lake Rd., Eau Claire, 269/782-2540, www.indianlakehills.com, daily Apr.-Oct., $31-39 pp w/cart).

Bird-Watching

Those who seek sanctuary find it at the **Sarett Nature Center** (2300 Benton Center Rd., Benton Harbor, 269/927-4832, www.sarett.com, 9am-5pm Tues.-Fri., 10am-5pm Sat., 1pm-5pm Sun., donation suggested). These 800 acres along the Paw Paw River northeast of Benton Harbor comprise a number of natural habitats, including upland meadows, swamp forests, and lowland marshes. As a nod to bird-watchers, the property contains many benches, elevated towers, and five miles of trails, which are open sunrise-sunset every day. A naturalist is usually on hand to answer questions. Ask about the full schedule of demonstrations, nature walks, workshops, and classes.

Boating and Fishing

Like most of the towns along the Southwest Coast, St. Joseph and Benton Harbor share both a shipping past and a modern-day boating fever, as evidenced by the 30 colorful boat sculptures throughout downtown St. Joseph and by the full-service **Pier 1000 Marina** (1000 Riverview Dr., 269/927-4471, www.pier1000.com) in adjacent Benton Harbor. There's nothing quite like sailing off across the blue expanse of Lake Michigan on a cloudless summer day.

But, even if you don't have your own boat, you can still enjoy venturing out on the water. **Headhunter Charters** (10034 Painter School Rd., Berrien Center, 269/921-6997, www.headhuntersportfishing.com, rates vary) specializes in year-round, open-water sportfishing charters on Lake Michigan and guided river trips for salmon and steelhead on the St. Joseph River.

ACCOMMODATIONS AND FOOD

Overlooking Lake Michigan, **C The Boulevard Inn & Bistro** (521 Lake Blvd., St. Joseph, 269/983-6600 or 800/875-660, www.theboulevardinn.com, $125-200 d) provides spacious suites, a genteel decor, and a super restaurant **Bistro on the the Boulevard** (269/983-3882, 6:30am-9:30am, 11:30am-2pm, and 5pm-9pm Mon.-Thurs., 6:30am-9:30am, 11:30am-2pm, and 5pm-10pm Fri., 7:30am-10am and 5pm-10pm Sat., 7:30am-10am, 11am-2pm, and 5pm-9pm Sun., $8-31) that offers breakfast, lunch, and dinner daily.

Dinner can be especially wonderful here; take a seat on the lovely outdoor terrace, order the chef's three-course special, select from one of the world's most outstanding restaurant wine lists, and enjoy the incredible lake views below. As a bonus, The Boulevard is within easy walking distance of shops, restaurants, and beaches.

The **South Cliff Inn** (1900 Lakeshore Dr., St. Joseph, 269/983-4881, www.southcliffinn.com, $85-229 d) is a gracious English-inspired bed-and-breakfast with seven sun-filled rooms that also overlook the big lake. It's run by charming Bill Swisher, who left behind a 10-year career as director of a probate court to open the inn.

If you'd feel more comfortable in a chain hotel, you'll find several in the area. Benton Harbor has at least two options: **Howard Johnson** (798 Ferguson Dr., 269/927-1172, www.hojo.com, $94-150 d) and **Courtyard St. Joseph/Benton Harbor** (1592 Mall Dr., 269/925-3000, www.marriott.com, $120-200 d). **Comfort Inn & Suites** (153 Ampey Rd., Paw Paw, 269/655-0303, www.comfortinn.com, $85-100 d) is in the heart of southwestern Michigan's wine country.

As for area vittles, **Schu's Grill & Bar** (501 Pleasant St., 269/983-7248, www.schus.com, 11am-10pm Mon.-Thurs., 11am-11pm Fri.-Sat., 11am-9pm Sun., $8-22) has quickly become a St. Joseph institution, with great sandwiches, soups, and brews in a pub-style setting above the waterfront. For morning coffee and baked goods, head for **Caffe Tosi** (516 Pleasant St., St. Joseph, 269/983-3354, 7am-8pm Mon.-Fri., 8am-8pm Sat., 8am-4pm Sun., $4-9).

Camping

For a real bargain, there are two excellent campgrounds in the vicinity. The **Dune Lake Campground** (80855 CR-376, Coloma, 269/764-8941, www.dunelakecampground.com, $27-30 daily) welcomes RVs and tents to a picturesque area not far from Lake Michigan. Farther inland, **Shamrock Park** (9385 Old US-31 S., Berrien Springs, 269/473-5691, www.shamrockpark.net, $20-30 daily), a year-round camping and fishing park in the heart of wine country, provides easy access to several of the wineries in the Lake Michigan Shore Wine Country. For those without a tent or an RV, both campgrounds also offer rental cabins.

INFORMATION AND SERVICES

For more information about St. Joseph, Benton Harbor, and the surrounding area, contact the **Southwestern Michigan Tourist Council** (2300 Pipestone Rd., Benton Harbor, 269/925-6301, www.swmichigan. org, 8:30am-5pm Mon.-Fri.), the **Coloma-Watervliet Area Chamber of Commerce** (209 N. Paw Paw St., Coloma, 269/468-9160, www.coloma-watervliet.org, 9am-5pm Mon.-Fri.), or the **Four Flags Area Council on Tourism** (321 E. Main St., Niles, 269/684-7444, www.fourflagsarea.org, 10am-3pm Tues. and Thurs.). For local news and weather, consult the *Herald-Palladium* (www.herald-palladium.com). For county information, contact the **Berrien County Administration** (www.berriencounty.org).

For mailing needs, visit the **St. Joseph post office** (205 Main St., 269/983-1579, www.usps.com); Benton Harbor has several locations, too. Both towns also have necessary services like groceries, dentists, and banks, including a few branches of **Fifth Third Bank** (www.53.com).

In case of an emergency, dial **911** from any cell or public phone. For medical services, visit the **Lakeland Regional Medical Center** (1234 Napier Ave., St. Joseph, 269/983-8300, www.lakelandhealth.org). If necessary, you can fill prescriptions at **Rite Aid** in Benton Harbor (1701 S. M-139, 269/927-3101, www.riteaid.com).

GETTING THERE AND AROUND

Amtrak (800/872-7245, www.amtrak.com) offers rail service between Chicago and St. Joseph (410½ Vine St.), both **Greyhound** (269/925-1121 or 800/231-2222, www.greyhound.com) and **Indian Trails** (800/292-3831, www.indiantrails.com) provide bus service to Benton Harbor at 2412 South M-139 and 2413 South M-139, respectively, and the **Kalamazoo/Battle Creek International Airport** (AZO, 5235 Portage Rd., Kalamazoo, 269/388-3668, www.azoairport.com) isn't too far east via I-94. Still, exploring St. Joseph, Benton Harbor, and the surrounding wine country is infinitely easier with a vehicle.

Whether you're coming from Detroit or Chicago, you can take I-94 almost directly to the St. Joseph/Benton Harbor area. From downtown Detroit, for instance, you can simply take M-10 North and I-75 South, merge onto I-96 West, continue onto M-14 West, and follow I-94 West toward the coast; without traffic, the 186-mile trip usually requires 2.75 hours. From Chicago, meanwhile, you can reach Benton Harbor by following I-90 East and I-94 East through Illinois and Indiana, crossing the Michigan state line, taking exit 28 for M-139 North/Scottdale Road, and continuing on M-139 North and Pipestone Road into downtown Benton Harbor; without traffic, the 100-mile trip will take about 1.75 hours. Just be advised that, en route from the Windy City, parts of I-90 East and I-94 East serve as the Indiana Toll Road. Of course, once you reach the St. Joseph/Benton Harbor area, you can easily access the wineries and tasting rooms along the Lake Michigan Shore Wine Trail via routes like I-94, I-196, US-31, and US-12.

THE SOUTHWEST COAST

South Haven

Once the center of Michigan's "fruit belt," the South Haven area is still a leading producer of blueberries and peaches. Lake Michigan can take credit for the area's well-drained soil and the moderating temperature effects of the prevailing west winds. Southwest Michigan's fruit belt had its origins in the 1850s, when St. Joseph and Benton Harbor farmers noticed that their peaches survived the severe winters that killed off other crops in the rest of the state. Fresh fruit was in high demand in bustling Chicago, and by the 1860s, crops were being shipped across the lake almost as fast as they could be picked.

Eventually, fruit farming and fruit-related industries spread throughout much of Van Buren and Berrien Counties. South Haven became famous for its peach crop; at the turn of the 20th century, some 144,000 acres were devoted to peaches, more than all the other fruit crops combined. But freezes during the 1920s led many farmers to abandon peaches in favor of heartier apples. More recently, blueberries have gained popularity, with the area around South Haven emerging as the world's leading blueberry producer. In July (National Blueberry Month), you'll spot blueberry stands along rural roadsides.

South Haven proper is known for its beautiful beaches and scenic fishing port, which prompted the *London Financial Times* to call it "one of the most picturesque and charming small fishing ports you could hope to find." In summer, the population of this lakeside town swells from roughly 4,400 to nearly 20,000, as visitors fill the historic inns that line North Shore Drive, stroll along the walks and shops that parallel the Black River near its mouth, and sunbathe on the long arc of sand beach that rims the town's northwestern edge. The town also offers its share of museums, festivals, golf courses, and other outdoor pleasures, including the trailhead of the Kal-Haven Trail, popular among hikers and bikers.

SIGHTS
Beaches
Seven lovely beaches line the Lake Michigan shore, north and south of where the Black River opens into the great lake. **North Beach,** situated on the northern bank of the river, is a hot spot for summertime beachgoers, with its volleyball courts and concession stand. For swimmers who enjoy a few less people and a little more quiet, **Packard Park Beach** farther north might be your best bet. But, for those eager to sunbathe, watch passing boats, and take a stroll toward the vibrant red-and-black **South Haven South Pier Lighthouse Light, South Beach** is definitely the place for you. Established in 1903 at the end of the South Pier and accessible via a sturdy catwalk, the cylindrical lighthouse is still active today; of course, most visitors just enjoy walking along the picturesque pier for an up-close glimpse.

Museums
The **Michigan Maritime Museum** (260 Dyckman Ave., 269/637-8078, www.michiganmaritimemuseum.org, 10am-5pm daily, $5 adults, $4 seniors, $3.50 students, children under 6 free) features a variety of maritime displays, some of which chronicle the U.S. Coast Guard and the commercial fishers who plied the local waters. Another intriguing attraction is the **Michigan Flywheelers Museum** (06285 68th St., 269/639-2010, www.michiganflywheelers.org, 10am-3pm Wed. and Sat.-Sun. Memorial Day-Labor Day), dedicated to the preservation of antique gas engines, steam engines, and tractors. In early September, the museum hosts its annual Antique Engine and Tractor Show, which includes historical demonstrations and a flea market as well as the usual parades, games, and crafts.

Van Buren State Park
South of South Haven, **Van Buren State Park** (23960 Ruggles Rd., 269/637-2788, daily,

© LAURA MARTONE

anchored near South Haven's South Beach

annual $11 Recreation Passport for Michigan residents or $8.40 day-use fee/$30.50 yearly Recreation Passport for nonresidents required) boasts some of the best water views in this part of the state. The high, wooded sand dunes of the 400-acre park hide a narrow opening that leads to the property's main attraction: the limitless blue waters of Lake Michigan, edged by a broad sweep of fine, black-speckled sand. "No Trespassing" signs on the huge barrier dunes hopefully prevent human erosion from adding to the natural wear of the fragile sand mountains.

ENTERTAINMENT AND EVENTS
The Arts
In addition to displaying a wide array of visual arts, the **South Haven Center for the Arts** (600 Phoenix St., 269/637-1041, www.southhavenarts.org, 10am-5pm Tues.-Thurs., 10am-4pm Fri., 1pm-4pm Sat.-Sun., event prices vary) hosts numerous concerts each year, showcasing styles as varied as Brazilian jazz, Celtic and classical music, blues, and folk.

National Blueberry Festival
South Haven hosts several different events during the year, but the town's probably best known for its longstanding National Blueberry Festival (www.blueberryfestival.com), which takes place in early August. Besides standard fare like raffles, pageants, parades, and the like, this four-day event does its best to celebrate the blessed fruit with blueberry pie-eating contests, blueberry pancake breakfasts, and blueberry-related cooking demonstrations.

SHOPPING
While South Haven has a few whimsical shops—such as **Decadent Dogs** (505 Phoenix Rd., 269/639-0716, www.decadentdogs.com, 10am-7pm Sun.-Thurs., 10am-9pm Fri.-Sat. May-Sept., 10am-5:30pm Sun.-Thurs., 10am-7pm Fri.-Sat. Oct.-Apr.), a terrific place to pamper your pooch with glitzy collars, fancy treat jars, and the like—shopping in these parts is all

THE SOUTHWEST COAST

about the fruit. For blueberries and blueberry products—including everything from jellies to plush toys—check out **The Blueberry Store** (525 Phoenix Rd., 269/637-6322 or 877/654-2400, www.theblueberrystore.com, 10am-7pm Mon.-Sat., 10am-6pm Sun. in spring/summer, shorter hours in fall/winter).

In addition, there are several farms, markets, and orchards in the vicinity, including the **South Haven Farmers' Market** (546 Phoenix St., 8am-2pm Sat. May-mid-Oct.), a smorgasbord of locally grown seasonal produce behind Dyckman Park. Northeast of South Haven, you'll find **McIntosh Apple Orchards** (6431 107th Ave., 708/878-3734, www.mcintoshorchards.com, Fri.-Sun. Apr.-June, daily July-Aug., Wed.-Sun. Sept.-Dec.), a 76-acre orchard and winery that's home to 26 different apple varieties. Here, you can purchase a myriad of homegrown products, including traditional hard cider.

SPORTS AND RECREATION
Golf
Golfers shouldn't miss playing a round at **HawksHead** (523 HawksNest Dr., 269/639-2121, www.hawksheadlinks.com, daily Apr.-Oct., $30-75 pp), once an asparagus farm that has now become one of the state's highest-ranked resorts, with a fine restaurant, a luxurious inn, and a championship course overlooking Lake Michigan. Another excellent choice is **Beeches Golf Club** (09601 68th St., 269/637-2600, www.beechesgolfclub.com, daily Apr.-Oct., $25-54 pp w/cart), which offers five sets of tee boxes, sandy waste areas on the front nine holes, and water hazards on the back nine—a challenge for almost any player.

Hiking and Biking
The **Kal-Haven Trail** (www.friendsofkalhaventrail.org), open to hiking and biking, stretches from South Haven to Kalamazoo along the abandoned Kalamazoo & South Haven Railroad, which existed from 1870 to 1970. There are several access points along the 34-mile route, which passes through the towns of Grand Junction, Bloomingdale, Gobles, and Kendall. The trail is also popular among bird-watchers, cross-country skiers, and snowmobilers. Trail passes ($3 individuals or $7 families daily, $15 individuals or $35 families yearly) are required for use of the trail; they can be purchased at various stores, restaurants, and museums, as well as the South Haven Visitors Bureau.

Diving
Given the shipping histories of the towns along the Southwest Coast, including St. Joseph, South Haven, Saugatuck, Holland, and Grand Haven, it's no surprise that underwater shipwrecks line the Lake Michigan shore. Established in 1999, the **Southwest Michigan Underwater Preserve** comprises at least 15 shipwrecks and geological formations between New Buffalo and Holland, with the greatest concentration of sites near South Haven. Some of the more popular ones include the *Rockaway*, a 107-foot schooner lost in a storm while transporting lumber from Ludington to Benton Harbor, and the *Havana*, a 92-foot yacht that sank in heavy seas en route from Chicago to Holland. Divers are welcome to explore these and other fascinating relics, though it's strongly advised that they bring along a compass, tow a warning flag, and watch out for obstacles that could cause entanglement. For more information, contact the **Michigan Underwater Preserve Council** (MUPC, 800/970-8717, www.michiganpreserves.org).

ACCOMMODATIONS AND FOOD
South Haven has no shortage of lodgings, from campgrounds to luxurious resorts. The **Old Harbor Inn** (515 Williams St., 269/637-8480, www.oldharborinn.com, $90-300 d) is part of a New England-style waterfront shopping village on the banks of the Black River—a great location, with extras like a friendly bar.

The Last Resort B&B Inn (86 N. Shore Dr., 269/637-8943, www.lastresortinn.com, early May-Oct., $125-295 d) was, ironically, South Haven's first resort. A few rooms have been updated with whirlpool suites, but the place has a funky, laid-back feel to it, largely due to its artist/owner, Mary Hammer. All rooms and suites offer views of Lake Michigan or the garden.

Lake Bluff Inn & Suites (76648 11th Ave., 269/637-8531, www.lakebluffinnandsuites. com, $99-269 d) is a well-kept waterfront resort that has been expanded over the years. It sits on a lovely bluff-top site south of South Haven, with outdoor pools, an indoor hot tub, a playground, and wireless Internet access.

Clementine's (500 Phoenix St., 269/637-4755, www.ohmydarling.com, 11am-10pm Mon.-Thurs., 11am-11pm Fri.-Sat., noon-10pm Sun., $8-19), originally a bank, is now a beloved family-owned restaurant. Don't miss the old pictures of Lake Michigan steamers and their captains and crews on the walls. The magnificently carved bar spent its first life on one of the many steamboats that once frequented the city. Almost everything on the menu has a clever, countrified moniker, but specialties include the Golden Garter (a fried pork sandwich) and the Tugboat Annie (charbroiled steak smothered with mushrooms, crab, shrimp, and mozzarella).

Camping

Like the area's other waterfront state parks, **Van Buren State Park** (23960 Ruggles Rd., 269/637-2788, daily, annual $11 Recreation Passport for Michigan residents or $8.40 da-use fee/$30.50 yearly Recreation Passport for nonresidents required) draws visitors because it offers a beach as well as the wooded dunes of Lake Michigan. Its 220 modern sites ($16-23 daily) are a five-minute walk from the beach and frequently fill on summer weekends. For reservations, which are highly recommended, call 800/447-2757 or visit www. michigan.gov/dnr.

For fancier environs, you can opt for the **Sunny Brook RV Resort** (68300 CR-388, 888/499-5253, www.sunnybrookrvresort.com, mid-Apr.-Oct., $35-45 daily), which includes a pool, a laundry and bathhouse, hiking trails, and a fishing lake.

INFORMATION AND SERVICES

For more information about South Haven, contact the **South Haven Van Buren Co. & Visitors Bureau** (546 Phoenix St., 269/637-5252 or 800/764-2836, www.southhaven.org, 9am-5pm Mon.-Fri., 10am-3pm Sat., noon-3pm Sun., shorter hours in winter) or the **Greater South Haven Chamber of Commerce** (606 Phillips St., 269/637-5171, www.southhavenmi.com, 9am-5pm Mon.-Fri.). For county information, contact the **Van Buren County Community Center** (www.vbco.org).

For mailing needs, visit the **South Haven post office** (336 Broadway St., 269/637-1283, www.usps.com). If you need an ATM, you'll find several branches of **Fifth Third Bank** (www.53.com) in the area, including one in South Haven and another in nearby Bangor.

In case of an emergency, dial **911** from any cell or public phone. For medical services, visit the **South Haven Community Hospital** (955 S. Bailey Ave., 269/637-5271, www.shch. org); prescriptions can be filled at the **Walmart Supercenter** (201 73rd St., 269/637-7802, www.walmart.com).

GETTING THERE AND AROUND

Although there are no direct flights to South Haven, you can get pretty close by flying into **Kalamazoo/Battle Creek International Airport** (AZO, 5235 Portage Rd., Kalamazoo, 269/388-3668, www.azoairport.com). From there, you can then rent a car and head west on I-94, merge onto US-131 North, and take M-43 West to downtown South Haven. **Amtrak** (800/872-7245, www.amtrak.com), meanwhile, offers rail service between Chicago and Bangor (541 Railroad St.), which lies about 11 miles (19 minutes) southeast of South Haven via M-43 West.

To reach South Haven directly, you can either hop a bus, via **Greyhound** (269/637-2944 or 800/231-2222, www.greyhound. com) or **Indian Trails** (800/292-3831, www. indiantrails.com), to the town's bus center at 1210 Phoenix Road or, as most travelers

THE SOUTHWEST COAST

do, embark on a road trip. If you're driving from elsewhere along the coast or from the towns in Michigan's Heartland, you'll more than likely get here via US-31, I-196, I-94, or M-43. From Grand Rapids, for instance, you can just follow I-196 West and Phoenix Road to downtown South Haven, a 58-mile trip that usually takes about 54 minutes. From Kalamazoo, meanwhile, M-43 West offers direct access to downtown South Haven, a 39-mile trip that normally takes about 55 minutes. If, on the other hand, you're headed from Chicago, you can simply follow I-90 East and I-94 East through Illinois and Indiana, cross the Michigan state line, continue onto I-196 North/US-31 North, and take Phoenix Road into downtown South Haven; without traffic, the 123-mile trip should take about two hours. Just be advised that, en route from the Windy City, parts of I-90 East and I-94 East serve as the Indiana Toll Road. Of course, once you reach downtown South Haven, it's easy enough to get around via car, bike, or your own two feet.

Saugatuck and Douglas

Some claim success has spoiled Saugatuck. Visit on a summer weekend, and you may be inclined to agree, when the city's narrow streets fill with much of what urban refugees are looking to escape: long lines in restaurants, shops overstuffed with designer threads, and beaches clogged with humanity. But come in any other season—or even midweek in summer—and Saugatuck reveals its real charm. The streets quiet down; you can linger over the excellent local cuisine and rich arts scene. And the folks who run the village's many fine B&Bs kick back and remember why they originally got into the business.

Saugatuck ("river's mouth" in the parlance of the Potawatomi tribe that settled the area) grew up in a fine natural setting—near the mouth of the wide Kalamazoo River, tucked between steep, rolling Lake Michigan dunes immediately west and lush, green orchards immediately east. Lumber interests discovered the region in the mid-1800s. Soon, it was home to a thriving mix of sawmills, factories, and the people to support them. Saugatuck, in fact, produced the majority of the lumber used to rebuild Chicago after the Great Fire in 1871.

When the trees inevitably disappeared, so did much of the city. The lack of trees proved especially fateful to a neighboring village known as Singapore. Without the windbreak the trees provided, blowing sand carried by the prevailing western winds eventually buried the city. Today, this ghost town lives on in local lore and in stories told by area tour guides.

While Singapore became the stuff of legend, Saugatuck survived and found new life as an art colony. In 1911, artists from the Art Institute of Chicago, less than two hours away, began sponsoring a summer art camp. Lured by the warm breezes and picturesque location, other creative types soon followed, earning Saugatuck an early reputation as Michigan's "Art Coast." Today, the Ox-Bow School of the Arts is still open to the public June-August and includes galleries, demonstrations, and changing exhibitions.

Douglas, Saugatuck's nearest neighbor, has also evolved over the years. Established in 1851 as a port for ships carrying lumber and produce to Chicago and other cities in the Great Lakes area, this small village-by-the-sea is now a popular vacation spot. Together, Saugatuck and Douglas have become two of the state's premier resort towns, boasting historic homes, quaint eateries, unique shops, and, of course, art galleries galore.

SIGHTS
◖ Art Galleries
The area's reputation as an "Art Coast" has attracted over 20 galleries within Saugatuck, Douglas, and Fennville. Notable stops

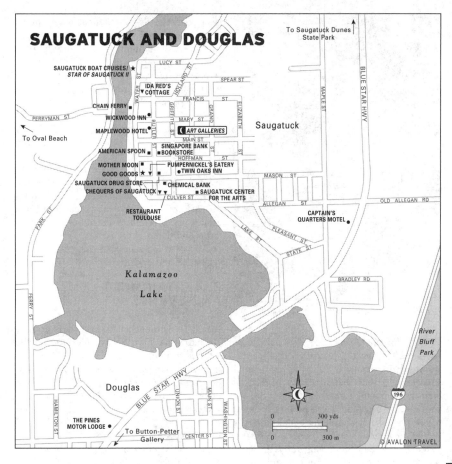

SAUGATUCK AND DOUGLAS

To Saugatuck Dunes State Park

SAUGATUCK BOAT CRUISES/ ★
STAR OF SAUGATUCK II

LUCY ST

SPEAR ST

BLUE STAR HWY

IDA RED'S
▼ COTTAGE

FRANCIS ST

CHAIN FERRY
WICKWOOD INN

MARY ST

MAPLEWOOD HOTEL

ART GALLERIES

Saugatuck

MAIN ST

AMERICAN SPOON

SINGAPORE BANK
BOOKSTORE

HOFFMAN ST

MOTHER MOON
GOOD GOODS ★

PUMPERNICKEL'S EATERY
TWIN OAKS INN

MASON ST

SAUGATUCK DRUG STORE
CHEQUERS OF SAUGATUCK

CHEMICAL BANK
SAUGATUCK CENTER
FOR THE ARTS

CULVER ST

ALLEGAN ST

OLD ALLEGAN RD

RESTAURANT
TOULOUSE

CAPTAIN'S
QUARTERS MOTEL

To Oval Beach

PERRYMAN ST

PARK ST

Kalamazoo
Lake

LAKE ST

PLEASANT ST

STATE ST

BRADLEY RD

FERRY ST

River
Bluff
Park

Douglas

BLUE STAR HWY

HAMILTON ST

THE PINES
MOTOR LODGE

To Button-Petter
Gallery

CENTER ST

196

0   300 yds

0   300 m

© AVALON TRAVEL

include the **Button-Petter Gallery** (161 N. Blue Star Hwy., Douglas, 269/857-2175, www.buttonpettergallery.com, 11am-5pm Fri.-Sun.), the convergence of two longstanding fine art galleries, offering a wide array of paintings, ceramics, sculptures, glasswork, and prints, and the eclectic **Good Goods** (106 Mason St., Saugatuck, 269/857-1557, www.goodgoods.com, 10am-6pm Sun.-Wed., 10am-7pm Thurs., 10am-10pm Fri.-Sat.), housed in a restored Victorian boardinghouse. Good Goods is the only place in town where you can pick up a one-of-a-kind piece by one of the area's founding artists,

Sylvia Randolph, who was amazingly prolific into her 90s. Between South Haven and Saugatuck, you'll also encounter the **Blue Coast Artists** (www.bluecoastartists.com, locations and hours vary), a group of 12 artists who allow visitors a behind-the-scenes look into their studios and galleries every spring, summer, and fall; some are even open year-round by appointment.

Beaches and Parks

If you're seeking a little more solitude, head for 1,000-acre **Saugatuck Dunes State Park** (269/637-2788, daily, annual $11 Recreation

© LAURA MARTONE

the sculpture garden behind Good Goods

Passport for Michigan residents or $8.40 day-use fee/$30.50 yearly Recreation Passport for nonresidents required). Despite 2.5 miles of undeveloped beach and dunes and 14 miles of well-marked trails (some winding to the top of the dunes for fantastic views), only about 40,000 people visit annually—making it the least visited park along this popular shoreline. Just a few miles north of Saugatuck, the park, which has no office or campground, offers easy-to-reach serenity in stark contrast to the downtown district.

Just a few steps from the shop-lined streets of Saugatuck, the frilly gingerbread **Chain Ferry** (269/857-2603, www.saugatuck.com, Memorial Day-Labor Day) shuttles visitors across the Kalamazoo River to the sandy Lake Michigan shore at **Oval Beach.** Families flock to this popular beach, filling the broad ribbon of sand and scaling Mount Baldhead, the steep dune that rises between town and the beach.

Tours

The two-level sternwheeler docked on the riverfront, the **Star of Saugatuck II,** offers cruises along the Kalamazoo River. Along the way, she passes beautiful homes, including one that once belonged to gangster Al Capone. (Keep in mind that in the Midwest, Capone apparently lived in as many places as Lincoln slept.) It operates May-October. For schedules, contact **Saugatuck Boat Cruises** (269/857-4261, www.saugatuckboatcruises.com, $19 adults, $8.50 children 6-12, $5.50 children 3-5, children under 3 free).

If you prefer land-based tours, consider **Saugatuck Dune Rides** (269/857-2253, www.saugatuckduneride.com, hours vary, $18 adults, $10 children 3-10). Expert guides lead small groups on 40-minute rides through the area's impressive dunes, sharing tales of the lost town of Singapore and educating visitors about local vegetation and wildlife.

ENTERTAINMENT AND EVENTS
The Arts

Visual arts are not Saugatuck's only creative claim to fame. The **Saugatuck Center for the Arts** (400 Culver St., 269/857-2399, www.sc4a.org, hours and prices vary) has, in addition to paintings and other artistic exhibitions, two theater spaces that present concerts, films, and comedy shows.

Festivals and Events

If possible, try to visit Saugatuck during one of its summertime festivals and art fairs. One that you should definitely not miss is the **Waterfront Film Festival** (various venues, 269/857-8351, www.waterfrontfilm.org, $10/film). In mid-June, this well-respected film fest brings a bit of Hollywood to Saugatuck. For one weekend, filmgoers, actors, producers, and directors converge for outstanding independent films from around the country, all screened in a casual setting.

SHOPPING

The Saugatuck/Douglas area offers some of the best shopping in western Michigan, with an eclectic mix of more than 70 stores and 30

touring the Kalamazoo River aboard the *Star of Saugatuck II*

© LAURA MARTONE

art galleries, most housed in well-kept 19th-century storefronts. The stylish merchandise ranges from highbrow antiques and trendy housewares to more campy fare.

Most of Saugatuck's shops are clustered along Butler, the main street. Two highlights include **American Spoon** (308 Butler St., 269/857-3084, www.spoon.com, 10am-6pm Mon.-Thurs., 10am-8pm Fri.-Sat., 11am-5pm Sun.), a Petoskey-based operation that specializes in fruit spreads and other gourmet foodstuffs, and the **Singapore Bank Bookstore** (317 Butler St., 269/857-3785, 10am-6pm daily), saved from the sands when it was moved here. Incense, jewelry, and metaphysical books are the specialty at **Mother Moon** (127 Hoffman St., 269/857-4407, www.magicalmothermoon.com, hours vary).

If trendiness threatens to overwhelm you, head for a breather at the **Saugatuck Drug Store** (201 Butler St., 269/857-2300, 9am-6pm Mon.-Sat., 10am-5pm Sun.), which has lured parched tourists and locals since 1913 with phosphates and other authentic treats.

For fresh produce, head to nearby Fennville, where family-operated **Crane Orchards** (6054 124th Ave., 269/561-8651, www.craneorchards.com, 10am-6pm daily summer and fall) offers an outstanding U-pick orchard, boasting sweet cherries in June, peaches in July or August, and apples in the fall. On-site diversions include hayrides, and a 20-acre corn maze. Almost more popular is **Crane's Pie Pantry Restaurant** (6054 124th Ave., 269/561-2297, www.cranespiepantry.com, 11am-4pm Tues.-Sun. Jan.-Mar., 11am-5pm daily Apr., 9am-8pm Mon.-Sat. and 11am-8pm Sun. May-Oct., 10am-6pm Tues.-Sat. and 11am-6pm Sun. Nov.-Dec., $4-10), which serves up thick sandwiches on homemade bread and Lue Crane's signature pies.

SPORTS AND RECREATION
Golf
For golfers, there are few nicer courses than the **Ravines Golf Club** (3520 Palmer Dr., Saugatuck, 269/857-1616, www.ravinesgolfclub.com, daily Apr.-Oct., $40-75 pp w/cart). In 2008, *Golf Digest* rated this Arnold Palmer-designed signature golf course, which opened to the public in 1999, as one of the "Best Places to Play" and as "The Best Conditioned Course in the State."

Horseback Riding
You might enjoy a pleasant horseback ride at the **Wild West Ranch** (2855 36th St., Allegan, 269/673-3539, www.4horserides.com, daily, $25-50 adults, $20-40 children), which offers a 1-hour trip past a natural wetland, a 1.5-hour trip through the woods, or a 2-hour trip across scenic hills. If you or your children need something a little tamer, you can always opt for a pony ride, a hayride, or, in winter, a sleigh ride.

ACCOMMODATIONS
With at least 30 bed-and-breakfasts in the area, Saugatuck has fast become one of the B&B capitals of the Midwest. The 1860 Victorian-style

THE SOUTHWEST COAST

CLAES OLDENBURG: AN OX-BOW ALUMNUS

Founded in 1910 along the shores of Lake Michigan, Saugatuck's **Ox-Bow** (3435 Rupprecht Way, 269/857-5811, www.ox-bow.org), a summer art school and artists' residency, has long inspired visual artists with its 115-acre campus of pristine forests, dunes, marshes, and historic buildings. Affiliated with the School of the Art Institute of Chicago, Ox-Bow offers courses in ceramics, glass, painting, drawing, papermaking, print, sculpture, and other artistic disciplines, from performance to photography. Not surprisingly, this prestigious school has lured many distinguished students, teachers, visiting artists, and board members over the years, from painter/sculptor Max Kahn to puppeteer Jim Henson – who, according to author Kit Lane (in her 1997 book *Painting the Town: A History of Art in Saugatuck and Douglas*), supposedly created an early version of his Kermit the Frog character amid Ox-Bow's pastoral splendor.

Claes Oldenburg, perhaps Ox-Bow's most famous alumnus, arrived in 1953 as a student. The son of a diplomat, Oldenburg was born in Sweden in 1929. As a child, he immigrated with his family to America, where he lived in New York and Chicago, and eventually studied literature and art history at Yale University. Back in the Windy City, he worked as a newspaper reporter while taking lessons at the Art Institute of Chicago. By 1953, he'd become a naturalized U.S. citizen and opened his own art studio.

During his summer at Ox-Bow, he further honed his artistic skills, dabbling in oil painting and staging his first "happening" – a choreographed combination of music, dance, dramatics, and poetry for which he and other artists became famous during the late 1950s and early 1960s. At Ox-Bow's annual end-of-summer farewell, Oldenburg planned a series of sulfur-bomb explosions over the lagoon to illuminate a barge carrying students dressed as priests and scantily clad maidens.

Following his Ox-Bow experience, Oldenburg sold his first art pieces at Chicago's annual 57th Street Art Fair. In 1956, he returned to New York and met numerous fellow artists, including Allan Kaprow and Robert Whitman, who introduced him to the world of interactive, performance-art "happenings." His first wife, model Pat Muschinski, frequently performed in his shows.

Of course, Oldenburg is probably best known as a pop-art sculptor, famous for his soft, oversized sculptures of food, such as apple cores, and public art installations featuring large replicas of everyday objects, including clothespins. Although initially dismissed as ridiculous, Oldenburg's colossal creations have since gained appreciation for their whimsy and insight.

Since 1976, Oldenburg has collaborated with his second wife, Dutch American pop sculptor Coosje van Bruggen. Together, they have created more than 40 colorful, large-scale projects for urban environments as varied as Miami, Philadelphia, Los Angeles, Tokyo, Barcelona, and the Netherlands. For more information, visit www.oldenburgvanbruggen.com.

Twin Oaks Inn (227 Griffith St., 269/857-1600, $110-150 d) is among the friendliest of the inns, with spacious rooms, portable cribs, and pull-out beds for families.

An 1860s Greek Revival building adjacent to the Saugatuck village square has served as a luxury resort hotel for more than 135 years. Today, it does business as the **Maplewood Hotel** (428 Butler St., 269/857-1771, www.maplewoodhotel.com, $140-275 d), with 15 antiques-filled bedrooms in the heart of the city's shops, galleries, and restaurants. Some suites have amenities like double whirlpool tubs and fireplaces. Breakfast is served in the Burr Tillstrom Dining Room, named for former Saugatuck resident and the creator of *Kukla, Fran, and Ollie* (a once-popular children's puppet show).

The **Wickwood Inn** (510 Butler St., Saugatuck, 800/385-1174, www.wickwood-inn.com, $189-489 d) is owned by Julee Rosso, co-author of *The Silver Palate* cookbook series, who treats guests at her bed-and-breakfast with

© LAURA MARTONE

the Twin Oaks Inn

seasonal menus she creates herself. But that's not the only special touch at this art-filled inn, recognized by numerous magazines. The 11 guest rooms are lavishly decorated with English and French country antiques, featherbeds, and antique linens.

For more economical options, head away from the water and toward the Blue Star Highway, where you'll find simple motels like the **Captain's Quarters Motel** (3242 Blue Star Hwy., Saugatuck, 269/857-2525, $50-125 d) or **The Pines Motor Lodge** (56 Blue Star Hwy., Douglas, 269/857-5211, www.thepinesmotorlodge.com, $70-205 d).

FOOD

Locals flock to **Ida Red's Cottage** (645 Water St., Saugatuck, 269/857-5803, 8am-2pm Wed.-Sun., $5-12) for the best breakfast in town, served all day. Specialties include dishes with a Greek or Italian flair, like the delectable Italian sausage omelets. Pick up an overstuffed sandwich and a few pastries for a carryout picnic at **Pumpernickel's Eatery** (202 Butler St., Saugatuck, 269/857-1196, www.pumpernickelssaugatuck.com, 8am-4pm daily, $6-9), though you may want to eat there when you spot the restaurant's great patio and sun deck.

◖ **Chequers of Saugatuck** (220 Culver St., Saugatuck, 269/857-1868, 11:30am-9pm Mon.-Thurs., 11:30am-10pm Fri.-Sat., noon-9pm Sun., $12-24) is a bit of London in western Michigan, with a pub-like atmosphere of dark paneled walls, stained glass, and lots of leather. Classic Brit-inspired grub includes shepherd's pie, fish and chips, and bangers and mash. There's also a good variety of ales and beer. Reservations are not accepted, so expect a wait at peak hours.

The **Restaurant Toulouse** (248 Culver St., Saugatuck, 269/857-1561, 5pm-10pm Thurs.-Fri., 11am-10pm Sat.-Sun., $16-26) features French country cuisine in a Provençal-inspired setting, complete with tableside fireplaces and live jazz on Saturday. Specialties include escargot, cassoulet, rack of lamb, and a killer chocolate fondue. At times, though, the service here can be rather slow. Prepare yourself for a long meal.

INFORMATION AND SERVICES

For more information about Saugatuck, Douglas, and surrounding towns, contact the **Saugatuck/Douglas Convention & Visitors Bureau** (2902 Blue Star Hwy., Saugatuck, 269/857-1701, www.saugatuck.com, 9am-5pm Mon.-Fri.), the **Saugatuck/Douglas Area Business Association** (269/857-1620, www.saugatuckdouglas.com), the **Greater Fennville Chamber of Commerce** (www.greaterfennville.com), or the **Allegan County Tourist Council** (888/425-5342, www.visitallegancounty.com). For local or county news, refer to the *Commercial Record* or the *Allegan County News* (both accessible at www.allegannews.com). For gay-related events and businesses in the area, visit www.gaysaugatuckdouglas.com.

Despite their small size, Saugatuck and Douglas offer plenty of practical services, from pharmacies to post offices. You'll find several banks in the area, too, including **Chemical Bank** (249 Mason St., Saugatuck, 269/857-2116, www.chemicalbankmi.com).

In case of an emergency, dial **911** from any cell or public phone. For medical services, head 10 miles north to the **Holland Hospital** (602 Michigan Ave., Holland, 616/392-5141, www.hollandhospital.org).

GETTING THERE AND AROUND

There are three major airports near Saugatuck and Douglas: the **Kalamazoo/Battle Creek International Airport** (AZO, 5235 Portage Rd., Kalamazoo, 269/388-3668, www.azoairport.com), the **Gerald R. Ford International Airport** (GRR, 5500 44th St. SE, Grand Rapids, 616/233-6000, www.grr.org), and the **Muskegon County Airport** (MKG, 99 Sinclair Dr., Muskegon, 231/798-4596, www.muskegonairport.com). All offer reputable rental car services, so reaching the "Art Coast" is a snap, even for those without their own vehicle. From Kalamazoo, which also has an **Amtrak train station** (459 N. Burdick St., 800/872-7245, www.amtrak.com), you can take the US-131 Business Route, merge onto US-131 North, continue onto M-89 West, and follow CR-A2/Blue Star Highway to downtown Saugatuck; without traffic, the 52-mile trip should last little more than an hour. From Grand Rapids, which also has an **Amtrak train station** (431 Wealthy St. SW), you can simply follow I-196 West to CR-A2/Blue Star Highway, a 40-mile trip that usually takes about 39 minutes. From Muskegon, meanwhile, you can just head south on US-31, through Grand Haven and Holland, to the Saugatuck/Douglas area; without traffic, the 47-mile trip should take less than an hour.

If, on the other hand, you're headed from Chicago, you can simply follow I-90 East and I-94 East through Illinois and Indiana, cross the Michigan state line, continue onto I-196 North/US-31 North, and take CR-A2/Blue Star Highway into downtown Saugatuck; without traffic, the 141-mile trip should take roughly 2.25 hours. Just be advised that, en route from the Windy City, parts of I-90 East and I-94 East serve as the Indiana Toll Road. Of course, once you reach downtown Saugatuck, it's easy enough to get around via car, bike, or your own two feet. It's also a snap to access the adjacent town of Douglas, which lies about a mile south on CR-A2/Blue Star Highway, just across Kalamazoo Lake.

Camping

Grand Haven State Park (1001 Harbor Ave., 616/847-1309, daily, annual $11 Recreation Passport for Michigan residents or $8.40 day-use fee/$30.50 yearly Recreation Passport for nonresidents required) offers a spacious campground. There are 174 modern sites ($16-29 daily), mostly in an open area near the water, as well as clean restrooms. For reservations, which are highly recommended, call 800/447-2757 or visit www.michigan.gov/dnr.

INFORMATION AND SERVICES

For more information about the Grand Haven area, contact the **Grand Haven Area Convention & Visitors Bureau** (1 S. Harbor Dr., 800/303-4092, www.visitgrandhaven. com, 9:30am-5pm Mon., 8am-5pm Tues.-Fri. year-round, 10am-2pm Sat. summer only) or the **Grand Haven Chamber of Commerce** (1 S. Harbor Dr., 616/842-4910, www.grand-havenchamber.org, 9:30am-5pm Mon., 8am-5pm Tues.-Fri. year-round, 10am-2pm Sat. summer only). For local news and events, pick up a copy of the **Grand Haven Tribune** (www. grandhaventribune.com).

The Grand Haven area offers a wide range of services necessary to travelers, including groceries, pharmacies, banks, and post offices. In case of an emergency, dial **911** from any cell or public phone. For medical services, consult the **North Ottawa Community Hospital** (1309 Sheldon Rd., 616/842-3600, www.noch.org).

GETTING THERE AND AROUND

As with Benton Harbor and South Haven, Grand Haven is situated on the Lake Michigan coast, which means that it's easily accessible via private boat. Visitors can also reach the town by flying into one of two nearby airports—the **Gerald R. Ford International Airport** (GRR, 5500 44th St. SE, Grand Rapids, 616/233-6000, www. grr.org) or the **Muskegon County Airport** (MKG, 99 Sinclair Dr., Muskegon, 231/798-4596, www.muskegonairport.com). At either airport, you can then rent a vehicle from one of several national rental agencies, before driving toward the coast. From the Grand Rapids airport, for instance, you'd head to I-96 West, merge onto M-104 West, and take US-31 South to Grand Haven, a 47-mile trip that, without traffic, will take about 52 minutes. From the Muskegon airport, meanwhile, you can take surface streets to access US-31 South, which will guide you to downtown Grand Haven, a 9-mile trip that will normally take 14 minutes.

Of course, whether you rent a car or drive your own, it's easy to reach Grand Haven via US-31, a route that traces the entire western coast of the Lower Peninsula, from the Indiana border to just north of Petoskey. It's even fairly simple to reach Grand Haven from Chicago, from which you'll follow I-90 East and I-94 East through Illinois and Indiana, cross the Michigan state line, and continue onto I-196 North/US-31 North, toward downtown Grand Haven; without traffic, the 172-mile trip will require less than three hours. Just be advised that, en route from the Windy City, parts of I-90 East and I-94 East serve as the Indiana Toll Road. Of course, once you reach downtown Grand Haven, it's easy enough to get around via car, bike, or your own two feet.

Muskegon and Vicinity

The largest town along this stretch of Lake Michigan shoreline, with more than 37,000 year-round residents, Muskegon has its roots in white pine. The deep Muskegon River, which flows through town, into Lake Muskegon, and toward Lake Michigan, proved the perfect route for transporting timber from the rich inland pine forests to the city's sawmills.

Muskegon's first sawmill went up in 1837. In the following 50 years, the frontier town grew at a feverish pace. By the 1880s, it was known throughout the world as a lumber metropolis, home to 47 sawmills and at least as many saloons, dance halls, and gambling joints—earning the city nicknames that ranged from "Lumber Queen of the North" to the more unsavory "Red Light Queen."

Muskegon was unprepared for the day just a decade or so later when the area's timber was tapped. Mills soon closed or were mysteriously torched. By the 1890s, the region's lumber industry and population declined steadily. By the 1950s, the city teetered on the brink of ruin—until tourists took over where timber left off. After decades of decline in industry and self-image, Muskegon has finally risen from the sawdust. While many parts of the city still have a tattered feel, visitors to Muskegon focus on its benefits, which include more than 26 miles of Lake Michigan shoreline, western Michigan's most extensive lakeshore park system, outstanding cultural and historical resources, a popular amusement park, and a lively multiethnic population.

SIGHTS
Historic Sites

The lumber barons in Muskegon left behind

Muskegon's Hackley & Hume Historic Site

© MUSKEGON COUNTY CVB

still active today, and often called the Pere Marquette Lighthouse, given its position on the south side of the Muskegon Lake Channel, near Pere Marquette Beach.

In winter, Muskegon State Park is best known for its **Muskegon Winter Sports Complex** (231/744-9629, www.msports.org, 10am-10pm daily in winter, prices vary), which offers ski and snowshoe rentals, houses an ice-skating rink, and includes one of the few luge runs in the nation. On winter weekends, you can reserve a spot for a quick lesson and give it a try yourself. Speeds reach up to 40 miles per hour, careening down the ice-covered wooden chute—and seem terribly faster on a sled made of wood, metal, and canvas. The luge is open on weekends only, beginning in mid-December; a day's pass includes a sled, helmet, and coach. First-timers are fully supervised. The park is also a favorite among cross-country skiers, who find some of the longest lighted trails in the state. The area usually enjoys a long season, thanks to reliable lake-effect snows.

The **Gillette Sand Dune Visitor Center** at **P. J. Hoffmaster State Park** (6585 Lake Harbor Rd., 231/798-3711, daily, annual $11 Recreation Passport for Michigan residents or $8.40 day-use fee/$30.50 yearly Recreation Passport for nonresidents required) gives an excellent introduction to dune history and ecology. Slide shows, dioramas, and colorful displays demonstrate the natural forces that shaped and continue to shape the face of these majestic mountains of sand. Besides the center, the 1,200-acre park contains 2 miles of shoreline, towering dunes that stand guard over a sandy beach, deep forests, interdunal valleys, 10 miles of hiking and cross-country trails (also popular with snowshoers in winter), and a very good campground.

Michigan's Adventure

Muskegon also has plenty to offer for those looking for more commercial amusements. Together, **Michigan's Adventure Amusement Park** and **Wild Water Adventure Water Park**

(4750 Whitehall Rd., 231/766-3377, www.miadventure.com, times vary seasonally, $27 pp plus parking) make up the state's largest amusement and water park, with more than 60 rides and attractions, including seven roller coasters and several pools and waterslides. The newest roller coaster, Thunderhawk, is the state's first and only suspended coaster; it's the steel complement to the park's longtime favorite, Shivering Timbers, a 125-foot-tall wooden coaster that's routinely considered one of the best in America.

FESTIVALS

In late June, the **Taste of Muskegon** (Western Ave., www.tasteofmuskegon.com, 11am-8pm Sat., 11am-6pm Sun., free to enter, $1-5 for food items), a relatively new diversion, offers a two-day celebration of the region's cuisine, with the area's best restaurants and bakeries serving their specialties to crowds of willing gourmands. Since all the proceeds benefit the Muskegon Main Street organization and Make a Wish Foundation of Michigan, you can fill your belly while knowing you're helping two good causes.

SPORTS AND RECREATION
Golf

If you're hankering to play a casual round of golf in a gorgeous setting, visit the **Stonegate Golf Club** (4100 Sweeter Rd., Twin Lake, 231/744-7200, www.stonegategolfclub.com, daily Apr.-Oct., $35-59 pp w/o cart). In addition to a round of golf, Stonegate provides golf training and a beautiful bar and grill, popular for its famous fish fry every Friday night.

Hiking and Biking

The 25-mile-long **Musketawa Trail** (www.musketawatrail.com) is a multiuse recreational pathway that links Marne in eastern Ottawa County to Muskegon. Passing amid a myriad of farmlands, wetlands, creeks, and villages, it offers hikers and biking enthusiasts a marvelous scenic tour of the area. Horseback riders, in-line skaters, and nature lovers frequent the

Musketawa, too, and in winter, it's popular among cross-country skiers and snowmobilers.

ACCOMMODATIONS

Overlooking Muskegon Lake, the € **Port City Victorian Inn** (1259 Lakeshore Dr., 231/759-0205, www.portcityinn.com, $150-225 d), a Queen Anne-style bed-and-breakfast built in 1877, has five guest rooms and a rooftop balcony with terrific views of the lake. It's open year-round. The **Holiday Inn Muskegon Harbor** (939 3rd St., 231/722-0100 or 877/863-4780, www.ichotelsgroup.com, $100-125 d) offers a convenient location in the heart of Muskegon. Amenities include an indoor pool and sauna.

Camping

Muskegon State Park (3560 Memorial Dr., North Muskegon, 231/744-3480, daily, annual $11 Recreation Passport for Michigan residents or $8.40 day-use fee/$30.50 yearly Recreation Passport for nonresidents required) has three campgrounds with a total of 247 sites ($16-28 daily). Tents and RV campers are welcome here; the campsites are equipped with 50-amp electricity, and there are modern restrooms available. The Lake Michigan Campground is especially nice. While not on the water, it's protected by tall maples and beaches and tucked behind dunes, with an easy walk to the beach. For reservations, which are definitely recommended in summer, call 800/447-2757 or visit www.michigan.gov/dnr.

FOOD

Adjacent to Muskegon's Shoreline Inn along the shores of Muskegon Lake, **The Lakehouse Waterfront Grille** (750 Terrace Point Blvd., 231/722-4461, www.thelakehousemi.com, 11am-midnight Sun.-Thurs., 11am-2am Fri.-Sat., $14-35) offers casual dining with an unpretentious vibe and gorgeous views. Given its extensive wine list, amazing house specials, and outdoor deck, you'll be hard-pressed to find a better dining experience in the area.

INFORMATION AND SERVICES

For more information about the Muskegon area, contact the **Muskegon County Convention & Visitors Bureau** (610 W. Western Ave., 231/724-3100, www.visitmuskegon.org, 8am-5pm Mon.-Fri.) or the **Muskegon Area Chamber of Commerce** (380 W. Western Ave., 231/722-3751, www.muskegon.org, 8:30am-5pm Mon.-Fri.). For government information, visit www.co.muskegon.mi.us. For local news, pick up a copy of the *Muskegon Chronicle* (www.mlive.com/chronicle).

As the Southwest Coast's largest city, Muskegon has no shortage of services for travelers. **Meijer** (www.meijer.com), a Midwestern superstore chain, offers three locations in the Muskegon area; here, you can fill prescriptions, get film processed, and pick up all manner of supplies. For mailing needs, you'll find several **post offices** in Muskegon; consult www.usps.com for locations and hours. If you're looking for an ATM, you'll find plenty here; consult **Comerica Bank** (www.comerica.com) or **PNC** (www.pnc.com) for locations.

In case of an emergency, dial **911** from any cell or public phone. For medical services, consult the **Mercy Health Partners** (231/672-2000, www.mghp.com), which has two campuses in Muskegon.

GETTING THERE AND AROUND

Travelers can reach Muskegon via boat, bus, plane, or vehicle. The pet-friendly *Lake Express* (1918 Lakeshore Dr., 866/914-1010, www.lake-express.com, one-way $82.50 adults, $74 students, military personnel, and seniors 65 and over, $26 children 5-17, children under 5 free), the first high-speed ferry to operate on the Great Lakes, has transported passengers and vehicles across Lake Michigan, between Milwaukee and Muskegon, since 2004. Naturally, though, private boats can also access Muskegon Lake. Meanwhile, **Greyhound** (351 Morris Ave., 231/722-6048 or 800/231-2222, www.greyhound.com) provides bus service to

Muskegon, and United Airlines offers flights from Chicago to **Muskegon County Airport** (MKG, 99 Sinclair Dr., 231/798-4596, www.muskegonairport.com), where you can typically rent a vehicle from one of six major rental car agencies. From the airport, you can also get a ride from **Express Transportation** (231/571-0741), which typically charges $17 for a trip to downtown Muskegon, $60 to reach Holland, and $85 for the journey to Grand Rapids.

Of course, as with the rest of the Southwest Coast, having a car is essential. Whether you're coming from Traverse City, which lies 147 miles to the north, or Benton Harbor, which lies about 90 miles to the south, US-31 is one of the most convenient routes to the Muskegon area. From Lansing and Grand Rapids, meanwhile, you'd simply take I-96 West to reach Muskegon. If, on the other hand, you're headed from downtown Detroit, you'll have to cross almost the entire width of the Lower Peninsula via a series of routes: M-10 North, I-696 West, I-96 West, and the US-31 North Business Route. Without traffic, the 197-mile trip should take less than three hours. It's even fairly simple to reach Muskegon from Chicago, from which you'll follow I-90 East and I-94 East through Illinois and Indiana, cross the Michigan state line, continue onto I-196 North/US-31 North, and take the US-31 North Business Route toward the downtown area; without traffic, the 187-mile trip will require less than three hours. Just be advised that, en route from the Windy City, parts of I-90 East and I-94 East serve as the Indiana Toll Road. Once in Muskegon, you'll be pleased to know that the city has decent public transportation, provided by the **Muskegon Area Transit System** (MATS, 231/724-6420, www.matsbus.com, one-way $1.25 pp, $0.60 seniors and disabled individuals, children under 6 free).

WHITEHALL AND MONTAGUE

About 12 miles north of Muskegon, the sleepy twin towns of Whitehall and Montague are friendly rivals. Both sit on US-31 at the head of White Lake, both have hospitable inns and old-fashioned general stores, and both fill up with summer people during the high season. Friendly and unfussy, they're good places to wander in and out of nautical- and country-themed stores, watch the swans in the White River marsh, enjoy a root beer at the Dog 'n' Suds, and take in the sunsets and sailboats at the marinas that ring White Lake.

Sights

Operated by the administration of Muskegon State Park farther south, **Duck Lake State Park** (3560 Memorial Dr., North Muskegon, 231/744-3480, daily, annual $11 Recreation Passport for Michigan residents or $8.40 day-use fee/$30.50 yearly Recreation Passport for nonresidents required) is a 728-acre day-use property, stretching along the northern shore of Duck Lake, adjacent to Lake Michigan. Swimmers, anglers, hikers, cross-country skiers, and snowmobilers all favor this less traveled place. Besides a picnic area, a restroom building, and a boat launch, there are few amenities here, but it's still worth a look if you're in the White Lake area.

Another interesting attraction is the **White River Light Station Museum** (6199 Murray Rd., Whitehall, 231/894-8265, www.whiteriverlightstation.org, 10am-5pm Tues.-Sun. late May-Oct., by appointment Nov.-late May, $4 adults, $2 children 2-12, children under 2 free). Visitors can climb the spiral staircase to the top of the 1875 lighthouse (deactivated in 1960), where spectacular views of Lake Michigan and the White Lake Channel await. Down below, the museum features stories, artifacts, photographs, and paintings that depict western Michigan's fascinating maritime heritage.

Recreation and Camping

The **Hart-Montague Trail** stretches 22 miles along the former C&O Railroad route between Hart and Montague. The smooth paved surface is popular for hiking, biking, and in-line skating. It leads north from Montague, passing through high sandy hills and orchards

© MUSKEGON COUNTY CVB

the White River Light Station Museum in Whitehall

between Muskegon and Ludington, an area renowned as one of America's top producers of apples, tart cherries, and Christmas trees. Small towns along the trail have a rural 1940s feel; a map available at trailheads lists area restaurants, B&Bs, and bike rentals. For more information about the trail, contact **Silver Lake State Park** (9679 W. State Park Rd., Mears, 231/873-3083).

Famous as a logging river, the **White River** offers some wonderful paddling—the river feels more remote than many of the longer and better-known rivers farther north. On early morning and late afternoon floats, you'll share the waters with blue herons, sandhill cranes, and an occasional beaver. The narrow river winds between steep, forested banks, across marshy flats, and through the Manistee National Forest, a hardwood and conifer forest that hasn't seen a logger since the 19th century. Access points to the river can be hard to find; one of the easiest solutions is

to arrange for a rental through the **Happy Mohawk Canoe Livery** (735 Fruitvale Rd., Montague, 231/894-4209, www.happymohawk.com, hours vary, $33-54 canoes, $27-57 kayaks, $80 rafts, $13 tubes), the only full-service provider of watercraft on the White River. The livery rents canoes, kayaks, inner tubes, and rafts for trips ranging 1-7 hours in length. Happy Mohawk also owns the nearby ◖ **White River RV Park & Campground** (735 Fruitvale Rd., Montague, 231/894-4708, www.whiterivercampground.com, May-mid-Oct., $26-43 sites, $129-179 cabins) in a heavily wooded valley near little Sand Creek. In addition to 235 premium and rustic campsites, the facility includes camping cabins along the creek, a heated pool, a wading creek, hiking trails, basketball and volleyball courts, and several playgrounds.

Information and Services

For more information about Whitehall and Montague, contact the **White Lake Area**

Chamber of Commerce & Visitors Bureau
(124 Hanson St., Whitehall, 231/893-4585,
www.whitelake.org, 9am-5pm Mon.-Fri., 9am-
3pm Sat., noon-2pm Sun.). For local news and
events, consult the *White Lake Beacon* (www.
whitelakebeacon.com).

If you require postal, banking, dental,
medical, automotive repair, or other services
during your stay, you'll find several friendly
businesses in these adjacent towns, not to
mention in nearby Muskegon. In case of an
emergency, dial **911** from any cell or public
phone.

Getting There and Around

Whitehall and Montague lie just a mile west of
US-31, so you can easily reach them via car—
whether you're traveling south from Traverse
City or north from Indiana. Since downtown
Muskegon is only 18 miles south of Whitehall,
you can also arrive by plane, bus, or ferry, rent
a car at **Muskegon County Airport** (MKG, 99
Sinclair Dr., Muskegon, 231/798-4596, www.
muskegonairport.com), and head north on US-
31; without traffic, the 24-mile trip from the
airport to downtown Whitehall will take about
a half hour.

THE SOUTHWEST COAST

TRAVERSE CITY AND NORTHWEST MICHIGAN

Although the entire state is defined by water, perhaps no region is more dramatically contoured by lakes, bays, and rivers than the northwestern corner of Michigan's Lower Peninsula, especially the coast surrounding Traverse City, the area's largest town and the self-proclaimed "Cherry Capital of the World." The aquamarine waters of Lake Michigan mingle with two stunning coastal bays: Grand Traverse Bay, a majestic, 32-mile-long inlet partially bisected by the slender Old Mission Peninsula, and Little Traverse Bay, situated farther north near Petoskey, a town famous for its high concentration of Petoskey stones, the fossilized coral rock that was named Michigan's state stone in 1965.

On summer weekends, the lakeside towns of Traverse City, Charlevoix, and Petoskey seem to grow exponentially. While some fear the overdevelopment that's encroached upon this area in recent years, visitors continue to flock to the coast, embracing a wide array of diversions, including windsurfing, fishing charters, bike trails, chic restaurants and galleries, golf and ski resorts, and old-fashioned downtown shopping districts. Along the coast, visitors can also admire a number of historic lighthouses, from the 1858 Beaver Head Lighthouse on Beaver Island to the picture-perfect 1870 Mission Point Lighthouse amid Grand Traverse Bay. Beyond the many islands and breezy shores of Lake Michigan, numerous inland lakes pepper this diverse region.

Outdoor enthusiasts embrace the pristine beaches and clear waters of Northwest Michigan, a breathtaking area that's also home to many state parks, several state forests,

HIGHLIGHTS

© AVALON TRAVEL

LOOK FOR **◖** TO FIND RECOMMENDED SIGHTS, ACTIVITIES, DINING, AND LODGING.

◖ National Cherry Festival: This annual celebration of Michigan's booming cherry industry attracts over 500,000 participants every July. Activities include cherry pie-eating and pit-spitting contests, a grand buffet, a golf tournament, and a cherry-related farmers market (page 226).

◖ Traverse City Film Festival: Since 2005, Michigan's premier film festival – cofounded by filmmaker Michael Moore – has lured thousands of filmmakers and cinema lovers to Traverse City for a week of eclectic screenings, panel discussions, parties, and musical performances (page 227).

◖ Interlochen Center for the Arts: Interlochen has, for more than 85 years, cultivated a passion for the arts. Besides offering a summer camp for young artists and year-round programs for adults, this renowned institute invites visitors to attend dance performances, film screenings, art exhibitions, and more (page 234).

◖ Sleeping Bear Dunes National Lakeshore: This one-of-a-kind national park features some of the largest freshwater dunes in the world, not to mention two isolated islands in Lake Michigan. Climb the dunes, explore historic buildings, and pursue a wide array of outdoor activities, from hiking to kayaking to scuba diving (page 235).

◖ Wineries of Grand Traverse Bay: Wineries and tasting rooms pepper the Leelanau and Old Mission Peninsulas, the destinations of choice for countless connoisseurs (page 243).

◖ Loda Lake National Wildflower Sanctuary: Nestled within the Manistee National Forest, north of White Cloud, this is the only wildflower sanctuary ever established in a U.S. national forest. Stroll through oak-maple woodlands, old pine plantations, and a shrub swamp boasting a slew of plant species (page 249).

and the expansive Manistee National Forest. Located along the western edge of the Leelanau Peninsula—known for its scenic, award-winning wineries—lies another natural wonder, Sleeping Bear Dunes National Lakeshore, one of the Midwest's finest natural escapes and a popular destination for anglers, hikers, bikers,

skiers, kayakers, and amateur geologists. While there's plenty to keep anyone occupied, the most eye-catching features are the pyramidal dunes themselves, some of which rise over 400 feet high, constituting the largest freshwater dunes in the world and offering an unparalleled view of Glen Lake and the surrounding hills.

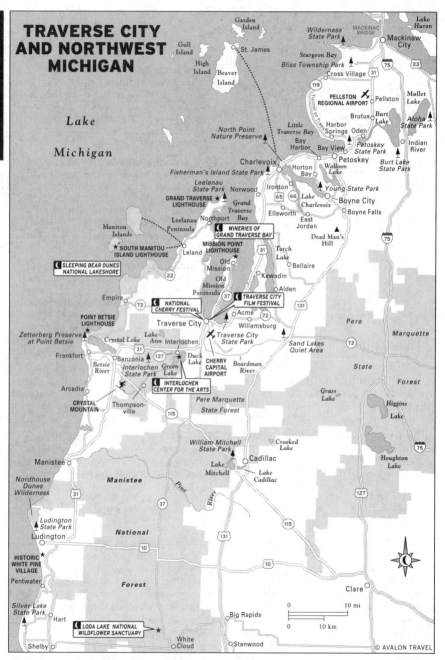

TRAVERSE CITY AND NORTHWEST MICHIGAN

Lake Michigan

Garden Island

Gull Island

High Island

Beaver Island

St. James

MACKINAC BRIDGE

Lake Huron

Mackinaw City

Wilderness State Park

Sturgeon Bay

Bliss Township Park

Cross Village

PELLSTON REGIONAL AIRPORT

Pellston

Mullet Lake

Brutus

Burt Lake

Aloha State Park

Indian River

Tunnel of Trees

North Point Nature Preserve

Little Traverse Bay

Bay Harbor

Harbor Springs

Bay View

Oden

Petoskey

Petoskey State Park

Burt Lake State Park

Charlevoix

Fisherman's Island State Park

Horton Bay

Walloon Lake

Leelanau State Park

Norwood

Ironton

Young State Park

★ GRAND TRAVERSE LIGHTHOUSE

Grand Traverse Bay

65

66

Lake Charlevoix

Boyne City

Boyne Falls

Leelanau Peninsula

Northport

Ellsworth

East Jordan

Dead Man's Hill

Manitou Islands

▲ WINERIES OF GRAND TRAVERSE BAY

MISSION POINT LIGHTHOUSE

★ SOUTH MANITOU ISLAND LIGHTHOUSE

Leland

31

Old Mission

Torch Lake

Bellaire

☾ SLEEPING BEAR DUNES NATIONAL LAKESHORE

22

Old Mission Peninsula

Kewadin

Alden

Empire

72

▲ NATIONAL CHERRY FESTIVAL

37

☾ TRAVERSE CITY FILM FESTIVAL

131

Pere

Marquette

Acme

72

POINT BETSIE LIGHTHOUSE

Traverse City

Willamsburg

Zetterberg Preserve at Point Betsie

Crystal Lake

Lake Ann

Interlochen

Traverse City State Park

Sand Lakes Quiet Area

72

Frankfort

31

Benzonia

137

Duck Lake

CHERRY CAPITAL AIRPORT

Boardman River

State

Betsie River

Interlochen State Park

Green Lake

▲ INTERLOCHEN CENTER FOR THE ARTS

Grass Lake

Forest

Arcadia

CRYSTAL MOUNTAIN

Thompsonville

Pere Marquette State Forest

Higgins Lake

115

Manistee

Manistee

William Mitchell State Park

Crooked Lake

75

Houghton Lake

127

Nordhouse Dunes Wilderness

31

37

Pine

Lake Mitchell

Cadillac

Lake Cadillac

115

☾ Ludington State Park

Ludington

National

River

131

10

HISTORIC WHITE PINE VILLAGE

Pentwater

Forest

Clare

Silver Lake State Park

Hart

☾ LODA LAKE NATIONAL WILDFLOWER SANCTUARY

White Cloud

Big Rapids

0   10 mi

0   10 km

Shelby

Stanwood

© AVALON TRAVEL

© TRAVERSE CITY TOURISM

hiking near the South Manitou Island Lighthouse

PLANNING YOUR TIME

Extending from the southern edge of Manistee National Forest to the Mackinac Bridge, Northwest Michigan is indeed a sprawling region. Although you can reach the area via boat, bus, or plane, you'll find it easier to navigate with a vehicle—whether your own or a rented one. By car, you can get here via US-31 from Muskegon, US-131 from Grand Rapids, US-10 from Midland, and I-75 from the Upper Peninsula.

If your schedule's tight, plan a weekend getaway to Traverse City. Two weeks, however, will ensure time to experience more than just the Cherry Capital, including Sleeping Bear Dunes, the Leelanau Peninsula, Manistee National Forest, Beaver Island, and several coastal towns, beaches, and golf resorts.

Summer is exceedingly popular in Northwest Michigan, especially in the resort towns and during the area's annual festivals. So, if you aren't a fan of crowds, try to come in spring, fall, or winter. After all, even during

the off-season, the region will appeal to art lovers, golfing enthusiasts, beachcombers, wine connoisseurs, cross-country skiers, and many other fun-seekers.

For more details about Northwest Michigan, contact the **West Michigan Tourist Association** (WMTA, 741 Kenmoor Ave., Ste. E, Grand Rapids, 616/245-2217, www.wmta. org).

HISTORY

Traverse City has been hosting visitors ever since the French explorers and fur traders passed through the area in the 1600s, soon spreading word of the treacherous canoe passage across the gaping mouth of the bay, *la grande traversée*. Since then, the Traverse region has attracted everyone from James Jesse Strang, a self-proclaimed king who set his sights on ruling Beaver Island, to a family called the Hemingways, who summered for decades on the shores of Walloon Lake.

But it was the Victorian "resorters" who left an indelible mark. Summer visitors began trickling in around the 1860s, escaping hot and sticky Midwestern cities for the lake's crisp breezes and gentle shores. Soon, they were flooding into communities like Charlevoix and Petoskey, by steamship and by train. The "old money" of Chicago, Detroit, and Cleveland built exclusive summer homes. The simply rich stayed in grand pastel-painted hotels. Good Christians came to the church-run camps, which soon evolved from canvas tents to frilly Victorian cottages that remain well preserved today. Decade after decade, they attended Sousa concerts in the park, sailed dinghies across the harbor, and sipped lemonade on verandas overlooking the beautiful blue-green bays.

Today, the two bays, Grand Traverse Bay and Little Traverse Bay, anchor one of the state's most popular vacation areas, where the air is still crisp and clean, and the waters are still clear and accessible. Like elsewhere, development is a hot-button issue, as slick developments for urban visitors push aside the quaint cottages and small-town life that made everyone want to visit here in the first place. The populations of lakeside Traverse City, Charlevoix, and Petoskey can grow several-fold on a good July weekend. Legions of "designer" golf resorts, blue-ribbon fly-fishing rivers, back-road biking routes, and some of the Midwest's largest ski resorts have drawn visitors inland, too.

But for all this activity, the region's past still weaves into the scene—the lyrical French names, the proud old lighthouses, the industrialists' homes, the century-old family farms. Like the great dunes that ignore park boundaries and drift across the newly paved park roads, past and present jumble together here, some parts planned, other parts as wild as the wind.

Nowhere does that seem more apparent than on Beaver Island. Irish immigrants arrived here in the 1840s, fleeing the potato famine and looking for new opportunities. They built Beaver Island into one of the premier commercial fisheries on the Great Lakes, ringing the hooked harbor at St. James with docks, net sheds, and icehouses. At about the same time, a man named Jesse Strang arrived. A New Yorker who challenged Brigham Young and claimed to be the leader of the Mormons, he brought his faithful to Beaver Island, where he proclaimed himself king, took five wives,

began a newspaper, pushed the Irish off their land, and eventually was assassinated by two of his followers.

The Irish reclaimed their island, the population soared to nearly 2,000 by the turn of the 20th century, and today, more than a third of the island's 660 year-round residents are descendants of the original Irish immigrant families. It's no wonder, then, that St. Patrick's Day is one of the island's most celebrated holidays.

The parasitic lamprey eel and overfishing pretty much ruined the commercial fishing trade, and the island's other main industry, logging, disappeared when ships converted from wood-burning engines to fossil fuels. Today, residents earn their living coaxing a few crops out of the rocky, sandy soil or, more commonly, by running service businesses that make a lion's share of their annual wages in July and August. By and large, residents encourage the summer tourist trade and the business visitors bring to the island. There's more of a battle regarding those who build summer cottages. While the building trades are a mainstay of the island economy and many welcome the jobs new construction provides, plenty of others oppose development. It's the universal controversy, though, fought in rural areas all over the continent.

Traverse City and Vicinity

Traverse City sits at the foot of Grand Traverse Bay, a body of water with incredible color and clarity. From blue to green to aquamarine, it shifts hues like a chameleon warming in the sun. The bay, not surprisingly, remains the top vacation draw in Traverse City. In summer months, this water lover's playground hums with activity—filled with kayaks, fishing boats, Jet Skis, sailboards, cruising sailboats, and twin-masted tall ships—and the sand beaches fill up with sunbathers and volleyball players.

Though its population swells from 14,900 to nearly 300,000 in summer

months—especially during the National Cherry Festival—Traverse City has managed to accomplish what few "vacation towns" have: It remains a real community, where services like hardware stores and quick-print shops still operate alongside the gift shops and galleries. Locals actually use their pretty downtown area, and peaceful neighborhoods still thrive just a few blocks away. Traverse City has style *and* substance. Oh, there's no doubt tourism drives the economy here, but Traverse City's strong sense of place makes it all the more appealing to residents and visitors alike.

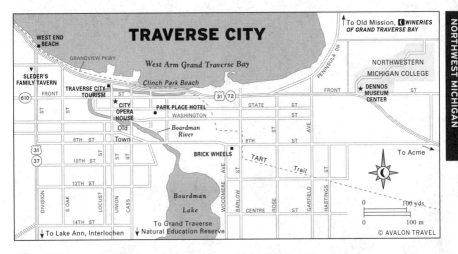

SIGHTS
Historic Sites and Museums

Downtown Traverse City abounds in Victorian architecture and historic buildings. One must-see is the 1892 red-brick **City Opera House** (106 E. Front St., 231/941-8082, www.city-operahouse.org), which is currently being restored to its Victorian splendor. Visitors can better appreciate the lovely theater by attending one of its regularly scheduled concerts, comedy shows, and other events.

On the campus of Northwestern Michigan College, the **Dennos Museum Center** (1701 E. Front St., 231/995-1055, www.dennosmuseum.org, 10am-5pm Mon.-Sat., 1pm-5pm Sun., $6 adults, $4 children) is a wonderful find. It houses one of the nation's finest collections of Inuit art, along with interactive exhibits in the Discovery Gallery that combine art, science, and technology.

In nearby Acme, the **Music House Museum** (7377 US-31 N, 231/938-9300, www.musichouse.org, 10am-4pm Mon.-Sat., noon-4pm Sun. May-Oct., 10am-4pm Fri.-Sat., noon-4pm Sun. Nov.-Dec., $10 adults, $3 children 6-15) is another surprise, showcasing a vast array of rare antique musical instruments, from 1870 to 1930. Its collection includes music boxes, jukeboxes, nickelodeons, pipe organs, and a hand-carved Belgian dance organ.

Old Mission Peninsula

The Old Mission Peninsula pierces north from Traverse City, a narrow sliver of land that neatly divides Grand Traverse Bay in two. This whale-back ridge stretches 22 miles, a quiet agrarian landscape cross-hatched with cherry orchards and vineyards. Nowhere else on earth grows more cherries per acre than the Old Mission Peninsula, where the surrounding waters, insulating snows, and cool summer air form the perfect microclimate for raising fruit. Veer off M-37 onto almost any country road to wander past the pretty, peaceful orchards.

Grapes also thrive on the Old Mission Peninsula, creating a burgeoning winemaking industry (www.wineriesofoldmission.com). (Though locals like to tell you it's because the peninsula sits at the same latitude as Bordeaux, France, they really should thank the moderating effects of the lake.) Most of the eight wineries here offer tours and tastings, and visiting them brings an extra benefit: The ridgetop roads of the Old Mission Peninsula come with incredible views that often take in both arms of Grand Traverse Bay.

Chateau Grand Traverse (12239 Center Rd., 231/223-7355 or 800/283-0247, www.cgtwines.com, 10am-7pm Mon.-Sat., 10am-6pm Sun. Memorial Day-Labor Day, 10am-6pm Mon.-Sat., 10am-5pm Sun. early Sept.-Oct.,

the City Opera House

10am-5pm daily Nov.-May), located nine miles north of Traverse City on M-37, was a pioneer in bringing European vinifera wines to the Midwest. It has a beautiful tasting room, with wonderful bay views, for tasting its internationally award-winning rieslings and ice wines. In addition, the winery offers tours as well as luxurious accommodations in its hilltop inn.

Just east of Bowers Harbor, **Bowers Harbor Vineyards** (2896 Bowers Harbor Rd., 231/223-7615 or 800/616-7615, www.bowersharbor.com, 10:30am-6pm Mon.-Sat., noon-6pm Sun. May-Oct., 10:30am-5pm Mon.-Sat., noon-5pm Sun. Nov.-Apr.) is a small, friendly, family-run winery, with a year-round tasting room.

Chateau Chantal (15900 Rue de Vin, 231/223-4110 or 800/969-4009, www.chateauchantal.com, 11am-8pm Mon.-Sat., 11am-6pm Sun. Memorial Day-Labor Day, 11am-7pm Mon.-Sat., 11am-6pm Sun. early Sept.-Oct., 11am-5pm daily Nov.-June) includes both a tasting room and a B&B in a

French chateau-inspired winery high on a hill. Winery tours are offered during the summer months; inexpensive wine-tastings are available all year. **Peninsula Cellars** (11480 Center Rd., 231/933-9787, www.peninsulacellars. com, 10am-6pm Mon.-Sat., noon-6pm Sun.) is one of the peninsula's newer wineries, with a tasting room in a converted 1896 schoolhouse.

The peninsula was named for the mission first built near its tip in 1829 by a Presbyterian minister who came from Mackinac to convert the Ojibwa and Ottawa. The **Mission Church** on M-37 in Old Mission is a replica, but it houses the original bell. A few displays tell the peninsula's early history and evolution into a fruit-growing region. Nearby, the 1842 **Dougherty House,** the region's first frame building, is the real thing. Once home to Reverend Peter Dougherty and his family, the homestead is currently undergoing restoration, after which the house and surrounding acreage will be open to the public. For more information about the Dougherty Homestead, consult the **Old Mission Peninsula Historical Society**

© LAURA MARTONE

the stunning view from Chateau Chantal

(www.omphistoricalsociety.org). In the meantime, you can stop by the **Old Mission General Store** (18250 Mission Rd., 231/223-4310), a 19th-century trading post filled with all manner of candy, wine, deli meats, and other supplies. After gathering your provisions, head east around Old Mission Harbor to **Haserot Beach,** a lovely curve of sand near the small protected harbor, ideal for a beachside picnic.

The **Mission Point Lighthouse** stands sentinel over the point, a pretty structure dating to 1870, along with its white clapboard keeper's home (now privately owned). The state has acquired several hundred acres around the lighthouse, including much of the rocky beach, land set aside for a possible future state park.

Beaches and Tours

The Old Mission Peninsula divides Grand Traverse Bay into two "arms." The West Arm (or West Bay) is the larger and deeper of the two, home to marinas, the bay's tall ship cruises, and a few commercial enterprises. The East Arm (or East Bay) is shallower, warmer, and ringed with sugary sand at its south end—prompting lodging and water-sports ventures along its shores.

Along with all the wonderful beaches on the Leelanau Peninsula, Traverse City has several right downtown. Most popular is **Clinch Park Beach** on West Bay, east of Union Street. A little farther west, at the foot of Division, **West End Beach** is the place to head for volleyball. On East Bay, **Bayside Park** has 600 feet of sand beach and a bathhouse, just off US-31 near the Acme turnoff.

The *Nauti-Cat* (231/947-1730, www. nauti-cat.com) offers varied cruises on West Bay aboard a 47-foot catamaran. The open-deck arrangement allows for up to 43 guests. Prices range from $15 for a 90-minute kids' cruise to $35 for a champagne sunset cruise. Reservations are recommended, but walk-ons are accepted if there's space. An authentic replica of an 18th-century wooden schooner, the *Tall Ship Manitou* (Dockside Plaza, 13390 S. West Bay Shore Dr., 231/941-2000,

© DANIEL MARTONE

sailing on the *Tall Ship Manitou*

www.tallshipsailing.com, $34-42 adults, $18-26 children) sets sail three times daily in July and August, cruising West Bay.

FESTIVALS
🄲 National Cherry Festival
Without question, Traverse City's largest event is the **National Cherry Festival** (800/968-3380, www.cherryfestival.org, prices vary), which takes place every July in various locations throughout downtown Traverse City. First held in 1925, this annual celebration of Michigan's cherry industry attracts over 500,000 participants, who come for the parades and fireworks, live entertainment, turtle races, cherry pie-eating contests, a grand cherry-themed buffet, and a cherry farmers market. Participants will be able to taste a wide array of cherry-enhanced

TRAVERSE CITY ALE TRAIL

Traverse City has become quite a beer lover's oasis. Even the Travel Channel has taken note, recently including Traverse City on its list of the "top seven beer destinations." *DRAFT Magazine*, meanwhile, named it one of three "emerging beer towns" in 2012. To celebrate the city's booming craft beer scene, the powers-that-be have created the **Traverse City Ale Trail** (www.tcaletrail. com), also known as the TC Ale Trail, a fun way to experience eight different microbreweries in the Traverse City area. To do so, you simply need to pick up a free TC Ale Trail passport at any of the participating breweries, most hotels and restaurants, or the Traverse City Visitors Bureau on West Grandview Parkway. Then, as you visit each of the featured breweries, just collect a unique stamp with any purchase. When you've visited all eight, return your completed passport to **The Filling Station Microbrewery** for a free, commemorative silicone pint glass. For an extra-credit prize, be sure to make a pit stop at the **Grand Traverse Distillery** (781 Industrial Cir., Ste. 5, 231/947-8635, www. grandtraversedistillery.com, 11:30am-5:30pm Mon.-Sat., noon-4pm Sun.), Michigan's oldest and largest vodka and whiskey distillery. Just remember that, given the spread-out nature

of these breweries, you'll probably need to access them via vehicle, so be sure to drink and drive responsibly.

Here are the eight breweries that you'll encounter along the TC Ale Trail:
- **Beggars Brewery** (4177 Village Park Dr., Ste. C, www.beggarsbrewery.com): Established in 2011, this small production brewery and tap room is one of the newest to join the ranks of Traverse City's craft beer scene. As of late 2013, though, it had yet to open, so until it does, its stamp won't be required to complete your passport.
- **Brewery Ferment** (511 S. Union St., 231/735-8113, www.breweryferment.com, 3pm-10pm Mon.-Thurs., 3pm-midnight Fri., noon-midnight Sat.): Housed within a century-old building, this casual neighborhood spot offers a handful of flagship and specialty taps, such as the Old Town Brown, plus tasty bar snacks.
- **The Filling Station Microbrewery** (642 Railroad Pl., 231/946-8168, http://thefillingstationmicrobrewery.com, 11:30am-11pm Mon.-Thurs., 11:30am-midnight Fri.-Sat., noon-10pm Sun.): Situated in the city's historic railroad district, this casual pub provides handcrafted ales, wood-fired

cuisine and cherry wines, produced by local wineries.

One of the busiest days, but well worth the fuss, is the first Sunday of the festival, when an air show features the astonishing flying skills of the U.S. Navy Blue Angels. Get there early, and plan to be camped out in the same spot for much of the day. If you're feeling really lucky, try entering the cherry pit-spitting contest, always a crowd pleaser.

◖ Traverse City Film Festival

The state's premier film event, the **Traverse City Film Festival** (various venues, 231/392-1134, www.traversecityfilmfest.org, tickets $10-75 pp), brings a bit of Hollywood to northern Michigan. Cofounded in 2005 by Academy Award-winning filmmaker Michael

Moore, the festival lures more and more celebrities, filmmakers, and cinema buffs every summer (usually at the end of July or beginning of August). For an entire week, the festival showcases eclectic film screenings, informative panel discussions, various parties, and live musical performances; it also offers a terrific opportunity to see a few of your favorite movie stars in person.

SHOPPING

Traverse City's main east-west avenue, **Front Street,** is lined with dozens of cafés, galleries, and shops, offering everything from nautical home furnishings to cherry pies. Cobblestone **Union Street** marks Old Town, a growing area of arts and antiques.

If you have a desire for local produce and

---

flatbreads, fresh salads, and pleasant views of adjacent Boardman Lake.

- **Jolly Pumpkin** (13512 Peninsula Dr., 231/223-4333, www.jollypumpkin.com, 11:30am-9pm Sun.-Thurs., 11:30am-10pm Fri.-Sat.): Located in a cottage-like setting on the Old Mission Peninsula, this popular restaurant, microbrewery, and distillery serves local artisan fare as well as spirits distilled on-site, wines from area vineyards, and craft beers.

- **Mackinaw Brewing Company** (161 E. Front St., 231/933-1100, www.mackinawbrewing.com, 11am-10pm Mon.-Thurs., 11am-11pm Fri.-Sat., noon-10pm Sun.): Founded in 1997 and housed within the historic Beale Building, MBC was actually the first brewpub to open in downtown Traverse City. Besides offering wine, spirits, and a full menu of salads, sandwiches, steaks, fish, and smoked meats, it features house-brewed beers, such as the Peninsula Pale Ale and Harvest Moon Oatmeal Stout.

- **North Peak Brewing Company** (400 W. Front St., 231/941-7325, www.northpeak.com, 11am-11pm Mon.-Thurs., 11am-midnight Fri.-Sat., noon-10pm Sun.): Established in 1995, North Peak prepares handcrafted beers,

from the Mission Point Porter to Shirley's Irish Stout, in an on-site brewery. It also offers a full menu of soups, salads, sandwiches, hearth-baked pizzas, steaks, ribs, pasta dishes, and well-prepared local fish.

- **Right Brain Brewery** (225 E. 16th St., 231/944-1239, www.rightbrainbrewery.com, noon-11pm Mon.-Thurs., 11am-midnight Fri.-Sat., noon-9pm Sun.): Recently named one of the "top five local breweries in the nation," Right Brain definitely has an unpretentious atmosphere. This popular brewery is known for making award-winning, culinary-inspired beers, such as the creamy Smooth Operator and the CEO Stout, not to mention rotating signature, Belgian, and premium taps. While here, you can also sample hefty waffle sandwiches.

- **The Workshop Brewing Company** (221 Garland St., Ste. A, 231/421-8977, www.traversecityworkshop.com, 11am-10pm Mon.-Thurs., 11am-midnight Fri.-Sat., 11am-10pm Sun.): Relatively new to Traverse City, this innovative, ecofriendly brewery offers a welcoming atmosphere, a wide array of traditional, seasonal, and oak-aged beers, and several tasty, one-hander sandwiches that complement the beers.

© DANIEL MARTONE

canine jumping competition at the National Cherry Festival

other goodies, from soaps to soup mixes, browse the **Traverse City Sara Hardy Farmers Market** (www.traversecityfarmers-market.com, 8am-noon Sat. May, 8am-noon Sat. and Wed. June-Oct.), along the banks of the Boardman River, between Union and Cass Streets.. Depending on the season, you'll find all manner of veggies, fruits, and flowers—and you can always count on the reliable muffin crop.

SPORTS AND RECREATION
Golf

Award-winning golf courses abound in the Traverse region, just a few minutes away from Traverse City. About three miles from town, **Elmbrook Golf Course** (1750 Townline Rd., 231/946-9180, www.elmbrookgolf.com, daily Apr.-Oct., $32 pp w/cart) is an older, unpretentious course, with lots of hills, valleys, and views of Grand Traverse Bay.

In Acme, about five minutes east of Traverse City on US-31, you'll find one of the state's finest golfing destinations. The 900-acre **Grand Traverse Resort and Spa** (100 Grand Traverse Village Blvd., 231/534-6000, www.grandtraverseresort.com, daily Apr.-Oct., $35-140 pp) features two signature

courses: The Bear, a famously humbling course designed by Jack Nicklaus, with minute greens and deep, deep bunkers, and the Gary Player-designed Wolverine, a watery course with views of Grand Traverse Bay. Both tend to overshadow Spruce Run, the resort's other fine championship course, which, though less challenging, is equally stunning. Set amid an evergreen forest, Spruce Run can even be appreciated by bird-watchers; ducks, swans, and blue herons abound here. In addition to the courses, the resort provides comfortable accommodations, decent dining, a top-notch spa, an indoor water park, and a 24-hour dog care facility.

East of Acme, the rolling pine forests and old orchards of **High Pointe Golf Club** (5555 Arnold Rd., Williamsburg, 231/267-9900, daily Apr.-Oct., $30-79 pp w/cart) once earned it a spot among *Golf Magazine*'s 100 favorites. Meanwhile, the views of picturesque Torch Lake add an extra challenge to keeping your head down at the **A-Ga-Ming Golf Resort** (627 A-Ga-Ming Dr., Kewadin, 231/264-5081, www.a-ga-ming.com, daily Apr.-Oct., $20-84 pp), which is situated north of Acme via US-31 and offers two 18-hole courses: Torch and the relatively new Sundance.

MICHAEL MOORE'S SALUTE TO FILM

Perhaps Michigan's most infamous son, Michael Francis Moore was born in Flint in 1954. Years after studying journalism at the University of Michigan-Flint, Moore turned to filmmaking. His first film, *Roger & Me* (1989), was lauded by some as a biting indictment of the automotive industry, and has been considered by others as the start of Moore's truth-bending, politically charged style of filmmaking. In equal measure, he's been called a documentary filmmaker and a propaganda artist. Some of his rather slanted films include *The Big One* (1997), another exposé about greedy executives and callous politicians; the Oscar-winning *Bowling for Columbine* (2002), an exploration of America's violent culture; *Fahrenheit 9/11* (2004), Moore's take on how the Bush administration used the tragic 9/11 events to push its war agenda; *Sicko* (2007), a comparison of America's healthcare industry to others around the world; and *Capitalism: A Love Story* (2009), an indictment of corporate interests and how their dogged pursuit of high profits has negatively impacted the rest of society.

No matter what you might think of Moore's controversial films, his contribution to Michigan's modern culture is undeniable. In 2005, Moore – along with photographer John Robert Williams and author Doug Stanton – established the **Traverse City Film Festival (TCFF),** a charitable, educational organization whose stated purpose is to preserve one of America's few native art forms: cinema. The festival, which owns and operates a year-round arthouse movie theater in the Cherry Capital (a theater that was generously donated to TCFF in 2007 by the Rotary Charities of Traverse City), also lures filmmakers and cinema buffs from around the world to its annual film festival, which usually occurs in late July or early August. This event, which has quickly become one of northern Michigan's biggest attractions, features panel discussions about the film industry in addition to screenings that include foreign flicks, American independent films, documentaries, and classic movies. Just be advised that, unlike most film festivals in the United States, TCFF doesn't accept submissions, which means that the films are often handpicked with a purpose, sometimes to serve Moore's extremely liberal agenda. For more information about the Traverse City Film Festival, visit www.traversecityfilmfest.org or call 231/392-1134.

Perhaps you'll find it surprising that the quiet countryside southwest of Traverse City is home to one of the best public golf courses in the state, but it's indeed true. Situated alongside a gorgeous stretch of Lake Michigan shoreline and accessible via M-22, the 18-hole **Arcadia Bluffs Golf Club** (14710 Northwood Hwy., Arcadia, 231/889-3001, www.arcadiabluffs.com, daily Apr.-Nov., $75-180 pp) promises incredible views of the glistening lake, plus a pro shop and seasonal restaurant in the Nantucket-style clubhouse.

For a somewhat less challenging golf game, stop by **Pirate's Cove Adventure Park** (1710 US-31 N, 231/938-9599, www.piratescove. net, 10am-11pm daily Apr.-Oct., $7.95 adults, $7.50 children), where families can play at one of the finest miniature-golf chains in the country. At this award-winning theme park, players can learn about infamous pirates while navigating their way through caves, over footbridges, beneath cascading waterfalls, and alongside wrecked pirate ships. The complex offers two 18-hole courses in addition to bumper boats, racing go-carts, and a water coaster.

Hiking and Biking

Here's the happy general rule about the Traverse Bay region: Downhill ski resorts seem to morph into golf resorts, and cross-country skiing trails often become mountain biking trails.

As proof, the **Pere Marquette State Forest** has a couple of "pathways" in the Traverse City area that double as cross-country and mountain biking trails. You may hike them, too, of course. Most widely known is the 15.6-mile

North American VASA Trail (www.vasa.org). The VASA (named after Swedish King Gustav Vasa) has challenging climbs and descents. Take US-31 toward Acme, turn right onto Bunker Hill Road, drive 1.5 miles, then turn right again onto Bartlett to reach the trailhead.

The **Sand Lakes Quiet Area** is a classic northwoods area of small lakes, forest, and meadow about 10 miles east of Traverse City. Ten miles of trails loop through the 2,500 acres of terrain, which is moderately hilly—pleasant, but nothing extreme. For more information on biking, hiking, and camping in the Pere Marquette State Forest, call or stop by the **Michigan Department of Natural Resources's district office** (970 Emerson Rd., 231/922-5280).

For getting around Traverse City and reaching various trailheads on your bike, you can avoid busy US-31 by using the 10.5-mile **Traverse Area Recreation Trail** (TART, www.traversetrails.org). This off-road path shares a railroad right-of-way. It currently extends from US-72 at the West Bay beach to the Acme area, with plans to continue expanding it eastward.

The entire Traverse region offers fantastic back-road cycling. The **Cherry Capital Cycling Club** (231/941-2453, www.cherrycapitalcyclingclub.org) has mapped out zillions of options on its *Bicycle Map of Northwest Michigan,* printed on coated stock that can take a lot of abuse. It's available for $7 at local bike shops like **Brick Wheels** (736 E. 8th St., 231/947-4274, www.brickwheels.com, daily). This full-service shop has knowledgeable employees and rents road bikes, mountain bikes, and in-line skates.

Bird-Watching

A few miles south of Traverse City on Cass Road, the **Grand Traverse Nature Education Reserve** maintains 435 acres along the Boardman River and the Sabin and Boardman Ponds. Though just outside of town, this surprisingly peaceful area includes five miles of self-guided nature trails (no bikes) that wind along the river and cross through marshes and grasslands. The Traverse Bay region attracts particularly large populations of mute swans, and a pair frequently nests here, gliding gracefully across the glassy ponds. Farther upstream on the Boardman, large stands of oak crown a steep bluff climbing up from the river and another small flowage, **Brown Bridge Pond.** Stairs and trails lead out to observation platforms and down to the water's edge.

Canoeing and Fishing

What's that island in the West Arm, you ask? It's **Power Island,** a 200-acre nature preserve owned by the city, with beaches and five miles of hiking trails. For paddlers and other boaters, it's a fun destination for an afternoon picnic, but on weekends, it often becomes a local party spot.

Grand Traverse Bay isn't the only show in town. The beautiful **Boardman River** twists gently through Grand Traverse County before melting into the West Arm at Traverse City. The Boardman offers excellent fly-fishing and canoeing. Generally, its upper stretches run deeper and are better for paddling.

Skiing

West of Thompsonville on M-115, **Crystal Mountain** (12500 Crystal Mountain Dr., 231/378-2623, www.crystalmountain.com) began as a downhill skiing destination but has evolved into much more. While it still offers plenty of downhill—45 runs on two camel-humped slopes—it really shines in the cross-country department. Nordic skiers ride a chairlift from the Nordic Center to the top of the downhill slopes, where a trailhead leads to 25 miles of impeccably groomed cross-country terrain—a combination of gentle pathways and roller-coaster rides that weave all over the resort's 1,500 acres of land. The network is truly one of the finest in the Midwest.

Crystal Mountain invested wisely in its architecture, with pretty villas and tasteful condos scattered all around the property. Rates begin at about $120 but vary widely depending on unit and time of visit. Ski or golf packages are usually your best deal. In summer, Crystal's 36 holes of golf are the main draw, but it also offers clay tennis courts, indoor

© TRAVERSE CITY TOURISM

Ranch Rudolf near the Boardman River

and outdoor pools, and other resort amenities. Some of those great cross-country trails welcome mountain bikes in spring—more than 10 miles of intermediate and advanced terrain overlooking the Betsie River Valley, along with 13 more miles in the nearby state forest.

ACCOMMODATIONS

The Traverse City area has more than 5,000 rooms, everything from inexpensive motels to deluxe resorts. The **Traverse City Tourism** (101 W. Grandview Pkwy., 231/947-1120, www.visittraversecity.com) has a good directory and can help you narrow down your choices. In summer months, you'd be wise to show up with a reservation.

Lots of mom-and-pop motels and chain operations line US-31 along East Bay, Traverse City's original tourist stretch, known as the "miracle mile." Some newer ones have nudged onto this desirable real estate, like the **Pointes North Beachfront Resort Hotel** (2211 US-31 N, 800/968-3422, www.pointesnorth.com, $150-289 d). It has 300 feet of private beach, a waterfront pool, balconies, and in-room mini-kitchens. You'll save money by staying on the other side of US-31, of course, and plenty of

public beaches mean you can still get to the water easily enough. The **Traverse Bay Inn** (2300 US-31 N, 800/968-2646, www.traverse-bayhotels.com, $149-199 d) is a tidy and pleasant older motel, with an outdoor hot tub and pool, and some fancier new suites with kitchens and fireplaces. It gets bonus points for allowing dogs.

It's not on the water, but the upper floors of the **C Park Place Hotel** (300 E. State St., 231/946-5000, www.park-place-hotel.com, $105-276 d) come with incredible views of Grand Traverse Bay. This 1870s downtown landmark was in sad disrepair in 1989, when the local Rotary club purchased it and poured $10 million into renovations. (The Traverse City Rotary is believed to be the wealthiest in the nation, after it discovered oil on property it owned.) The club did a fabulous job restoring the Park Place to its turn-of-the-20th-century opulence.

Outside of town, the pet-friendly, year-round **Ellis Lake Resort** (8440 US-31 S, Interlochen, 231/276-9502, www.ellislakeresort.com, $78-249 d) offers cozy, smoke-free cabins housing private bathrooms and fully equipped kitchens, just 10 minutes from Traverse City. Built in 1939, the cabins are definitely in need of renovation, but some guests appreciate the rustic nature of the place, including the private outdoor yards equipped with picnic tables and campfire pits. While here, guests can enjoy an outdoor hot tub, a small playground, and a variety of other activities, from croquet and volleyball to hiking and snowshoeing. There's also a private 70-acre lake with a swimming beach; guests are also free to use the resort's canoes, rowboats, and paddleboat, and anglers may appreciate the bounty of bass, perch, bluegill, and pike here. Of course, if you're a light sleeper, you probably won't be happy at Ellis Lake; despite the bucolic setting, the property lies very close to the highway. **Ranch Rudolf** (6841 Brown Bridge Rd., Traverse City, 231/947-9529, www.ranchrudolf.com, $68-150 d) has motel units and a lodge with fireplaces, but the draw here is the location: 12 miles from Traverse City in the Pere Marquette State Forest on the shores of the Boardman River. There's paddling and fly-fishing right outside the door. Tent and RV sites are also available.

To the east of Traverse City, golfers and relaxation-seekers often flock to the **Grand Traverse Resort and Spa** (100 Grand Traverse Village Blvd., Acme, 231/534-6000 or 800/236-1577, www.grandtraverseresort.com, $135-439 d), a 900-acre spread that offers access to three signature golf courses, three unique restaurants, a sports bar, a wine-tasting room, a luxurious spa, a health club, a private beach, several swimming pools, and a wide range of well-appointed rooms, suites, condominiums, and resort homes. Given such amenities, plus stunning area views and a complimentary shuttle service to the nearby Turtle Creek Casino & Hotel, it's no wonder that the Grand Traverse Resort is also a popular spot for weddings.

Camping

You won't find a quiet nature retreat, but if you're looking for clean and convenient camping, then **Traverse City State Park** (1132 US-31 N, 231/922-5270, annual $11 Recreation Passport for Michigan residents or $8.40 day-use fee/$30.50 yearly Recreation Passport for nonresidents required) fits the bill. Just two miles east of downtown, the park has 343 modern sites ($27 daily) in a suburbanish

setting, grassy with shade trees. A pedestrian overpass will get you across busy US-31 to the main feature of the park: a grassy picnic area and a quarter mile of beach on Grand Traverse Bay. Though pretty, the stretch of sand can quickly become unpleasantly jammed on a summer weekend. Camp here for convenience, maybe, but head elsewhere for a day at the beach—the region has plenty of better choices. For reservations at the state park campground, contact the **Michigan Department of Natural Resources** (800/447-2757, www.michigan.gov/dnr).

You'll find more peace and seclusion at the many rustic campgrounds in the **Pere Marquette State Forest** just a few miles east of town. One to consider is **Arbutus Lake 4** (231/922-5280, $15 daily), with 50 sites on a pretty chain of lakes. From US-31 near the state park, take Four Mile Road south to North Arbutus Road.

FOOD

Traverse City is thick with good restaurants, from simple to elegant. **Apache Trout Grill** (13671 S. West Bay Shore Dr., 231/947-7079, www.apachetroutgrill.com, 10am-10pm daily, $8.50-28) is a casual spot overlooking the West Arm, featuring "northern waters" fish specialties partnered with distinctive sauces.

Sleder's Family Tavern (717 Randolph St., 231/947-9213, www.sleders.com, 11am-11pm Mon.-Thurs., 11am-midnight Fri.-Sat., noon-9pm Sun., $8-17) has been around since 1882, an institution known for its burgers and ribs, and its gorgeous original mahogany and cherry bar.

On the Old Mission Peninsula, the **Boathouse Restaurant** (14039 Peninsula Dr., 231/223-4030, www.boathouseonwestbay.com, 4pm-9pm Mon.-Thurs., 4pm-10pm Fri.-Sun., $36-75) is one of the region's most highly touted restaurants, with fine, diverse cuisine in a nautical atmosphere overlooking the Bowers Harbor marina. The nearby **◖ Mission Table at Bowers Harbor Inn** (13512 Peninsula Dr., 231/223-4222, www.missiontable.net, 5pm-9pm Sun.-Thurs., 5pm-10pm Fri.-Sat., $20-36) offers elegant dining in an 1880s mansion, complete with a resident ghost and an excellent wine list. Specialties include pan-seared diver scallops and smoked jowl.

For something quite different, try the Asian-inspired **Red Ginger** (237 E. Front St., 231/944-1733, www.eatatginger.com, 5pm-10pm Mon.-Thurs., 5pm-11pm Fri.-Sat., $9-32). Featuring flavors from Chinese, Thai, Vietnamese, Japanese, and other Asian cuisines, the Red Ginger is easily the best Asian restaurant in northern Michigan. If you go on a Monday, you can enjoy some live jazz while dining on Red Ginger dragon rolls and sake-glazed sea bass.

INFORMATION AND SERVICES

For more information about Traverse City, contact the **Traverse City Tourism** (101 W. Grandview Pkwy., 231/947-1120, www.visittraversecity.com, 8am-9pm Mon.-Fri., 9am-5pm Sat., noon-6pm Sun.). Stop by the visitors center to pick up maps and brochures, talk to a volunteer staff member about area activities, and check out rotating exhibits that feature the area's culture, history, and environment. You can also consult the **Traverse City Area Chamber of Commerce** (202 E. Grandview Pkwy., 231/947-5075, www.tcchamber.org). For regional news and events, pick up a copy of the *Traverse City Record-Eagle* (www.record-eagle.com) or *Traverse* magazine (www.mynorth.com).

To learn more about the Old Mission Peninsula, visit www.oldmission.com. For details about Benzie County, contact the **Benzie County Visitors Bureau** (826 Michigan Ave., Benzonia, 800/882-5801, www.visitbenzie.com, 9am-5pm Mon.-Fri.).

As Northwest Michigan's largest town, Traverse City offers an assortment of necessary services, including groceries, laundries, banks, and post offices. In case of an emergency requiring police, fire, or ambulance services, dial **911** from any cell or public phone. For medical assistance, consult **Munson Healthcare** (www.munsonhealthcare.org), which offers

several locations in the area, including **Munson Medical Center** (1105 6th St., Traverse City, 231/935-5000).

GETTING THERE AND AROUND

As with many towns and cities throughout Michigan, there are several ways to reach Traverse City. One option is to fly into **Cherry Capital Airport** (TVC, 727 Fly Don't Dr., Traverse City, 231/947-2250, www.tvcairport.com), which offers service from Detroit and Minneapolis on Delta Air Lines and from Chicago on American Airlines and United Airlines. From there, you can hire a taxi from **Cherry Capital Cab** (231/941-8294, www.cherrycapitalcab.com), a 24-hour company that charges $2.40 per pickup, plus $2.80 per mile. Typically, each trip costs an extra $1 for each passenger beyond the first two, and there's also a $5 fee for each pet or bike on-board, not to mention a stopping charge of $0.60 per minute. As an alternative, you can also rent a vehicle from one of five national rental car companies stationed at the airport, which lies about four miles southeast of downtown Traverse City.

Given its location on Grand Traverse Bay, it's also possible to access Traverse City via boat. A journey via bus is also an option. After all, both **Greyhound** (231/946-5180 or 800/231-2222, www.greyhound.com) and **Indian Trails** (800/292-3831, www.indiantrails.com) provide regular service to the **Bay Area Transportation Authority** (BATA, 115 Hall St., 231/941-2324 or 231/778-1025, www.bata.net, one-way $1.50-3 adults, $0.75-1.50 seniors 60 and over, students, and disabled individuals), which, in turn, offers year-round public transportation throughout Grand Traverse and Leelanau Counties. Of course, Traverse City is also a friendly town toward bikers and pedestrians. Many travelers, however, depend on their vehicles to reach the Cherry Capital and explore its environs, and luckily, you can reach the region's biggest town from a variety of directions. From Sault Ste. Marie, for instance, you can simply take I-75 South, cross the Mackinac Bridge (for which you'll have to pay a toll), and merge onto

US-31 South, which will take you directly to Traverse City; without traffic, the 160-mile trip will take about three hours. From downtown Detroit, meanwhile, you can take I-375 North, merge onto I-75 North, follow the I-75 Business Route to M-72 West, and continue onto US-31 South; without traffic, the 256-mile trip will require about four hours.

If, conversely, you're headed from Chicago, just follow I-90 East and I-94 East through Illinois and Indiana, cross the Michigan state line, continue onto I-196 North/US-31 North and I-196 East, merge onto US-131 North toward Cadillac, and take M-113 West and various surface streets to downtown Traverse City; without traffic, the 318-mile trip should take less than five hours. Just be advised that, en route from the Windy City, parts of I-90 East and I-94 East serve as the Indiana Toll Road.

◖ INTERLOCHEN CENTER FOR THE ARTS

South of town, the summertime bustle of Traverse City quickly fades into rolling farmland and woodlots. Incongruously tucked within this rural landscape, 14 miles southwest of Traverse City on M-137, the **Interlochen Center for the Arts** (4000 M-137, Interlochen, 231/276-7200, www.interlochen.org) operates a renowned school on a 1,200-acre campus under a tall canopy of pines. For over 85 years, Interlochen has cultivated a passion for the arts, with year-round programs for adults and a yearly summer camp for young artists, during which nearly 2,500 gifted students come to explore music, dance, theater, film, literature, and visual arts. Audiences can also appreciate Interlochen; throughout the year, this acclaimed institute offers hundreds of concerts, readings, dance and theatrical performances, film screenings, and art exhibitions. Its lineup of musicians and entertainers has always been diverse and impressive, ranging from Itzhak Perlman to the Neville Brothers.

INTERLOCHEN STATE PARK

Not far from the Interlochen school, 187-acre **Interlochen State Park** (M-137,

231/276-9511, annual $11 Recreation Passport for Michigan residents or $8.40 day-use fee/$30.50 yearly Recreation Passport for nonresidents required) fans out between Green Lake and Duck Lake, preserving one of the area's few remaining stands of virgin white pine. Thanks to the park's location near Traverse City and Interlochen, its campsites are the main draw. They're very nice ones, too, clustered around the lakeshores with many nice lake views. The modern campground, with the bulk of the park's 480 campsites, is on Duck Lake. Several dozen rustic sites are across the park on Green Lake. Both fill up in summer, so reserve a site ahead of time. For reservations, call 800/447-2757 or visit www.michigan.gov/dnr.

BENZIE COUNTY

Unspoiled Benzie County stretches from west of Traverse City to the port of Frankfort, a hilly region dotted with lakes and bisected by two pristine rivers, the Platte and the Betsie.

The six miles of trails in the **Lake Ann Pathway** offer plenty to see, taking you past Lake Ann, some smaller lakes, a stretch of the Platte River, bogs, and natural springs. The hilly terrain is pleasant for hiking, mountain biking, or cross-country skiing. Part of the Pere Marquette State Forest, it also has a very nice rustic campground with 30 shady, grass-covered sites and a swimming beach on Lake Ann. Follow US-31 west from Traverse City to Reynolds Road (4.5 miles past the turnoff to Interlochen). Turn right and drive 4 miles to the campground and trailheads.

The **Betsie River** wanders across Benzie County, eventually growing into a broad bay at Frankfort. Popular among anglers for trout and lake salmon, it is also a pretty paddling spot. From a put-in at Grass Lake, it's a 44-mile float to Betsie Lake near the Lake Michigan shore, largely through undeveloped state forest. There are several other public launches for a shorter trip.

West of Benzonia, the Betsie passes through the private wildlife sanctuary of **Gwen Frostic Prints** (231/882-5505, www.gwenfrostic.com,

9am-4:30pm Mon.-Sat., 10am-4pm Sun., free). Frostic's studio is an eclectic building of wood, stone, glass, and cement, where a dozen old Heidelberg presses clank away, cranking out Frostic's woodblock prints and poetry. Frostic, who died in 2001, was a woman of bold spirit, whose works paid homage to nature and independence. This intriguing shop has note cards, books, and more.

At Frankfort, the Betsie River flows into Betsie Lake, which forms a remarkably well-protected harbor in Lake Michigan. A crude wooden cross at the river's mouth marks the site of French explorer Père Jacques Marquette's death in 1675. Researchers now believe that the French voyageurs who wrote in their journals of the "Rivière du Père Marquette" were describing the Betsie. From here, you might be able to spot the offshore **Frankfort North Breakwater Light.**

North of Frankfort at Point Betsie, the 1858 **Point Betsie Lighthouse** (231/352-7644 or 231/352-7666, www.pointbetsie.org, 10:30am-4:30pm Sat., 12:30pm-4:30pm Sun., $4 adults, $2 children) perches atop a dune, with waves practically lapping at its base, a tenuous but highly scenic setting. The lighthouse was automated in 1984. The **Zetterberg Preserve at Point Betsie** stretches south from the lighthouse, 71 acres of wonderfully undeveloped duneland, with barren sand beach, scrubby pines, and low-lying dunes.

The Leelanau Peninsula

A ragged land of hills, lakes, and scribbled shoreline straggling northward between Lake Michigan and Grand Traverse Bay, the Leelanau Peninsula has long held a grip on writers and artists (novelist Jim Harrison, among others, makes his home here). Maybe it's the dramatic dichotomy of the place: On its western shore, the oh-so-grand dunes, rising directly up from the lake's surface; inland, a soft and pretty landscape, a muted watercolor of red barns, white farmhouses, and Queen Anne's lace waving in the roadside ditches.

All kinds of people will tell you that Leelanau is an Indian word meaning "land of delights," a description that certainly fits this varied peninsula. The only problem is, the word never existed in the language of the area's Ottawa Indians; they never even used the letter "L." Henry Schoolcraft, the white man who explored the Lake Michigan coast in the 1820s, most likely named it, giving it an "Indian-sounding" name. "Leelanau" can be anything you want it to be—just like your time here.

Leelanau County begins just west of Traverse City, and the county line stretches 30 miles straight west to the Sleeping Bear Dunes and Lake Michigan. Everything above that line is the Leelanau, a 28-mile-long peninsula that includes 98 miles of Great Lakes shoreline, 142 inland lakes and ponds, 58 miles of streams, and numerous award-winning wineries. Roads twist along with the contours of the hills, luring you toward farm stands and onto dirt roads that can't possibly go anywhere you intended to go.

As local author Bill Mulligan has noted, "The meandering expanse of water, woods, and sand of Leelanau is a nice counterweight to the exuberance of Traverse City." So meander.

◖ SLEEPING BEAR DUNES NATIONAL LAKESHORE

Glaciers and a millennium of wind and water sculpted the Sleeping Bear Dunes, rimming this corner of Michigan with a crust of sand and gravel, like salt on a margarita glass. Beach dunes line the southern part of the national seashore, the classic hillocks of sand you might picture when you think of dunes, created by the prevailing west winds carrying sand to low-lying shores.

But it's the perched dunes that claim center stage here, immense pyramids of sand spiking

NORTHWEST MICHIGAN

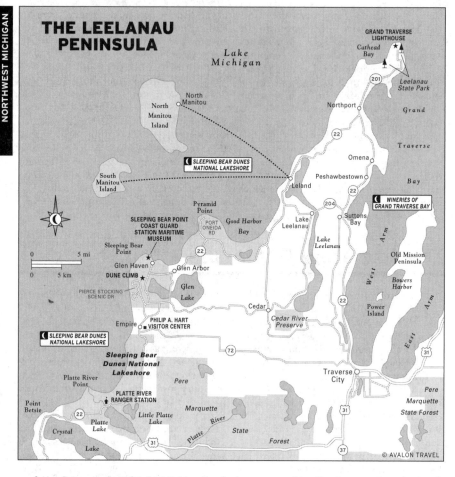

THE LEELANAU PENINSULA

up from the very edge of Lake Michigan and climbing at an impossible angle toward the sky. Glaciers first carried these mountains of sand and gravel to what is now the shoreline; nature continues the process, with waves eroding the great dunes and westerlies building them up again. At their highest, the perched dunes once topped out at about 600 feet. Today, Sleeping Bear measures closer to 400 feet, still the largest freshwater dune in the world.

To borrow an old cliché, words really *can't* describe the Sleeping Bear Dunes. They can

be a sunny, friendly playground, with squealing children tumbling down the Dune Climb. They can be lunar-like and desolate, a bleak desert on a January day. They can be pale and white-hot at noon, then glow in peaches and pinks like white zinfandel at sunset.

But they are always spectacular. Today, the **Sleeping Bear Dunes National Lakeshore** (9922 Front St., Empire, 231/326-5134, www. nps.gov/slbe, visitors center 8am-6pm daily Memorial Day-Labor Day, 8:30am-4pm daily early Sept.-late May, dunes 24 hours daily, $10

© DANIEL MARTONE

the popular Dune Climb in Sleeping Bear Dunes National Lakeshore

vehicles, $5 individuals, children under 16 free), established in 1977, encompasses nearly 72,000 acres, including 35 miles of Lake Michigan shoreline, North and South Manitou Islands, lakes, rivers, beech and maple forest, waving dune grasses, and those unforgettable dunes. It's truly a magnificent landscape, unlike anything else on the continent.

Empire Area

Situated beside Lake Michigan, Empire is home to the state's newest lighthouse, the cylindrical **Robert Manning Memorial Lighthouse,** erected in 1991 to honor a longtime resident. South of Empire, the **Empire Bluff Trail** winds through forest before erupting into a clearing, for a dramatic vantage point of the big dunes some 5 miles north. In 0.75 mile, the trail dead-ends at a high bluff overlooking the water, so clear you can often see schools of big lake trout. Farther south, **Platte River Point** improves on a great day at the beach with a perfect setting, a sandy spit bordered by Lake Michigan and the mouth of the Platte River. Rent an inner tube from **Riverside Canoe Trips** (5042 Scenic Hwy., Honor, 231/325-5622, www.canoemichigan.com, 8am-7pm daily) on M-22 at the Platte River Bridge and enjoy the popular sport of launching in the river and shooting out into the lake.

Pierce Stocking Scenic Drive

"I used to have a recurrent nightmare that there was a big highway across the top of the dunes and at the topmost point, a Holiday Inn," writes Kathleen Stocking in *Letters from the Leelanau.* "Now, except for the Holiday Inn, that prescient dream has materialized."

Ironically, the drive is named for Stocking's father, a lumberman who owned much of the land that is now a national park. For those of us who didn't grow up with the dunes as our backyard, this 7.4-mile paved loop that winds through the woods and atop a stretch of dune is less offensive. In fact, it could be argued that it keeps people from traipsing over fragile dune plants for views. Either way, the extremely

LEGEND OF THE SLEEPING BEAR

According to the Ojibwa Indians that formerly inhabited the Great Lakes region, a terrible forest fire once raged in what is now Wisconsin, along the shores of Lake Michigan. In an effort to flee the conflagration, a mother bear and her two cubs tried to swim across the enormous lake, toward present-day Michigan. When the mother reached the far shore, she climbed to the top of a bluff to await her cubs, who had grown tired and lagged behind.

As she waited, the sands collected around her, creating Sleeping Bear Dune, the largest in what eventually became **Sleeping Bear Dunes National Lakeshore** in 1977. Though the cubs sadly drowned in the lake, the Great Spirit took pity on the grieving mother and raised her children from the depths as North and South Manitou Islands, which lie offshore and are also part of the national park.

popular route *is* there, with scenic overlooks of Glen Lake, the dunes, and Lake Michigan.

The drive offers access to the **Cottonwood Trail,** a 1.5-mile, sandy, self-guided walk that educates visitors about the ecology and diverse plant life in the dunes. The drive also leads you to the **Lake Michigan Overlook,** a platform 450 feet above the water with views stretching to Point Betsie, 15 miles south, and 54 miles across to Wisconsin. Though the park service discourages it—having seen too many sprained ankles, broken arms, and close cardiac calls—you can slide your way down the dune here, though it's a steep, long, exhausting climb back up, about an hour's worth of crawling.

That's why the park service points visitors instead to the nearby **Dune Climb,** a more manageable 130-foot dune that Mother Nature conveniently deposited on the lee side of the plateau. It's the perfect place to let kids run off their energy, or to climb up for a fine view of shimmering Glen Lake. Even hardier souls can continue on the **Dunes Trail,** a challenging, 3.5-mile hike that extends from the Dune Climb, across several rugged dunes, to the sandy shores of Lake Michigan and back.

Glen Haven Area

In sleepy Glen Haven, the park service operates a nifty museum in the old lifesaving station. In summer months, the **Sleeping Bear Point Coast Guard Station Maritime Museum** (11am-5pm daily mid-May-Sept., noon-5pm

Sat.-Sun. Oct., free) depicts the work of the U.S. Lifesaving Service, the forerunner of the U.S. Coast Guard. Exhibits include lifesaving boats and the cannon used to shoot lifelines out to the sinking vessels, while video programs illustrate the drill and the rigorous life the crews led. They got a regular workout: Some 50 ships wrecked along this passage between the mainland and the nearby Manitou Islands, one of the busiest routes on the Great Lakes in the mid-19th century, since it offered a convenient shortcut between Mackinac Island and Chicago. The station originally sat a few miles west at Sleeping Bear Point, but was moved here in 1931 when the ever-omnipotent dunes threatened to bury it.

East on M-109, **Glen Arbor** occupies a small patch of private real estate completely surrounded by the national park, Lake Michigan, and Glen Lake. It caters to the tourist trade with mostly tasteful galleries and craft shops, and also has a grocery for reloading the picnic supplies. Cherry lovers shouldn't miss **Cherry Republic** (6026 Lake St., 800/206-6949, www.cherryrepublic.com, 9am-9pm daily), which bills itself as "the largest exclusive retailer of cherry products in the United States." You'll find cherry baked goods, cherry sodas, chocolate-covered cherries, cherry salsas, cherry jam . . . well, you get the idea.

Near Glen Arbor, the **Pyramid Point** hiking trail is a hilly 2.7-mile loop that leads to the park's northernmost point, with a high lookout

KERRY KELLY/NPS

Glen Haven

over Lake Michigan and Sleeping Bear Bay. To reach the trailhead, take M-22 three miles east of Glen Arbor to Port Oneida Road.

North and South Manitou Islands

Lying about 17 miles off the mainland, the Manitous comprise more than 20,000 acres of once-developed land that has largely been reclaimed by nature and now is managed as part of Sleeping Bear Dunes National Lakeshore. South Manitou is the smaller (5,260 acres) and more accessible of the two, serviced by passenger ferry from Leland daily in summer months. The same ferry also stops at North Manitou five times a week in July and August, fewer times in spring and fall. The trip to either island takes about 90 minutes. No cars, bikes, or pets are permitted. For schedule information and reservations, contact **Manitou Island Transit** (Leland, 231/256-9061, www.leelanau.com/manitou, round-trip $35 adults, $20 children under 13). The islands have potable water at a few locations, but no other services. Even day hikers should pack a lunch.

South Manitou Island was first settled in the 1830s. Islanders made a living by farming and logging, supplying food and fuel to the wood-burning steamers that traveled through the busy Manitou Passage. Farming was exceptional on South Manitou. Isolated from alien pollens, it proved the perfect place to produce crops and experiment with hybrid seeds, and was soon highly respected in agricultural circles. A South Manitou rye crop won first prize in an international exposition in 1920; by the 1940s, most of Michigan's bean crop came from South Manitou seed. By the 1960s, though, the island had become mostly a summer cottage getaway, and, a decade later, the National Park Service began condemning and buying up the land for a national lakeshore.

Today, visitors can arrange for a tour ($8 adults, $5 children) through the ferry company, a 90-minute trip in an open-air truck that follows abandoned roads to farmsteads, a schoolhouse, and a cemetery. Near the ferry dock, a small visitors center in the old village post office has displays on island history. Nearby,

© DANIEL MARTONE

the original Cherry Republic in Glen Arbor

the 1872 **South Manitou Island Lighthouse** is open on summer afternoons, allowing you to scale the 100-foot tower.

Hikers and backpackers will want to get farther afield, though. The island has 10 miles of marked hiking trails that lead to some interesting sights. Day hikers will have to move right along, but they can make the 6-mile round-trip to check out the wreck of the *Francisco Morazan* and still make it back in time for the afternoon ferry. Like many ships that failed to navigate the tricky Manitou Passage, this Liberian freighter ran aground in 1960. Its battered skeleton lies largely above the water's surface, just a few hundred yards offshore.

Nearby, a side trail winds through a grove of virgin cedars, some more than 500 years old. Deemed too isolated to log, the slow-growing trees are the largest of their kind left in North America, some measuring more than 15 feet around and nearly 90 feet tall. Another half mile west, the state's most remote dunes tower over the western shore, 300-foot perched dunes similar to those on the mainland.

To properly enjoy all the island has to offer, of course, you need to spend more than an afternoon. Camping is permitted only at three rustic campsites; reservations are required.

Like South Manitou, **North Manitou Island** was once a farming and logging community, then a summer getaway. Acquired by the National Park Service in 1984, it still has some patches of private property. But otherwise, this large island is even less developed than its southern neighbor. Those who come here do so to camp, hike, and explore the abandoned buildings.

North Manitou receives far fewer visitors than South Manitou—until fall hunting season, anyway. Nine deer were introduced here in the 1920s in the hopes of developing a herd large enough to hunt. Boy, did that work! In 1981, more than 2,000 deer roamed the island, decimating the vegetation so much that the island's forests had an "open park-like appearance," according to the park service. Today, it manages the herd by issuing hunting permits.

North Manitou has only one water source

© DANIEL MARTONE

Leland's historic "Fishtown" district

and one small rustic campground near the ferry dock; backcountry camping is permitted throughout the island's public property. Backcountry permits, though free, are required.

For camping permits and more information on the Manitous, contact **Sleeping Bear Dunes National Lakeshore** (231/326-5134, www.nps.gov/slbe).

LELAND TO NORTHPORT

The restored **"Fishtown"** at Leland's harbor is probably one of the most photographed spots in all of Michigan, a collection of 19th-century weathered gray fish shanties lined up on the docks. Whether you find it charming or obnoxious pretty much pegs your feelings about development—or reveals you as a local who remembers what the harbor looked like before the gift shops came to town. For many Leelanau residents, slicked-up Leland is a sad commentary on how tourism is erasing a simpler lifestyle.

Leland was a diverse industrial center in the mid-1800s, with two sawmills, a gristmill,

an iron smelter, and a flourishing commercial fishing trade. By the early 1900s, eight fisheries were operating out of Leland. Where the Carp River spills into Lake Michigan, they built shanties along the docks, which they used to store ice, repair nets, and house equipment. Once common in ports all over the Great Lakes, most of these complexes completely disappeared when commercial fishing declined in the mid-1900s.

In Leland, the shanties happily remain, lined up on the docks right out of a historical photo. **Carlson's Fishery** (205 W. River, 231/256-9801, www.carlsonsfish.com, 9am-6pm daily) still operates here, with its sturdy snub-nosed boats tied up to the pier and a shop that sells fresh fillets and smoked trout out of a long deli case. Most of the other shanties, though, now house gift shops and galleries, and the fishnets dry in the sun solely for the benefit of the summer tourist trade.

Though it's undeniably touristy, Leland is also undeniably attractive. The Carp River rolls by, where you can gaze down at the steelhead schooling in the waters. And whether or not you care for the shops, appreciate the fact that no one tore down these neat old buildings.

East of Leland lies lengthy Lake Leelanau. Popular with anglers, the lake is also a good spot for paddlers, especially at the **Cedar River Preserve** (Leelanau Conservancy, 231/256-9665, www.theconservancy.com) along its southern shore, part of the Pere Marquette State Forest. Launch a canoe partway up the eastern shore, where Lake Leelanau Road intersects Bingham Road.

North of Leland, handsome **Peterson Park** sits high atop a bluff overlooking Lake Michigan, with picnic tables, a playground, and a great vantage point for the area's renowned sunsets. A steep staircase leads to a rocky beach, a good spot to hunt for Petoskey stones. Take M-201 to Peterson Park Road and turn left. For swimming, **Christmas Cove** offers a perfect arc of sugar-sand beach near the tip of the peninsula. To find it, follow M-201 north from Northport; just after it joins CR-640, turn left on Kilcherman Road, which leads to Christmas Cove Road.

With a fine horseshoe harbor in the protected waters of Grand Traverse Bay, it's not surprising that **Northport** was one of the first spots settled on the Leelanau. Catholic missionaries established a village there in 1849, bringing with them several area Ottawa families that they had successfully converted to Christianity. Within 20 years, Northport was the county seat, overseeing a population of 2,500, and had a thriving commercial fishing industry. At the turn of the 20th century, it built a fancy resort hotel with room for 250 guests; within five years, the uninsured building burned to the ground. Today, Northport is popular with pleasure boaters, who still appreciate its snug harbor, and shoppers, who cruise its cute little downtown, a row of revamped 1860s buildings filled with eclectic antiques and clothing shops.

LEELANAU STATE PARK

Split into two units at the tip of the Leelanau Peninsula, the 1,350-acre **Leelanau State Park**

(15310 N. Lighthouse Point Rd., Northport, 231/386-5422 in summer or 231/922-5270 in winter, annual $11 Recreation Passport for Michigan residents or $8.40 day-use fee/$30.50 yearly Recreation Passport for nonresidents required) is a wonderful surprise: While the northern unit, with its lighthouse and campground, is very popular, most visitors seem to ignore its southern portion—meaning you can often have its lovely beaches and trails all to yourself.

In the southern unit, low dunes and more than a mile of sand beach curve along Cathead Bay. It's a mile walk from the parking area through maple and beech forest to get to the water, so it rarely draws a crowd. The park's 8.5 miles of walking trails radiate out from the same parking area. The **Mud Lake Tour** circles a wetland area and small lake, a good choice in spring and fall when waterfowl migrate through the area. The **Lake Michigan Trail** leads to the water, but don't skip the short side trail to the overlook—a stairway climbs up a dune for a breathtaking view of North Manitou Island. To reach the southern unit, follow CR-629 north and turn left just after Woolsey Airport.

Five miles north, the **Grand Traverse Lighthouse** (15500 N. Lighthouse Point Rd., Northport, 231/386-7195, www.grandtraverse-lighthouse.com, 10am-6pm daily June-Aug., noon-4pm daily May and Sept.-Oct., $4 adults, $2 children) presides over the park's northern unit at the peninsula's tip. Built in 1858, the pretty white brick tower looks woefully small for the huge expanse of water that surrounds it. (The Coast Guard thought so, too; the light was decommissioned in 1972, replaced by a more pedestrian—but taller—steel tower churning away down on the beach.) Today, visitors can stroll through the on-site museum or climb the tower when the lighthouse is open.

SUTTONS BAY

Once a town largely inhabited by immigrant laborers from the fruit orchards, Suttons Bay has gotten fancier and wealthier along with the rest of the Leelanau Peninsula. With mechanization, there simply aren't that many laborers anymore, and the desirable real estate—on Grand Traverse Bay, just 12 miles from Traverse City, with views of the cross-hatched orchards of the Old Mission Peninsula—was just too good to leave alone. These days, Suttons Bay has almost become a suburb of Traverse City. Residents have worked hard to maintain the community's own personality, though, with colorfully painted storefronts and old-fashioned red telephone booths along St. Joseph's Avenue (M-22). Suttons Bay's downtown boasts a restored movie theater, all manner of galleries and boutiques, and some of the best restaurants in the Grand Traverse region.

◖ WINERIES OF GRAND TRAVERSE BAY

As on the Old Mission Peninsula, the surrounding waters of Lake Michigan have a moderating effect on the Leelanau Peninsula, providing a surprisingly fruitful climate for growing cherries, apples, peaches, and wine grapes. Slow-changing lake temperatures keep things nice and cool during the growing season; come winter, they insulate the delicate trees and vines from killing deep freezes.

Michigan leads the nation in cherry production, and the Leelanau accounts for a quarter of that crop. And while Michigan's grape harvest isn't yet ready to challenge California's, a few of its wines have been. Leelanau (and Old Mission Peninsula) wineries regularly produce award-winning vintages, especially rieslings, which do particularly well in this climate, and chardonnays. Sure, you can still find some overly sweet cherry wines, but serious vintners are letting their wines do the talking, and winning over new converts every year. Some 25 wineries now make their home on the Leelanau Peninsula, and most offer both tours and tastings. For the latest information about this winemaking region, consult the **Leelanau Peninsula Vintner's Association** (www.lpwines.com).

Leelanau Cellars

Leelanau Cellars (7161 N. West Bay Shore Dr., Omena, 231/386-5201, www.leelanaucellars.com, 10am-6pm Mon.-Sat., noon-6pm Sun.) is the largest winery on the peninsula, producing 65,000 gallons of vinifera, hybrid, and fruit wines each year. Highest honors go to its Tall Ship chardonnay.

L. Mawby Vineyards

L. Mawby Vineyards (4519 S. Elm Valley Rd., Suttons Bay, 231/271-3522, www.lmawby.com, noon-6pm Thurs.-Sat.) is one of the region's smallest wineries—with a big reputation, especially for its sparkling wines and oak-barrel-fermented dry whites. Larry Mawby produces about 3,000 cases a year, with a goal to "keep things small enough to do what I want to do—make great wine with minimal intervention." He brings a creative flair to the winemaking business, evidenced in the artful wine labels designed by his wife, artist Peggy Core. From Suttons Bay, follow CR-633 south to Elm Valley Road.

Boskydel Vineyard

Boskydel Vineyard (7501 E. Otto Rd., Lake Leelanau, 231/256-7272, www.boskydel.com, noon-6pm daily) was the first vineyard in the Grand Traverse region, with French hybrid grapes first planted in 1964. Today, the winery produces about 2,500 cases a year—mostly semi-dry red and white table wines—from its vineyards sloping down toward Lake Michigan. The winery is two miles south of Lake Leelanau on CR-41.

Good Harbor Vineyards

Some consider Bruce Simpson's dry white chardonnay and pinot gris the finest wines to come out of the Traverse Bay region. An informative self-guided tour at **Good Harbor Vineyards** (34 S. Manitou Trail, 231/256-7165, www.goodharbor.com, 11am-5pm Mon.-Sat., noon-5pm Sun. May-Nov.), three miles south of Leland on M-22 in Lake Leelanau, explains how he's done it.

Chateau Fontaine Vineyards & Winery

Stop by **Chateau Fontaine Vineyards & Winery** (2290 S. French Rd., Lake Leelanau,

sampling wines at Black Star Farms

231/256-0000, www.chateaufontaine.com, noon-5pm Wed.-Sun. June-Oct., noon-5pm Sat.-Sun. May and Nov.-Dec.), a long-ago potato farm and cow pasture now transformed into 30 acres of grapevines. They produce chardonnay, pinot gris, and a "Woodland White," among others.

Black Star Farms

In Suttons Bay, you'll find **Black Star Farms** (10844 E. Revold Rd., 231/944-1271, www.blackstarfarms.com, 10am-6pm Mon.-Sat., noon-5pm Sun. May-Nov., 11am-5pm Mon.-Sat., noon-5pm Sun. Dec.-Apr.), billed as "an agricultural destination." This fascinating winery, distillery, creamery, and farmers market also offers a welcoming tasting room and a luxurious bed-and-breakfast.

More Wineries

Take special note of several other locales in Suttons Bay, including **Raftshol Vineyards** (1865 N. West Bay Shore Dr., 231/271-5650,

11am-6pm Mon.-Sat., noon-6pm Sun.), a former dairy enterprise and cherry orchard that now produces over 1,000 cases of bordeaux varietal red wines annually.

Owned by a cardiologist with a special interest in Michigan's agriculture, **Chateau de Leelanau Vineyard & Winery** (5048 S. West Bay Shore Dr., 231/271-8888, www.chateaudeleelanau.com, 11am-6pm Mon.-Sat., noon-5pm Sun. May-Oct., by appointment Mon.-Wed., noon-5pm Thurs.-Sun. Nov.-Apr.) presents a tasting room and retail store not far from Grand Traverse Bay.

Established in 1996, the **Ciccone Vineyard & Winery** (10343 E. Hilltop Rd., 231/271-5553, www.cicconevineyard.com, noon-5pm Sat. Jan.-Mar., noon-5pm Thurs.-Sun. Apr.-May, noon-6pm daily June-Oct., noon-5pm Tues.-Sat. Nov.-Dec.), owned by Madonna's father, is a Tuscan-inspired winery and tasting room. For a $5 fee, you can purchase a Ciccone wine glass and up to five tastings of the vintner's choice.

EVENTS

The Leelanau Peninsula is home to a myriad of art festivals, culinary events, and seasonal gatherings. One curious event occurs in late September, the annual **Harvest Stompede Vineyard Run & Walk,** which features a race through Leelanau's vineyards as well as a tour of area wineries. During the weekend, visitors are able to sample wines, gourmet pastas, and other culinary delights. For more information, consult the **Leelanau Peninsula Vintner's Association** (www.lpwines.com).

DIVING

The waters around North Manitou Island, South Manitou Island, and the Sleeping Bear Dunes are rife with historic dock ruins and shipwrecks, making the **Manitou Passage Underwater Preserve** a fascinating place for scuba divers. Besides the popular *Francisco Morazan* wreck near the south end of South Manitou Island, divers enjoy exploring the artifacts that abound on the *Walter L. Frost*, a wooden steamer that ran aground in 1905, only to be further wrecked in 1960 when the *Morazan* landed on top of it. For more information, contact the **Michigan Underwater Preserve Council** (800/970-8717, www.michiganpreserves.org).

ACCOMMODATIONS AND FOOD

If your budget won't allow a stay at **❰ Black Star Farms** (10844 E. Revold Rd., Suttons Bay, 231/944-1271, www.blackstarfarms.com, $150-395 d)—a winery, creamery, market, and luxurious B&B—you'll be happy to know that the region also accommodates campers. The rustic campground at **Leelanau State Park** (15310 N. Lighthouse Point Rd., Northport, 231/386-5422 in summer or 231/922-5270 in winter, annual $11 Recreation Passport for Michigan residents or $8.40 day-use fee/$30.50 yearly Recreation Passport for nonresidents required) has 52 wonderful sites ($15 daily), with several right along the water and several more with water views. Though the campground is extremely popular in summer, most sites offer a fair amount of seclusion.

In Leland, a couple of restaurants overlook the river and Fishtown, including **❰ The Cove** (111 River St., 231/256-9834, www.thecoveland.com, 11:30am-9pm daily, $9-26), featuring seafood chowder, fish stew, and fresh fish specials. A block or two farther upstream, across M-22 (the main drag), **The Bluebird Restaurant & Bar** (102 River St., 231/256-9081, www.leelanau.com/bluebird, 11:30am-9pm Tues.-Sun., $6-14) is a well-known dinner spot, with reasonably priced seafood dishes, homemade soups, and a decent wine list. Meanwhile, Lake Leelanau is home to **Dick's Pour House** (103 W. Philip St., 231/256-9912, www.dickspourhouse.com, 11:30am-10pm Sun.-Thurs., 11:30am-11pm Fri.-Sat. in summer, 11:30am-8pm Sun.-Thurs., 11:30am-9pm Fri.-Sat. in winter, $7-16), where you can sample pizza, sandwiches, soups, pies, and a Friday fish fry.

INFORMATION AND SERVICES

For more information about the Leelanau Peninsula, contact the **Traverse City Convention & Visitors Bureau** (101 W. Grandview Pkwy., 231/947-1120, www.visittraversecity.com, 8am-9pm Mon.-Fri., 9am-5pm Sat., noon-6pm Sun.). You can also consult the **Leelanau Peninsula Chamber of Commerce** (5046 S. West Bay Shore Dr., Ste. G, Suttons Bay, 231/271-9895, www.leelanauchamber.com), **Leelanau Communications** (113 N. Main, Leland, 231/256-2829, www.leelanau.com), the **Leland Michigan Chamber of Commerce** (231/256-0079, www.lelandmi.com), the **Suttons Bay Area Chamber of Commerce** (231/271-5077, www.suttonsbayarea.com), and **The Third Coast Traveler** (www.thetctraveler.com).

If you require other services while traveling across the Leelanau Peninsula, remember that nearby Traverse City offers everything you might need, from groceries to hospitals. If an emergency occurs, don't hesitate to dial **911** from any phone.

GETTING THERE AND AROUND

To reach the Leelanau Peninsula, many travelers first arrive in Traverse City, usually via their own vehicles. Of course, it's also possible to reach Traverse City by flying into **Cherry Capital Airport** (TVC, 727 Fly Don't Dr., Traverse City, 231/947-2250, www.tvcairport.com) or coming by bus via **Greyhound** (231/946-5180 or 800/231-2222, www.greyhound.com) or **Indian Trails** (800/292-3831, www.indiantrails.com). From there, you can then rent a vehicle (or rely on your own) and head west on M-72 to Empire, where you'll find the headquarters of Sleeping Bear Dunes National Lakeshore; the 24-mile trip from Traverse City to Empire usually takes about a half hour. From Traverse City, you can also explore the wineries of the Leelanau Peninsula by heading north on M-22, which actually traces the perimeter of the peninsula, passing through towns like Suttons Bay, Northport, Leland, Glen Arbor, and Empire. To give you an idea of the distances here, know that it takes about 42 minutes to cover the 29 miles between Traverse City and Northport via M-22. Of course, if you'd rather not drive, you can also rely on the **Bay Area Transportation Authority** (BATA, 231/941-2324 or 231/778-1025, www.bata.net, one-way $1.50-3 adults, $0.75-1.50 seniors 60 and over, students, and disabled individuals) to navigate the peninsula.

Manistee to Cadillac

As you continue south along the Lake Michigan shoreline, towns grow sparser, summer crowds thin, and beaches climb into windswept dunes. If you're looking for a quiet beach walk or a mellow waterfront town without a full parade of activities and attractions, this may be the stretch of shore for you. Even farther south lies the Manistee National Forest, which is surrounded by towns like Ludington and Pentwater and contains several inland lakes, miles of hiking possibilities, and a wildflower sanctuary.

MANISTEE

Manistee's slogan is "Manistee: A Great Place to Be." While the city's downtown is a charming mix of historic logging buildings and ornate Victorian mansions, much of the credit for that claim goes to the wonderful Manistee National Forest that lies just outside the city limits. In fact, the national forest is such a part of Manistee's psyche that the city honors it with the annual **Manistee National Forest Festival** each July. Manistee serves as a good base camp for exploring the forest, as well as an

© JIM PARKIN | DREAMSTIME.COM

the Manistee North Pierhead Light

exceptionally lovely and untouched stretch of Lake Michigan shoreline. Before you head south, though, stop by the **Manistee North Pierhead Light,** erected in 1927 and still active today.

LUDINGTON

Because of its midpoint position on Lake Michigan and its ample supply of lumber, Ludington enjoyed a boom as a busy port during the latter half of the 19th century. (Originally named Père Marquette in honor of the missionary explorer who died here in 1675, the city later changed its name to reflect the influence of its more recent founder, James Ludington, a lumber baron.) Today, visitors are drawn to its enormous expanse of sugar-sand beach. As you'll see from the busy marina in the heart of town, fishing and boating are the pulse of this appealing community. Take special note of the white pyramidal lighthouse, the 1924 **Ludington North Pierhead Light,** which replaced a much older lighthouse at the end of the breakwater.

Historic White Pine Village

Opened in 1976, the **Historic White Pine Village** (1687 S. Lakeshore Dr., 231/843-4808, www.historicwhitepinevillage.org, 10am-5pm Tues.-Sat., 1pm-5pm Sun. Memorial Day-Labor Day, 10am-5pm Tues.-Sat. early-late May and Labor Day-mid-Oct., closed mid-Oct.-Apr., $9 adults, $6 children 6-17, children under 6 free) presents 30 buildings and historic sites, dedicated to preserving Mason County's past. It's worth bringing the whole family for this educational yet fun-filled tour. The old-fashioned ice cream parlor is an especially big hit with young travelers.

Ludington State Park

Ludington State Park (8800 W. M-116, 231/843-8671, www.ludingtonfriends.com, annual $11 Recreation Passport for Michigan residents or $8.40 day-use fee/$30.50 yearly Recreation Passport for nonresidents required) is one of the state's finest outdoor playgrounds and one of the largest state parks in the Lower

© DANIEL MARTONE

enjoying the waters of Ludington State Park

Peninsula. Attendance ranks in the top 10 of all Michigan state parks, with good reason. The park encompasses more than 5,300 acres of beautiful beaches, almost six miles of Lake Michigan shoreline, dunes and forests that wrap around picnic areas, biking and hiking paths, three campgrounds, an interesting interpretive center, an inland lake, and a canoe trail.

The park occupies a wide strip of land between Lake Michigan and Hamlin Lake, straddling the Big Sable River, which connects them. The numerous trails that lace the park's interior are among the finest foot paths in the Lower Peninsula. They offer everything from a leisurely half-hour stroll to a rather strenuous six-mile round-trip trek to the 1867 **Big Sable Point Lighthouse** (www.bigsablelighthouse. org, 10am-5pm daily May-Oct., $2 adults, $1 children 12-18), painted in tiers of black and white, and standing guard over Big Sable Point. Trudging through sand is tiring on the calves, but the view from the top of the tower makes it all worth it.

PENTWATER AND SILVER LAKE

Once considered a sleepy town along the Lake Michigan shore, the Victorian logging town of Pentwater ticks along at a pleasant—but not frantic—summer pace. On Hancock Street, Pentwater's main drag, visitors prowl through a growing number of antiques shops, searching for turn-of-the-20th-century treasures and nautical artifacts. A parade of pleasure boats purr through the boat channel that links Pentwater Lake and Lake Michigan, accompanied by folks strolling along the Channel Lane Park walkway. On the north side of the boat channel, **Charles Mears State Park** (400 W. Lowell St., 231/869-2051, annual $11 Recreation Passport for Michigan residents or $8.40 day-use fee/$30.50 yearly Recreation Passport for nonresidents required) seems more like a city beach than a state park.

Between Silver Lake and Lake Michigan lie more than 2,000 acres of unspoiled and ever-shifting sand dunes, remnants of the glaciers that once scrubbed this landscape. They are one of the largest deposits of dunes on the shores of Lake Michigan, acre after acre of ridges and valleys of wind-blown sand that are void of trees, scrub, or, in many places, even dune grass. Most of the dunes are protected as **Silver Lake State Park** (9679 W. State Park Rd., 231/873-3083, annual $11 Recreation Passport for Michigan residents or $8.40 day-use fee/$30.50 yearly Recreation Passport for nonresidents required), with hiking trails that climb high sand hills and weave through grasses and stunted trees. The park and dunes are located on one of the westernmost spots of the state's shoreline, a broad point that extends more than seven miles out from the main shore. From here, you can visit the 1874 **Little Sable Point Light,** a tall brick conical structure preserved by the park.

The Wood family once owned most of this land, and sold it to the state in 1973. They retained the right to use about 700 acres at the park's south end to operate **Mac Wood's Dune Rides** (629 N. 18th Ave., Mears, 231/873-2817, www.macwoodsdunerides.com, daily mid-May-Oct., $17 adults, $11 children 3-11). Visitors load into hybrid buggy/trucks for a seven-mile drive through the dunes, roaring up and down hills and splashing along the Lake Michigan surf line. While it's easy to question this kind of use of the dunes, the operation does make an effort to help visitors understand and appreciate the region's unique ecology.

MANISTEE NATIONAL FOREST

Manistee National Forest (231/775-2421, www.fs.usda.gov) stretches from Manistee south to Muskegon, over a half-million acres of woods, beaches, dunes, and two fine paddling rivers, the Pine and Pere Marquette. Most notable of the national forest's many attractions is the **Nordhouse Dunes Wilderness,** a 3,450-acre swath of untouched dunes and dune forest. It is the only federally designated wilderness in Michigan's Lower Peninsula, and the only federal dune wilderness in the nation.

The wilderness area includes 3 miles of isolated Lake Michigan beach, where dunes reach more than 140 feet. From the beach, 10 miles of hiking trails spin inland. Because they are minimally signed, bring a map and compass, along with plenty of water. Backcountry camping is permitted in the wilderness more than 200 feet from the waterline. The adjacent Nordhouse Dunes Recreation Area offers a modern campground with potable water.

Hikers should seek out the **Manistee River Trail,** a 10-mile route that follows the east bank of the Manistee River. The trail offers plenty of diversity, scaling steep slopes, meandering through pine and hardwood forest, dipping through ferny glades and crossing several creeks. It is open to foot traffic only. The north trailhead is near the south end of the Hodenpyl Dam, which lies east of Manistee. Pick up a map at the **ranger office** (412 Red Apple Rd., Manistee, 231/723-2211).

For paddlers, the **Pine National Scenic River** serves up lots of twists and turns, and some Class II rapids as well. There are four access sites within the national forest, each with toilets, water, grills, and parking areas. Rent canoes from **Horina Canoe & Kayak Rental** (9889 M-37, Wellston, 231/862-3470, www.horinacanoe.com, $42 daily). The wonderfully clear **Pere Marquette River,** also a national scenic river, is great for both canoeing and fishing, with healthy populations of brown trout, steelhead, and salmon. The navigable stretch within the national forest is more than 43 miles long, with several access points.

Loda Lake National Wildflower Sanctuary

Nestled within the Manistee National Forest, between the towns of Brohman and White Cloud, the **Loda Lake National Wildflower Sanctuary** (www.fs.usda.gov/hmnf, 24 hours daily, $5 daily, $15 weekly) is the only sanctuary of its kind ever established in a U.S. national forest. Although the sanctuary is open year-round, it's not maintained in winter, and the ideal months for seeing wildflowers are April-September. During this time, nature lovers can take a self-guided tour through oak-maple woodlands, old pine plantations, and

THE RULES OF LODA LAKE

Situated in Manistee National Forest in the northwestern part of Michigan's Lower Peninsula, **Loda Lake National Wildflower Sanctuary** is the only one of its kind in America's national forest system. Supported by the Federated Garden Clubs of Michigan for more than seven decades, the sanctuary welcomes visitors all year long, though it's particularly popular May-August. While several diversions are allowed here, including hiking, hunting, boating, snowshoeing, and cross-country skiing, certain restrictions do apply. So, bear the following rules in mind on your next visit to Loda Lake:

- Do not bring bicycles, llamas, pack and saddle animals, snowmobiles, and other motorized vehicles into the sanctuary.

- Keep your dogs leashed at all times.

- Remember that hiking and foot travel are only permitted on official trails.

- Do not pick or remove wildflowers.

- Use only dead and down wood for fires.

- Build fires in grills and fire rings only.

- Do not camp overnight in the sanctuary.

For more information about **Loda Lake National Wildflower Sanctuary** (800/821-6263, www.fs.usda.gov/hmnf), contact the **Baldwin/White Cloud Ranger Station** (P.O. Box Drawer D, Baldwin, MI 49304, 231/745-4631).

a shrub swamp, boasting a slew of wildflowers and other plant species, from columbine to witch hazel to huckleberries. A detailed brochure is available from the **Baldwin/White Cloud Ranger District** (650 N. Michigan Ave., Baldwin, 231/745-4631, 8am-4:30pm daily mid-May-mid-Sept., 8am-4:30pm Mon.-Fri. mid-Sept.-mid-May). To reach the sanctuary,

© LODA LAKE NATIONAL WILDFLOWER SANCTUARY

nodding lady's tresses in the Loda Lake National Wildflower Sanctuary

head north from White Cloud on M-37 for 6.8 miles; the sanctuary will be on your left.

CADILLAC

It may share a name with the luxury car maker, but snowmobiles, not Caddies, are the preferred means of transportation in the forest and lake country surrounding Cadillac. An intricate web of trails links the city with routes through the Manistee National Forest. In summer, much of the same crowd turns to fishing. The city of 10,270 sits on the shore of large 1,150-acre Lake Cadillac, which is linked by canal to even larger Lake Mitchell. Both are known for excellent northern pike and walleye fishing. The canal was originally built by loggers, who grew tired of the twisting, shallow river that originally traversed the wetlands between the two lakes.

Situated between the two lakes, **William Mitchell State Park** (6093 E. M-115, Cadillac, 231/775-7911, annual $11 Recreation Passport for Michigan residents or $8.40 day use

fee/$30.50 yearly Recreation Passport for non-residents required) is a dream come true for anglers and pleasure boaters. Some of its 221 modern campsites ($27-29 daily) are in fact on the canal itself, where boats can be tied up right next to your tent or RV. The park maintains a boat launch on Lake Cadillac, as well as swimming beaches on both lakes. There's a short nature trail skirting a wetlands area with an observation tower. Visit early in the morning to observe the active birds here. Though it's pretty, be aware that this park and both of its lakes tend to be extremely busy throughout the summer. Those looking for a peaceful retreat will likely be disappointed by the buzz of activity, but if that doesn't scare you away, be sure to reserve a spot well in advance by calling 800/447-2757 or visiting www.michigan.gov/dnr.

GOLF

Situated in Mecosta County, east of Manistee National Forest and accessible via US-131, the courses of **The Resorts of Tullymore & St. Ives** (9900 St. Ives Dr., Stanwood, 231/972-4837, www.tullymoregolf.com, daily Apr.-Oct., $75-160 pp) are popular among golfers of all skill levels. This fine resort, which you'll find on the road between Grand Rapids and Cadillac, offers two marvelous 18-hole courses, an Irish pub, and two fine restaurants.

ACCOMMODATIONS

In Manistee, the **Days Inn** (1462 US-31 S, 231/723-8385, www.daysinn.com, $92-115 d) offers an indoor pool and spa, and a nice location at the south end of town near the scenic riverwalk. Just steps from Lake Michigan and downtown Ludington, **Snyder's Shoreline Inn** (903 W. Ludington Ave., 231/845-1261, www.snydersshoreinn.com, mid-May-Oct., $59-309 d) offers a variety of rooms and cottages. ❮❮ **The Lamplighter Bed & Breakfast** (602 E. Ludington Ave., Ludington, 231/843-9792, www.ludington-michigan.com, $125-170 d) is a Victorian-inspired inn housed within an 1894 home, with five guest rooms and original paintings, lithographs, and antiques throughout. On Hamlin Lake, **Sauble Resort** (3443

N. Stearns, Ludington, 231/843-8497, www. saubleresort.com, $67-165 d) presents house-keeping cottages overlooking the dunes, not far from Ludington State Park.

Camping

Ludington State Park (8800 W. M-116, 231/843-2423, annual $11 Recreation Passport for Michigan residents or $8.40 day-use fee/$30.50 yearly Recreation Passport for nonresidents required) offers 354 sites ($16-29 daily) in four campgrounds, as well as three rustic mini-cabins; call 800/447-2757 or visit www.michigan.gov/dnr for reservations. The **Mason County Campground** (5906 W. Chauvez Rd., Ludington, 231/845-7609, $35 daily) has 50 modern sites and a wooded picnic area set among tall trees. A paved path leads visitors to Vista Point, a scenic overlook above Lake Michigan.

FOOD

While in Manistee, stop by the **Boathouse Grill** (440 River St., 231/723-2300, 11am-11pm Thurs.-Sat., 11am-10pm Sun.-Wed., $7-18), which serves comfort foods like chicken pot pie or crispy pan-fried lake perch. If the weather is nice, try to get a table on the patio overlooking the Manistee River. In Ludington, the **Jamesport Brewing Company** (410 S. James St., 231/845-2522, www.jamesportbrewingcompany.com, 11:30am-9pm Sun.-Thurs., 11:30am-10pm Fri.-Sat., $6-24) offers a wide array of salads, burgers, and other bar favorites, along with handcrafted beers.

INFORMATION AND SERVICES

For more information about this area, contact the **Manistee Convention & Visitors Bureau** (www.visitmanisteecounty.com), the **Manistee Area Chamber of Commerce** (11 Cypress St., Manistee, 800/288-2286, www.manisteechamber.com), the **Ludington Area Convention and Visitors Bureau** (5300 W. US-10, Ludington, 800/542-4600, www.pureludington.com), the **Pentwater Chamber of Commerce** (231/869-4150, www.pentwater.

org), the **Hart-Silver Lake/Mears Chamber & Visitors Bureau** (2388 N. Comfort Dr., Hart, 231/873-2247, www.thinkdunes.com), the **Newaygo County Convention & Visitors Bureau** (4686 S. Evergreen, Newaygo, 231/652-9298, www.newaygocountytourism.com), the **Mecosta County Area Convention & Visitors Bureau** (246 N. State, Big Rapids, 231/796-7640, www.bigrapids.org), and the **Cadillac Area Visitors Bureau** (222 Lake St., Cadillac, 231/775-0657, www.cadillacmichigan.com).

The towns along this route offer a limited number of services. For a bit more, head north to Traverse City, which offers everything from groceries to banks. If an emergency occurs, don't hesitate to dial **911** from any phone or visit **Mercy Hospital Cadillac** (400 Hobart St., 231/876-7200, www.munsonhealthcare.org).

GETTING THERE AND AROUND

To reach the towns and counties south of Traverse City, you can fly into **Cherry Capital Airport** (TVC, 727 Fly Don't Dr., Traverse City, 231/947-2250, www.tvcairport.com) or come by bus via **Greyhound** (231/946-5180 or 800/231-2222, www.greyhound.com) or **Indian Trails** (800/292-3831, www.indiantrails.com), after which you can rent a car and simply head south. From Traverse City, you can reach Manistee, Ludington, and the Pentwater area via US-31, cut through the Manistee National Forest on M-20, and drive north to Cadillac via US-131. Of course, it's also possible to reach the towns of Cadillac and Big Rapids (which lies about 42 miles south of Cadillac via US-131) directly by bus, courtesy of both Greyhound and Indian Trails.

Most travelers, however, will probably venture to this region via car, and luckily, there are plenty of helpful routes available. From Muskegon, for instance, you can access Pentwater, Ludington, and Manistee via US-31 North; without traffic, the 45-mile journey to Pentwater will usually take about 47 minutes, while the 59-mile trip to Ludington and the 83-mile trip to Manistee will take about 60 minutes and 80 minutes, respectively. From

Petoskey, meanwhile, you can access Cadillac via US-131 South, a 91-mile trip that usually takes less than two hours.

Lake Michigan Carferry

Ludington is also home to the Great Lakes' only authentic passenger steamship, offering two round-trip sailings each day in summer between Ludington and Manitowoc, Wisconsin. This historic carferry, the 410-foot-long SS *Badger* (701 Maritime Dr., Ludington, 920/684-0888 or 800/841-4243, www.ssbadger.com, round-trip $121 adults, $109 seniors 65 and over, $39 children 5-15, one-way $69 adults, $62 seniors 65 and over, $24 children 5-15, $86 pickup campers, $69 cars, vans, and pickups, $38 motorcycles, $6 bikes, children under 5 free), is the sole survivor of the fleet of auto/train/passenger ferries that once plowed across Lake Michigan, linking Midwestern cities like Chicago, Muskegon, and Milwaukee. The first steamer, the *Pere Marquette,* was hailed as a "titan of size and power." These hard-working vessels were owned by the railroads, and were even equipped with rails in their holds, so they could load boxcars as well as automobiles and passengers. The *Badger* operates daily mid-May-mid-October, though reservations are strongly recommended. Note, too, that pets must remain in your vehicle or in a ventilated kennel (which you must provide) on the car deck—a practice that's not recommended during the hot summer months. Also bear in mind that, for security reasons, you cannot access your vehicle during the crossing.

Charlevoix and Vicinity

Woodland Indians were likely the first to settle in present-day Charlevoix (SHAR-luh-voy), summering along the Lake Michigan shores some 4,000 years ago. But it was a French missionary who gave the town its name. Pierre François-Xavier de Charlevoix traveled through the region in the early 1700s, surreptitiously searching for the fabled Northwest Passage without tipping off the British. He never found a passage, of course, but that hasn't stopped boats from gathering in this yachter's paradise.

Nestled between Grand Traverse Bay and Little Traverse Bay, Charlevoix was practically destined to become a vacation spot. Along with the inherent appeal of Lake Michigan, Charlevoix also sidles up against lovely Lake Charlevoix, a clear, wishbone-shaped lake that draws anglers and pleasure boaters.

Inland, along the north arm of Lake Charlevoix toward Horton Bay, the land crumples like a fallen soufflé. This is lake country, river country, trout-fishing country, the boyhood backyard of a young Ernest Hemingway, whose family spent summers on nearby Walloon Lake. Just a few miles from the summer throngs that can descend on Charlevoix, much of Charlevoix County ticks along at a much mellower pace, the kind of place that inspires you to drift downstream in a canoe, make a few casts from a quiet bank, or pedal the two-lanes that twist through the region.

Or really get away from it all on Beaver Island, which you can reach by ferry or plane from Charlevoix. Originally settled by the Irish, it became a Mormon stronghold in the 1840s, ruled by a self-proclaimed king who was eventually assassinated by two of his followers. Things are considerably tamer on the island today, a sandy, wooded retreat with an Irish flavor and a decidedly somnolent air. Like much of the region, it's just the kind of place to spark creativity, maybe even inspire prose. Hey, it worked for Hemingway.

SIGHTS
Downtown

"Charlevoix the Beautiful," they call this nautical town of 3,000, wedged on an isthmus between Lake Michigan and Round Lake, which

© CHARLEVOIX AREA CVB

the Charlevoix harbor at night

opens to large Lake Charlevoix. With flowers flanking Bridge Street (US-31), a walkway along the Pine River linking the lakes, gleaming yachts with clanging halyards, screeching gulls, and yacht shops, Charlevoix *is* pretty beautiful.

Downtown Charlevoix also can be crammed on a summer weekend, so do yourself a favor: If you don't arrive by boat (as many do), leave the car at your hotel or on the edge of town and walk. This is a town meant for strolling, and you can enjoy nearly all of its sights on foot.

Bridge Street is Charlevoix's main drag, lined with restaurants, galleries, gift shops, and 50,000 petunias (planted by volunteers each spring, and watered by volunteers with a donated tank truck). For a free directory, stop by the **Charlevoix Area Convention & Visitors Bureau** (109 Mason St., 231/547-2101 or 800/367-8557, www.visitcharlevoix.com).

Toward the north end of the shopping district, a lift bridge rises on the half hour to allow tall-masted boats to travel the **Pine River Channel** from Lake Michigan to Round

Lake, essentially a yacht basin that connects to much larger Lake Charlevoix. A lovely walkway lit with Victorian-style lamps lines both sides of the channel between Bridge Street and Lake Michigan. Follow the north side to reach the long pier that extends far out into Lake Michigan. To your right, Michigan Avenue parallels the lakeshore, where stately old homes preside over the waterfront.

Follow the south side of the walkway to the **South Pierhead Lighthouse** and **Lake Michigan Beach,** with fine white sand, changing rooms, a playground, and a picnic area. The woods behind the beach have some short walking trails. Cross the street that parallels the beach, Park Avenue, to check out the weird elfin architecture of **Earl Young** scattered throughout this pleasant neighborhood. Young, a local real estate agent and self-taught home designer, constructed or remodeled two dozen homes in the 1930s and 1940s, many in the triangular block bordered by Park, Clinton, and Grant. Young used natural materials like enormous lake boulders to build his odd mushroom-shaped homes, topping them with curved cedar shake roofs. They're tucked amid Victorians, and it looks like Smurfs have invaded the neighborhood.

Young was also selected to design the Weathervane Terrace Inn and Stafford's Weathervane Restaurant along the channel. Rock walls and massive fireplaces characterize the designs; the restaurant's fireplace features a nine-ton keystone shaped like the state of Michigan. The local convention and visitors bureau has a map that directs you to Charlevoix's Young homes.

On the east side of Bridge Street, **East Park** fronts the bustling marina and city docks on Round Lake. This is a fun spot to grab a sandwich and watch the comings and goings of all the boat business. Even better, pick up some smoked fish from **John Cross Fisheries** (209 Belvedere Ave., 231/547-2532, 9am-5pm Mon.-Sat., 9am-4pm Sun.). One of the last commercial fisheries left in the area, it sells fresh walleye, perch, lake trout, and whitefish, which it also supplies to local restaurants. You can also buy smoked whitefish or trout by the chunk.

Northern Charlevoix

Around the southern end of Round Lake, the grounds of the century-old **Belvedere Club** spread across a high hill, overlooking both Round Lake and Lake Charlevoix. Founded by Baptists from Kalamazoo in the 1870s, the Belvedere Club was planned as a summer resort community, mirroring the Methodists' successful Bay View near Petoskey. Wealthy summer folk built homes in the opulent fashion of the day, with verandas, dormers, and gabled roofs. Today, many of the homes are occupied in summer by the grandchildren and great-grandchildren of the original owners. Though the streets through still-private Belvedere are closed in July and August, you can get a glimpse of the neighborhood from Ferry Avenue along Lake Charlevoix.

Inspired by the Belvedere Club, the First Congregational Church of Chicago formed a similar community on the north side of the Pine River Channel. As with the Belvedere, the

Chicago Club is closed to the public. Check out its fancy Victorians from East Dixon Avenue. As a bonus, this road also leads you to **Depot Beach,** a popular swimming beach, playground, and picnic area on Lake Charlevoix.

North of the city pier is Mt. McSauba Recreation Area, a municipal ski facility. At its northern end, Mt. McSauba shares a boundary with the **North Point Nature Preserve** (Mt. McSauba Rd. and Pleasant St., 231/347-0991, www.landtrust.org). The 27-acre preserve was purchased with funds raised by the people of Charlevoix, with help from the Michigan Natural Resources Trust Fund. Today, it offers several steep nature trails through hardwood forest and a pretty stretch of fairly secluded sand, home to threatened plant species like Pitcher's thistle. To reach the preserve, take US-31 north to Mercer Road, turn left onto Mt. McSauba Road, and turn right before the dirt road. The preserve will be on your left. For more information, contact the **Little Traverse Conservancy** (3264 Powell Rd., Harbor Springs, 231/347-0991, www.landtrust.org).

CHARLEVOIX VENETIAN FESTIVAL

Like several other communities along the Lake Michigan coast, Charlevoix presents its own **Venetian Festival** (231/547-3872, www.venetianfestival.com, free) in summer. Begun in 1930 as a simple candlelight boat parade, Charlevoix's version has grown to be the highlight of the season. Usually occurring in late July, the weeklong Charlevoix Venetian Festival offers daily events, from live concerts to athletic competitions, within the town's waterfront parks, in Round Lake Harbor, and on Lake Charlevoix, attracting tens of thousands of visitors each year. The annual event culminates in a beautiful Venetian Boat Parade on Round Lake, followed by a terrific fireworks display.

SHOPPING

Charlevoix's quaint downtown district offers its share of equally quaint shops. For unique children's clothing, check out **Ga Ga For Kids**

(323 Bridge St., 231/547-1600, 9am-6pm daily). Another fine clothing store is just down the street at the **Claymore Shop** (411 Bridge St., 231/237-0400, 9am-6pm daily). Exuding a "shop around the corner" vibe, the **Round Lake Bookstore** (107 Mason St., 231/547-2699, 10am-7pm daily) offers a great sampling of works by regional authors.

RECREATION
Hiking and Biking
The **Little Traverse Wheelway** extends for approximately 29 miles from Charlevoix to Harbor Springs. The trail is ideal for hiking, jogging, bicycling, and in-line skating. Horses and snowmobiles, however, are not permitted. The trail begins at the intersection of Division and Mt. McSauba Roads on the north side of Charlevoix.

Boating
Situated between Lake Michigan and several other inland lakes, Charlevoix is truly a boater's paradise. In fact, the area has three principal centers for boating: the Jordan River, Lake Charlevoix, and, of course, Lake Michigan, which has several access sites along the coast. Boaters and canoeists can access the Jordan River in East Jordan, at Old State Road, Webster's Bridge, and Roger's Bridge. Lake Charlevoix, meanwhile, presents lovely swimming beaches and several access points for boaters and anglers. Pleasure cruisers can view several sights along the Lake Charlevoix shoreline, from some of the area's most beautiful homes to an old shipwreck at Oyster Bay.

Skiing
About a half mile north of the city pier lies the **Mt. McSauba Recreation Area** (231/547-3253), one of the state's few municipal ski facilities. Overlooking Lake Michigan, it lures downhill and cross-country skiers. Other popular wintertime activities include snowboarding, snowshoeing, sledding, and ice skating. The groomed 1.2-mile cross-country trail is even lit at night.

ACCOMMODATIONS AND FOOD
Accommodations
Charlevoix can get pretty busy, especially during the summer months, so make reservations early before coming into town. That said, Charlevoix has loads of lodging possibilities, from basic motels on US-31 to swanky condos along the waterfront.

The **Edgewater Inn** (100 Michigan Ave., 231/547-6044, www.edgewater-charlevoix. com, $89-389 d) has suites on Round Lake and amenities like an indoor/outdoor pool and full kitchen facilities. The **€ Weathervane Terrace Inn & Suites** (111 Pine River Ln., 231/547-9955, www.weathervane-chx.com, $59-299 d) sits directly on the channel, offering an outdoor pool and hot tub as well as views of Lake Michigan and Round Lake. The **Charlevoix Inn & Suites** (800 Petoskey Ave., 231/547-0300, www.charlevoixinnandsuites. com, $50-150 d) offers less expensive accommodations, with an indoor pool and proximity to Lake Charlevoix beaches.

Food
The **€ Stafford's Weathervane Restaurant** (106 Pine River Ln., 231/547-4311, www.staffords.com, 11am-8:30pm Sun.-Thurs., 11am-9:30pm Fri.-Sat., $10-25) is one of Charlevoix's best restaurants, in terms of both food and location. Affiliated with the Stafford restaurants of Petoskey, it specializes in planked whitefish and steaks, and overlooks the Pine River Channel. Outside seating is available for lunch and dinner. **Terry's** (101 Antrim St., 231/547-2799, www.terrysofcharlevoix.com, 5pm-close daily, $23-36) is frequented for its fresh walleye and whitefish.

INFORMATION AND SERVICES
Information
For more information about the Charlevoix area, contact the **Charlevoix Area Chamber of Commerce** (109 Mason St., 231/547-2101, www.charlevoix.org, 9am-5pm Mon.-Fri.), the **Charlevoix Area Convention & Visitors**

NORTHWEST MICHIGAN

© LAURA MARTONE

Stafford's Weathervane Restaurant in Charlevoix

Bureau (109 Mason St., 231/547-2101 or 800/367-8557, www.visitcharlevoix.com), or the **Petoskey Area Visitors Bureau** (401 E. Mitchell St., 231/348-2755, www.boynecountry.com, 8am-4pm Mon.-Fri.). For local news and events, consult the *Charlevoix Courier* (www.charlevoixcourier.com).

Services

Charlevoix may be a small town, but it still has its share of necessary services, such as beauty salons, pharmacies, and banks. There are even several **post offices** in the area, including one near downtown Charlevoix (6700 M-66 N., 231/547-2631, www.usps.com). For medical services, consult the **Charlevoix Area Hospital** (14700 Lakeshore Dr., 231/547-4024, www.cah.org). If an emergency occurs, don't hesitate to call **911** from any phone.

GETTING THERE AND AROUND

Travelers can access Charlevoix in a variety of ways. One option is to fly into **Cherry Capital**

Airport (TVC, 727 Fly Don't Dr., Traverse City, 231/947-2250, www.tvcairport.com) or **Pellston Regional Airport** (PLN, 1395 US-31, Pellston, 231/539-8441 or 231/539-8442, www.pellstonairport.com), rent a vehicle, and take US-31 to Charlevoix. From the Traverse City airport, you'll take CR-620, 3 Mile Road, and US-31 North to reach Charlevoix; without traffic, the 48-mile trip usually takes about 55 minutes. From the Pellston airport, meanwhile, you'll take US-31 South along the coast to Charlevoix; without traffic, the 36-mile trip should take about 47 minutes. Another possibility is to arrive via bus; after all, both **Greyhound** (800/231-2222, www.greyhound.com) and **Indian Trails** (800/292-3831, www.indiantrails.com) provide service to the **Beaver Island Boat Company** (103 Bridge Park Dr., 888/446-4095, www.bibco.com) in downtown Charlevoix. With several marinas in the area, it's also possible to arrive in Charlevoix by boat.

Of course, most visitors come via car, which is an ideal way to explore the surrounding towns and lakes. From Sault Ste. Marie, for instance, you'll take I-75 South, cross the Mackinac Bridge (a toll bridge), and merge onto US-31 South to reach Charlevoix, a 110-mile trip that normally takes about 2 hours. From downtown Detroit, meanwhile, you can follow I-375 North to I-75 North, take M-32 West and various surface streets to M-66 North, and continue to US-31 North; without traffic, the 274-mile trip will require about 4.25 hours. No matter how you reach Charlevoix, though, you can easily get around town via car, bike, or foot. In addition, some travelers choose to rely on the **Charlevoix Cab Co.** (231/547-9700, www.charlevoixcab.com), which offers 24-hour service around Charlevoix County.

FISHERMAN'S ISLAND STATE PARK

Five miles south of Charlevoix off US-31, **Fisherman's Island State Park** (16480 Bells Bay Rd., 231/547-6641, annual $11 Recreation Passport for Michigan residents or $8.40 day-use fee/$30.50 yearly Recreation Passport for nonresidents required) does indeed encompass a little 10-acre offshore island, but most visitors come to enjoy its five miles of lakeshore and wooded dunes. With long stretches of soft sand and exceptionally clear water, it's a particularly good spot to hunt for Petoskey stones.

There's evidence that Woodland Indians inhabited Fisherman's Island more than 1,000 years ago. In the early 1900s, one enterprising Charlevoix innkeeper planned a casino for the site. But those plans died with the property owner, and the state eventually acquired the island and nearby shoreline, naming it a state park in 1978. Today, the small island is inhabited only by birds and insects. Wading or swimming to it is not recommended, since a strong current often rushes between the island and mainland.

The park is nearly divided in two by a parcel of private property in its middle. The northern portion is the more popular of the two state park sections, with five miles of hiking trails, a pretty day-use area, and 81 rustic campsites. Most are nice, private sites in the woods near

the water; if you're really lucky, you'll snag one of the dozen or so sites right on the beach.

To reach the day-use area, hike the marked trail along the dune ridge, or drive south on the park road past the campgrounds. It has grills, picnic tables, outhouses, and a trail leading across bubbling Inwood Creek to the beach. On a clear day, you can see the tip of the Leelanau Peninsula from this fine stretch of beach, and you'll often be treated to a spectacular sunset. For real solitude, access the southern end of the park from the town of Norwood, 11 miles south on US-31. Follow signs to Norwood Township Park on the shoreline, then trace the double track into the state park. (Driving is not recommended if it's wet.) You're likely to have the beach and old truck trails all to yourself.

LAKE CHARLEVOIX
Horton Bay

Several authors and artists have roots in northern Michigan, but none as celebrated as Ernest Hemingway. Hemingway spent his childhood summers at the family cottage on nearby Walloon Lake, fished the waters of Lake Charlevoix, hunted on the point at Horton Bay, and once escaped a game warden by fleeing across the lake's north arm to the point between the arms, now known as Hemingway Point.

The tiny town of Horton Bay, on Boyne City Road about 10 miles east of Charlevoix, played a special role in Hemingway's life. He whiled away summer afternoons on the front steps of the classic false-front, white-clapboard general store, which he describes in his short story "Up in Michigan." (He drew on many of his surroundings, in fact, for his Nick Adams short stories.) Later, he married his first wife, Hadley Richardson, at Horton Bay's Congregational Church.

Today, the **Horton Bay General Store** (5115 Boyne City Rd., 231/582-7827, www.hortonbaygeneralstore.com, 8am-5pm daily, $9-18) is preserved more as a shrine to Hemingway than a store and eatery—light on foodstuffs but heavy on Hemingway nostalgia. Built in 1876, the cavernous building is filled with Hemingway photos, novels, even a copy of his

1922 marriage certificate. There's a small lunch counter and a few assorted groceries. But it's the charming old building itself that draws you in. Steeped in literary history, its inviting front porch is still a great place to while away a summer afternoon.

Boyne City

At the foot of Lake Charlevoix, pleasant and relaxing Boyne City was once a loud industrial town. In the 19th century, Boyne City thrived as a regional logging center, with 90 miles of railroad track and several hundred logging cars linking the town to the surrounding logging camps and feeding its hungry sawmills. Tanneries also became big business at the turn of the 20th century, using bark from the hemlock tree to tan leather. One Boyne City tannery produced six million pounds of shoe leather annually.

Boyne City has done a fine job preserving some of its historic buildings, with a main street that looks like it could be in the Wild West. The best example is the **Wolverine-Dilworth Inn** (300 Water St.), a 1911 landmark and former hotel, boasting a spacious veranda, a terrazzo tile lobby with fireplace, and a saloon-style dining room.

Boyne Mountain

Six miles southeast of Boyne City in Boyne Falls, Everett Kircher carved out his own piece of history at Boyne Mountain (1 Boyne Mountain Rd., Boyne Falls, 231/549-6000 or 800/462-6963, www.boyne.com). A Studebaker dealer from the Detroit area, Kircher figured out that Detroit's booming auto industry would make for a lot of wealthy Michigan residents, many of whom would be looking for a place to vacation. He obtained some farmland near Boyne Falls and proceeded to develop the area's first downhill ski resort. Boyne Mountain opened in 1947.

Over the years, the visionary Kircher became known for "firsts"—the Midwest's first chairlift in 1948, the nation's first freestyle skiing exhibition in 1961, the world's first quad chairlift in 1967, the state's first high-speed quad in

1990, and the nation's first six-person chair in 1992. Kircher was the first to perfect artificial snowmaking, and Boyne's patented snowguns are used at resorts all over the world. Olympic ski planners still contact Boyne for snowmaking consultation.

Even in his 80s, Everett Kircher would come to Boyne headquarters in Boyne Falls nearly every day, overseeing a privately held ski/golf enterprise that seems to grow exponentially every year. In the tightly consolidated ski industry, Boyne is a player: It owns three impressive ski resorts in Michigan. The company's not doing too badly in the golf industry department either, with its spectacular Bay Harbor development near Petoskey.

By those standards, Boyne Mountain seems almost quaint, but it is an extremely popular resort in summer and winter. The ski area offers over 40 runs, including the Disciples Ridge area, which features some of the steepest pitches in the state. The property also has over 20 miles of groomed and tracked trails for cross-country skiing, which double as mountain biking trails. Come summer, two 18-hole golf courses help fill Boyne Mountain's 600-plus rooms (and its jumbo 30-person outdoor hot tub).

Jordan River

You'll better understand Ernest Hemingway's love for this land after passing a little time along the Jordan River, which empties into Lake Charlevoix's south arm. Look for the small wooden canoe signs that signify access points, like the one along Alba Road near the Charlevoix-Antrim county line. Here, the Jordan rolls silently northward, the pale brown of hospital coffee, framed by weeping willows and grassy banks. Though anglers hate to advertise it, the Jordan is one of the finest trout streams in the state.

The Jordan River valley cuts a wide swath through the landscape south of Lake Charlevoix, and nowhere is the view more dramatic than from **Dead Man's Hill,** off US-131 south of Boyne Falls. Two miles south of M-32 West, watch for Dead Man's Hill Road; turn west and travel 1.5 miles or so to the end. Here, the flat country lane suddenly falls away to reveal a marvelous valley more than 1,000 feet below: The Jordan straggles through a woodland of pines interspersed with beech and maple, reaching out across the lowlands like spider veins.

The morbid name is in reference to Stanley Graczyk, a 21-year-old logger who, in 1910, mistakenly drove his team of horses up the hill and right over the edge. Whoops. Dead Man's Hill is also the trailhead for the **Jordan River Pathway,** which loops 18 miles through the valley floor. There's a marked 3-mile loop, too. Maps are available at the trailhead.

Ironton Ferry

Up M-66, the tiny **Ironton Ferry** (6:30am-10pm daily, $3.25 vehicles, $0.50 pedestrians) chugs its way from Ironton across the narrows of Lake Charlevoix's south arm to Hemingway Point—a distance of about 100 yards. The U.S. flag flies gallantly from the *Charlevoix's* white steel pilothouse; a sign sternly warns auto passengers—all three of them—that "We will not be responsible for vehicles left unattended"—a difficult task, considering you can't even open the car door wide enough to get out. The funky little ferry even made the "Ripley's Believe It or Not" newspaper feature, noting that its captain traveled more than 15,000 miles without ever being more than 1,000 feet from home.

It is efficient. The *Charlevoix* takes just two minutes to follow its cable to the far shore, and just a little over four minutes to unload, reload, and be back again—but saves a 15-mile trip around the south arm of the lake. People have found it to be a worthwhile service since 1876. Its "1884 Rates for Ferriage" are still posted: "Double Teams, 0.30; Single Teams, 0.20; Beast, 0.10 except sheep; Sheep, 0.10 up to 6, 0.05 over 6; footmen, 0.05 without beast."

ELLSWORTH AND VICINITY

Eleven miles south of Charlevoix on CR-65, Ellsworth wouldn't be much more than a wide spot in the road but for a couple of very notable exceptions: The Rowe Inn Restaurant and Tapawingo. These two restaurants have

put unlikely Ellsworth on the map, with rave reviews in national publications like *Gourmet* and *Wine Spectator.* Unfortunately, a poor economic climate forced Tapawingo to close its doors in 2009, but happily, **The Rowe Inn** (6303 E. Jordan Rd., 231/588-7351 or 866/432-5873, www.roweinn.com, 5pm-close Mon.-Sat., noon-2pm and 5pm-close Sun., $20-39) remains. With a rather rustic decor and one-of-a-kind entrées like duck magret with port-cinnamon sauce, The Rowe has attracted quite a following. Its distinctive menu—thick with rich local ingredients like duck, veal, trout, morels, and fresh berries—and the largest and most outstanding wine cellar in Michigan have earned it a spot among the nation's top restaurants.

Shanty Creek

If you're looking for a year-round destination that accommodates a yen for golf, hiking, biking, winter sports, and much more, consider visiting **Shanty Creek Resorts** (1 Shanty Creek Rd., Bellaire, 800/678-4111, www.shantycreek.com), a half-hour's drive south of Charlevoix. Separated into three villages—Cedar River, Schuss, and Summit—this enormous 4,500-acre swath of land features several dining, lodging, and spa options, three award-winning golf courses, numerous downhill skiing runs, and a fantastic trail network for cross-country skiers and mountain bikers.

The main draw here is golfing ($18-108 pp), which is usually available April-October, weather depending. Summit Village, which offers a newly renovated hotel and conference center, also presents two favored courses: **The Legend,** designed by Arnold Palmer and named the best course in the Midwest by readers of *Golf Magazine,* and the more wide-open **Summit Golf Course,** the resort's original course. In addition, Summit Village boasts heated indoor and outdoor pools, a spa and fitness center, and a downhill ski area with a dozen slopes.

Five minutes away, Schuss Mountain offers more advanced skiing, with 37 runs, three terrain parks, and seven lifts. Its Bavarian-style base area is smaller, with a scattering of villas and condos. This village also has its share of other diversions, including the challenging **Schuss Mountain Golf Course,** set amid abundant wetlands and rolling hills.

The newest resort, Cedar River Village, houses 14 condos, over 70 luxurious suites, two restaurants, and **Cedar River Golf Course,** situated amid verdant hills and peaceful waters. Between the three resorts, over 13 miles of groomed and tracked cross-country trails wind through hilly terrain and hardwood forest. In summer, many of those same trails become prime mountain biking terrain. The network includes beginner to expert trails, some made even more difficult by the area's sandy terrain.

BEAVER ISLAND

Traveling to Beaver Island is kind of slow, rather expensive, and there isn't much to do when you get there. There is no must-see attraction and no particularly spectacular scenery on this flat, wooded island. Nope, Beaver Island ticks along at a rather sleepy, predictable pace: The bank opens every Tuesday 9am-1pm. The ferry brings the mail. When Island Airways arrives from Charlevoix, everybody leaving pretty much knows everybody arriving.

If this sounds hopelessly dull, then don't go to Beaver Island. There is precious little in the way of formal entertainment on Beaver, save for some occasional Irish music and beer drinking at the Shamrock Bar. Though it ranks as the largest island in Michigan—13 miles long and 6 miles wide—you won't find any towns outside the port of St. James, just simple cottages and 100 miles of sandy roads.

On the other hand, if the inherent isolation and somnolent pace appeal to you, then by all means, go. Stranded 18 miles from the nearest Lower Peninsula shoreline, Beaver Island is the most remote inhabited island in the Great

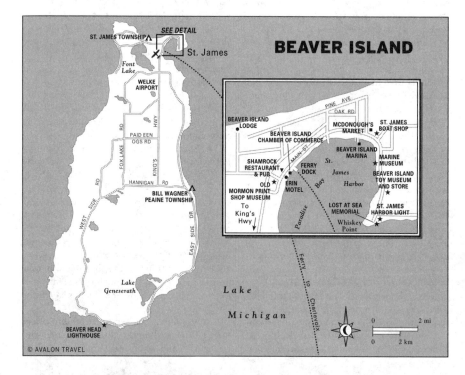

Lakes, offering what may be a quintessential glimpse of island life: unhurried, unbothered, unaffected by whim and fashion. You make your own entertainment here, and it can be delightful. Bike a quiet road to an even quieter beach. Explore the island's quirky history at a couple of terrific little museums. Buy a local a cup of coffee and talk island politics. Paddle a kayak to another island in the Beaver archipelago. Take off your watch.

Sights

Beaver Island activity centers around St. James on hook-shaped Beaver Harbor, which many locals still call by its 19th-century name, Paradise Bay. This is where the ferry lands, and where you'll find the sum of the island's commercial development. Everything in St. James is within walking distance.

You can pick up much of the island's colorful history and character without ever leaving the harbor. The **Shamrock Restaurant & Pub** (26245 Main St., 231/448-2278, www. shamrockbarrestaurant.com, 11am-9pm daily, $12-19) is the most popular spot in town for a burger, beer, and island news. At the **St. James Boat Shop** (38230 Michigan, 231/448-2365, www.stjamesboatshop.com), Bill Freese builds gorgeous wood-strip canoes and kayaks, along with beautiful handmade wooden buckets.

From the boat shop, it's just a short walk to Whiskey Point, the **Lost at Sea memorial,** and the **St. James Harbor Light,** marking the entrance to this well-protected natural harbor. The 19th-century light was "manned" for years by Beaver Island native Elizabeth Whitney Williams, the only woman light keeper on the Great Lakes.

The southern half of the island has far more public land than the northern half, much of it a state wildlife research area. It has several small lakes, bogs, unimproved roads, and trails that are fun to explore, especially if you have a mountain bike. Fish in **Lake Geneserath,** swim at several sandy beaches on the southern shore, or check out the **Beaver Head Lighthouse** near the island's southern tip, a pretty cream-brick house and tower built in 1858, one of the oldest

on all the Great Lakes. Back in the 1920s, thrill-seekers from Charlevoix drove across the thick lake ice, headed for Beaver Island. When a thick fog left them completely disoriented, the keeper guided them to safety with the light's fog signal.

If you plan to explore Beaver Island on your own, pick up two maps in St. James first: the comprehensive island map available at **McDonough's Market** (38240 Michigan Ave., 231/448-2736, www.mcdonoughsmarket.com) and a small history map, available at the chamber of commerce. It points out several noteworthy attractions that you can seek out on your own.

Kayaking

Eleven other islands scatter around Beaver's northern half, an inviting archipelago for sea kayakers. The islands range in distance from Garden (2 miles away) to Gull (11 miles). Garden, practically due north from St. James, is probably the most intriguing for paddlers, with several protected bays and inlets. High Island, four miles west, has bluffs along the western shore rising to 240 feet. Most of High and Garden are public land, part of the **Beaver Islands State Wildlife Research Area.** Some of the smaller islands are privately owned or otherwise off-limits to preserve nesting sites. For more information, contact the **Gaylord DNR Operations Service Center** (Wildlife Office, 1732 W. M-32, Gaylord, 989/732-3541, www.michigan.gov/dnr).

The **Inland Seas School of Kayaking** (231/448-2221, www.inlandseaskayaking.com) offers instruction and guided tours. If you plan to do any inter-island paddling, observe all the usual safety precautions, watch the weather, and make sure you have a good nautical chart. The open waters of the Great Lakes are not for amateurs.

Accommodations

There are several motels, lodges, B&Bs, and cabins for rent on the island. Near the ferry dock, the **Erin Motel** (231/448-2240, $69-99 d) overlooks the water with a sand beach. The

Beaver Island Lodge (231/448-2396, www. beaverislandlodge.com, $120-190 d) sits along a secluded stretch of beach west of town, with nice rooms and an on-site restaurant.

The island has two rustic campgrounds (with pit toilets and water), both on the lakeshore. The **St. James Township Campground** is on the north side of the island one mile from town, and has 12 sites. The **Bill Wagner Peaine Township Campground,** with 22 sites, is along the east shore, seven miles south of town. Both are $10 per night (no reservations). There are two grocery stores and a handful of restaurants on the island.

Information and Services
For information about Beaver Island's services, businesses, and lodging options, contact the **Beaver Island Chamber of Commerce** (231/448-2505, www.beaverisland.org). For local news and events, consult the monthly *Beaver Beacon* (www.beaverisland.net).

Getting There and Around
Commercial transportation to Beaver Island is available only from Charlevoix, which lies about 32 miles away. The **Beaver Island Boat Company** (103 Bridge Park Dr., 231/547-2311 or 888/446-4095, www.bibco.com, one-way $24-29 adults, $12-17 children 5-14, children under 5 free, $25 canoes or kayaks, $10 bikes, rates vary for pets and vehicles) makes scheduled trips April-December, with two trips daily during most of the summer. It takes a little over two hours each way, and the 95-foot-long *Beaver Islander* or 130-foot-long *Emerald Isle* can be a bit of a rough ride in choppy waters. Reservations are recommended for passengers and required for autos. If you take the first ferry in the morning, you can make Beaver Island a day trip of six hours or so, returning on the late afternoon ferry. Of course, the time constraints will limit you to exploring just a small portion of the island.

Island Airways (111 Airport Dr., 800/524-6895, www.islandairways.com, one-way $47 adults, $44 seniors 65 and over, $33 children 2-9, children under 2 and small pets free, $23 large pets, $10 bikes), meanwhile, provides daily air service from Charlevoix in a little 10-seater. The flight takes about 20 minutes, and reservations are required.

In truth, it's probably not necessary to have a car on Beaver Island. Though the island is quite large and has more than 100 miles of roads, downtown St. James is ideal for walking and biking. In addition, many accommodations provide transportation from the dock or airport; if there's something specific you want to see (such as the lighthouse on the southern shore), you can usually rent a vehicle for about $55 daily from **Gordon's Auto Rentals and Clinic** (231/448-2438). Just remember to reserve ahead of time.

Petoskey and Vicinity

Petoskey (puh-TOS-kee) was originally settled by the Ottawa Indians in the 1700s and takes its name from a local Native American, Petosega. With bountiful fishing and hunting, the region was a desirable place to live, and Ottawa and Ojibwa tribes thrived here. In the 1800s, the federal government negotiated more equitably with local tribes than it did elsewhere in the young nation; tribes were given the first choice of land (albeit their land!) until 1875.

White settlers began arriving in the 1850s, establishing logging operations along the Bear River, the name the town used until 1873. With a sawmill, a lime quarry, and other enterprises along the river and Little Traverse Bay, Bear River quickly became an industrial town of buzzing saws and belching smoke.

But the town began changing with the arrival of the railroad in 1873. Lured north by the beautiful Lake Michigan waters and cool northern air, residents from southern Great Lakes cities like Chicago and Detroit began migrating to Petoskey, gradually converting its industrial squalor to an elegant summer getaway. The artesian springs that bubbled throughout town and their "health-giving waters" only encouraged Petoskey's growth.

By the turn of the 20th century, Petoskey's downtown was filled with fine shops and 13 grand resort hotels like the Arlington, with its imposing columns, dance hall, and 24-foot-wide veranda. At its heyday in 1900, three trains a day stopped at the Arlington, which could sleep 800—surpassed only by the rival Grand Hotel on Mackinac Island. Unfortunately, the Arlington burned to the ground in 1915, the same fate that met almost every single one of Petoskey's grand resorts— The Jewel, The Imperial, the City Hotel. Only the Perry Hotel, made of expensive brick, still stands.

Thankfully, plenty of other historic buildings still stand in the Petoskey area, a city that wisely realized early the value of protecting them. From its well-preserved Gaslight District to the entire Victorian neighborhood of Bay View, Petoskey maintains the charm of the grand resort era, along with the natural resources that brought summer visitors here in the first place. Equally appealing to anglers, boaters, shoppers, golfers, and skiers, the town has so far been able to balance its need for tourism with its desire for preservation, but only time and resolve will determine if it will last. In 1996, the National Trust for Historic Preservation listed Petoskey as one of 10 national historic treasures most worthy of fighting for, warning that "retail, roadway, and residential sprawl threaten the town's historic character and pastoral setting."

SIGHTS
Gaslight District
Though growth indeed threatens Petoskey— busy US-31 slices right between downtown and the waterfront—it remains a charming city for vacationers, with a downtown made for strolling. The Gaslight District anchors the downtown, an eight-block area of well-preserved Victorian brick storefronts filled with shops

Petoskey's historic Gaslight District

and restaurants that has drawn shoppers since the early 1900s. A low-interest loan program sponsored by the regional chamber of commerce encourages their preservation and renovation. Centered around Lake and Howard Streets, the district mixes high-brow boutiques with bookstores, art galleries, antiques haunts, and homegrown souvenir shops.

Crooked Tree Arts Center

If you enjoy strolling through art galleries, then you're in luck. Despite its relatively small size, Petoskey's Gaslight District boasts several worthy choices. One such option is the **Crooked Tree Arts Center** (CTAC, 461 E. Mitchell St., 231/347-4337, www.crookedtree.org, 9am-5pm Mon.-Tues. and Thurs.-Fri., 10am-5pm Wed., 10am-4pm Sat., free). Founded in 1971 as the Crooked Tree Arts Council, the CTAC was established for three reasons: to bring more culture to northern Michiganders, support local and regional artists, and form an umbrella organization that could provide cultural services to the people of both Charlevoix and Emmet

Counties. Initially, the CTAC operated out of members' homes—that is, until 1978, when the old United Methodist Church in downtown Petoskey became available for purchase. Built in 1890, the church soon became the official home of the CTAC, and today, the multicolored building is hard to ignore. It's also hard to dismiss all the artistic and educational activities that take place inside, including dance and visual arts classes, wine-tasting events, live concerts, and theatrical performances. Of course, you're also welcome to wander through the onsite art galleries, which house rotating exhibits that feature the paintings, photographs, sculptures, and other creations of many Michigan-based artists. Recent exhibits, for instance, have showcased Robert deJonge's images of the state's scenic shorelines and a colorful collection of children's book illustrations, donated by Francis Molson, a retired English professor from Central Michigan University.

Of course, the CTAC isn't Petoskey's only attraction for art lovers. Only a few blocks to the north, you'll encounter **Stafford's Gallery of Art & History** (410 Rose St., 231/347-0142, www.staffords.com, 10am-6pm Mon.-Sat., 10am-4pm Sun., free), which is located behind the historic Stafford's Perry Hotel. Housed in an old warehouse building that was once a 1930s-era icehouse, a meat-packing company, an ice cream plant, and, from 1969 to 2007, Longton Hall Antiques, this spacious fine art gallery presents a wide assortment of watercolor and oil paintings, photographs, sculptures, jewelry, gifts, and original prints by nearly 40 Michigan artists. Recent offerings have included Valerie Thomson's impressionistic landscapes of northern Michigan locales; Michael McPeak's photographs, which are curiously printed on light-penetrating silk; John Riepma's colorful, hand-blown glass sculptures; Janet Lewandowski's whimsical, wool-based "steampunk" dolls; and Tera Jackson's dichroic glass rings, pendants, necklaces, and earrings. Here, you may also spot antiques as well as Stafford's exclusive collection of artifacts and photographs that represent the history of downtown Petoskey from the late

© LAURA MARTONE

the Crooked Tree Arts Center

19th century to the early 20th century, with an emphasis on the nearly two dozen hotels that once dominated this area.

Little Traverse History Museum

Near the intersection of Petoskey and Bay Streets, follow the pedestrian tunnel under US-31 to **Bayfront Park,** which merges with **Sunset Park** to the east, offering a vast green space along the waterfront. Once the center of Petoskey's sawmill operations, now this beautifully renovated area comprises a marina, a walkway along the Bear River, one of the area's historic mineral springs, and the fine **Little Traverse History Museum** (231/347-2620, www.petoskeymuseum.org, 10am-4pm Mon.-Sat. Memorial Day-mid-Oct., $3 adults, children under 11 free) in the restored rail depot.

The museum is crammed full of interesting displays, including a photo collection of Petoskey's old hotels and an exhibit detailing the sad tale of the passenger pigeon, which migrated to the Little Traverse Bay area by the billions (yes, *billions*) in the 1870s. Accounts tell of the skies blackening when the birds were in flight, with individual flocks stretching for miles and miles. Alas, the nesting habits and docile nature of the pigeons made them easy to hunt by simply clubbing them to death in their nests. Entrepreneurs did so with glee, since their meat was considered a delicacy. By the 1870s, entire steamships were loaded with pigeons for delivery to urban restaurants in the southern Great Lakes. In less than 25 years, the passenger pigeon had completely disappeared from the region; by 1914, it became officially extinct.

Probably the museum's most popular display is the collection of Ernest Hemingway memorabilia. Hemingway's family began vacationing on nearby Walloon Lake when Hemingway was just a boy, and the family still owns a couple of acres of land there. After he was injured in World War I, Hemingway recuperated in Petoskey, living in a rooming house at the corner of State and Woodland Streets in 1919-1920. Here, he gathered material and began drafting *Torrents of Spring,* which alludes to several Petoskey locations. The museum's display includes first editions of that classic novel as well as *For Whom the Bell Tolls* and *A Farewell to Arms.*

Hemingway overshadows Petoskey's other famous author, Bruce Catton, who won a Pulitzer Prize in 1954 for his Civil War account *A Stillness at Appomattox.* The Little Traverse History Museum gives him his due.

Near the museum, you can pick up the **Top of Michigan trail,** a 15-mile paved, off-road path that stretches from Bay Harbor through Petoskey to Harbor Springs. Several other trails radiate off this route, creating a network of 180 miles of multiuse recreation pathways between Charlevoix and Mackinaw City. Trail maps are available at the Petoskey Area Visitors Bureau.

ENTERTAINMENT

Just outside town, the **Odawa Casino Resort** (1760 Lears Rd., 877/442-6464, www.odawacasino.com, 24 hours daily) provides a 300,000-square-foot entertainment complex, with gaming, restaurants, and a theater that books big-name talent on a regular basis. They also have O zone, a state-of-the-art nightclub that compares to many of the hot spots in Vegas.

SHOPPING

Petoskey's delightful Gaslight District offers a wide assortment of shops. **American Spoon** (411 E. Lake St., 231/347-1738, www.spoon.com, 9am-7pm daily) offers an assortment of delicious jams, sauces, and more, all made from local produce and other fresh ingredients. Check out the adjacent café for delicious sandwiches made with their sauces. **McLean & Eakin Booksellers** (307 E. Lake St., 231/347-1180, www.mcleanandeakin.com, 9am-8pm Mon.-Sat., 10am-5pm Sun.) offers an eclectic assortment of titles and regularly hosts educational and literary events. If antiques are more your style, stop in at **Longton Hall Antiques** (329 Bay St., 231/347-9672, www.longtonhallantiques.com, 9am-7pm Mon.-Sat., 11am-5pm Sun.).

locally made condiments at American Spoon

SPORTS AND RECREATION
Golf

While the area around Traverse City and Charlevoix boasts several terrific courses, the Petoskey/Harbor Springs area has no shortage of great golf either. Several lodgings even offer packages and will reserve tee times.

Best known are the four courses at **Boyne Highlands Resort** (600 Highland Dr., 231/526-3000 or 800/462-6963, www.boyne. com, daily May-Oct., $40-145 pp), a ski/golf resort a few miles north of Harbor Springs: The Moor, the Donald Ross Memorial, The Heather, and the Arthur Hills. *Golf Magazine* considers The Heather course, designed by Robert Trent Jones, one of the top courses in the country, with lots of sculpted bunkers and water hazards (and cool global positioning systems on the carts to feed you yardage information). The Ross Memorial course is a perennial favorite. It re-creates several of the most famous holes throughout the world designed by Ross, considered by many to be the "father of golf course architecture."

Boyne also operates the **Crooked Tree Golf Club** (Bay Harbor, 231/439-4030 or 800/462-6963, www.boyne.com, $35-65 pp), a British-style course overlooking Little Traverse Bay near Petoskey. In Harbor Springs, the **Harbor Point Golf Course** (8475 S. Lake Shore Dr., 231/526-2951, www.harborpointgolfclub.com, $55 pp w/cart) had been an exclusive private club since 1896; it's now open to the public in the spring and fall months and considered a favorite walking course by *Golf Digest*.

Near Burt Lake in Brutus, **Hidden River Golf & Casting Club** (7688 Maple River Rd., 231/529-4653, www.hiddenriver.com, daily Apr.-Oct., $40-91 pp) offers classic "up north" scenery, with tall stands of pine and hardwoods and the meandering Maple River; this resort is also popular for fly-fishing.

Winter Activities

Nub's Nob (500 Nubs Nob Rd., Harbor Springs, 231/526-2131, www.nubsnob.com, lift tickets $41-69 pp) often gets overshadowed by the Boynes, but it has its own loyal following.

© DANIEL MARTONE

The well-protected, wooded slopes (blocked from cold winter winds) are best known for short and steep faces like Twilight Zone and Scarface, but its 23 trails and 427-foot vertical drop have plenty of beginner and intermediate terrain, too. If Boyne Highlands gets crowded, this is the place to escape.

ACCOMMODATIONS AND FOOD

Accommodations

Petoskey offers an enormous array of lodgings, from basic motels along US-31 to resort complexes to condo units that are especially convenient for families or groups.

Unless you're on a tight budget, opt for a stay at the lemon chiffon-colored **Stafford's Perry Hotel** (100 Lewis St., 231/347-4000, www.staffords.com, $99-319 d), which overlooks Little Traverse Bay and dates back to 1899. Today, it's run by successful local innkeeper/restaurateur Stafford Smith, who has done a wonderful job of updating the venerable old building while retaining every bit of its charm. Rates are reasonable for such a treasure. The Perry also features three separate dining choices, if you just want to relax and don't feel like wandering around town.

The **Terrace Inn** (1549 Glendale, 800/530-9898, www.theterraceinn.com, $79-189 d) provides an elegant bed-and-breakfast experience in a turn-of-the-20th-century building. If you're on a tighter budget, try the **Econo Lodge South** (1859 US-131 S, 231/348-3324, www.econolodge.com, $59-150 d).

Food

Petoskey also offers a superb array of dining options, especially in the downtown area. Since 1875, the historic **City Park Grill** (432 E. Lake St., 231/347-0101, www.cityparkgrill.com, 11:30am-9pm Mon.-Thurs. and Sun., 11:30am-10pm Fri.-Sat., extended bar hours, $7-24) has lured residents and visitors alike, despite several transformations over the years. Today, patrons come for the happy-hour specials and live weekend music in the adjacent bar, plus an eclectic restaurant menu that includes shellfish

© LAURA MARTONE

Stafford's Perry Hotel in Petoskey

chowder, jambalaya, almond-crusted whitefish, and filet mignon with blue cheese sauce. Another delectable downtown eatery is **Grand Traverse Pie Company** (316 E. Mitchell St., 231/348-4060, www.gtpie.com, 7am-6:30pm Mon.-Sat., $4-13), part of a statewide chain that offers scrumptious soups, salads, sandwiches, quiches, and, naturally, pies—from the Suttons Bay Blueberry to the Glen Haven Peach Crumb.

INFORMATION AND SERVICES

Information

For more information about the Petoskey area, contact the **Petoskey Area Visitors Bureau** (401 E. Mitchell St., 231/348-2755, www.boynecountry.com, 8am-4pm Mon.-Fri.) or the **Petoskey Regional Chamber of Commerce** (401 E. Mitchell St., 231/347-4150, www.petoskey.com). For local news and events, consult the *Petoskey News-Review* (www.petoskeynews.com).

Services

Though a relatively small town, Petoskey still has its share of necessary services, from post offices to pharmacies. For banking needs, contact **Chase** (www.chase.com) and **Fifth Third Bank** (www.53.com), both of which have several branches in Petoskey. For medical services, consult the **Northern Michigan Regional Hospital** (416 Connable Ave., 800/248-6777, www.northernhealth.org). If an emergency occurs, don't hesitate to call **911** from any phone.

GETTING THERE AND AROUND

As with other coastal resort towns in the northwestern part of Michigan's Lower Peninsula, Petoskey isn't terribly hard to reach. First of all, given its position beside Little Traverse Bay, it's obviously accessible by boat. In addition, visitors can reach Petoskey via bus; both **Greyhound** (231/439-0747 or 800/231-2222, www.greyhound.com) and **Indian Trails** (800/292-3831, www.indiantrails.com) regularly stop in town, specifically in front of the

restaurant located at 2286 Harbor Petoskey Road.

Another option is to fly into the region. Nearby airports include **Pellston Regional Airport** (PLN, 1395 US-31, Pellston, 231/539-8441 or 231/539-8442, www.pellstonairport.com), which is located northeast of Petoskey and offers commuter service from Detroit via Delta Air Lines, and **Cherry Capital Airport** (TVC, 727 Fly Don't Dr., Traverse City, 231/947-2250, www.tvcairport.com), which is situated in Traverse City and offers commuter service from Detroit and Minneapolis via Delta Air Lines and from Chicago via United Airlines and American Airlines. From either airport, you can rent a vehicle and take US-31 to Petoskey. From the Pellston airport, for instance, you'll take US-31 South to downtown Petoskey; without traffic, the 20-mile trip should take about 28 minutes. From the Traverse City airport, meanwhile, you'll take CR-620, 3 Mile Road, and US-31 North to reach Petoskey; without traffic, the 65-mile trip usually takes about 80 minutes.

Of course, most visitors come by car, which is an ideal way to explore the surrounding towns and lakes. From Sault Ste. Marie, for instance, you'll take I-75 South, cross the Mackinac Bridge (a toll bridge), and merge onto US-31 South to reach Petoskey, a 93-mile trip that normally takes about 1.75 hours. From downtown Detroit, meanwhile, you can follow I-375 North to I-75 North, take M-32 West, follow US-131 North, and continue to US-31 North toward downtown Petoskey; without traffic, the 268-mile trip will require about 4 hours. No matter how you reach Petoskey, though, you can easily get around town via car, bike, or foot.

LITTLE TRAVERSE BAY

North of the Leelanau Peninsula and just a half hour south of the Straits of Mackinac, Little Traverse Bay delves due east nine miles, forming a picture-perfect bay ringed by bluffs, fine sand, and well-protected harbors. Well-known Petoskey, with its historic downtown Gaslight District, sits at the foot of the bay, justifiably drawing many of the area's visitors. But golfers, skiers, anglers, and wanderers will find plenty to enjoy in this appealing and compact region, too.

LAKE MICHIGAN SHORE
Bay Harbor

A couple of miles west of downtown Petoskey, Bay Harbor represents the nation's largest land reclamation project, a stunning example of what foresight and $100 million can accomplish. Stretching five miles along the shore of Little Traverse Bay and encompassing more than 1,100 acres, this beautiful chunk of real estate spent its last life as, of all things, a cement plant. When the plant closed in 1981, it left behind a scarred, barren landscape that sat untouched for a decade.

But from industrial squalor comes impressive luxury. With the combined resources of CMS Energy (the Jackson, Michigan, parent company of a large utility) and ski-industry giant Boyne, Bay Harbor has shaped up into one of the nation's most spectacular resort communities. The **Bay Harbor Yacht Club,** with little touches like a compass rose made of inlaid cherrywood, overlooks a deepwater port (the old quarry) with nearly 500 slips, including 120 for public transient use. An equestrian club entertains the horsy set. Multimillion-dollar homes dot the property, at a low density that maintains a breezy, resort feel. Public parks buffer Bay Harbor on both sides.

Acclaimed golf designer Arthur Hills has created **The Links, The Preserve,** and **The Quarry golf courses** (5800 Coastal Ridge Dr., 231/439-4085, www.bayharborgolf. com, $39-159 pp), 27 holes that ramble atop 160-foot bluffs, over natural sand dunes, and along the shoreline for more than two miles. Eight holes hug the water—more, Boyne developers like to tell you, than at Pebble Beach. Completed in 1998, it was almost immediately named the eighth-best public course in the nation by *Golf Magazine.*

Bay View

Adjacent to Petoskey on the east side of town, Bay View looks like a Hollywood set for a Victorian romance. This amazing community includes 430 Victorian homes, most built before the 1900s, a riot of gingerbread trim and cotton-candy colors. All are on the National Historic Register, and represent the largest single collection of historic homes in the country.

Bay View was founded by the Methodist Church in 1875, a summer-only religious retreat that took some inspiration from the Chautaqua movement in the East. Summers at Bay View were filled with lectures, recitals, craft classes, and religious programs. Over the years, speakers included such notable names as Booker T. Washington, Helen Keller, and William Jennings Bryan.

Originally a tent community, Bay View's canvas lodgings were slowly replaced by Victorian cottages, many with grand views of Little Traverse Bay. Bay View residents were not an extremely wealthy lot; the homes come in all shapes and sizes, lined up in tidy rows in a shady, park-like campus. Residents own their cottages but lease the land from the Methodist Church.

Today, Bay View remains a quiet enclave, still hosting a full roster of courses, concerts, and other events. While many residents are descendants of Bay View's founding families, the strict religious focus has been diluted. The biggest emphasis now, it seems, is on carefully preserving Bay View's slice of history. (Even minor renovations require approval by the Bay View Association.) Plan a stroll or a bike ride through this calm, gentle place for a true taste of another era.

Petoskey State Park

Just beyond Bay View, **Petoskey State Park** (2475 M-119, Petoskey, 231/347-2311, annual $11 Recreation Passport for Michigan residents or $8.40 day-use fee/$30.50 yearly Recreation Passport for nonresidents required) bends along the east end of Little Traverse Bay. Though quite small at 300 acres, the park nonetheless offers a nice dose of nature right smack between the summertime bustle of Petoskey and Harbor Springs. Its main attraction is its mile-long

PETOSKEY STONES

Michigan's official state stone isn't really a stone at all, but a chunk of fossilized coral more than 350 million years old. Coral reefs once thrived in the warm-water seas that covered northern Michigan from Grand Traverse Bay to Alpena on present-day Lake Huron. They are characterized by the distinct honeycomb pattern that covers them. Petoskey stones are common enough that they don't have much real value, but are prized nonetheless by rockhounds and anyone looking for a true local souvenir.

When dry, Petoskey stones often look like, well, ordinary stones, typically with a dusty gray-brown hue. Their unique pattern, however, becomes more apparent when they're wet and especially when polished. Since the stones are quite soft, locals suggest polishing them by hand with 220-grit wet sandpaper, then repeating the process with 400-grit and 600-grit sandpaper. Rock tumblers are not recommended.

Hunt for Petoskey stones along public beaches almost anywhere in the Traverse Bay region. Some of the more productive spots include Fisherman's Island State Park south of Charlevoix and Petoskey State Park beside Little Traverse Bay. You also can find Petoskey stones, polished up and often crafted into jewelry, at gift shops throughout the northwestern part of Michigan's Lower Peninsula.

---

beach, with soft sand and enough rocks to keep people on the hunt for Petoskey stones. (The coral pattern appears most clearly when wet, so dip a promising-looking stone in the water.) Try to look up occasionally; the beach has great views of Petoskey and Harbor Springs, and can serve up some terrific sunsets.

Climb the 0.7-mile **Old Baldy Trail** for an even better view from the top of a dune. The park's only other hiking trail, the **Portage Trail,** is an easy 2.8-mile loop that winds south to a little inland lake. It's groomed in winter for cross-country skiing.

Nearly 200 modern campsites are tucked behind some small dunes, mostly wooded sites with good privacy. Sites along the southern loop are closer to the bay, with a few prime (though more public) sites right on the water.

Harbor Springs

Just before Petoskey State Park, US-31 veers inland toward Mackinaw City and the straits. To stay along the water, turn west on M-119, which follows the curve of Little Traverse Bay and traces the Lower Peninsula's final stretch of Lake Michigan shoreline.

If you were to imagine the quintessential summer resort getaway, it might look a lot like genteel Harbor Springs on the north side of Little Traverse Bay: a deep, clear harbor tucked against a high, wooded bluff, ringed with grand estates and white church spires and, for good measure, gleaming yachts bobbing at anchor.

Harbor Springs, in fact, has the deepest natural harbor on all of the Great Lakes, which made it a natural stopping point for the large passenger steamers in the early 1900s. Several artesian wells added to its appeal, making it a popular destination for those seeking healthful air and water. Families like the Fords and the Gambles (of "Proctor and" fame) decided Harbor Springs looked pretty good and helped create exclusive resort communities like Harbor Point and Wequetonsing, where crisp white mansions line up across crisp emerald lawns.

Those "old money" communities still thrive, now inhabited largely by younger generations of Fords and Gambles. Harbor Point remains the more exclusive of the two, with homes topping $10 million hidden away behind gates. The only way in and out is by foot or carriage; even cars are banned from the point. You can walk, bike, or drive through Wequetonsing (WEE-kwee to the locals), where homes have wonderfully nostalgic names like Summer Set and Brookside, and long lines of Adirondack chairs line up on porches, just in case 10 or 12 friends drop by for gin and tonics.

It all makes for an interesting diversity, where ultra-wealthy Old Guard, younger trust-funders, vacationing families, and hired help all commingle easily in the delightfully tidy downtown. Of course, Harbor Springs has no strip malls, no sprawl, no ugly franchise signs.

Shopping is a popular sport in Harbor Springs, which hosts an appealing mix of galleries, tony boutiques, and distinctive handmade crafts. Start your exploring at Main and State. Also check out the **Harbor Springs History Museum** (349 E. Main St., 231/526-9771, www.harborspringshistory.org, 11am-3pm Fri.-Sat., by appointment 9am-5pm Tues.-Thurs., 9am-11am and 3pm-5pm Fri., $5 adults, $3 seniors and children), which uses photographs, artifacts, and hands-on activities to explore the area's history, from the influence of the Odawa Indians to the emergence of the ski industry. Here, you'll also learn about famous former residents, such as Andrew J. Blackbird, an Odawa chief who lived here in the mid-1800s. The town's first postmaster, Blackbird wrote books about Indian language, legends, and adapting to white civilization.

The harborfront is a natural for strolling, with ample benches and a swimming beach at **Zorn Park** near the west end. (Hardy bathers only—the harbor's water is *cold*.) For a more natural beach, the **Thorne Swift Nature Preserve** (231/347-0991 or 231/526-6401, www.landtrust.org) offers a quiet 300-foot sand beach and dune observation deck with a wonderful bay view. Other trails wind through cedar lowlands, with trees canted and curved at crazy angles, and are marked with interpretive signs. A protected holding of the very active Little Traverse Conservancy, Thorne Swift has a naturalist on duty daily Memorial Day-Labor Day. Pick a breezy day to visit, since bugs can be zealous here in summer months. To reach the preserve from Harbor Springs, head northwest on M-119 for 3.8 miles and then follow Lower Shore Drive for a half-mile. The preserve sign will be on your left.

Tunnel of Trees

The stretch of M-119 from Harbor Springs to Cross Village is considered one of the prettiest drives in Michigan, and deserves the distinction. The narrow lane twists and turns as it follows Lake Michigan from high atop a bluff, with furtive views of the water and the Beaver Island archipelago. Yet it is the trees that take top billing, arching overhead to form a sun-dappled tunnel. The effect is spectacular on autumn afternoons, when the fiery oranges and bronzes glow in the angled sunlight like hot coals.

In spring, trilliums form a blanket of white on the forest floor. Spring also offers a few more deep blue glimpses of the lake, since the trees usually are not fully leafed out until late May. And any season is a good time to spot wildlife. One trip up the corkscrewy road tallied five deer, 15 wild turkeys, and countless grouse.

Try to bike or drive this road during the week, or at least early or late in the day, when traffic should be lighter. The combination of narrow blacktop, blind curves, no shoulders, and lots of wildlife means you'll need to keep a close eye on the road. The more cars there are, the less scenery you can enjoy.

Legs Inn

Even if you've traveled far and wide, it's doubtful you've ever encountered anything like the **Legs Inn** (6425 N. Lake Shore Dr., Cross Village, 231/526-2281, www.legsinn.com, 11am-9pm daily, $14-25). Part ethnic restaurant, part eclectic folk art display, this is a weird and fascinating place to explore. Outside is strange enough, a roadside building with a facade of fieldstone, accented with bizarre-looking totems and carved wooden legs spiking up from the roof (hence, the "legs" name).

But that's nothing compared with the interior, where the bar is a dark and mysterious den crammed with twisted driftwood, roots, and stumps-turned-cocktail tables. Seemingly every square inch has been carved into fanciful shapes, weird faces, and indescribable animals—and more and more seem to appear as your eyes adjust to the darkness. The theme carries through to the dining rooms, though not with such intensity. These areas are brighter and warmer, with picture windows overlooking gardens and distant views of Lake Michigan.

Legs Inn was created by Stanley Smolak, a Polish immigrant who moved to Cross Village from Chicago in the 1920s. He became enamored with the local land and its native people. He befriended the local Ottawa tribes, still thriving here in the 1920s, and was accepted enough into their culture that they gave him an Indian name, Chief White Cloud. Inspired by their art, he began carving. Soon, word of his restaurant and his relations with the Indians made Smolak a celebrity back in Poland.

With its eccentric decor, it's almost easy to overlook the food at the Legs Inn, but you shouldn't. It offers a wonderful array of Polish cooking, with rich soups, thick stews, and popular Polish specialties like pierogies. Even the drink menu offers Polish vodkas and Polish meads, made from honey and fruit juices. This is authentic stuff—many of the cook staff are immigrants themselves. They'll smile and nod and feed you like long-lost relatives.

Sturgeon Bay

M-119 ends at Cross Village, but continue northeast on Scenic Route 1 along Sturgeon Bay to reach **Bliss Township Park,** with low dunes and a pretty sand beach, great for swimming and sunsets. Far enough away from Petoskey and the Straits of Mackinac, it rarely draws a crowd.

Sturgeon Bay also offers the best big-water windsurfing in the area, with an easy shore break and generally warmer water than Little Traverse Bay. Bliss Township Park is a wonderful launch in southwest through north winds. A second launch is about a mile north of the township beach, just where the road makes a hard right. Watch for poison ivy. Advanced sailors looking for big waves should check out the boat launch in Cross Village—good in west through north winds.

Wilderness State Park

North of Cross Village near the top of the "mitten," Waugoshance Point stretches west out into Lake Michigan and dribbles off into a series of islands. This is the spectacular setting for **Wilderness State Park** (903 Wilderness Park Dr., Carp Lake, 231/436-5381, annual $11 Recreation Passport for Michigan residents or $8.40 day-use fee/$30.50 yearly Recreation Passport for nonresidents required), the second-largest state park in the Lower Peninsula. Aptly named, it occupies more than 7,500 acres of largely undeveloped land, including more than 26 miles of Lake Michigan shoreline. Considering that it sits just 15 minutes away from the Straits of Mackinac, it offers remarkable solitude.

As proof, this is one of the nesting sites of the endangered piping plover. (When the birds are nesting in late spring and early summer, part of the point is closed to visitors.) About 100 other bird species also nest or migrate through Wilderness State Park, making it a favorite of bird-watchers. Anglers also gather here, with notable bass fishing especially in the grassy beds along the southern shore of the point. The park has a boat launch near the campgrounds and day-use area.

The park offers a wide range of topography, with sandy beaches and rocky limestone ledges along the shore. Inland, 12 miles of trails (mostly old truck trails) wind through cedars, pines, and birches. A gravel road leads toward the end of the point, open to autos. To hike there, you can follow the northern shoreline for two miles, unless the endangered piping plovers are nesting. Depending on weather conditions and water depths, it's often possible to wade to Temperance Island—a fun mini-adventure.

Wilderness State Park has two large campgrounds with 250 sites, five rustic cabins, and 24-bunk lodges for rent ($12-69 daily). The Lakeshore Campground sits on Big Stone Bay in an open, grassy setting, with several sites right along the water. Just across the park road, the Pines Campground has more shaded, private sites in the, uh, pines.

MACKINAC ISLAND AND NORTHEAST MICHIGAN

Commonly called the Sunrise Side, the northeastern part of Michigan's Lower Peninsula is perhaps its most under-appreciated region—which is a shame given the untamed beauty that abounds here. Of course, year-round residents and seasonal vacationers value the tranquility of this less traveled place, so most are grateful that development has been slower here than in other parts of Michigan.

The area's remarkable woods—including sizable Hartwick Pines State Park—lure a wide array of recreationists, from hikers in summer to hunters in winter, while the region's many lakes, such as Higgins Lake south of Grayling, attract numerous anglers, boaters, and canoeists. Wildlife enthusiasts relish Northeast Michigan, too—it's common to spot scurrying foxes amid the underbrush, curious deer along country roads, bald eagles circling above the coves, and majestic elk stalking through the Pigeon River Country State Forest, home to the largest free-roaming elk herd east of the Mississippi River.

Although many locals live here all year long—even during the splendid, if bitter cold, winters—more come during the summer months, escaping humid places like Chicago and Florida. Dwelling in vacation cottages that line the roads and encircle the area's idyllic lakes, these seasonal residents spend their summers playing golf, shopping for antiques, fishing for walleye, and picking wild blueberries.

A superb way to experience the hinterlands of Northeast Michigan is, ironically, via the road. The 22-mile River Road Scenic Byway showcases the high cliffs, white pines, and wooded

HIGHLIGHTS

LOOK FOR ◖ TO FIND RECOMMENDED SIGHTS, ACTIVITIES, DINING, AND LODGING.

◖ **Grand Hotel:** Opened in 1887, this gorgeous hotel is a timeless piece of American history, boasting the world's longest porch and a guest list that's included at least five U.S. presidents (page 285).

◖ **Diving in Thunder Bay:** Scuba divers will discover a wealth of artifacts in the 448-square-mile Thunder Bay National Marine Sanctuary and Underwater Preserve. "Shipwreck Alley" is the unfortunate resting place of more than 80 historic vessels (page 297).

◖ **Canoeing on the Au Sable River:** Home to North America's longest nonstop canoe marathon, the Au Sable is one of the most picturesque rivers in Michigan (page 302).

◖ **Houghton and Higgins Lakes:** These sizable inland lakes, two of the state's largest, offer seven swimming beaches, nearly a dozen access sites for boaters and anglers in summer, and the possibility of ice fishing for walleye, pike, bass, and bluegill in winter (page 307).

◖ **Hartwick Pines State Park:** One of the largest state parks also preserves the state's largest remaining stand of virgin white pines. View forestry exhibits, experience a former logging camp, explore trails, and observe a variety of wildlife (page 312).

◖ **Colonial Michilimackinac State Historic Park:** Just south of the Mackinac Bridge lies this reconstruction of the original Fort Michilimackinac, a French fur-trading village and military outpost established in 1715. Costumed soldiers, traders, and colonial ladies demonstrate skills of the late 18th century (page 277).

◖ **Golfing in Gaylord:** Golfers will find a wide assortment of options in the northern half of the Lower Peninsula, especially in the area around Gaylord, which offers a high concentration of championship golf courses, with challenging holes, scenic views, and fine lodgings (page 315).

lakes of the Au Sable River Valley. Meanwhile, the Sunrise Side Coastal Highway (US-23) stretches for 200 miles along the Lake Huron shoreline, from Standish to the Mackinac Bridge. Along the way, motorists can experience quaint coastal towns, inviting beaches, and lovely lighthouses. These stunning drives are especially wonderful in the fall, when the trees are ablaze with spectacular colors.

Situated just north of the mainland lies Mackinac Island, a nostalgic destination claimed by both the Upper and Lower Peninsulas. Although most of the island is preserved as a state park, about 20 percent of it

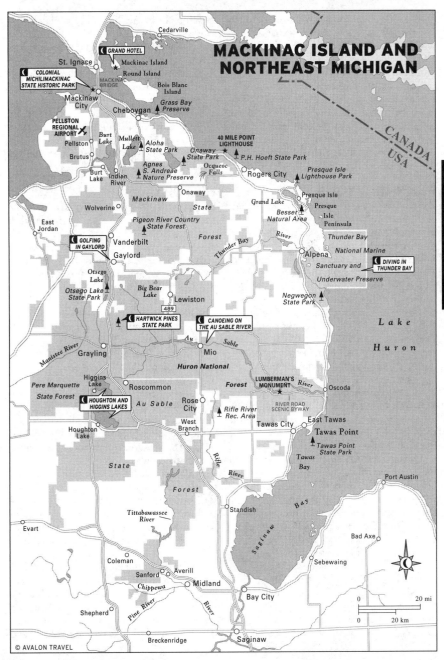

NORTHEAST MICHIGAN

MACKINAC ISLAND AND NORTHEAST MICHIGAN

CANADA
USA

Cedarville

GRAND HOTEL

St. Ignace
Mackinac Island
Round Island
MACKINAC BRIDGE
Bois Blanc Island

COLONIAL MICHILIMACKINAC STATE HISTORIC PARK

Mackinaw City

Cheboygan
Grass Bay Preserve

PELLSTON REGIONAL AIRPORT

Burt Lake
Mullett Lake
Aloha State Park

40 MILE POINT LIGHTHOUSE

Pellston
Onaway State Park
P.H. Hoeft State Park

Brutus
Agnes S. Andreae Nature Preserve
Ocqueoc Falls
Rogers City

Burt Lake
Indian River
Presque Isle Lighthouse Park

Mackinaw
Onaway
Grand Lake
Presque Isle

Wolverine
Besser Natural Area
Presque Isle Peninsula

East Jordan
State
Thunder Bay

Pigeon River Country State Forest
Forest
River

GOLFING IN GAYLORD
Vanderbilt
Alpena
Thunder Bay National Marine

Gaylord
Thunder Bay
DIVING IN THUNDER BAY

Otsego Lake
Sanctuary and Underwater Preserve

Otsego Lake State Park
Big Bear Lake
Lewiston
Negwegon State Park

489

HARTWICK PINES STATE PARK
CANOEING ON THE AU SABLE RIVER

Au
Sable

Manistee River
Grayling
Mio

Huron National

Higgins Lake
Roscommon
Forest
LUMBERMAN'S MONUMENT
River
Oscoda

Pere Marquette State Forest
HOUGHTON AND HIGGINS LAKES
Au Sable
Rose City
RIVER ROAD SCENIC BYWAY

Houghton Lake
West Branch
Rifle River Rec. Area
Tawas City
East Tawas
Tawas Point

State
Tawas Point State Park

Tawas Bay

Forest
Port Austin

Tittabawassee River
Standish
Saginaw Bay

Evart
Bad Axe

Coleman
Sebewaing

Sanford
Averill
Midland

Chippewa
Pine River
River

Shepherd
Bay City

0   20 mi

0   20 km

Breckenridge
Saginaw

© AVALON TRAVEL

has become a year-round tourist mecca, offering boat docks, historic sites, enchanting hotels, and intriguing attractions like the Original Butterfly House & Insect World. Since automobiles are banned here, bikes, horses, and carriages are the preferred modes of transportation—just another facet of the island's yesteryear vibe. Mackinac Island might be, at times, teeming with "fudgies" (a local term for tourists), but its charms are unmistakable, and it's definitely worth a look after exploring the wilds of Northeast Michigan.

PLANNING YOUR TIME

For those who prefer small towns, the solitude of the great outdoors, and winter activities like snowmobiling, Northeast Michigan is an ideal precursor to visiting the even wilder and more isolated Upper Peninsula. In the summer, it's also a good spot to avoid the crowded beaches and resort towns along Lake Michigan. Of course, that doesn't mean you won't encounter plenty of folks on the area's championship golf courses, near inland lakes during summer weekends, and on Mackinac Island throughout the year. You will, however, likely avoid crowds during the off-season, November-March.

To hit the highlights of Northeast Michigan, you'll need a minimum of three days, including a day trip to Mackinac Island. A whole week will give you a better chance to tour the historic coastline and explore the interior's impressive forests and lakes.

Two main roads cut through the Huron shore region. US-23 hugs the coastline from Standish to the Straits of Mackinac, offering vistas and villages along the way. I-75 is the quicker, though less scenic, route, heading north from Bay City, through Grayling and Gaylord, to the Mackinac Bridge.

For those not driving to Northeast Michigan (or arriving via private boat), consider taking a Greyhound bus to towns like Cheboygan, Rogers City, Alpena, Tawas City, Grayling, and Gaylord. It's also possible to fly into the Pellston Regional Airport and Alpena County Regional Airport, both of which are

served by Delta Air Lines. If you plan on exploring several areas in this spread-out region, it's advisable to rent a vehicle as soon as you arrive.

Tourism folks market the Huron shore region as the state's "Sunrise Side." For more information about Northeast Michigan, consult **Travel Michigan** (Michigan Economic Development Corporation, 300 N. Washington Sq., Lansing, 888/784-7328, www.michigan.org) or the **Northern Michigan Tourist Association** (www.travelnorth.org).

HISTORY

In appearance, Northeast Michigan has come nearly full circle in 200 years. Its first inhabitants were Native Americans, who left the land much as they found it, until the Europeans arrived in the 17th century. By the mid-1800s, logging companies that had exhausted the nation's eastern forests had moved on to Michigan's fertile ground, making it the largest lumber-producing state in the country between 1850 and 1910, with an estimated 700 logging camps and more than 2,000 mills.

Before the rush of settlers to Michigan in the 1830s, more than 13 million of the state's 37 million acres were covered with white pine. These majestic trees thrived in sandy soil, grew up to 200 feet tall, and could live an incredible 500 years. By 1900, however, all that was left of these once awe-inspiring forests were stumps. Logging had devastated the terrain, leaving behind a wasteland.

In 1909, the federal government established the Huron National Forest, the first of many such preserves that sought to repair years of damage. More than a century later, much of this region is once again forested, and it's possible to hike for miles through towering, whispering pines.

Mackinac Island, of course, has its own unique history. The Ojibwa and Ottawa peoples called it Michilimackinac, which some scholars claim means "The Great Turtle," an apt description for this hump of limestone. The Indians summered here, hunting, fishing, and trading some of their catch for grains and produce from other tribes.

French missionaries were the first Europeans to settle in the area, erecting a mission in nearby St. Ignace in 1671. The French were also the first whites to exploit the rich fur harvest, establishing a trading post in St. Ignace in the late 1600s. In 1715, they erected Fort Michilimackinac in Mackinaw City. The British, meanwhile, were also eager to expand their territory. They regularly skirmished with the French, and Fort Michilimackinac traded hands more than once—that is, until the 1763 Treaty of Paris gave all French land east of the Mississippi to Great Britain.

Upstart colonists became the new enemy. In 1780, the British commander abandoned Fort Michilimackinac in favor of Mackinac Island, where the high limestone bluffs offered better protection from attack. Though American troops never came, they won the fort anyway, gaining title to the northern territory after the American Revolution. Still, the British refused to turn over the fort until 1796.

During the War of 1812, British troops landed at the northern end of the island in early morning darkness, dragged a couple of cannons up the bluff and aimed them at Fort Mackinac below. The surprised Americans surrendered without firing a single shot. The British once again controlled Fort Mackinac until 1814,

when the Treaty of Ghent passed the land back to the United States once and for all.

In 1817, John Jacob Astor set up the American Fur Company here, bartering with the Indians for beaver pelts and storing them in warehouses on the island. Until overhunting decimated the fur industry and commercial fishing became the area's mainstay, Astor ranked as the richest man in the United States.

By the second half of the 19th century, Mackinac Island had evolved from a battleground to a gracious getaway. Wealthy Midwesterners, who had heard about the island's lovely waters and clean air, began arriving by lake steamer to summer here. Hotels sprang up, soon followed by private homes along the bluffs—30-room Victorian "cottages," complete with carriage houses, stables, and servants' quarters.

To minimize its potentially destructive impact, the automobile was banned from Mackinac Island as quickly as it arrived. Today, roughly 600 horses are stabled on the island in summer, used for hauling freight, pulling carriages, and private recreation. The horses, carts, carriages, bicycle fleets, and well-preserved Victorians all blend to give Mackinac the magical, frozen-in-time feel that has turned it into one of the most popular vacation spots in the Midwest.

Mackinaw City

Although some may consider it a tourist trap, Mackinaw City offers more than just strip malls and souvenir shops. Despite overdevelopment, the town has several things to recommend it—namely, a maritime museum, a lighthouse, two excellent historic parks, several fudge shops, numerous hotel rooms, terrific views of the Great Lakes, and, of course, ferry service to Mackinac Island.

SIGHTS
C Colonial Michilimackinac State Historic Park

Archaeologists have been uncovering treasures since 1959 on the site of this 18th-century fur-trading post, believed to be the nation's longest-running archaeological dig. It was long a well-traveled Indian hunting and trading ground, and the French built a post here in 1715. The French exploited the Indians, bribing them with gifts and alcohol,

a period gardener at Colonial Michilimackinac State Historic Park

and encouraging them to work in the fur trade. Though the unfortunate relationship led many Indians to abandon their traditional way of life, the two groups rarely fought. Instead, the French feuded with the British, who sought to expand their landholdings in the region. For the next 65 years, the fort along the straits alternately fell under French and British control.

The fort's most violent episode occurred while it was under British rule. In 1763, Pontiac, the Ottawa war chief, ordered an attack on British posts all over Michigan, an attempt to drive the growing British population out of their native land. While Pontiac laid siege to Detroit, local Ojibwa stormed the fort, killing all but 13 soldiers. In the end, though, it was the feisty colonists who sent the British fleeing from Fort Michilimackinac. They dismantled what they could and burned the rest to the ground in 1780, opting for a new, more-defensible post on nearby Mackinac Island.

Today, **Colonial Michilimackinac State Historic Park** (102 W. Straits Ave., 231/436-4100, www.mackinacparks.com, 9am-6pm daily June-Aug., 9am-4pm daily May and Sept.-mid-Oct., $10 adults, $6.25 children 5-17), located just west of the Mackinac Bridge, portrays the lives of both the Indians and European settlers, with costumed interpreters reenacting daily life at an Indian encampment and a stockaded fort. Displays include many of the artifacts unearthed by archaeologists. Interpreters demonstrate various crafts and skills, from cooking and weaving to cleaning weapons. Interpreters are quite knowledgeable and able to answer most visitors' questions. Don't miss the underground archaeological tunnel exhibit, "Treasures from the Sand."

Historic Mill Creek Discovery Park

Today, this exceptionally pretty glen and rushing stream creates a pleasant oasis for visitors, but it once was an innovative industrial site. When the British made plans to move from Fort Michilimackinac to Mackinac Island, Scotsman Robert Campbell recognized their imminent need for lumber. He purchased 640 acres of the land around the only waterway in the area with enough flow to power a sawmill. He built the mill in 1790 and later added a blacksmith shop and gristmill.

The site was no longer profitable when the fort ceased operation, so it was abandoned in the mid-1800s. Since the 1970s, archaeologists and historians have worked together to re-create the water-powered sawmill on its original site. Today, visitors to the 625-acre **Historic Mill Creek Discovery Park** (9001 US-23, 231/436-4100, www.mackinacparks.com, 9am-5pm daily June-Aug., 9am-4pm daily May and Sept.-mid-Oct., $7.50 adults, $4.50 children 5-17) can see the splashing waterwheel in action and visit the Orientation Center, which has an audiovisual presentation and displays on other artifacts uncovered during the dig. Make sure to walk the park's 1.5 miles of trails, which wind along the creek and mill pond, rising up to scenic overlooks with views of the straits and Mackinac Island.

Old Mackinac Point Lighthouse

Located on a point just east of the Mackinac Bridge, this 1892 cream-brick light guided ships through the busy Straits of Mackinac for nearly 70 years. When the Mackinac Bridge was completed in 1957, it became obsolete, since vessels could range on the bridge's high lights instead of the diminutive 40-foot tower. Today, the charming **Old Mackinac Point Lighthouse** (9am-5pm daily June-Aug., 9am-4pm daily May and Sept.-mid-Oct., $6 adults, $3.50 children 5-17), topped with a cherry-red roof, houses a maritime museum, part of Colonial Michilimackinac State Historic Park. A schooner and other ships are docked and on display. The lighthouse grounds serve as their own delightful little park, with impressive views of the Mackinac Bridge as well as picnic tables scattered around a tidy lawn.

From here, you can reach several island and offshore reef lights via boat—though you should take care in these potentially dangerous waters. Two of the most interesting are the 1874 **Spectacle Reef Light,** an impressive example of a monolithic stone lighthouse, and the 1895 **Round Island Light** in the Straits of Mackinac.

the Old Mackinac Point Lighthouse

Mackinac Bridgemen Museum

It's not slick or fancy, but the small **Bridgemen Museum** (231 E. Central, 231/436-8751, 8am-midnight daily May-Oct., free) above Mama Mia's Pizza is loaded with tidbits and artifacts on the construction of the $100 million Mackinac Bridge. A very well-done video documents the bridge's design and construction. For more information about the bridge itself, consult the **Mackinac Bridge Authority** (www.mackinacbridge.org).

Lighthouse Tours

Although a self-guided tour of Michigan's lighthouses can be a delightful way to pass a few days in the Great Lakes State, the experience can be even more enlightening with a well-informed guide. Besides shuttling tourists to and from Mackinac Island, **Shepler's Mackinac Island Ferry** (800/828-6157, www.sheplersferry.com) also offers lighthouse cruises ($52.50 adults, $27.50 children 5-12). Departing from Mackinaw City, these trips guide passengers amid lighthouses and shipwrecks that would be difficult for most people to reach otherwise. Along the way, passengers are treated to historical tales that provide an informative context for the lighthouses that still stand today. The eastbound cruise features offshore lights like Round Island Light and the privately owned Bois Blanc Island Light, while the westbound cruise highlights structures such as the red-and-white-striped White Shoal Light and the 1873 St. Helena Island Lighthouse.

SHOPPING

Although Mackinaw City isn't as high on shoppers' lists as, for instance, the resort towns along Lake Michigan, it does have its share of decent shops. Of course, no area is quite as pleasant as **Mackinaw Crossings** (248 S. Huron Ave., 231/436-5030, www.mackinawcrossings.com, shop hours vary), a tidy open-air collection of restaurants and stores. Here, you can find everything from **To Bead or Not to Bead,** which offers handmade jewelry and beads for creating your own accessories, to the **Great Lakes**

Mackinaw City shops

© DANIEL MARTONE

Bear Factory, where children (and adults) can customize their very own stuffed teddy bears.

ACCOMMODATIONS AND FOOD

With the Straits of Mackinac a major tourism draw, Mackinaw City alone has more than 3,000 rooms. For a variety of amenities, check out the **Comfort Inn Lakeside** (611 S. Huron Ave., 231/436-5057, www.comfortinn.com, $158-220 d) or the **Ramada Inn Waterfront** (723 S. Huron Ave., 231/436-5055, www.ramadainn.com, $48-278 d).

In between sightseeing and shopping, grab a bite to eat at one of the numerous area restaurants. Step back a couple of centuries at the **Dixie Saloon** (401 E. Central Ave., 231/436-5449, www.dixiesaloon.com, 11am-9pm Sun.-Thurs., 11am-11pm Fri.-Sat., $6-24), a historic landmark. Try the potato-encrusted walleye or the fried perch, both of which are locally caught. For something a little more elegant, stop by **The Lighthouse Restaurant** (618 S. Huron Ave., 231/436-5191, 11am-9pm daily,

$10-49), with its prime rib, lobster, and excellent wine list.

INFORMATION AND SERVICES

For more information about Mackinaw City, contact the **Mackinaw Area Visitors Bureau** (231/436-5664, www.mackinawcity.com). While you won't find a ton of services here, there is indeed a small grocery, a post office, and a 24-hour ATM at **Citizens National Bank** (580 S. Nicolet St., 231/436-5271, www.cnbismybank.com). In case of a police-related or medical emergency, dial **911** from any cell or public phone.

GETTING THERE AND AROUND

While Mackinaw City may not have any airports, train stations, or bus centers of its own, it's still not terribly difficult to reach the Lower Peninsula's northernmost town. **Pellston Regional Airport** (PLN, 1395 US-31, Pellston, 231/539-8441 or 231/539-8442, www.pellstonairport.com), for instance, offers commuter service from Detroit via Delta Air Lines. From there, you can rent a vehicle from Avis or Hertz, take US-31 North, merge onto I-75 North, and head north to downtown Mackinaw City; without traffic, the 16-mile trip should take about 20 minutes. With advance reservations, you can also hop aboard a van or shuttle bus via **Mackinaw Shuttle** (231/539-7005 or 888/349-8294, www.mackinawshuttle.com), which regularly transports passengers from the Pellston airport to Mackinaw City as well as other towns in northern Michigan, from Traverse City and Petoskey in the Lower Peninsula to St. Ignace and Sault Ste. Marie in the Upper Peninsula.

Of course, many visitors come to Michigan by car, and luckily, it's possible to reach Mackinaw City from a variety of directions, usually via US-31, I-75, or US-23. From Sault Ste. Marie, for instance, you can simply take I-75 South to St. Ignace, cross the Mackinac Bridge (for which you'll have to pay a toll), and take exit 338 toward US-23; the 59-mile trip typically takes about an hour. From Traverse City, meanwhile, you can take US-31 North, merge onto I-75 North, and take exit 338 toward South Nicolet Street; without traffic, the 103-mile trip should take roughly two hours. Even downtown Detroit is closer to Mackinaw City than one might think; the 289-mile journey is predominantly a direct route via I-75 North, and without traffic, it usually takes about four hours to make the trip "up north."

If, on the other hand, you're coming from Chicago, you'll just take I-90 East and I-94 East through Illinois and Indiana, cross the Michigan state line, continue onto I-196 North/US-31 North and I-196 East, merge onto US-131 North, follow CR-42 and M-32 East, and take I-75 North to exit 338; without traffic, the 406-mile trip will require at least six hours. Just be advised that, en route from the Windy City, parts of I-90 East and I-94 East serve as the Indiana Toll Road. Still, no matter how you reach Mackinaw City, you may be happy to know that it's a fairly small town, so just park your vehicle and take a pleasant stroll amid the downtown shops and eateries.

Mackinac Island

Linking Lakes Huron and Michigan, the Straits of Mackinac (MAK-i-naw) have been a crossroads of the Great Lakes for hundreds of years, a key waterway for hunting, fishing, trading, and transportation. The four-mile-wide straits also sever Michigan in two, both emotionally and geographically. Until the 1950s, the only way across was by ferry, effectively blocking the development of the Upper Peninsula and creating half-day backups at the ferry dock during prime hunting and fishing seasons.

Today, the magnificent five-mile-long Mackinac Bridge stitches the state together, allowing a free flow between the Upper and Lower Peninsulas. But the straits, now a key vacation area for much of the Midwest, continue to lure people, and many come specifically for Mackinac Island.

No place name in Michigan conjures up as much history, attention, and affection as the tiny parcel known as Mackinac Island. Over the centuries, the 2,200-acre island has been a sacred ground for the Native Americans who summered here, an important base for French fur trappers, a fort for British soldiers, and a gilded summer retreat for the wealthiest of Victorian-era industrialists.

It is the Victorian era that Mackinac chose to preserve, from the exquisite 1887 Grand Hotel, with its 660-foot-long porch stretching across the hillside, to the clopping of the horse-drawn carriages down the vehicle-free streets. Yes, it can seem touristy at first blush. Yes, it can be crowded. But Mackinac Island can also be irrepressibly charming, all buffed up and neatly packaged, the state's heirloom jewel.

Some of the criticism lobbed at Mackinac is based on misconception, anyway. For starters, Mackinac is more than the tangle of fudge and souvenir shops that greet you at the ferry dock. A full 80 percent of the island is a state park, comprising a restored 18th-century fort, undeveloped woodlands, crisscrossing trails, rare wildflowers, and sculpted limestone outcroppings.

Secondly, Mackinac Island has far more lodging choices than the famous Grand Hotel. Many are moderately priced. Plan to spend at least one night, so you have a little time to wander around and get past the cliché. Mackinac doesn't lend itself well to a cursory glance. Like those wealthy resorters knew, it's a wonderful place to retreat from the pulls of the real world.

SIGHTS
Downtown

Everyone wants to wander among the four blocks of shops and restaurants on Main Street. The ferry docks themselves are particularly interesting. At the Arnold Transit dock, you can sneak a peek at the day-to-day grunt work of Mackinac, like workers unloading carton after carton of vegetables from the ferry and reloading them by hand onto drays (wagons) for horse-drawn delivery to area restaurants. Even the UPS man does his route via bike, pulling a cart loaded with packages.

Once you've done the Main Street stroll and nibbled your requisite hunk of fudge (there's a reason tourists are known as "fudgies"), make the most of your visit by getting off the main drag. You can get a good taste of what the island has to offer on a carriage tour with **Mackinac Island Carriage Tours** (906/847-3307, www.mict.com, 9am-4pm daily May-Oct., $25 adults, $10 children 5-12), located across from the Arnold Transit ferry dock. The pleasant narrated tour takes about two hours, rambling along at a relaxing pace past the Grand Hotel, Arch Rock, Skull Cave, Fort Mackinac, and most of the island's other key sights. This locally owned business is the world's largest horse and buggy livery, with more than 300 horses, mostly crosses of beefy Percherons, Belgians, and Clydesdales.

One block inland from Main, some of Mackinac's original residences line up on

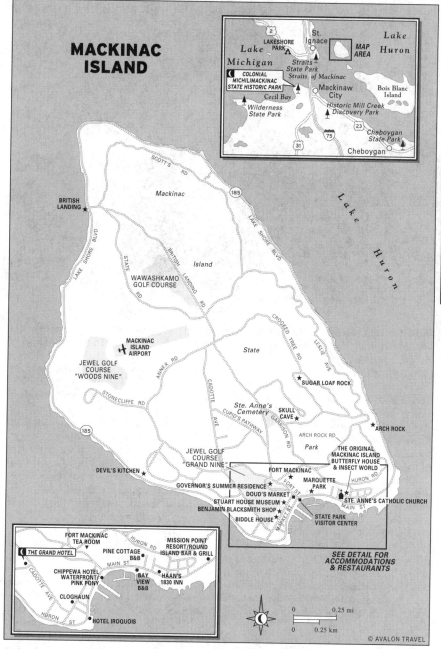

MACKINAC ISLAND

NORTHEAST MICHIGAN

Lake Michigan

Lake Huron

2

St. Ignace

LAKESHORE PARK

MAP AREA

Straits State Park

Straits of Mackinac

COLONIAL MICHILIMACKINAC STATE HISTORIC PARK

Cecil Bay

Mackinaw City

Bois Blanc Island

Wilderness State Park

Historic Mill Creek Discovery Park

23

Cheboygan State Park

31

75

Cheboygan

SCOTT'S RD

Mackinac

185

LAKE SHORE BLVD

BRITISH LANDING

Lake Huron

LAKE SHORE BLVD

STATE

BRITISH LANDING RD

Island

WAWASHKAMO GOLF COURSE

MACKINAC ISLAND AIRPORT

RD

JEWEL GOLF COURSE "WOODS NINE"

STONECLIFFE RD

ANNEX RD

CADOTTE AVE

State

CROOKED TREE RD

LESLIE AVE

★ SUGAR LOAF ROCK

185

Ste. Anne's Cemetery

CUPID'S PATHWAY

GARRISON RD

SKULL CAVE ★

ARCH ROCK RD

★ ARCH ROCK

JEWEL GOLF COURSE "GRAND NINE"

Park

THE ORIGINAL MACKINAC ISLAND BUTTERFLY HOUSE & INSECT WORLD

DEVIL'S KITCHEN ★

FORT MACKINAC ★

GOVERNOR'S SUMMER RESIDENCE ★

DOUD'S MARKET ★

STUART HOUSE MUSEUM ★

BENJAMIN BLACKSMITH SHOP ★

BIDDLE HOUSE ★

MARQUETTE PARK

HURON RD

FORT ST

MARKET ST

★ STE. ANNE'S CATHOLIC CHURCH

MAIN ST

STATE PARK VISITOR CENTER

SEE DETAIL FOR ACCOMMODATIONS & RESTAURANTS

FORT MACKINAC TEA ROOM

HURON RD

MISSION POINT RESORT/ROUND ISLAND BAR & GRILL

THE GRAND HOTEL

PINE COTTAGE B&B

MAIN ST

CHIPPEWA HOTEL WATERFRONT PINK PONY

CADOTTE AVE

BAY VIEW B&B

HAAN'S 1830 INN

CLOGHAUN

HURON ST

HOTEL IROQUOIS

0   0.25 mi
0   0.25 km

© AVALON TRAVEL

© MACKINAC ISLAND TOURISM BUREAU

a horse-drawn carriage ride on Mackinac Island

Market Street. Much quieter than frenetic Main, Market has several interesting stops for visitors. The headquarters of the American Fur Company, John Jacob Astor's empire, is now the **Stuart House Museum** (34 Market St., 9am-4pm daily May-late Oct., donation suggested). The 1817 building retains much of its original decor, including fur company ledgers, fur weighing scales, and other artifacts. The museum is operated by the City of Mackinac Island.

A block west, knowledgeable interpreters demonstrate spinning at **Biddle House** and blacksmithing at the **Benjamin Blacksmith Shop** (both 11am-4pm daily mid-May-late Oct.). These and other historic buildings are part of the state park, and are included with the admission ticket to Fort Mackinac. For current information, stop by the park visitors center across from Marquette Park on Huron Street, or contact **Mackinac State Historic Parks** (213/436-4100, www.mackinacparks. com, 11am-4pm daily).

From Marquette Park, follow Fort Street up the hill to the **Governor's Residence** at the corner of Fort and East Bluff Road. The state purchased the "cottage" in the 1940s. It is the official summer residence of the governor, though the amount of time actually spent here varies from governor to governor. The house is open for tours on Wednesday mornings.

Some of the island's more impressive "cottages" line up along **East Bluff.** Wander east from the governor's mansion to see some of these Victorian marvels. Happily, most survived the Depression era—when they could be purchased for pennies on the dollar, of course. Today, they're well cared for and worth $1 million plus. (And remember, most are summer homes only!)

Work your way down one of the sets of public steps to the lakefront. Main Street has become Huron Street here. Continue your walk east, passing smaller but no less appealing cottages and homes. Many are skirted with geraniums and lilacs, the island's signature flowers. Behind Ste. Anne's Catholic Church, seek out the **Original Mackinac Island Butterfly House**

& Insect World (906/847-3972, www.original-butterflyhouse.com, 10am-7pm daily Memorial Day-Labor Day, $9 adults, $4.50 children 5-12), tucked away on McGulpin Street.

Owner Doug Beardsley used to use his greenhouses to grow thousands of geraniums for the Grand Hotel and others. He relied on biodynamic growing methods, releasing beneficial insects to care for his plants rather than chemical sprays. When economics made his small greenhouse less viable, he stuck with his insects. After hearing about a butterfly house in Europe, Beardsley added some different host plants and began ordering pupa from around the world. Now hundreds of butterflies fly freely in his greenhouse/atrium, some nearly six inches long. You can observe them up close on walls and plants, or sit still long enough and they'll land on you.

The engaging Beardsley hopes his attraction will help convince gardeners to wean themselves off herbicides and pesticides. He sells helpful insects to control garden pests like aphids and will give you ideas for attracting butterflies to your own garden. (Host plants like milkweed and cabbage, where butterflies like to lay their eggs, will work best. "Think of it as planting a caterpillar garden, not a butterfly garden," he says.)

◖ Grand Hotel

The **Grand Hotel** (286 Grand Ave., 906/847-3331 or 800/334-7263, www.grandhotel.com) has become practically synonymous with Mackinac Island, a gracious edifice built on a truly grand scale. It is the largest summer resort in the world, operating early May-late October. Its famous 660-foot-long covered front porch gets decked out each spring with 2,000 geraniums planted in seven *tons* of potting soil. Its 11 restaurants and bars serve as many as 4,000 meals a day. Its impeccable grounds offer guests every amenity, from saddle horses to designer golf to swimming in the outdoor pool made famous by the 1940s swimming actress, Esther Williams, who filmed *This Time for Keeps* here.

But opulence is what the railroads and

a busy day on Mackinac Island

costumed guides atop Fort Mackinac

steamships were after when they formed a consortium and built the Grand Hotel in 1887, dragging construction materials across the frozen waters by horse and mule. The wealthiest of all Mackinac Island visitors stayed here, of course, high on the hill.

Yet unlike other turn-of-the-20th-century resorts that burned to the ground or grew dogeared and faded, the Grand Hotel has managed to maintain its grace and dignity over the years. It still hosts all manner of celebrities and politicians—five U.S. presidents to date—and still offers a sip of the Gilded Age, with high tea in the parlor each afternoon and demitasse served after dinner each evening. Room rates still include a five-course dinner in the soaring main dining room, and jackets/ties and skirts/dresses are still the required attire.

The Grand Hotel's time-capsule setting prompted director Jeannot Szwarc to choose it as the location for the 1980 film *Somewhere in Time,* starring Christopher Reeve, Jane Seymour, and Christopher Plummer. Curiously, the movie has developed a huge

following; its fan club reunites at the hotel each year in late October.

While room rates can get outright astronomical, they can be a worthwhile splurge if you enjoy this kind of thing. What the heck—take high tea, loll in the beautifully landscaped pool, or dance to the swing orchestra in the Terrace Room. Nonguests can sneak a peek at the hotel's public areas and grounds for a not-unreasonable $10. (It's needed to thin the sightseers more than anything.) Highly recommended are a stroll through the grounds, filled with Victorian gardens—24,000 tulips in spring!—and a visit to the snazzy Cupola Bar, with views halfway to Wisconsin.

Fort Mackinac

Located at the crest of the bluff, whitewashed **Fort Mackinac** (231/436-4100, 9am-5pm daily mid-May-mid-Oct., $10 adults, $6.25 children 6-17) is worth a visit for the views alone, presiding over—as forts do—the downtown, the marina, and Lake Huron. But there's also plenty to see at this military outpost, which the British and Americans haggled over for nearly 40 years.

Along with peering over the parapets, you can wander in and out of 14 buildings within the fort. The barracks, officers' quarters, post hospital, and others are filled with interpretive displays and decorated in period decor. Costumed guides lead all sorts of reenactments, including musket firings and cannon salutes. A short audiovisual presentation, "The Heritage of Mackinac," does a good job of presenting basic history.

Mackinac Island State Park

Often overshadowed by other visitor attractions, Mackinac Island's natural history has attracted scientific observation for over 200 years. In the early 19th century, botanists discovered several species completely new to science, including the dwarf lake iris, still found predominantly in the Straits of Mackinac region.

Early scientists also marveled at the island's distinctive geology, mostly brecciated limestone that has been sculpted by eons of wind and waves. The result is some dramatic rock formations, like the giant inland slab of limestone called Sugar Loaf Rock, the lakeside caves of Devil's Kitchen, and impressive Arch Rock, which rises nearly 150 feet above the eastern shore and spans some 50 feet.

In recognition of the park's distinctive natural curiosities and growing tourism, the U.S. government created Mackinac National Park in 1875—following Yellowstone as the nation's second national park. Twenty years later, it was returned to Michigan and became **Mackinac Island State Park** (906/847-3328, www.mackinacparks.com, park 24 hours daily, visitor's center 9am-4pm daily early May-early June and mid-Aug.-early Oct., 9am-6pm daily early June-mid-Aug., free), Michigan's first state park. For more information about the state park, head to the Mackinac Island Visitor's Center, on the south side of Main Street, across from Marquette Park.

SHOPPING

Although shopping isn't a huge activity here, the island does present a few unique browsing options. The **Island Scrimshander** (906/847-3792, www.scrimshanders.com, 9am-4pm daily May-Oct.), for instance, offers amazing engraved trinkets. You should also check out **La Galerie** (906/847-6311, 9am-4pm daily May-Oct.), with its line of Pandora jewelry and Christopher Radko ornaments.

RECREATION

Walk, run, bike, or ride a horse, but make sure you get out of downtown to really see Mackinac Island. You'll be surprised how quickly you can leave any crowds behind as you set out on the paved eight-mile path that circles the island. The trail never wanders far from the pleasant shoreline and passes many of the island's natural features, which are well marked. Traveling clockwise, the first you'll reach is Devil's Kitchen; heading in the opposite direction, you'll arrive first at Arch Rock, the most dramatic of all Mackinac limestone oddities.

About halfway around, on the island's northwestern side lies **British Landing,** where British soldiers sneaked onto the island in 1812. They hiked across Mackinac's interior, totally surprising the American garrison stationed at the fort (and apparently looking the other way), and recaptured the island. Today, the landing is a good spot for a picnic or short break (water and restrooms available). There's a small **nature center** here, staffed in summer months by a helpful naturalist. Hike the short nature trail, which has several interpretive signs as it weaves up a bluff.

British Landing is also a good spot from which to head inland and explore the island's interior. British Landing Road bisects the island and links up with Garrison Road near Skull Cave, leading to the fort. It's a hilly, three-mile trip from shore to shore. British Landing Road is considered a major road by Mackinac standards, meaning you'll share it with carriages. On bike or foot, you'll have endless other options—at last count, Mackinac had some 140 miles of trails and footpaths.

Pick up a free *Mackinac Island Map,* available all over town, and venture off. The map marks the location of old cemeteries, rock formations, and such, but it's even more appealing to just explore the smaller trails on your own and discover pretty, peaceful Mackinac. Everything's well marked, and you can't really get lost anyway—you're on a small island, after all.

ACCOMMODATIONS

Along with the ◖ **Grand Hotel** (286 Grand Ave., 906/847-3331 or 800/334-7263, www.grandhotel.com, $275-805 d), there are plenty of grand and graceful places to stay on Mackinac Island. Yes, rates can be high, but don't dismiss staying on Mackinac; you can find reasonable rates at smaller B&Bs and apartments, the latter of which often have good deals for weeklong stays. The options here tip both ends of the scale.

The venerable **Chippewa Hotel Waterfront** (7221-103 Main St., 906/847-3341 or 866/847-6575, www.chippewahotel.com, $100-575 d) is a classy and comfortable place to stay, with a location in the heart of the island, overlooking the marina. The 24-person lakeside hot

MACKINAC'S MIGRANT VISITORS

While the Straits of Mackinac usually serve as a mighty barrier for many of the mammals that dwell on Mackinac Island, Michigan winters can indeed alter the situation, allowing some of the larger mammals, such as wolves, bears, and deer, to reach the mainland via an ice bridge. So, unlike the isolated isles of warmer climates, this 2,200-acre island is less of a biological vacuum. In fact, many of its seasonal visitors are migrant birds, who use this popular migration spot as a resort habitat in the spring, while en route to summer homes in the north.

Although Mackinac Island also attracts seasonal recreationists, such as hikers and bikers, bird-watchers are especially fond of this enchanted place. In late April and early May, you'll spot golden eagles, bald eagles, red-tailed hawks, and broad-winged hawks flying above. Yellow warblers, American redstarts, and indigo buntings arrive in summer. Along the shoreline, you might also see herrings, cormorants, great blue herons, loons, and Canadian geese. Even wintertime guests will be treated to bird sightings: Beautiful snowy owls and great gray owls often fly south from the Arctic to savor the comparatively warmer climate of Mackinac Island.

Of course, some bird species stay here year-round, including cardinals, blue jays, black-capped chickadees, and large red-crested woodpeckers. The difference between them and many other native inhabitants is that they're here by choice. They can spread their wings and leave at any time – unlike coyotes, for instance, which must wait for an ice bridge to form before making their escape.

tub alone may be worth the stay. Meanwhile, the **Hotel Iroquois** (7485 Main St., 906/847-3321, www.iroquoishotel.com, $215-495 d, suites $395-1,075) offers 46 well-appointed guest rooms and suites, including the two-bedroom Lighthouse Suite, which features spectacular views of Round Island Light. Besides private baths, cable television, and complimentary wireless Internet service, this lovely hotel provides direct access to a private sunbathing beach as well as the Carriage House, one of the island's finest restaurants.

The **Mission Point Resort** (6633 Main St., 906/847-3312 or 800/833-7711, www.missionpoint.com, $149-599 d) may have Mackinac's very best location, spread across 18 acres at the island's southeastern tip. Though not from the Victorian era—it was built in the 1950s by the Moral Rearmament Movement, a post-World War II patriotic group—the sprawling, bright-white resort is attractive and well maintained, with beautiful lawns lined with Adirondack chairs. Amenities include an outdoor pool, tennis and volleyball courts, and loads of children's activities.

From May through October, visitors can opt for a stay at the unique **Jacob Wendell House Bed & Breakfast** (231/818-0334, www.jacobwendellhouse.com, $89-295 d), situated on Main Street, within walking distance of the downtown shopping area and marina. Built in 1846, this picturesque, Federal-style B&B offers four lovely bedrooms, each of which features a full private bath, plus access to a spacious living room, a formal dining room, and a comfortable kitchen.

If you're looking for a more economical place to stay on the island, the year-round **Pontiac Lodge** (1346 Hoban St., 906/847-3364, www.pontiaclodge.com, $65-180 d) features 10 simply furnished rooms as well as three apartments, ideal for families. Conveniently situated near the ferry dock, this comfortable hotel also boasts an on-site eatery, the Village Inn Restaurant.

FOOD

One of the best dining deals on the island is the **Fort Mackinac Tea Room** (906/847-3328, www.grandhotel.com, 11am-3pm daily June-Sept., $8-14), located in the lower level of the Officers' Stone Quarters within the fort.

Surrounded by thick masonry walls, the tea room serves up both a great atmosphere and delicious food, with good soups, salads, and sandwiches prepared by Grand Hotel chefs. Opt for a spot on the terrace since the high setting is outstanding, and forts were not exactly designed for expansive views.

Of course, everyone has to hit the **Pink Pony** (7221-103 Main St., 906/847-3341, www. chippewahotel.com, 8am-1:30am daily, $7-34) at least sometime during a Mackinac visit. Located in the Chippewa Hotel overlooking the marina, this is *the* party place following the famed Chicago-to-Mac yacht race. The food's terrific, too, with various omelets for breakfast, yummy salads and sandwiches on the lunch menu, and steaks, seafood, and ribs for dinner.

Another tasty downtown option is **The Yankee Rebel Tavern** (1493 Astor St., 906/847-6249, www.yankeerebeltavern.com, 10:30am-midnight daily, $14-32), which serves American-style comfort food, from traditional pot roast to pistachio-encrusted whitefish. Named after the famous underdog horse from 1938, the nearby **Seabiscuit Café** (906/847-3611, www.seabiscuitcafe.com, 10am-2am daily Apr.-Oct., $10-22) prepares some colorfully named appetizers, such as the Painted Pony Macaroni or the War Admiral Hot Wings, plus various salads, sandwiches, and heartier meals, ranging from curry chicken to baby back ribs.

Sooner or later, however, you'll succumb to fudge, a visitor treat since Victorian tourism days. In fact, fudge shops pepper the downtown shopping area. One of the oldest, **Murdick's Fudge** (7363 Main St., 906/847-3530, www. originalmurdicksfudge.com), established in 1887, has a prime Main Street location, where you can buy a sizable slab to take or mail home, or just a small sliver to nibble during your downtown stroll. After all, a little bit goes a long way.

INFORMATION AND SERVICES

For more information about Mackinac Island, contact the helpful **Mackinac Island Tourism Bureau** (7274 Main St., 877/847-0086, www. mackinacisland.org, 9am-5pm daily), which is located across from the Arnold Transit ferry dock. For further information, consult www. mackinac.com or pick up a copy of the weekly *Mackinac Island Town Crier* (www.mackinacislandnews.com).

Mackinac Island offers a limited amount of services, including a couple of groceries, one post office, and a small police department. For banking needs, stop by the **Central Savings Bank** (21 Hoban St., 906/847-3759, www. centralsavingsbank.com). In case of a medical emergency, dial **911** from any phone or consult the **Mackinac Island Medical Center** (906/847-3582, www.mackinacstraitshealth.org), which offers an on-call staff 24 hours daily.

GETTING THERE AND AROUND
Getting There

More than a million people visit Mackinac Island every year, so getting here isn't a problem. One option is to fly into **Pellston Regional Airport** (PLN, 1395 US-31, Pellston, 231/539-8441 or 231/539-8442, www.pellstonairport. com), then either charter a flight to the island through **Great Lakes Air, Inc.** (906/643-7165, www.greatlakesair.net, one-way $28 adults, $14 children 4-12, children under 4 free) or use the **Mackinaw Shuttle** (231/539-7005 or 888/349-8294, www.mackinawshuttle.com) to reach the ferry docks in Mackinaw City or St. Ignace. If you're coming from somewhere else in Michigan, you can also reach the ferry docks by private vehicle.

No matter what, though, you'll find that there are in fact three ferry services that can zip you across the Straits of Mackinac in less than 20 minutes: the **Arnold Transit Co.** (906/847-3351 or 800/542-8528, www.arnoldline.com, round-trip $23 adults, $12 children 5-12, children under 5 free, $8 bikes), **Shepler's Mackinac Island Ferry** (231/436-5023, 906/643-9440, or 800/828-6157, www. sheplersferry.com, late Apr.-Oct., round-trip $25 adults, $13 children 5-12, children under 5 free, $8 bikes), and **Star Line** (800/638-9892,

biking on Mackinac Island

www.mackinacferry.com, round-trip $25 adults, $13 children 5-12, children under 5 free, $8 bikes).

During the main tourist season—May-October—they operate several times daily. Only one, the longstanding Arnold Transit, in operation since 1878, offers service November-April (from St. Ignace only). Since much of the island shuts down for the winter, you'll find it a little more challenging to reach Mackinac between December and March.

No matter which ferry you choose, it will deposit you at the southern end of the island, in the heart of the hotels and shops lining Main Street, which follows the curve of the waterfront. It's a wild scene: Dock workers load luggage onto pull-carts and carriages, flocks of bikers dodge horse-drawn buggies, and pedestrians stream up and down the road eating fudge and window-shopping.

Getting Around

Navigating Mackinac Island isn't tough, though you'll have to do it without a motorized vehicle. Cars, after all, aren't allowed on the island. Instead, you can rely on horse-drawn "taxis," which are available from **Mackinac Island Carriage Tours** (906/847-3323 or 906/847-3307, www.mict.com, $4.75-7.25 pp) 24 hours daily during the summer months; November-April, such services are available by appointment. If you enjoy walking and hiking, however, you can easily traverse Mackinac on foot; in fact, it's a wonderfully scenic place for casual strolls and all-day hikes.

The island is also a terrific locale for biking. Bike rentals are available all over downtown; the **Mackinac Island Bike Shop** (906/847-6337, www.bikemackinac.com), for instance, rents mountain bikes, cruisers, tandems, and tag-a-longs for $7-12 hourly or $30-70 daily. All bikes are available in men's and women's styles, and kids' bikes are available, too. It's also possible to rent pet carriers, strollers, and wheelchairs. Equipment varies greatly, though, so look before you pay. Of course, if you plan to do much biking, you'll likely be happier with your own bike, since you can transport it on the ferry. Just remember that you'll want a hybrid or mountain bike to negotiate most interior trails, and be sure to bring your own helmet.

Cheboygan and Vicinity

With a population of 4,800, Cheboygan ranks as one of the largest cities along Lake Huron. While the town offers history buffs a few interesting sites, including a 19th-century opera house, it mainly appeals to outdoor enthusiasts, who venture beyond the city limits to explore surrounding lakes, rivers, and forests. Boaters and anglers especially focus their gaze inland, where a 45-mile-long waterway links Lake Huron with several large inland lakes, ending just shy of Lake Michigan's Little Traverse Bay. Cheboygan sits at the mouth of this popular waterway, welcoming boaters with open arms. Hikers, bird-watchers, and other lovers of the outdoors will find plenty to interest them here, too.

SIGHTS
Historic Sites and Lighthouses

The **Cheboygan History Center** (427 Court St., 231/627-9597, www.cheboyganhistorycenter.org, 1pm-4pm Tues.-Sat. Memorial Day-Sept., $2 pp) was built in 1882 and served as the county jail and local sheriff's home until 1969. The two-story brick structure houses a parlor, kitchen, schoolroom, and bedroom in period style, with an adjacent building that contains logging and marine displays.

The city's **Opera House** (403 N. Huron, 231/627-5841, www.theoperahouse.org, 10am-4pm daily, $2) once entertained the likes of Mary Pickford and Annie Oakley. Built in 1877 and later rebuilt after an 1888 fire, the Victorian-style theater serves as a stage for local entertainment and is open for tours in summer.

From the boardwalk in **Gordon Turner Park** at the northern end of Huron Street, you can gaze out over one of the largest cattail marshes in the Great Lakes. A nesting ground for more than 50 species, it's a favorite of bird-watchers. From the boardwalk and nearby fisherman's walkway, you also can see the Mackinac Bridge as well as Round and Bois Blanc Islands. Visitors might also appreciate the quaint 1884

Cheboygan Crib Light, an octagonal structure that, when deactivated, was relocated from the mouth of the Cheboygan River to the base of the west breakwater on Lake Huron. Now, the pretty white-and-red lighthouse is an ideal stop for photographers.

Parks and Preserves

Cheboygan's **Grass Bay Preserve** contains a rare find in the Great Lakes—one of the finest examples of an original interdunal wetland habitat, characterized by beach pools, marshes, flats, and wetlands, all separated by low dunes. Owned by The Nature Conservancy, this delicate ecosystem comprises a great diversity of plants, including more than 25 species of orchids and 11 types of conifers. Four of the species—dwarf lake iris, Lake Huron tansy, Pitcher's thistle, and Houghton's goldenrod—grow only on the Lake Huron and Lake Michigan shores.

The Nature Conservancy considers Grass Bay its best property in Michigan. The preserve's original 80 acres have grown to more than 830, including a one-mile stretch of Lake Huron shore. From May to September, Grass Bay is noted for its carpet of wildflowers, including lady's slipper, Indian paintbrush, blue harebell, and sundews. The best way to take them all in is from one of the park's two short trails, which wander through an aspen/birch forest and across old shoreline ridges to the beach. Note, however, that this is private—and very fragile—land. Parking can be hard to find, too—most visitors use lots on US-23 (ask first). For more information, contact **The Nature Conservancy** (517/316-0300, www.nature.org)

RECREATION

For hikers and cross-country skiers, the **Wildwood Hills Pathway** on Wildwood Road in nearby Indian River offers almost complete isolation. Three well-marked trails—ranging

4-9 miles in length—take visitors deep into the heart of a northern Michigan second-growth forest and cross high, rolling hills in the Mackinac State Forest just a few miles south of Burt Lake.

Two trailheads on Wildwood Road provide access to the pathway, leading into a dense forest of hardwoods and evergreens. Along the way, the only companion you'll likely have is the wind through the trees, an occasional bird-call, and a curious chipmunk or two. Trail system maps are located at the trailheads and most major intersections.

The swift and turbulent Pigeon River, designated by the state as a natural river, is the highlight of the **Agnes S. Andreae Nature Preserve.** Located in Indian River, the beautifully secluded 27-acre preserve includes 2,000 feet of Pigeon River frontage. On the river's west side, a lowland stand of cedar bordering the riverbank rises to high bluffs covered with conifers and dense hardwoods. There are no designated trails, but hikers and cross-country skiers find well-worn tracks to follow and other trails that border the river. Like many other tracts in this undeveloped part of the state, the preserve is owned by the **Little Traverse Conservancy** (3264 Powell Rd., Harbor Springs, 231/347-0991, www.landtrust.org).

ACCOMMODATIONS AND FOOD

There are several decent motels in the Cheboygan area, such as the **Best Western River Terrace Motel** (847 S. Main St., 231/627-5688, www.bestwesternmichigan.com, $143-169 d), with most rooms overlooking the Cheboygan River. You can also camp at **Cheboygan State Park** (4490 Beach Rd., 616/627-2811, annual $11 Recreation Passport for Michigan residents or $8.40 day-use fee/$30.50 yearly Recreation Passport for non-residents required), at one of 78 modern sites ($12-27 daily) along Lake Huron's Duncan Bay. The area is a favorite among anglers, but there's not much in the way of swimming at the campground; instead, head for the park's

day-use area, four miles away, which has a sandy beach and bathhouse.

For good food served up with interesting history, try the **Hack-Ma-Tack Inn & Restaurant** (8131 Beebe Rd., 231/625-2919, www.hackmatackinn.com, 5pm-10pm daily May-mid-Oct., $18-50), housed in a rustic 1894 lodge overlooking the Cheboygan River. Whitefish is the specialty.

INFORMATION AND SERVICES

For more information about Cheboygan, contact the **Cheboygan Area Chamber of Commerce** (124 N. Main St., 231/627-7183, www.cheboygan.com, 9am-5pm Mon.-Fri.). For local news and events, consult the **Cheboygan Daily Tribune** (www.cheboygannews.com).

Cheboygan offers most of the services that travelers might require. Here, you'll find groceries, banks, even a **post office** (200 N. Main St., 231/627-9898, www.usps.com). In case of a police-related or medical emergency, dial **911** from any phone. For medical assistance, visit the **Cheboygan Memorial Hospital** (748 S. Main St., 231/627-5601, www.cheboygan-hospital.org).

GETTING THERE AND AROUND

From **Pellston Regional Airport** (PLN, 1395 US-31, Pellston, 231/539-8441 or 231/539-8442, www.pellstonairport.com), you can rent a car, head north on US-31, and take CR-66 east to Cheboygan. Without traffic, the 20-mile trip should take about 24 minutes. As an alternative, you can take a bus directly to Cheboygan (309 E. State St.) via **Greyhound** (800/231-2222, www.greyhound.com) or **Indian Trails** (800/292-3831, www.indiantrails.com).

Of course, if you're already traversing Michigan by car, you can reach Cheboygan via several convenient routes, including M-27, M-33, or US-23. From Sault Ste. Marie, for instance, simply merge onto I-75 South, cross the

Mackinac Bridge (for which you'll have to pay a toll), and continue onto US-23 South to downtown Cheboygan, a 74-mile trip that usually takes about 80 minutes. From Traverse City, meanwhile, you can take M-72 East to US-131 North, continue onto CR-42 and M-32 East, merge onto I-75 North, and follow Levering Road to Cheboygan, a 114-mile trip that normally takes about two hours. Even downtown Detroit is only four hours away; simply follow I-375 North to I-75 North, continue north for 275 miles, and take Levering Road to Cheboygan—a journey that, in all, will cover about 284 miles. Then, once in Cheboygan, you can easily get around via car, bike, or foot.

THE INLAND WATERWAY

The geography of this region was kind to the early Indians and French voyageurs traversing the Lower Peninsula: A chain of lakes and rivers forms a 45-mile water route, very nearly linking Lakes Michigan and Huron. The route was safer and faster than traveling on the big lakes, and certainly beat the heck out of portaging. Today, the inland waterway remains extremely popular, mostly for fishing and recreational boating. Narrower portions are dredged to a depth of five feet and a width of 30 feet. Boats up to 30 feet long can join in on what sometimes looks like a nautical parade.

Burt Lake State Park

Big Burt Lake is the focus of its namesake **state park** (6635 State Dr., Indian River, 231/238-9392, annual $11 Recreation Passport for Michigan residents or $8.40 day-use fee/$30.50 yearly Recreation Passport for nonresidents required), located at the lake's southern end. Anglers flock to this 10-mile-long lake, known as one of the best fisheries in the state for walleye, panfish, and bass—but especially walleye. Swimmers seek it out, too, since a soft sand beach runs the entire length of the park. The park has two boat launches, one located next to

a popular campground with 375 modern sites ($22 daily). The park offers little in the way of hiking, but does have a nifty observation tower that gives you a great view of the lake.

Mullett Lake

Popular with anglers, Mullett Lake also has a lesser-known claim to fame: the origin of the term *kemosabe,* used by Tonto in *The Lone Ranger.* Yep, it's true—according to the diehard research of Cecil Adams, anyway, who authors "The Straight Dope," a quirky factfinding column that began in the *Chicago Reader* and has appeared in alternative weeklies around the country.

Adams's research revealed that the word *kemosabe* appears to have originated with Jim Jewell, a director for *The Lone Ranger.* Jewell had stated in an interview that he took the term from Kamp Kee-Mo-Sah-Bee, a boys' camp in Mackinac, Michigan. According to Jewell, *kee-mo-sah-bee* translates to "trusty scout."

Speaking of name mysteries, no one really knows why a small town on the east end of Mullett Lake was originally named Aloha Depot. Today, it's the site of **Aloha State Park** (231/625-2522, annual $11 Recreation Passport for Michigan residents or $8.40 day-use fee/$30.50 yearly Recreation Passport for nonresidents required), a small 100-acre state park that primarily consists of a boat launch and 295-site campground ($14 daily). Not particularly picturesque by Michigan standards, most sites sit in a relatively open setting, with just a handful directly on the water.

Along with neighboring Burt Lake, pretty Mullett Lake is one of the most popular and productive fishing lakes in the state. Anglers vie for walleye and northern pike, but larger stuff lurks down there as well: In 1974, Mullett produced a 193-pound sturgeon, a scaly, longnosed creature that hasn't evolved much since prehistoric times. Think about that while you're taking a dip.

Rogers City to Alpena

Driving along the picturesque Lake Huron shore, you'll encounter several slow-moving communities, including Rogers City, home to lovely lighthouses, parks, and beaches, and Alpena, a larger city favored by outdoor enthusiasts for its wildlife sanctuary and underwater preserve.

Despite its beautiful beaches, few travelers visit Rogers City, a quiet town of about 2,800, better known as home to the world's largest limestone quarry. The Huron shore's limestone was formed by ancient seas that once covered most of the state. Full of coral-forming organisms, they eventually created large limestone deposits, one of which nears the earth's surface in Rogers City. In 1907, tests found that the limestone was unusually pure, ideal for making steel and many chemicals. The Michigan Limestone and Chemical Company was formed a year later, and subsequently purchased by U.S. Steel. Nearly four miles long and roughly three miles wide, the quarry is expected to produce well into the 21st century.

Alpena, protected by the deep curve of Thunder Bay, is the largest city north of Bay City on the Lake Huron shore, yet has always been tinged by a lack of respect. When surveyed in 1839, a deed to the land was offered to anyone in the survey party in lieu of summer wages, but few took the offer. At the time, the area was considered mostly a desolate cedar swamp.

Not long after, however, the intrepid Daniel Carter arrived with his wife and young daughter and built a log cabin, becoming the town's first white settler. By 1857, a store and boardinghouse had popped up, and in 1859, Alpena became the site of the county's first steam-powered sawmill. Before long, some 20 lumber and shingle mills buzzed life into the growing town.

Today, the town's economy relies on a large cement industry. But for visitors, it also offers the chance to enjoy the natural beauty of the Great Lakes without the trendy development and gentrification that have taken over so many of the old resort towns on the opposite side of the state.

Part of the reason visitors have overlooked Alpena is because it's not that easy to reach. More than 70 miles from the nearest interstate, it remains an unpretentious working-class town of corner bars and friendly residents. For decades, diversified industries, including paper mills, cement plants, and an Air Force base, meant that the area didn't have to seek out the tourist trade the way other areas have.

But with its bread-and-butter industries gone, Alpena has learned to promote its assets. And there's plenty worth promoting, including two lightly visited state parks with several miles of Lake Huron shoreline, a handsome marina, an impressive museum, northern Michigan's only year-round professional theater, and a fascinating underwater preserve with more than 80 shipwrecks.

SIGHTS
Besser Museum for Northeast Michigan

The excellent **Besser Museum for Northeast Michigan** (491 Johnson St., Alpena, 989/356-2202, www.bessermuseum.org, 10am-5pm daily, $5 adults, $3 children) combines art, history, and science on two levels. The museum's highlight is the "Gallery of Early Man," a collection of Great Lakes Native American artifacts considered one of the finest in the country. To the probable dismay of archaeologists, the collection, which numbers more than 60,000 pieces, was gathered by Gerald Haltiner, a local state highway worker, and his museum-curator son, Robert.

The museum purchased the collection from the Haltiners in the 1970s and is working closely with local Native American tribes to review the collection with repatriation in mind. Some of its most intriguing artifacts are the copper items that date back more than 7,000

© DANIEL MARTONE

Alpena's Besser Museum for Northeast Michigan

years, made by a people known only as the Copper Culture. The museum's Sky Theater Planetarium puts on changing shows, many with Native American themes, throughout the year.

Alpena Wildlife Sanctuary

Alpena Wildlife Sanctuary (Wildlife Sanctuary Board, 989/595-3919 or 989/354-1770, www.alpena.mi.us), on US-23 within the Alpena city limits, has been a favorite sanctuary of hikers, paddlers, anglers, and nature lovers since it was established in 1938 by the Michigan Conservation Department. The 500-acre refuge bordering the Thunder Bay River contains a large expanse of wetlands, an island with fishing platforms, and a viewing platform that overlooks the river. According to the Thunder Bay Audubon Society, more than 130 different species of birds have been spotted here. Year-round residents include Canada geese and mute swans; spring migration brings others, including buffleheads, canvasbacks, whistling swans, and more.

Lighthouses

Travelers who find the Huron shore lacking in comparison with the state's Lake Michigan shore change their minds after a visit to the **40 Mile Point Lighthouse.** Seven miles north of Rogers City on US-23, a limitless expanse of blue water sweeps in a 180-degree arc to the horizon. A gently sloping beach proves just right for wading, sandcastle building, and swimming. The 52-foot-tall lighthouse, built in 1897, stands guard as a reminder that Huron can, and does, turn dangerous. Though not open to the public, it is a favorite of photographers.

Other lighthouses along this stretch include the 1905 **Middle Island Lighthouse** and the 1832 **Thunder Bay Island Light,** both accessible via boat. In Alpena, you won't need a vessel to view the 1914 **Alpena Light,** a skeletal red structure near the Thunder Bay River.

Beaches and Parks

Many rate **P. H. Hoeft State Park** (US-23 N, Rogers City, 989/734-2543, annual $11

© DANIEL MARTONE

the 40 Mile Point Lighthouse near Rogers City

Recreation Passport for Michigan residents or $8.40 day-use fee/$30.50 yearly Recreation Passport for nonresidents required) as the most beautiful state park along Michigan's Lake Huron shore. It's easy to see why. With a mile-long swath of soft, white sand, low rolling dunes, and a mixed hardwood/conifer forest, it offers a breathtaking, simple beauty. Surprisingly, it's also one of the least visited state parks in the Lower Peninsula. Even the 144-site modern campground ($22 daily), set against mature pines and hardwoods with lots of shade and privacy, sits half empty most of the time. Head directly for sites 1-33, located just a few steps from the beach. One cabin and four rent-a-tents are also available.

Behind the park's picnic area lies an almost totally undeveloped area, with dunes and woods that abound in wildlife and vegetation. Naturalists can search for the more than 40 species of wildflowers that grow here, including many orchids and irises rare in the state and North America. More than four miles of trails loop through the area for hikers and cross-country skiers.

From Rogers City, it's just 11 miles west on M-68 to the Lower Peninsula's only major waterfall. **Ocqueoc (Sacred Water) Falls** cascades over a series of two- to six-foot drops. The picturesque site is a favorite of picnickers, sunbathers, and swimmers. A seven-mile trail for hikers and cross-country skiers starts next to the falls.

Just a few hundred yards away, the **Bicentennial Pathway** (created in 1976) loops through the deep woods and over the gently rolling hills of the Mackinaw State Forest. The pathway's three loops measure 3, 4, and 6.5 miles and are well used by area hikers. Bed down at the **Ocqueoc Falls State Forest Campground,** across M-68.

Just north of Rogers City on US-23, **Seagull Point Park** (193 E. Michigan Ave.) draws visitors to its beautiful beach, curved like a scimitar. A wide band of soft sand and a gradual slope into Lake Huron create a perfect spot for beachcombers, sunbathers, and families. Behind the beach, a two-mile interpretive trail winds through a series of low dunes, with signs along the route that identify the area's natural history and accompanying flora and fauna. Near the park, the **Herman Vogler Conservation Area** (240 W. Erie St., Rogers City, 989/734-4000) provides a quiet, car-free area on the Trout River. Five miles of nature trails are open to cross-country skiing in the winter.

Negwegon State Park (Ossineke, 989/724-5126, annual $11 Recreation Passport for Michigan residents or $8.40 day-use fee/$30.50 yearly Recreation Passport for nonresidents required) is the carefully guarded secret of a number of outdoor lovers. What exactly are they hiding? Some of the most beautiful and most isolated beaches on Lake Huron. The 2,469-acre park's shoreline stretches for more than six miles, a lovely string of bays and coves.

Named after Chippewa chief Negwegon, the park also offers three hiking trails named after Native American tribes: the Algonquin, Chippewa, and Potawatomi. The 10 miles of trails skirt the shoreline and loop through a heavily wooded interior. A serene retreat, this isolated park offers natural beauty to hikers and backpackers willing to trade conveniences for quiet, contemplative walks along 8 miles of Lake Huron shoreline. Note: There are no camping or picnic facilities here.

Between this park and the considerably smaller **Harrisville State Park** (248 State Park Rd., Harrisville, 989/724-5126, annual $11 Recreation Passport for Michigan residents or $8.40 day-use fee/$30.50 yearly Recreation Passport for nonresidents required) is one of several lighthouses along the Lake Huron shore. The gleaming white **Sturgeon Point Lighthouse** (989/727-4703, www.alconahistoricalsociety.com, 11am-4pm Fri.-Sat. Memorial Day-Sept., free), built in 1869, is still active today—as both a lighthouse and a maritime museum. The grounds are open to the public year-round.

◖ DIVING IN THUNDER BAY

Divers have their own sanctuary just off the Alpena shore. Here, the **Thunder Bay National Marine Sanctuary and Underwater Preserve** thrills divers with its clear waters, interesting underwater limestone formations, and shipwrecks. Rocky islands and hazardous shoals proved treacherous for mariners; the preserve protects some 80 shipwrecks, 14 of which can be explored with the help of a wreck-diving charter. Among the most popular are the *Nordmeer,* a German steel steamer that sank in 1966, and the *Montana,* a 235-foot steamer that burned and sank in 1914. **Thunder Bay Scuba** (413 S. Ripley Blvd., Alpena, 989/356-6228, www.tbscuba.com, 9am-5:30pm Mon.-Fri., 10am-2pm Sat.-Sun.) offers charter diving services for about $44 per day, departing from Alpena's city marina.

The state established the Thunder Bay National Marine Sanctuary and Underwater Preserve—more than 288 protected miles in all—in 1981, largely to prohibit divers from removing artifacts from the site. In October 2000, the state preserve was also designated a national marine sanctuary, a status that grants it federal funding and additional resources for scientific and archaeological study. For more information, contact the **Michigan Underwater Preserve Council** (800/970-8717, www.michiganpreserves.org).

ACCOMMODATIONS AND FOOD

Lodging choices are pretty limited in Rogers City. The best place in town (and the only place with an indoor pool) is the 43-room **Driftwood Motel** (540 W. 3rd St., 989/734-4777, $49-99 d), which overlooks Lake Huron. Adjacent to the motel, the **Waters Edge Restaurant** (530 N. 3rd St., 989/734-4747, 11am-10pm daily, $9-23) serves up Lake Huron views and fish dishes.

Hotels and restaurants in Alpena have a funky, nostalgic vibe, as if you've been transported back to the 1950s or 1960s. Chief among them are the **40 Winks Motel** (1021 S. State Ave., 989/354-5622, www.40winksmotel.com, $49-69 d), with simple rooms opposite Lake Huron.

NORTHEAST MICHIGAN

OMER IN THE NEWS

Located along the Sunrise Side Coastal Highway (US-23), Omer is one of the tiniest towns in Michigan. In fact, a sign posted at the city limit even claims that it's "Michigan's smallest city." Founded as a logging town in the mid-1860s and originally called Rifle River Mills, the town was renamed by the first postmaster, who wanted to call it Homer. When, however, he discovered that Michigan already had a town named Homer — southeast of Marshall — he dropped the "H," and the town of Omer was incorporated as a city in the early 20th century.

With a current population of just over 300, Omer has little to recommend it to travelers — except, perhaps, its proximity to the Rifle River. Still, the town is curious for at least one other reason. It was near here that, in August 1998, Timothy Joseph Boomer, a 24-year-old engineer, was canoeing with friends when he fell into the water and began yelling a long string of expletives in the presence of a man, his wife, and their two young children. A sheriff's deputy, who heard the shouts downstream, ticketed Boomer for violating an 1897 law that claimed anyone using immoral or obscene language within earshot of a woman or child could be charged with a misdemeanor. An Arenac County jury found Boomer guilty of the charge, and though a district judge ruled the ban on cursing in front of women unconstitutional, he left intact the provision concerning children. Boomer was fined $75 and ordered to work in a child-care program, but the sentence was postponed during the appeals process.

The case of the "cussing canoeist" sparked a nationwide debate about free speech and public behavior. While some protested the vague nature of the law — which could leave the question of what constitutes "indecent" language up for interpretation — others defended the need to regulate improper conduct, especially in front of children. Needless to say, the American Civil Liberties Union (ACLU) was only too quick to handle the case, and in 2002, the Michigan Court of Appeals successfully overturned the 105-year-old law. Afterward, the "cussing canoeist," who had initially admitted to using only a few choice words (not the alleged string of them), decided to be more careful about what he said in public.

INFORMATION AND SERVICES

For more information about this area, contact the **Rogers City Chamber of Commerce** (292 S. Bradley Hwy., Rogers City, 989/734-2535, www.rogerscity.com) or the **Alpena Area Convention & Visitors Bureau** (235 W. Chisholm St., Alpena, 800/425-7362, www.alpenacvb.com). For local news, consult the *Presque Isle County Advance* (www.piadvance.com) or the *Alpena News* (www.thealpenanews.com).

Between Rogers City and Alpena, you're likely to find the services you need, from groceries and pharmacies to banks and post offices. In case of a medical emergency, dial **911** from any phone or consult **Alpena Regional Medical Center** (1501 W. Chisholm St.,

Alpena, 989/356-7000, www.alpenaregionalmedicalcenter.org).

GETTING THERE AND AROUND

To reach Alpena, some travelers may choose to fly; luckily, Delta Air Lines offers commuter service to the **Alpena County Regional Airport** (APN, 1617 Airport Rd., Alpena, 989/354-2907, www.alpenaairport.com), where you can either hail a cab or rent a car. From there, you can then drive (or be driven) to Rogers City by taking M-32 West, M-65 North, and US-23 North to West Erie Street, a 37-mile trip that will usually take about 44 minutes. As an alternative, you can ride a bus to this part of northeastern Michigan; after all, both **Greyhound** (989/734-4903 or 800/231-2222, www.greyhound.com) and **Indian Trails**

(800/292-3831, www.indiantrails.com) provide service to Rogers City (285 S. Bradley) as well as Alpena (1141 N. US-23).

Of course, it's probably easier (and cheaper) to reach this area via car. From I-75, take M-68 to Rogers City or M-32 to Alpena. Both towns can also be accessed via US-23 along the coast. To get an idea of how long it might take to reach this area, consider the trip between Sault Ste. Marie and Rogers City: From the Soo, you'll take I-75 South, cross the Mackinac Bridge (a toll bridge), merge onto US-23 South, and continue on the Sunrise Side Coastal Highway (US-23) to Rogers City, a 115-mile trip that typically takes about two hours. From Traverse City, meanwhile, you can take M-72 East to M-66 North/US-131 North, continue onto Mancelona Road and Old State Road, follow Meridian Line Road for 4 miles, and then take M-32 East to Alpena, a 128-mile trip that will usually take 2.5 hours. You can also access this area from downtown Detroit by taking I-375 North to I-75 North, merging onto US-23 North, and following the Sunrise Side Coastal Highway to Alpena; without traffic, the 243-mile trip should take less than four hours. No matter how you reach these two coastal towns, though, you can easily get around via car, bike, or foot.

PRESQUE ISLE

It would be easy to pass the Presque Isle peninsula and never know it was there. Easy, but a mistake. This almost completely undiscovered resort area off the beaten path between Rogers City and Alpena features two of the jewels in the region's crown. Both are well worth driving out of the way to see.

On a map, the peninsula looks like a beckoning finger (*presqu'île* means "peninsula"—"almost an island"—in French). Two classic lighthouses perch at the tip of the strangely shaped peninsula, including the tallest lighthouse on the Great Lakes.

Inside the **Old Presque Isle Lighthouse complex** (5295 E. Grand Lake Rd., 989/595-6979 or 989/595-5419, www.presqueislelighthouses.org, 9am-6pm daily May-Oct., free),

which consists of a light tower and a nearby keeper's dwelling, exhibits and displays relate the history of Great Lakes shipping and light keeping. Artifacts and antiques that range from wooden doors from a shipwreck to an old pump organ that visitors can play. Built in 1840, the lighthouse was used for 30 years until it was replaced by a new light a mile north. But no automatic light can provide the view you'll get from the parapet surrounding the lantern room, reached by a trip up the two-story tower's winding steps.

The **New Presque Isle Lighthouse and Museum** (4500 E. Grand Lake Rd., 989/595-5419 or 989/595-9917, www.presqueislelighthouses.org, 9am-6pm daily May-Oct., free) dates to 1870. Trees had grown to obscure the older, shorter lighthouse; the "new" one stretches to 113 feet, the tallest on all the Great Lakes. Situated in the middle of 100-acre **Presque Isle Lighthouse Park,** the tower and restored light keeper's house look much as they did more than a century ago. Inside, a caretaker—a descendant of generations of

the New Presque Isle Lighthouse and Museum

© DANIEL MARTONE

Great Lakes sailors—plays the part of a turn-of-the-20th-century light keeper on special occasions.

The park's fine nature trails begin at the lighthouse and circle the peninsula's tip. The trails border rugged shoreline, then weave in and out of evergreens and hardwoods, before reaching the peninsula's tip and a sweeping view of Lake Huron from a rocky beach.

Besser Natural Area, now part of **Rockport State Recreation Area** (annual $11 Recreation Passport for Michigan residents or $8.40 day use fee/$30.50 yearly Recreation Passport for nonresidents required), offers an intriguing mix of attractions: nearly a mile of wild, undeveloped Lake Huron shoreline, a ghost town, a sunken ship, and one of the few remaining stands of virgin white pine left in the state.

Reach the 134-acre preserve by taking Grand Lake Road six miles southeast of Presque Isle. For more information, contact **Harrisville State Park** (989/724-5126).

The boom-and-bust logging industry both created and destroyed the ghost town of Bell, which once included a school, a sawmill, a store, a saloon, and several houses during the 1880s. A one-mile self-guided trail leads through a magnificent stand of virgin white pine and passes the ghost town and a tiny inland lagoon, the graveyard for an unnamed small vessel. Halfway along the trail, a plaque honors Jesse Besser, who donated this land to the state in 1966 as a memorial to Michigan's lumbermen. The trail continues through a dark cedar forest before emerging on Lake Huron's shore.

Oscoda to West Branch

Farther along the Lake Huron shore, several towns serve as gateways to incredible outdoor delights, including Oscoda, popular among canoeists, and Tawas City, a favorite among bird-watchers.

Oscoda sits at the mouth of the Au Sable River, famed as a trout stream and navigable by canoe as far as Grayling and Roscommon. The waterway played a prominent part in the state's early pine-logging days. At its most populous, the city's population numbered more than 23,000, and the river was filled with pine logs on their way to the sawmills. While the logs were plentiful, Oscoda grew unchecked. With the depletion of the resource, though, its population began to shrink. Finally, nature put an abrupt end to the city's logging boom: A forest fire swept through in 1911, reducing the city's heyday to ashes. The current population is roughly 900.

As for Tawas City, its name derives from Otawas, the name of an important Chippewa chief. He's honored in this stretch of Lake Huron shore many times over. The twin cities of Tawas City and East Tawas straddle the

Tawas River, which empties into Tawas Bay, formed by a crooked finger of land called—you guessed it—Tawas Point.

Today, local festivals, such as February's Perchville U.S.A., reveal the area's popularity with anglers. Visitors can watch the boat-filled bay in Tawas Point State Park, which occupies the fishhook-shaped Tawas Point. It's a favorite of naturalists, as much for the ever-changing landscape created by wind and waves during annual winter storms as for some of the best bird-watching in the state.

West of Tawas City, West Branch is a small town with quaint Victorian-style architecture, a downtown shopping district, and an outlet mall. It's also not far from a popular recreation area, the Huron National Forest, and the road to Houghton and Higgins Lakes.

SIGHTS
Beaches and Parks
Opposite the large beach on the shore of Tawas Bay, part of 183-acre **Tawas Point State Park** (686 Tawas Beach Rd., East Tawas, 989/362-5041, daily, annual $11 Recreation Passport for

Michigan residents or $8.40 day-use fee/$30.50 yearly Recreation Passport for nonresidents required), the white Victorian-style 1876 **Tawas Point Lighthouse** is undoubtedly the park's most-photographed feature and a favorite among lovers of these classic lights. One of the state's most well-maintained lighthouses, it is often open to the public for self-guided tours. Not far away, bird-watchers gather at the day-use area and nature trail. A checklist of birds spotted in the park lists more than 250, with 31 species of warblers and 17 species of waterfowl.

In summer, swimmers favor this park for its white sand and warm, shallow waters. Anglers and hikers appreciate Tawas Point, too. Here, you'll also find a playground, a picnic area, public restrooms, a spacious campground, and gorgeous sunsets.

From the state park, history buffs can take a self-guided 68-mile driving tour amid key historical, natural, and cultural features west of the park, including the site of a 1984 forest fire, a 1,000-acre marsh that nurtures deer and other wildlife, the 1917 Foote Dam, a former Air Force base, and the Lumberman's Monument, a bronze statue erected in 1931 on the high scenic banks of the Au Sable River. Dedicated to the pioneer spirit and efforts of Michigan lumbermen, the monument isn't far from a visitors center, whose exhibits relate to Michigan's logging era. For more information, pick up brochures at the park office. Here, you can also learn more about the **Highbanks Trail,** a seven-mile, ungroomed route about 14 miles west of Oscoda that traces the bluffs along the southern shore of the Au Sable River and offers scenic views of the popular canoeing waterway and surrounding wildlife. This hiking trail, which is free to utilize and favored by cross-country skiers in winter also provides access to sites like the 14-foot-tall Lumberman's Monument and the Canoer's Memorial, which was erected in 1950 to honor marathon canoe racing.

Rifle River Recreation Area

Inner tubes seem to be the transportation option of choice on the slower-moving Rifle River, which meanders from the **Rifle River Recreation Area** (2550 E. Rose City Rd., Lupton, 989/473-2258, annual $11 Recreation Passport for Michigan residents or $8.40 day use fee/$30.50 yearly Recreation Passport for nonresidents required), about 15 miles northeast of West Branch, to Saginaw Bay, some 90 miles south. Paddlers shouldn't overlook the Rifle, though, since it flows through Devoe Lake, one of five paddle-only lakes in this spacious preserve.

The 4,449 acres that now make up the Rifle River Recreation Area were once part of the private hunting preserve of H. M. Jewett, an early auto-industry tycoon. Today, most of the visitors who are hoping to leave with a catch are bagging bass and other varieties of fish, not four-legged game.

The recreation area includes several miles of paved and packed-dirt trails that travel across one-lane bridges, past forest-fringed lakes, and up several high hills that reveal vistas of tangled stands of cedar. For a great view, head for **Ridge Road,** a dirt track that passes over the park's highest elevations. Those who like to hike can follow 14 miles of picturesque trails that cut through some of the park's most breathtaking terrain.

Visitors can stay at a choice of on-site accommodations, including both rustic and modern campsites as well as five "frontier-style" cabins, all located in secluded areas far from campgrounds and day-trippers. The cabins have vault toilets, hand pumps, and only basic furnishings. In winter, the park is a popular spot for cross-country skiing, ice fishing, and snowmobiling.

SHOPPING

Needless to say, shopping isn't why most people come to the southern reaches of Northeast Michigan. But not all the attractions in this area are of the natural kind. In a seemingly unlikely place, the **Tanger Outlets Center** (2990 Cook Rd., West Branch, 989/345-2594, www.tangeroutlet.com, 9am-9pm Mon.-Sat., 10am-7pm Sun.) offers an enormous variety of mainstream shopping choices, everything from a Gap Outlet to a Bath & Body Works store. The outlet mall lies east of I-75.

CANOEING ON THE AU SABLE RIVER

While anglers often try their luck on the Au Sable, paddlers may appreciate the river even more. The **AuSable River Canoe Marathon** (www.ausablecanoemarathon.org) starts in Grayling and ends in Oscoda. For canoe rentals, try **Oscoda Canoe Rental** (678 W. River Rd., 989/739-9040, www.oscodacanoe. com, 8am-4pm daily, $25-45 pp) or **Hunt's Canoes & Miniature Golf** (711 Lake St., Oscoda, 989/739-4408, www.huntscanoes. com, $18-40 pp).

Trips on the *Au Sable River Queen* (1775 W. River Rd., Oscoda, 989/739-7351, www. ausableriverqueen.net, 10am-5pm daily, $14 pp) depart from Foote Dam daily in season. The tours are especially popular during fall color, and reservations are recommended.

ACCOMMODATIONS AND FOOD

The **Redwood Motor Lodge** (3111 N. US-23, Oscoda, 989/739-2021, $54-127 d) offers standard motel rooms and cottages near Lake Huron. Also on Lake Huron, the **Rest-All Inn** (4270 N. US-23, Oscoda, 989/739-8822, www.restallinnoscoda.com, $59-109 d) has clean motel rooms (some with microwaves and refrigerators), a beach, and a playground.

In West Branch, stay at the **LogHaven Bed, Breakfast, and Barn** (1550 McGregor Rd., 989/685-3527, www.loghavenbbb.com, $125 d), where you'll find comfortable rooms, private baths, hearty country-style breakfasts, and a place to stable horses. It's a perfect home base for exploring the area's hiking, horseback riding, snowmobiling, and cross-country skiing trails.

Michigan's state parks offer consistently good campgrounds. **Tawas Point State Park** (686 Tawas Beach Rd., East Tawas, 989/362-5041, annual $11 Recreation Passport for Michigan residents or $8.40 day-use fee/$30.50

© BORCHERS CANOE LIVERY

Paddlers favor the Au Sable River.

yearly Recreation Passport for nonresidents required) is no exception, with 210 campsites ($27 daily) and a large sand beach.

While you won't find any gourmet hideaways in the area, restaurants offer good, stick-to-the-ribs food in generous portions. One good option is **Wiltse's Brew Pub and Family Restaurant** (5606 N. F-41, Oscoda, 989/739-2231, www.wiltsebrewpub.com, 8am-12:30am Mon.-Sat., 8am-9pm Sun., $12-27), where you can order up a homemade brew to wash down the chicken dishes and steaks cut to order.

INFORMATION AND SERVICES

For more information about the area, contact the **Oscoda Area Convention & Visitors Bureau** (P.O. Box 572, Oscoda, MI 48750, 989/739-0900, www.oscoda.com), the **Oscoda-AuSable Chamber of Commerce** (4440 N. US-23, Oscoda, 800/235-4625, www.oscodachamber.com), the **Tawas Bay Tourist & Convention Bureau** (877/868-2927, www.tawasbay.com), the **Tawas Area Chamber of Commerce** (402 E. Lake St., Tawas City, 800/558-2927, www.tawas.com), or the **West Branch-Ogemaw County Travelers & Visitors Bureau** (422 W. Houghton Ave., West Branch, 989/345-2821, www.visitwestbranch.com).

Although you won't find a ton of services in these smaller towns, basics like groceries, banks, and post offices won't be too hard to find. If an emergency occurs, dial **911** or consult **St. Joseph Health System** (200 Hemlock, Tawas City, 800/362-9404, www.sjhsys.org).

GETTING THERE AND AROUND

Despite the relatively remote nature of Oscoda, Tawas City, and West Branch, it's not terribly hard to reach this part of northeastern Michigan. For one thing, you could always fly into the area. Both **Alpena County Regional Airport** (APN, 1617 Airport Rd., Alpena, 989/354-2907, www.alpenaairport.com) and **MBS International Airport** (MBS, 8500 Garfield Rd., Freeland, 989/695-5555, www.mbsairport.org) offer commuter flights via

Delta Air Lines; from both airports, you can then easily rent a car and head to your specific destination. From the Alpena airport, for instance, you can take M-32 East and various surface streets to reach US-23 South, which will lead you directly to Oscoda, a 54-mile trip that usually takes about an hour. From the Freeland airport, meanwhile, you can follow US-10 East to I-75 North, take exit 212, and continue on the I-75 Business Route and M-55 West to West Branch, a 64-mile trip that will typically take about an hour. In addition, both **Greyhound** (800/231-2222, www.greyhound.com) and **Indian Trails** (800/292-3831, www.indiantrails.com) provide bus service to Tawas City (989/362-6120, 1020 W. Lake St.), which is located between West Branch and Oscoda, as well as **Standish** (220 E. Cedar St., 989/846-4613), which lies about 27 miles southeast of West Branch via I-75 and roughly 36 miles southwest of Tawas City via US-23.

Naturally, given the spread-out nature of this region, your best bet will probably be to drive here yourself. From Detroit, for instance, you can reach West Branch by taking I-375 North, merging onto I-75 North, and following the I-75 Business Route and M-55 West into town; without traffic, the 165-mile trip should take about 2.5 hours. Similarly, you can access West Branch from Sault Ste. Marie, via I-75 South, which crosses the Mackinac Bridge (a toll bridge), and M-55 East, a 183-mile trip that, without traffic, will take roughly 2.75 hours. From West Branch, you can then take M-55 East directly to Tawas City, a 37-mile trip that will normally require about 45 minutes, and from Tawas City, you can continue to Oscoda via US-23 North, a 16-mile trip that will usually take about 20 minutes. Once you've arrived in the region, you can get around in a number of ways, including by car, bike, foot, or canoe.

HURON NATIONAL FOREST

Oscoda also is known as the gateway to the **Huron National Forest** (Huron Shores Ranger Station, 5761 N. Skeel Rd., 989/739-0728), which covers most of the acreage between

PADDLING TIPS

Given the bounty of rivers, inland lakes, and coastal waters in and around Michigan, it's no surprise that canoeing and kayaking are popular activities in the Great Lakes State. Options range from short, hour-long canoe trips on the Au Sable River to multiday kayaking journeys around Isle Royale National Park. Though some enthusiasts bring their vessels with them, you can easily rent a variety of canoes and kayaks at several different outfitters, from Ann Arbor to Marquette. In addition, many hotels and resorts offer complimentary canoes and kayaks to their guests.

Paddling throughout Michigan can be a rewarding experience, but it can also be dangerous if you're ill-prepared. High winds and strong currents can make paddling conditions challenging; in fact, while beginners are welcome to give paddling a try, it's helpful if you've had at least some experience before attempting it here. No matter what your experience level, however, the following guidelines are necessary for all canoeists and kayakers to remember:

- Ensure that you've had proper instruction for the vessel that you plan to use.
- Check the daily weather forecast, especially predicted wind speeds, beforehand.
- Be aware of tidal conditions, currents, and water levels; under normal circumstances, you should allow for a minimum paddling time of two miles per hour.

- Inform someone on shore of your plans, especially your intended destination and expected return time; leave a float plan with a responsible individual, place a copy of the plan in a visible spot in your vehicle, and contact the onshore person when you do, in fact, return.
- Arrange to have a vehicle (if not yours) and dry clothes waiting at your take-out point.
- Secure a spare paddle to your vessel.
- Place your keys, identification, money, and other valuables in a waterproof bag and secure the bag to the vessel.
- Apply sunscreen, even on cloudy days, and insect repellent.
- Wear appropriate clothing for weather and water conditions.
- Have a readily accessible, personal flotation device (PFD) with attached whistle for each occupant; children under six must wear PFDs at all times.
- Bring plenty of food and drinking water (one gallon/person/day) in nonbreakable, watertight containers.
- Bring a cell phone in case of an emergency, but don't rely solely on said phone, as reception can be sporadic in the backcountry and offshore waters.

Oscoda to the east and Grayling to the west. Together, the Manistee National Forest in the western part of the state and the Huron National Forest cover more than 950,000 acres in the northern part of the Lower Peninsula. The scenic Au Sable River flows through the Huron National Forest and was once used to float logs to the sawmills in East Tawas and Oscoda; now, of course, it's more popular with paddlers.

The national forest is favored by a wide range of outdoor enthusiasts, including morel hunters who visit in the spring, backpackers, swimmers, and cross-country skiers. Trout fishing is a good bet in most lakes and streams, as well as in the legendary Au Sable River.

The forest's famous **River Road Scenic Byway** runs 22 miles along the southern bank of the Au Sable. The byway passes some of the most spectacular scenery in the eastern Lower Peninsula, and provides stunning vistas of tree-banked reservoirs and views of wildlife that include everything from bald eagles to spawning salmon. Along the way, you'll also pass the **Lumberman's Monument,** a 9-foot bronze statue that depicts the area's early loggers and overlooks the river valley 10 miles northwest of East Tawas. A visitors center here houses

- Pack up all trash and store it on board until you can dispose of it properly at your trip's end.

- Leave all historical resources, plants, birds, and marine creatures as you find them.

- Respect all wildlife; do not approach, harass, or feed any animals that you see.

- Be considerate of anglers and other paddlers, avoid crossing fishing lines, and stay to the right of motorboats.

- If you're taking an overnight paddling trip and plan to camp somewhere, be sure to camp on durable surfaces away from the water, and minimize the impact from campfires (if they're even allowed where you're staying).

Besides the items already mentioned, you should bring the following essentials with you:

- anchor (if you plan to snorkel or camp) and some rope

- area maps and NOAA nautical charts

- bilge pump and sponge

- binoculars

- camera and extra batteries

- compass or GPS

- duct tape

- extra waterproof bags

- first-aid kit

- insect repellent

- lip balm with SPF

- long-sleeved shirt for extra protection

- pocketknife or multipurpose tool

- repair kit

- signaling devices such as a flashlight, flare, mirror, or air horn

- sunglasses

- sunscreen

- 360-degree light for operating your vessel at night

- towels, extra clothing, and extra shoes in a waterproof bag

- VHF or weather radio to monitor weather forecasts

- wide-brimmed hat

For more information about canoeing and kayaking in Michigan, including paddling destinations and liveries, consult the **Michigan Department of Natural Resources** (DNR, Parks and Recreation Division, 517/284-7275, www.michigan.gov/dnr) and the **Michigan Association of Paddlesport Providers** (MAPP, www.michigancanoe.com), or visit www.canoeingmichiganrivers.com.

NORTHEAST MICHIGAN

interpretive displays that explore the logging legacy. Just a short walk away, a cliff plummets in a near-vertical 160-foot drop to the Au Sable River below. It offers jaw-dropping views of the valley and marks the beginning of the **Stairway to Discovery,** an unusual interpretive nature trail that descends 260 steps to the river and earns distinction as the nation's only nature trail located entirely on a staircase.

Also in the national forest, the **Tuttle Marsh Wildlife Management Area,** about seven miles west of Au Sable, was created in the spring of 1990 as a cooperative effort by the U.S. Forest Service, the state's Department of Natural Resources, and Ducks Unlimited. Once an area filled with sad-looking shrubs and scattered patches of grass, the wetlands now attract a significant number of migrating waterfowl, shorebirds, and sandhill cranes, as well as muskrats, minks, beavers, and bald eagles.

Backpackers looking for a wilderness camping experience should try the **Hoist Lakes Trail System.** Backcountry camping is allowed just about anywhere in this large, rugged area of more than 10,000 acres. Nearly 20 miles of trails (hiking only) wander through second-growth forest over gently rolling wooded terrain, around marshes, past beaver floodings,

THE TINY BIRD WITH THE HUGE FOLLOWING

To call **Kirtland's warbler** endangered is an understatement – save for parts of Wisconsin and Canada, several counties in Michigan's Upper and northern Lower Peninsulas, especially the region around the Au Sable River between Grayling and Mio, are the only places in the world where the bird is known to breed today. The world population is estimated at less than 1,400 pairs.

A tiny blue-gray songbird with a yellow breast, Kirtland's warbler winters in the Bahamas, then returns to the Au Sable River area, where it subsists on insects and blueberries and searches for the proper habitat to suit its picky nesting requirements: young stands of jack pine with small grassy clearings. It builds nests on the low-lying branches of jack pines between 5 and 20 feet high; when the trees get much higher, the warbler seeks out younger trees.

The bird's precarious plight is a classic case of habitat loss. When forest fires occur naturally, jack pines are one of the first trees to regenerate in burned areas. But decades of logging and fire suppression led to fewer forest fires, which in turn led to fewer young jack pines. To help the warbler, the U.S. Forest Service, the U.S. Fish and Wildlife Service, the Michigan Department of Natural Resources,

and other government agencies now do nature's job, cultivating, harvesting, and re-planting acres of jack pines in the **Kirtland's Warbler Wildlife Management Area, in** order to keep an ample supply of young trees suitable for the warbler's nesting needs. Environmentalists also assist the warbler by controlling the region's population of brown-headed cowbirds, which routinely take over warbler nests and outcompete their nest-mates for food.

Not surprisingly, the bird's breeding grounds are off-limits to the public during the May-August nesting season. From mid-May through late June, however, guided, three-hour tours (7am daily, $10 pp) are led by the U.S. Forest Service, beginning at the Mio Ranger Station, and from mid-May through early July, the U.S. Fish and Wildlife Service and Michigan Audubon Society jointly offer guided tours (7am Mon.-Fri., 7am and 11am Sat.-Sun. and holidays, free) of the same area, usually departing from the Ramada Inn in Grayling. Of course, actual sightings aren't guaranteed. For more information about the tours, contact the **Forest Service's Mio Ranger Station** (989/826-3252) or **Seney National Wildlife Refuge** (906/586-9851).

and across streams. The forest teems with deer, bears, coyotes, foxes, owls, hawks, and songbirds, along with turkeys, woodcocks, grouse, and other game birds. Fishing includes good numbers of bass and panfish. The 6.1-mile **Reid Lake Foot Travel Area** marks another great hiking area surrounded by some of the forest's most imposing hardwoods.

About 10 miles west of East Tawas, the **Corsair Trail System** bills itself as "Michigan's Cross-Country Ski Capital," but it is equally popular with hikers and backpackers. Also part of the Huron National Forest, the well-marked trail system (groomed in winter) includes more than 15 loops totaling 44 miles. One writer described this sprawling complex as

"a web spun by a spider high on LSD." Choose-your-own adventures range from a short jaunt along Silver Creek to a two-day trek through the entire system.

Full of rolling hills, deep glacial potholes, and a beautiful hardwood forest, the **Island Lake Recreation Area** offers a quiet and beautiful alternative to the more heavily used recreation areas. You'll find it seven miles north of Rose City via M-33 and CR-486. Out of the way and relatively small, it hides a swimming beach, a 17-site campground, and a 65-acre lake that supports perch, bluegills, and large- and smallmouth bass. A self-guiding nature trail explains the area's natural history and notes points of interest along the way.

◖ HOUGHTON AND HIGGINS LAKES

Near the southern end of Northeast Michigan, in Roscommon County, lie two of the state's largest inland lakes—22,000-acre Houghton Lake and 10,200-acre Higgins Lake—both of which entice plenty of anglers, boaters, canoeists, swimmers, hikers, and campers during the summer months. In winter, this area is also popular among hunters, ice fishers, and cross-country skiers.

Beaches

Both lakes present a number of terrific beaches. On Higgins Lake, you'll find the **North Higgins Lake State Park Day Use Area,** situated on North Higgins Lake Drive, and the **South Higgins Lake State Park Day Use Area,** located on CR-100. Each offers a sandy swimming beach, a bathhouse, a playground, picnic shelters, and a boat launch. You'll need an annual Recreation Passport ($11 residents/$30.50 nonresidents) or a day-use pass ($8.40) in order to utilize either of these beaches.

Meanwhile, on Houghton Lake, you'll discover the **Roscommon Township Beach** (Sanford St.), which has a pleasant sandy beach on the south shore, ideal for swimmers of all ages. The area also offers a sheltered picnic area, a small playground, and restrooms.

Boating and Fishing

Houghton and Higgins Lakes are both well known among boaters, canoeists, and anglers. Together, the two enormous lakes offer a dozen launch sites and tons of water to explore. Although Houghton and Higgins are particularly ideal for those with their own canoes, kayaks, and fishing boats, several facilities do rent boats as well. For more information about renting pontoon and fishing boats, check out **Houghton Lake Marina** (13710 W. Shore Dr., 989/422-7257). It's a terrific way for those without boats of their own to enjoy drifting around the lake, savoring the sunshine, or trying their luck at snagging bass, bluegill, walleye, and pike.

Accommodations and Food

You'll find a decent variety of lodgings in the area, including chain hotels. The **Comfort Inn** (200 Cloverleaf Ln., Houghton Lake, 989/422-7829, www.comfortinn.com, $63-149 d) and the **Comfort Suites Lakeside** (100 Clearview Dr., Houghton Lake, 989/422-4000, www.comfortsuiteslakeside.com, $139-350 d) each offer terrific access to the lakes as well as numerous water-related amenities, such as canoeing packages and watercraft rentals. Comfort Suites also features a 9,000-square-foot water park, a boat dock, and the Blue Bayou Restaurant and Lounge, with a deck bar that overlooks the majestic lake.

Houghton and Higgins Lakes both have numerous campgrounds, too, some catering to RVs, others allowing both tent and RV camping. On Houghton Lake, you'll find the **Houghton Lake Travel Park Campground** (370 Cloverleaf Ln., Houghton Lake, 989/422-3931, www.houghtonlaketravelparkcampground.com, Apr.-Oct., $30-43 daily), which has something for everyone. On Higgins Lake, check out the **Higgins Lake KOA** (3800 W. Federal Hwy., Roscommon, 989/275-8151, www.koa.com, $28-34 daily).

After a long day of boating, fishing, swimming, or exploring the area, satisfy your hunger at the nearby **Buccilli's Pizza** (2949 W. Houghton Lake Dr., Houghton Lake, 989/366-5374, www.buccillispizza.com, 11am-10pm daily, $5-19), which offers tasty pizza for dine-in, takeout, or delivery.

Information and Services

For more information about Houghton and Higgins Lakes, contact the **Houghton Lake Area Tourism & Convention Bureau** (9091 W. Lake City Rd., Houghton Lake, 989/422-2002 or 800/676-5330, www.visithoughton-lake.com). If you require other services, such as banks and groceries, your best bet would probably be to drive north on I-75 to Grayling or Gaylord.

Getting There and Around

The easiest way to reach the lakes is via car.

From West Branch, for instance, you can simply take M-55 West, merge onto I-75 North/M-55 West, and continue onto M-55 West, which hugs the southern shore of Houghton Lake; the 28-mile trip from West Branch to the town of Houghton Lake usually takes about a half hour. From Grayling, meanwhile, you can reach North Higgins Lake State Park by heading south on I-75, continuing onto US-127 South, and turning left onto North Higgins Lake Drive, a 13-mile trip that usually takes about 16 minutes. Once you reach the lakes, you can explore the area via boat, bike, or foot.

Grayling Area

From Bay City, I-75 cuts across the northeastern part of the state until it bisects the North Country near Grayling. Several clean, clear, and immensely popular rivers—most notably, the Au Sable and the Manistee—corkscrew their way through the region, making Grayling the hub of one of the Lower Peninsula's leading recreational areas.

First classified in 1884, the grayling once was the only game fish to inhabit the upper Au Sable system. Related to trout and salmon and characterized by a long, wavy dorsal fin, grayling were considered both a fine sporting fish and a delicious eating fish—a fatal combination. The thrill of landing one drew the attention of sportfishers near and far, who came by railroad to Grayling, soon a bustling center of fishing trips. With no regulations at the time, anglers snatched grayling from area rivers by the thousands. The wanton fishing, combined with the declining water quality caused by riverbank erosion from logging, put a quick end to the species. Grayling were rare in Grayling by 1900 and extinct by 1930.

Alas, the town's namesake fish may be gone, but we've learned a few lessons about protecting species and their habitat along the way. Today, Grayling offers some of the finest trout fishing in the Midwest—even the nation—and is a key destination for anglers, canoeists, hunters, hikers, mountain bikers, cross-country skiing enthusiasts, and snowmobilers.

RECREATION
Hiking and Biking
Popular with equestrians, hikers, cross-country skiers, and snowshoers, the 220-mile **Michigan Shore-to-Shore Riding and Hiking Trail** traverses the entire Lower Peninsula. In this area, it skirts the north end of the George Mason River Retreat Area, passing through pine plantations, stands of hardwood, and along the gentle Au Sable. Other good area access points include the McKinley Trail Camp in Oscoda and across from the Curtisville Store in Glennie.

The rolling terrain of Crawford County makes for some great mountain biking, and even better, the local tourism council actually encourages it—a rare thing in the Midwest. The Grayling Visitors Bureau recommends the following near Grayling: **Michigan Cross Country Cycle Trail**, a great technical singletrack that "goes for miles and miles." Access it where it crosses Military Road, 0.5 mile north of the North Higgins Lake State Park exit off US-27. Also check out the **Hanson Hills Recreation Area** (7601 Old Lake Rd., Grayling, 989/348-9266, www.hanson-hills.org, $2 donation suggested), which offers challenging terrain that includes some sandy stretches, and **Wakely Lake**, situated 10 miles east of Grayling via M-72 and featuring three loops of 4.5, 5, and 7 miles. To secure a required parking pass for the Wakely Lake area, contact the **Mio Ranger District** (107 McKinley Rd., Mio, 989/826-3252, www.fs.usda.gov, 8am-4:30pm Mon.-Fri.) of the Huron National Forest.

Canoeing
Scenic streams crisscross the forests around

Grayling. The Boardman, Manistee, Pine, Rifle, and Au Sable Rivers meander through wetlands, across dunes, and past tree-covered hills. Canoeing ranks among the area's most popular pastimes, with a number of liveries offering adventures on the Au Sable and other area rivers. Even novice paddlers can handle the easygoing currents of these waterways as they scan the shoreline for deer, beavers, black bears, and winsome river otters. The area's canoe liveries are concentrated in Grayling.

Flowing east out of Grayling, the Au Sable coils through the **Au Sable State Forest.** Designated a state natural river with stretches of the main stream protected as a national wild and scenic river, the Au Sable flows past wooded islands and stretches of white sand. At night, weary paddlers can bed down at one of several state and national forest campgrounds along the river's shore. For day-trippers, the most popular take-outs are at Stephan Landing (about a 4-hour leisurely paddle from Grayling) and Wakely Landing, a 5.5-hour trip at a similar pace.

Recognized for its excellent trout fishing and often overlooked by paddlers is the Au Sable's South Branch, in which you can also launch a boat. You'll find landings at Chase Bridge on the south end and at Smith Bridge, 11 miles to the north.

The Au Sable can be a victim of its own success, though, with raucous crowds sometimes floating the river en masse on hot summer weekends. If you're looking for a party, this is the place, but be aware that local authorities watch for intoxication carefully and fine liberally. (Glass containers, kegs, and Styrofoam coolers are prohibited on the Au Sable to keep down the partying and the littering.) If you're looking for a more peaceful experience, avoid the party set by departing during the week or arranging to paddle a stretch farther outside Grayling, if you can talk an outfitter into it. Alternatively, many paddlers find the Manistee River less of a scene. For a complete list of liveries in the Grayling region, contact the **Grayling Visitors Bureau** (213 N. James St., 800/937-8837, www.grayling-mi.com).

As a testament to its paddling popularity, Grayling is the site of one of the country's few canoeing festivals, the **AuSable River Canoe Marathon** (www.ausablecanoemarathon.org). Held in late July, the 120-mile route runs from Grayling to Oscoda on Lake Huron and ranks as North America's longest and most difficult nonstop canoe race. An estimated 30,000 fans turn out, many following the world-class athletes in the grueling race down the river, which requires some 55,000 paddle strokes and more than 14 hours to complete. It's worth going just to watch the thrilling 9am shotgun start, when more than 50 teams carrying canoes on their heads race through downtown Grayling to the launch site.

Fishing

Fly-fishing enthusiasts from all over the country make the pilgrimage to the Au Sable, where the combination of spring-fed waters, clean gravel river bottoms, and all the right insect hatches make for stellar trout fishing. All along the area's rivers, you'll spot anglers plying their sport, standing midstream in hip waders, unfurling a long arc of lemon-colored line across the river with their fly rods, or casting from a flat-bottom Au Sable riverboat specifically designed for drifting these shallow waters. Many congregate just east of town in a 10-mile catch-and-release area known as "the holy waters."

While the Grayling Visitors Bureau will help you link up with fishing guides, you also can try your luck from shore. (Obtain a license—available at local shops and gas stations—and check fishing regulations first.) Both the Manistee and Au Sable pass through several miles of state and federal lands, so you won't have much trouble finding public access.

Farther southeast, the Rifle River and its upper tributaries have earned reputations for yielding good catches of brown, rainbow, and brook trout. Some steelhead and chinook salmon are caught on the river's upper reaches, and pike, bass, and panfish are pulled from the dozen or so lakes and ponds in Rifle River Recreation Area, many of which have public access sites.

REBUILDING AMERICA: THE CIVILIAN CONSERVATION CORPS

By 1933, the United States was cracked deeply by the Great Depression. One after another, factories and businesses shut down. Lines at soup kitchens straggled around city blocks. Nearly 14 million Americans were unemployed.

Along with an economy in ruin, President Franklin D. Roosevelt saw an environment in ruin as well. While virgin forests had once covered 800 million acres of the United States, old growth had dwindled to just 100 million acres. Erosion had ruined more than 100 million acres of the nation's tillable land, and more was eroding at an alarming rate.

In March 1933, President Roosevelt asked Congress for the power to create the Civilian Conservation Corps (CCC). A New Deal program, the proposed corps would recruit 250,000 unemployed, unmarried young men to work on federal- and state-owned land for "the prevention of forest fires, floods, and soil erosion, plant, pest and disease control."

As proposed, the Labor Department would recruit the young men, while the War Department would run the program, housing, clothing, and feeding the men in work camps, and paying them a monthly stipend of $30–$25 of which had to be sent home to their families. The Department of Agriculture and Interior planned the work projects, which included reforesting cutover land, preventing fires, developing state parks, and building dams, bridges, and roads. Along with the field work, education was a hallmark of the CCC. Camps helped members obtain their high school diplomas, and provided supplemental training in at least 30 different vocations.

The program was not without controversy. Some criticized the cost; others balked at the idea of military control over labor, comparing it to fascism and Hitlerism. Still others contended young men should be with their families, or, as Michigan congressman Fred Crawford suggested, at work in farm fields rather than in "some camp in the woods to participate in a face-lifting operation on Mother Earth."

But Roosevelt saw it differently. Through the CCC, he believed two invaluable and impoverished resources – the nation's young men

ACCOMMODATIONS AND FOOD

For paddlers, you can't do better than 🅒 **Penrod's Au Sable River Resort** (100 Maple St., 888/467-4837, www.penrodscanoe.com, $60-96 d), where cute cabins line a peaceful bend in the river. Penrod's adjacent paddle-sport center rents canoes, kayaks, and mountain bikes, and offers shuttle service for river trips. If you care more about location than amenities and are coming to fish, **Gates Au Sable Lodge** (471 Stephan Bridge Rd., 989/348-8462, www.gateslodge.com, $90 d) has motel-style rooms with a perfect setting right on the banks of the Au Sable. Also right on the Au Sable, **Borchers Au Sable Canoe Livery with Bed & Breakfast** (101 Maple St., 989/348-4921, www.canoeborchers.com,

$78-98 d) invites you to slow to the pace of the river on its wraparound porch.

Hungry hunters, paddlers, and bird-watchers head to **Spikes Keg O Nails** (301 N. James St., 989/348-7113, www.spikes-grayling.com, 10am-1:30am Mon.-Sat., noon-1:30am Sun., $6-19) for a burger. Try the "World Famous Spikeburger," topped with everything.

Camping

You'll find plenty of good, inexpensive public campgrounds in the Grayling area. **Hartwick Pines State Park** (4216 Ranger Rd., 989/348-7068, annual $11 Recreation Passport for Michigan residents or $8.40 day-use fee/$30.50 yearly Recreation Passport for nonresidents required) in Grayling offers clean, modern sites ($16-33 daily) that fill up fast. You might find and its land – could be brought together in an attempt to save both. In his message to Congress, Roosevelt declared that "we face a future of soil erosion and timber famine" and that the CCC would "conserve our precious national resources" and "pay dividends to the present and future generations."

The measure was easily passed, and so was Roosevelt's goal of 250,000 workers. On April 17, 1933, the nation's first CCC camp opened in the George Washington National Forest in Virginia. By July 1, 250,000 men were at work in more than 1,460 camps –t he fastest large-scale mobilization of men (including World War I) in U.S. history. By 1935, "Roosevelt's Tree Army" had ballooned to more than 500,000 workers.

Evidence of the CCC's work remains apparent throughout the Great Lakes region. CCC workers eradicated white pine blister rust in Minnesota, built fire towers and fire roads in Wisconsin, and improved hundreds of miles of fishing streams in Michigan. They built park shelters in Ohio, campgrounds in Indiana, and trails in Illinois. They planted thousands of acres of trees, fought countless wildfires, and built hundreds of bridges and buildings. They even

moved moose from Isle Royale to the Upper Peninsula for wildlife studies.

By 1936, the CCC was above reproach, supported by more than 80 percent of Americans and even endorsed by Roosevelt's political opponents. With the bombing of Pearl Harbor in 1941, however, the nation soon had a more pressing duty for its young men. The nation's entry into World War II, along with an improving economy, meant the end of the CCC by 1942. But its legacy, like the trees it planted, continues to grow in our nation's parks and forests.

The **Civilian Conservation Corps Museum** (11747 N. Higgins Lake Dr., Roscommon, 989/348-6178, www.michigan.gov/cccmuseum, 10am-4pm daily Memorial Day-Labor Day, free) uses various photographs, artifacts, and outdoor exhibits to tell the story of Michigan's CCC crews. Situated in North Higgins Lake State Park, the CCC Museum celebrates the efforts of more than 100,000 young men who strived to improve Michigan's forests during the Great Depression. Just note that, although the museum itself is free to visit, you'll need to pay a day-use fee or show your annual Recreation Passport to enter the state park.

a little more solitude (and fewer RVs) at the **Au Sable State Forest** (5.5 miles east of Grayling via N. Down River Rd., 989/826-3211, annual $11 Recreation Passport for Michigan residents or $8.40 day-use fee/$30.50 yearly Recreation Passport for nonresidents required), which offers several rustic campgrounds ($13 daily).

INFORMATION AND SERVICES

For more information, contact the **Grayling Visitors Bureau** (213 N. James St., 800/937-8837, www.grayling-mi.com). Grayling has a limited number of services; if necessary, you can always head north to Gaylord to stock up on supplies prior to an outing in the great outdoors. If an emergency occurs, dial **911** from any cell or public phone.

GETTING THERE AND AROUND

While **Greyhound** (989/348-8682 or 800/231-2222, www.greyhound.com) and **Indian Trails** (800/292-3831, www.indiantrails.com) both provide bus service to Grayling (500 Norway St.), most visitors arrive via car, truck, motorcycle, or RV. Given that the town sits at the junction of I-75 and M-72—and not far north from where I-75 and US-127 converge—it's easy to reach whether you're headed from Detroit to the southeast, Mackinaw City to the north, Traverse City to the west, or Chicago to the southwest. From downtown Detroit, for instance, you can simply take I-375 North, I-75 North, and the I-75 Business Route to reach Grayling; without traffic, the 205-mile trip requires less than three hours. From Mackinaw

City, you can access Grayling via I-75 South, an 85-mile trip that usually takes about 80 minutes, while from Traverse City, you can typically reach Grayling, which lies 51 miles away, in about an hour via M-72 East. If, on the other hand, you're venturing here from Chicago, just follow I-90 East and I-94 East through Illinois and Indiana, cross the Michigan state line, continue onto I-196 North/US-31 North and I-196 East, merge onto US-131 North toward Cadillac, and take M-72 East to Grayling. Just be advised that, en route from the Windy City, parts of I-90 East and I-94 East serve as the Indiana Toll Road. No matter how you reach Grayling, though, you can easily get around by car, bike, and, to a certain extent, foot.

GEORGE MASON RIVER RETREAT AREA

George Mason, an area industrialist, so loved this area that he bequeathed 1,500 acres to the state for its preservation in 1954. Located about 15 miles east of Grayling on Canoe Harbor Road, the George Mason River Retreat Area is considered part of the Au Sable State Forest. Subsequent land acquisitions have nearly tripled the size of this natural area, which provides ample opportunity to fish, canoe, or hike for free along a stretch of the South Branch of the Au Sable River. For more information about the George Mason River Retreat Area, which is open year-round, contact the **Roscommon Field Office** (989/275-4622) of the Michigan Department of Natural Resources (www.michigan.gov/dnr).

◖ HARTWICK PINES STATE PARK

The majestic white pine may be the state tree, but few virgin stands remain today. One of the last can be seen at the **Hartwick Pines State Park** (4216 Ranger Rd., 989/348-7068, annual $11 Recreation Passport for Michigan residents or $8.40 day-use fee/$30.50 yearly Recreation Passport for nonresidents required), one of the largest parks in the state. A century ago, more than 13 million of the state's 38 million acres were covered with the majestic trees, but by the

early 1900s more than 160 billion board feet of timber had been harvested. By the 1920s, these once majestic forests were denuded wastelands.

More than 250,000 visitors stroll through the pines annually, marveling at trees that have been here since before the Revolutionary War. Long a popular stop for vacationers heading north, the state park has been improved over the years, with a superb visitors center, a walkway to the pines that's accessible to both wheelchairs and strollers, and a steam sawmill that's part of an extensive logging museum area. The park is also the site of the **Hartwick Pines State Forest Festivals:** four different events held throughout the summer, including **Sawdust Days, Wood Shaving Days, Black Iron Days,** and **Old Time Days.**

The park's **Michigan Forest Visitors Center** boasts a 100-seat auditorium; a 14-minute audiovisual show on "The Forest: Michigan's Renewable Resource," which is presented every 30 minutes; and an exhibit hall that concentrates on forest management. Ironically, many of the displays were funded by forestry products companies, so don't expect to see explorations of the negative environmental effects of logging.

The 49-acre virgin tract of white and red pines is the main attraction. Reaching as high as 10 stories, the majestic trees were slated for cutting in the mid-1890s. Fortunately for us, the logging company charged with felling the trees was forced to suspend operations due to economic problems. In 1927, the trees and the surrounding 8,000 acres were purchased from the lumber company and donated to the state for a park.

The self-guided **Old Growth Forest Trail** connects the pines with the visitors center, a 1.25-mile blacktopped path that weaves among the regal giants, including the Monarch. Once the tract's largest specimen at 155 feet, a windstorm destroyed the top 40 feet of the now-diseased and dying tree. Part of nature's cycle, several other immense white pines tower nearby, ready to take its place in the record books.

The pines and museums overshadow the rest

of the park, but don't overlook it yourself. With more than 9,600 acres, it offers plenty to do besides admire tall trees. Signs and other displays mark the eight-mile **Scenic Drive,** about two miles north of the main entrance, encouraging visitors to explore the woods and natural world around them. Hiking and biking trails include 17 miles of easy trails open to mountain bikes in summer and cross-country skiers in winter. The Au Sable River Trail (no bikes) is one of the loveliest. It crosses the East Branch of the legendary river and passes a rare forest of virgin hemlock, saved from the saw by a sudden drop in the price of its bark, which was once used for tanning leather. The two-mile Mertz Grade Nature Trail loops through the park and past an old logging railroad grade before linking up with the Virgin Pines Trail behind the visitors center.

Open year-round, the park is especially popular in the spring, when wildflowers bloom, and in the early fall, when the colorful hardwoods explode in a riot of fiery reds, yellows, and oranges.

Gaylord Area

North of Grayling on I-75, Gaylord was officially organized in 1875 as "Otsego," an Indian word that means "beautiful lake." Located at the north end of long, skinny Otsego Lake, Gaylord remains a basically rural village with a year-round population of roughly 3,600. But its topography lures vacationers by the thousands.

Gaylord sits on the highest point in southern Michigan, which inspired the town to morph itself into "the Alpine Village." Its Main Street is decorated with balconies, blossoming window boxes, even a glockenspiel on the Glen's Market grocery store. And while more Polish and German descendants reside here than Swiss, the townspeople happily don dirndls and lederhosen each July during the annual Alpenfest. Some visitors come for the culture, but Gaylord offers plenty of outdoor attractions as well—from world-class golf to accessible lakes to bugling elk.

SIGHTS
Call of the Wild Museum

While this unassuming museum has been around for decades (during which the displays haven't changed all that much), the **Call of the Wild Museum** (850 S. Wisconsin Ave., 989/732-4336, www.gocallofthewild.com, 9am-9pm daily June 15-Labor Day, 9:30am-6pm Mon.-Sat. Sept.-mid-June, $7 adults, $4.50 children 5-13) is still a terrific place to take your children for a little while. Many of its wildlife displays come packed with audio features, bringing the animals to life. Creepy, yet fascinating, the two projected images of Joseph Bailly help to educate visitors about what life was like in the early 1800s, when he (one of the area's first trappers) initially ventured into the Michigan area.

Otsego Lake State Park

Established in 1920, **Otsego Lake State Park** (7136 Old 27 S, 989/732-5485) is a boating enthusiast's dream. The lake itself is long and wide, allowing ample room for boats and all manner of other water sports. This park has been a popular, family-friendly destination for nine decades.

ALPENFEST

You can't miss the distinctive architecture that's earned Gaylord its "Alpine Village" moniker. To celebrate the community's Alpine heritage, part of Main Street is blocked off every July for the annual **Alpenfest** (989/732-6333, www.gaylordalpenfest.com). Established in the mid-1960s, the five-day event features traditional dancing, costumed musicians, yodeling and pie-eating contests, an "Edelweiss" sing-along, and plenty of ethnic food, from sauerkraut to strudel to pasties, in addition to carnival favorites like hot dogs, ice cream, and, yes, beer.

MICHIGAN'S ELK

© GAYLORD AREA CTB

Once a common sight in the Lower Peninsula, the eastern elk disappeared from Michigan in the late 1870s. Biologists made several attempts to reintroduce the animal to the state throughout the early 1900s, but it wasn't until the successful release of seven Rocky Mountain elk in 1918 that the mammals once again were seen regularly in northeastern Michigan.

Wildlife biologists today believe that the region's elk are descendants of those early animals. They roam a 600-square-mile area primarily east and north of Gaylord in Otsego, Cheboygan, Presque Isle, and Montmorency Counties. The heaviest concentration is north of Gaylord in the 95,000-acre **Pigeon River**

Country State Forest (9966 Twin Lakes Rd., Vanderbilt, 989/983-4101).

The best way to plan a visit is to stop by the Pigeon River forestry field office off Sturgeon Valley Road. To reach the office from Vanderbilt, drive east on Sturgeon Valley Road about 13 miles (past a prime elk-viewing site), turn left onto Hardwood Lake Road, and continue for about one mile to the office. Although the office hours vary seasonally, the staff, when present, will provide helpful maps and suggest ideal areas and times to view the elk. That said, fall rutting season often proves to be the most spectacular, when the bulls throw their heads back and fill the forests with eerie bugling sounds, their distinctive mating call.

© DANIEL MARTONE

NORTHEAST MICHIGAN

the Call of the Wild Museum

The open-air "Alpenstrasse," an arts-and-crafts village showcases the wares of more than 60 Michigan artists and artisans. The town even makes room for several amusement park rides and carnival games.

SPORTS AND RECREATION
◖ Golf

But Gaylord is best known for its golf, boasting the largest number of courses in the state: more than 20, with more on the drawing board all the time. The area around Gaylord, in fact, has emerged as America's premier golf mecca, with the thickest concentration of designer courses anywhere in the United States, including those by well-known designers such as Robert Trent Jones Sr., Tom Fazio, and Al Watrous.

If you have the time, consider visiting at least three of the area's favored golf clubs. Head first to Onaway, on M-68, where you'll find the **Black Lake Golf Club** (2800 Maxon Rd., 989/733-4653, www.blacklakegolf.com, daily Apr.-Oct., $55-70 pp). Operated by the UAW, this magnificent golf course is part of the union's 1,000-acre family center, which sits astride picturesque Black Lake.

Another winning choice is **Garland Lodge & Resort** (4700 N. Red Oak Rd., Lewiston, 989/786-2211 or 877/442-7526, www.garlandusa.com, daily May-Oct., $75-120 pp). Considered one of the state's most beautiful resorts, this longstanding option presents four magnificent golf courses amid the woods of northeastern Michigan.

Lastly, schedule a tee time at the lovely **Treetops Resort** (3962 Wilkinson Rd., Gaylord, 989/732-6711 or 888/873-3867, www.treetops.com, daily Apr.-Oct., $45-135 pp). This year-round resort keeps visitors busy with downhill skiing in winter, activities like tennis and biking in summer, and, of course, five stunning golf courses.

Hiking
The Shingle Mill Pathway links up with the **High Country Pathway,** an 80-mile route that snakes east through state land in four counties, passing through a wilderness of rolling hills and

© DANIEL MARTONE

an Alpenfest crowd

several creeks feeding the Black River. A side trail leads to Shoepac Lake and the Sinkholes Pathway, where the land is pitted with dry sinkholes and sinkhole lakes, formed when underground limestone caves collapsed.

Elk may be the main attraction at the Pigeon River Country State Forest, but beavers bring visitors to the **Big Bear Lake Nature Pathway,** 17 miles east of Gaylord. Part of the Mackinaw State Forest trail system, the pathway's two loops total just over 2 miles and lead through a variety of landscape and habitats home to deer, porcupines, woodcocks, waterfowl, and beavers. The shorter, 0.8-mile Beaver Lodge Loop circles a pond with an active beaver colony. The longer Eagles Roost Trail carves a wide, 2-mile loop that threads its way through upland hardwoods and through a dense stand of aspen and an open area carpeted with wildflowers in the summer. Both trails begin and end at the **Big Bear Lake State Forest Campground** (989/732-3541, $15 daily), on the north shore of Big Bear Lake, accessible via Bear Lake Road.

Snowmobiling

Gaylord is the crossroads of many snowmobiling trails (www.visitgaylord.com/snowmobile). With over 150 inches of average snowfall a year, Gaylord is a snowmobiler's dream. Many of the state's best trails either start or pass through the area. If you're looking for a great ride, the **Gaylord-Frederic-Grayling-Blue Bear Loop** will give you a two- to four-day adventure.

ACCOMMODATIONS AND FOOD

The Gaylord area is best known for its golf resorts, and they can offer some good package deals, especially for families. **◖Garland Lodge & Resort** (4700 N. Red Oak Rd., Lewiston, 989/786-2211, www.garlandusa.com, $99-499 d) has a lot of stay-and-play deals where golf is included in the price. If you're just looking for a simple motel room, you'll find several of the usual chains—Super 8, Days Inn, Comfort Inn, etc.—near I-75.

The same Greek American family has

the Garland Lodge & Resort

been running the **Sugar Bowl** (216 W. Main St., 989/732-5524, 7am-11pm daily, $6-22) since 1919. Specialties include Lake Superior whitefish, scampi, Athenian chicken, and other favorite ethnic dishes, all prepared on an open hearth. Tip: They serve morel mushroom dishes in season, usually May. Don't miss the vintage photos of historic Gaylord on the walls.

Gobbler's Famous Turkey Dinners (900 S. Otsego, 989/732-9005, 10am-9pm daily, $5-14) prepares more than 80,000 pounds of bird annually, all from scratch and served with mashed potatoes, biscuits, gravy, and dressing. The portion sizes are legendary. There's also hand-breaded fresh fish and barbecued ribs if you don't do turkey.

Between Gaylord and Lewiston is the single-traffic-light town of Johannesburg, where you'll find **C Paul's Pub** (10757 E. M-32, 989/732-5005, www.paulspubandcatering. com, 10am-midnight Mon.-Thurs., 10am-2am Fri.-Sat., 8am-midnight Sun., $6-28), with its wide assortment of beers and the best fried

perch in Michigan. They also have quite the Sunday brunch, but get here early. This local favorite can get pretty busy on the weekends.

Camping
Pigeon River Country State Forest (off Sturgeon Valley Rd., 989/983-4101, $15 daily) offers 29 rustic sites in a nice secluded setting. For waterfront sites, try **Otsego Lake State Park** (7136 Old 27 S, 989/732-5485, annual $11 Recreation Passport for Michigan residents or $8.40 day-use fee/$30.50 yearly Recreation Passport for nonresidents required), with 206 sites ($16-26 daily) on or near Otsego Lake.

INFORMATION AND SERVICES
For more information about the Gaylord area, contact the **Gaylord Area Convention & Tourism Bureau** (101 W. Main St., 989/732-4000, www.gaylordmichigan.net). For local news, consult the *Gaylord Herald Times* (www.gaylordheraldtimes.com).

Despite its relatively small size, Gaylord offers a wide range of services, including a post office, several banks and gas stations, and numerous stores, from Wal-Mart to Home Depot to Glen's Market. If a medical emergency occurs during your visit, dial **911** or consult **Otsego Memorial Hospital** (825 N. Center Ave., 989/731-2100, www.myomh.org).

GETTING THERE AND AROUND
While **Greyhound** (989/732-9063 or 800/231-2222, www.greyhound.com) and **Indian Trails** (800/292-3831, www.indiantrails.com) both provide bus service to Gaylord (1041 W. Main St.), most visitors arrive via car, truck, motorcycle, or RV. After all, given that the town sits at the junction of I-75 and M-32, it's an easy place to reach whether you're coming from Detroit, Sault Ste. Marie, Traverse City, or Chicago. From downtown Detroit, for instance, you can simply follow I-375 North and I-75 North to reach Gaylord; without traffic, the 232-mile

© DANIEL MARTONE

Paul's Pub in Johannesburg

trip takes about 3.25 hours. From Sault Ste. Marie, you can access Gaylord via I-75 South, which crosses the Mackinac Bridge (a toll bridge) before continuing south to Gaylord, a 116-mile trip that usually takes less than 2 hours, while from Traverse City, you can simply take M-72 East, US-131 North, CR-42, and M-32 East to reach Gaylord, a 62-mile trip that typically takes about 80 minutes.

If, on the other hand, you're venturing here from Chicago, just follow I-90 East and I-94 East through Illinois and Indiana, cross the Michigan state line, continue onto I-196 North/US-31 North and I-196 East, merge onto US-131 North toward Cadillac, and take CR-42 and M-32 East to Gaylord. Just be advised that, en route from the Windy City, parts of I-90 East and I-94 East serve as the Indiana Toll Road. Note that, no matter how you reach Gaylord, you can easily get around by car, bike, and, to a certain extent, foot.

PIGEON RIVER COUNTRY STATE FOREST

With a shaggy chocolate mane and a crown of showy antlers, the eastern elk may be Michigan's most spectacular mammal, sometimes weighing in at close to 1,000 pounds. Elk are rare in the Midwest, but about 1,000 of them—the largest free-roaming elk herd east of the Mississippi River—populate this state forest and the surrounding countryside.

Although its primary draw is the opportunity to spot the elk herd, this 97,000-acre state forest north of Gaylord has miles of hiking trails, good fishing, and scenic rustic campgrounds. The **Shingle Mill Pathway** passes through deep woods and across rolling, hilly terrain. Keep an eye out for the forest's "other" wildlife, which includes bears, coyotes, bobcats, beavers, otters, woodcocks, turkeys, bald eagles, ospreys, loons, and blue herons. For more information on the state forest, stop by the **Pigeon River forestry field office** (off Sturgeon Valley Rd., 989/983-4101).

EASTERN UPPER PENINSULA

A short drive across the Mackinac Bridge, from the Lower to the Upper Peninsula, can feel like a journey between two very disparate countries. Despite the presence of sizable towns like St. Ignace and Sault Ste. Marie, the eclectic eastern half of this enormous, sparsely populated peninsula epitomizes the very definition of "wilderness," illustrated by its rushing rivers, thunderous cascades, dramatic cliffs, deserted beaches, and vast tracts of forested terrain.

Although there are several ways to reach the U.P., most travelers utilize "Big Mac," the only link between the northern and southern parts of Michigan. From the south, the first stop is St. Ignace, a former fur-trading town that now offers a variety of attractions, from an Ojibwa history museum to a casino. Via I-75, the eastern U.P.'s largest city, Sault Ste. Marie, lies only 50 miles north. Here, travelers will find a unique maritime attraction: the Soo Locks, an engineering marvel that has allowed safe passage between Lake Superior and the other Great Lakes for roughly 160 years.

Those seeking a more untamed landscape should head west, where over a million acres of protected state and federal land—including the enormous Hiawatha National Forest—await. From the highway, many of these coniferous woods look the same—the "real" peninsula is accessible via more challenging routes. Of course, the difficulty of reaching such breathtaking places is part of the reward. Every season, adventure seekers are lured to these remote forests and wetlands to share the open space with native deer, foxes, black bears, and bald eagles—the true "locals" of these parts.

HIGHLIGHTS

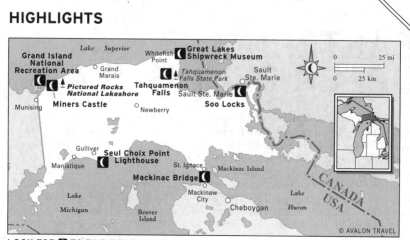

LOOK FOR ◖ TO FIND RECOMMENDED SIGHTS, ACTIVITIES, DINING, AND LODGING.

◖ **Mackinac Bridge:** Once you've crossed the "Mighty Mac," make a quick stop in lovely Bridge View Park, where you can snap pictures of this engineering marvel, one of the longest suspension bridges in the world (page 323).

◖ **Seul Choix Point Lighthouse:** Michigan's lengthy coastline is dotted with dozens of historic lighthouses, some of which are open to the public. If you only have time to visit one in the U.P., head to Seul Choix Point southeast of Gulliver, where you'll find a seasonal museum and a supposedly haunted lighthouse (page 330).

◖ **Grand Island National Recreation Area:** For those who aren't ready to brave the isolation of Isle Royale, Grand Island offers its own treasures, including sandy beaches, sandstone cliffs, historic lighthouses, and clear, if frigid, Lake Superior waters. Better yet, it's only a half mile from the mainland (page 336).

◖ **Miners Castle:** The Pictured Rocks National Lakeshore presents windswept beaches, gorgeous waterfalls, and tall sand-

stone cliffs – including the park's most famous formation, which overlooks the seemingly endless Lake Superior (page 338).

◖ **Great Lakes Shipwreck Museum:** This is the only museum dedicated to the dangers of maritime transport on the Great Lakes. Exhibits include various artifacts from "Lake Superior's Shipwreck Coast," such as a bronze bell recovered from the famous *Edmund Fitzgerald* shipwreck (page 347).

◖ **Tahquamenon Falls:** This nearly 50,000-acre, year-round state park preserves one of the largest waterfall systems east of the Mississippi River. Take a scenic train ride and narrated riverboat cruise to these impressive cascades (page 348).

◖ **Soo Locks:** This marvelous structure allows the passage of massive freighters between Lake Superior and the other Great Lakes, the world's largest waterway traffic system. Boat tours guide visitors along this international shoreline (page 352).

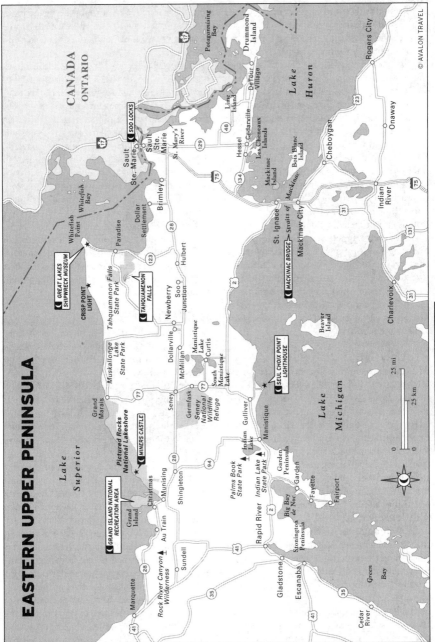

EASTERN UPPER PENINSULA

© AVALON TRAVEL

The peninsula's wild interior, once depleted by the 19th-century logging industry, also contains a variety of stunning lakes and waterways. In the summer, boaters and anglers flock to the Manistique Lakes, while paddlers relish exploring serpentine rivers like the Two Hearted.

Of course, the most well-visited areas lie along the perimeter. The southern shore, beside Lake Michigan, contains nostalgic towns, sheltered harbors, and historic sites like the haunted Seul Choix Point Lighthouse. While the northern shore, along Lake Superior, contains its share of man-made highlights, its most well-known destinations are of the natural variety, such as Pictured Rocks National Lakeshore and Tahquamenon Falls, one of the largest waterfalls east of the Mississippi River.

Sadly, the rugged shoreline along Lake Superior is also known as the "Graveyard of the Great Lakes"—an 80-mile stretch that has witnessed the wreckage of more than 300 ships, the memories of which are preserved within the Great Lakes Shipwreck Museum, the Alger Underwater Preserve, and the Whitefish Point Underwater Preserve.

PLANNING YOUR TIME

Airports, bus stations, and public transit systems are few and far between in the Upper Peninsula, so while it's possible to reach the eastern half by flying into Escanaba, Marquette, or Sault Ste. Marie, you'll definitely require a car to explore much of the area. Though not a compact region, the eastern U.P. is relatively easy to navigate via its main routes, such as I-75 between St. Ignace and Canada, US-2 along Lake Michigan, M-28 from I-75 to Munising, and M-123 between I-75, Paradise, and Newberry.

At minimum, you'll need at least four days to visit St. Ignace, Sault Ste. Marie, Pictured Rocks, and the attractions near Whitefish Bay. A week or more will be necessary for die-hard outdoor enthusiasts or those interested in exploring the Lake Michigan shoreline and inland lakes. Although you don't have to worry about crowds in much of this region, you do have to bear the seasons in mind. In general,

the U.P. is much harsher than Michigan's lower half. Summer here is cooler, especially in the evening, and winter tends to come faster and stay longer.

Pictured Rocks' tourist season, for instance, is short. Most of the park's 594,000 annual visitors come in July and August when they're most likely to enjoy daytime temperatures in the 70s. Visit in June and you'll share the park with fewer people, but the black flies and mosquitoes often aren't worth the trade-off. May and September may be the park's finest months. No matter when you go, though, pack plenty of warm clothes, just in case—and try to avoid swimming in Lake Superior, which is bone-numbing all year long.

For more information about the communities and attractions within the eastern U.P., consult the **Upper Peninsula Travel & Recreation Association** (UPTRA, P.O. Box 400, Iron Mountain, MI 49801, 906/774-5480 or 800/562-7134, www.uptravel.com).

HISTORY

As with other parts of Michigan, the history of the eastern U.P. was defined by its Native American cultures, the 19th-century logging industry, and the Great Lakes' use as a major shipping route. Names like Chippewa County, old logging towns like Blaney Park, and the presence of numerous lighthouses and shipwrecks along the Lake Michigan and Lake Superior shorelines are evidence of this diverse past.

Of course, the two main towns in the eastern U.P. have their own interesting histories. St. Ignace was founded by Father Marquette in 1671 and named for St. Ignatius of Loyola. Once the bustling hub of the 17th-century French fur trade, St. Ignace witnessed even more growth in the 1800s, as the logging and fishing industries prospered. The lumber industry came to an abrupt halt in the early 20th century, when the U.P.'s forests were nearly depleted of their timber. Although railroad ferries made it easier for travelers to cross the Straits of Mackinac from lower Michigan, it was the opening of the Mackinac Bridge in 1957 that improved the town's fortunes, facilitating the flow of tourists.

Even older is Sault Ste. Marie, which was first settled by the Ojibwa Indians in the 1500s. After discovering a rich supply of whitefish in the turbulent waters, they established a permanent settlement along the shore. The Ojibwa lived here for more than 300 years, but the combination of warring Iroquois—forced west by European immigrants—and the ever-growing European settlement of Sault Ste. Marie (founded in 1668) eventually drove the Ojibwa from the region.

By the early 1800s, Michigan's northern reaches were increasingly being settled, and people were discovering the bounty of natural resources—copper, iron, lumber, grain—ringing the shores of Lake Superior. The only problem was those rapids. For decades, ship cargo had to be unloaded by hand, portaged around the rapids by horses and mules pulling carts, then reloaded onto another boat. In 1839, the American Fur Company built a short railroad line, which eased the job, but it remained backbreaking and exceedingly slow. While shipping was booming on the lower Great Lakes, Superior remained largely isolated, its cargo backed up by the rapids.

Eastern industrialists began lobbying for government-funded locks. Locals, however, opposed such a project, fearing the loss of their portaging business. The town managed to stave off the inevitable until 1852, when President Millard Fillmore signed a bill authorizing the first lock at Sault Ste. Marie. In 1855, the State Lock opened, a system of two 350-foot-long locks. In the first year, nearly 12,000 tons of iron ore passed through the locks; within a decade, that figure grew to more than 120,000 tons. By World War I, the nation's hunger for iron and copper, coupled with the opening of vast iron mines in Minnesota's Mesabi Range, made the Soo Locks the busiest shipping canal in the world.

Soon after the completion of the State Lock, the burgeoning commercial traffic indicated that more locks were needed. The 515-foot Weitzel Lock opened in 1881. Since then, a succession of locks have been built, to handle both the traffic and the increasing size of Great Lakes-area ships. Today, three U.S. locks are in operation (there's a fourth, smaller lock on the Canadian side), including the 1,200-foot Poe Lock built in 1968 to accommodate the huge vessels now common on the Great Lakes.

Nowadays, Sault Ste. Marie is inseparable from the locks that shaped its past. Although Lake Superior State University and the Ojibwa-owned Kewadin Casinos are two of the area's largest employers, tourism remains a staple of the economy—with many of those visitors coming specifically to see the parade of commerce that incessantly passes through town.

St. Ignace and Vicinity

The St. Ignace (IG-nus) economy benefits from two groups of tourists: those stopping by on their way to Upper Peninsula destinations, and those using it as a base for Mackinac Island day trips and area exploration. Along with a large supply of lodgings, restaurants, and services, the city at the north end of the Mackinac Bridge has a few attractions of its own, including museums, parks, even a casino. To the east, you'll also find several islands worth a look.

SIGHTS
◀ Mackinac Bridge

Opened in late 1957, the Mackinac Bridge was built to link Michigan's two disparate peninsulas. Presently, "Mighty Mac" is the third-longest suspension bridge in the world. Once you've crossed the five-mile-long bridge (one-way toll $4), between Mackinaw City and St. Ignace, make a quick stop at lovely **Bridge View Park,** where you can snap pictures of this modern engineering marvel. The eight-acre grounds include an observation building and several picnic pavilions. For more information about the bridge, consult the **Mackinac Bridge Authority** (www.mackinacbridge.org).

Father Marquette National Memorial

High above the Straits of Mackinac, in **Straits State Park** (720 Church St., 906/643-8620, annual $11 Recreation Passport for Michigan residents or $8.40 day-use fee/$30.50 yearly Recreation Passport for nonresidents required), west of I-75 and south of US-2, this open-air site commemorates French explorer and Jesuit missionary Jacques Marquette. In the 1660s and 1670s, Marquette paddled through the Great Lakes, founding dozens of cities—including Sault Ste. Marie and St. Ignace—along the way. Next, Marquette linked up with Louis Joliet and paddled another several thousand miles, thus becoming the first white explorers of the Mississippi. Walking trails at the **Father Marquette National Memorial** (www.michigan.gov/dnr, 9:30am-5pm daily Memorial Day-Labor Day) feature interpretive signs that discuss Marquette's Great Lakes travels and the impact that geography had on the area's settlement.

Museum of Ojibwa Culture

In contrast to the Father Marquette memorial, the excellent **Museum of Ojibwa Culture** (500 N. State, 906/643-9161, 10am-6pm daily, $2 adults, $1 children under 13) tells the story of the Ojibwa and the effect that the European explorers had on their culture. Ironically, the museum is on the presumed site of Father Marquette's grave and the site of his Jesuit mission.

Displays housed in a former Catholic church include artifacts from archaeological digs on the grounds (some dating to 6000 BC), explanations of how the Ojibwa adapted and survived in the area's sometimes harsh climate, and a discussion of how they allied with the French fur traders, though it greatly diminished their traditional way of life. The Huron boardwalk follows the shoreline, with interpretive signs

explaining the role of the bay in the area's settlement.

ENTERTAINMENT

St. Ignace might not be the hottest nightlife spot in Michigan, but you will find at least one round-the-clock entertainment venue. The **Kewadin Casino** (3015 Mackinac Trail, 800/539-2346, www.kewadin.com) promises Las Vegas-style gaming 24 hours daily and top-notch live entertainment on Friday and Saturday nights. Situated on the shores of Lake Huron, the casino resort also offers an 81-room hotel with plenty of amenities. Kewadin has four other casinos in the eastern Upper Peninsula, in the towns of Hessel, Manistique, Christmas, and Sault Ste. Marie.

ACCOMMODATIONS

The St. Ignace area offers plenty of lodgings, from simple motels to full-service resorts. If you're looking for an inexpensive choice, **America's Best Value Inns** (1074 N. State St., 906/643-7777, www.americasbestvalueinnstignace.com, $59-76 d) offers basic rooms at a good value. For something a little fancier, stay at the **Kewadin Casino** (3015 Mackinac Trail, 800/539-2346, www.kewadin.com, $70-89 d), which offers an 81-room hotel, an indoor pool, a fitness center, and a game room. Unfortunately, pets aren't allowed.

Camping

The St. Ignace area provides campers lots of options, especially if you want to stay somewhere with some seclusion but still be close to the area's many attractions. Just a couple of miles west of the bridge, the **Lakeshore Park Campground** (416 Pointe La Barbe, 906/643-9522, www.lakeshoreparkcampground.com, $25-40 daily) has RV sites, tent spaces, and easy access to Lake Michigan. **Straits State Park** (720 Church St., 906/643-8620, annual $11 Recreation Passport for Michigan residents or $8.40 day-use fee/$30.50 yearly Recreation Passport for nonresidents required) may not be particularly peaceful, but the 270 modern and semi-modern sites ($16-28 daily) are clean and

THE BUILDING OF "BIG MAC"

© DANIEL MARTONE

"Big Mac," the link between Michigan's two peninsulas

A bridge across the Straits of Mackinac, connecting the Lower and Upper Peninsulas of Michigan, was first proposed in 1884. It remained a point of debate for decades. Detractors believed that such a structure – required to span nearly five miles of open water – was an impossible feat. But "the people of Michigan built the world's greatest bridge," wrote bridge designer David B. Steinman. "They built it in the face of discouragement, of faintheartedness on the part of many of their leaders, of warnings that the rocks in the straits were too soft, the ice too thick, the winds too strong, the rates of interest on the bonds too high, and the whole concept too big."

Steinman and his supporters proved the detractors wrong. After three years of construction and $99 million, the Mackinac Bridge opened on November 1, 1957. It was, and is, an engineering marvel, one of the longest suspension bridges in the world and definitely the longest in the Western Hemisphere. Some 33 underwater foundations support the five-mile-long steel structure. It is designed to withstand anything Mother Nature can dish out, including winds of up to 600 miles per hour!

Granted, it can be unnerving to drive across the Mackinac Bridge, which visibly bows as much as 30 feet in strong crosswinds. The 552-foot-high towers are designed to give, too, swaying as much as 15 feet. Not everyone appreciates the engineering show; bridge workers take over the wheel numerous times each year for drivers too terrified to cross the bridge themselves.

But for most, the Mackinac Bridge is Michigan's pride and joy. Not only do hotel rooms with bridge views command premium rates, but also the bridge opened up the Upper Peninsula to the hundreds of cars that used to form a huge snarl waiting for the ferry. (Especially during fall hunting season, the wait to cross the straits could stretch to six hours or more.) Today, it's just a matter of handing over $4 (or more, if you're driving a bus, motorhome, tractor trailer, or other commercial vehicle) and keeping both hands on the wheel – and all of Michigan is yours to explore, linked together as one.

For more information about "Big Mac," which serves over 4.2 million vehicles annually, contact the **Mackinac Bridge Authority** (N 415 I-75, St. Ignace, www.mackinacbridge.org).

convenient. Aim for the nicely wooded sites right on the straits, which offer great views of the bridge. To reach the park, take I-75 to US-2 and exit at Church Street, then follow Church south for a half mile. For camping reservations, call 800/447-2757 or visit www. michigan.gov/dnr.

FOOD

When you're craving a bite to eat, consider the Kewadin Casino's two dining options: the **Horseshoe Bay Restaurant** (7am-9pm Sun.-Thurs., 7am-midnight Fri.-Sat. May-Oct., 7am-8pm Sun.-Thurs., 7am-10pm Fri.-Sat. Nov.-Apr., $6-25) and the **White Tail Sports Bar & Grill** (7am-9pm Sun.-Thurs., 7am-midnight Fri.-Sat. May-Oct., 7am-8pm Sun.-Thurs., 7am-10pm Fri.-Sat. Nov.-Apr., $9-16). You can also stop by the **Mackinac Grille** (251 S. State St., 906/643-7482, www. mackinacgrille.com, 10:30am-midnight daily, $8-16), where you can sample everything from ribs to burritos.

INFORMATION AND SERVICES

For more information about St. Ignace, contact the **St. Ignace Visitors Bureau** (6 Spring St., Ste. 100, 800/338-6660, www.stignace.com) or the **St. Ignace Chamber of Commerce** (560 N. State St., 906/643-8717, www.saintignace. org). St. Ignace offers numerous services for travelers, from groceries to banks. In case of an emergency, dial **911** from any phone, or visit the **Mackinac Straits Hospital & Health Center** (220 Burdette St., 906/643-8585, www.mshosp.org).

GETTING THERE AND AROUND

The easiest way to reach St. Ignace is via car. From the Lower Peninsula, simply cross the Mackinac Bridge; you'll find St. Ignace at the northern end of "Big Mac." If you're already in the U.P., simply head east from Manistique via US-2, an 87-mile trip that, without traffic, will take about 90 minutes, or drive south from Sault Ste. Marie via I-75,

a 52-mile trip that usually takes about 53 minutes.

If you have no car of your own, just hop aboard a **Greyhound** (800/231-2222, www. greyhound.com) or **Indian Trails** (800/292-3831, www.indiantrails.com) bus to St. Ignace (700 US-2 W., 906/643-1531), or fly into one of several regional airports, where you can typically rent a vehicle from a national chain. From **Pellston Regional Airport** (PLN, 1395 US-31, Pellston, 231/539-8441 or 231/539-8442, www.pellstonairport.com) in the Lower Peninsula, for instance, take US-31 North, merge onto I-75 North, and cross the Mackinac Bridge (where you'll have to pay a toll); without traffic, the 22-minute trip will take about a half hour. In the Upper Peninsula, meanwhile, you can fly into **Chippewa County International Airport** (CIU, 5019 W. Airport Dr., Kincheloe, 906/495-5631, www.airciu.com) near Sault Ste. Marie and then take I-75 South to St. Ignace, a 36-mile trip that normally takes about 37 minutes. As an alternative, you can land at **Sawyer International Airport** (MQT, 125 G Ave., Gwinn, 906/346-3308, www.sawyerairport. com) near Marquette and then follow M-94 East to M-28 East to M-77 South to US-2 East, a 157-mile trip that, without traffic, will require about three hours. Then, once in St. Ignace, you can easily get around via car, bike, or foot.

LAKE HURON SHORE

East of I-75, the Upper Peninsula narrows and dribbles off into a series of peninsulas, points, and islands. The area has a simple, pretty feel, the kind of place where casual biking, beach-combing, and picnicking set the pace for a summer day, though there are few true destinations. In fact, the whole area is often over-looked by guidebooks—which is just fine with the locals and summer cottage owners.

M-134, between I-75 and Drummond Island, is a lovely stretch. This pretty and un-usually peaceful road skims along the Lake Huron shore, past coastal villages, rocky bays, and pine-studded islands. **DeTour Village** marks the end of the road and the end of the U.P. mainland. This small village has long

EASTERN UPPER PENINSULA

© ELIZABETH FELS

a marina near Lake Huron

served an important navigational role for ships heading up and down the St. Mary's. Many ships squeeze through DeTour Passage here, the narrow waterway between the point and Drummond Island. They make a turn, or detour, to chart a course from the St. Mary's River to the Straits of Mackinac. When Detroit was still a blank spot on the map, DeTour Village was busy guiding ships, with a navigational light as far back as 1848. It remains a pleasant place to watch the ship traffic.

Les Cheneaux Islands

"The Snows," everyone calls them, though the real name for these islands is Les Cheneaux (lay shen-O), French for "The Channels." And there are channels aplenty. Like shards of glass, 36 long and narrow islands lie splintered just off the U.P.'s southeastern shore, forming a maze of calm channels and protected bays in northern Lake Huron. Not surprisingly, this area is a delight for boaters. Tall sailboats, classic cabin cruisers, and simple canoes all share these waters, as they have for more than a century.

The best way to see Les Cheneaux, of course, is to get out on the water. Aside from the pretty wooded islands themselves, part of the fun is eyeing the beautiful old boathouses that dot the shorelines, especially on Marquette Island. If you've got your own craft, you'll find launches in Hessel and Cedarville, the only two towns in the area. Though the waters are protected and normally quite safe, be sure to bring a chart, or at least a map provided by local businesses. The various bays, channels, and points can be confusing for a newcomer.

Drummond Island

Few would likely guess that low-key Drummond is, in fact, the largest U.S. island in the Great Lakes. About 66 percent of Drummond Island is state-owned; the rest is largely owned by summer residents, who swell the island's population to about 5,000 in July and August. You'd never know it—life in this fishing-oriented place is focused along the shore, which you can rarely see from the island's few roads.

With sandy beaches, inland lakes, cedar swamps, hardwood forests, and open meadows, Drummond Island boasts remarkably diverse animal and plant habitat. Loons, bobcats, moose, and wolves all roam here, and various orchid species grow wild on the island. Biking is a fun way to explore Drummond, since M-134 dissolves into a variety of doubletracks and, eventually, single-track. Kayaking is even better. The fjord-like bays and 150 miles of ragged shoreline make this a magical place to paddle.

For such a mellow island, you might be surprised to run across **The Rock** (Drummond Island Resort and Conference Center, 800/999-6343, www.drummondisland.com, daily Apr.-Oct., $35-59 pp w/cart), a spectacular designer golf course completed in 1990 by then-owner Tom Monaghan, owner of the Domino's Pizza chain. The first-rate course makes fine use of the natural environment, its holes weaving through woods and limestone outcroppings.

Accommodations and Camping

Along the Lake Huron shore near Cedarville, t **Spring Lodge & Cottages** (916 Park Ave., Cedarville, 906/484-2282 or 800/480-2165, www.springlodge.com, May-Oct.) has a wonderful location in the heart of Les Cheneaux. Large and well-kept grounds house cottages, most overlooking the water. In nearby Hessel, you can stay at year-round **C Hessel on the Lake** (210 Island View Rd., 906/484-2440, www.hesselonthelake.com, $125-235 d), which offers 11 fully equipped cottages.

Stay in luxury at the **Drummond Island Resort and Conference Center** (Drummond Island, 800/999-6343, www.drummondisland.com, $147-202 d), a grandiose retreat with handsome log-lodge rooms and several private cottages. Guests have access to all resort facilities, including tennis courts, a restaurant, and a golf course.

The island's best camping is at **Drummond Island Township Park** (906/493-5245 or 800/737-8666), which lies about six miles from

a peaceful morning at Hessel on the Lake

© DENIS FOX

the ferry dock. This rustic campground contains 46 pretty RV and tent sites tucked within the woods on Potagannissing Bay. Many of the sites have electric service; other amenities include picnic tables, fire pits, outhouses, water wells, a sandy beach, and a boat ramp.

Information and Services

For more information about the Lake Huron shore, contact the **DeTour Area Chamber of Commerce** (DeTour Village, 906/297-5987, www.detourvillage.com), the **Les Cheneaux Islands Tourist Association** (Cedarville, 888/364-7526, www.lescheneaux.org), and the **Drummond Island Tourism Association** (Drummond Island, 906/493-5245, www.drummondislandchamber.com). Services are limited here; head south to St. Ignace for groceries and other needs. In case of an emergency, dial **911** from any phone, or visit the **Mackinac Straits Hospital & Health Center** (220 Burdette St., St. Ignace, 906/643-8585, www.mshosp.org).

Getting There and Around

From St. Ignace, you can reach Les Cheneaux Islands by driving north on I-75 and then east on M-134 to Hessel, where you'll need a private boat to access this cluster of small islands; the 29-mile trip between St. Ignace and Hessel will take about a half hour. To reach Drummond Island from St. Ignace, you'll also utilize I-75 North and M-134 East, but pass through Hessel and continue for another 27 miles (30 minutes) to DeTour Village, where you can hop aboard the **Drummond Island ferry** (906/322-5511, www.eupta.net, from Drummond Island 6:10am-5:10am daily, from DeTour Village 6:40am-5:40am daily, $2 adults, $1 seniors 65 and over and students). Besides people, the ferry also accommodates motorcycles, cars, pickups, motorhomes, off-road vehicles, and snowmobiles.

Once you reach Drummond and Les Cheneaux Islands, you can get around via foot, bike, kayak, canoe, boat, and off-road vehicle. Naturally, snowshoeing, snowmobiling, and cross-country skiing are popular modes of transport during the winter months, and, of course, Drummond Island also welcomes cars, trucks, and other vehicles.

Manistique Area

Four factors created the logging legacy that once dominated the southern reaches of the U.P.: vast stands of timber, wide rivers for transporting logs, well-protected harbors, and a building frenzy that began in southern Great Lakes-area ports like Chicago and stretched west across the treeless prairie. Devastating clear-cuts and diminished demand ended the region's logging boom by the early 20th century, but those well-protected ports and deep harbors still serve the area well, as busy shipping centers and enviable fishing waters.

These ports can be accessed via US-2, which traces the incomparable Lake Michigan shore west of St. Ignace. One such town, Manistique, sits where the corkscrewing Manistique River, which pours through the sloughs of the Lake Superior State Forest, empties into Lake Michigan. A community of about 3,050, Manistique offers proximity to historic sites and good swimming beaches, and it serves as an ideal home base for anglers, boaters, hikers, and other recreationists.

DOWNTOWN MANISTIQUE

Manistique presents a few curiosities for history buffs. The **siphon bridge,** built across the Manistique River in 1919, is a strange engineering feat, partially supported by the water underneath it. In fact, the roadway sits four feet below water level. Its construction was prompted by a paper mill just upstream, which needed to dam the river for its water needs, thus raising the river.

Also interesting is the historic **Manistique Water Tower,** a fancy neoclassical brick

THE MOOSE CAPITAL OF MICHIGAN

Northeast of the Manistique Lakes and Seney National Wildlife Refuge lies the village of Newberry, a gateway town to the impressive Tahquamenon Falls. Surrounded by acres of state and national forestland, Newberry also serves as a terrific home base for hikers, bird-watchers, anglers, off-road enthusiasts, and snowmobilers.

The town also has another claim to fame. In 2002, Michigan's state legislature designated Newberry the official "Moose Capital of Michigan." There are, after all, more moose sight-ings in Luce County than in any other place in the state. So, while the majestic moose tend to be elusive creatures, your chances of seeing one in the wild are fairly high in the Newberry area. Just remember to keep your distance, snap photos from afar, and report any moose sightings to the **Newberry Area Chamber of Commerce** (P.O. Box 308, Newberry, MI 49868, 906/293-5562 or 800/831-7292, www. newberrychamber.net, 9:30am-4:30pm Mon.-Fri.), which is located just south of the intersec-tion of M-28 and M-123.

structure built in 1922, now serving as the town's landmark. From the boardwalk, stroll-ers can view the vivid red **Manistique East Breakwater Light,** constructed in 1916 and still operational today.

[SEUL CHOIX POINT LIGHTHOUSE

East of Gulliver, a road leads you down a point to this 1895 light, a worthwhile detour. Pronounced "sis SHWA" or "sel SHWA"— French for "Only Choice"—the **Seul Choix Point Lighthouse** (672 N. West Gulliver Lake Rd., 906/283-3183, www.greatlake-lighthouse.com, 10am-6pm daily Memorial Day-mid-Oct., donation suggested) sits at the end of a finger of land that once offered Native Americans and French fur traders the "only choice" for hiding from storms along this stretch of Lake Michigan shoreline.

The Gulliver Historical Society has done a splendid job of restoring the light and creating a maritime museum in the fog signal building. (It includes an admirable scale model of the lighthouse, made by hand with thousands of miniature bricks.) Climb the tower for great views of much of northern Lake Michigan. You have a good chance of seeing ship traffic, since Port Inland, just to the east, is an impor-tant commercial port. There's also a chance that you'll have an otherworldly experience while touring the site. Over the years, visitors and employees have reported odd occurrences at the lighthouse complex, such as phan-tom footsteps, unexplained smells (like cigar smoke), and misplaced items. Some believe that the spirit of a former lighthouse keeper is still in residence.

To reach Seul Choix from Manistique, follow US-2 East for 12.6 miles to Gulliver, head south on CR-432 for 4.3 miles, and con-tinue south on CR-431/Seul Choix Road for 4.1 miles to the lighthouse. Without traffic, the entire 21-mile trip will take you about 43 minutes.

THE BAYS DE NOC

At Green Bay's northern end, two large penin-sulas—Stonington and Garden—hang down from the U.P., forming Little Bay de Noc and Big Bay de Noc. More than 200 miles of won-derfully protected and undulating shoreline, combined with the region's temperate climate, make for outstanding fishing for northern pike, perch, lake salmon, rainbow trout, smallmouth bass, and especially tasty walleye.

Stonington Peninsula

The quiet Stonington Peninsula is largely ignored by tourists, lacking accessible sand beaches or commercial attractions. It is a soft and peaceful place, with smooth slabs of

© FLORA EHRLICH/123RF.COM

Seul Choix Point Lighthouse

bedrock shoreline and sunny meadows that have reclaimed abandoned farmland. To explore the 15-mile-long peninsula, follow US-2 west of Manistique and turn south on CR-513 or CR-511. The Hiawatha National Forest manages a nice stretch of shoreline along the peninsula's west side, with numerous hiking trails.

The peninsula preserves several stands of old-growth hemlocks, hardwoods, and pines. One of the most notable examples is now protected as the **Squaw Creek Old Growth Area,** part of the Hiawatha National Forest. Though not virgin timber, loggers in the 19th century practiced selective cutting (quite unusual in those days) and left behind several large trees, now huge. Trails are few—just a couple of abandoned logging roads open only to foot traffic. Walking is easy, however, since the high shade canopy created by the trees crowds out the underbrush usually found in the woods.

The peninsula is also an excellent spot for bird-watchers, since the Stonington is a favorite migration stopping point for songbirds. Watch

the water's edge for great blue herons. These grand birds stand straight and motionless in the water for several minutes, then quickly snatch unsuspecting fish out of the shallows.

Garden Peninsula

Like the Stonington Peninsula, the Garden Peninsula is a quiet, peaceful point of land, filled with little-used blacktopped roads perfect for biking, and a handful of sleepy farms and orchards. The main road down the peninsula is M-183, accessed off US-2. As it traces the eastern shore of Big Bay de Noc, M-183 passes through the tiny hamlet of Garden. Along with a few shops, it's home to a commercial fishery at the end of Little Harbor Road, where you can buy some fresh catch.

By far the peninsula's most notable attraction—and rightly so—is the 711-acre **Fayette Historic State Park** (13700 13.25 Ln., 906/644-2603, annual $11 Recreation Passport for Michigan residents or $8.40 day-use fee/$30.50 yearly Recreation Passport for nonresidents required). If you make time for just one stop in this part of the U.P., make it this outstanding state park. Once the site of a large smelting operation, Fayette's limestone furnaces converted raw iron ore from U.P. mines into pig iron that was loaded onto barges bound for Escanaba. In the 1880s, stinky, industrial Fayette boasted a population of 500, and its loud, hot blast furnaces cranked away seven days a week. By 1891, nearby forests that fueled the furnace were all but depleted, and more efficient steelmaking methods came into vogue. The furnace shut down, and the town died with it.

Nearly a century later, Fayette was reborn as a wonderfully restored historic site and state park. Today, Fayette is surely one of the nation's most scenic ghost towns, its dozen limestone buildings tucked along the sheer white bluffs and deep, clear waters of Snail Shell Harbor. Start at the visitors center, which gives a good historical overview and features a helpful scale model of the village. You can wander in and out of the hotel, opera house, homes, and other buildings, some intact, some more decayed.

MANISTIQUE LAKES

Near the convergence of H-33 and H-42, the town of Curtis serves as the base camp for the Manistique Lakes Area. Three lakes—North Manistique, Big Manistique, and South Manistique—combine to offer almost 16,000 acres of shallow, warm waters that are extremely popular with boaters, swimmers, and anglers. Big Manistique, one of the largest lakes in the U.P., is just 5-10 feet deep, and best known for its perch and bass fishing. To reach the town of Curtis from Manistique, take US-2 East for 30.6 miles, turn left onto H-33/Manistique Lakes Road, and head north for 7.4 miles to Main Street. Without traffic, the 38-mile trip should take about 50 minutes. For more information, contact the **Manistique Lakes Area Tourism Bureau** (800/860-3819, www.curtismi.com).

THE FOX RIVER

In 1919, Ernest Hemingway stepped off a train in Seney, asked for directions to a good trout stream, and was directed up an old railroad grade to the east branch of the Fox. Where truth meets fiction we'll never know, but Hemingway's U.P. travels resulted in "Big Two-Hearted River," his Nick Adams tale about fishing on what was really the Fox. (The more lyrical Big Two Hearted actually flows about 25 miles to the northeast.) Consequently, the Fox has always carried a special cachet in the U.P. and among trout fishers.

The **Fox River Pathway** was no doubt prompted by perennial interest in Hemingway's river. The route stretches 27 miles from Seney north to just shy of Pictured Rocks National Lakeshore and, by U.P. standards, is really nothing that special. Its most appealing stretch—especially for anglers looking for fishing access—is the southern end, where the trail parallels the main river for 10 miles. Farther north, it follows the Little Fox and the west branch. Heading north, the trail traverses the Kingston Plains, where loggers left behind "stump prairies." Markers along the route provide information about the area's logging history.

SENEY NATIONAL WILDLIFE REFUGE

Seney was the center of action in the 1880s, both in and out of the woods. Situated along a railroad siding and the shores of the Fox River—used to transport the logs—it became an important transit point. Turns out, the local economy also revolved around drinking, whoring, and gambling. Seney was sensationalized in the national press, right along with Tombstone and other wild towns in the Wild West.

The problem was that Seney never had the huge fertile forests so common elsewhere in Michigan. Glaciers scrubbed this swath of the central U.P. flat, creating a patchwork of rivers, wetlands, and rocky, sandy soil. The red and white pines that did grow here were leveled in just a few short years; soon, loggers were settling for the less valuable hardwoods and small conifers, burning the scrub as they went. Shortly after the turn of the 20th century, they moved on, leaving behind the denuded land and vast "stump prairies."

Optimistic farmers followed the quickly departed loggers. They burned the brush and went to great lengths to drain the wetlands, digging miles of 20-foot ditches. Yet their hopes were quickly buried by the area's poor soils, and they, too, departed almost as quickly as they came. But the fires had a more lasting effect, scarring the fragile soil deeply.

Eventually, humans began to help this beleaguered land. The immense **Seney National Wildlife Refuge** (www.fws.gov/refuge/seney) now manages and protects more than 95,000 acres immediately west of M-77, restoring the wetlands with an intricate series of dikes and control ponds in what began as a Civilian Conservation Corps project in the 1930s. While humans on foot or bike can access much of this preserve via an extensive network of maintenance roads, the sanctuary offers plenty of seclusion for its inhabitants. More than 200 species of birds and nearly 50 species of mammals have been recorded here, including bald eagles, trumpeter swans, loons, even the occasional moose or wolf. Whether you're a dedicated bird-watcher or a casual observer, Seney is a wonderful place to get into and among a fascinating array of wildlife.

Start your tour at the **visitors center** (906/586-9851, 9am-5pm daily mid-May-mid-Oct.), five miles south of the town of Seney on M-77. A 15-minute audiovisual program, interactive exhibits, and printed materials give you a good overview of what you can expect (or at least look for) in the refuge. From the center, the 1.2-mile **Pine Ridge Nature Trail** allows for a quick foray into wetland habitat.

Biking

Many visitors to Seney never get out of their cars and beyond the Marshland Drive, which is a shame. A bike is really the way to experience Seney. Bikes are welcome on more than 100 miles of gravel and dirt maintenance roads, which are closed to all motorized traffic except refuge vehicles. Though you won't find any technical rides, a bike allows you to cover a lot of ground and is quiet enough not to spook much of the wildlife. Besides, there's something magical about spinning down a gravel road amid chirping and twittering, with nothing but waving grasses and glinting ponds surrounding you for miles. No off-road riding is permitted in the refuge.

ACCOMMODATIONS

Several nice mom-and-pop motels are managing to hang on along US-2, though they're getting more and more competition from chains. Let's hope places like the **Star Motel** (1142 E. Lakeshore Dr., Manistique, 906/341-5363, $34-62 d) continue to fend off the big boys. Located a mile east of Manistique on US-2, this tidy, vintage 1950s-era motel has large rooms, meticulous owners, and a nice setting on the lake. It allows well-behaved dogs, too.

The gracious **Celibeth House Bed & Breakfast** (M-77 Rt. 1, Blaney Park, 906/283-3409, www.celibethhousebnb.com, $75-125 d), once a lumber baron's home, is a fine out-of-the-way relaxation spot, or a good base for day trips to Pictured Rocks National Lakeshore, Seney National Wildlife Refuge, Lake Michigan beaches, and more. You're welcome to explore the inn's grounds, which cover 85 acres and include a small lake, beaver ponds, woods, and meadows. A horde of hummingbirds frequenting the backyard bird feeders practically guarantees a wildlife encounter.

Camping

Camping is readily available at dozens of rustic campgrounds within the **Hiawatha National Forest** (2727 N. Lincoln Rd., Escanaba, 906/786-4062, www.fs.usda.gov/hiawatha, $12-18 daily). A particularly nice one is the very secluded—and difficult to reach—Portage Bay campground on the Garden Peninsula's eastern shore. It's southeast of Garden, at the end of Portage Bay Road.

INFORMATION AND SERVICES

For more information about the area around Manistique and Seney, contact the **Manistique Tourism Council** (800/342-4282, www.visit-manistique.com), the **Bays de Noc Convention & Visitors Bureau** (230 Ludington St., Escanaba, 906/789-7862, www.travelbaysde-noc.com), and the **Manistique Lakes Area Tourism Bureau** (Curtis, 800/860-3819, www.curtismi.com). For services like banks and groceries, your best bet would be Manistique, though you'll find a better selection in major towns like Marquette and Sault Ste. Marie. If an emergency occurs, dial **911** from any phone. Even in remote areas, help will surely come—though it might take awhile.

GETTING THERE AND AROUND

The closest airport to this region is **Delta County Airport** (ESC, 3300 Airport Rd., Escanaba, 906/786-4902, www.deltacoun-tymi.org), which offers limited service via Delta Air Lines. As an alternative, you can fly into **Sawyer International Airport** (MQT, 125 G Ave., Gwinn, 906/346-3308, www.sawyerair-port.com) near Marquette, where luckily you can rent a vehicle from national chains like Budget and Alamo. After all, most travelers will find it easier to venture across the U.P. by car. From the Sawyer airport, for instance, you can reach Manistique via M-94 East, US-41 South, and US-2 East, an 83-mile trip that will take about 90 minutes. From St. Ignace, meanwhile, you can reach Manistique directly via US-2 West, an 87-mile trip that, without traffic, will also take about 90 minutes. From Manistique, you can then reach the town of Seney—which lies between the Fox River, Seney National Wildlife Refuge, and the Manistique Lakes—via US-2 East, M-77 North, and M-28, a 40-mile trip that will take about 45 minutes. As with most towns in the U.P., Manistique and Seney are both easily navigable by foot, bike, and vehicle.

Munising Area

When it comes to enticing visitors, nature dealt Munising, situated on the U.P.'s northern coast, a royal flush. The town of 2,330 curves around the belly of protected Munising Bay. The Grand Island National Recreation Area looms just offshore, in expansive Lake Superior. Pictured Rocks National Lakeshore begins at the edge of town and stretches for over 40 miles east. The Hiawatha National Forest spills across the forests to the south and west. So, obviously, if you're looking for outdoor activities, Munising's got all the right cards. M-28 leads you right to the heart of town, where you'll find restaurants, mom-and-pop motels, and the ferry dock for cruises to Pictured Rocks.

SIGHTS
Historic Sites
If you do just one thing in the Munising area, make it the marvelous two-hour **Glass Bottom Boat Tours** (1204 Commercial St., 906/387-4477, www.shipwrecktours.com, June-Sept., $32 adults, $12 children under 13). Pete Lindquist, an experienced local who also operates a dive charter, came up with the idea of installing viewing wells in the hulls of a couple of tour boats, so even nondivers can marvel at the area's shallow-water shipwrecks.

The view through the 8- to 10-foot-long windows is truly remarkable. The boat glides directly over shipwrecks, some in as little as 28 feet of water. They fill the viewing windows like historic paintings, perfectly visible in the clear water and looking close enough to touch. On the *Bermuda*, you can easily make out deck lines, hatches, even piles of iron ore lying on the deck. Weather permitting, the tour visits three shipwrecks, dating from 1860 to 1926. Along the way, Lindquist's knowledgeable crew also shares history and points out features (including the wooden East Channel Light) along the shore of Grand Island.

Waterfalls
The Munising area is thick with waterfalls, and many are easy to reach. The **Munising Visitors Bureau** (422 E. Munising Ave., 906/387-2138, www.munising.org) prints a waterfall map that will direct you to most of them. Nearby Pictured Rocks National Lakeshore also has several notable falls.

The Tannery Creek spills over **Olson Falls** and **Memorial Falls** just on the northeast edge of town. Follow H-58 (Washington Street) northeast out of town, and watch for a small wooden staircase on the right side of the road, across from the road to Sand Point and the National Park Service headquarters. (If you've come by car, note that you can't park alongside the road here, so you'll have to park in Munising or Pictured Rocks National Lakeshore and venture here on foot or via bike.) Climb the stairs and follow the trail through a small canyon to Olson , also known as Tannery Falls.. To reach Memorial Falls, it's easiest to return to H-58, turn right on Nestor Street, and follow the signs.

Right on the outskirts of town, M-28 leads east to **Horseshoe Falls** (turn east on Prospect Street) and **Aiger Falls,** which spills down along the highway. The impressive **Wagner Falls** is right in the same area, just off M-94 near the junction of M-94 and M-28. It's a well-marked spot, operated by the state park system as a scenic site. Though it feels secluded, 20-foot Wagner Falls is just a few minutes' walk from the parking area. Continue up the streamside trail past the main falls to a second cascade.

About 20 miles west of Munising, wonderful **Laughing Whitefish Falls** has also been protected as a state park scenic site. Here, water plunges 30 feet over hard dolomite rock ledges, then continues rolling and frothing at least twice that far to the bottom of a gorge. To reach Laughing Whitefish Falls, follow M-94 west from Munising to Sundell, then go north on Dorsey Road for 2.5 miles.

SHOPPING

Aluminum snowshoes now dominate the sport, but for beauty and tradition, they simply can't match white-ash-and-rawhide snowshoes. In **Shingleton,** 25 miles west of Seney on M-28, workers at **Iversons Snowshoe & Furniture** (E-12559 Mill St., 906/452-6370, www.iversons-snowshoes.com, 10am-4pm Mon.-Fri.) shape by hand strips of local ash into those classic snowshoe frames. Iversons also makes rustic furniture and trout fishing nets.

DIVING

When loggers were felling the vast stands of pine across the central Upper Peninsula in the 1800s, Munising grew into a busy port, with schooners carrying loads of timber to the growing cities of the southern Great Lakes and iron ore to an ever-growing number of factories. Yet the narrow and shoaly passage between the mainland and Grand Island, and along the Pictured Rocks shoreline, was the downfall of many ships; their skeletons litter the lake floor here.

The **Alger Underwater Preserve** covers 113 square miles, from just west of Grand Island to Au Sable Point near the east end of Pictured Rocks National Lakeshore. Nearly a dozen ships lie here, well preserved in Lake Superior's cold, fresh water. Some wrecks, like the 19th-century *Bermuda* and the 145-foot *Smith Moore,* lie upright and nearly intact. The Alger Underwater Preserve marks many of the dive sites with buoys and helps ensure that they will be protected from poachers—it's a felony to remove or disturb artifacts within any Great Lakes underwater preserve.

Several factors combine to make the Alger Underwater Preserve one of the finest sport-diving locations in the Midwest. There are several wrecks concentrated in one area; the cold, fresh water keeps them from deteriorating; many wrecks are in very shallow water, as little as 20 feet deep; visibility is excellent, usually a minimum of 25 feet and sometimes twice that; and Grand Island helps moderate the cold water temperatures. "It's one of the best wreck diving sites for beginners that I can imagine," notes Pete Lindquist, who operates a dive charter in Munising.

Just offshore from the Munising High School, an **underwater museum** among dock ruins includes underwater signs that interpret large maritime artifacts. The Alger Underwater Preserve also attracts divers for its sea caves in about 20 feet of water, where sandstone cliffs have been eroded by wave action. To arrange a dive charter, contact **Lake Superior Shipwreck Diving** (1204 Commercial St., Munising, 906/387-4477, www.shipwrecktours.com).

ACCOMMODATIONS

The **Sunset Resort Motel** (1315 E. Bay, 906/387-4574, www.sunsetmotelonthebay.com, $69-109 d) has a great location right on Munising Bay at the east end of town. Some rooms have kitchenettes. Unlike most commercial strips, the one along M-28 on Munising's near east side is still within walking distance of downtown and the waterfront. It has some nice chain offerings like the **Days Inn** (420 E. M-28, 906/387-2493, www.daysinn.com, $89-129 d), the best of the chains with a close-in location and an indoor pool.

Camping

For ultimate convenience but with a sense of

seclusion, the Hiawatha National Forest's **Bay Furnace** (906/786-4062, www.fs.usda.gov/hiawatha, $12-18 daily) is a good choice. Just west of Munising, north of M-28, it offers 50 rustic sites with a very nice setting next to Lake Superior and overlooking Grand Island. Some sites almost have their own private stretch of beach, and a short cross-country ski trail at the campground's north end gives campers a little extra breathing room.

FOOD

For a town on the edge of a national park that presumably gets a fair amount of tourist traffic, Munising has surprisingly little in the way of dining. Try **Sydney's Restaurant & Shark Bay Bar** (400 Cedar St., 906/387-4067, www.sydneysrestaurant.com, 6am-11pm Mon.-Thurs., 6am-2am Fri.-Sat., 6am-10pm Sun., $6-24) for fresh whitefish and lake trout, as well as steaks and a Friday seafood buffet, served with an Australian touch. **Muldoon's Pasties & Gifts** (1246 W. M-28, 906/387-5880, www.muldoonspasties.com, 10am-6pm daily) is the best spot in town for a fresh, authentic taste of this potpie-type meal, a U.P. classic.

INFORMATION AND SERVICES

For more information about Munising, contact the **Munising Visitors Bureau** (422 E. Munising Ave., 906/387-2138, www.munising.org). Although you'll find a limited amount of supplies in Munising, you might want to head west to Marquette for a wider range of services. In case of an emergency, however, don't hesitate to dial **911** from any cell or public phone.

GETTING THERE AND AROUND

To reach Munising, you can first fly into **Sawyer International Airport** (MQT, 125 G Ave., Gwinn, 906/346-3308, www.sawyerairport.com), which offers limited service from Detroit and Chicago via Delta Air Lines and American Eagle. From there, you can simply rent a vehicle from several major car rental agencies, head west on M-94, and turn left onto M-28 West, a 42-mile trip that will take about 50 minutes. If you're already driving across the Upper Peninsula, you can access Munising from Marquette via M-28 East, a 43-mile trip that will take roughly 50 minutes. From Sault Ste. Marie, meanwhile, take I-75 South to exit 386, and then follow M-28 West to Munising, a 122-mile trip that will require about 2.25 hours.

◀ GRAND ISLAND NATIONAL RECREATION AREA

Though it's just a 10-minute ferry ride from Munising, the surrounding Lake Superior waters effectively isolate Grand Island. Owned since 1901 by the Cleveland Cliffs Iron Company, the 13,000-acre, largely wooded island was maintained for decades as a private hunting playground for the firm's executives and stockholders. In 1989, the Hiawatha National Forest purchased all but 40 acres of Grand Island and proclaimed it a national recreation area. Except for those few patches of private property, you have the entire island—roughly the size of Manhattan—for hiking, beachcombing, mountain biking, and camping.

With its status as a national recreation area, Grand Island will likely see more development than the rest of the Hiawatha National Forest. Since 1989, the Forest Service has generated mountains of paperwork developing various management plans and putting them out for public comment. Ideas range from leaving the island in its natural state to developing roads, lodges, and other visitor amenities.

So far, a few compromises have been reached. Autos are not allowed on the island except with special permission or those rare few owned by island landholders. Van tours now operate under special permit, bumping along a few dirt roads on the island's southern half. ATVs are allowed October-mid-April; mountain bikes are permitted anytime on all public-land trails. Pets are allowed on leash. Note that drinking water is not available anywhere on the island.

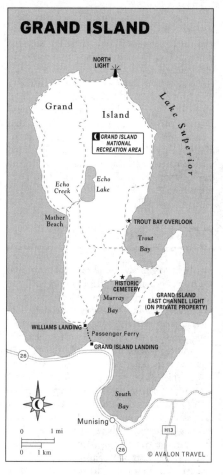

GRAND ISLAND

NORTH LIGHT

Grand   Island

Lake Superior

GRAND ISLAND NATIONAL RECREATION AREA

Echo Creek

Echo Lake

Mather Beach

★ TROUT BAY OVERLOOK

Trout Bay

★ HISTORIC CEMETERY

Murray Bay

GRAND ISLAND EAST CHANNEL LIGHT (ON PRIVATE PROPERTY) ★

WILLIAMS LANDING ■

Passenger Ferry

■ GRAND ISLAND LANDING

28

South Bay

Munising ○

0   1 mi
0   1 km

H13

28

© AVALON TRAVEL

Sights and Recreation

About 50 miles of trails crisscross Grand Island, mostly old roadbeds. If you're just visiting for a day, a mountain bike is the only way you'll have time to see the entire island: It's about a 23-mile trip around the perimeter. In fact, it's probably one of the best mountain bike routes in the U.P. for the nontechnical rider, with wide grassy paths cutting through hardwood forests, passing under towering pines, shinnying up against Lake Superior shorelines, and rewarding you with grand views of wilderness bays and the distant Pictured Rocks.

Both hikers and bikers can reach **Murray Bay,** about two miles from the ferry dock at the southern end of the island. Murray Bay has a nice day-use area and sand beach nestled in a grove of pines. There are also two campsites here, but the location near the ferry dock means you'll have less privacy than elsewhere on the island.

Don't miss the nearby **historic cemetery,** where you can pick up a little history and examine the gravestones of various shipwreck victims and the island's first white settlers. Grand Island had long been a summering ground for the Ojibwa when Abraham Williams arrived in the 1840s to establish a trading post. He raised a family and died on the island in 1873 at the rather amazing age of 81. Today, only the descendants of Williams and their spouses can be buried here.

North of Murray Bay, the island sprouts a tombolo off its southeastern corner known as "the thumb." This landmass wraps north and forms **Trout Bay,** a lovely spot ringed with honey-hued beaches and sandstone cliffs. Watch for the low profile of loons bobbing in calm waters. Trout Bay is home to the island's four other developed campsites, and you could camp a long time before finding another site this pretty.

Camping

There are no reservations, fees, or permits required for camping on Grand Island. The island has two designated campgrounds at Murray Bay (two sites) and Trout Bay (four sites), offering the relative luxury of pit toilets and fire rings. Backcountry camping is permitted throughout the island as long as you stay off the tombolo, off private property, and at least 100 feet away from lakes, streams, cliffs, trails, roads, and natural research areas. No ground fires are permitted. And remember, there is no drinking water anywhere on the island, so come prepared.

Information

For more information about Grand Island, contact the **Munising Ranger District** (Hiawatha

EASTERN UPPER PENINSULA

National Forest, 400 E. Munising Ave., 906/387-3700, www.grandislandmi.com).

Getting There and Around

A **passenger ferry** travels from Munising to Grand Island (906/387-3503, www.grandislandmi.com, times vary Memorial Day-early Oct., $15 adults, $10 children 6-12). The ferry's departure point is about two miles west of downtown near Powell Point. Follow M-28 West and watch for the signs. Even if you're planning just a day trip, you'd be wise to pack some warm clothing and a method for purifying water. Rough weather can cancel ferry service at any time; similarly, probably more than one hiker or biker has lost track of time and missed the last ferry. There is a ship-to-shore radio at Williams Landing in the event of an emergency.

Altran Bus Service (530 E. Munising Ave., 906/387-4845, $16 adults, $8 children) offers two- to three-hour van tours of Grand Island June-early October. The tour makes six stops on the southern end of the island, including Echo Lake, the Trout Bay Overlook, and Mather Beach, an excellent swimming beach where Echo Creek empties into Lake Superior.

Pictured Rocks National Lakeshore

Lake Superior takes center stage at this national park, just 3 miles wide but spanning more than 40 miles along this magnificent lake, from Munising to Grand Marais. Pictured Rocks derives its name from the sandstone bluffs that rise 200 feet directly up from the water's surface. Washed in shades of pink, red, and green due to the mineral-rich water that seeps from the rock, these famous bluffs extend for more than 15 miles, at times sculpted into caves, arches, and castle-like turrets. The national lakeshore also features a lesser-known, but equally spectacular, stretch of shoreline called the Grand Sable Banks, where 200-foot-high sand dunes are hemmed by a 12-mile ribbon of sand and pebble beach. If that's not enough, you'll also find lakes, forest trails, waterfalls, a lighthouse, and other historic attractions—plenty of reasons to put Pictured Rocks at the top of the list for anyone visiting the eastern U.P.

SIGHTS
Munising Falls

Just inside the park's western boundary, a short trail leads to 50-foot Munising Falls, which spills into a narrow gorge before emptying into Lake Superior's Munising Bay. The highlight of this spot used to be the trail that led hikers behind the falls, but erosion problems prompted its closure. It's still worth a stop here, though, for the falls and the adjacent **interpretive center,** which offers a glimpse of this peaceful area's history, home to a belching pig iron furnace in the 1860s. Munising Falls also marks the west trailhead for the **Lakeshore Trail,** a 43-mile segment of the North Country National Scenic Trail, which spans seven states from New York to North Dakota. The Lakeshore Trail runs the length of the Pictured Rocks National Lakeshore—predictably, never far from the water's edge. The park's eastern trailhead lies near Sable Falls.

Past Munising Falls, the paved access road ends at **Sand Point,** home of the national lakeshore headquarters. While the headquarters primarily houses offices (not visitor services), it displays some interesting Coast Guard and shipwreck artifacts on its grounds. Sand Point has a small beach and a boat ramp, a good spot to launch a small craft for exploring nearby Grand Island.

◖ Miners Castle

The sandstone cliffs five miles northeast of Munising Falls are known as Miners Castle,

GREGG BRUFF/NPS

a coastal arch at Pictured Rocks National Lakeshore

for the turret-like shape caused by wind and wave erosion. The nine-story-high rock formation is impressive and ranks as one of the park's most popular attractions, despite a 2006 collapse of one of the signature "turrets." Boardwalks and steps lead you to two viewing platforms out on the rock, where you can peer down into the gloriously clear waters of Lake Superior. If that entices you to do a little beachcombing and wading, a nearby trail leads down some steps through the pines to inviting **Miners Beach.**

To reach Miners Castle, follow H-58 east from Munising to the well-marked turnoff for Miners Castle Road. Before you reach the Miners Castle formation itself, you'll see another sign on Miners Castle Road directing you to Miners Falls. It's a one-mile walk to this pleasant cascade, where Miners Creek tumbles 40 feet over a rocky escarpment.

Chapel Basin Area

Continuing northeast on H-58, the next auto-accessible route into the heart of the park is at Melstrand, where the gravel/dirt Chapel Road bumps six miles toward the shore and another park highlight, the Chapel Basin area. Park your car here and you'll find plenty to entertain you during a long day hike or a weekend: three waterfalls, a deep inland lake, Superior beaches, and a good hiking loop.

Chapel Falls is the key attraction, as evidenced by the wide paved pathway that leads 1.5 miles to the falls. Amid a pale birch forest, frothing water drops like a horsetail some 90 feet into a deep gorge and Chapel Lake below. Continue past the falls to reach Chapel Beach in another 1.75 miles, where you'll find a backcountry campground. From here, you can turn right to Chapel Rock and follow the Lakeshore Trail 1.5 miles to Spray Falls, one of the least visited and loveliest waterfalls in the park, where Spray Creek drops over the sandstone cliffs right into Lake Superior.

If you turn left instead of right at Chapel

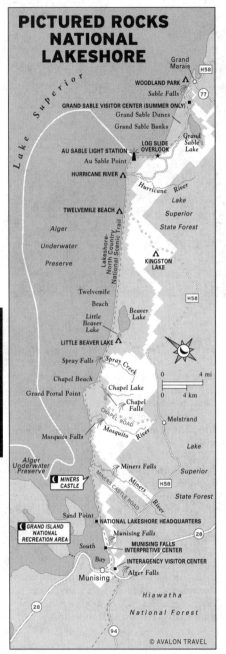

PICTURED ROCKS NATIONAL LAKESHORE

Grand Marais

WOODLAND PARK
Sable Falls
GRAND SABLE VISITOR CENTER (SUMMER ONLY)
Grand Sable Dunes
Grand Sable Banks
LOG SLIDE OVERLOOK
Grand Sable Lake
AU SABLE LIGHT STATION
Au Sable Point
HURRICANE RIVER
Hurricane River
Lake Superior State Forest
TWELVEMILE BEACH
Alger
Underwater
Preserve
KINGSTON LAKE
Lakeshore-North Country National Scenic Trail
Twelvemile Beach
Little Beaver Lake
Beaver Lake
LITTLE BEAVER LAKE
Spray Falls
Spray Creek
Chapel Beach
Grand Portal Point
Chapel Lake
Chapel Falls
CHAPEL ROAD
Mosquito Falls
Mosquito River
Melstrand
Lake Superior State Forest
Miners Falls
Alger Underwater Preserve
MINERS CASTLE
MINERS CASTLE ROAD
Miners River
Sand Point
GRAND ISLAND NATIONAL RECREATION AREA
NATIONAL LAKESHORE HEADQUARTERS
Munising Falls
South Bay
MUNISING FALLS INTERPRETIVE CENTER
INTERAGENCY VISITOR CENTER
Alger Falls
Munising
Hiawatha National Forest

Lake Superior

0   4 mi
0   4 km

© AVALON TRAVEL

Beach, you can make a 10-mile loop around Chapel Basin. Along the way, you'll pass Grand Portal Point—another significant Pictured Rocks landmark—before returning to the parking area. Don't leave Chapel Basin without a visit to Mosquito Falls, a little farther inland off Chapel Road. The Mosquito River spills over a series of ledges, creating an accessible and calm enough waterfall for wading and soaking fatigued hiking feet. A trail leads to various sections of the falls and links up with the Lakeshore Trail.

Beaver Lake

Located near the center of the park, 800-acre Beaver Lake is the largest inland lake in Pictured Rocks. Anglers are drawn to the lake and the tributaries that feed it, especially for trout. Little Beaver Lake, connected by a small channel, has a boat launch. Boats are limited to 10 horsepower or less, making this a pleasant waterway for paddlers. Little Beaver has one of the park's three auto-accessible campgrounds, with eight sites available on a first-come, first-served basis. Be aware that wetlands cover much of the land between Beaver Lake and Lake Superior, so bugs can be a problem here, especially in June and early July.

Two good hiking trails leave from the campground. The short and pleasant 0.7-mile **White Pine Trail** is a self-guided nature trail that circles through a 300-year-old pine forest. The 5-mile **Beaver Basin Loop Trail** makes a lap around Little Beaver and Big Beaver Lakes, then follows the Lake Superior shore past sea caves cut by the lake's pounding waves. Boardwalks skirt the wetlands before returning you to the trailhead.

Twelvemile Beach

An icon near the Twelvemile Beach campground says it all: Indicating that this is a permitted beach area, it shows a swimmer not in the usual "crawl" position, but with water lapping at the ankles. In other words, the water

© L. DIGGS OF PICTURE THIS...

Munising Falls

Just about five miles farther up the beach (or H-58) lies the auto-accessible **Hurricane River campground,** where the Hurricane River spills into Lake Superior.

Au Sable Point

It's a 1.5-mile walk along the Lakeshore Trail from the Hurricane River campground to the **Au Sable Light Station** at Au Sable Point. Built in 1874, the 87-foot brick light and its keepers did yeoman's duty for decades—warning ships away from the rocky shoals that extend out for nearly a mile and create shallows of just 6-30 feet. Nonetheless, at least 10 steamers were wrecked here. As you walk the trail from the campground, look for parts of the shipwrecks just offshore, often poking out of the sand bottom and easily visible in the gin-clear water. The light was automated in 1958 and recently restored.

Grand Sable Dunes

Just east of Au Sable Point, the **Log Slide Overlook** marks the spot of a once-busy logging operation. In the late 1800s, loggers used this high point—some 300 feet above Lake Superior—to send freshly cut logs down to the water's edge where they were loaded on Great Lakes schooners. Today, you can stand on a platform and simply marvel at the view, with the lighthouse to your left, the great dunes to your right, and the brilliant blue of the big lake filling the horizon. If you're in the mood for some exercise, the two-mile stretch of the **North Country National Scenic Trail** from the Log Slide to the Au Sable Light Station is one of the park's most scenic hikes.

The Grand Sable Banks and Dunes (*grand sable* is French for "big sands") stretch for nearly five miles from the overlook, glacial banks of gravel supporting the huge mounds of sand. They are magnificent when viewed from a distance, glowing gold and rising up abruptly from the cobalt waters of Lake Superior. In many areas, especially near the

here is damn *cold*. Swim if you dare, but wading is really more realistic.

Which is what keeps Twelvemile Beach the pristine, stunning ribbon of sand that it is. After all, if such a perfect beach boasted 75°F water, it would be overrun with stereos, Jet Skis, and zinc oxide. Instead, it's a beach where you can stroll for hours with only the company of peregrine falcons, bald eagles, deer wandering down for a drink, even the occasional black bear snorting around in the sand.

The **Twelvemile Beach campground** is easy to reach, just a short drive off H-58 through a pretty birch forest. Many of the 37 campsites string out along a bluff over the beach—come midweek (or early on Saturday, often a turnover day) for one of the choice spots. Some are larger than the average house lot and undoubtedly have a better view. Well-placed stairs deposit campers and picnickers at lake level. The campground also has a nice day-use area at its east end.

© DANIEL MARTONE

Miners Castle at Pictured Rocks National Lakeshore

overlook, the dunes are free of grasses and plants, so you can play around on them without fear of damaging fragile plant life or causing erosion. Though park officials discourage it for safety reasons, no one will stop you from flopping on your butt and rocketing down the slope. Be aware, though, that the climb back up takes a lot longer!

Most people, however, choose to explore the dunes from the eastern end. Near the Grand Sable Visitors Center, a trail winds across the top of the dunes, where marram grass, beach pea, and sand cherry cling to the sand for dear life. (Be careful to stay on the trail here.) Interpretive signs discuss the plants' tenuous hold on the environment. The trail to **Sable Falls** also leaves from the visitors center, a half-mile walk largely composed of steps. As you work your way downhill, you'll be treated to several views of this exceptionally pretty cascade, which drops in tiers through a narrow canyon and out to a

rocky Lake Superior beach. Across H-58, the sandy shores and often warm waters of **Grand Sable Lake** make this a wonderful spot for a swim or picnic.

Grand Marais

Though not part of Pictured Rocks National Lakeshore, sweet little Grand Marais marks the park's eastern boundary and is an excellent jumping-off point for a visit to the national lakeshore. This sleepy New England-style village is worth a visit of its own for its simple windswept beauty. With an outstanding natural harbor—rather rare on Lake Superior's southern shore—Grand Marais was originally settled by fishermen. Loggers soon followed, when sawmills were built here in the 1860s and 1870s to handle the logging that went on just south of here.

Today, commercial fishing remains an economic factor (though an increasingly difficult way to make a living), but a little bit of tourism

THE FACTS ABOUT PICTURED ROCKS

Encompassing more than 73,000 acres in Michigan's Upper Peninsula, **Pictured Rocks National Lakeshore** extends for 42 miles along the southern shore of Lake Superior. It was designated a Michigan state historic site in February 1965, only to be upgraded to the country's first national lakeshore in October 1966. Since then, annual visitation has steadily increased, and in 2012, the park welcomed nearly 594,000 visitors. Here are some other fun facts about Pictured Rocks:

- Pictured Rocks National Lakeshore was named for the varied hues observed in the sandstone cliffs alongside Lake Superior. Caused by mineral seepage, these colors can range from red and orange (iron) to green and blue (copper) to black (manganese) to white (lime).

- In modern times, no pictographs or petroglyphs have been spotted within the park's 42 miles of Lake Superior shoreline. Because the sandstone bedrock here is relatively soft and prone to large collapses, it's unlikely that any rock paintings or carvings from the past would have survived.

- During the summer months, temperatures are commonly in the 70s and 80s (degrees Fahrenheit), though 90-degree days are possible. In the winter, meanwhile, temperatures are usually below freezing.

- Generally speaking, black fly season runs mid-May–mid-June; of course, other biting insects, such as mosquitoes, no-see-ums, deer flies, horse flies, and stable flies, can also be an issue during the summer, so be sure to bring insect repellent and protective clothing.

- While the peak color season is hard to predict, fall colors are usually at their most vibrant in late September or early October. If you hope to see them, you should plan your visit for the earlier end of the season; the longer you wait, after all, the more probable it is that heavy rainfall or unexpected winds will dislodge many of the leaves.

- Pets, which must be kept on six-foot leashes at all times, are only permitted in designated areas, such as picnic areas, drive-in campgrounds, and certain beach areas, like Sand Point and Miners Beach; they are not, however, allowed in the backcountry.

- Although small backpacking stoves may be used at individual campsites, campfires are only permitted in the community metal fire rings within certain campgrounds. They are forbidden, for instance, in the Mosquito River and Chapel Beach Campgrounds. Where allowed, you must keep your fire small, use only dead, fallen wood, and douse it before leaving the site.

- Unfortunately, cell phone service isn't available throughout much of the park.

- Visitors may hand-pick, for personal use only, any wild blueberries, mushrooms, apples, and other native fruits and berries found in the park; there is, however, a limit of one gallon per person for all but the apples, of which each person can gather up to five gallons per week.

If you're curious about other aspects of the park, including the rules pertaining to visitors, contact the headquarters of **Pictured Rocks National Lakeshore** (N8391 Sand Point Rd., P.O. Box 40, Munising, MI 49862, 906/387-2607, www.nps.gov/piro).

Grand Sable Dunes at Pictured Rocks National Lakeshore

GREGG BRUFF/NPS

EASTERN UPPER PENINSULA

is what keeps the town slowly ticking along. The downtown huddles around the harbor, which, incidentally, is a good spot for kayakers to play in the surf on a north to east wind. The few streets here offer some arts-and-crafts shops and a handful of clean, inexpensive motels and restaurants.

KAYAKING

For paddlers, an even better alternative to really experience the grandeur of this shoreline is in a sea kayak. Safety warnings cannot be overemphasized, however. Only experienced paddlers should venture out on their own, and only in a closed cockpit (i.e., no canoes) and after scrupulously monitoring weather conditions. Paddlers can get themselves into serious trouble along Pictured Rocks, caught in sudden summer squalls along the 15-mile rock wall with nowhere to hide. Having said that, sea kayaking along Pictured Rocks ranks as one of the finest paddles on all the Great Lakes.

Kayak rentals (and longer trips to Grand Island and Isle Royale) are available. **Great Northern Adventures** (906/225-8687, www.greatnorthernadventures.com) also offers guided paddling trips, from one-day excursions along Pictured Rocks to multiday trips that combine kayaking with hiking and mountain biking on nearby Grand Island.

ACCOMMODATIONS

Open year-round, the smoke-free **Beach Park Motel** (E21795 Randolph St., Grand Marais, 906/494-2681 or 906/250-7985, $80 d) offers 14 large rooms, all of which have full bathrooms, cable television, wireless Internet access, microwaves, small refrigerators, and waterfront views. Guests can also partake of the free continental breakfasts and complimentary beach cruiser bike rentals. In addition, pets are welcome for an extra $10 fee. As a bonus, the motel is situated a block east of H-77 on Randolph, which means that it's within easy walking distance to everything in town.

East of H-77 on Wilson Street, **The Voyageurs Motel** (906/494-2389, http://voyageursmotel.grandmaraismichigan.com, $59-129 d) sits atop a ridge overlooking Grand Marais Harbor. Nice rooms with mini-fridges and a sauna/whirlpool facility make this a good choice.

Camping

Pictured Rocks has three auto-accessible campgrounds—Beaver Lake, Twelvemile Beach, and Hurricane River—with water and pit toilets. No reservations are accepted, and fees are $10 per night. Backcountry camping is permitted only at designated hike-in sites, mostly along the Lakeshore Trail. A $15 permit is required, good for 1-6 campers, and for any number of nights. Most sites do not have water or toilets. Camping is also available in Munising, Grand Marais, and the Lake Superior State Forest, which borders Pictured Rocks to the south.

FOOD

Grand Marais has a couple of good finds in the food department, both right downtown on H-77. The **Sportsman's Restaurant** (N14260 Lake Ave., 906/494-2800, 8am-10pm Mon.-Sat., $6-24) is more distinctive than its name suggests, with good fish dishes, salads, and homemade soups, as well as plenty of burgers and steaks.

 Lake Superior Brewing Company (N14283 Lake Ave., 906/494-2337, 9am-2am daily, $4-18) does the microbrewery tradition proud, with homemade brews like Sandstone Pale Ale and Granite Brown, as well as sandwiches, soups, and great homemade pizzas.

INFORMATION AND SERVICES

For general information, contact the **Pictured Rocks National Lakeshore headquarters** (906/387-2607, www.nps.gov/piro, 8am-4:30pm Mon.-Fri.). Pictured Rocks also operates several visitor centers, including seasonal ones near Miners Castle and Grand Sable

Dunes. Stop at one of these centers before beginning your trip—they have on-duty rangers, excellent maps, informative displays, and historical information that will enhance your visit. Some have small but decent bookstores, too. The **Pictured Rocks National Lakeshore/ Hiawatha National Forest Interagency Visitor Center** (400 E. Munising Ave., 906/387-3700, 9am-4:30pm daily Memorial Day weekend-Sept., 9am-4:30pm Mon.-Sat. Oct.-late May) is another option.

GETTING THERE AND AROUND
H-58 provides access to the park, winding roughly along the park's southern boundary for about 49 miles and linking Munising and Grand Marais. A large stretch of the road— from Beaver Lake to the Grand Sable Dunes— is unpaved and can deteriorate into washboard rough enough to jar your dental work loose. So, leave the '55 T-bird at home and plan your time accordingly—it's about an 80-minute trip from one end to the other.

Lake Superior Shore

Traveling east from Pictured Rocks National Lakeshore, you leave behind the grand bluffs, enormous dunes, and well-marked attractions for the unknown. Like many U.P. roads, the sometimes paved, often gravel, H-58 winds through the trees, giving few clues as to what lies beyond the pines and hardwoods. The land flattens out here—a far less dramatic landscape than the nearby Pictured Rocks area—so many visitors just pass on by. That's good news for those looking for simple solitude, since these woods hide little-used hiking trails, scenic paddling rivers, undeveloped stretches of Lake Superior shoreline, and all kinds of secluded lakes and campsites known only by regulars. Of course, if you continue along the meandering county roads to Whitefish Bay, you'll find some of the U.P.'s more popular sights, including towering waterfalls and a shipwreck museum.

SIGHTS
Lake Superior State Forest
H-58 passes largely through state forest land, which encompasses much of the Lake Superior shoreline, extends six or seven miles inland in many places, and serves as a buffer zone protecting Pictured Rocks. Several other "truck trails" spin off gravel H-58, sandy roads that are *usually* well marked at intersections and quite navigable. They can be confusing, however, so

venture off onto them with a good map or at least a good sense of direction.

Muskallonge Lake State Park
Wedged on a quarter-mile strip of land between Lake Superior and Muskallonge Lake, **Muskallonge Lake State Park** (30042 CR-407, Newberry, 906/658-3338, annual $11 Recreation Passport for Michigan residents or $8.40 day use fee/$30.50 yearly Recreation Passport for nonresidents required) occupies the site of the old Deer Park township, once home to a sawmill, a hotel, and no doubt a saloon or two. Today, a couple of fishing resorts represent the only commerce in this remote area 18 miles east of Grand Marais.

Water is the draw here. The park's two miles of Lake Superior frontage is wonderfully secluded, with low, grass-covered dunes stretching off to the east and west, and no visible development in either direction. It offers peace, quiet, and good rockhounding, especially for agates. Muskallonge Lake is stocked by the Department of Natural Resources and produces good fishing opportunities for northern pike, walleye, smallmouth bass, and perch. Because the lake is relatively shallow, it warms up enough for comfortable swimming—a rarity in much of the U.P., which accounts for this park's somewhat surprising popularity in summer.

EASTERN UPPER PENINSULA

THE MEMORY AND THE MYSTERY OF THE *EDMUND FITZGERALD*

In early November 1975, the 729-foot-long lake carrier *Edmund Fitzgerald* departed Superior, Wisconsin, loaded with 26,000 tons of taconite pellets, bound for the port of Detroit and area steel mills. Launched in 1958, the *Fitzgerald* had a long and profitable record for the Columbia Line, the ship's Milwaukee-based owner. This was to be one of the last trips across Lake Superior before the shipping lanes and Soo Locks shut down for the season.

The *Fitzgerald* had rounded the Keweenaw Peninsula when, at dusk on November 10, one of the worst storms in 30 years screamed across Lake Superior. Winds howled at 90 miles an hour, whipping the immense lake into 30-foot-high seas. The *Fitzgerald* was prepared for bad weather from the northeast; Superior was notorious for her November gales. Like the captain of the 767-foot *Arthur M. Anderson* traveling nearby, the captain of the *Fitzgerald* had chosen to follow a more protected route across the lake, some 20-40 miles farther north than usual.

Just 10 miles apart, the two captains had been in intermittent visual and radio contact, discussing the perilous weather, which had dangerously shifted from northeast to northwest. At 7:10pm, the *Fitzgerald* captain radioed, "We are holding our own." Then abruptly at 7:15, radio contact was lost. Turning to his radar, the captain of the *Anderson* stared in disbelief: The *Fitzgerald* had completely disappeared off the screen. A 729-foot-long lake carrier and all 29 hands simply vanished, without a single distress call, without a trace.

When the storm cleared, the wreck of the *Edmund Fitzgerald* was found in 530 feet of water, just 17 miles from the shelter of Whitefish Bay. She lay at the bottom in two pieces, 170 feet apart, with debris scattered over three acres—evidence of the force with which the massive hull hit bottom. Many believe the *Fitzgerald* torpedoed bow first, which would have meant nearly 200 feet of the ship was towering above the water's surface at impact.

But even after four decades, an exhaustive Coast Guard investigation, and several dives to the site, no one really knows what happened. Theories abound, of course. The Coast Guard's best deduction is that the ship took on water through leaking hatches, then developed a list and was swamped by the storm's huge waves. Others believe that, outside the normal shipping lane, she scraped bottom on uncharted shoals. Still others believe the warm taconite pellets weakened the structure of the ship, causing it to snap in two when caught between two particularly enormous waves.

Not surprisingly, such controversy has sparked numerous books, articles, and films over the ensuing years, plus a 1976 ballad, "The Wreck of the Edmund Fitzgerald," by Canadian folk singer Gordon Lightfoot. No doubt, however, new books and articles will continue to be written, new songs and films inspired by the mysterious shipwreck, and new theories put forth.

Meanwhile, the *Edmund Fitzgerald* remains in its grave at the bottom of the lake, along with all its victims, whose bodies were never recovered. It ranks as the worst modern-day disaster on the Great Lakes (and perhaps the most controversial as well), a constant reminder of the power of these inland seas.

For further details about this tragedy, or to view the bronze bell recovered from the *Fitzgerald* shipwreck, visit the seasonal **Great Lakes Shipwreck Museum** (18335 N. Whitefish Point Rd., Paradise, 888/492-3747, www.shipwreckmuseum.com, 10am-6pm daily May-Oct., $13 adults, $9 children 5-17, children under 5 free).

Crisp Point Life Saving Station

If lighthouses are your thing, here's a truly obscure one to add to the list. The 58-foot Crisp Point Light sits on a tiny arc of land 14 miles west of Whitefish Point, an isolated, unbroken stretch of Lake Superior shoreline. Though an automated light took over duty decades ago, the handsome 1904 tower and adjacent home still stand. The buildings definitely need work, but the tower was recently painted, so there's some movement afoot for their preservation. You'll need a map to find the light—and a four-wheel-drive vehicle wouldn't hurt either. (Don't attempt the last couple of miles if the ground is wet.) The light is about nine miles east of the mouth of the Two Hearted. Reach it from the west on CR-412, or from the east via the Farm Truck Road truck trail off M-123.

Whitefish Point

"The searchers all say they'd have made Whitefish Bay if they'd put 15 more miles behind her." Singer/songwriter Gordon Lightfoot immortalized the ill-fated ore carrier *Edmund Fitzgerald* for the masses, but locals here need no reminders. Less than 20 miles from Whitefish Point and the safety of Whitefish Bay, the huge laker and all 29 hands on board were swallowed up in mere minutes by a fierce November squall in 1975.

On Lake Superior—the largest and fiercest of the Great Lakes—northwest storms can build over 200 miles of cold, open water. They unleash their full fury on the 80-mile stretch of water from Grand Marais to Whitefish Point (hence the nickname, the "Graveyard of the Great Lakes"). Whitefish Point has long served as a beacon for mariners, a narrow finger of land reaching toward Ontario and forming the protected waters of Whitefish Bay, one of the few safe havens on the big lake.

◖ Great Lakes Shipwreck Museum

To commemorate the many ships that failed to round that point of safety, Whitefish Point is now the proper home of the **Great Lakes Shipwreck Museum** (18335 N. Whitefish Point Rd., Paradise, 888/492-3747, www.shipwreckmuseum.com, 10am-6pm daily May-Oct., $13 adults, $9 children 5-17, children under 5 free). With dim lighting and appropriately haunting music, this fine, compact museum traces the history of Great Lakes commerce and the disasters that sometimes accompanied it. Several shipwrecks are chronicled here, each with a scale model, photos or drawings, artifacts from the wreck, and a description of how and why it went down. Most compelling is the *Edmund Fitzgerald* display, complete with a life preserver and the ship's huge bell, recovered in a 1994 expedition led by museum founder Tom Farnquist, an accomplished diver and underwater photographer.

Housed in the former Coast Guard station, the museum also includes the restored light keeper's home, a theater showing an excellent short film about the *Fitzgerald* dive, and an interesting gift shop with nautical charts, prints, books, and more. To reach it, take M-123 to Paradise and follow Whitefish Point Road 11 miles north. The museum alone makes this out-of-the-way point a worthy detour.

Whitefish Point Light Station

Whitefish Point first beamed a warning light in 1849, and has done so ever since, making it the oldest operating light station on all of Lake Superior. Marking the bay's entry, the Whitefish Point Light Station is a utilitarian-looking 80-foot steel structure supported by a framework of steel girders. Though it looks relatively modern, the light actually dates to 1902. The beefy design was considered an extraordinary engineering experiment at the time, but one deemed necessary to withstand the gales that frequently batter this exposed landscape. It was automated in 1970 and continues to do yeoman's duty.

© LAURA MARTONE

Tahquamenon Falls State Park

◖ Tahquamenon Falls

West of Newberry, the headwaters of the Tahquamenon bubble up from underground and begin a gentle roll through stands of pine and vast wetlands. Rambling and twisting northeast through Luce County, the river grows wide and majestic by the time it enters its namesake state park. Then, with the roar of a freight train and the power of a fire hose, it suddenly plummets over a 50-foot drop, creating a golden fountain of water 200 feet wide.

As much as 50,000 gallons of water per second gush over the Upper Tahquamenon, making it the second-largest falls (by volume) east of the Mississippi, outdone only by Niagara. Adding to Tahquamenon's majesty are its distinctive colors—bronze headwaters from the tannic acid of decaying cedars and hemlocks that line its banks, and bright white foam from the water's high salt content.

Accessing Tahquamenon Falls is easy, since both the Upper Falls and Lower Falls lie within **Tahquamenon Falls State Park** (41382 W. M-123, Paradise, 906/492-3415,

annual $11 Recreation Passport for Michigan residents or $8.40 day use fee/$30.50 yearly Recreation Passport for nonresidents required), which has provided short, well-marked paths to prime viewing sites. At the Upper Falls, follow the trail to the right and down the 74 steps to an observation deck, which brings you so close you can feel the falls' thundering power and the cool mist on your face. The view provides a dual glimpse of the placid waters above and the furious frothing below. Four miles downstream, accessible via the **Tahquamenon River Trail,** the Lower Falls plunge over a series of cascades. The best vantage point is from a small island midriver; a state park concessionaire obliges visitors by renting canoes and rowboats to make the short crossing.

With the dramatic centerpiece of Tahquamenon Falls, it's easy to overlook the rest of this nearly 50,000-acre state park, Michigan's second largest. In sharp contrast to the often frenzied crowds at the falls (more than half a million people per year, the greatest of any U.P. state park), the vast majority of the park remains peaceful, etched with 25 miles of little-used hiking trails. From the Upper Falls, the Giant Pines Loop passes through a stand of white pines before crossing M-123. Once on the north side of the highway, link up with the Clark Lake Loop, a 5.6-mile hike that traces the southern shoreline of the shallow lake.

The final 16 miles of the Tahquamenon River wind through the park, spilling into Lake Superior's Whitefish Bay at its eastern end. Fishing for muskie and walleye is usually quite good in the pools below the Lower Falls. Also consider joining the fleet of runabouts and anglers in waders near the mouth of the river, where trout often school.

It's possible to paddle nearly all 94 miles of the Tahquamenon. A popular put-in is off CR-415 north of McMillan, but you'll start off through several buggy miles of wetlands. A better choice is about 10 miles downstream, off CR-405 at Dollarville, where you'll also avoid portaging around the Dollarville Dam. Beyond Newberry, you'll be treated to a pristine paddle, since no roads come anywhere near the river. Watch the banks for bears, deer, and other wildlife. Naturally, you'll have to portage around the falls, but then you can follow the river to its mouth without any other interruptions.

TAHQUAMENON FALLS TOURS

For another look at the river and falls, you may want to plan a day for the **Toonerville Trolley and Riverboat** (Soo Junction, 906/876-2311, mid-June-mid-Oct., $45 adults, $29 children 9-15, $20 children 4-8). It's much more appealing than its cheesy name suggests, and a good way to experience a remote stretch of the river. Departing from Soo Junction near Newberry (watch for a sign on M-28), a narrow-gauge train chugs its way five miles along an old logging route, through roadless spruce and maple forest, tamarack lowlands, and peat bogs. In about a half hour, the train sighs to a stop deep in the woods at the Tahquamenon's banks. Here, you'll transfer to a large tour boat and cruise downstream nearly two hours toward

the falls. Just as the river begins to roil and boil, the boat docks on the river's south shore, and guests walk the last half mile to the falls. It's a nifty trip, one that has been in operation since long before there was a state park providing easy access to the falls. Originally, the tour operator—the grandfather of present-day owner Kris Stewart—used a Model T truck with train wheels to reach the river.

Curley Lewis Memorial Highway

This twisting, scenic road (also called Lakeshore Drive) follows the curve of Lake Superior's Whitefish Bay from M-123 east 20 miles or so to Sault Ste. Marie. It's almost an attraction in itself, passing through the Hiawatha National Forest, offering up plenty of water views and a handful of worthwhile stops.

Pendills Creek National Fish Hatchery

Four miles west of tiny Dollar Settlement, the federally run **Pendills Creek Fish Hatchery** (21990 W. Trout Ln., Brimley, 906/437-5231, www.fws.gov/midwest, 9am-5pm Mon.-Fri., free) raises thousands of lake trout that grow up to tempt anglers in Lakes Superior, Michigan, and Huron. Visitors can wander around the tanks to peer down at the hundreds of wriggling trout fry (the raceways are covered to keep birds and other predators from helping themselves to a free lunch) and the breeder trout that weigh in at 15 pounds or more.

Point Iroquois Light Station and Museum

Continuing east, don't miss a chance to climb the tower at the **Point Iroquois Light Station** (906/437-5272, 9am-5pm daily mid-May-mid-Oct., free), where Whitefish Bay narrows into the St. Mary's River. Since 1855, a beacon here has helped guide ships through this extremely difficult passage, where reefs lurk near the Canadian shore and the rock walls of Point Iroquois threaten on the Michigan side. In 1870, the original wooden light tower was replaced with the present one, a classic

the Point Iroquois Light Station

white-painted brick structure. A keeper's home was added in 1902.

With fewer and fewer lighthouses open to the public, it's fun to climb the iron spiral staircase for a freighter-captain's view of the river, the bay, and frequent shipping traffic. Stop in the adjacent light keeper's home, too, where the local historical society has restored some rooms to illustrate the life of a light keeper; other rooms feature displays and old photos. The lighthouse and adjacent beach are now part of the Hiawatha National Forest, which should help ensure continued protection.

Mission Hill Overlook

This is the kind of road where every view is better than the last. As the highway curves south, watch for the turnoff to the west marking this terrific overlook. Drive up the sand and gravel road for grand, sweeping views of the river and bay, Ontario's Laurentian Mountains, the cityscape of Sault Ste. Marie, freighters that look like toy ships, the Point Iroquois Light, and, just below, Spectacle Lake.

RECREATION
Bird-Watching

A needed resting spot for birds migrating across Lake Superior, **Whitefish Point** is a bird-watcher's dream. Beginning with the hawk migration April-late fall, the point attracts an amazing variety of birds. Eagles, loons, songbirds, waterfowl, owls, some unusual arctic species like arctic loons and arctic terns, and more all pass through, some 300 species in all. Even if you're not a birding enthusiast, plan to spend some time at this lovely point, where you can wander the sand beaches, watch the birds, and keep an eye out for the big lakers that pass quite close to shore as they round the point. Bring along binoculars and an extra jacket.

Canoeing

The Two Hearted is a fine canoeing river, clean and clear and usually quite mellow—except in spring when, depending on snowmelt, it can crank out some pretty serious white water. A state-designated wilderness river, the Two Hearted winds through pine and hardwood forest; the only signs of civilization you're likely to see are a handful of cottages at the river's mouth. It offers plenty of low banks and sandbars, so picnic spots are easy to find. The Two Hearted is also a widely regarded blue-ribbon trout stream, so be prepared for plenty of anglers when the season opens in April.

Put in at the High Bridge State Forest Campground on CR-407 for a 23-mile trip to the mouth. (You'll find two state forest campgrounds and other camping sites along the route.) Alternatively, you can hook up with **Two Hearted Canoe Trips** (CR-423, Newberry, 906/658-3357), a livery based out of the Rainbow Lodge at the river's mouth. It operates trips ranging from a couple of hours to three days. A popular half-day trip departs from the Reed and Green Bridge (east of Muskallonge Lake State Park on CR-410) and takes out at Lake Superior.

Diving

For experienced divers, the **Whitefish Point Underwater Preserve** offers a fantastic array of wrecks—18 steamers and schooners littered all around the point. (The *Edmund Fitzgerald* is not among them.) Good visibility is a hallmark of this 376-acre preserve. Most wrecks lie in deep water, though—ranging 40-270 feet—and in an area with few protected harbors. Needless to say, only very experienced divers and boaters should consider this spot. For information on area dive services, contact the **Paradise Area Tourism Council** (906/492-3927, www.paradisemi.org).

ACCOMMODATIONS

While there are plenty of chain hotels from which to choose, the area also has some smaller, more interesting lodgings. **Curley's Paradise Motel** (M-123 at Whitefish Point, 906/492-3445, $49-129 d) has nice standard rooms.

Ask about their cottages and home rentals. To the south, you'll find the **Evening Star Motel** (7475 M-123, Newberry, 906/293-8342, www.theeveningstarmotel.com, $49-89 d), which boasts 40 clean rooms, some with kitchenettes. The property also has an indoor heated pool, so bring your swimsuit.

Camping

There are many campgrounds along the Lake Superior shoreline, including the **Mouth of the Two Hearted River Campground** (906/293-3293, $15 daily), where you'll find rustic sites in the state forest. You can also pitch your tent at the **High Bridge State Forest Campground** (906/293-3293, $13 daily), only 10 miles from Pine Stump and 24 miles from Newberry.

INFORMATION AND SERVICES

For more information about the Lake Superior shore, consult the **Upper Peninsula Travel & Recreation Association** (UPTRA, P.O. Box 400, Iron Mountain, MI 49801, 906/774-5480 or 800/562-7134, www.uptravel.com). If you require services like banks, post offices, groceries, and medical care, consider heading to more sizable towns like St. Ignace or Sault Ste. Marie. In an emergency, dial **911** from any phone.

GETTING THERE AND AROUND

Although you can certainly hike, bike, and go horseback riding in the Upper Peninsula, the easiest (or at least quickest) way to navigate this part of the eastern U.P. is definitely via car. From Munising, head east on H-58, which leads to several county roads. To reach the eastern part of this shoreline, take M-123 North from Newberry to Paradise, a 37-mile trip that, without traffic or other major obstacles, will take about 41 minutes.

Sault Ste. Marie and Vicinity

The second-largest city in the Upper Peninsula, Sault Ste. Marie serves as a striking contrast to the surrounding hinterlands of northern Michigan. With a population of 14,200, this historic city is well worth a visit, especially to view the boat traffic through the famous Soo Locks that link Lakes Superior and Huron. At the foot of Whitefish Bay, grand Lake Superior narrows to a close at the St. Mary's River, the sole waterway that connects it to the other Great Lakes. With Superior 21 feet higher than the others, the St. Mary's naturally erupted into a series of falls and rapids near Sault Ste. Marie. *Sault,* pronounced "SOO" (and often spelled that way as a city nickname), means "falling water," a name given by early French explorers. While in town, you should consider hopping across the river to Canada, where you'll find Sault Ste. Marie's sister city, considerably larger and also known as Sault Ste. Marie.

SIGHTS
◖ Soo Locks

Nearly every visitor to the Soo makes a pilgrimage to the locks, right in the heart of downtown at the end of Ashmun Street (Business I-75). The city has wisely dressed up this area beautifully, with lovely **Brady Park.** Blue freighter signs mark the **Locks Park Walkway,** which wanders along Water Street and is dotted with interpretive plaques that share the city's history.

In the heart of the rather formal park, the U.S. Army Corps of Engineers manages the locks and a **visitors center** (Portage Ave.,

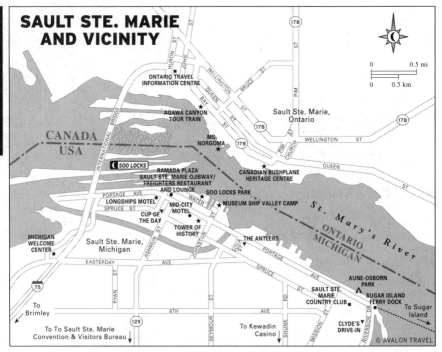

© TOURISM SAULT STE. MARIE

Sault Ste. Marie

906/932-1472, 9am-9pm daily, free), next to a raised **viewing platform** that lets you peer down on the action. Start at the visitors center to make sense of what's happening. Here, a moving model shows how the locks raise and lower ships by opening and closing the gates of a lock chamber and allowing water to rush in or rush out. No pumps are required; the water simply seeks its own level. Other displays explain the construction of the locks. A knowledgeable staff with a P.A. system, along with video cameras upriver, notify you about approaching vessels. In the summer months, you can usually count on a ship coming through every hour or so. The visitors center will have the day's shipping schedule, but be aware that times can change depending on weather conditions and other factors.

It's easy to while away an hour or two watching the ships as they slither into the locks with seemingly just inches to spare. Summer evenings are especially pleasant, when you'll likely have the platform to yourself to watch the illuminated ships. If you're lucky, you might see a "saltie," an oceangoing vessel that's likely hauling grain to foreign ports. Overall, the three most plentiful Great Lakes shipments are iron ore (for steelmaking), limestone (a purifying agent for steelmaking, also used in construction and papermaking), and coal (for power plants).

The locks and viewing platform are open throughout the Great Lakes shipping season, which runs March 25-January 15. Those are the official dates, between which the locks cease operation for maintenance; ice buildup on Superior sometimes affects the length of the shipping season, too. The visitors center is open mid-May-mid-November.

SOO LOCKS BOAT TOURS
After viewing the locks, you can "lock through" yourself on one of these extremely popular tours. The two-hour trip takes you through both the American and Canadian locks and travels along both cities' waterfronts. At busy times, you'll be in the midst of freighter traffic, dwarfed by their enormous steel hulls. The

large passenger boats have both heated and open deck areas. The **Soo Locks Boat Tours** (1157 E. Portage Ave. or 515 E. Portage Ave., 906/632-6301, www.soolocks.com, times vary, $24 adults, $11 children 5-12) depart daily early May-mid-October beginning at 9am.

Other Downtown Attractions

After watching the big Great Lakes boats, the **Museum Ship *Valley Camp*** (501 E. Water St., 906/632-3658, www.thevalleycamp.com, hours vary, $23.75 adults, $11.75 children 6-16) gives you a chance to see what it was like to live and work aboard a giant steamer. This 550-foot steamship logged more than a million miles on the Great Lakes, hauling ore, coal, and stone from 1907 to the mid-1970s. Now, it's permanently docked five blocks east of the Soo Locks. Visitors can tour the pilothouse, engine room, main deck, crew quarters, coal bunker, and more. Throughout, the ship has a number of aquariums and maritime displays, some better than others. Most popular: a display on the sinking of the *Edmund Fitzgerald,* including two tattered lifeboats found empty and drifting on the lake. All in all, it's well worth a couple of hours. Make sure to stop at the museum shop, housed in a separate building next to the parking lot. It has an excellent selection of maritime books and videos.

Like many observation towers, the **Tower of History** (326 E. Portage Ave., 906/632-3658, www.saulthistoricsites.com, 10am-5pm Mon.-Sat., noon-5pm Sun. mid-May-June and Sept.-Oct., 9:30am-5:30pm Mon.-Sat., 10am-5pm Sun. July-Aug., $7 adults, $3.50 children 5-17, children under 5 free), which lies a few blocks east of the Soo Locks, doesn't quite blend with the landscape. Though it's essentially a stark 21-story concrete monolith, the tower presents a wonderful 360-degree view of the twin Soos, St. Mary's River, Lake Superior, and the forests rolling off in the distance. Enjoy the views from an open-air deck; just remember to bring a jacket. The tower also includes a few small exhibit areas and a theater showing documentary videos. Happily, there is an elevator to the top.

The **River of History Museum** (209 E. Portage Ave., 906/632-1999 or 906/632-3658, www.riverofhistory.org, 11am-5pm Mon.-Sat. mid-May-mid-Oct., $7 adults, $3.50 children 5-17) uses the St. Mary's River as the framework for telling the story of the region's history. Life-sized dioramas depict things like Native Americans spearfishing in the rapids and a French fur trapper's cabin. The museum incorporates lots of sound in its displays: dripping ice from melting glaciers, roaring rapids, and Ojibwa elders passing down legends.

I-500 SNOWMOBILE RACE

Founded in 1968, the **International 500 Snowmobile Race** (906/635-1500, www.i-500.com) has become one of the world's largest and longest snowmobile races. Usually occurring in the beginning of February, this annual event lures thousands of snowmobilers to Sault Ste. Marie, where they speed around a one-mile oval course, competing against one another for an impressive purse, nowadays close to $40,000. Visitors, too, relish this frenzied spectacle, one you're unlikely to see in many places.

ACCOMMODATIONS

Now part of the Ramada chain, the rather plush **C Ramada Plaza Sault Ste. Marie Ojibway** (240 W. Portage Ave., 906/632-4100, www.ramada.com, $99-179 d) has the nicest accommodations in town, and the best location, too, overlooking the St. Mary's River and the locks. Ask for an upper-level, north-facing room. The elegant 1928 building has been well restored, with large rooms, an indoor pool, a whirlpool, and the Freighters restaurant. Ask about packages for a better deal.

For the same good location but for less money, try the **Longships Motel** (427 W. Portage Ave., 888/690-2422, www.longshipsmotel.net, $59-99 d), a clean and comfortable mom-and-pop-style motel with a fine spot across from Locks Park. There are plenty of chain hotels near I-75, but they are nowhere near the locks or other downtown walking attractions.

Camping

Right in Sault Ste. Marie, there's a modern, 65-site municipal campground at **Aune-Osborn Park** (1225 E. Portage Ave., 906/632-3268, mid-May-mid-Oct., $20-22) on the St. Mary's River near the Sugar Island ferry dock. Just east of Brimley, **Brimley State Park** (9200 W. 6 Mile Rd., 906/248-3422, annual $11 Recreation Passport for Michigan residents or $8.40 day-use fee/$30.50 yearly Recreation Passport for nonresidents required) offers about a mile of sandy Lake Superior beach, a large modern campground ($16-23 daily), and not a whole lot else. Still, it's a good choice for anyone looking for an easy place to set up camp to enjoy the Soo and other nearby attractions. This is a popular park, so consider making reservations (800/447-2757) if you're aiming for a summer weekend.

FOOD

Start your day at **Cup of the Day** (406 Ashmun St., 906/635-7272, www.cupoftheday.com, 7:15am-6pm Mon.-Fri., 8:30am-3pm Sat., $4-6) for good coffee drinks, a juice bar, and sandwiches and salads at lunchtime. In the Ojibway Hotel, **Freighters Restaurant and Lounge** (240 W. Portage Ave., 906/632-4100, 8am-9pm daily, $4-24) offers a wall of glass overlooking the locks and a very nice menu featuring steaks and seafood, especially local fish. This is a great spot for a good breakfast, too.

INFORMATION AND SERVICES

For more information about the Sault Ste. Marie area, contact the **Sault Ste. Marie Convention & Visitors Bureau** (536 Ashmun St., 906/632-3366, www.saultstemarie.com). For local news, consult the *Sault Ste. Marie Evening News* (www.sooeveningnews.com).

The Sault Ste. Marie area offers its share of services, including banks, groceries, post offices, and more. Just ask the locals for directions—they're a friendly bunch. In case of an emergency that requires police, fire, or ambulance services, dial **911** from any cell or public phone.

GETTING THERE AND AROUND

While it's possible to fly into **Sault Ste. Marie Airport** (YAM, 475 Airport Rd., Sault Ste. Marie, Canada, 705/779-3031, www.saultairport.com) in Ontario, Canada, and cross the **International Bridge** (www.michigan.gov/mdot, $3 passenger vehicles and motorcycles, $4.50-6 vehicles w/trailers, $5.50 recreational vehicles, $8-44 commercial trucks) to Sault Ste. Marie, Michigan, many travelers may prefer to fly into the Upper Peninsula's **Chippewa County International Airport** (CIU, 5019 W. Airport Dr., Kincheloe, 906/495-5631, www.airciu.com). From there, you can then rent a car via Avis and head north on I-75 to Sault Ste. Marie, a 21-mile trip that will take about 25 minutes on a traffic-free day. Incidentally, you can also reach Sault Ste. Marie via bus; **Greyhound** (800/231-2222, www.greyhound.com) and **Indian Trails** (800/292-3831, www.indiantrails.com) both offer regular service to the **Eastern Upper Peninsula Transportation Authority** (EUPTA, 4001 I-75 Business Spur, 906/632-8643, 7am-4pm Mon.-Fri.).

Of course, most travelers will reach the Soo from some other part of Michigan. From the Lower Peninsula, for instance, you'd simply head north on I-75, cross the Mackinac Bridge, and continue about 51 miles north of St. Ignace. From the western U.P., you'll probably just head east on M-28 or US-2, both of which connect to I-75 North. If you have the time, you can even embrace the 463-mile, seven-hour route from Chicago to Sault Ste. Marie, which will involve I-90 East, I-94 East, I-196 North, US-131 North, M-32 East, and I-75 North; just be advised that you'll encounter toll booths on the I-90 East and I-94 East through Indiana, as well as I-75 North in Michigan (for use of the Mackinac Bridge).

However you manage to reach Sault Ste. Marie, though, you'll be able to walk, bike, and drive around the city rather easily. If it's late and you're unable to drive, you can also rely on a taxi. The **Taxi Cab Co.** (906/632-5555), for instance, often transports tipsy passengers from the Kewadin Casino back to their hotels.

SAULT STE. MARIE, ONTARIO

Just across the International Bridge lies the Soo's sister city in Ontario, also named Sault Ste. Marie. With a population of roughly 67,600, it's the larger of the two cities, home to a huge steel plant and paper company. But along with these industries, Sault Ste. Marie, Ontario, also has a lot to offer visitors. Downtown, a lovely **boardwalk** rambles along the river for a mile or so, beginning at the bridge and extending east past fishing platforms, shops, and the MS *Norgoma*, the last passenger cruise ship built for the Great Lakes, now a museum. On Wednesday and Saturday, there's a farmers market near the tented pavilion.

One of the most popular visitor attractions is the **Agawa Canyon Tour Train** (129 Bay St., 800/242-9287, www.agawacanyontourtrain. com, times vary, $73 adults, $64 seniors, $32 children 5-18, $25 children under 5), a seven-hour round-trip through the scenic wooded gorge of the Agawa Canyon. The daylong tour includes a two-hour stopover in the canyon, where you can hike to lookouts, visit waterfalls, wander along the river, or just hang out in the grassy picnic area. The train trip is even more popular in the fall color season, which usually runs mid-September-mid-October, and in winter when it is known as the "Snow Train" (and during which the two-hour layover is eliminated).

Reach Ontario via the three-mile-long **International Bridge** ($3 passenger vehicles and motorcycles, $4.50-6 vehicles with trailers, $5.50 recreational vehicles, $8-44 commercial trucks). Nowadays, U.S. citizens need to show either a passport or an official birth certificate with photo identification, such as a driver's license. You can exchange money and pick up maps and other useful area information at the travel center at the foot of the bridge.

Information

For more information about Sault Ste. Marie in Canada, contact **Tourism Sault Ste. Marie** (800/461-6020, www.saulttourism.com).

WESTERN UPPER PENINSULA

As with other parts of Michigan, town names found throughout the western half of the Upper Peninsula reveal the region's diverse history. Some monikers, such as Mohawk and Menominee, refer to the Native American tribes that once dwelled amid these remote lands. Other names signify words used by the Chippewa Indians, such as Escanaba ("Flat Rock"), Negaunee ("Pioneer"), and Ishpeming ("High Ground"). Many more, however, highlight the area's former mining industries; names like Copper Harbor, Copper City, Ironwood, Iron River, Iron Mountain, and Mineral Hills are nearly all that's left of the copper and iron ore operations that thrived here from the mid-19th to the early 20th centuries.

Following the Copper Rush of 1840, which eventually yielded more mineral wealth than California's better publicized gold rush, and the discovery of iron ore four years later, the U.P. flourished, employing thousands of eager Americans and European immigrants, resulting in the construction of numerous cities, and creating millionaires virtually overnight. Timber was also an important commodity in the U.P., but eventually all three industries declined during the 20th century. Nowadays, the only remnants of this mineral-rich past are the aptly named cities, enormous mansions, abandoned mines, ghost towns, and occasional caveins that occur beneath homes and streets.

In many respects, the wilderness has reclaimed the land, much of which has been preserved in the form of regional, state, and national parks and forests, including the Porcupine Mountains Wilderness State Park

HIGHLIGHTS

LOOK FOR 🌙 TO FIND RECOMMENDED SIGHTS, ACTIVITIES, DINING, AND LODGING.

🌙 **Isle Royale Boat Tours:** For those not ready to venture alone into Isle Royale National Park, the MV *Sandy* offers seasonal boat tours that guide visitors around this isolated archipelago, taking in sights like the Rock Harbor Lighthouse, the Edisen Fishery, Pine Mountain, and Lookout Louise (page 363).

🌙 **Fort Wilkins Historic State Park:** Near the tip of the Keweenaw Peninsula, you'll find this historical recreation area, where visitors can stroll, bike, or ski along a four-mile nature trail, explore a restored 1844 military outpost, view one of the oldest lighthouses on Lake Superior, and watch costumed interpreters demonstrate the peninsula's history (page 369).

🌙 **Quincy Mine:** This former copper mine, once one of the world's richest, offers visitors a fascinating glimpse into a bygone era; informative excursions include a visit to the on-site museum, a video tour of the towering shaft house, a guided stroll through the 1894 hoist engine building, and an expert-led tram ride to the underground mine (page 372).

🌙 **Porcupine Mountains Wilderness State Park:** Hikers, mountain bikers, anglers, canoeists, and cross-country skiers can explore towering trees, secluded lakes, wild rivers, and sights like the Lake of the Clouds Overlook (page 379).

🌙 **Ironwood-Area Downhill Skiing:** The Upper Peninsula contains several fantastic downhill ski resorts. In fact, the mountainous region around Ironwood boasts three solid choices, all of which offer lessons for first-timers, not to mention plenty of snow-covered slopes throughout the Porcupine Mountains (page 383).

🌙 **Iron County Historical Museum:** The U.P.'s largest outdoor museum presents an assortment of exhibits, including wildlife art, early mining equipment, an 85-foot-long miniature logging camp, a former mining site, and several old log cabins (page 386).

and Ottawa National Forest, where there are miles of hiking, mountain biking, and cross-country skiing trails; where cell phone signals rarely, if ever, exist; where the chance of seeing moose, timber wolves, and black bears is high; and where the summer sun might not set until 11pm.

While tourism has never thrived here as in the Lower Peninsula, it seems that every year more and more people are discovering this region's unspoiled beauty and cultural attractions, including several museums in and around Marquette, the U.P.'s largest city, as well as the various heritage sites that make up

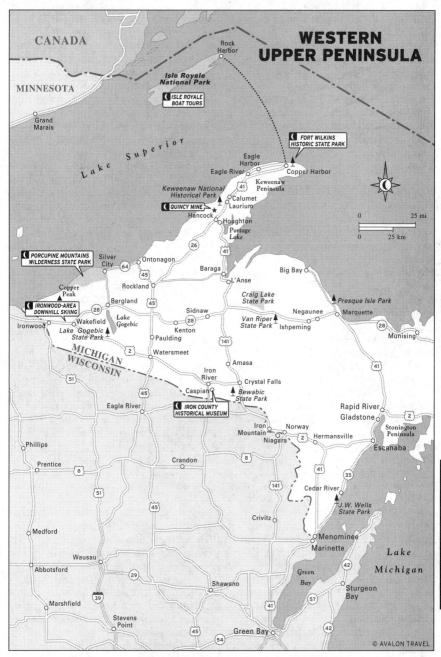

the Keweenaw National Historical Park, established in 1992. Outdoor enthusiasts travel to the western U.P. and nearby Isle Royale National Park, an isolated, road-free archipelago in Lake Superior, to savor the region's cornucopia of wild rivers, majestic waterfalls, desolate beaches, remote lakes, downhill ski resorts, and surprisingly tall mountains (by Midwestern standards), including 1,979-foot Mount Arvon east of L'Anse. For those seeking solitude, history, and challenging winters, this is an ideal destination.

PLANNING YOUR TIME

The western Upper Peninsula is even less compact than the eastern half, especially when you consider places like isolated Isle Royale, the protruding Keweenaw Peninsula, and the stretch between Escanaba and Menominee. The easiest way to traverse this vast region is via vehicle. Of course, you'll need to rely on canoes, bikes, boats, horses, or your own feet if you want to explore the wilderness.

Luckily, several major highways snake across this region. From Wisconsin, take US-2 East or US-51 North to Ironwood, US-45 North to Watersmeet, US-141 North to Iron Mountain, and US-41 North to Menominee. From the Mackinac Bridge, head west on US-2 to Escanaba, or drive north on I-75 and take M-28 West to Marquette. Either US-41 North or M-26 North can guide you onto and up the Keweenaw Peninsula, from which ferries and small planes can take you to Isle Royale.

Although much of the western U.P. comprises untamed land, with sizable towns few and far between, it is possible to reach this part of Michigan via commercial transportation. Greyhound serves several towns, including Hancock, Ironwood, Iron River, Iron Mountain, Escanaba, and Marquette. The region's primary airport is Sawyer International Airport, south of Marquette; it's served by Delta Air Lines and American Eagle. Smaller airports also exist in the Houghton, Ironwood, and Escanaba areas.

Still, the relative difficulty of reaching the western U.P. promises fewer tourists throughout the year—which is ideal for those seeking solitude. So, your seasonal interests will likely determine when you decide to visit this region and how long you plan to stay. If you intend to hit the highlights of Isle Royale, the Keweenaw Peninsula, and Marquette, then three days should be sufficient. A week or more is necessary for those who appreciate the great outdoors; after all, average visitors can spend at least three days just exploring Isle Royale.

During your visit to the western U.P., you should keep in mind the matter of time zones. While most of the Upper Peninsula, like the Lower Peninsula, is situated in the Eastern Time Zone (ET), the four counties bordering Wisconsin—Gogebic, Iron, Dickinson, and Menominee—are in the Central Time Zone (CT).

For more information about this area, consult the **Western U.P. Convention & Visitor Bureau** (P.O. Box 706, Ironwood, MI 49938, 906/932-4850 or 800/522-5657, www.explore-westernup.com).

HISTORY

Raking off the back of the Upper Peninsula like a ragged dorsal fin, the Keweenaw (KEE-wuh-naw) Peninsula, though once home to the Copper Culture Indians, was quickly shunned by early European immigrants: It was, after all, hopelessly remote, not to mention nearly engulfed by Lake Superior, smothered in snows half the year, and blanketed by impenetrable forests, which grew out of untillable rock and infertile sand. They dismissed it as nothing more than a wasteland, even more so than the rest of the U.P.

But then, in 1840, state geologist Douglass Houghton confirmed the presence of copper. Vast deposits of pure, native copper, much of it right near the surface, there for the taking. The young United States had an insatiable appetite for the metal: first, for new industrial machinery and, later, for Civil War hardware, electrical wiring, and other innovations. Houghton's find was as good as gold. Actually, it was even better than gold.

The Copper Rush began almost overnight,

first with prospectors, then large mining enterprises flooding the "wasteland" of the Keweenaw. It was the nation's first mineral rush. Copper employed thousands of immigrant laborers, built cities, made millionaires, and prompted extravagant luxuries like opera houses and "copper baron" mansions. Before it was over, King Copper generated more than $9.6 billion—10 times more money than the California gold rush.

The Keweenaw's copper legacy still looms large, but now in the form of abandoned mines, ghost towns buried in the forest, and the odd juxtaposition of lavish buildings in almost forgotten towns. After it was neglected for most of the 20th century, a slow pull finally began in the 1970s to preserve the Keweenaw's copper heritage. The result is the Keweenaw National Historical Park, established in 1992 (and still in development). To be sure, a lot of rich history has been demolished, thrown away, or crushed under the weight of winter snows. But an astounding amount remains, too.

The Keweenaw Peninsula might have its roots in veins of copper, but much of the rest of the western Upper Peninsula traces its heritage to iron. You can read it in the town names—Iron Mountain, Iron River, National Mine, Mineral Hills—and see it on the faces of the residents, an ethnically diverse mix descended from the melting pot of immigrant mine workers. The U.P.'s iron industry stretched from the western border east some 150 miles to the Lake Superior port of Marquette and the Lake Michigan port of Escanaba. It comprised three major ranges: the Gogebic Range, with operations centered around Ironwood; the Menominee Range, based largely around the

Iron River and Iron Mountain areas; and the Marquette Range, encompassing Marquette and the Ishpeming/Negaunee area.

Federal surveyors first discovered iron ore in 1844, near present-day Iron River. As workers systematically surveyed this strange landmass recently acquired by Michigan, their compasses swung wildly near Negaunee, where iron ore was so plentiful it was visible even on the surface, intertwined in the roots of a fallen tree. The tree is the official symbol of the city of Negaunee, which itself became completely intertwined with the rise and fall of the iron industry.

Aside from a handful of small mining operations, the unfathomable wealth of the Upper Peninsula's iron remained largely untapped for several decades, until the ever-expanding web of railroad lines reached the area. In the 1870s, the arrival of the railroad prompted the development of the first major mines in the Menominee Range. A few years later, the Gogebic Range opened. Many of the early mines were open-pit affairs, but soon the need for iron ore drove miners deeper and deeper underground. Today, communities like Ishpeming sit atop a swiss-cheese patch of earth riddled with mine shafts; occasionally, tracts of land sink, leaving behind tilted and abandoned houses.

World War II and its insatiable demand for iron drove area mines to peak production, eventually depleting some of them. By the 1960s and 1970s, the western U.P. iron ranges grew quiet after shipping out nearly two billion tons of ore. All underground iron mines in the U.P. closed by 1978, hurt by foreign steelmakers and the use of more and more plastics in manufacturing.

Isle Royale National Park

Stranded in the vast waters of Lake Superior, Isle Royale is perhaps the model of what a national park is supposed to be—wild, rugged, and remote. No roads touch the 45-mile-long island, and its only contact with the outside world remains ship-to-shore radio. One of the least visited parks in the National Park Service system, Isle Royale's yearly attendance is less than a single weekend's worth at Yellowstone.

Civilization on Isle Royale (ROY-al) is concentrated in two small developments at opposite ends of the island. Windigo, on the southwest end, includes an information center, a grocery, and a marina. Rock Harbor, near the northeast end, offers the same, plus a no-frills lodge and restaurant across from the ferry dock, and a handful of cabins overlooking fingerlike Tobin Harbor. The rest of the island is backcountry, 210 square miles of forested foot trails, rocky bluffs, quiet lakes, and wilderness campsites.

Those who make the trek by boat or seaplane to Isle Royale come primarily to hike its 165 miles of trails, fish its 46 inland lakes, and paddle its saw-toothed shoreline. Wildlife viewing is popular, too, especially for the moose that swam across from Ontario several decades back, and the eastern timber wolves that later followed their prey across on the pack ice. Though the wolves are notoriously elusive, you can pretty much bet that your wildlife sightings will outnumber your human ones on Isle Royale.

The geography of Isle Royale is inseparable from the water that surrounds it. Along with its namesake island—the largest in Lake Superior—Isle Royale National Park actually consists of an archipelago of some 400 islands, all of them remnants of the same landmass. More than 80 percent of the national park lies underwater, beneath shallow ponds, bogs, inland lakes, and the clear, cold water of Lake Superior. And here's some trivia: Ryan Island, located on Isle Royale's Siskiwit Lake, is the largest island in the largest lake on the largest island in the largest freshwater lake in the world.

The islands' wildlife, especially the moose and wolf populations, have been a draw for many naturalists and tourists alike. Populations for both animals have fluctuated rather dramatically over the decades. Moose, which numbered more than 1,000 in 2002, plummeted to less than 400 in 2007, mainly due to increasingly warm summers, which caused the moose to eat less and fatal ticks to thrive. As of early 2010, the population has risen to more than 500.

Still, hikers have a decent chance of spotting the 1,000-pound mammals, which often feed in ponds and lowlands or along inland lakeshores. Hidden Lake, across Tobin Harbor south of Lookout Louise, is an exceptionally good spot, since moose have a taste for its mineral licks. If you're lucky enough to come upon a moose, give it very, very wide berth. Although they look cartoonish and friendly, moose can be exceptionally dangerous if approached too closely—especially cows with calves or males during the fall rutting season—capable of inflicting lethal blows with their hooves.

The wolf population, too, has dwindled, in part because of hot summers and the lessening of their food supply. The wolves, which numbered around 19 in early 2010, tend to hide out in the remote southwestern corner of the island. Only the rare backpacker ever spots one of the shy and stealthy creatures, and many a wolf howl heard at night is probably the haunting call of a loon. But the notion that wolves are there, somewhere—perhaps even watching from deep in the forest—is compelling enough for most, especially those lucky enough to spot a paw print across the trail.

While many national parks struggle with their fate as islands of wilderness surrounded by a more developed world, Isle Royale has the advantage of a much larger buffer zone protecting it from outside encroachment and influence. As a result, it is one of the most closely managed holdings in the national park system. That's good or bad depending on your opinion of the park service, but it does present some unique opportunities for protecting the wilderness. For starters, it is one of the few parks that already regulate the number of visitors who pass through their "gates." Though logistics have done a sufficient job of keeping numbers down thus far, the National Park Service only has to cut back on ferry service or campsites to slow the flow.

Limited access also allows the park service to enforce rules more effectively. Dogs, for example, are not allowed on the island for fear they might bring rabies and other diseases to the island's wolf pack. Arrive with a poodle on your powerboat—even if it never sets paw on the dock—and you will be quickly waved off the island. Thumbs-down also to wheeled vehicles like mountain bikes or canoe carts. (Exceptions are made for wheelchairs.) The park service also takes great pains to preserve its backcountry solitude, with a park brochure reminding hikers to "refrain from loud conversation," "avoid songfests," and "select equipment of subtle natural tones rather than conspicuous colorful gear."

◖ BOAT TOURS

The park service shuttles visitors to various island attractions on its 25-passenger **MV Sandy** (906/482-0984, www.nps.gov/isro, June-early Sept., $17-49.50 adults, $17-28 children under 12). The *Sandy* makes several different trips in season. One four-mile boat ride takes passengers to the Hidden Lake Trailhead, where they're asked to debark and then guided on a two-mile round-trip hike past Hidden Lake, up 320 feet, to **Lookout Louise.** From here, visitors can view the southern shore of Canada and the northern shore of Isle Royale.

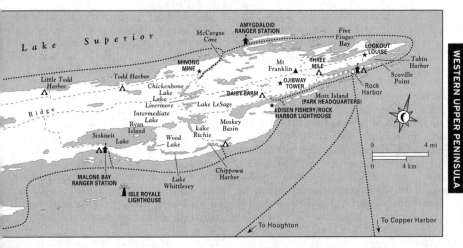

FACTOIDS ABOUT ISLE ROYALE

Established in 1940, **Isle Royale National Park** may be one of the least visited units of the national park system, but that certainly doesn't mean it's not worth experiencing. Centered around 45-mile-long Isle Royale, the largest island in Lake Superior, the park also encompasses about 400 smaller islands as well as all submerged lands within a 4.5-mile radius of the archipelago. In 1980, it was designated an International Biosphere Reserve, and today, it appeals to hikers, backpackers, boaters, anglers, kayakers, canoeists, scuba divers, and wildlife watchers, especially those hoping to spot a moose or a wolf. Here are some other curious factoids about Isle Royale:

- The highest point on Isle Royale is Mount Desor, which stands 1,394 feet above sea level.

- Ryan Island is the largest island found in Siskiwit Lake, which is the largest lake on Isle Royale, which, in turn, is the largest island in Lake Superior, which just happens to be the largest freshwater lake in the world.

- Mosquitoes and black flies can be a major park nuisance late May-late July, so be sure to bring insect repellent and protective clothing.

- Dogs, cats, and other pets (save for service animals) aren't allowed on any islands or boats within the park boundaries, mainly because they can disturb wildlife and transmit diseases, especially to wolves. Any visitor spotted bringing a pet to Isle Royale will be turned away immediately.

- Vehicles, bicycles, and other wheeled devices (save for wheelchairs) aren't permitted in Isle Royale National Park; the only approved modes of transportation include hiking, boating, canoeing, and kayaking.

- Visitors must avoid disturbing wild animals at all times, which means that, if you hope to observe or photograph them during your visit, you'll have to rely on binoculars or a zoom lens from a safe distance.

If you're curious about other aspects of the park, including the rules pertaining to visitors, contact the headquarters of Isle Royale National Park (800 E. Lakeshore Dr., Houghton, 906/482-0984, www.nps.gov/isro).

Another trip heads across the mouth of Moskey Basin to the historic fishery of Peter and Laura Edisen, restored to show what life was like for the commercial fisheries that once thrived on the island. From **Edisen Fishery,** it's a short quarter-mile walk to the stout and simple **Rock Harbor Lighthouse,** a white edifice built in 1855 to guide ships to Isle Royale's then-busy copper ports.

Other tours feature out-of-the-way destinations such as Middle Island Passage and Starvation Point. History buffs, too, will enjoy these tours. Besides viewing the Rock Harbor Lighthouse, you can also select a tour to see the Passage Island Lighthouse, the historic Minong Mine, and the site of the *Monarch* shipwreck.

RECREATION
Hiking

Several day hikes are doable if you choose to "motel camp" in Rock Harbor. Don't miss **Scoville Point,** a 4.2-mile loop with interpretive signs that traces a rocky finger of land east of Rock Harbor. Another popular short hike is the 3.8-mile loop to **Suzy's Cave,** formed by the wave action of a once much-deeper Lake Superior. **Lookout Louise,** north of Tobin Harbor, offers one of the island's most spectacular views, looking out over its ragged northeastern shoreline. If you've got a canoe, it's a short paddle and short 2-mile hike. Without a canoe, it's a fine hike along lovely Tobin Harbor and the eastern end of the Greenstone Ridge, but you'll have to retrace your steps to return to Rock Harbor, about a 20-mile trek in all.

For another all-day hike, follow the Lake Superior shoreline to the Daisy Farm campground and the Ojibway Trail, which heads north and brings you to the **Ojibway Tower,** an air-monitoring station. The tower marks the highest spot on the eastern end of the island, and you can climb its steps (but not enter the tower room) for an unmatched view of the island's interior lakes and bays on both the north and south sides of the island. Travel back via the Greenstone Ridge and along Tobin Harbor for a varied 18-mile hike that will take you through blueberry patches, wildflower meadows, and serene shorelines. For a similar but shorter hike of about 10 miles, turn north at the Three Mile campground to ascend Mount Franklin, another high point on the Greenstone Ridge.

Canoeing

For paddlers, Isle Royale is a dream destination, a nook-and-cranny wilderness of rocky islands, secluded coves, and quiet bays interrupted only by the low call of a loon. First-time visitors can't do better than the **Five Fingers,** the collection of fjord-like harbors and rocky promontories on the east end of the island. Not only is it well protected (except from northeasterlies), it offers some of the finest and most characteristic Isle Royale scenery and solitude. Though Isle Royale is generally better suited to kayaks, open canoes can handle these waters in calm weather.

For kayaks, the entire island offers paddling opportunities, though some areas require long stretches of paddling without good shoreline access. Note that open-water passages on Lake Superior should be attempted by experienced paddlers only, and are not at all recommended in an open boat like a canoe. Capsizing in Lake Superior is not an unfortunate experience, it is a life-threatening one. With waters rarely exceeding temperatures in the 40s, hypothermia can occur in a matter of minutes. There are many places where you can rent canoes, 14-foot fishing boats, and outboard motors at Windigo and Rock Harbor.

ACCOMMODATIONS AND FOOD

Those just looking for a quiet island stay and some swell day hikes can set up a base in comfort at the **Rock Harbor Lodge** (906/337-4993 May-Sept. or 866/644-2003 Oct.-Apr., http://rockharborlodge.com, $237-271 d). Lodge rooms are pretty much your basic motel-style accommodations, but they sit right at the water's edge with a glorious view of nearby islands and the open waters of Lake Superior. You'll pay for this little slice of civilization in the wilderness, but the rate does include one half-day use of a canoe and three meals at the lodge dining room. (Dinner often features fresh lake trout from the restored Edisen Fishery.) Guests also have use of an adjacent day lodge with a comfy wood-burning fireplace. Nearby housekeeping cottages include small kitchens, one double bed, and one bunk bed. While you can call about reservations year-round, the lodge is only open Memorial Day-Labor Day, and yes, reservations are a must.

Rock Harbor's **Lighthouse Restaurant** (7am-8:30am, noon-1:30pm, and 5:30pm-7:30pm daily late May-early Sept., $10-37) is open to the public, and its meals taste like a gourmet feast after a week of freeze-dried fare. The on-site **Greenstone Grill** (7am-7:30pm daily late May-early Sept., $5-15) is also a good option for hungry hikers; the fare there consists of burgers, sandwiches, pizza, and a wide assortment of regional beer and wine. Meanwhile, the **Marina Store** (9am-5pm daily) in Rock Harbor carries a good supply of food, camping supplies, film, fuel, and pretty much any other travel essential that you forgot to pack.

Camping

If you want to see more of the island, camping is the way to do it. Rustic campsites are located throughout Isle Royale, with three types of sites available: tent sites for 1-3 tents, group sites for parties of 7-10 campers, and three-sided shelters that hold up to six people. You must obtain a free camping permit from the Windigo Ranger

Station when you arrive, outlining your itinerary, but you can't obtain a reservation. All sites are available on a first-come, first-served basis. Should you reach a site at the end of the day and find it full (this can happen at sites a day's hike from Rock Harbor, especially in August), the unwritten rules say double up. No one expects you to hike off into the dwindling light to the next campsite.

INFORMATION AND SERVICES

For general information about the park, including camping and transportation options, contact **Isle Royale National Park** (906/482-0984 or 906/482-0986, www.nps.gov/isro). You'll find few services (and probably no cell phone reception) on the islands, so be sure to stock up on supplies in Houghton or Copper Harbor before heading to Isle Royale.

Isle Royale was one of the first national parks to charge a "park user fee." Daily fees are $4 per person per day. If you're traveling to the island by ferry or seaplane, the concessionaire will collect your fee. If you're traveling by private boat, you can pay at the ranger station at Windigo or Rock Harbor, or at the **Houghton Visitor Center** (800 E. Lakeshore Dr., 906/482-0984, 8am-6pm Mon.-Fri., 11am-6pm Sat. June-mid-Aug., 8am-4:30pm Mon.-Fri., 2pm-4pm Sat. mid-Aug.-mid-Sept., 8:15am-4:15pm Mon.-Fri. mid-Sept.-May) prior to your departure. Also, remember that Isle Royale is one of the few national parks to close during the winter, November-mid-April. This is due, of course, to extreme weather conditions, wildlife protection, and visitor safety.

GETTING THERE AND AROUND

Your options for accessing Isle Royale are seaplane, ferry, or personal boat. The National Park Service operates the largest ferry, the 165-foot MV *Ranger III*. Usually operating end of May-mid-September, it departs from Houghton twice a week, at 9am on Tuesday and Friday, on the five-hour passage to Rock Harbor (one-way $53-63 adults, $23 children

7-11, children under 7 free), and makes the return trip to Houghton at 9am on Wednesday and Saturday. It costs extra to transport canoes, kayaks, boats, and outboard motors. Make reservations through the national park (906/482-0984, www.nps.gov/isro).

A faster but more expensive boat, the 65-foot MV *Voyageur II*, travels from Grand Portage, Minnesota, to Windigo in two hours (one-way $67 adults, $46 children 4-11, children under 4 free), then continues on to Rock Harbor. On its way to Rock Harbor, it circumnavigates the island, offering drop-off and pickup service along the way, making for a slow but interesting trip. For additional fees, it can also carry canoes, kayaks, bikes, and extra gear or luggage. Make arrangements through **Grand Portage-Isle Royale Transportation Line, Inc.** (218/475-0024 May-Oct. or 651/653-5872 Nov.-Apr., www.isleroyaleboats.com) and ask about inter-island trip rates; remember, too, that you'll also have to pay a daily user fee ($4 adults, children under 12 free) to access the national park.

Generally speaking, seaplane service from Houghton is the most expensive but quickest way to reach Isle Royale—though the 35-minute flight is often delayed by wind and fog. From mid-May to mid-September, the plane flies on scheduled trips between Houghton County Memorial Airport and the protected bays at Windigo and Rock Harbor. It can carry up to four passengers (round-trip $299 pp, one-way $199 pp, children under 2 free), plus their luggage. Note, however, that you won't be able to bring stove fuel on board, though you can purchase it at one of the park stores on the island. Reservations are required for these flights, and the rates do not include the daily user fee ($4 adults, children under 12 free) required to access the national park. For more information, contact **Royale Air Service, Inc.** (218/721-0405, www.royaleairservice.com).

Once you've arrived in Isle Royale National Park, you'll have little choice regarding transportation. For most visitors, hiking or kayaking are the optimal modes for getting around the islands.

The Keweenaw Peninsula

South of Isle Royale, the enormous Keweenaw Peninsula juts out from the northern coast of the Upper Peninsula. Here, you'll find several former mining towns, a few inland lakes, and Keweenaw National Historical Park, comprising numerous historic attractions.

The Keweenaw is home to some of the Midwest's most distinctive geology and oldest exposed rock. Part of the Precambrian Canadian Shield, the peninsula was created more than 2 billion years ago by spewing volcanoes and colliding continents. Much later, about 1.2 billion years ago, the hardened crust broke apart. More lava began seeping out through fissures, forming bedrock called basalt. For hundreds of years, the basalt piled up thicker and thicker; groundwater percolated in,

too, filling the bubbles and cracks with minerals, creating the Keweenaw's vast deposits of pure copper.

Eventually, the basalt layers sank, forming a basin surrounded by tilted, uplifted rock. These high spots today are visible as the Keweenaw Mountain Range, the spine that runs the length of the peninsula and across Isle Royale. Consequently, the basalt found throughout the Keweenaw is believed to be among the oldest—perhaps *the* oldest—exposed volcanic rock on earth.

Though the Keweenaw's variety of minerals is not particularly vast, it contains some unusual gemstones in substantial quantity. Rock hounds seek out three in particular: porcelaneous datolite, mohawkite, and chlorastrolite.

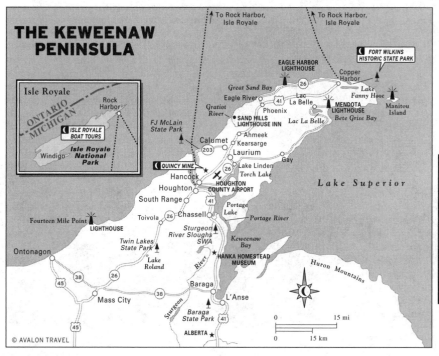

WESTERN UPPER PENINSULA

Chlorastrolite is more commonly known as the Isle Royale greenstone, a tortoiseshell-patterned rock rarely found elsewhere in the world. The peninsula's beaches are also a good place to hunt for agates, thomsonite, epidote, zeolites, red feldspar, and others. Area mineral shops are excellent sources for guidebooks and hunting tips.

COPPER HARBOR AND VICINITY

Wedged between Lake Superior to the north and long and lovely Lake Fanny Hooe to the south, Copper Harbor marks the end of the road in the Keweenaw Peninsula. Literally. Even US-41 peters out here, circling in a loop some 1,990 miles from its other terminus in Miami. The tip of the peninsula probably draws people precisely because it is the end of the road. And when they get there, they discover one of the Upper Peninsula's most scenic natural areas and one of its most appealing little towns.

Downtown

Tiny Copper Harbor, population 108, offers more than you might expect from its size. If shopping is your thing, check out the locally made copper plates, bowls, vases, and jewelry at **Studio 41** (260 4th St., 906/289-4808, www.studio41copper.com, 10am-6pm daily). Rock hounds, meanwhile, will appreciate **Swede's Gift Shop** (260 3rd St., 906/289-4596, 9am-5pm daily May-Oct.), which offers a decent selection of local minerals, plus handcrafted jewelry, paintings, copper artwork, and Scandinavian gifts. In downtown Copper Harbor, you'll also find a year-round grocery, the Gas Lite General Store (39 Gratiot St., 906/289-4652, hours vary daily), which packs a lot into a small space. Although the prices may run a bit higher than in other parts of Michigan, it's a convenient and friendly place to stock up on a variety of supplies, from beer and produce to area maps and fishing licenses—pretty much everything you might need for a campout, a cabin stay, or a trip to Isle Royale. Besides, it would likely be just as expensive, at least when you factor in fuel costs, to return to the stores of Houghton or Calumet.

© KEWEENAW PENINSULA CHAMBER OF COMMERCE

the Copper Harbor Lighthouse on the Keweenaw Peninsula

WESTERN UPPER PENINSULA

THE GIPPER OF LAURIUM

Born in Laurium on the Keweenaw Peninsula, George Gipp (1895-1920) attended Notre Dame University on a baseball scholarship. There, famed football coach Knute Rockne, recognizing an innate athletic talent, lured him onto the gridiron, where Gipp excelled as a runner, passer, punter, kicker, defensive back, and kick returner. During his collegiate career, he amassed over 8,200 yards in rushing, passing, kickoffs, and punts, and scored more than 150 points, including numerous touchdowns. Despite his incredible football skills, his first love remained baseball; in fact, he continued to play centerfield for Notre Dame's team and planned to join the Chicago Cubs following graduation.

In 1920, Gipp was named Notre Dame University's first all-American football player, but he didn't have long to celebrate the honor. Following a winning game against Northwestern on November 20, he contracted pneumonia and died on December 14. Though he was celebrated for his talent, grace, humor, generosity, and leadership skills, it is undoubtedly his final words that have sustained his legend. From his deathbed, he supposedly told his coach: "I've got to go, Rock. It's all right. I'm not afraid. Some time, Rock, when the team is up against it, when things are wrong and the breaks are beating the boys, tell them to go in there with all they've got and win just one for the Gipper. I don't know where I'll be then, Rock. But I'll know about it, and I'll be happy." The Gipper's inspiring story was made famous by Ronald Reagan in the film *Knute Rockne: All American* (1940), which solidified Gipp's legacy in the minds and hearts of many a football fan.

Boat Tours

Unfortunately, you can't reach the **Copper Harbor Lighthouse** (906/289-4215, annual $11 Recreation Passport for Michigan residents or $8.40 day use fee/$30.50 yearly Recreation Passport for nonresidents required), part of Fort Wilkins Historic State Park, by land since adjacent property owners refuse to grant right-of-way. As a result, the park service has arranged for boat tours (906/289-4966, May-Oct., $15 adults, $10 children under 12) of the light and keeper's house, which contains a small worthwhile museum.

Just wandering around the lovely rocky point is worth the trip. It was on this point, by the way, where Douglass Houghton first spotted a thick green stripe in the rock indicating the presence of copper, a discovery that unleashed the Keweenaw's copper boom. The 90-minute tour leaves from the municipal marina several times daily. Also ask about sunset cruises.

◖ Fort Wilkins Historic State Park

The history of **Fort Wilkins** (15223 US-41, 906/289-4215, annual $11 Recreation Passport for Michigan residents or $8.40 day use fee/$30.50 yearly Recreation Passport for nonresidents required, campsites $16-25 daily) reads like one of those overblown military spending stories of the 20th century. With miners pouring north during the Copper Rush, the federal government feared fighting would surely erupt between miners and the local Indian tribes, and ordered the construction of a garrisoned fort. In 1844, they sent troops of more than 100 men, who built barracks, a mess hall, a hospital, and other buildings behind a tall stockade fence, then hunkered down to fend off the fighting. Only no fighting ever erupted, and winters proved long, cold, and desolate. By the following year, half the troops were pulled out and sent south, where the country faced the threat of war with Mexico. By 1846, the rest were gone.

Today, Fort Wilkins stands as one of a few wooden forts remaining east of the Mississippi, with 16 whitewashed buildings wonderfully restored and filled with exhibits of life on the northern frontier. From mid-June to late

August, costumed "inhabitants" even re-create military life. Along with the fort, the state park includes rocky and scenic Lake Superior frontage, a few short hiking trails, the 1866 Copper Harbor Lighthouse, and an excellent campground on Lake Fanny Hooe.

Brockway Mountain Drive

Dubbed "the most beautiful road in Michigan," this 10-mile route traces the spine of a high ridge between Copper Harbor and Eagle Harbor. Rising 735 feet above Lake Superior, it is the highest paved road between the Rockies and Allegheny Mountains. A parking area midway allows you to stop and soak in the panorama of Lake Superior and the rolling forests of the Keweenaw, an incredible vista no matter how many times you've seen it. Watch for ravens, bald eagles, and peregrine falcons—which sometimes soar below you. Traveling west to east, the end of the drive is marked by a picture-postcard shot of Copper Harbor, tucked between Lake Superior and Lake Fanny Hooe. From this drive, you might catch a glimpse of the 1871 **Eagle Harbor Light,** now site of a maritime museum (10am-5pm daily mid-June-early Oct., $4 adults, children free) operated by the Keweenaw County Historical Society.

CALUMET

At the height of the Keweenaw's copper-mining glory, the Calumet and Hecla Consolidated Copper Company, operating largely in Calumet, proved the grandest operation of all. At the turn of the 20th century, C&H employed some 11,000 workers, who extracted more than 1.5 billion tons of copper from a web of mines tunneled out under Calumet. Striking red sandstone buildings with false fronts and cornices lined the 12-square-block downtown, filled with elegant shops, soaring churches, some 70 saloons, even a lavish theater that attracted the nation's leading vaudeville stars. The city buzzed day and night both above—and belowground.

After mining died, no one ever bothered to "modernize" Calumet. As a result, downtown

the Eagle Harbor Light beside Lake Superior

Calumet is a marvel of architecture from the early 1900s, and was a deciding factor in the area earning national historical park status.

Downtown Calumet

Thanks to the national historical park and renewed civic pride, downtown Calumet looks more like a movie set every day. Ugly 1960s facades are coming down off the elegant sandstone and brick buildings, and new money is coming in to further restore and preserve them. To appreciate this architectural bonanza, stop by the **Keeweenaw Convention & Visitors Bureau** (56638 Calumet Ave., 906/337-4579, www.keweenaw.info, 9am-5pm Mon.-Fri.) to pick up a walking tour guide. A few stops of particular note: The **Union Building,** at 5th and Red Jacket, was home to one of the area's first banks in 1888 and remains in excellent shape, with a decorative metal cornice. **Shute's Bar** (322 6th St.) doesn't look that special on the outside, but the interior preserves ornate plaster ceilings and a magnificent back bar with a stained-glass canopy. The **Red Jacket Town Hall and Opera House,** now called the **Historic Calumet Theater** (340 6th St., 906/337-2610, $4 adults, $1.50 children 6-12), was the pride of the community. The theater portion, added in 1898 as the first municipally owned theater in the country, was a showy extravagance of plaster rococo in cream, crimson, green, and gilt. It even had electric lights!

Coppertown USA

The mine's pattern shop, where wooden patterns were made as molds for machine parts, now serves as the home of **Coppertown USA** (Red Jacket Rd., 906/337-4354, 10am-5pm Mon.-Sat., 12:30pm-4pm Sun. June-mid-Oct., $3 adults, $1 children 12-18), a privately run museum (and national park cooperating site) that traces the region's copper industry. It includes loads of artifacts, a display of area minerals, a replica of a mining captain's office, a diorama of Native American mining, and more, with all the exhibits close enough to really examine.

HOUGHTON AND HANCOCK

When the hip outdoor sporting magazine *Outside* listed Houghton (HOE-ton) among America's "next wave of dream towns," you knew times were a-changin.' Ho-where? Well, turns out *Outside* may have something here. Houghton—and the adjacent city of Hancock—not only offers great sporting diversions, it boasts a quirky ethnic flair, streets lined with beautifully preserved early-1900s buildings, and a university to add a dollop of culture and liveliness. If you find old mining ruins intriguing instead of ugly, then the Houghton and Hancock area is downright pretty, too.

Houghton (population 7,700) and Hancock (population 4,600) face each other across the Portage Waterway, with homes and churches tumbling down steep 500-foot bluffs. (Especially on the Hancock side, streets can be downright unnerving, rivaling those in San Francisco for pitch.) The Portage Waterway effectively slices the Keweenaw in two, a 21-mile passage that saves boaters the 100-mile trip around the peninsula.

A unique lift bridge spans the waterway to link Houghton and Hancock, its huge center section rising like an elevator to let water traffic pass. Today, the Portage Waterway largely serves pleasure boaters and the 165-foot *Ranger III,* the ferry that transports hikers to Isle Royale National Park, 70 miles northwest. Houghton and Hancock are considered the gateways to the Keweenaw and to Isle Royale—but visitors just whizzing through will miss an appealing slice of the region.

Downtown

You can conduct your own historic walking tour of Houghton by strolling down **Shelden Avenue,** the city's main street. Tall facades of red brick and red sandstone line the street, like the **Douglass House Hotel** (517 Shelden Ave.), built in 1860 as a luxury hotel and dining establishment for travelers through the Portage Waterway. An addition in 1899 provided the lavish building you see today. The

the historic Union Building in downtown Calumet

Finnish-American Heritage Center (601 Quincy St., 906/487-7367, 9am-5pm daily, free) maintains a gallery open to the public that features Finnish artists, as well as archives of the area's Finnish settlement.

◖ Quincy Mine

Just north of Hancock, the mammoth shaft house of the **Quincy Mine** (49750 US-41, 906/482-3101, www.quincymine.com, 9:30am-5pm Fri.-Sun. May, 9:30am-5pm daily June-mid-Oct., group tours by appointment mid-Oct.-Apr., $10-18 adults, $10-17 seniors 55 and over, $5-9 children 6-12, children under 6 free) dominates the skyline. The Quincy ranked as one of the world's richest copper mines in the late 1800s, producing over a billion pounds of copper. Today, a few of its buildings still stand, and the land beneath it remains stitched with the shafts that stretched more than 1.5 miles deep— 92 levels!—and 2 miles wide.

From the hoist house, the tour starts with a rather dramatic ride in a glass-enclosed tram down the side of a steep hill. Views of Houghton and Hancock are terrific as the tram descends to an entrance to the mine, an adit at Level 7. A tractor carries you a couple thousand feet into the mine, where guides demonstrate mining techniques and give you a feel for what it was like to work deep inside the earth, in a drippy, damp environment with only hand tools and candles.

BARAGA AND L'ANSE

While Baraga and L'Anse suffer from stuttering economies, the Keweenaw Bay Indian Community economy is on the upswing. Ojibwa tribal leaders here were among the first to profit from treaty rights that allow them to establish gaming on tribal lands along Keweenaw Bay. Today, the popular **Ojibwa Casino and Resort** (16449 Michigan Ave., 906/353-6333, www.ojibwacasino.com) generates millions of dollars in revenues and feeds much-needed tax dollars into the local economy. Other tribes have followed suit and opened successful casinos throughout the U.P. and the northern Lower Peninsula. Consequently, tribal governments now wield considerable influence in the region.

On a more traditional note, the tribe also hosts a colorful **powwow** each July, a traditional celebration of dancing and drumming. On the eastern shore of Keweenaw Bay, north of L'Anse, you can visit an Ojibwa burial ground from the mid-1800s, with spirit houses marking graves. These small shelters held offerings of food, provisions to help sustain the soul on its journey to the afterlife.

KEWEENAW NATIONAL HISTORICAL PARK

The **Keweenaw National Historical Park** (headquarters: 25970 Red Jacket Rd., Calumet, 906/337-3168, www.nps.gov/kewe, 9am-5pm Mon.-Fri.) is not so much a place on a map but a place in time. The state's newest national park, it was established in 1992 "to

© KEWEENAW PENINSULA CHAMBER OF COMMERCE

the former mining town of Hancock

commemorate the heritage of copper mining on the Keweenaw Peninsula—its mines, its machinery, and its people."

Rather than a park with simply defined boundaries, the Keweenaw National Historical Park consists of historical attractions throughout the Keweenaw. Two units anchor the park—the Quincy Unit at the Quincy Mine in Hancock and the Calumet Unit in historic downtown Calumet—but some of this land remains in private ownership. The National Park Service owns just a limited amount of land to preserve key sites and conduct interpretive activities. In addition, the park has designated "cooperating sites" throughout the peninsula, including mine tours and museums that will remain in private ownership, but will continue to benefit from increased visibility and federal monies.

GHOST TOWNS

Ghost towns litter the Keweenaw, faded testament to the boom-and-bust days of copper. The ruins of old mines and stamping plants

(facilities that separated copper from rock) line M-26 between Hancock and Calumet. The gray piles of residue are mine tailings or stamping plant leftovers called "stamp sand." Several bona fide ghost towns hide in the woods, too, especially between Calumet and Copper Harbor. At **Central** (watch for the small brown sign on US-41 about 11 miles north of Mohawk), an exceptionally rich mine produced nearly $10 million by 1898; the surrounding town grew to 1,200. Today, nature has all but reclaimed Central, with just a few clapboard houses creaking in the breeze. Turn right near the top of the hill for a look at the mine ruins and rows of house foundations. Watch where you're walking.

Just south of Copper Harbor on US-41, another sign announces your "arrival" in **Mandan,** directing you down a dirt road disappearing into birches. Follow it south for about 50 yards and homes suddenly erupt out of the woods, lined up in a tidy row. Welcome to Mandan, the last stop on a trolley line from Hancock.

WESTERN UPPER PENINSULA

DAN JOHNSON/NPS

the Quincy Mine hoist house

FESTIVALS AND EVENTS

Despite its relative isolation from the rest of Michigan, the Keweenaw Peninsula plays host to numerous events and celebrations throughout the year. In winter, residents honor the frigid temperatures with ice-fishing derbies, cross-country skiing races, a winter carnival on the campus of Michigan Technological University, and **Heikinpäivä** (www.pasty.com/heikki), a Finnish American festival that takes place around January 19 every year, mainly in Houghton. Presenting traditional Finnish crafts, music, cuisine, and more, this annual event honors the Finnish culture that helped build this area and remains a significant part of it today. In Hancock alone, 40 percent of the population still claims Finnish ancestry.

Of course, the milder months are even busier on the Keweenaw Peninsula. Between May's **International Migratory Bird Day Festival** (www.keweenawimbd.org) in Copper Harbor and the **Houghton County Fair** (www.houghtoncountyfair.com) every August, you'll surely find something to do on the Keweenaw all through the summer. Of course, besides bike races, art fairs, and heritage events, one of the most popular annual events is Houghton's **Bridgefest** (906/370-2399, www.bridgefestfun.com), a mid-June celebration of the Portage Lake Lift Bridge—or perhaps just an excuse for the community to enjoy live concerts, sporting events, boat tours, arts-and-crafts exhibits, fireworks displays, and a seafood festival, where even live lobster is part of the fun.

RECREATION

Anglers and hunters increasingly find themselves sharing the backwoods and waters with hikers, mountain bikers, and paddlers.

Hiking and Biking

Mountain bikers new to the area can hardly believe the wealth of terrific trails in the Keweenaw, literally hundreds of miles of old mining and logging roads, overgrown double-track routes, and technical single-track. They loop through towering pines to backwoods waterfalls, to otherwise inaccessible Lake Superior

DAN JOHNSON/NPS

heritage site at Keweenaw National Historical Park

shorelines, even past ghost towns now buried deep in the woods. (Consider it fair warning that many trails also peter out and stop in the middle of nowhere.)

Vast tracts of land in the Keweenaw are privately owned by large corporations—some mining firms, but mostly paper companies. In exchange for a break in state taxes, the companies allow public use of the land for recreation, including hiking, fishing, and mountain biking. Still, for liability reasons, some outfitters and bike shops are loath to hand out maps or "endorse" these lands for riding. If you ask, though, most bike shops tend to be quite helpful about suggesting trails, especially the **Keweenaw Adventure Company** (145 Gratiot St., Copper Harbor, 906/289-4303, www.keweenawadventure.com), a company that began in 1994 and now helps to organize the annual **Copper Harbor Fat Tire Festival,** a mountain biking race in late summer.

Canoeing and Kayaking

This growing sport is at its finest in the Keweenaw, where you have plenty of islands, rock formations, and wilderness coastlines to explore. The **Keweenaw Adventure Company** (145 Gratiot St., Copper Harbor, 906/289-4303, www.keweenawadventure.com) rents kayaks, guides trips, and offers lessons. Beginners should try the 2.5-hour introductory paddle, which includes novice dry-land instruction and a fine little trip around the harbor and along the Lake Superior shoreline. The Keweenaw Adventure Company also offers some daylong trips around the peninsula—to Horseshoe Harbor, Agate Harbor, and the mouth of the Montreal River—as scheduling permits.

Rivers in the Keweenaw tend to be pretty bony, so white-water kayaking is limited (though this varies with the year's precipitation). Sea kayaking, on the other hand, is outstanding, the perfect way to access bluffs, caves, sea stacks, and rocky islands all along the Lake Superior shoreline. The Keweenaw Water Trail, still under development, guides small craft around the peninsula and through the Portage Waterway. Isle Royale makes for

WESTERN UPPER PENINSULA

an excellent paddling destination, too, and the ferries will transport kayaks and canoes for an additional fee. Canoeing is popular on inland lakes, but open boats are not recommended on Lake Superior.

Diving

The cold, clear freshwater of Lake Superior offers outstanding visibility for divers. Though there isn't much to look at in the way of plant and animal life—the cold waters make for a pretty sterile-looking environment—the waters provide plenty of entertainment in the form of interesting underwater geologic formations and shipwrecks.

Ships have been running aground for well over a hundred years around the Keeweenaw Peninsula, a navigational hazard if there ever was one. Within the 103-square-mile **Keweenaw Underwater Preserve,** divers can explore the *Tioga,* a freighter that ran aground near Eagle River in 1919, and the *City of St. Joseph,* which met its fate north of Eagle Harbor in 1942. Both ships lie in less than 40 feet of water, with large sections of the hull, deck machinery, and other artifacts clearly visible.

One of the Upper Peninsula's oldest shipwrecks, the *John Jacob Astor,* lies just offshore from Copper Harbor, near the Fort Wilkins State Park Lighthouse Overlook. An Underwater Trail marks the location of the rudder, anchor, and other remnants of the *Astor,* which sank in 1844. For more information, contact the **Michigan Underwater Preserve Council** (MUPC, 800/970-8717, www.michiganpreserves.org).

Winter Activities

A giant snow gauge on US-41 south of Phoenix proudly marks the Keweenaw's record snowfall, a staggering 390.4 inches in the winter of 1977-78. It wasn't an aberration; the surrounding waters of Lake Superior routinely generate colossal lake-effect snows, often averaging over 300 inches. That reliable snowfall, combined with the remarkable local terrain, makes the Keweenaw a haven for snowmobilers, skiers, and snowshoers. Downhill skiers can check out

Michigan's most challenging terrain at **Mount Bohemia** (100 Lac La Belle Rd., 231/420-5405, www.mtbohemia.com, 10:30am-4:30pm Mon.-Fri., 9:30am-5pm Sat.-Sun., $52 lift tickets) near Lac La Belle. Although lodging is available at the resort year-round, weather conditions determine the actual skiing season, which, depending on the snowfall, can begin in December.

ACCOMMODATIONS

Located high on a ridge above Copper Harbor, the log lodge and cabins of the ◖ **Keweenaw Mountain Lodge** (US-41, 906/289-4403, www.atthelodge.com, early May-late Oct., $95-169 d) were built as a public works project in the 1930s. Take advantage of breakfast, lunch, and dinner in the grand dining lodge as well as the scenic nine-hole golf course. The helpful staff can arrange hiking, biking, bird-watching, kayaking, charter fishing, and lighthouse excursions. Reservations at the resort can be tough. Try to snag a private log cabin, equipped with a fireplace and, in some cases, a whirlpool, rather than one of the eight less inspired motel rooms (which were added much later than the other buildings).

The no-frills rooms at the **King Copper Motel** (Copper Harbor, 906/289-4214, www.kingcoppermotel.com, $50-100 d) come with great views of the harbor. Just a few steps from the ferry dock, this is a perfect spot for a warm shower and a real bed after a hard-core week on Isle Royale.

For a truly unforgettable experience, consider spending the night at the ◖ **Sand Hills Lighthouse Inn** (5 Mile Point Rd., Ahmeek, 906/337-1744, www.sandhillslighthouseinn.com, $135-200 d), a beautifully preserved lighthouse constructed in 1917 and now serving as a year-round Victorian-style bed-and-breakfast. Listed on the National Register of Historic Places, this romantic spot offers eight lovely rooms, each with a roomy bed and private bathroom. Two of the chambers even have whirlpool bathtubs and a balcony overlooking Lake Superior.

The **Wonderland Motel and Cabins** (787 Lake Linden Ave., Laurium, 906/337-4511,

$50-75 d) offers decent budget-friendly accommodations, complete with kitchens in the cabins. For such a small metropolitan area, Houghton's lodgings run a bit on the pricey side. A good mom-and-pop operation is the **Downtowner Motel** (110 Shelden Ave., 906/482-4421, $69-99 d). **Carla's Lake Shore Motel** (14258 US-41, Baraga, 906/353-6256, www.carlasinn.com, $52-58 d) has clean, inexpensive rooms with a view of Keweenaw Bay, and it gets bonus points for allowing your pooch.

Camping

Fort Wilkins Historic State Park (15223 US-41, Copper Harbor, 906/289-4215, annual $11 Recreation Passport for Michigan residents or $8.40 day-use fee/$30.50 yearly Recreation Passport for nonresidents required) has 159 modern sites ($16-25 daily) in two campgrounds, both on Lake Fanny Hooe. Many sites sit along the water and offer decent privacy. For reservations, call 800/447-2757.

West of Ahmeek, the **Sunset Bay RV Resort & Campground** (2701 Sunset Bay Beach Rd., Eagle River, 906/337-2494 June-Oct. or 941/232-4832 Nov.-May, www.sunsetbay.com, $22-27 daily) indeed offers a fine view of the sunset from your tent flap. Many of its 12 tent sites and 18 RV spaces sit on Lake Superior. Three cabins, modern restrooms, a laundry and dump station, a nice swimming beach, a small boat launch, several hiking trails, and wireless Internet access are also available. Keep in mind that many locals simply head out into the woods on weekends and set up camp near a favorite stretch of beach or river. If you choose to do the same, respect "No Trespassing" signs and observe all backcountry camping practices (such as burying waste, hanging packs, etc.).

Sunsets get top billing at **McLain State Park** (18350 M-203, Hancock, 906/482-0278, annual $11 Recreation Passport for Michigan residents or $8.40 day-use fee/$30.50 yearly nonresident motor vehicle permit required), where the sky often glows in peaches and pinks before the sun melts into Lake Superior. As at most Michigan state parks, the campsites ($16-26 daily) and cabins ($60 daily) are fine, too,

and many come with those waterfront views. Follow M-203 seven miles north of Hancock. For reservations, call 800/447-2757.

FOOD

The **Pines** (174 Gratiot St., 906/289-4222, www.pinesresort.net, 8am-9pm daily, $4-15), a small café in downtown Copper Harbor, is great for rainy-day breakfasts, with its homemade cinnamon rolls and crackling fireplace. Delicious soups, sandwiches, and local fish specialties keep folks coming all day. The adjacent **Zik's Bar** (906/289-4222, 10:30am-close) is the hangout for Copper Harbor locals.

In Eagle Harbor, the **Shoreline Resort Café** (122 Front St., 906/289-4441, www.shorelineresort.com, 7am-2pm daily Memorial Day-mid-Oct.) draws 'em in for homemade pies, but there's plenty of other home-style cooking—like soups, sandwiches, and well-prepared fresh lake trout—to make it worth the stop. **Fitzgerald's Restaurant** (5033 Front St., Eagle Harbor, 906/337-0666, 11am-9pm daily, $9-27), located in the Eagle River Inn, offers upscale dining overlooking Lake Superior. The menu features Black Angus steaks, fresh fish and seafood, inventive vegetarian dishes, and a comprehensive wine list.

Combine a college town with a large ethnic population, and you'll conjure up a good range of eating options in the Houghton/Hancock area. **Marie's Deli & Restaurant** (518 Shelden Ave., Houghton, 906/482-8650, 9am-9pm daily, $4-16) is a terrific find—the place for homemade breads, soups, sandwiches, salads, vegetarian options, and lots of Middle Eastern dishes like kibbie and spinach pies, reflecting the Lebanese heritage of its cheery owner. It's a good value at breakfast, lunch, and dinner.

INFORMATION AND SERVICES

For more information about the Keweenaw Peninsula, including attractions and lodging, contact the **Keweenaw Convention & Visitors Bureau** (56638 Calumet Ave., Calumet, 906/337-4579, www.keweenaw.info, 9am-5pm Mon.-Fri.) or the **Keweenaw Peninsula**

Chamber of Commerce (902 College Ave., Houghton, 906/482-5240, www.keweenaw. org, 9am-6pm Mon.-Fri.). If you're hankering for a dose of local news, consult the daily *Mining Gazette* (www.mininggazette.com).

The twin towns of Houghton and Hancock represent the area's largest population center, where you'll find the lion's share of area services, like medical care, public transportation, and post offices. They also serve as the unofficial gateway to the Keweenaw, even though they sit halfway up the peninsula. In case of an emergency while visiting the Keweenaw, dial **911** from any cell or public phone. For medical assistance, consult **Portage Health** (906/483-1000, www.portagehealth.org), which offers facilities in Houghton and Hancock.

GETTING THERE AND AROUND

Bus service can be spotty throughout the Upper Peninsula, but particularly in the Keweenaw Peninsula; nevertheless, you can rely on both **Greyhound** (800/231-2222, www.greyhound. com) and **Indian Trails** (800/292-3831, www. indiantrails.com) to access towns like Hancock (125 Quincy St., 906/483-0093) and L'Anse (102 N. Main St., 906/524-6400). Of course,

you can also opt to fly into **Houghton County Memorial Airport** (CMX, 23810 Airpark Blvd., Calumet, 906/482-3970, www.houghtoncounty.org), though it can indeed be an expensive way to go. You might also choose to fly into **Sawyer International Airport** (MQT, 125 G Ave., Gwinn, 906/346-3308, www.sawyerairport.com) near Marquette, where you can then rent a vehicle and head to the Keweenaw Peninsula via US-41 North/M-28 West.

In truth, most travelers venture to and around the Keweenaw Peninsula by vehicle, utilizing two main routes: US-41 North and M-26 North. If you choose to drive as well, be advised that many secondary roads in the Keweenaw are dirt or gravel, and for old logging roads and other questionable routes, a four-wheel-drive vehicle is highly recommended. To give you an idea of the distances in this region, realize that, via US-41 North from Marquette, it will normally take you 75 minutes to cover the 68 miles to L'Anse, 80 minutes to traverse the 72 miles to Baraga, almost 2 hours to travel the 100 miles to Houghton and Hancock, a little over 2 hours to make the 112-mile trip to Calumet, and roughly 2.75 hours to reach Copper Harbor, which lies about 146 miles northwest of Marquette.

Ontonagon to Ironwood

From Ontonagon to Ironwood, once thriving mining communities, stretches some of the most untamed wilderness in all of Michigan. This western edge of the Upper Peninsula is definitely a recreationist's dream, favored for fishing, canoeing, hunting, hiking, and snowmobiling.

Come November, Lake Superior snows inundate the region, marketed to downhill skiers throughout the Midwest as "Big Snow Country." Many visitors never get past the area's well-known downhill resorts and the homely stretch of US-2 that links them. It's their loss, because when the snow melts, a beautiful landscape emerges of inland lakes and rivers for fishing and paddling, and hundreds of miles of national

forest trails for hiking and biking. After all, even in Big Snow Country, it stops snowing eventually—at least for a few months, anyway.

ONTONAGON

The Ontonagon Boulder was pried from its namesake riverbank a few miles upstream from the Lake Superior shoreline community of Ontonagon. Today, the two-ton mass of native copper resides at the Smithsonian, and Ontonagon's mining heritage thrives now only in museums—especially since the nearby copper mine and smelter in White Pine closed in 1995. (Nowadays, White Pine is little more than a creepy ghost town of 1950s tract housing.)

Check out Ontonagon's happier heyday at the worthwhile **Ontonagon County Historical Society Museum** (422 River St., 906/884-6165, www.ontonagonmuseum.com, 11am-4pm Thurs.-Sat. Jan.-Apr., 10am-5pm Mon.-Sat., 10am-2pm Sun. May-Sept., 10am-5pm Tues.-Sat. Oct.-Dec., free), a lavender building on M-38, downtown's main street. The historical society's biggest project these days has been restoring the 1866 **Ontonagon Light,** which replaced one of Lake Superior's first lighthouses, built in 1853.

◖ PORCUPINE MOUNTAINS WILDERNESS STATE PARK

Anchored along the Lake Superior shore in the northwest corner of the U.P., **Porcupine Mountains Wilderness State Park** (33303 Headquarters Rd., Ontonagon, 906/885-5275, annual $11 Recreation Passport for Michigan residents or $8.40 day-use fee/$30.50 yearly nonresident motor vehicle permit required) covers 59,020 acres, the largest in Michigan's excellent state park system. The Porcupine Mountains were considered as a national park site in the 1940s, but were quickly preserved as a state park in 1945 when loggers threatened to get to work on their virgin timber before the federal government took action.

Someone once decided that this rumpled landscape of low mountains and tall pines looked like the silhouette of a porcupine. Hmm. But the name stuck, endearingly dubbed "the Porkies." It is a mecca for casual hikers and hard-core backpackers alike, home to 90-plus miles of well-marked, well-maintained trails—more than you'll find in many national parks, and certainly more than you'll find in most of the Great Lakes region.

And in this case, bigger also means better. The park preserves vast stands of virgin hemlock, pine, and hardwoods—the largest tract of virgin hardwoods between the Rockies and Adirondacks, in fact—secluded lakes, wild rivers, and some of the Midwest's highest peaks. (Summit Peak tops out at 1,958 feet.) Unlike most state parks, the Porkies are large enough to provide a sense of wilderness and serenity, an escape from the civilized world.

Hiking

Many park visitors head immediately for the justly famous **Lake of the Clouds Overlook.** From the parking lot at the end of M-107, it's just a few steps to the overlook, where the placid lake slices a long sliver of blue through a thick mat of jade forest hundreds of feet below. The view is the stuff postcards are made of and is probably the most photographed scene in the U.P.

The overlook also serves as the trailhead for some of the park's most rugged and scenic routes. To properly soak in the Lake of the Clouds view, hike the aptly named **Escarpment Trail,** which winds east and skims over Cloud Peak and Cuyahoga Peak. Bordered by a sheer cliff, the four-mile trail is considered by many to be the most beautiful in the park. Allow ample time to stop and enjoy the shimmering lake and valley floor spreading out around you.

Long before the Porcupine Mountains were preserved for their virgin timber and natural beauty, miners harvested the rich minerals buried in their bedrock. At the east end of the park, the **Union Mine Trail** provides a glimpse into the 1840s, when the Porkies pulsed with the excitement of the area's copper rush. Marked with white mine shovels to indicate points of interest, this self-guided interpretive trail forms a one-mile loop along the spring-fed Union River and the site of an old copper mine, now largely swallowed by nature. In the shadow of lofty hemlocks, you'll see how miners tunneled shafts into the riverbank and learn about their life in the wilderness—a wilderness still untamed today.

In winter, the park's many hiking trails double as cross-country skiing trails. Just be careful of the higher ones. On days when the strong north wind is blowing, you'll feel the windchill all the way from Canada.

Camping

Campers have their choice of two campgrounds ($14-25 daily), both with a number of sites overlooking Lake Superior: Union Bay (with full hookups and modern restrooms), at the east end of the park, or rustic Presque Isle (no hookups), near the mouth of the Presque Isle River on the park's western edge. In addition, three rustic campgrounds (called "outposts") with 3-8 sites each are located off the South Boundary Road, accessible by car, but with no facilities. They tend to offer more privacy than the actual campgrounds.

As another option, the park offers 19 hike-in rustic cabins ($60 daily). These are great retreats after a day on the trail. They come with 2-8 bunks, mattresses, a woodstove, basic utensils, and protection from the elements, but no electricity or running water. Bring your own stove for cooking. Cabins situated on inland lakes even come with a rowboat, so you can finish the day with a lazy drift across the water. Three yurts ($60 daily) and a lodge are also available. Reserve any of these as much as a year in advance (800/447-2757).

Information

Start your visit at the park's **visitors center** at the junction of M-107 and South Boundary Road. Rangers on duty can provide you with maps and suggest trails. A gift shop has topo maps and a good selection of nature guidebooks.

Getting There and Around

Two roads lead to Porcupine Mountains Wilderness State Park, the headquarters of which lies about 58 miles northeast of Ironwood. From Wakefield, you can simply head north on CR-519, which leads to the park's western edge and the Presque Isle River Area, a 17-mile trip that will take you about a half hour. From Bergland, meanwhile, you can reach the park headquarters by taking M-64 North through Ottawa National Forest and

A DYNASTY OF PINE

In the mid-1800s, a young and growing United States suddenly had an insatiable appetite for lumber. Settlers, moving west into the treeless plains, needed lumber to build their new towns; burgeoning cities needed lumber to build more homes and businesses; and railroads needed lumber as they laid mile after mile of track to connect it all. Michigan's natural resources proved the perfect mix to fuel a hungry nation. Immense white pines and other conifers grew thick and tall across the Upper Peninsula and more than half of the Lower Peninsula. Rivers honeycombed through these vast forests, providing a route to the Great Lakes, which in turn connected the northern wilderness to Chicago, Detroit, and other railroad centers in the south. Mother Nature had created the perfect delivery system for the logging industry.

Around 1850, logging camps began springing up deep in the woods, from the western U.P. to the shores of Lake Huron. Young men streamed north, some of them farm laborers looking for winter wages, others newly arrived immigrants looking to gain a foothold in their new homeland. The lumberjacks worked by hand, with axe and saw, tree after tree, acre after acre. The logging camps operated pri-

marily in the winter months, when it was easier to transport the huge logs. Workers hauled the logs from the woods to the river's edge, branded the ends with the lumber company's mark, and stacked them there until spring.

In spring, when the ice melted, the colorful and chaotic log drives began. Thousands of logs were shoved into northern rivers, guided downstream by daredevil workers known as "river pigs," who danced across the dangerous mass of moving wood, using hooks, poles, and sometimes dynamite to dislodge log jams. It was the most dangerous job in the trade; with one misstep, river pigs ended up crushed between tons of logs or trapped underwater.

Once at the mills, the jumble of logs was sorted according to the mill owner's mark and floated into mill storage ponds. From there, buzzing sawmills sliced the logs into lumber and loaded them onto lumber schooners – and later, barges and steamers – headed primarily to Chicago, the nation's largest lumber market and railroad hub.

In its heyday, the logging industry generated billions of feet of lumber and billions of dollars. Lumber companies made all sorts of proclamations: Michigan mills asserted that arriving at Lake Superior, where the road converges with M-107 (also known as West 107th Engineers Memorial Highway) near the park's eastern boundary. From here, you can simply turn left onto M-107, head toward the park headquarters, or continue toward the Lake of the Clouds Scenic Area; the 30-mile trip between Bergland and the park headquarters will require about 40 minutes. Incidentally, South Boundary Road connects CR-519 and M-64 along, yes, the southern end of the park.

OTTAWA NATIONAL FOREST

Although backpackers could get lost amid the deep woods of Ottawa, and anglers favor Lake Gogebic east of Ironwood, visitors should be sure to visit the **Sturgeon River Gorge Wilderness Area.** The Sturgeon River, a federally designated wild and scenic river, travels a circuitous route through much of Baraga County before bleeding into Portage Lake near Chassell. One of three wilderness areas within the national forest, the Sturgeon River Gorge Wilderness protects 14,000 acres that surround this river and its tributaries. The highlight is west of US-41 and south of M-38, where the river cuts and tumbles through a magnificent 300-foot-high gorge. To reach it, follow Forest Road 2200 north from Sidnaw. Follow signs onto Forest Road 2270 to reach a parking area and foot trail that winds down about a half mile or so to a cascade and the river. Continue west from the parking area on Forest Road 2270 to reach Silver Mountain, with stone steps that lead to a remarkable valley view. Come in fall for a fiery display by the abundant maple forest.

they produced enough lumber to lay an inch-thick plank across the state. Success stories were everywhere. A sawmill in Hermansville, Michigan, came up with the idea of tongue-and-groove flooring, and quickly became the largest flooring plant in the country, crafting the floors for the Mormon Temple in Salt Lake City and the main lodge in Yellowstone National Park. Timber barons' homes were marvels of hand-carved mahogany, gold-leaf inlay, and cut-crystal chandeliers.

But the era that everyone thought would last forever lasted less than 50 years. By 1900, nearly all the big trees were gone – a scorched, denuded landscape of stump prairies left in their place. When farmers were able to convert some of the southernmost pineries into useful crop land, ambitious entrepreneurs sought to do the same in the north. A newspaper publisher in Menominee, Michigan, extolled the virtues of the Upper Peninsula's cutover land for farming or ranching. "No matter where the first Garden of Eden was located," he proclaimed, "the present one is in the Upper Peninsula."

Thousands of hard-working folks were lured north by the promise of cheap land in exchange for the back-breaking labor of removing pine stumps and tilling the soil. But by the late 1920s, their work proved futile. Nearly half the U.P. was tax-delinquent cutover land. Ranches had failed. Most farms had failed. The stock market had crashed, and the nation's economy was in shambles.

The federal government took a different approach. In 1911, it established the first national forests in Michigan and Wisconsin, setting aside land and creating tree nurseries as a first step in reestablishing the Midwest's great forests. The Civilian Conservation Corps (CCC), established in 1933, continued the reforestation efforts, planting trees, fighting fires, and nursing the remaining great forests back to health.

Although we can never re-create the magnificent old-growth forests of yesteryear, pines once again stretch skyward across Michigan. Logging continues, too, though usually with sophisticated forest management and reforestation practices that help ensure the livelihood of the state's important lumber and paper industries. And a few stands of virgin old-growth timber remain, giving us an awe-inspiring glimpse of a lost Michigan landscape.

WESTERN UPPER PENINSULA

The U.S. Forest Service has marked few trails within the wilderness area, which, of course, is its appeal for those who love the backcountry. Several grown-over logging roads wind through the area for hikers who want to explore on their own. (A topo map is an absolute necessity.) Camping is permitted throughout the wilderness, and you can find some pretty choice spots out there.

Information

To make sense of what the Ottawa has to offer, start with a map. You can pick up a small brochure or large topo map at **Ottawa National Forest Headquarters** (E6248 US-2, Ironwood, 906/932-1330, 9am-6pm Mon.-Fri.). Other district offices, in Ontonagon and Watersmeet, may have maps and brochures, but budget cuts have forced them to curtail other visitor services.

IRONWOOD AREA

With mammoth Lake Superior providing the requisite moisture, the northwestern corner of the U.P. isn't exaggerating when it markets itself as "Big Snow Country." Cool air moving across the warmer waters of Lake Superior creates lake-effect snows when it hits land, generating an average of 200 inches per season. This combines nicely with the area's rugged hills and Midwestern mountains, home to many of the Midwest's largest downhill ski resorts. As a result, the western U.P., especially around Ironwood, is one of the Upper Peninsula's more heavily marketed tourism areas, luring sizable crowds of skiers up I-39/US-51 every weekend from Wisconsin and the Chicago area.

Cross-country skiers and, increasingly, snowshoers also take advantage of the abundant snows. Gogebic County has more dedicated Nordic skiing resorts than you'll find elsewhere in the Upper Peninsula. And the Ottawa National Forest offers a dizzying array of terrain for those seeking solitude. The U.P. never overlooks snowmobiling, though, and you'll see plenty of trucks pulling snowmobiles; snowmobile routes radiating out from Lake Gogebic seem especially popular. To avoid them, ask state park/national forest officials about the proximity of snowmobiling trails where you plan to set out.

Follow M-505 north from Ironwood to reach **Little Girl's Point,** an area favorite. Perched high on a bluff over Lake Superior, this county park features a sand beach, a boat launch, picnic tables, grills, and fantastic views—the Porcupine Mountains to the east, the Apostle Islands to the west.

From Little Girl's Point, continue west on M-505 to reach **Superior Falls.** The rushing Montreal River puts on its final spectacular show here, plummeting more than 40 feet, then squeezing through a narrow gorge before spilling into Lake Superior a short distance away. You can also reach it by taking US-2 about 11 miles west from Ironwood and turning north on W-122. (You'll travel through Wisconsin and back into Michigan in the process.) In about 4.8 miles, watch for a small brown sign that directs you west into a small parking area near a Northern States Power substation. From here, it's a short walk to the falls. You also can continue down the path past the falls to Lake Superior, a fine sunset spot.

SYLVANIA WILDERNESS AND RECREATION AREA

Sylvania protects its assets well—36 crystalline glacial lakes hidden among thick stands of massive, old-growth trees. For anglers who dream of landing that once-in-a-lifetime smallmouth bass, for paddlers who yearn to glide across deep, quiet waters and along untrammeled shoreline, for hikers who wish to travel under a towering canopy of trees and hear nothing more than the haunting whistle of a loon, Sylvania can be a truly magical place.

One of three wilderness areas within the national forest, Sylvania stretches across 18,300 acres near Watersmeet, an area roughly bordered by US-2 to the north, US-45 to the east, and the Wisconsin border to the south. The adjacent Sylvania Recreation Area acts as a buffer, an additional 3,000 acres of lakes and woodlands with a few developed services like a drive-in campground, nice beach, flush toilets, and running water.

Once viewed as just another tract of good timber, Sylvania's fate turned in the late 1890s, when a lumberman who purchased 80 acres near the south end of Clark Lake decided it was too lovely to cut, and instead kept it as his personal fishing retreat. He invited his wealthy buddies—some of them executives of U.S. Steel—who also were captivated by the land. Together, they purchased several thousand additional acres and formed the private Sylvania Club.

Begin a trip to Sylvania with a call or visit to the **Ottawa Visitors Center** (906/358-4724, 10am-4pm Wed.-Sat.), at the intersection of US-2 and US-45 in Watersmeet. The staff can help you with maps, regulations, campsite reservations, and other information. Sylvania's rules can be quite unique—especially fishing regulations—so take time to ask questions and read through the materials rangers provide. To reach Sylvania itself, follow US-2 west about four miles from the visitors center and turn south on Thousand Island Lake Road. Travel about four miles, following signs to reach the entrance building. All visitors are required to register upon arrival.

The entrance sits in the recreation area, near the drive-in campground on Clark Lake. If you intend to travel into the wilderness area, plan on treating your own water; you'll find water pumps only in the recreation area. Cookstoves are highly encouraged, too, to lessen the number of feet tramping through the forest in search of dead wood. During summer months, make sure you also have ample bug dope or, better yet, a head net to combat mosquitoes and black flies.

RECREATION
Biking
There are many tantalizing mountain biking opportunities in the western Upper Peninsula: 200 miles of trails in three networks with routes ranging from tame gravel roads to single-track trails deep in the woods. As a bonus, many link up with waterfalls, remote lakes, and historical features.

Near Marenisco in Gogebic County, the **Pomeroy/Henry Lake network** offers 100 miles of gentle rides on wide gravel roads around a national forest area peppered with small lakes. It's a good choice for families. The **Ehlco network,** just south of the Porcupine Mountains Wilderness State Park, includes more single-track deep in the forest, on grass or dirt paths. Arguably the best of the three is the one located outside the national forest: the **Iron County system.** Trails radiating out of Hurley lead you past waterfalls, large flowages, and old mining relics like the Plummer headframe near Pence. Good interpretive signs help make sense of historic sites. Routes in this system range from gravel roads to terrific single-track, though it's not clear from the map which is which.

Canoeing and Kayaking
Seven major river systems flow within the forest, a staggering 1,000 miles of navigable waters for paddlers. Congress has designated more than 300 of those miles as wild and scenic or recreational rivers, leaving them largely in a pristine state. In general, rivers like the Ontonagon and Presque Isle offer quiet water in their southern reaches, winding through relatively flat woodlands. North of M-28, they begin a more rugged descent through hills and bluffs, requiring higher skills and boats appropriate for white water. For strong paddlers with good white-water skills, these rivers offer some of the finest paddling in the Midwest.

Of course, all of this can change depending on rainfall and the time of the year. Rivers that normally flow gently can be torrents in the spring. Always check with U.S. Forest Service officials, such as the supervisor's office of the **Ottawa National Forest** (E6248 US-2, Ironwood, 906/932-1330, www.fs.usda. gov), before setting out. For maps, brochures, and permits, you can also stop by a district ranger office, such as the **Ontonagon Ranger District** (1209 Rockland Rd., Ontonagon, 906/884-2085).

◀ Downhill Skiing
The area's three major downhill ski resorts— Big Powderhorn, Blackjack, and Indianhead— line up conveniently along a short stretch of US-2 just east of Ironwood. All welcome downhill skiers and snowboarders.

© PETOSKEY AREA VISITORS BUREAU

downhill skiing in Michigan

Heading east from Ironwood, the first resort you'll reach is **Big Powderhorn Mountain** (N11375 Powderhorn Rd., Bessemer, 906/932-4838, www.bigpowderhorn.net, lift tickets $31-45 pp). Powderhorn's 33 downhill runs wrap across two faces, with 700 feet of vertical drop and nine double chairlifts. Perhaps more than the others, Big Powderhorn Mountain caters to families with affordable lift tickets, mostly tame runs, and plenty of ski-in/ski-out lodgings bordering its slopes.

Also in Bessemer, the smaller, family-run **Blackjack Ski Resort** (N11251 Blackjack Rd., 888/906-9835, www.skiblackjack.com, lift tickets $28-40 pp), with its 20 trails, carves out a niche in the market by making the most of its terrain. Cameron Run and Spillway often are left ungroomed and offer up good bump skiing, and it's arguably the best resort around for snowboarders, with the area's best half-pipe and a great terrain park on Broad Ax.

A few more miles down the road bring you to the **Indianhead Mountain Resort** (500 Indianhead Rd., Wakefield, 800/346-3426, www.indianheadmtn.com, lift tickets $34-46 pp), the area's largest resort with 638 feet of vertical, nine chairlifts, two T-bars, and 29 runs. Indianhead offers some of the region's most challenging (although overly groomed) skiing, and pleasant runs that wind for more than a mile through the woods.

Cross-Country Skiing
Active Backwoods Retreats (E5299 W. Pioneer Rd., 906/932-3502, $10 adults, $8 children 11-17, $5 children under 11) grooms 25 miles of trails for skating and striding, on hundreds of acres of private land three miles south of Ironwood. A warming hut, lessons, and rentals are available.

Between Ironwood and Bessemer, take Section 12 Road north from US-2 to reach **Wolverine Nordic Trails.** Situated on private land and maintained by volunteers, its 9.3 miles of groomed trails wind through the hilly country south of the Big Powderhorn ski area. You can, in fact, ride one of Powderhorn's chairlifts ($2 pp) to access the network. Otherwise, begin at the lot with the warming hut on Sunset Road off Section 12 Road. Donations are requested.

ACCOMMODATIONS
You'll find a string of motels along M-64 between Silver City and Ontonagon. Many are plain, somewhat tired mom-and-pop-type places, but they work just fine after a long day outdoors. **Tomlinson's Rainbow Lodging** (2900 M-64, Silver City, 906/885-5348, $79-189 d) offers motel rooms and cottages on the shores of Lake Superior, with a private sand beach. Some units have whirlpools and kitchen facilities. Pets are welcome.

You'll also find a large selection of mom-and-pop motels along US-2, many of which have great deals and clean, comfortable, if simple, rooms. A good choice is the **Sandpiper Motel** (1200 E. Cloverland Dr., Ironwood, 906/932-2000, $39-79 d). Reserve well ahead of time during ski season. Meanwhile, the larger area ski resorts offer slopeside (or near-slopeside) accommodations, ranging from dormitories to simple motel rooms to deluxe condominiums. The ◖**Indianhead Mountain Resort** (500 Indianhead Rd., Wakefield,

800/346-3426, www.indianheadmtn.com, $105-483 d) offers some of the nicest rooms and condos (and the closest to what you might find in Aspen).

Camping

The **Ottawa National Forest** (E6248 US-2, Ironwood, 906/932-1330, www.fs.usda.gov, free-$17 daily) maintains 27 auto-accessible campgrounds, all with tent pads, fire grates, and toilet facilities. Many are located along rivers and lakes. Most tend to be quite rustic and secluded, with the exception of Black River Harbor, Sylvania, and Bobcat Lake. A few, like Black River Harbor, require a fee and allow reservations.

FOOD

If you get hungry while exploring the area, head to Ontonagon, where you'll find **Syl's Café** (713 River, 906/884-2522, 7am-7pm daily, $4-9), a classic small-town café with some of the best pasties around. Their breakfasts are so big, you may not need to eat for the rest of the day. In Ironwood, you may spot what looks like a classic corner tavern, but **Don & GG's** (1300 E. Cloverland Dr., 906/932-2312, 11am-9pm Mon.-Thurs., 11am-10pm Fri.-Sat., 11am-8pm Sun., $5-14) might surprise you with its vegetarian dishes and smoked trout salad. Don't worry—you can still get burgers and chicken dinners, too.

INFORMATION AND SERVICES

While many of the area's small communities have chambers of commerce that can help with lodging and other services, the area's most comprehensive source of tourism information is the **Western U.P. Convention & Visitor Bureau** (Ironwood, 906/932-4850, www.westernup. info). Of course, if you need more specific details, you can also consult the **Ontonagon County Chamber of Commerce** (Ontonagon, 906/884-4735, www.ontonagonmi.org), the **Lake Gogebic Area Chamber of Commerce** (Bergland, 888/464-3242, www.lakegogebicarea.com), and the **Ironwood Area Chamber**

of Commerce (150 N. Lowell, Ironwood, 906/932-1122, www.ironwoodmi.org).

While the towns in this part of the U.P. offer limited services, such as local banks and small groceries, you'd be better off stopping first in larger towns like Marquette and Escanaba. There, you'll find a better selection of supplies and services before venturing into the western wilderness. In case of an emergency, however, don't hesitate to dial **911** from any phone.

GETTING THERE AND AROUND

Although the western U.P. has a couple of small airports, in places like Calumet and Escanaba (both of which offer commuter service via either United Airlines or Delta Air Lines), most air travelers prefer **Sawyer International Airport** (MQT, 125 G Ave., Gwinn, 906/346-3308, www.sawyerairport.com) near Marquette. From there, you can rent a vehicle and head west to Ontonagon, taking Kelly Johnson Memorial Drive to M-553 North, following CR-480 to M-28 West/US-41 North, and continuing onto M-38 West; without traffic, the 122-mile trip will take you roughly 2.25 hours. From the Sawyer airport, you can also reach Ironwood via a similar route to M-28 West, from which you'll turn south onto US-2 West; without traffic, this 154-mile trip will require about 3 hours.

Beyond area airports, **Greyhound** (800/231-2222, www.greyhound.com) and **Indian Trails** (800/292-3831, www.indiantrails.com) both offer limited bus service to Ironwood (235 E. McLeod Ave., 906/932-0346), but honestly, most travelers prefer to arrive in the western U.P. via car and traverse the region in much the same manner. From Sault Ste. Marie, for instance, just head south via I-75, follow M-28 West, and take M-38 West to Ontonagon; without traffic, the 278-mile trip should take about 5 hours. From St. Ignace, meanwhile, you can reach Ironwood by heading west on US-2, taking M-77 North, continuing on M-28 West, and hopping back onto US-2 West; without traffic, the 306-mile trip usually takes about 5.5 hours.

Iron River to Iron Mountain

The Menominee Range is an anomaly in the Upper Peninsula, the only area not within rock-tossing distance of one of the Great Lakes. Roughly encompassing Iron, Dickinson, and Menominee Counties (all in the Central Time Zone), as well as the southern reaches of Baraga County, it is a land of deep forests and literally thousands of inland lakes.

Tourists tend to pass right though the region, which admittedly doesn't look like much from US-2, the main thoroughfare. But that thin strip of development masks an astounding amount of untrammeled wilderness. As proof, wolves thrive here (without any human assistance) because the region provides exactly the habitat wolves need: large tracts of land not sliced up by roads where they can avoid civilization, and plenty of large prey in the form of the region's abundant white-tailed deer.

Iron County's population centers around Iron River and Crystal Falls, the picturesque county seat 15 miles to the east. Both retain their small-town charm. The heart of Dickinson County, meanwhile, is Iron Mountain. Iron River and Iron Mountain, both former iron-mining centers, now offer visitors several historical museums, a couple of downhill ski slopes, and areas ideal for anglers, canoeists, and kayakers.

SIGHTS

◖ Iron County Historical Museum

You won't find a lot of dramatic lighting and fancy display cases at the **Iron County Historical Museum** (M-189, Caspian, 906/265-2617, www.ironcountymuseum.com, 10am-4pm Mon.-Sat., 10am-1pm Sun. mid-May-Oct., $8 pp), two miles south of US-2. What you will find is an interesting, appealing, and eclectic blend of local history and culture at this rambling, funky, and homegrown museum. Located on the site of the productive Caspian iron mine—whose rusting headframe still looms over the complex—it runs largely on

donated money and donated time. In the main museum building, displays cover everything from Native American history to logging, mining, and sporting equipment and kitchenware from the early 1900s. The perennial favorite display is the mechanized iron mine and railroad model. For five cents, a miniature ore skip hauls rocks to the surface and loads them on the railroad. Outside, several relocated buildings occupy the grounds, including a streetcar barn and the streetcar that once traveled between the mines in Caspian and Iron River.

Bewabic State Park

A small but pleasant chain of lakes is the highlight of **Bewabic State Park** (720 Idlewild Rd., Crystal Falls, 906/875-3324, annual $11 Recreation Passport for Michigan residents or $8.40 day-use fee/$30.50 yearly nonresident motor vehicle permit required), located five miles west of Crystal Falls. Boaters can put in at the first of the Fortune Lakes and make their way to Fourth Lake, an easy day's paddling adventure. Though First Lake can be somewhat frenetic on summer weekends, the waters get quieter and downright pristine as you proceed down the chain. Most of the shoreline is dotted with cottages, though you can camp on state-owned land bordering Third Lake. Fishing for perch and bass is best on First Lake, the largest (192 acres) and deepest (72 feet). Paddlers can escape fishing boats by darting under the low US-2 bridge to Mud Lake. The park itself has a modern 137-site campground ($10-20 daily) with good privacy, a small stretch of sandy beach, tennis courts, and other amenities. For reservations, call 800/447-2757.

Iron Mountain

Iron Mountain was first settled in about 1880 and reached its heyday soon after, when vast deposits of iron were discovered underfoot. The Chapin Mine—located near present-day US-2 and Kent Avenue on the north end of downtown—helped boost the town's population to almost 8,000 by 1890. Italian immigrants led the melting-pot mix working at the Chapin Mine, and Italian neighborhoods still thrive around the old mine on Iron Mountain's north side—as evidenced by a mouthwatering supply of Italian restaurants and corner markets.

The long-abandoned Chapin Mine still serves an important role, this time as a magnet for brown bats. An estimated two million bats winter in the shaft, protected from predators yet able to enter and exit freely, thanks to bat-friendly grates installed at the mine entrance. As the weather turns cool (usually sometime in September), the bats congregate all around Iron Mountain before retreating to the mine, an amazing sight.

While iron mining seems to dominate the city's psyche, Henry Ford added to the economic mix in the 1920s, when he bought up huge tracts of nearby forest and built his first company sawmill on land southwest of town, which he dubbed Kingsford (named for Iron Mountain's Ford dealer, Edward Kingsford). Soon Ford's Kingsford empire included the main plant for making floorboards for the Model T, residential developments for workers, an airport, a refinery, even a plant to make newfangled charcoal briquettes. All of it eventually closed or was sold off, including the briquette plant, which relocated to Oakland, California, and still manufactures the ever-popular Kingsford charcoal briquettes.

Iron Mountain's Chapin Mine once led Menominee Range mining production, but it was also one of the wettest mines ever worked. In 1893, an immense steam-operated pump was put to work, a 54-foot-high, 725-ton behemoth—the largest in the world at the time. Though electric pumps replaced it just 20 years later, the pump survives intact at the **Cornish Pump and Mining Museum** (300 Kent St., Iron Mountain, 906/774-1086, www.menominee-museum.com, 9am-5pm Mon.-Sat., noon-4pm Sun. Memorial Day-Labor Day, $2 pp). Along with the impressive pump, this comprehensive museum includes a good-sized collection of mining equipment, photos, and clothing; a small theater; and, arguably the most compelling display of all, the story of the World War II gliders built by Henry Ford's nearby Kingsford plant, used to quietly deploy troops behind enemy lines.

ACCOMMODATIONS AND FOOD

The ◖ **Lakeshore Motel** (1257 Lalley Rd., Iron River, 906/265-3611, www.lakeshore-motelicelake.com, $42-68 d) sits on the edge of spring-fed Ice Lake (just east of downtown Iron River on US-2), with tidy motel rooms, some with kitchenette units. This is a great find, complete with a sand beach and boat launch.

In Iron Mountain, the **Pine Mountain Resort** (N3332 Pine Mountain Rd., 906/774-2747, www.pinemountainresort.com, $60-90 d) anchors a full-service ski and golf resort on the northwest side of town, complete with a dining room, an indoor pool, an outdoor pool, a sauna, tennis courts, and trails ideal for hiking and mountain biking. Choose from standard lodge rooms or condominiums.

The namesake of **Alice's** (402 W. Adams St., Iron River, 906/265-4764, 11am-8pm daily, $8-14) produces Italian specialties just as her immigrant mother did before her, with homemade ravioli and other pasta dishes, gnocchi (Italian dumplings), and soups.

Italian is the way to go if you've decided to eat out in Iron Mountain. Homemade ravioli, slow-roasted pork, Italian sausage, Roma red sauce . . . you'll find it all in the town's unassuming Italian eateries. **Bimbo's Wine Press** (314 E. Main, 906/774-8420, 11am-10pm daily, $5-14) dishes out mouthwatering Italian sandwiches like *porketta* for incredibly reasonable prices.

INFORMATION AND SERVICES

For more information about the Iron River and Iron Mountain areas, contact the **Iron County Chamber of Commerce** (50 E. Genesee St., Iron River, 906/265-3822, www.iron.org or www.ironcountylodging.com, 9am-5pm

Mon.-Fri.) or the **Tourism Association of the Dickinson County Area** (600 S. Stephenson Ave., Iron Mountain, 800/236-2447, www.ironmountain.org). Remember that, unlike most of Michigan, both Iron and Dickinson Counties are situated in the Central Time Zone (CT).

While the towns in this part of the U.P. offer limited services, such as local banks and small groceries, you'd be better off stopping first in larger towns like Marquette and Escanaba. There, you'll find a better selection of supplies and services before venturing into the western wilderness. In case of an emergency, however, don't hesitate to dial **911** from any phone.

GETTING THERE AND AROUND

Although the western U.P. has a couple of small airports, in places like Calumet and Escanaba (both of which offer commuter service via either United Airlines or Delta Air Lines), most air travelers prefer **Sawyer International Airport** (MQT, 125 G Ave., Gwinn, 906/346-3308, www.sawyerairport.com) near Marquette. From there, you can rent a vehicle and head to Iron River by taking Kelly Johnson Memorial Drive to M-553 North, following CR-480 to M-28 West/US-41 North, continuing onto M-95 South and M-69 West, and taking US-2 West into town; without

traffic, the 96-mile trip will take you roughly 2 hours. From the Sawyer airport, you can also reach Iron Mountain via a similar route to M-28 West/US-41 North, from which you'll turn left onto M-95 South, drive 49 miles, and continue for 3.3 miles on M-95 South/US-141 South/US-2 East; without traffic, this 87-mile trip will require about 1.75 hours.

Beyond area airports, **Greyhound** (800/231-2222, www.greyhound.com) and **Indian Trails** (800/292-3831, www.indiantrails.com) both offer limited bus service to Iron River (211 E. Cayuga St. for Greyhound, 239 W. Adams St. for Indian Trails) and Iron Mountain (710 Norway St., 906/774-0266), but frankly, most travelers prefer to arrive in the western U.P. via car and traverse the region in much the same way. Luckily, both Iron River and Iron Mountain are situated along US-2, so either can be easily reached from other parts of the Upper Peninsula. From St. Ignace, for instance, you can access Iron River by heading west on US-2 for about 149 miles, turning right onto M-69 West, continuing for about 65 miles, and again following US-2 West for 15 miles; without traffic, the 229-mile trip will take roughly 4.25 hours. From Ironwood, meanwhile, you can reach Iron Mountain via US-2 East, which briefly passes through Wisconsin; without traffic, the 127-mile trip will take about 2.25 hours.

Menominee to Escanaba

Spiking south like a canine tooth between Wisconsin and the waters of Green Bay, the triangle of land comprising Menominee County and southern Delta County has been dubbed the peninsula's "banana belt." Well, it does have the U.P.'s most temperate climate, thanks to the warm (okay, relatively warm) waters of protected Green Bay, and the lightest snowfall in the entire U.P.—just 50 inches a year on average, a quarter of what typically falls on the rest of the Upper Peninsula. M-35 traces the shore of

Green Bay, from Menominee, a handsome community near the Wisconsin border, to Escanaba, a sizable town by U.P. standards, with a downtown district of shops, restaurants, and historic structures.

SIGHTS
Menominee
The Menominee River spills into Green Bay between the twin cities of Marinette, Wisconsin, and Menominee, Michigan, once the region's richest lumber port. The bustling business

district centers on 1st Street along the waterfront. Happily, most of the late 19th-century brick and sandstone buildings have survived intact, and renovation and restoration is underway on many of them. You can explore the **historic district,** guided by a walking tour brochure available at the **Spies Public Library** (940 1st St.). Its 1905 beaux arts facade happens to be one of the tour's most handsome buildings. A growing number of shops and restaurants along 1st Street are adding new life to this pleasant area.

The waterfront district is also home to bayside parks, easily accessible on foot. **Victory Park** stretches along the water between 6th and 10th Avenues, flanked by a new marina and a band shell that hosts summer concerts on Tuesday and Thursday evenings. For a longer walk or bike ride, head south along the water to the **Tourist Park** swimming beach. Farther south, the **Menominee North Pier Light** marks the entrance to Menominee Harbor with a beacon at the end of a rocky breakwater.

Escanaba and Gladstone

A metropolis for these parts, Escanaba and neighboring Gladstone (just a few miles north) are home to some 17,480 people, serving as the industrial and commercial center for the south-central Upper Peninsula. The natural deepwater port gave Escanaba its start back in the Civil War days, when a hastily built rail line linked the iron mines in Negaunee with the port, to bring coveted raw materials to the weaponsmakers and railroad builders of the Union Army. Today, Escanaba's modern ore port still ships iron, now in the form of iron/clay taconite pellets, to steelmakers in Indiana and Ohio.

Downtown Escanaba focuses on Ludington Street, an east-west route that runs from M-35 to the waterfront. The town's landmark is the **House of Ludington,** a grand old Queen Anne resort hotel built in 1865. The building's imposing facade continues to anchor the downtown.

At the foot of Ludington Street, lovely **Ludington Park** offers paved pathways along the water and to a small island (in-line skates

© BENKRUT | DREAMSTIME.COM

the Sand Point Lighthouse in Escanaba

WESTERN UPPER PENINSULA

permitted), interpretive signs explaining local history, a band shell that hosts concerts on Wednesday evenings in summer, a playground, a beach, tennis courts, and a boat launch. One of the park's most popular attractions is the **Sand Point Lighthouse** (16 Water Plant Rd., 906/786-3763, 9am-5pm daily June-Sept., $2 pp), an 1867 brick light that was restored and reopened as a museum in 1990 by the Delta County Historical Society. It was a big job. In the 1940s, the Coast Guard remodeled the obsolete light for staff housing, removing the lantern room and lopping off the top 10 feet of the tower.

ACCOMMODATIONS AND FOOD

The typical sprawl of chain motels runs along M-35 between Escanaba and Gladstone, but some nice family-owned operations are still holding their own along the waterfront. The **Terrace Bay Resort** (7146 P Rd., Gladstone, 906/786-7554, www.terracebay.com, $79-149 d), on Little Bay de Noc between Escanaba and Gladstone, has nice, clean motel rooms with great bay views. The 200-acre resort complex includes an 18-hole golf course, indoor and outdoor pools, tennis courts, a game room, and more. To find Terrace Bay, watch for the signs on US-41 south of Gladstone. For vittles, try the **House of Ludington** (223 Ludington St., Escanaba, 906/786-6300, www.houseofludington.com, $55-85 d), a historic, Queen Anne-style hotel built by E. Gaynor in 1864 and now offering comfortable rooms with private bathrooms, cable television, and air conditioning. In addition, The nostalgic, family-operated hotel features two restaurants: the casual **Emerald Dining Room** (5pm-8pm Tues.-Thurs., 5pm-9pm Fri.-Sat., $6-12) and the more formal **King George Dining Room** (5pm-8pm Tues.-Thurs., 5pm-9pm Fri.-Sat., $6-12).

INFORMATION AND SERVICES

For general information, your best source is the large and comprehensive **Michigan Welcome Center** (906/863-6496, www.michigan.gov/mdot, 8am-4:30pm daily May-Oct., 8am-4:30pm Tues.-Sat. Nov.-Apr.) in Menominee. The picturesque log building, which is located on US-41 near the state line (just north of the bridge), provides ample local and statewide visitor information. For more specific details about the region, consult the **Bays de Noc Convention & Visitors Bureau** (230 Ludington St., Escanaba, 906/789-7862, www.travelbaysdenoc.com) or the **Delta Chamber of Commerce** (230 Ludington St., Escanaba, 906/786-2192, www.deltami.org, 9am-5pm Mon.-Fri.). Remember that Menominee County is in the Central Time Zone (CT), like neighboring Wisconsin. When you cross the line into Delta County, however, you're back on Eastern Time (ET), with the rest of Michigan.

Escanaba offers plenty of services for travelers, though you might find more in the way of supplies farther north in Marquette. In case of an emergency, however, you can always dial **911** from any phone or visit the **OSF St. Francis Hospital** (3401 Ludington St., Escanaba, 906/786-5707, www.osfstfrancis.org).

GETTING THERE AND AROUND

The closest airport to this region is **Delta County Airport** (ESC, 3300 Airport Rd., Escanaba, 906/786-4902, www.deltacountymi.org), which offers limited service via Delta Air Lines. In addition, **Greyhound** (906/789-7030 or 800/231-2222, www.greyhound.com) and **Indian Trails** (800/292-3831, www.indiantrails.com) both provide limited bus service to Escanaba's **Delta Area Transit Authority** (DATA, 2901 N. 27th Ave., 906/786-1186, www.databus.org). Still, the most common way to visit Menominee and Delta Counties is via car. From St. Ignace, for instance, you can take US-2 West directly to Escanaba, a 142-mile trip that will normally take you about 2.5 hours; note that, also via US-2 West, the town of Gladstone lies about 133 miles from St. Ignace. Meanwhile, you can also reach Escanaba from Marquette by taking M-28 East, continuing onto US-41

South, and following US-2 West/US-41 South into town; without traffic, the 67-mile trip will take you roughly 75 minutes. From Escanaba, you can access Menominee via M-35 South, a 55-mile trip that usually takes about an hour.

Once you reach this region, you'll probably want to rely on your car to get around, but walking and biking are certainly viable options in Escanaba, Gladstone, Menominee, and other small towns. Of course, if you're sick of driving around the Upper Peninsula, you can always opt for the bus service provided by DATA (one-way $2-16 adults, $1-8 seniors, students, and disabled individuals). There are routes in both Escanaba and Gladstone, though service is also available for up to 30 miles beyond the city limits of both towns.

Marquette and Vicinity

With 21,500 hardy year-round souls, Marquette is distinguished as the largest city in Michigan's Upper Peninsula. Tucked in a well-protected natural harbor nearly midway across the U.P.'s northern shore, it grew and still thrives largely because of its location—an important Lake Superior port for the iron industry, and a rather central location that has helped it evolve into the U.P.'s center of commerce and government. In short, Marquette is definitely worth a visit—whether you plan to explore the historic architecture of its waterfront district or rest up before heading into the rugged hills, forests, and rivers that lie just beyond the city limits.

SIGHTS

Third Street, running north-south, and Washington, running east-west, represent Marquette's main cross streets, and where they meet is a good area to begin an exploration of the downtown. This puts you in the heart of the shopping and historic district. Buildings like the 1902 **Marquette County Courthouse** (3rd St. and Baraga) and the 1927 **MFC First National Bank** (101 W. Washington St.) showcase the city's affinity for **beaux arts architecture.** Step inside the courthouse for a better look, and also to check out a display about Michigan Supreme Court justice and author John Voelker. Better known by his pen name, Robert Traver, the Ishpeming native wrote *Anatomy of a Murder,* among other works. Scenes from the popular 1959 movie starring Jimmy Stewart were filmed here, as well as in nearby Big Bay, where the actual murder occurred.

The **Marquette Regional History Center** (145 W. Spring St., 906/226-3571, www.marquettehistory.org, 10am-5pm Mon.-Tues. and Thurs.-Fri., 10am-8pm Wed., 10am-3pm Sat., $7 adults, $6 seniors, $3 students, $2 children under 13) features artifacts from prehistoric to contemporary times, and is overseen by the oldest historical society in the U.P.

Another highlight here is the **Marquette Maritime Museum** (300 Lakeshore Blvd., 906/226-2006, http://mqtmaritimemuseum.com, 10am-5pm daily late May-mid-Oct., $7 adults, $5 children under 13), which preserves the city's maritime history and honors its submarine veterans, with exhibits such as a lighthouse lens collection and a silent service memorial. The museum also offers tours of the 1866 **Marquette Harbor Lighthouse.**

SHOPPING

Downtown Marquette is home to several distinctive shops worth a bit of browsing time. One pleasant stop is **Book World** (136 W. Washington St., 906/228-9490, www.bookworldstores.com, 9am-9pm Mon.-Sat., 9am-5pm Sun.), which offers a decent selection of local and regional titles. The U.P.'s Scandinavian heritage also looms large in Marquette's shopping district. **Scandinavian Gifts** (1025 N. 3rd St., 906/225-1993,

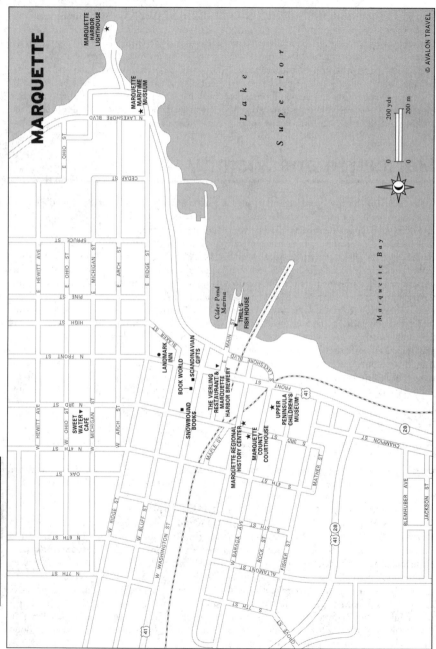

MARQUETTE

MARQUETTE HARBOR LIGHTHOUSE

MARQUETTE MARITIME MUSEUM

N LAKESHORE BLVD

E OHIO ST

CEDAR ST

SPRUCE ST

E HEWITT AVE
E OHIO ST
MICHIGAN ST
E ARCH ST
E RIDGE ST

PINE ST

HIGH ST

N FRONT ST

BAKER ST

LANDMARK INN

BOOK WORLD

SCANDINAVIAN GIFTS

Cider Pond Marina

THILL'S FISH HOUSE

MAIN ST

E LAKESHORE BLVD

THE VIERLING RESTAURANT & MARQUETTE HARBOR BREWERY

FRONT ST

SWEET WATER CAFE

SNOWBOUND BOOKS

W HEWITT AVE
W OHIO ST
N 3RD ST
W ARCH ST
MICHIGAN ST

N 4TH ST

MAPLE ST

MARQUETTE REGIONAL HISTORY CENTER

MARQUETTE COUNTY COURTHOUSE

UPPER PENINSULA CHILDREN'S MUSEUM

41

28

S 3RD ST

S 4TH ST

MATHER ST

CHAMPION ST

OAK ST

N 5TH ST

W RIDGE ST

W BLUFF ST

W WASHINGTON ST

N 6TH ST

W BARAGA AVE

ROCK ST

FISHER ST

S 5TH ST

ALTAMONT ST

41 28

BLEMHUBER AVE

JACKSON ST

GROVE ST

S 7TH ST

N 7TH ST

41

Lake Superior

Marquette Bay

200 yds
200 m
0
0

© AVALON TRAVEL

the Marquette Harbor Lighthouse

9am-7pm daily) showcases the sleek and simple lines of classic Scandinavian design in its selection of glassware and silver (lots of Norwegian sweaters, too).

RECREATION
Hiking and Biking

A thumb of land thrust out into the big lake, **Presque Isle Park,** about four miles north of downtown off Lakeshore Boulevard, is a microcosm of the area's beauty: rocky red bluffs, tall pines, and lovely Lake Superior vistas. You can drive through the 323-acre park, but you'd do better to get out and stroll or ski along its many trails. Watch for albino deer (white-tailed deer lacking pigment), which survive in this protected setting. Near the park's entrance, there's a playground, a picnic area, tennis courts, a marina, and a good spot from which to watch the huge 800-foot freighters arrive at the towering railroad ore dock. Also at the entrance of the park, you can pick up the **Marquette Bicycle Path,** a paved route that hugs the shoreline all the way to Harvey,

offering access to downtown and the Northern Michigan University campus.

Skiing

Among skiers and snowboarders, **Marquette Mountain** (4501 M-553, 906/225-1155, www. marquettemountain.com, lift tickets $30-35 pp) gets the thumbs-up for its 600-foot vertical drop, one of the highest in the state. The 23 trails may not be exceptionally long, but they offer good variety—including bumps and tree runs—and the half-pipe and terrain park grow and improve every year. Located just three miles south of town on M-553, it's popular all week long among local residents and college students. Night skiing is offered Tuesday-Sunday in season, which usually runs about mid-November-early April.

ACCOMMODATIONS

The best spot in Marquette is easily the ◖**Landmark Inn** (230 N. Front St., 906/228-2580, www.thelandmarkinn.com, $124-269 d). Built in the 1930s as the Northland Hotel, it

NORTH COUNTRY NATIONAL SCENIC TRAIL

When completed, the 4,600-mile North Country National Scenic Trail will be the longest continuous off-road hiking trail in the United States. Eventually, it will link communities, forests, and prairies across seven northern states, including New York, Pennsylvania, Ohio, Michigan, Wisconsin, Minnesota, and North Dakota. Much of the trail is already open to hikers, cross-country skiers, and other nonmotorized recreationists, though access to bikers and equestrians depends on the land management guidelines of each section. In general, the trail can be accessed at all times and during all seasons, although regional and seasonal closures can occur at the discretion of local landowners and land managers.

Not surprisingly, the Great Lakes State contains the largest percentage of the North Country Trail, linking Michigan's southern border to the Wisconsin state line alongside the western Upper Peninsula. All told, it traverses the Heartland, the Grand Traverse Bay region, the Mackinac Bridge, Pictured Rocks National Lakeshore, Marquette, and three national forests. Maps are available from the **North Country Trail Association** (229 E. Main St., Lowell, 866/445-

3628, www.northcountrytrail.org), and although there's no specific fee for using the trail, recreationists may need to secure backcountry permits in areas like Pictured Rocks National Lakeshore, or pay entrance fees in places like Wilderness State Park near Petoskey. Also, be aware that "Big Mac" can only be crossed on foot during the famous Labor Day Bridge Walk; otherwise, you'll need to contact the **Mackinac Bridge Authority** (N 415 I-75, St. Ignace, www. mackinacbridge.org) for permission.

For more information about the trail, consult the **National Park Service** (North Country National Scenic Trail, P.O. Box 288, Lowell, MI 49331, 616/340-2004, www.nps. gov/noco), the **Michigan Department of Natural Resources** (Forest Resources, P.O. Box 30452, Lansing, MI 48909, 517/284-5900, www.michigan.gov/dnr), or the three participating units of the **U.S. Forest Service** (www. fs.fed.us): **Huron-Manistee National Forest** (1755 S. Mitchell St., Cadillac, 800/821-6263), **Hiawatha National Forest** (820 Rains Dr., Gladstone, 906/428-5800), and **Ottawa National Forest** (E6248 US-2, Ironwood, 906/932-1330).

hosted such luminaries as Amelia Earhart and Abbott and Costello. After falling into disrepair and eventually closing in the 1980s, it now has been beautifully remodeled and reopened as the Landmark. For not much more than you'd pay for a basic franchise motel room, you get a taste of history, a touch of elegance, and a primo location: Lake Superior on one side, downtown Marquette on the other.

There's also a surprisingly good and varied choice of lodgings in tiny Big Bay. Probably the best known is the **Big Bay Point Lighthouse Bed and Breakfast** (3 Lighthouse Rd., 906/345-9957, http://bigbaylighthouse.com, $125-190 d). As a lighthouse, it naturally occupies a dramatic position on a rocky point just a few miles from the town of Big Bay. The red-brick lighthouse keeper's home, attached to the 1896 light, has been restored and retrofitted

with seven very comfortable guest rooms, all with private baths. Five have Lake Superior views. The inn has extensive grounds, more than 43 acres and a half mile of shoreline, set far back from busy roads and hustle and bustle. Guests are welcome to use the sauna, climb the light tower, or relax in the living room, where owners Linda and Jeff Gamble have collected loads of lighthouse lore and history. Reserve well in advance.

Camping

Van Riper State Park (851 CR-Ake, Champion, 906/339-4461, annual $11 Recreation Passport for Michigan residents or $8.40 day-use fee/$30.50 yearly nonresident motor vehicle permit required) offers 187 easily accessible modern and rustic campsites ($14-23 daily), although within earshot of US-41.

The 1,044-acre park also has several hiking and cross-country skiing trails as well as a fine sand beach along Lake Michigamme, which is considerably warmer than Lake Superior. Reserve well in advance by phoning 800/447-2757 or visiting www.michigan.gov/dnr.

FOOD

For a city its size, Marquette has a very good selection of quality, locally owned restaurants. The **Vierling Restaurant & Marquette Harbor Brewery** (119 S. Front St., 906/228-3533, www.thevierling.com, 11am-10pm Mon.-Sat., $8-27) stands out for its consistently good food, century-old decor, and interesting views of the Marquette Harbor ore docks. (Ask for a table near the large windows in back.) The menu offers a lot of variety, including vegetarian dishes, whitefish served five ways, and excellent breakfasts, soups, and sandwiches. The microbrewery downstairs features British-style ales and stouts.

In Big Bay, stop by the **Lumberjack Tavern** (202 Bensinger St., 906/345-9912, restaurant noon-10pm daily, bar noon-2am daily, $5-14), which has a large local following. Once used as a backdrop for the Otto Preminger film *Anatomy of a Murder* (1959), this homey joint offers homemade pizza and specialty beers.

INFORMATION AND SERVICES

For more information about Marquette and its surrounding areas, contact the **Marquette Country Convention & Visitors Bureau** (337 W. Washington St., 906/228-7749, www.marquettecountry.org, 9am-5pm daily). For local news, refer to the *Mining Journal* (www.miningjournal.net).

As the largest city in the U.P., Marquette has a wide array of banks, groceries, pharmacies, gas stations, and other necessary services. In case of a medical emergency, dial 911 from any phone or contact the **Marquette General Health System** (580 W. College Ave., 906/228-9440, www.mgh.org). Remember that Marquette is situated in the Eastern Time Zone (ET).

GETTING THERE AND AROUND

As the Upper Peninsula's largest city, Marquette is one of the easiest places to reach in the western U.P. First of all, you can fly directly into **Sawyer International Airport** (MQT, 125 G Ave., Gwinn, 906/346-3308, www.sawyerairport.com), rent a vehicle from several major car rental agencies, and head north on M-553 to Marquette, an 18-mile trip that, without traffic, will take about 25 minutes. In addition, **Greyhound** (800/231-2222, www.greyhound.com) and **Indian Trails** (800/292-3831, www.indiantrails.com) both offer bus service to Marquette (1325 Commerce Dr., 906/228-8393).

Of course, most travelers simply drive to the city and its environs. From Sault Ste. Marie, for instance, you can take I-75 South, followed by M-28 West, to Marquette, a 165-mile trip that will usually take about three hours. From Detroit, meanwhile, you can just head north on I-75, cross the Mackinac Bridge (where you'll have to pay a toll), merge onto US-2 West, and follow M-77 North and M-28 West to Marquette; without traffic, the 455-mile trip will take roughly seven hours. Given Marquette's location near the middle of Michigan's Upper Peninsula, it's actually quicker to access the city from Chicago by taking I-90 West and I-94 West, continuing onto I-43 North and WI-172 West in Wisconsin, entering Michigan via US-41 North, and taking M-35 North, US-2 East, and US-41 North to Marquette; without traffic, the 383-mile trip should take less than 6.5 hours. Just be advised that you'll encounter toll booths on I-94 West.

However you manage to reach Marquette, though, you'll be able to walk, bike, and drive around the city rather easily. Of course, you can also park the car and rely on the **Marquette Transit Authority** (Marq-Tran, 906/225-1112, www.marqtran.com), which provides wheelchair-accessible service to destinations throughout Marquette County, including Negaunee and Ishpeming, every day of the year. Typically, a one-way ride in the greater Marquette area (6:45am-6:30pm Mon.-Fri., 8:45am-6:30pm

Sat., 9am-4pm Sun.) is $2.60 for adults and $1.30 for students, seniors, and disabled individuals; as with many public transit systems, though, monthly passes ($66 adults, $33 students and disabled individuals) are also available.

NEGAUNEE AND ISHPEMING

In many ways, these twin towns 15 miles west of Marquette represent the heart of the iron range. One of the Upper Peninsula's earliest iron mines, the Jackson Mine, opened here in 1847; the nearby Empire and Tilden Mines mark the end of the era, the last operating iron mines in the range.

Ishpeming and Negaunee pretty much faded right along with the glory days of mining. The economy never quite recovered from the closing of the area mines in the 1960s, and the once-vital downtowns were further displaced by the commercial strips along US-41, which passes just north of the towns. But anyone who enjoys tidbits of history will find these towns intriguing, with their leftover ornate storefronts, ramshackle antiques shops, and fenced-off cave-in areas—where the land once and for all has succumbed to its mining heritage.

Sights

One of the finest museums in the Upper Peninsula, the state-run **Michigan Iron Industry Museum** (73 Forge Rd., Negaunee, 906/475-7857, 9:30am-4:30pm daily, free) is well worth the short detour off US-41 to its picturesque location along the Carp River. The spot wasn't chosen for its scenery; it marks the site of one of the area's earliest iron forges, built in 1848. This small facility packs a lot of information and well-done displays into a single exhibit hall. It tells the story of Michigan's $48 billion iron mining and smelting industry, which dwarfed the California gold rush ($955 million), Michigan's lucrative logging industry ($4.4 billion), and even Michigan's venerable copper mining empire ($9.6 billion). You'll learn how iron prompted the development of dozens of port towns and the giant 1,000-foot ore freighters that now ply the Great Lakes. The "Technology Timeline" traces the advancements of exploration, working conditions, and mining methods.

Few people think of Ishpeming as the center of the U.S. ski industry, but a lot of those big resorts in the Rockies can trace America's interest in the sport to Michigan. Michigan residents—many of them Scandinavian immigrants—established the Ishpeming Ski Club in 1887, one of the oldest continuously operating clubs in the nation, and organized the country's first ski jumping competition in 1888. Everett Kircher, visionary founder of Michigan's Boyne Mountain resort, invented the first successful snowmaking machine. Hence, Ishpeming was chosen as the site of the **U.S. Ski and Snowboard Hall of Fame and Museum** (610 Palms Ave., 906/485-6323, www.skihall.com, 10am-5pm Mon.-Sat., free) the official hall of fame, just like the Football Hall of Fame in Canton, Ohio, and the Baseball Hall of Fame in Cooperstown, New York.

The museum, on US-41 between 2nd and 3rd Streets, covers the sport from *way* back, beginning with a replica of a 4,000-year-old ski and pole found in Sweden. Most interesting are the displays of early ski equipment (including early poles, which "often doubled as weapons"), the evolution of chairlifts, and an account of the skiing soldiers of the 10th Mountain Division, who played an important role in the mountains of Italy during World War II. The Hall of Fame plaques offer insightful short biographies of those who shaped the sport, from racers to resort owners to, ahem, orthopedic surgeons.

Recreation

In summer, the entire area is part of the comprehensive **Range Mountain Bike Trail System,** with more than 25 miles of trails stretching from Teal Lake to Lake Sally, south of Suicide Bowl. Routes are covered in the *Marquette Region Hike and Bike Trail Guide,* available from local shops or the **Marquette Country Convention & Visitors Bureau** (337 W. Washington St., Marquette, 906/228-7749, www.marquettecountry.org, 9am-5pm daily).

JACQUES MARQUETTE: EXPLORER EXTRAORDINAIRE

A Jesuit missionary and explorer from France, Jacques Marquette (1637-1675) established a mission among the Ottawa at St. Ignace. He and his fellow traveler Louis Joliet were probably the first white men to explore much of the Great Lakes region and the Upper Mississippi.

Born in Laon, France, Marquette joined the Jesuit order in 1656 and spent the next decade studying and teaching in France. In 1666, Jesuit priests sent him to New France (present-day Quebec) as a missionary. Like many Jesuits, he lived among the Native Americans and studied their languages. In 1671, he was appointed missionary to the Ottawa tribe and established the St. Ignace mission on the northern shore of the Straits of Mackinac.

In 1672, French explorer Louis Joliet arrived at the mission, sent by the governor of New France, Comte de Frontenac, to search for a trade route to the Far East. From the Native Americans, they had heard about a great waterway, Missi Sipi ("Big River"), which they thought might flow into the Pacific Ocean. Marquette, with his knowledge of Native American languages, was to accompany Joliet.

Marquette, Joliet, and five other Frenchmen set out in canoes across the northern shore of Lake Michigan in May 1673. They traveled down Green Bay and up the Fox River in present-day Wisconsin, where local Native Americans led them to a portage to the Wisconsin River. The team followed the Wisconsin to its confluence with the Mississippi and explored the Mississippi all the way to the Arkansas River.

They grew alarmed by both the swiftness of the water and word from the Indians about white men downstream. Fearing they would be attacked by Spaniards and deducing that the southerly flow of the river would not lead to the Pacific, the explorers turned back. They paddled the Illinois River to the Chicago River, then followed the western shore of Lake Michigan to Green Bay – a staggering journey of more than 2,900 miles. Along the way, they peaceably communicated with dozens of Native American tribes.

An ailing Marquette spent the winter at a mission in Wisconsin, returning to Illinois the following spring to work with Native Americans that he had met along his voyage. In 1675, he died on Lake Michigan near present-day Ludington, Michigan, en route to St. Ignace. Marquette and Joliet's exploration added greatly to the European knowledge of North American geography. Of course, the Native Americans who treated him so well would later suffer when that new knowledge spurred increasing European settlement.

© NEFTALI77/123RF.COM

The explorations of Jacques Marquette and Louis Joliet are commemorated on a United States postage stamp.

WESTERN UPPER PENINSULA

Down Wind Sports (514 N. 3rd St., Marquette, 906/226-7112, www.downwindsports.com, 9am-7pm Mon.-Thurs., 9am-8pm Fri., 9am-5pm Sat., 11am-3pm Sun.) is a great local source for information on mountain biking, white-water kayaking, sea kayaking, rock climbing, and more. The shop also hosts weekly climbing outings, mountain bike rides, and river trips in the summer months. Down Wind sells a full line of sporting equipment, including kayaks, skis, and snowshoes, and has rentals available.

THE HURON MOUNTAINS

Ask 10 people where the Huron Mountains begin and end, and you're likely to get 10 different answers. But everyone will agree that they fall within the fuzzy boundaries of Lake Superior to the north and east, and US-41 to the south and west. That's a swath of land some 50 miles wide by 25 miles long, where the terrain rises into rugged hills and, yes, even mountains. Mount Arvon, about 15 miles due east of L'Anse, tops out at 1,979 feet, the highest point in the state.

Look at a map, and you'll see it's an intriguing parcel of land, virtually devoid of towns and roads. What the Huron Mountains do have, however, includes washboard peaks and valleys, virgin white pine forests, hundreds of lakes, the headwaters of a half-dozen classic wilderness rivers, dazzling waterfalls, far more wildlife than people, and utter silence. Even by U.P. standards, it's a rugged, remarkable place.

The preservation wasn't the result of happy accident; beginning around the 1880s, the Huron Mountains became the wilderness retreat of choice for several millionaire industrialists. Cyrus McCormick, head of the lucrative farm implement company that would become International Harvester, amassed a huge wilderness estate around White Deer Lake, now part of the Ottawa National Forest's McCormick Tract Wilderness Area. Frederick Miller of Miller Brewing owned his piece of wilderness at Craig Lake, now a wilderness state park. Dozens of others owned "camps" at the Huron

Mountain Club, an organization so exclusive, even Henry Ford was turned downed for membership when he first applied. The members easily had enough clout to stop construction of a road that was to link L'Anse with Big Bay—CR-550 abruptly ends west of Big Bay at a gate and security guard house.

Today, the 25,000-acre enclave is shared mostly by the descendants of those original members, who quietly protect and preserve this spectacular landholding. Though locals grumble about the lack of access onto the property (remember, trespassing is considered a right here), no one can argue that the Huron Mountain Club has proved to be an exceptional steward of the land. It kept away the loggers, the miners, and the developers, leaving what some consider the most magnificent wilderness remaining in the state, maybe even in the entire Midwest. Within its boundaries lie towering virgin pines, blue-ribbon trout streams, pristine lakes, and waterfalls that don't even appear on maps. If the club should ever come up for sale, government officials admit (albeit off the record) that they would clamor to turn it into a state or national park.

In the meantime, the rest of us have to be content simply knowing that such wonderful natural beauty is there, and lovingly protected. Besides, there's plenty of Huron Mountains wilderness open to the public—more than enough to go around for those who are fortunate and smart enough to explore this special place.

Big Bay Area

Many people approach the Huron Mountains from the east, where CR-550 climbs 30 miles out of Marquette to the tiny town of Big Bay, population 270. Sited above Lake Independence and within minutes of Lake Superior, Big Bay is a scrappy little place, where residents take pride in their simple life on the fringes of wilderness. The town has swung from prosperity to near-ghost-town status more than once, first as a bustling logging outpost, then as one of Henry Ford's company towns, home to busy sawmills. More recently, residents joke about how the local bank, well aware of the town's volatile economy, was loath to loan money to Big Bay businesses; while the town's 20 businesses are thriving, the bank closed down. Folks now frequent Big Bay for its Huron Mountains access, Lake Superior harbor, Lake Independence fishing, and unique lodgings.

McCormick Wilderness

Once the private wilderness retreat of Cyrus McCormick, whose father invented the reaping machine, this 27-square-mile tract of wilderness was willed to the U.S. Forest Service by the McCormick family in 1967. Today, it remains in pristine wilderness condition—remote, undeveloped, and largely unused. In other words, perfect for backcountry hiking and camping. No-trace camping is permitted throughout the wilderness area. For more information, contact the **Ottawa National Forest Ranger District** (4810 E. M-28, Kenton, 906/852-3500, 9am-5pm daily).

To access the McCormick Tract, follow US-41/M-28 west from Marquette about 50 miles to Champion. Just after you cross the Peshekee River, follow the first paved road north. This is CR-607, also called the Peshekee Grade or the Huron Bay Grade. In about 10 miles, you'll see a sign for Arfelin Lake; take the next road to your right and watch for a sign and small parking area.

Once you've arrived, you'll be pretty much on your own to explore this rugged terrain of high hills, rivers, muskeg, and bedrock outcroppings. Don't expect marked and maintained hiking trails. This tract is wild, so with the exception of a well-worn path to White Deer Lake (where the McCormicks' lodge once stood), you'll mostly be traveling cross-country. A compass and topo map are absolute necessities. Wildlife sightings can be excellent—the state's largest moose herd roams here, which in turn has attracted predators like the elusive gray wolf. You're not likely to see a wolf, but may be treated to its hollow wail at your camp some evening.

BACKGROUND

The Land

GEOLOGY AND GEOGRAPHY

Many eons ago, a combination of cataclysmic volcanic eruptions and soupy tropical seas initially formed what we now know as Michigan. In the northern part of the state, around Lake Superior and northern Lake Huron, erupting volcanoes laid down thick layers of basalt, which later tilted and faulted, forming the area's rugged, rocky topography of mountain ranges and steep shorelines.

Farther south, a shallow sea covered the vast Michigan Basin, an area that now encompasses the lower four Great Lakes. Over millions of years, sand, shells, and other detritus compacted into thick layers of sedimentary rock, the limestone, dolomite, sandstone, and shale now found from the shores of northern Lake Michigan to the state's southern border.

Much later, powerful glaciers added their indelible touch to the Michigan landscape, the last one as recently as 12,000 years ago. Four separate ice sheets scraped across the region, scouring out depressions that became lakes, lowlands, and ragged shorelines. When the ice melted and glaciers retreated, the water filled vast basins and created the modern-day Great Lakes.

Michigan comprises three distinct land

KERRY KELLY/NPS

Lake Michigan

regions: the Superior Uplands, Northern Highlands, and Great Lakes Plains. The Superior Uplands span the western two-thirds of the Upper Peninsula, the region formed by ancient volcanic activity. It is a landscape of dramatic beauty, characterized by rugged basalt cliffs and thick boreal forests of fir, spruce, and birch—all part of the vast Canadian Shield that dips down from the Arctic, across portions of the northern Great Lakes region, and up the west side of Hudson Bay in a giant horseshoe. Much of the region rises more than 1,000 feet above sea level, including the state's highest natural point, Mount Arvon, which tops out at 1,979 feet. The Superior Uplands harbor some of the nation's richest sources of minerals, especially copper and iron ore deposits.

South of the Superior Uplands lie the Northern Highlands, covering the eastern Upper Peninsula and the northern Lower Peninsula. Here, basalt bedrock gives way to sandstone and limestone, and boreal forests segue into pine and hardwoods. Once heavily logged for its vast, valuable stands of white and red pine, the Northern Highlands area is now prized by recreationists for its woods, water, and wildlife.

The Great Lakes Plains stretch across southern Michigan (as well as southern Wisconsin and northern Ohio). This region received the full brunt of the ice age and its powerful glaciers, which left behind a flattened landscape of sandy lakebeds, wetlands, prairies, and fertile topsoil, making it Michigan's primary farming region for a variety of fruit and vegetable crops.

Geographically, no other state is so distinctly divided. Michigan consists of two separate landmasses, the Lower Peninsula and the Upper Peninsula, circled by Lakes Michigan, Superior, Huron, and Erie, and connected by the Mackinac Bridge, which spans five miles across the Straits of Mackinac.

Ask Michiganders to give you directions in the Lower Peninsula, and odds are that they'll hold up a right hand and use their palm to pinpoint locales within the state. Shaped like a mitten, the Lower Peninsula is 286 miles long and 220 miles wide, with the landmass jutting out into Lake Huron universally dubbed "the Thumb."

The Upper Peninsula, which extends for 215 miles from north to south, shares a border with northeastern Wisconsin, then stretches east for 334 miles between Lakes Superior and Michigan, and reaches a third Great Lake, Huron, where it terminates at Drummond Island. Also considered part of the U.P. is 46-mile-long Isle Royale, the largest island in Lake Superior. The entire Isle Royale archipelago is a national park, one of the most remote and least-visited in the national park system.

Altogether, Michigan's landmass (including inland lakes) covers 58,530 square miles, making it the second-largest state east of the Mississippi. But it is water that defines Michigan and helps to make it the 11th-largest state in America. Along with its 3,288-mile shoreline—second only to Alaska—it encompasses more than 11,000 lakes, over 36,000 miles of rivers, and nearly 200 named waterfalls, and boasts 16 federally designated Wild and Scenic Rivers. Each peninsula is also home to a national lakeshore: Pictured Rocks in the Upper and Sleeping Bear Dunes in the Lower.

It's no wonder, then, that many of Michigan's nicknames—the Great Lakes State, Water Wonderland, Land of Hiawatha—accurately describe this most beautiful of Midwestern states.

CLIMATE

It's difficult to make any generalizations about Michigan's climate, given that its two peninsulas cover a lot of latitude, and the Great Lakes tend to complicate weather patterns. Still, the state's weather is probably more moderate than you think, since the ever-looming Great Lakes cool the hot summer air and warm the cold winter winds.

Michigan has four distinct seasons. Summers require shorts and T-shirts almost everywhere (except near Lake Superior, where you'll want a sweatshirt handy). July and August temperatures average in the 80s in the Lower Peninsula and the 70s in the Upper Peninsula. Come December through February,

they drop to the 30s in the L.P. and the 20s in the U.P. (Temperatures listed here are in degrees Fahrenheit.)

But don't take any of this too seriously. You can enjoy springlike skiing conditions in the U.P. in February, or freeze to death at Thanksgiving. You may swelter on a summer hike through the woods, then grab for your fleece on a Great Lakes beach. Michigan is anything but predictable.

The Lake Effect

The Great Lakes act like insulators—slow to warm up, slow to cool down. That's what allows for Michigan's valuable fruit harvest: Lake Michigan moderates springtime temperatures, so fruit trees and vines aren't usually tempted to bud until the threat of frost has passed.

The Great Lakes also have a dramatic effect on snowfall. Dry winter air travels over the Great Lakes on the prevailing western winds, absorbing moisture. When this air hits land, it dumps its load of precipitation in the form of snow. Weather people refer to this phenomenon as lake-effect snows, which can be surprisingly localized—hence, the reason you'll find many of Michigan's ski resorts clustered along the western edge of the state.

The prevailing western breezes also affect water temperatures, most noticeably on Lake Michigan. In summer, the warm surface waters tend to blow right into those nice, sandy beaches along the lake's eastern edge. While Lake Michigan is rarely warm enough for swimming on the Wisconsin side, it can be downright pleasant in Michigan—as evidenced by the numerous popular beaches lining the state.

Lake Superior is another story. Temperatures on this deep, huge, northern lake never climb out of the 40s, save for the occasional shallow bay. "No one's ever drowned in Lake Superior," the saying goes. "They all die of hypothermia first."

Freshwater freezes faster than saltwater, and the Great Lakes will often freeze over from land to several miles out. The ice gets thick enough for brave souls to snowmobile to the islands, especially nearby ones like Mackinac. The commercial shipping season shuts down

TWO STATES IN ONE

the Mackinac Bridge

© DANIEL MARTONE

Is it a case of sibling rivalry or a marriage of irreconcilable differences? That's what many outsiders may wonder about the Upper and Lower Peninsulas of Michigan, which are a five-mile bridge and a world apart. Many L.P. residents dismiss the U.P. as a bug-infested backwoods filled with yokels. Not surprisingly, U.P. residents (who proudly call themselves "Yoopers") find the generalizations rather insulting, especially when those same L.P. folks seem to enjoy the U.P.'s woods, wildlife, and beaches while on vacation.

That the two are even joined as a single state is a bit of a lark. The Michigan Territory actually wound up with the U.P. as a consolation prize, part of a deal struck with Ohio in 1837. Both Michigan and Ohio had fought for control of the "Toledo Strip," a valuable port on Lake Erie. To earn admission to the Union, the Michigan Territory was forced by Congress to relinquish all rights to the Toledo Strip in exchange for the "barren wasteland" of the Upper Peninsula. Michigan got the last laugh, though, when priceless quantities of iron ore and copper were discovered in its bedrock just a few years later.

Much of the rivalry is good-natured; Yoopers, for instance, joke about blowing up the Mackinac Bridge and display bumper stickers portraying a giant U.P. with a tiny L.P. dangling from its eastern end. Yet there is some truth to the squabble. Yoopers feel that they pay taxes to a distant state capital and receive very little in return – save for perhaps another protected land or wildlife program, of which they already have plenty. Occasionally, U.P. residents launch pseudo-serious drives to declare sovereignty from the rest of Michigan. As Da Yoopers, a musical comedy troupe from Ishpeming, sings, "Dear Mr. Governor, you better turn us loose/ We asked you for some rest stops, instead you sent us moose/The honeymoon is over, the declaration's written/We'll take what's above the bridge, and you can keep the mitten."

Miners Falls, one of Michigan's nearly 200 waterfalls

leading from some houses to the sidewalk—no need to shovel those front walks in winter until there's at least 24 inches on the ground. Ladders nailed to roofs are there for a reason, too. When accumulated snows threaten to collapse the roof, the ladders give a foothold from which to clear off the stuff.

You should be aware of a dangerous little thing called the windchill factor, when cold temperatures are coupled with biting winds. If it's 5°F outside, a 15-mph wind will make it feel like -25°F. Besides being exceedingly uncomfortable, it means that you're at an even greater risk for frostbite and hypothermia. Weather forecasts tend to warn you about the windchill factor, but not always; remember to consider both the temperature and the wind speed when dressing for the outdoors.

That said, many people welcome Michigan's winter, which constitutes a huge piece of the state's tourism pie. Few other areas in the Midwest can offer as reliable a season for skiing, snowboarding, snowmobiling, ice fishing, ice skating, and snowshoeing. Of course, sitting around a fire or soaking in a hot tub is acceptable behavior, too.

mid-January-late March, but bad weather often hampers it for much longer. Commercial ships regularly pound through ice up to a foot thick; more than that, and they rely on the U.S. Coast Guard's *Mackinaw,* a 240-foot, reinforced ship that was named after its namesake, commissioned in June 2006, and principally designed for ramming a passage through ice.

Michigan Winters

You can usually count on snow and cold temperatures in northern Michigan Thanksgiving-Easter. If you want reliable snow, head to the Upper Peninsula. While the Detroit area averages about 43 inches of snow a year, the U.P. gets blanketed with more than 150 inches annually.

U.P. snows are legendary, especially in the Keweenaw Peninsula, where 300-inch winters have been known to occur. (Sticking far out into Lake Superior, it *really* gets nailed with lake-effect snows.) In summer, you'll often notice curious elevated, pier-like contraptions

AVERAGE TEMPERATURES

(High/Low °F)

Month	Detroit	Marquette
January	32/19	25/13
February	35/21	28/14
March	46/29	36/22
April	59/39	47/33
May	70/49	59/43
June	79/60	68/52
July	84/64	74/59
August	81/63	74/59
September	74/55	67/52
October	62/43	54/41
November	49/34	40/29
December	36/24	29/18

Flora and Fauna

TREES AND PLANTS

There's a reason that the white pine is the state tree: Vast stands of it once covered the northern portions of the state, making Michigan the nation's leading lumber center. Michigan pine largely rebuilt Chicago after the Great Fire and supplied a hungry nation as it expanded westward across the treeless plains.

Today, a few tracts of virgin white pine, red pine, and cedar remain in Michigan, magnificent species scraping the sky several stories above. Much of Michigan's original prime logging land is now second-growth pines, many growing tall again. Today's logging operations still clear-cut, but in much smaller sections, and are increasingly turning to selective-cutting methods.

Along with pines in the north, much of the state is covered in hardwoods, especially oak, maple, aspen, and birch. Since Michigan has few native prairies, except in the southwestern corner of the state, many of its plant species are woodland varieties, including columbine, iris, aster, blazing star, various berries, and several species of orchids. Along the coastal dunes, milkweed and wormwood thrive.

MAMMALS AND BIRDS

Though it's called the Wolverine State, there's no evidence that wolverines ever lived in Michigan—just a lot of tall tales about how it acquired the nickname. Most likely, early fur traders brought wolverine pelts to the numerous trading posts here.

With more than half the state forested, Michigan harbors lots of red foxes, skunks, squirrels, badgers, raccoons, porcupines, minks, muskrats, bats, and other small mammals. The state has a huge—and problematic—population of white-tailed deer throughout various areas, and a very healthy number of black bears in its northern reaches. Elk can be found in the northeastern portion of the L.P., part of a successful reintroduction program. Wolves, moose, bobcats, and cougars live in secluded areas of the U.P.

Some 300 kinds of birds also live in the state, including such notable species as bald eagles, peregrine falcons, loons, swans, herons, and dozens of songbirds. Hunting is popular for game birds, such as ducks, geese, grouse, and pheasant. Michigan lies on a major migratory pathway, so it offers excellent bird-watching in spring and fall. Of special note is the hawk migration, as thousands fly between the southern Lower Peninsula and Canada.

REPTILES, AMPHIBIANS, AND FISH

The backwoods and lakeshores of Michigan are rife with reptiles and amphibians, including numerous varieties of toads, frogs, salamanders, and snakes. With so much water, fish thrive here, too, in both the Great Lakes and inland waters. Though commercial fishing has decreased dramatically in the last few decades (the result of overfishing and the accidental introduction of the lamprey eel and zebra mussel), sportfishing remains popular on the Great Lakes, for chinook salmon, coho, steelhead, lake trout, and brown trout. On inland waters, the walleye and yellow perch are prized for flavor, while the muskie and northern pike are considered top sport fish. Bass and trout can also be found within inland lakes. Additionally, Michigan has several blue-ribbon streams, especially near Traverse City and Grayling in the Lower Peninsula, and in the eastern U.P.

INSECTS AND ARACHNIDS

While parts of Michigan lie along the migratory route of the stunning monarch butterfly, the state also has its share of pesky insects. There's a reason that you may spot those corny T-shirts proclaiming the mosquito as the Michigan state bird. The first hatch of mosquitoes usually occurs in early June (depending on

Raccoons and other mammals abound in the woods of northern Michigan.

travel companion. Like mosquitoes, black flies don't usually pose any health risk but have a nasty bite—somewhere between a mosquito bite and a bee sting on the pain scale. Black flies look like houseflies on steroids. They tend to be worst in the deep woods and in early summer. U.P. black flies can be the stuff of legend; anyone planning time in the back-country there would be wise to carry the nas-tiest repellent that they can find, and pack a head net, too.

The wilds of Michigan are also favored by a variety of beetles, including the multicolored Asian lady beetle, which was imported in the early 20th century to control other insect pests. You might also encounter spiders on your hikes through the Great Lakes State. Be especially careful of the black widow and the extremely rare brown recluse; the bites of both are poison-ous and painful.

REINTRODUCTION PROGRAMS

Michigan has had great success with reintro-ducing two large mammals to the state. The eastern elk, once common in Michigan, had disappeared from the state by 1875. In 1918, state officials relocated seven Rocky Mountain elk to Cheboygan County in the northeastern Lower Peninsula. Today, more than 900 Rocky Mountain elk roam the woods and meadows of a four-county area. The largest concentra-tion lies within the Pigeon River Country State Forest near Vanderbilt.

In the mid-1980s, moose were reintroduced to a remote area south of the U.P.'s Huron Mountains, where officials released a total of 59 moose from Ontario, Canada, in two separate operations. Most interesting was the method of reintroduction: Wildlife biologists airlifted the moose one by one in a sling dangling beneath a helicopter to a base camp where they were trucked 600 miles to the Huron Mountains. Van Riper State Park near Champion has an interesting display with photos of the infamous "moose lifts." It worked: Today, about 430 re-portedly roam the western U.P., while less than 100 inhabit the eastern half.

local weather conditions), and the little buggers immediately discover their love for humans. Unless they're carrying a harmful disease like the West Nile virus, they won't seriously injure you, but their sting will cause a small, itchy lump. Most populous in woods and low-lying wet areas, and most active at dusk, mosquitoes can persist all summer, but tend to be less of a problem as the season wears on, especially if conditions are dry.

Your best way to avoid them is to stay in a breeze, and wear long pants and long sleeves. Many people swear by repellent; the stuff with deet is most effective, but studies have linked it with various health risks. If you choose to use repellent, be sure to wash your hands carefully before eating, and read the label warnings, es-pecially before applying it on small children. Some people also swear that eating a lot of garlic makes one less attractive to mosquitoes. (Probably to your hiking partners, too, but hey, this is about survival.)

Black flies can be an equally obnoxious

THREATENED PLANTS OF THE GREAT LAKES

In the summer, Michigan's forests, riverbanks, and beaches are rife with native ferns, weeds, and wildflowers. While some of these vibrant landscapes remain relatively intact, others have long suffered from human encroachment. As a result, the following endemic plants are at risk for extinction, due to habitat loss or destruction:

- **American hart's-tongue fern** – once prevalent throughout the U.P.'s Hiawatha National Forest, now threatened by development, recreational activities, and former logging and quarrying practices

- **Dwarf lake iris** – once prevalent throughout the U.P.'s Hiawatha National Forest and along the northern shores of Lakes Michigan and Huron, now threatened by development, off-road vehicle use, and tourism

- **Eastern prairie fringed orchid** – once prevalent throughout Michigan's prairies and wetlands, now threatened by agricultural practices

- **Houghton's goldenrod** – once prevalent along the sandy shores of Lakes Michigan and Huron, now threatened by human coastal activities

- **Lakeside daisy** – once prevalent in the U.P.'s Hiawatha National Forest, now threatened by limestone quarrying

- **Michigan monkey-flower** – once prevalent along Michigan's streams and lakeshores, now endangered by recreational and residential development

- **Pitcher's thistle** – once prevalent amid Michigan's coastal dunes, now threatened by development, road construction, and recreational activities

While enjoying Michigan's great outdoors, take care not to disturb these and other precious natural resources. For further information, consult the **U.S. Fish & Wildlife Service** (www.fws.gov) or **The Nature Conservancy** (www.nature.org).

ENDANGERED SPECIES

At last count, Michigan was home to roughly 130 threatened or endangered animals and insects, and more than 275 plant species. One of the ones that didn't make it was the passenger pigeon. Michigan was one of the premier places in the world to watch the passenger pigeon migration, which would literally blacken the skies as hundreds of thousands of birds took flight. Unfortunately, their meat became a delicacy and they were easy to hunt, a combination that wiped out the species nationwide by 1914.

Many hope that a happier ending will result for the gray wolf. With plenty of deer to eat and few roads and people to disturb them, wolves have repopulated the Upper Peninsula without help from humans, strolling over from Minnesota or across the ice from Ontario. The wolves that originally populated Isle Royale, for instance, came across the ice in the late 1940s. Sadly, though, the Isle Royale wolves have recently declined in number, from a high of 50 in 1980 to less than 10 today. Of course, the population throughout the Upper Peninsula is currently on an upswing: From three wolves back in 1989, the population has since grown to more than 650 today. As a result, though, a battle now rages between naturalists, who want the gray wolf to remain on the federal endangered species list, and U.P. residents, who have long pleaded for management efforts, including the use of lethal control against problem wolves, particularly those found on their properties.

History

MICHIGAN'S NATIVE PEOPLES

Buried under layers of glacial ice until about 10,000 years ago, the land that is now Michigan was inhospitable to many of the native cultures that thrived in much of the Midwest, like the Paleo and Archaic Indians. Some of the first signs of civilization can be found in the Upper Peninsula's Keweenaw Peninsula, where the Copper Culture Indians of about 5000-500 BC left evidence of their skill as prehistoric miners, devising ways to extract copper from bedrock and fashioning it into tools. Archaeologists believe that they may have been the world's earliest toolmakers.

Later, the Algonquin Indians migrated to the Great Lakes region from the banks of the St. Lawrence Seaway, probably after AD 1000. The Algonquins were divided into three tribes: the Ottawa (or Odawa), the Ojibwa (or Chippewa), and the Potawatomi. Together, they called themselves the Anishinabe ("first people") and named their new land Michi Gami ("large lake"). In and around that lake, they found the state's abundant wildlife—including fish, white-tailed deer, moose, elk, and black bear—and rich natural resources that nourished the tribes for centuries.

The three tribes coexisted peacefully, each moving to a different area. The Ottawa settled around Sault Ste. Marie, the Straits of Mackinac, and the Leelanau Peninsula; the Ojibwa moved west, along the shores of Lake Superior; and the Potawatomi headed south, to the southern half of the Lower Peninsula. They communicated regularly, and their peaceable relationship proved valuable when others came to their lands. Together, they successfully fought off the warring Iroquois, who came from the east in the 1600s, and presented themselves as a strong, unified people when the Europeans arrived.

FRENCH SETTLERS

Étienne Brulé, the first European to arrive on the state's soil (in 1615), was more interested in exploiting the land than worshiping it. Brulé was sent by Samuel de Champlain, lieutenant governor of New France, who hoped to find copper and a shortcut to the Far East. Brulé sent back reports recounting the land's untamed beauty and strange new flora and fauna.

Other opportunists soon followed. Some were after Michigan's rich supply of furs, others after the souls of what they saw as a godless land. Among the most famous of these early explorers was Father Jacques Marquette, who established the state's first permanent settlement at Sault Ste. Marie in 1668 and a second outpost at the straits of Michilimackinac in 1671. The French *coureurs de bois,* a loose term for unlicensed traders, provided a sharp contrast to the priests and nobility. Rugged individualists, they lived among the Native Americans, respected their customs, and hunted the region's rich stores of game.

Few efforts were made to establish a permanent settlement until 1696, when Antoine de la Mothe Cadillac (born Antoine Laumet) convinced France's King Louis XIV that the area was under threat from the British, who were forming alliances with the Native Americans, and that it would be a strategic stronghold for the French crown.

The king sent Cadillac and a 100-men-strong passel of priests, soldiers, and settlers to found Fort Pontchartrain du Détroit in 1701. Cadillac, in turn, persuaded several Native American tribes to form a sort of coalition and settle near the fort. Within a short time, thousands of Native Americans and several hundred French families lived nearby, many establishing narrow "ribbon farms" along the Detroit River. Known as *la ville détroit* ("the village at the strait"), it soon became an important trading

PONTIAC: HERO OF THE OTTAWA

The son of an Ojibwa mother and Ottawa father, Pontiac (1720-1769) eventually became the chief of the Ottawa, Ojibwa, and Potawatomi peoples in the Great Lakes region. He is best known for organizing the most powerful coalition in Native American history.

During the French and Indian War (1754-1763), Native Americans joined the French in their battles against the British over land claims in North America. Nonetheless, the British were able to drive the French out of their most lucrative fur-trading areas. In early 1763, Pontiac organized a Detroit-area conference for the many tribes of the Great Lakes and Ohio Valley and convinced them to join together to fend off the British. The far-reaching alliance was a remarkable achievement, considering how widespread and disparate the tribes were at the time.

Pontiac's diplomatic skills were matched by his military ones. In 1763, Pontiac's forces seized every British post between the Straits of Mackinac and western New York, save for two. The fort at Detroit proved their downfall. While some accounts claim Pontiac's plan to capture Detroit was exposed by a "half-breed" girl, his men did besiege the fort for five months, withdrawing only when the French cut off their supplies. Pontiac and his people retreated to their hunting grounds and eventually signed a peace treaty with the British at Detroit in 1765.

Despite pressure from the French to renew warfare, Pontiac lived among the British in peace until 1769, when he was mysteriously killed in Illinois by a Native American reportedly bribed by a British trader.

PUBLIC DOMAIN/ARTIST IMPRESSION BY JOHN MIX STANLEY

post and a strategic base for the area's continued settlement. Detroit remains the oldest city in the state and, perhaps surprisingly, among the oldest in the Midwest.

BRITISH SETTLERS

The area wasn't peaceful for long. As the fur trade became more lucrative, the intensity of the British and French animosity reached its peak, resulting in the French and Indian War in the mid-1700s. The war effectively ended the 145-year French era and, following the Treaty of Paris in 1763, ushered in British rule. Skirmishes continued, though, especially around the Straits of Mackinac. Today, museums and historic state parks in the area chronicle the events.

The British ruled the colony with an iron fist. While the French had treated the Native Americans with a certain amount of respect, the British allied themselves with tribes that were traditional enemies of those native to the area. The British actively discouraged settlement of the state's interior to protect their rich fur empire. In 1783, after the American Revolutionary War had ended, the Treaty of Paris passed the lands to the newly independent United States.

Jacques Marquette's 17th-century writings brought even more settlers, mostly fur traders such as John Jacob Astor. In the early 1800s, Astor's American Fur Company, headquartered on Mackinac Island, made him the richest man in the United States.

STATEHOOD

In 1825, New York's Erie Canal, which connected Albany on the Hudson River to Buffalo on Lake Erie, opened. This new water route enabled more and more whites to move westward and settle in the Michigan Territory. From 1820 to 1830, the population more than tripled, to just over 31,000. In January 1837, the burgeoning territory was awarded statehood, making Michigan the 26th state in the Union.

By 1840, more than 200,000 people had moved to Michigan. Early industry revolved around farming and agriculture, with lumber becoming a hugely successful enterprise in the later part of the century. Altogether, more than 160 billion feet of pine were cut and hauled from Michigan's northwoods by the 1890s—enough to build 10 million six-room houses. While the southern part of the state grew increasingly civilized, the northwoods were filled with wild and rollicking logging camps.

INDIAN REMOVAL ACT

In one of the saddest chapters in our nation's history, President Andrew Jackson signed the Indian Removal Act in 1830, giving the U.S. government permission to "trade" Native American lands east of the Mississippi for unspecified lands out west. The federal government claimed it was for the tribes' own protection, reporting—and correctly so—that whites would continue to surge into their homelands in the name of frontier expansion.

The Native Americans, of course, had no interest in leaving what had been their homeland for centuries. Tribes in northern Michigan were largely ignored by the federal Indian Bureau at first, most likely because the government found their lands undesirable at the time. Unfortunately, though, the Potawatomi, who lived on valuable farmland in southern

Michigan, were forcibly removed from their lands, and in reality, the federal government didn't leave the other tribes alone for long. By the mid-1800s, treaties "legally" took away more and more Native American land in both the Upper and Lower Peninsulas and established many of the reservations that exist today.

The new state government, however, did treat the tribes with a modicum of decency. In 1850, Native Americans were given the right to vote and even run for office in counties where the population was predominantly American Indian—a concession unheard of elsewhere for many years.

THE COPPER RUSH

In 1840, state geologist Douglass Houghton confirmed the presence of copper in the Upper Peninsula's Keweenaw Peninsula—vast deposits of pure, native copper, much of it right near the surface. The United States acquired the western half of the U.P.—and its mineral rights—from the Ojibwa in 1842, as prospectors began flooding toward the wild and remote Keweenaw. The young country had an insatiable appetite for the metal, first for new industrial machinery and, later, for Civil War hardware, electrical wiring, and other

STATE SYMBOLS

- State bird – American robin
- State fish – brook trout
- State flower – apple blossom
- State fossil – mastodon
- State game mammal – white-tailed deer
- State gem – Isle Royale greenstone
- State reptile – painted turtle
- State soil – Kalkaska sand
- State stone – Petoskey stone
- State tree – white pine
- State wildflower – dwarf lake iris

innovations. Houghton's find was nearly as good as gold.

The Copper Rush began almost overnight, first with prospectors, then with large mining enterprises swarming the Keweenaw. Lucky prospectors secured deck space on Great Lakes vessels, sailing up Lakes Huron and Michigan, then along the southern shore of Lake Superior. But hundreds of others straggled through the roadless wilderness, trudging overland through northern Wisconsin by snowshoe, or following rivers through thick forests to reach the fabled riches. It was the nation's first mineral rush. Copper employed thousands of immigrant laborers, built cities, made millionaires, and prompted extravagant luxuries like opera houses and "copper baron" mansions. Before it was over, King Copper generated more than $9.6 billion—10 times more money than the California Gold Rush.

The entire nation turned to the Keweenaw for its copper. From 1845 to 1895, the Keweenaw Peninsula produced 75 percent of U.S. copper; during the Civil War, it produced 90 percent. More than 400 mining companies operated in the Keweenaw over the course of the 19th century, and the resulting demand for labor drew immigrants from more than 30 countries—most notably, the British Isles and Scandinavia. With multiple cultures sharing the same mine shafts and communities, the Copper Country served as one of the nation's first true melting pots.

In the mid-1900s, however, virtually all the big mines disappeared, sealed up by economic conditions, leaving behind tattered houses and empty streets. They had extracted the easiest-to-reach copper; soon, newer mines in the southwestern United States and South America proved more cost-effective.

THE 20TH CENTURY AND THE RISE OF THE AUTOMOBILE

In the early 1900s, industrial giants like Kellogg and Dow were getting their start, giving rise to industries that flourish even today. Yet few innovations had as much influence on the state—or on the nation—as the "horseless carriage." Shortly after the turn of the century, it gave birth to the state's largest corporate citizens: Ford, Chrysler, and General Motors. As the entire nation grew dependent on their products, the powerful "Big Three" automakers would soon change the face of the state forever.

With the auto industry came thousands of well-paying jobs and, for most, an improved standard of living. Henry Ford's revolutionary $5-a-day wage attracted workers from across the country and around the world, making Detroit one of the country's richest melting pots. Agricultural workers from the Deep South, looking for a better wage, came north to work in the gleaming new factories. Many were African Americans, an influx that created the Detroit area's largest ethnic group.

As time passed, changing working conditions and a lack of employee representation in the auto factories spurred another American invention: the creation of the labor movement and the rise of unions.

THE 1930s-1950s

While labor unions have existed in Michigan since statehood, few were organized until the 1930s. A number of factors contributed to their growth, including auto industry automation, the uncertainties of the Great Depression, and the pro-labor New Deal environment. The most famous confrontation between labor and management was the 1936 sit-down strike in Flint, which led to General Motors accepting the United Auto Workers as the sole bargaining agent for its employees.

In contrast to the Depression, the 1950s were an era of great growth and prosperity. Only Florida and California attracted more people during the decade. The rise of the number of school-age children led, in part, to the greatest expansion of the state's educational system and the founding of new community colleges and other facilities of higher education. While plans to build a bridge connecting the state's two peninsulas had existed as early as 1884, it wasn't until the 1950s that the Mackinac Bridge Authority was founded and funds were raised. Work on the bridge began in 1954, one of the largest and most innovative engineering projects in the country. After more than three years of perilous construction over the turbulent Straits of Mackinac, "Big Mac" opened to the public on November 1, 1957, at last linking the two disparate halves of the state.

THE CIVIL RIGHTS ERA

Racial tensions have occasionally erupted into violence throughout Michigan's history, but few eras were as turbulent as the 1960s. The national struggle for social justice and equality came to a head in Michigan, in some of the state's worst race riots. Before state and federal troops restored a semblance of order in Detroit on July 23, 1967, 43 people had been killed, nearly 1,200 injured, and over 7,200 arrested. Damage to property topped $50 million. This tragic event was just one of several violent episodes that marred the era.

In some ways, the city of Detroit and the state of Michigan are still digging out from those indelible events. While the makeshift yellow fences that bordered riot sites have long been replaced by new development throughout the city, the psychological scars have proven harder to heal. Race relations are an ongoing, front-burner issue in Detroit, one of the most racially divided cities in the country. Always described as the metro area's largest "minority" group, African Americans are, in fact, no longer the minority at all, at least in a demographic sense: Detroit is roughly 83 percent African American.

CONTEMPORARY TIMES

Along with healing racial wounds, Michigan faces other challenges in the coming years. The state must wrestle with an increasingly poor urban population, growing concern with quality of life, and an overdependence on the ever-fluctuating fortunes of the automobile industry—even with the 2009 bailout by the federal government.

On the positive side, one of Michigan's enduring strengths is its abundant natural resources, including one of the nation's largest forest areas and a staggering supply of freshwater—a commodity that, in the long run, will probably prove more valuable than oil. With a 19th-century history of land scarred from clear-cutting virgin forests and lackadaisical mining practices, one hopes that Michigan has learned some lessons. Only time, however, will tell if the state chooses to protect or exploit its vast cache of natural riches.

Government and Economy

GOVERNMENT

Politically, the state has traditionally been a stronghold of the Republican Party. One of the major developments of the post-World War II years in Michigan, however, was the emergence of a competitive two-party political arena. Starting during the Depression, the Democratic Party made major inroads in the state.

Labor union leadership, including the powerful United Auto Workers, became much more active in postwar politics, reflecting the union's interest in larger social issues and quality of life outside the workplace. The electoral support of African Americans, whose population had more than doubled between 1940 and 1950, also helped strengthen the Democratic Party. In 1948, Democrat G. Mennen Williams won the first of what would be six terms as Michigan's governor.

Beginning in the 1950s and continuing through today, Michigan politics reflect a highly competitive two-party state. Among recent Michigan politicians in the spotlight was Governor Jennifer M. Granholm, who became the state's first female governor in 2002, following John Engler's 12-year term. As governor, Granholm worked to diversify Michigan's economy, expand educational opportunities for residents, and create universal access to affordable health care. Part of President Barack Obama's economic advisory team, Granholm was briefly considered for possible appointment to the U.S. Supreme Court in 2009.

Another curious case is former Detroit mayor Dennis Archer, a Democrat who took over from controversial mayor Coleman Young, also a Democrat, in 1994. While Young was best known for antagonizing the suburbs and championing the rights of urban African Americans, Archer proved to be much more of a peacemaker, striving to mend the seemingly insurmountable rift between the predominantly black city and its predominantly white suburbs. Unfortunately for some, however, he refused to run for reelection in 2001 and decided against vying for governor in 2010. Instead, Republican Rick Snyder, a venture capitalist from Ann Arbor, won the 2010 gubernatorial election. Since then, Snyder has garnered mixed reactions from Michiganders, particularly due to controversial measures like the 2011 Public

Employee Domestic Partner Benefit Restriction Act, which prevents the same-sex domestic partners of local and state government employees from receiving health benefits, and the 2012 Employee Free Choice Act, which provides that payment of union dues cannot be required as a condition of employment.

ECONOMY

Despite its patchwork of farm and field, Michigan remains a highly industrialized state. Heavy manufacturing leads its list of income-producing industries, followed by tourism and agriculture.

For almost two centuries, Michigan has been a mirror of the country's great industrial transition. As the state's economy has evolved from agriculture and fur trading to metals, logging, and, finally, automobile manufacturing, the state has ridden a roller coaster that shows no signs of stopping.

Ironically, the ups and downs that sometimes curse the state's economic fortunes are nothing new. Just as today's auto industry has

© CINDY LINDOW

a freighter at sunrise

MADE IN MICHIGAN

As you probably know, Henry Ford created the automobile assembly line in Michigan, which in turn prompted the nation's first mile of concrete highway in 1909 and its first freeway in 1942. Here are a few other notable Michiganders and their inventions:

- Melville Reuben Bissell – carpet sweeper
- Herbert Henry Dow – bromine extraction process

- Frank Daniel Gerber – prepared baby food
- William Redington Hewlett – audio oscillator
- Donald B. Keck – optical fiber
- Dr. John Harvey Kellogg – ready-made breakfast cereal
- Dr. William Erastus Upjohn – dissolvable pill
- James Vernor Sr. – ginger ale

experienced both wild success and dismal failure, so it was with the mining era in the Upper Peninsula, which left a legacy of fantastic wealth juxtaposed with depressed towns huddled around played-out mines. In the 1880s, just before the birth of the automobile, many Detroit residents thought that the city had already seen its greatest growth. Little did they know that in the city's workshops and laboratories, inventors were talking about a revolution.

Industry

Most Americans today need only look in their garages or on their kitchen tables to find evidence of Michigan's diversified economy. While a variety of businesses call Michigan home, the state will always be associated with the automobile industry. Michigan's largest town, nicknamed the "Motor City," and most of the state's economy are driven by the most enduring of American inventions.

With $5-a-day wages and innovative automated assembly lines, Henry Ford revolutionized the industrial world with his "horseless carriage." To this day, the "Big Three"—Ford, Chrysler, and General Motors—maintain world headquarters in metropolitan Detroit. Those corporations in turn spawned hundreds of auto-related businesses and legions of millionaires.

Outside of Detroit, industries are a bit more varied. To the west, Battle Creek is the cereal capital of the country, a place where the Kellogg brothers pioneered their new breakfast food at the Battle Creek Sanitarium. Grand Rapids has long been associated with the furniture industry. Midland is the home of Dow Chemical Company. Tiny Fremont claims Gerber, one of the world's best-known baby-food companies. Other Michigan exports include nonelectric machinery, appliances, pharmaceuticals, and lumber.

Agriculture

Beyond the larger cities, however, agriculture dominates. Farming remains an important presence in the state, with approximately 56,000 farms occupying a total of 10 million acres. Crops vary from asparagus to strawberries. The state ranks first in the nation in the production of tart cherries, dry black beans, blueberries, pickling cucumbers, geraniums, and petunias.

Other principal field crops include hay, oats, corn, rye, potatoes, soybeans, carrots, celery, wheat, and sugar beets. The western side of the state, which enjoys warmer temperatures modified by Lake Michigan, is known as the "Fruit Belt" and has made the state a leading producer of apples, plums, peaches, and sweet cherries. It also has proved surprisingly tolerant for growing wine grapes, and Michigan's winemaking industry continues to surprise people with its award-winning and ever-improving vintages.

Rounding out the state's wide-ranging agricultural products are fresh market and processing vegetables, mushrooms, potted eastern lilies, spearmint, milk, eggs, and poultry.

Logging and Mining

Farther north, the Upper Peninsula's economy was long based on logging and mining. Great fortunes were made in logging in the late 1800s, as Michigan's vast stands of virgin timber produced enough wood to lay an inch-thick plank across the state—with enough left over to cover Rhode Island, too. Few can even grasp the riches of Michigan's copper and iron mining industries, which each dwarfed the gold rush taking place in California. Michigan produced more than $9.6 billion in copper and a staggering $48 billion in iron, compared with $955 million from the gold rush. The riches and the miners disappeared as the most accessible deposits were exhausted and global economics began to play a role. Nearly all the U.P.'s mines shut down by the mid-1900s.

Tourism

Since the U.P.'s former industries folded, it has relied largely on tourism to maintain its sputtering economy, luring many visitors with its unsurpassed rugged beauty. Today, tourism is one of Michigan's largest income producers, accounting for over $17 billion in annual revenues and more than 150,000 jobs statewide. At one time, tourism was focused on the summer months, when beaches, festivals, and resort towns in the Lower Peninsula were most popular. Nowadays, however, the state is a four-season destination, attracting anglers in spring, hunters in autumn, and all manner of skiers, snowmobilers, and skaters in winter.

Shipping and Fishing

Just as semis rumble down the interstate highways, commercial ships transport commodities across the Great Lakes. Officially designated as the nation's "Fourth Seacoast" by Congress in 1970, the Great Lakes serve as a vital, economical transportation artery for the nation's commerce. Via the U.S.-flag fleet, about 125

underground at the Champion Mine, 1905

HENRY FORD AND THE HORSELESS CARRIAGE

Industrialist, billionaire, folk hero, preservationist, social engineer – these and many other labels exemplify Henry Ford's status as one of the most influential and complex Americans of the 20th century. While many schoolchildren learn the story of Ford's pioneering assembly line and the affordably priced Model T it spawned, most know little else of the automaker who rose from rural southeastern Michigan to become one of the world's richest and most powerful men.

Ford was born in 1863 on a prosperous farm in what is now Dearborn, a Detroit suburb. His was a typical rural 19th-century childhood, including endless chores and long lessons in a one-room school. From an early age, he was fascinated by machinery. He loved tinkering with watches and saw his first steam engine at 12. Four years later, he moved to Detroit to serve as a machinist's apprentice. At 18, he accepted an engineer position at the Edison Illuminating Company. In 1893, he was promoted to chief engineer and began tinkering with a crude iron contraption in his spare time – the first gasoline engine.

In 1894, Ford began his first automobile, the Quadricycle, in a small workshop behind his home. Two years later, he took it for its first test run and sold it for $200, later buying it back as a souvenir. By 1898, he'd quit his job at Edison to devote himself full-time to his dream of producing automobiles.

His first business venture, the Detroit Automobile Company, lasted just a year and was dissolved in 1901. His next effort fared only a little better, with Ford resigning in 1902 as president of the Henry Ford Company, which, under Henry Leland's leadership, developed into the Cadillac Motor Company.

Ford finally hit pay dirt with the Ford Motor Company, which he established in 1903 at age 40. The inexpensive, two-cylinder Model A and Model C sold so fast that, by 1905, the company was forced to move out of its original factory into larger quarters. Ford succeeded, in part, because he viewed the automobile not as a luxury, but as a tool that could ease the burden of everyday men. He strove to make his products as inexpensive as possible, believing that a low price tag and prompt service would please his customers more than flashy trim.

The car that put America on wheels was Ford's legendary Model T, which became the nation's workhorse. By 1925, the price had dropped to just $260, and sales climbed. More than 15 million were bought and sold. A major reason for the car's low cost was the rise of the assembly line – also pioneered by Ford. Waist-level workstations minimized the effort expended, and the line moved at the exact speed needed to mount a carburetor or lubricate a chassis. The assembly line cut production costs tremendously.

---

million tons of cargo travel across the lakes each year. Without them, many of the country's largest industries, including Michigan's auto manufacturing, couldn't survive.

With its hundreds of miles of Great Lakes shoreline and dozens of deepwater ports, Michigan is a key player in the Great Lakes transportation network. What's more, the Soo Locks that link Lakes Superior and Huron at Sault Ste. Marie rank as the largest and busiest lock system in the world.

Iron ore forms the foundation of the Great Lakes trade. In Upper Peninsula ports like Escanaba and Marquette, huge lake carriers as long as 1,000 feet load iron ore from nearby mines, then transport it to steelmaking centers in the southern Great Lakes, where the steel is, in turn, used by heavy manufacturers like Detroit's auto industry.

Heavy manufacturing also drives much of the demand for the second-largest cargo, limestone, which is used as a purifying agent

In 1914, Ford made yet another contribution: a profit-sharing plan that more than doubled the salaries of his workers to $5 per day. This reduced Ford's turnover and training costs and made him a national hero. People flocked to Detroit from around the world to work in his plants.

By 1918, Ford had become bored with the company and turned to other interests, including a failed attempt to end World War I and an unsuccessful bid for the U.S. Senate. Though his engineering skills were untouchable, some of his other habits were less sound. His company's "Sociological Department," established to monitor the conduct of workers, invaded the privacy of their homes. Too, Ford was condemned for his anti-Semitic beliefs and practices.

Ford's views grew increasingly rigid as he aged. Despite the fact that his $5-a-day plan made him a working-class hero, he voiced violent opposition to the formation of labor unions during the 1920s. This caused widespread unrest in his factories. Ford Motor Company, in fact, was the last of the major auto companies to sign with the United Auto Workers in 1941.

Since Ford, who died in 1947, amassed such enormous fame and wealth, it has been incorrectly assumed that he was the first to build a gas-powered car. That title belongs to George B. Selden of Rochester, New York, who applied for the first patent in 1879, the same year that Ford left the family farm. Problems with patents caused some of Ford's greatest frustrations, long after his original competitors were out of business.

While Ford is perhaps the best known of Michigan's motoring men, others also played key roles. Charles B. King, an engineer, drove the first gas-powered horseless carriage through the streets of Detroit in 1896, six months before Ford. That same year, Ransom Olds of Oldsmobile fame drove a gas-powered vehicle through downtown Lansing. A successful industrialist, Olds developed a steam-powered experimental vehicle as early as 1887. He made his greatest mark, however, in 1900 when he invented a tiny, motorized buggy known as a "Runabout." Other key figures include Dodge, Durant, Mott, and Sloan, all of whom played crucial, if often forgotten, parts in the history of the car.

Of today's "Big Three" – Ford Motor Company, General Motors, and the Chrysler Group – Ford is the only one still partially owned by the original family. Henry Ford was always at the center of his company, and his descendants remain involved today. William Clay Ford Jr., one of his great-grandsons, was named board chairman in 1999, the first Ford to hold the title in over 15 years. Today, following a five-year stint as Ford's chief executive officer, he serves as the company's executive chairman.

in steelmaking. The construction, chemical, and paper industries rely on limestone, too. Michigan has a good corner on the market: The limestone quarry in Rogers City, northwest of Alpena, ranks as the largest in the world.

Great Lakes shipping does face its share of competition, especially from overseas, in the form of imported finished products ranging from refrigerators to automobiles. That translates to a decrease in steel production here, which in turn reduces the need for iron ore shipments. Secondly, other transportation networks like trains and trucks compete with shipping for certain commodities. Despite such factors, shipping has proven to be a steady industry for the state, although its success may ultimately be hindered by two modern-day factors: low water levels and the state's relatively new ballast water discharge regulations, which are intended to stop the spread of invasive aquatic species.

People and Culture

While the Algonquins were the land's first inhabitants, today's Michiganders reflect a much more diverse population. The French "empire builders" were the first Europeans to come, and in due time, the British replaced the French. Early American settlers included a large group of Yankees from western New York and New England. From Europe came immigrants seeking a better life, including Finns, Swedes, Italians, and the Cornish who worked in the Upper Peninsula mines and lumber camps. Germans, the Irish, and the Dutch settled in the cities and the rich agricultural lands to the south. Later, the automobile industry attracted large numbers of immigrants from southern and eastern Europe and, later, a large influx of southern Americans. Between 1850 and 1900, the state's population increased by more than 600 percent.

Today, Michigan's residents number just under 9.9 million, making it the ninth most populous state in the United States. The vast majority of the state's residents live in the southern third of the Lower Peninsula, mostly near major cities. Just three counties—Wayne, Oakland, and Macomb, near Detroit—contain almost 40 percent of Michigan's entire population.

NATIVE AMERICANS

In most books about Michigan history, the land's first inhabitants are given little more than a cursory nod, a line or two that identifies the approximately 100,000 early Native Americans as belonging to the tribes of the "Three Fires"—the Ojibwa, Ottawa, and Potawatomi—collectively known as the Anishinabe. During the 1700s, other tribes included the Huron, also known as the Wyandotte, who came to southeastern Michigan from Ontario; the Sauk, who lived in the Saginaw River Valley; the Miami, who lived along the St. Joseph River; and the Menominee, who lived in parts of the Upper Peninsula.

The fact that Native Americans get little more than a footnote in many history books reflects a cultural ignorance throughout the nation. One of the few state museums to devote any space to the subject is the excellent Grand Rapids Public Museum, where a fine permanent exhibit ("Anishinabek: The People of This Place") traces the story of the Native Americans of western Michigan. While many tribes were being removed from their lands to reservations in Kansas and Oklahoma during the 1880s, Michigan's Anishinabe used skillful negotiation and hard work to remain in their homeland. Through video interviews, photographs borrowed from local families, and hundreds of artifacts, including clothing, tools, and decorative arts, the exhibition tells of the high price that the tribe paid to remain citizens of the state, and of its ongoing struggle to preserve and protect this heritage in a swiftly changing modern society.

Today, Michigan is home to one of the largest Native American populations in the country, estimated at 59,300, though it's hard to name an exact figure, since the label "Native American" can be defined in more than one way—by political, ethnic, or cultural criteria. Depending on how you count, Michigan may have the largest Indian population east of the Mississippi, and only a small percentage live on reservations. As with the state's general population, the majority of Michigan's Native Americans reside near Detroit and Grand Rapids.

There are a number of reservations in the state, including federally recognized tribes near Ontonagon, Baraga, L'Anse, Watersmeet, Wilson, Brimley, Sault Ste. Marie, Petoskey, Suttons Bay, Manistee, Mount Pleasant, Fulton, and Dowagiac. Some are authorized to operate their own tribal courts, which exercise exclusive jurisdiction over certain laws and civil matters involving Native Americans and events that occur on their reservations. In addition,

Native American tribal councils throughout the state provide a variety of outreach services, economic development initiatives, and cultural activities.

Many reservations have cultural centers, many tribes host powwows and festivals, and some even operate casinos. For details, check with local tourism bureaus or inquire at tribal headquarters, which are prominent buildings on most reservations.

THE IMMIGRANTS

Traveling Michigan's numerous rivers as early as the 1600s, the French fur traders, missionaries, and voyageurs were the area's first white settlers, establishing posts in far-flung areas across the state. The majority of white immigrants, however, didn't arrive until the early 1800s. Expatriate New Englanders were the first in the 1830s, grabbing up vast tracts of land in the state's southern counties. More and more settlers followed in the next two decades, in response to a European food shortage.

During the remaining 19th and early 20th centuries, refugees from at least 40 countries arrived in record numbers. Among them were the Germans, still the largest ethnic group in Michigan. In the early 1830s, the first families settled the Ann Arbor area and the Saginaw River valley town of Frankenmuth—now a major tourist destination, famous for its Bavarian festivals and all-you-can-eat chicken dinners.

Other early immigrants included the Dutch, Irish, and Poles, who continue to make up large chunks of the state's ethnic population. Concentrations of Dutch can still be found in Holland, a western city along Lake Michigan, where the tulip festival is one of the state's largest tourist attractions. Poles can be found throughout the state, most notably in Detroit's Hamtramck neighborhood. Not far away, the Irish settled Detroit's charming Corktown, the city's oldest neighborhood and the former home of the Detroit Tigers.

By the beginning of the 20th century, a new wave of immigrants poured into the state from southern and eastern Europe, including Austria, Hungary, Italy, and the Balkans. Their arrival coincided with Detroit's newest industry, and thousands of them went to work in the auto factories. More recent migrations included Africans, Asians, Latinos, and Middle Eastern immigrants.

Today, African Americans make up one of the most influential ethnic groups in Michigan, especially in Detroit. While the majority of blacks came from the American South to work in the auto industry, there has been an African American presence in the state since Jean de Sable traded furs in the 1600s.

From the 1830s to the 1860s, Michigan played an important role in the Underground Railroad, helping slaves escape north to Canada. Many escapees stayed in Michigan, mostly in the L.P.'s southwestern corner, where they started their own farms in towns like Benton Harbor. Still, the largest number of African Americans came to Michigan after 1910, leaving families in the Deep South to find better jobs in Detroit's factories.

One of the state's newest waves of immigrants has been from the Arab world, including Iraq, Jordan, Lebanon, and Syria. Today, Michigan has one of the largest groups of Arabic people living in cities such as Dearborn and Southfield, where it's not unusual to see storefront signs in Arabic and women in full headdress.

The immigrants of the Upper Peninsula vary greatly from those of the Lower Peninsula. The iron and copper mines lured many from Sweden, Finland, Italy, and England with promises of steady work and decent wages, despite difficult job conditions. Swedes and Finns in particular took to the U.P., at home with the area's woods and rushing rivers. Finnish names, foods, and the ubiquitous sauna can be found throughout the Keweenaw Peninsula, and Hancock remains largely Finnish, down to its street signs. Farther south, in Detroit, the Finnish Saarinen family helped develop Cranbrook, a well-known private school, arts community, and science center near Detroit.

Arts and Entertainment

FINE ARTS

While state tourism boosters have long sung the praises of Michigan's legendary sand and surf, they've only, in recent years, begun heavily promoting its considerable cultural riches. The majority of the arts scene is concentrated in its larger cities, including Detroit, Grand Rapids, and Traverse City. Yet the arts thrive from Kalamazoo to Kalkaska—both mainstream and underground cultures that plug along without much state government support. The neighboring towns of Saugatuck and Douglas, for example, rely heavily on arts-related tourism; their downtown streets virtually teem with visual art galleries.

Surprising as it might sound, the Detroit Institute of Arts is considered one of the country's top art museums, and the Cranbrook Academy of Art, in nearby Bloomfield Hills, is a huge educational community that pioneered the Finnish Modern school. Beyond the Detroit area, notable art museums include the University of Michigan Museum of Art in Ann Arbor, a city known for its galleries and excellent summertime art fair; the Flint Institute of Arts, which ranks second in size and scope only to the Detroit Institute of Arts; and the new Eli and Edythe Broad Art Museum at Michigan State University in East Lansing, noted for collections that span more than 5,000 years of art and history. In addition, the Marshall M. Fredericks Sculpture Museum, part of Saginaw Valley State University, contains one of the state's finest sculpture collections.

MUSEUMS

The Henry Ford, in Dearborn, ranks among the state's top tourism draws, with a funky collection that ranges from vintage washing machines to presidential limousines. Adjacent Greenfield Village is a patchwork quilt of 83 historic buildings, including Thomas Edison's Menlo Park laboratory and Noah Webster's home, where he wrote the first American dictionary. Detroit's Charles H. Wright Museum of African American History, meanwhile, is the largest of its kind in the world, filled with dramatic visual arts and historic artifacts.

Not surprisingly, many of the state's museums cover the lore and legends of the Great Lakes and the state's maritime industry. Belle Isle State Park, Detroit's 980-acre urban park, is home to the Dossin Great Lakes Museum, which includes a full-size freighter pilothouse and a massive anchor from the *Edmund Fitzgerald*, the Great Lakes ship that sank mysteriously in 1975.

In South Haven, the Michigan Maritime Museum traces the state's history from Native Americans to the 19th century, when huge freighters crossed Lake Michigan and the state's tourism industry began in earnest. In the Upper Peninsula, more stories can be found at Whitefish Point's Great Lakes Shipwreck Museum, which tells the haunting tales of the numerous ships that met their match in the area's frigid, turbulent waters. Also in the U.P., the U.S. Ski and Snowboard Hall of Fame and Museum in Ishpeming chronicles both sports, while neighboring Negaunee is home to the Michigan Iron Industry Museum, an excellent state-run facility on the site of one of Michigan's first iron forges.

LITERATURE

While most out-of-towners know about the famous musicians that hail from Detroit, few are perhaps aware of the many notable writers who, at times, have called the Great Lakes State home, including novelists Ernest Hemingway, Joyce Carol Oates, Elmore Leonard, and L. Frank Baum, author of *The Wonderful Wizard of Oz*. Some authors were even born here, including Petoskey's Bruce Catton, Kalamazoo's Edna Ferber, Port Huron's Terry McMillan, and Grayling's Jim Harrison, whose first collection of novellas,

THE HEIDELBERG PROJECT

Buses full of Japanese tourists are a strange sight in this rundown neighborhood on Detroit's east side, a part of the city better known for its crack houses than its tourist attractions – that is, until artist Tyree Guyton, who grew up on Heidelberg Street, began The Heidelberg Project (42 Watson St., Detroit, 313/974-6894, www.heidelberg.org), a remarkable piece of inner-city environmental art.

As a child, Guyton lived here in poverty, neglected, abused, and harassed for his growing interest in art. Only his grandfather encouraged him. Despite the odds, Guyton went on to study at Detroit's respected Center for Creative Studies (CCS), but he never forgot his roots. His first work was *Fun House,* created in 1986 from an abandoned house next door to his grandfather's duplex. He transformed the dilapidated frame structure with bright patches of color and covered it with old toys, dollhouses, picture frames, shoes, signs, and other urban castoffs. The Heidelberg Project grew to encompass most of Heidelberg Street between Mt. Elliott and Ellery Streets (which you can reach from downtown Detroit by taking Gratiot Avenue northeast to Mt. Elliott, turning right, and then turning right again on Heidelberg). It drew ac-

claim from newspapers and art journals as well as curators at the nearby Detroit Institute of Arts, but failed to win over neighbors and then-mayor Coleman Young, who regularly demolished Guyton's work along with vacant houses.

Former mayor Dennis Archer was more enlightened, and though he didn't openly encourage Guyton's work – perhaps Detroit's most controversial art project – he didn't discourage it either. Guyton's grandfather, who served as an unofficial tour guide, died in 1992. His neat duplex, known as the *Dotty Wotty House,* is now part of the project. It is dedicated to the memory of Guyton's grandfather and of Dr. Martin Luther King Jr. Despite arson and vandalism, The Heidelberg Project has endured, and improvements are on the horizon, including a grant-funded plan to transform the *House That Makes Sense* into the project's official center, featuring administrative offices, an exhibition space, a library, and a children's workshop. Though admission is free if you visit on your own, you should always respect the privacy of area residents and never approach individual structures without permission. Of course, guided group tours are also available, if reserved in advance.

Legends of the Fall, inspired an Academy Award-winning film. Meanwhile, Pulitzer Prize-winning poet Theodore Rothke was born in Saginaw, and former judge John D. Voelker, who wrote *Anatomy of a Murder* under his pen name, Robert Traver, spent his formative years in Ishpeming.

PERFORMING ARTS

In Motown, the restored Theater District is second only to Broadway in its number of available seats, with performances ranging from cutting-edge productions to the classics. Queen of the venues is the 5,000-seat Fox Theatre, a gloriously gaudy 1920s-era theater that defied the odds to survive until its 1988 restoration by Little Caesars magnate Mike Ilitch. Other Theater District highlights include the Music

Hall Center for the Performing Arts; the intimate 450-seat Gem Theatre; and the restored Detroit Opera House. The towns north of Detroit offer their own impressive performance venues, most notably The Whiting in Flint. Even farther north, in the town of Cheboygan, the historic Opera House was once a stop for luminaries such as Mary Pickford and Annie Oakley.

Detroit is one of the few large cities without a resident dance company. Ballets from around the world stop at the city's restored opera house, which sells out regularly, but you'll have a better chance of finding modern dance performances at university venues in Ann Arbor and East Lansing. Elsewhere in the state, dance events are held throughout the summer season.

MUSIC

While Michigan has spawned numerous musicians—including Aretha Franklin, the queen of soul, and Madonna, the queen of pop—American music has never been the same since Berry Gordy Jr. started a small recording studio in the 1950s, giving birth to the Motown Sound. Soon, this fresh, exciting creation was known worldwide, made famous by local talents like Smokey Robinson, Mary Wells, Diana Ross, Marvin Gaye, Gladys Knight, The Temptations, Stevie Wonder, and countless more. Their stories are told in the Motown Museum, also known as Hitsville U.S.A., where displays include everything from the legendary Studio A to flashy Supremes and Temptations costumes.

Classical fans flock to Saginaw's Temple Theatre, where the Saginaw Bay Symphony Orchestra regularly performs, or the Max M. Fisher Music Center, home to the 125-year-old Detroit Symphony Orchestra. Almost as old is the award-winning Grand Rapids Symphony, founded in 1930 and now featuring a wide array of classical and pops concerts. Here, you'll also find the impressive Grand Rapids Youth Symphony. Farther north, the Traverse Symphony Orchestra is one of the region's premier ensembles.

The lands around Traverse City and the Lake Michigan shore also provide plenty of inspiration for the 1,200-acre Interlochen Center for the Arts, a music academy and arts camp founded in 1928. During the summer, students from around the world come to practice and perform in a variety of open-air concerts, most of which are open to the public. Luckily, though, music lovers can also attend live performances, including musicals, throughout the year.

If you're an alternative music fan, plenty of options exist in lower Michigan. In the Detroit area, bands favor Saint Andrew's Hall and the Royal Oak Music Theatre, both known for their warm receptions to cutting-edge artists. Meanwhile, well-known folk artists usually add the Hill Auditorium in Ann Arbor to their list of dates, and fans of blues and jazz can find several hangouts in downtown Detroit.

CINEMA

Film entertainers have also made their mark in Michigan. Jeff Daniels may be a Hollywood type, but the Georgia native prefers to live in tiny Chelsea, a village west of Ann Arbor, where the actor-director founded the acclaimed Purple Rose Theatre Company (named after the Woody Allen film in which he starred). Other successful filmmakers and performers who were actually born in the Great Lakes State include producer Jerry Bruckheimer, directors Sam Raimi and Francis Ford Coppola, and actors Ellen Burstyn, Gilda Radner, Lily Tomlin, Timothy Busfield, Tom Selleck, Ernie Hudson, Tom Skerritt, J. K. Simmons, Lee Majors, George Peppard, and Piper Laurie, among others.

NIGHTLIFE

Michigan's larger cities have a full plate of nightlife options. On most nights and every weekend, you can choose from blues, jazz, alternative, rock, country, and everything in between. In Detroit, check out the free *Metro Times,* an alternative weekly that provides comprehensive entertainment listings (and is also known for its colorful personal ads). Another good bet is the entertainment section of the *Detroit Free Press,* which lists city events as well as dates throughout the state. Beyond Detroit, nightlife varies, but almost universally gears up in the summer season. From gay bars in Saugatuck to Nugent-lovers in Jackson, there's something for everyone.

INDIAN GAMING AND DETROIT CASINOS

As sovereign lands, Indian reservations are often able to offer high-stakes gambling that isn't legal elsewhere in the state. Michigan's first Indian-run casino opened in 1984. The Kings Club Casino in Bay Mills, since replaced by the Bay Mills Resort & Casinos, had just 15 blackjack tables and one dice table in a 2,400-square-foot room in the tribal center. While it wasn't

IGGY POP: THE GODFATHER OF PUNK

Born in Muskegon in 1947, James Newell Osterberg Jr. spent his early years in Ann Arbor, where he became a drummer for various high school bands. After dropping out of the University of Michigan, he moved to Chicago to study the blues. In the mid-1960s, he formed a band called the Psychedelic Stooges (for which he was the lead vocalist) and adopted the moniker Iggy Pop. In 1968, his band, now called the Stooges, signed with Elektra Records (also The Doors' label). Despite the explosive phenomenon of their unique sound — which eventually heralded the styles of punk rock and American heavy metal — their first two albums sold poorly, and Iggy's heroin addiction caused the group to disband.

His career rebounded when David Bowie decided to produce an album with him in England. Some of the original Stooges reunited, and the album, *Raw Power*, became a punk-rock landmark. Despite the album's success, Iggy's drug problem persisted, initiating a second breakup of the Stooges and stalling his career for several years.

Together, he and Bowie, his consistent friend and collaborator, tried to overcome their drug addictions. Iggy signed with RCA and, with Bowie's help, produced two acclaimed albums, *The Idiot* and *Lust for Life*, in 1977. After producing a third album with RCA, Iggy moved to Arista Records, with which he produced *New Values*, a partial Stooges reunion and not much of a commercial success. While promoting the album in Australia and New Zealand, Iggy displayed his characteristically irreverent, erratic behavior. After two subsequent album failures, however, he was dropped from the Arista label.

During the 1980s, Iggy's life continued to resemble a roller coaster. After another failed album, his fortunes improved with Bowie's cover of his song "China Girl." Subsequent royalties allowed Iggy to resolve his tax problems and take a three-year break, during which he tried to beat his heroin addiction. In 1986, his popular cover of "Real Wild Child" constituted one of his few brushes with major commercial success. His follow-up album, *Instinct*, resembled the guitar-based sound of the Stooges, and while punk-rock fans embraced it, his record label did not.

Iggy continued to perform during the 1990s, playing with musicians like Deborah Harry, contributing old songs to films like *Trainspotting* (1996), and even acting in a few movies. More recently, he's collaborated with the surviving members of the Stooges, appeared in various commercials and documentaries, and participated in music festivals around the world.

Over the years, Iggy has been noted for his extreme performance style. Inspired by Jim Morrison's antagonistic stage antics of the 1960s, he has been known to expose himself to the crowd, dive off the stage, and participate in other raucous activities. While Iggy's often been labeled a controversial performer, there's no doubt that he's an iconic figure in the world of modern music. His songs have been covered by the likes of Joan Jett and the Sex Pistols, and countless soundtracks, documentaries, commercials, and compilation albums have kept the mystique of Iggy and the Stooges alive — and to think that the "godfather of punk" got his start on the laid-back coast of southwestern Michigan. For more information, visit www.iggypop.com or www.iggypop.org.

Atlantic City, visitors quickly displayed their love of gambling, pouring millions of dollars into casino coffers. It started a gambling tradition that has escalated ever since.

There are roughly 25 Indian casinos in Michigan. They range from small, simple gambling halls to glitzy showplaces like Leelanau Sands in Peshawbestown. Many are open 24 hours daily and have become enormous tourism draws.

By the early 1990s, the state wanted in on the deal. In September 1993, Governor John Engler passed the first Tribal-State Gaming Compacts, giving the state 8 percent of net win income derived from games of chance. While providing the state government with easy cash, the success of Indian gaming has also given new power and influence to tribal governments.

Non-Indian groups were soon eager to seize a piece of this cash cow. In late 1996, Detroit voters approved a controversial referendum permitting non-Indian casino gambling within the city limits. After years of controversy, several casinos have opened in the Motor City, including the MGM Grand Detroit, the first-ever Las Vegas-style destination to open in a major metropolitan core.

Given the competition from Detroit, many of the Indian-owned facilities have expanded. Soaring Eagle, in Mount Pleasant, added a 514-room luxury hotel. The Kewadin complex in Sault Ste. Marie houses an incredible, 1,500-seat performance venue. Not surprisingly, even more tribes, many of whom live at or near the poverty level, are seeking to open casinos.

While the pros and cons of gambling remain an ethical debate, there's no arguing the positive effect gaming has had on the reservations' economies. Within the Indian community, gambling provides jobs and funds schools, health-care facilities, and cultural centers. Many overlook that it provides loads of economic benefits to those outside the Native American community, too, providing jobs for the building trades and tourism industry. Michigan residents and visitors, it seems, just can't spend enough on Lady Luck.

FAIRS AND FESTIVALS

Given the down-to-earth Midwestern vibe that permeates the state of Michigan, it's no wonder that fairs and festivals, especially family-friendly ones, abound here. All major towns and most small villages celebrate their unique culture with annual events, from music festivals to county fairs. While the summer months, in particular, are rife with such celebrations—from Traverse City's National Cherry Festival in July to the Detroit area's Woodward Dream Cruise in August—winter is not without its share of fun. Frankenmuth, for one, offers Zehnder's Snowfest in January, while Sault Ste. Marie hosts the I-500, the world's oldest snowmobile race, in late January or early February.

ESSENTIALS

Getting There

While international tourists will most likely arrive in Michigan via plane or by crossing the United States-Canada border, domestic travelers can reach the Great Lakes State by air, water, rail, or road. So, consider your budget and intended destinations before choosing the method that's right for your trip.

BY PLANE

The **Detroit Metropolitan-Wayne County Airport** (DTW, 1 Detroit Metropolitan Airport Tram, Detroit, 734/247-7678, www.metroairport.com), also known as the Detroit Metro Airport, is the state's biggest and busiest.

Given that 12 major airlines service this airport, you can fly from Detroit to almost anywhere in the United States and Canada, and to a surprising number of cities around the globe, from Amsterdam to Tokyo. Via **Delta Air Lines** (800/221-1212, www.delta.com), it's also possible to reach many of Michigan's commercial airports in the Lower and Upper Peninsulas, including Alpena County Regional (Alpena), Bishop International (Flint), Capital Region International (Lansing), Cherry Capital (Traverse City), Chippewa County International (near Sault Ste. Marie), Delta County (Escanaba), Gerald R. Ford

© LAURA MARTONE

International (Grand Rapids), Kalamazoo/ Battle Creek International (Kalamazoo), MBS International (Freeland), Pellston Regional (near Petoskey), and Sawyer International (near Marquette). For specific routes, flights, and rates, check with the airlines directly; among those servicing Detroit are, besides Delta, **American Airlines** (800/433-7300, www.aa.com), **Southwest Airlines** (800/435-9792, www.southwest.com), **United Airlines** (800/864-8331, www.united.com), and **US Airways** (800/428-4322, www.usairways.com). If you're looking for a flight to Canada, consider United, which can take you to both Sault Ste. Marie and Windsor; of course, **Air Canada** (888/247-2262, www.aircanada.com) is also a possibility. Since routes and carriers seem to change with the weather, your best bet is to call a travel agent or book your trip online (through such websites as www.orbitz.com, www.cheaptickets.com, www.expedia.com, www.travelocity.com, or www.kayak.com).

BY BOAT

Given that Michigan is surrounded by miles and miles of shoreline, it's no surprise that many visitors arrive via boat, and they'll find plenty of docks when they get here. The state's Parks and Recreation Division has established a network of over 90 protected public mooring facilities (fees vary) along the Great Lakes, a "marine highway" that ensures boaters are never far from a safe harbor. For a free copy of *The Handbook of Michigan Boating Laws and Responsibilities,* contact the **Michigan Department of Natural Resources** (Parks and Recreation Division, Mason Bldg., 3rd Fl., P.O. Box 30257, Lansing, MI 48909, 517/284-7275, www.michigan.gov/dnr) or download the inexpensive Kindle edition from Amazon.com.

Non-boaters, too, can arrive by water via the **SS *Badger*** (Lake Michigan Carferry, 701 Maritime Dr., Ludington, 920/684-0888 or 800/841-4243, www.ssbadger.com), the only authentic passenger steamship on the Great Lakes. The 410-foot-long ship ferries up to 600 passengers and 180 vehicles across Lake Michigan, from Manitowoc, Wisconsin, to Ludington, Michigan. The four-hour passage spares travelers from a congested auto trip through Chicago or a lengthy jaunt across the Upper Peninsula. Plus, it saves on gas and can be great fun.

Built in 1952, the SS *Badger* was one of seven railroad and passenger ferries crossing Lake Michigan; you can still see the railroad tracks that lead into the car deck. The *Badger* marked the end of an era; ferries were to the Great Lakes what steamboats were to the Mississippi. Today, it's the only ferry of its kind, and it's been quite inventive about making a go of it. Although it also transports loaded trucks and occasional business travelers, tourism is its bread and butter. The ship is comfortably outfitted with tables, chairs, a theater showing free movies, a cafeteria and snack bar, a gift shop, a video arcade, and small staterooms ($49 one-way). Equipped with twin berths, these are well worth it if you hope to catch some sleep. There's ample deck space and chaise lounges, if it's warm enough, and the crew even hosts children's activities, bingo, and interactive games. Satellite television and wireless Internet access are also available.

The *Badger* sails daily mid-May–mid-October. It departs Ludington at 9am (ET) and Manitowoc at 2pm (CT) from the beginning of the season to early June and from early September to the end of the season. From early June to early September, it offers two round-trip passages daily: one leaves Ludington at 9am (ET), arrives in Manitowoc at noon (CT), and departs for Ludington at 2pm (CT), and the other leaves Ludington at 8:30pm (ET), arrives in Manitowoc at 11:30pm (CT), and departs for Ludington at 1am (CT). Rates are $69 one-way or $121 round-trip for adults; $62 or $109 for seniors 65 and over; $24 or $39 for children 5-15; free for children under 5; $69 one-way for cars, vans, and pickups; $38 one-way for motorcycles; and $6 one-way for bicycles. There is a $5.95-per-foot charge for motorhomes and an $86 one-way fee for pickup campers. Pets must remain in your vehicle or in a ventilated kennel (which you must provide) on the car deck; this isn't recommended during

© OSELAND | DREAMSTIME.COM

the SS *Badger* crossing Lake Michigan

the hot summer months. For security reasons, you cannot access your vehicle during the crossing. Reservations are strongly recommended.

BY TRAIN

Amtrak (800/872-7245, www.amtrak.com), which has a hub in Chicago, runs three regular routes through the southern half of Michigan's Lower Peninsula. One Michigan route, the Pere Marquette, travels from Chicago through St. Joseph and Holland to Grand Rapids. A second route, the Blue Water, travels from Chicago to Kalamazoo, Battle Creek, East Lansing, Flint, Lapeer, and Port Huron. A third Chicago train, the Wolverine, splits at Battle Creek and heads for Jackson, Ann Arbor, Dearborn, Detroit, Royal Oak, Birmingham, and Pontiac. From Windsor and Sarnia, the Canadian cities adjacent to Detroit and Port Huron, respectively, you can hop aboard **VIA Rail Canada** (888/842-7245, www.viarail.ca), which offers service to Toronto, Vancouver, and roughly 450 other destinations throughout Canada.

BY BUS

Both **Greyhound** (800/231-2222, www.greyhound.com) and **Indian Trails** (800/292-3831, www.indiantrails.com) operate in most major Michigan cities, and plenty of smaller ones, too. It can be a very inexpensive way to travel if you've got the time. Traveling from Chicago to Marquette, for example, takes over 10 hours—but costs less than $100.

BY CAR

About a dozen major interstates and highways make it mighty efficient to zip into and around Michigan. I-75 stretches from the state's southern border at Toledo through Detroit and all the way north across the Mackinac Bridge to Sault Ste. Marie. I-69 cruises up the middle of the Lower Peninsula, from Indianapolis through Lansing, then east to Flint and Port Huron. I-94, which comes over from Chicago, traverses the southern tier of the state to Detroit. From I-94 just east of Benton Harbor, I-196 extends north along Lake Michigan and over to Grand Rapids, where I-96 heads east to Lansing and Detroit.

Major highways include US-31, which heads north from Indiana, follows the Lake Michigan shore as a major four-lane to Ludington, becomes a smaller two-lane in Traverse City and Petoskey, and merges with I-75 just south of the Mackinac Bridge. US-131, at first a small road near the southern border, becomes a major highway south of Kalamazoo, linking it to Grand Rapids, Cadillac, and Petoskey. US-127, which also begins as a small road near the southern border, heads north from Jackson to Lansing, connecting with I-75 south of Grayling. US-23, which extends north from

Toledo, passes through Ann Arbor, merges with I-75 in Flint, and splits off near Standish, becoming the Sunrise Side Coastal Highway, a scenic route that traces the Lake Huron shore all the way to Mackinaw City.

Meanwhile, two main east-west routes traverse the Upper Peninsula. M-28 is the northern route, starting at I-75 and passing through Munising and Marquette. US-2 is the southern route, starting in St. Ignace, passing through Escanaba, and heading west to Ironwood. Several north-south highways link the two. If you're traveling all the way from the U.P.'s eastern end to Ironwood, M-28 is usually faster.

Getting Around

BY PLANE

Regional airports pepper the entire state; even the Upper Peninsula has a number of options, including Delta County Airport (ESC) near Escanaba, a stop for Delta Air Lines. Hence, it's easy, though often expensive, to fly from one end of Michigan to the other.

In addition, it's possible to charter small planes to some of the surrounding islands. **Great Lakes Air, Inc.** (906/643-7165, www.greatlakesair.net, $28 adults, $14 children 4-12, children under 4 free), for example, offers service from St. Ignace to Mackinac Island, while **Royale Air Service** (218/721-0405, www.royaleairservice.com, mid-May-mid-Sept., $199 pp one-way, $299 pp round-trip, children under 2 free) provides the only air transportation to Isle Royale National Park, with scheduled trips between the Houghton County Memorial Airport and the protected bays at Windigo and Rock Harbor. Reservations are required for both services.

BY BOAT

Surrounded by four Great Lakes and filled with thousands of inland lakes and rivers, Michigan is a popular place for water-based travel during the summer. Visitors will find many

pleasure cruises throughout the state, including **Saugatuck Boat Cruises** (269/857-4261, www.saugatuckboatcruises.com, hours vary May-Oct., $19 adults, $8.50 children 6-12, $5.50 children 3-5, children under 3 free), offering trips down the Kalamazoo River, and the **Bavarian Belle** (866/808-2628, www.bavarianbelle.com, starting at 11am daily May-mid-Oct., $10 adults, $4 children 5-10, children under 5 free), which tours the Cass River in Frankenmuth.

To reach the islands that surround Michigan, boating is usually the best option. The **Beaver Island Boat Company** (231/547-2311 or 888/446-4095, www.bibco.com, hours vary Apr.-Dec., $24-29 adults, $12-17 children 5-14, children under 5 free, rates vary for pets and vehicles) links Charlevoix to Beaver Island, while **Shepler's Mackinac Island Ferry** (231/436-5023 or 800/828-6157, www.sheplersferry.com, late Apr.-Oct., $25 adults, $13 children 5-12, children under 5 free) connects St. Ignace and Mackinaw City to Mackinac Island. **Plaunt Transportation, Inc.** (231/627-2354 or 888/752-8687, www.bbiferry.com, hours vary daily May-Nov., $17 adults, $12 children 5-11, children under 5 free, rates vary for vehicles), meanwhile, provides service from Cheboygan to Bois Blanc Island, and the **Isle Royale Line** (906/289-4437, www.isleroyale.com, mid-May-Sept., round-trip $120-130 adults, $60-65 children under 12, $50 per canoe or kayak) operates between Copper Harbor and Isle Royale.

BY TRAIN

Besides Amtrak, which links several cities in Michigan's Lower Peninsula, the state boasts several authentic train tours. In the Upper Peninsula, the **Tahquamenon Falls Wilderness Excursion** (906/876-2311 or 888/778-7246, www.superiorsights.com/toonerville, hours vary mid-June-early Oct., $47 adults, $44.50 seniors 62 and over, $29 children 9-15, $20 children 4-8, children under 4 free) leads visitors on a scenic round-trip tour via riverboat and the Toonerville Trolley, a narrow-gauge railroad in operation since the late 1920s. In the Lower Peninsula, the **Southern Michigan Railroad** (517/456-7677 or 734/396-0416, www.southernmichiganrailroad.com, hours vary mid-May-Dec., round-trip $10-15 adults, $8-12 seniors 65 and over, $6-9 children 2-12, children under 2 free) offers seasonal and holiday train tours between Clinton and Tecumseh.

BY BUS

Most of Michigan's major towns and regions offer a public bus system. Beyond the **Detroit Department of Transportation** (313/933-1300 or 888/336-8287, www.ci.detroit.mi.us/ddot), others include **Thumb Area Transit** (989/269-2121 or 800/322-1125, www.tatbus.com), Lansing's **Capital Area Transportation Authority** (517/394-1000, www.cata.org), the **Muskegon Area Transit System** (231/724-6420, www.matsbus.com), Traverse City's **Bay Area Transportation Authority** (231/941-2324, www.bata.net), and the **Marquette Transit Authority** (906/225-1112, www.marqtran.com).

BY CAR

In Michigan, the birthplace of the automobile, the car is the preferred method of travel, never more apparent than on Friday afternoons May-October, when it seems about half the state's southern residents load up the car (or motorcycle) and head out on the highway—to hotels, resorts, cabins, and campgrounds "up north." Though it's best to avoid northbound highways on Friday and southbound ones on Sunday, Michigan—a state of remarkable diversity—is highly worthy of a road trip.

Roads here are plentiful and good. Along with interstates and federal highways, the state is crisscrossed with numerous state highways, marked on road maps by a circled number. In conversation, they are often preceded by an "M," as in, "Follow M-28 west to Marquette." County roads are marked with rectangles on most road maps. The state also has several toll bridges, including "Big Mac" between Mackinaw City and St. Ignace, and the four international bridges that link Canada to the cities of Detroit, Port Huron, and Sault Ste. Marie.

When planning a route in the Upper Peninsula, consult your map legend regarding road surfaces. All state and federal highways are paved and well maintained, as are most county roads and many secondary roads. But just be aware. Gravel and dirt roads can make for very slow going. For road construction updates, consult the **Michigan Department of Transportation** (State Transportation Building, 425 W. Ottawa St., P.O. Box 30050, Lansing, MI 48909, 517/373-2090, www.michigan.gov/mdot).

In Michigan, all drivers, front-seat passengers, and children 8-15 must wear seat belts. Children younger than age 8 or shorter than 4 feet, 9 inches must be properly buckled in a car seat or booster seat. Motorcyclists are required to wear helmets at all times, and all motorists must yield to emergency vehicles. In addition, you must always stop at railroad crossings when the lights are flashing and/or the crossing gates have been activated. Remember, too, that littering is against the law on state and federal highways. Unless otherwise posted, the maximum speed limit on Michigan's interstates and federal highways is usually 70 mph; on county roads and state highways, it's typically 55 mph.

Finally, there's a myth that driving a foreign

MILEAGE BETWEEN CITIES

Comprising two large peninsulas, Michigan is a bigger place than it appears on many maps. It can be deceptively far from point A to point B, especially if point A is, say, Kalamazoo and point B is Copper Harbor, which lies about 590 miles to the north. To put it into perspective, traveling roughly the same distance from Kalamazoo would take you to the outskirts of Kansas City or Washington DC. So, while traveling across Michigan, consider these common distances between Detroit, Marquette, Chicago, and various towns and cities throughout the state; note, however, that the estimated driving times do not take into account unexpected traffic.

DISTANCE FROM DETROIT TO:

- Bay City: 115 miles (1.75 hours)
- Benton Harbor: 186 miles (2.75 hours)
- Copper Harbor: 600 miles (9.75 hours)
- Grand Rapids: 158 miles (2.5 hours)
- Mackinaw City: 289 miles (4 hours)
- Marquette: 455 miles (7 hours)
- Sault Ste. Marie: 345 miles (5 hours)

- Traverse City: 256 miles (4 hours)

DISTANCE FROM MARQUETTE TO:

- Grayling: 251 miles (4.25 hours)
- Ironwood: 145 miles (2.75 hours)
- Lansing: 396 miles (6.25 hours)
- Muskegon: 409 miles (7 hours)
- Petoskey: 202 miles (3.75 hours)
- Port Huron: 456 miles (7.25 hours)
- Saginaw: 356 miles (5.75 hours)
- St. Ignace: 162 miles (3 hours)

DISTANCE FROM CHICAGO TO:

- Detroit: 283 miles (4.25 hours)
- Flint: 274 miles (4 hours)
- Gaylord: 349 miles (5.25 hours)
- Kalamazoo: 147 miles (2.25 hours)
- Marquette: 383 miles (6.5 hours)
- Saugatuck: 141 miles (2.25 hours)
- Sault Ste. Marie: 463 miles (7 hours)
- Traverse City: 318 miles (5 hours)

car is a potentially dangerous practice in Michigan. While that may have been true in the 1970s when the Japanese were doing serious damage to the U.S. auto industry, it's not the case today. These days, many "foreign" cars are made in the United States, and U.S. plants supply parts to foreign automakers, so it's often a moot point. But don't push it too far. For instance, you might not feel comfortable parking your Toyota in front of a tavern near the Flint GM truck plant, especially given Michigan's economic recession in recent years.

Taxi and Shuttle

Most of Michigan's major cities have taxi and shuttle services. Unless you're at an airport, however, you'll have to call ahead to arrange a ride. From the Detroit Metropolitan-Wayne County Airport, contact **Checker Cab** (313/963-7000, www.checkercab-det.com) or **Metro Airport Taxi** (800/745-5191, www.metroairporttaxi.org). Other services include Lansing's **Spartan Cab/Yellow Cab** (517/482-1444, www.capitoltransport.com), Traverse City's **Cherry Capital Cab** (231/941-8294, www.cherrycapitalcab.com), and the Upper Peninsula's **Checker Transport** (906/226-7777, www.checkertransport.com).

Rental Car

Rental cars are available at most commercial airports around the state. In smaller cities, you'll be limited to the big players like **Alamo** (888/233-8749, www.alamo.com), **Avis** (800/633-3469, www.avis.com), **Budget** (800/218-7992, www.budget.com), **Enterprise**

(800/261-7331, www.enterprise.com), **Hertz** (800/654-3131, www.hertz.com), and **National** (877/222-9058, www.nationalcar. com). Reservations are highly recommended; big cities do a huge volume, and small locales don't keep many cars on the lot. If you plan to explore the Upper Peninsula, ask about the company's policies regarding off-road driving. Many forbid you to leave the pavement, which can curtail your access to a lot of U.P. sights.

RV

Traversing Michigan via RV can be a wonderful way to see the state's diverse attractions and spend quality time with family and friends. If you don't have a motorhome or trailer of your own, you can easily rent one from various locations. For more information about RV rentals, contact **General RV Center** (888/436-7578, www.generalrv.com) and **Cruise America** (800/671-8042, www.cruiseamerica.com). For a list of Michigan's campgrounds and RV parks, consult the **Michigan Association of Recreation Vehicles and Campgrounds** (MARVAC, 2222 Association Dr., Okemos, 517/349-8881, www.marvac.org) or the **Association of RV Parks and Campgrounds Michigan** (ARVC, 4696 Orchard Manor Blvd., #11, Bay City, 989/619-2608, www.michcampgrounds.com).

WINTER DRIVING

Michigan roads are generally well maintained in winter, plowed free of snow, then salted or sanded. (Salt does a better job of melting, while sand is less destructive to the environment.) During or immediately after a storm, though, don't expect smooth sailing; it's often hard for road crews to keep up with conditions. County and city crews have a well-established hierarchy, first taking care of interstates, state highways, major thoroughfares, and roads to schools and hospitals, then addressing less vital routes. In the Upper Peninsula, many small roads are considered seasonal, which means they're not plowed or patrolled in winter. To check winter driving conditions before you travel, consult the **Michigan State Police** (333 S. Grand Ave., P.O. Box 30634, Lansing, MI 48909, 517/332-2521 or 800/525-5555, www.michigan.gov/msp).

If you're not used to driving in snow, don't learn on the road in a Michigan snowstorm. Drive slowly, allow lots of room between you and the car in front of you, and remember it may take a lot longer to stop than you're accustomed to. Tap your brakes lightly in succession to come to a stop; never stomp on them, or you'll send your car reeling into a "doughnut." If you have anti-lock brakes, apply steady pressure and let the system's computer do the work.

Chains or studded snow tires are not permitted on Michigan roads. Many residents do switch to snow tires, which have a heavier tread. If you have a rear-wheel-drive car, adding weight to the back end can greatly improve traction. Bags of sand or salt work well, and sand can be used if you get stuck.

Ice is considerably more dangerous than snow, since it provides even less traction and stopping ability. Especially beware of black ice—seemingly wet pavement that is actually glare ice. Watch for icy roads as rain turns to snow (called freezing rain), especially on bridges, where the cold air circulating above and below the road will cause it to freeze first. Ice also forms when lots of cars drive over a snowy surface (like a heavily traveled interstate), packing it down into a super-slick hardpack. On four-lane roads, the left lane usually looks snowier but may be less icy and, therefore, less slippery.

Equip your vehicle with a shovel, sand (or cat litter), and boots, in case you get stuck. Throw the sand/cat litter under the front tires for a front-wheel-drive car, the rear tires on a rear-wheel-drive car. Keep the tires straight and slowly apply the gas. Flooring it will only spin you deeper. Gently rocking the car forward and back, especially if you have someone who can push, works best.

Pack an emergency kit and make sure your car is in good mechanical condition before embarking upon your journey; check your batteries, fluids, and tire pressure. Keep a flashlight (with fresh batteries), flares, blankets, extra

© OSELAND | DREAMSTIME.COM

Even in winter, white-tailed deer can surprise motorists.

clothing, and a first-aid kit in your vehicle in case you have to spend the night in your car. It could save your life. Help may not always be on the way, especially in rural areas. If you spy a car hung up on a snowbank or in a ditch, try to offer a push or a ride to town (as long as your personal safety isn't in doubt).

DEER CROSSINGS

Several million deer inhabit Michigan, posing a significant threat to drivers. Thousands contribute to automobile accidents each year, some of them fatal. Deer behave erratically and will dart in front of your car with no warning. Be particularly alert at dawn and dusk, when deer are most active, and during the fall hunting season, when they're really unpredictable. Yellow-and-black "leaping deer" signs warn motorists of roadways where crossings are common, but they can occur virtually anywhere.

Deer may come from the woods or an open field, seemingly out of nowhere. If you see deer by the side of the road, slow down and get ready to stop. If you see a deer cross ahead of you, also slow down—where there's one deer, there are usually several. If you do hit a deer, notify the nearest law enforcement office immediately.

Visas and Officialdom

For U.S. citizens, a trip to Michigan is a snap. International travelers, however, should understand current American policies before heading here. With Canada so close to Detroit, Port Huron, and Sault Ste. Marie, it's helpful for all tourists to know the ins and outs of traveling between the two nations.

PASSPORTS AND VISAS

While international travelers are required to show a valid passport upon entering the United States, most citizens from Canada, Bermuda, and the 37 countries that are part of the Visa Waiver Program (VWP)—including France, Italy, Australia, Japan, and the United Kingdom—are allowed to travel to Michigan without a visa. Since January 2009, however, they have been required to apply to the Electronic System for Travel Authorization (ESTA) for approval to travel to the United States; as of September 2010, this formerly free system now costs $14 per registration application or renewal. All other temporary international travelers are required to secure a nonimmigrant visa before entering Michigan. For more information, consult the **U.S. Department of State's Bureau of Consular Affairs** (202/663-1225, http://travel.state.gov).

CUSTOMS

Upon entering Michigan, international travelers must declare any dollar amount over $10,000 as well as the value of any articles that will remain in the country, including gifts. A duty will be assessed for all imported goods; visitors are usually granted a $100 exemption. Illegal drugs, Cuban cigars, obscene items, toxic substances, and prescription drugs (without a prescription) are generally prohibited. In order to protect American agriculture, customs officials will confiscate certain produce, plants, seeds, nuts, meat, and other potentially dangerous biological products. For more information, consult the **U.S. Department of Homeland Security's U.S. Customs and Border Protection** (202/325-8000, www.cbp.gov).

EMBASSIES AND CONSULATES

While the embassies for most countries are located in Washington DC, some nations have consular offices in Detroit's Renaissance Center, including Canada (600 Renaissance Center, Ste. 1100, 313/567-2340, www.detroit.gc.ca, 8:30am-4:30pm Mon.-Fri.) and Japan (400 Renaissance Center, Ste. 1600, 313/567-0120, www.detroit.us.emb-japan.go.jp, 9am-5pm Mon.-Fri.). Other consulates are situated in nearby Chicago, including those of the United Kingdom (625 N. Michigan Ave., Ste. 2200, 312/970-3800, http://ukinusa.fco.gov.uk, by appt.), France (205 N. Michigan Ave., Ste. 3700, 312/327-5200, www.consulfrance-chicago.org, 9am-12:30pm Mon.-Thurs., 8:30am-12:30pm Fri.), Germany (676 N. Michigan Ave., Ste. 3200, 312/202-0480, www.germany.info, 8am-4:45pm Mon.-Thurs., 8am-noon Fri.), and Mexico (204 S. Ashland Ave., 312/738-2383, www.consulmexchicago.com). For a more comprehensive list of the foreign embassies and consulates in America, consult the **University of Michigan's International Center** (www.internationalcenter.umich.edu), specifically the "Travel Abroad Basics" section of the center's comprehensive website.

UNITED STATES-CANADA BORDER

Years ago, U.S. citizens were barely given a perfunctory glance upon crossing the Canadian border. Given today's more vigilant climate, however, they must now show either a valid U.S. passport or a certified birth certificate with photo identification (such as a driver's license) to enter Canada; bear in mind, though, that you must have a valid U.S. passport to return to the United States (in other words, a birth certificate and driver's license won't suffice). Unless you have a criminal record or decide to transport something suspicious, you'll probably just be asked about the purpose of your visit, then waved through. Pets require proof of proper vaccinations; plants and animal products will be confiscated. In addition, you must declare any alcohol or tobacco products, which could be taxed depending on the amount. Obscene materials, illegal drugs, and most weapons are prohibited from entering Canada.

With child abductions on the rise, border officials are especially concerned about protecting minors. If you're traveling with children, you must bring proper identification for them as well, such as a birth certificate or passport. If the children are not your own, you must provide written permission from a parent or legal guardian. If you are divorced or separated and traveling with your children, you must provide a copy of the legal custody agreement. For more information, consult **American Consular Services** (http://canada.usembassy.gov/consular_services.html).

Non-U.S. citizens must have a valid passport, too. If you're a citizen of a non-European country, you may also need a visa (obtained in advance from the Canadian Consulate). U.S. resident aliens will be asked to show a green card. For more information, consult the **Canada Border Services Agency** (www.cbsa-asfc.gc.ca).

Unless you travel between Michigan and Canada by plane or boat, you'll do so by bridge or tunnel. There are four toll bridges connecting Michigan and Ontario: the Ambassador Bridge from Detroit to Windsor (www.ambassadorbridge.com, $5 passenger vehicles and motorcycles, $10 buses), the Detroit-Windsor Tunnel (www.dwtunnel.com, $4.75 passenger and commercial vehicles, $8.50 buses), the Blue Water Bridge from Port Huron to Sarnia (www.michigan.gov/mdot, $3 passenger vehicles, $3.25 per truck/bus axle), and the International Bridge from Sault Ste. Marie to Sault Ste. Marie (www.michigan.gov/mdot, $3 passenger vehicles and motorcycles, $4.50-6 vehicles w/trailers, $5.50 recreational vehicles, $8-44 commercial trucks). If you do arrive by plane or boat, you're required to check in at the nearest customs station immediately upon arrival.

Sports and Recreation

SPECTATOR SPORTS

While Michigan boasts a variety of spectatorial teams—including minor-league baseball players like the Traverse City Beach Bums—most sports lovers flock to Detroit to watch the state's mega-professional teams in action. From September to December, football fans head to **Ford Field** (2000 Brush St., 313/262-2013) to cheer on the **Detroit Lions** (www.detroitlions.com). From April to October, baseball fans can see the **Detroit Tigers** (http://detroit.tigers.mlb.com) at **Comerica Park** (2100 Woodward Ave., 313/962-4000 or 866/668-4437). From October to April, hockey fans can catch the **Detroit Red Wings** (http://redwings.nhl.com) at **Joe Louis Arena** (19 Steve Yzerman Dr.,

313/396-7000 or 313/471-6606, www.olympiaentertainment.com). Basketball fans, meanwhile, can support the NBA's **Detroit Pistons** (www.nba.com/pistons) or the WNBA's **Detroit Shock** (www.wnba.com/shock) at **The Palace** (6 Championship Dr., Auburn Hills, 248/377-0100, www.palacenet.com) during the November-April season.

Of course, Michigan has some fantastic college teams, too. In Ann Arbor, fans of football, baseball, basketball, soccer, and other varsity sports can watch the **University of Michigan's Wolverines** (734/764-0247 or 866/296-6849, www.mgoblue.com) throughout the year. Meanwhile, **Michigan State University's Spartans** (517/355-1610 or 800/467-8283, www.msuspartans.com) regularly lure sports lovers to East Lansing.

GOLF

As it turns out, northern Michigan has both the perfect climate for turf-growing and a diverse terrain of hills and water views that make for great golf courses. Over the last few decades, golf course architects have noticed. Michigan is home to all kinds of nationally ranked courses, including several with designer names like Arnold Palmer, Robert Trent Jones, and Jack Nicklaus attached.

Traverse Bay, Mackinac Island, and the city of Oscoda on Lake Huron form a golden triangle of golf courses. Here, you'll find award-winners like The Bear at the Grand Traverse Resort and Spa near Traverse City, Cedar River at Shanty Creek Resorts in Bellaire, Signature at the Treetops Resort near Gaylord, Fountains at the Garland Lodge & Resort in Lewiston, and The Gailes at the Lakewood Shores Resort near Oscoda. Outside this "triangle," you'll find plenty of well-kept and challenging courses, too. (Note: Typically, golf rates refer to 18-hole play.) For more information, consult the **Golf Association of Michigan** (GAM, 24116 Research Dr., Farmington Hills, 248/478-9242, www.gam. org), peruse *Michigan Golf* (www.michigan-golfmagazine.com), or visit www.michigan-golf.com.

NATIONAL PARKS AND FORESTS

Michigan is home to four national forests, two national lakeshores, a national park, a national historical park, a national heritage area, and eight national wildlife refuges. This federal land is rather evenly divided between the two peninsulas, which can each claim two national forests and a national lakeshore. In the Upper Peninsula, **Pictured Rocks National Lakeshore** traces the Lake Superior coastline east of Marquette, while in the Lower Peninsula, **Sleeping Bear Dunes National Lakeshore** sits alongside Lake Michigan west of Traverse City. The L.P. also contains five

© GREATER LANSING CVB

Michigan is home to many nationally ranked golf courses.

wildlife refuges and the **MotorCities National Heritage Area** near Detroit, just as the U.P. boasts three wildlife refuges, the **Keweenaw National Historical Park,** and **Isle Royale National Park,** a 45-mile-long wilderness surrounded by the frigid waters of Lake Superior.

Save for key attractions like waterfalls or beaches, national forests are often overlooked as visitor destinations, yet they offer a remarkable range of activities for outdoor enthusiasts. Hiking trails tend to be little used. Campsites are more secluded, more rustic, and usually less crowded than in other places. Mountain biking, which is often forbidden on national park trails, is permitted on miles and miles of federal forest land, and inland lakes, which can be difficult to reach with a boat trailer, are often ideal for those looking for a quiet paddling experience.

The national forests also cover an astounding amount of real estate. The **Ottawa National Forest,** situated in the western U.P., contains nearly one million acres, while the **Hiawatha National Forest,** which comprises two units in the eastern U.P., adds another 895,000 acres. In the Lower Peninsula, the **Manistee National Forest** stretches from Cadillac to just north of Muskegon, an area of more than 540,000 acres, while the **Huron National Forest** covers roughly 439,000 acres in the northeastern section, encompassing lightly developed rivers like the Au Sable. To receive information about hiking, camping, paddling, and other activities, contact the **U.S. Forest Service** (202/205-1680, www.fs.fed.us) or each forest's headquarters: **Ottawa National Forest** (E6248 US-2, Ironwood, 906/932-1330), **Hiawatha National Forest** (2727 N. Lincoln Rd., Escanaba, 906/786-4062), and **Huron-Manistee National Forests** (1755 S. Mitchell St., Cadillac, 231/775-2421 or 800/821-6263). For more information about Michigan's national lakeshores or wildlife refuges, consult the **National Park Service** (202/208-3818, www.nps.gov) or the **U.S. Fish & Wildlife Service** (800/344-9453, www.fws.gov/refuges), respectively.

STATE PARKS AND FORESTS
State Parks

Michigan has an outstanding state park system. Well planned and well maintained, the parks showcase some of the state's most diverse and most beautiful land. Some state parks, like those along Lake Michigan, were clearly set aside for public access, while others preserve historic sites and state jewels like Mackinac Island and the Porcupine Mountains.

Currently, Michigan has more than 100 state parks and recreation areas, covering roughly 285,000 acres. The **Michigan Department of Natural Resources** (Parks and Recreation Division, Mason Bldg., 3rd Fl., Lansing, 517/284-7275, www.michigan.gov/dnr) publishes a handy brochure that includes regional maps as well as charts listing each park's amenities.

As of October 2010, Michigan residents can purchase, at the time of their vehicle plate registration, a Recreation Passport (www.michigan.gov/recreationpassport, $11 vehicles, $5 motorcycles), which allows access to all state parks, recreation areas, and boat launches during the period of the vehicle registration. For nonresidents, every entering vehicle, despite the number of passengers, must also have an annual Recreation Passport ($30.50); otherwise, you'll have to pay a day-use fee ($8.40) for any state park or recreation area that charges such fees.

There is an additional fee for camping ($10-17 daily for rustic campsites, $16-33 daily for modern campsites that include utility hookups, showers, and restrooms). For $45 per night, some parks also rent mini-cabins, tiny shelters that offer little more than a roof and four walls to protect against the elements. These book up fast, so reserve yours well ahead of time. A few parks, including Bald Mountain Recreation Area and Porcupine Mountains Wilderness State Park, rent rustic cabins ($60-80 daily), which are equipped with heaters and basic furniture, and are ideal for groups and terrific when bugs are particularly fierce. They're *extremely* popular during the summer months, so if you hope to get one, call in January. The same goes for the few tepees and tents ($30

STATE PARK EXPLORER PROGRAM

Every summer, campers and day-use visitors can participate in the State Park Explorer Program at 44 of Michigan's state parks and recreation areas. Equipped with field guides and hands-on materials, expert rangers and volunteers lead informal programs, nature hikes, and nighttime activities that feature each region's unique natural, cultural, and historical resources. These free programs, which are designed for children and adults alike, focus on a wide assortment of topics, including insects, frogs, birds, mammals, carnivorous plants, forests, ponds, and constellations.

Participating locales range from Van Riper State Park in the Upper Peninsula – where visitors can learn about native dragonflies, owls, black bears, wolves, and moose – to Warren Dunes State Park along Lake Michigan's southeastern shore – where guides explore coastal tides and the area's fossils, birds, and wildflowers. For program details and schedules, consult the **Michigan Department of Natural Resources** (www.michigan.gov/dnr).

---

daily) on offer at places like Baraga State Park and Interlochen State Park, as well as the yurts ($60 daily) available at Porcupine Mountains.

For a nonrefundable $8 fee, you can make a camping reservation at any park by calling 800/447-2757 or visiting www.midnrreservations.com. Though you can request a specific site, it isn't guaranteed. In summer, reservations are recommended at many state parks.

State Forests

Like national forests, state forests are a hidden gem for anyone looking for a quiet corner in the wild. Much of the state's forest land was actually acquired by default, picked up after the Depression when its owners couldn't pay the property taxes. Their loss was the public's gain—much of the property is exceptional, comprising rivers, waterfalls, lakes, beaches, and, naturally, forests. Altogether, it encompasses 3.9 million acres of land, the largest state forest system in the nation.

In the Lower Peninsula, you'll find **Pere Marquette State Forest** south of Traverse City, **Mackinaw State Forest** between Gaylord and Mackinaw City, and **Au Sable State Forest** between Grayling and Midland. In the Upper Peninsula, meanwhile, you can explore **Lake Superior State Forest** in the eastern half, **Escanaba River State Forest** in the central part, and **Copper Country State Forest**

on the western side. For more information, contact the **Michigan Department of Natural Resources** (517/284-7275, www.michigan.gov/dnr), and, for a nonrefundable $8 fee, you can make a camping reservation at any state forest campground by calling 800/447-2757 or visiting www.midnrreservations.com.

HIKING AND HORSEBACK RIDING

Given its bounty of national parks and lakeshores, federal and state forests, state parks, and whatever county land is set aside for public use, Michigan has almost unlimited offerings for hikers, especially in the Upper Peninsula. Where you go depends on your taste.

For backpackers, **Isle Royale National Park** in Lake Superior is an outstanding choice, free of roads and other development. Rustic campsites along the way allow you to hoof across the 45-mile-long island; water-taxi services can get you back to your starting point. A little less remote, **Porcupine Mountains Wilderness State Park** in the western U.P. also offers great backpacking in a rugged backcountry environment not normally associated with a state park.

Michigan also has lots of linear hiking trails, like the **Bay de Noc-Grand Island Trail,** which bisects the U.P., and the 220-mile-long **Michigan Shore-to-Shore Trail,** a hiking and horseback riding trail that stretches from

Empire on Lake Michigan to Oscoda on Lake Huron. For those seeking a real adventure, the **North Country National Scenic Trail** (www. northcountrytrail.org) traverses both the Upper and Lower Peninsulas as part of a 4,600-mile-long national trail that stretches from New York to North Dakota. In Michigan, hikers will encounter a wide array of sights along this trail, from the Fort Custer National Cemetery near Battle Creek to the cliffs of Pictured Rocks National Lakeshore to the trees of Ottawa National Forest.

For more information about hiking and horseback riding trails in Michigan, contact the **Michigan Trail Riders Association, Inc.** (MTRA, 5806 E. State Rd., Hale, 989/473-3205, www.mtra.org).

BIKING

With its rolling topography, stunning shorelines, and ample country roads, Michigan makes for a great biking destination. Some favorite areas for road riding include the wine country region near South Haven, the farmland around historic Marshall, and the lovely Leelanau Peninsula. For more information about suggested routes and bicycle tours, check with local tourism bureaus or consult the **League of Michigan Bicyclists** (LMB, 416 S. Cedar St., Ste. A, Lansing, 517/334-9100 or 888/642-4537, www.lmb.org), **Michigan Mountain Biking Association** (MMBA, www. mmba.org), or **Michigan Trails & Greenways Alliance** (MTGA, P.O. Box 27187, Lansing, MI 48909, 517/485-6022, www.michigan-trails.org).

Michigan leads the nation in the number of rails-to-trails, with over 50 old railroad beds converted into multiuse trails. Some, like the 41-mile **Bill Nichols Trail** on the U.P.'s Keweenaw Peninsula, are very rough, often still marked by old railroad ties and sharp mining rock. While spectacular, some of these more primitive trails are appropriate only for snowmobiles and all-terrain vehicles, but many are ideal for adventuresome mountain bikers hoping to experience wonderful wilderness terrain. At the other end of the spectrum, the 22-mile

Hart-Montague Bicycle Trail is paved, making it especially popular with families and in-line skaters. For more information, consult the **Rails-to-Trails Conservancy** (202/331-9696, www.railstotrails.org).

Unlike much of the Midwest, Michigan is kind to mountain bikers. Good technical mountain biking can be found in many state and national forests, and ski resorts in the Lower Peninsula have wisely courted mountain bikers by maintaining their cross-country trail networks for biking in the off-season.

As for the Upper Peninsula, you can pretty much consider it a giant mountain biking park. Between the national and state forests, you probably have more miles than you could ever ride, not to mention the hundreds of miles of old logging roads. Off-road riding in places like the Keweenaw and the Huron Mountains is the best you'll find between the Rockies and the Appalachians, and Michigan adds a little extra perk: some stunning Great Lakes views.

BIRD-WATCHING

Given Michigan's myriad forests, prairies, lakes, rivers, marshes, and beaches, it's no wonder that the state is rife with hundreds of avian species, including songbirds, raptors, shorebirds, and waterfowl. It's no wonder, too, that bird-watchers flock here, especially in the spring and fall, to observe them in action. Equipped with little more than binoculars and cameras, bird-watchers are welcome at many nature centers, state parks, wildlife refuges, bird sanctuaries, and other protected areas.

In Saginaw, the **Shiawassee National Wildlife Refuge** (www.fws.gov/refuges), which hosts over 270 bird species annually, provides trails, observation platforms, and bird species lists, while the **Whitefish Point Bird Observatory** (www.wpbo.org) near Paradise offers field trips for bird-watchers of all skill levels. For more information about Michigan's birds as well as birding tours and festivals, visit www.michiganbirding.com or consult **Michigan Audubon** (P.O. Box 15249, Lansing, MI 48901, 517/641-4277, www.michiganaudu-bon.org).

HUNTING

With its plentiful populations of deer, ducks, pheasants, turkeys, and other game, Michigan is definitely a hunter's paradise. Even black bears and elk can be legally hunted here. Hunting seasons, license requirements, and regulations vary depending upon the animal and region, so it's important to do your research ahead of time. For example, white-tailed deer (the state game mammal) can be hunted with bows October 1-mid-November and during December; firearms can only be used mid- to late November and throughout December.

For up-to-date regulations and to apply for specific licenses, consult the **Michigan Department of Natural Resources** (517/284-9453, www.michigan.gov/dnr). For hunting-related articles (including some by Ted Nugent, perhaps the state's most famous hunter), visit www.michigan-sportsman.com.

BOATING AND FISHING
Boating

In summer, boating is an exceedingly popular pastime in Michigan. Boaters cruise from port to port on the Great Lakes, sail around large bays like Grand Traverse and isolated areas like Beaver Island, water-ski on thousands of inland lakes, paddle the state's white-water rivers and quiet waters, cruise the inland waterway through Cheboygan County, and fish just about everywhere.

Small watercraft like canoes and fishing boats are readily available in many Michigan communities. For more information, contact the local chamber of commerce or tourism bureau in the area that you plan to visit. For larger watercraft, such as sailboats, contact the **Michigan Charter Boat Association** (MCBA, 800/622-2971, www.michigancharterboats.com).

If you plan to bring your own boat, consult the **Michigan Department of Natural Resources** (517/284-7275, www.michigan.gov/dnr), which provides maps, a listing of public marinas and harbors, a handbook of boating laws, and a harbor reservation system. State law requires that all boaters must carry a Coast

© PETOSKEY AREA VISITORS BUREAU

sailboats in Little Traverse Bay

Guard-approved life jacket—known as a personal flotation device (PFD)—for each person on board, regardless of the type of boat.

Canoeing and Kayaking

Michigan is a paddler's dream. You can canoe down several national wild and scenic rivers, surf waves along Lake Michigan's shoreline, sea kayak along Pictured Rocks or Isle Royale, or run white water. For mellow paddling, the Au Sable River is a perennial favorite, stretching from Grayling to Lake Huron. In late July, it's even the site of the annual 120-mile **AuSable River Canoe Marathon** (www.ausablecanoemarathon.org), which usually runs from Grayling to Oscoda.

Also in the northeastern Lower Peninsula is the less crowded Rifle River, east of West Branch. Other popular paddling rivers include the Platte and Betsie Rivers south of Traverse City, and the Sturgeon River in the Upper Peninsula. The U.P. also has several notable white-water rivers, including the beautiful Presque Isle River and the Ontonagon, both of which are designated wild and scenic rivers. For more information on paddling destinations and liveries, consult the **Michigan Association of Paddlesport Providers** (MAPP, www.michigancanoe.com).

Fishing

Fishing is deeply embedded in the state's psyche. It comes in all styles and seasons, too, from fly-fishing along a pristine stream in summer to hanging out in an ice-fishing shanty, watching a Lions-Packers game on a portable TV. The quantity of blue-ribbon trout streams is unrivaled this side of Montana—enough clear, swift, and rocky waters to keep you busy for weeks on end. The Fox, the Jordan, the Boardman . . . you'll find most of the best ones in the eastern U.P. and northern parts of the Lower Peninsula.

"Deep-sea" charters on the Great Lakes go after the big chinook salmon, coho salmon, and lake trout. Lake Michigan's Little Bay de Noc arguably offers the finest walleye fishing in the state, if not in all the Great Lakes.

Inland, literally thousands of lakes harbor walleye, northern pike, muskie, bass, and perch. Some of the most popular spots are the lakes around Cadillac and Indian River in the Lower Peninsula, and the Manistique Lakes chain and huge Lake Gogebic in the U.P.

But to avoid the people and the whine of outboards, you really should head for the dozens of small lakes in the U.P.'s Ottawa and Hiawatha National Forests, which are peaceful, harder to access, and teeming with fish. Some, like the 34 lakes of the Sylvania Wilderness and Recreation Area near Watersmeet, have special fishing regulations, so check with authorities. All Michigan waters require a valid Michigan fishing license. For fishing information, contact the **Michigan Department of Natural Resource** (Fisheries Division, P.O. Box 30446, Lansing, MI 48909, 517/373-1280 or 517/373-0908, www.michigan.gov/dnr). For additional information about fish species, fishing reports, river guides, and charters in your area, contact the **Michigan Charter Boat Association** (MCBA, 800/622-2971, www.michigancharterboats.com).

DIVING

Over a century ago, the Great Lakes were like today's interstates—the fastest and most efficient way to get around. Commodities like lumber and iron ore were hauled from the forests and mines to Great Lakes ports; passengers traveled on steamships from urban areas around the southern Great Lakes to imbibe the fresh, cool air of northern resorts.

Of course, the Great Lakes were also known for shallow reefs and violent storms, which led to hundreds of shipwrecks. Moreover, the fresh, cold, barnacle-free waters kept those shipwrecks from badly decaying. Many of them sit on the lake floor, undisturbed and almost unchanged.

Decades later, all of this comes as a delight to divers. Michigan has set aside 14 areas (where shipwrecks were particularly prevalent) as underwater preserves, protecting their historical significance and mapping them for divers. Together, they cover 2,300 square miles of Great Lakes bottomland—an area roughly the size of Delaware. Underwater preserves are located off Isle Royale, the Keweenaw Peninsula, Marquette, Munising, and Whitefish Point on Lake Superior; in the DeTour Passage, around the Straits of Mackinac, off Thunder Bay, and near Port Austin and Port Sanilac on Lake Huron; and around Grand Traverse Bay, along the Manitou Passage, and beside the western and southwestern shores on Lake Michigan.

Most of the popular dive sites are marked with buoys in summer by volunteers of the **Michigan Underwater Preserve Council, Inc.** (560 N. State St., St. Ignace, 800/970-8717, www.michiganpreserves.org), which also produces a biannual booklet. All the preserves are served by diving charters, which can be found through the **Michigan Charter Boat Association** (MCBA, 800/622-2971, www.michigancharterboats.com). For more information, you can also contact the chamber of commerce or tourism bureau near the preserve that you wish to visit.

BEACHES AND SWIMMING

For a state nearly surrounded by water, Michigan does not disappoint with its beaches. Public access is excellent. State parks and forests alone provide more than 140 miles of Great Lakes frontage; county and local parks offer countless more.

The western shore of the Lower Peninsula gets most of the attention; along this "Gold Coast," a wide, soft ribbon of sand stretches along Lake Michigan from the Indiana state line over 200 miles north to the tip of the Leelanau Peninsula, the longest freshwater beach in the world. With the prevailing western winds carrying warm surface water to these shores, Gold Coast beaches are comfortable for summertime bathing, too. Favorite spots include the immensely popular **Warren Dunes State Park,** near Michigan's southern border, and **Ludington State Park,** a six-mile-long sandy point wedged between Lake Michigan and inland Hamlin Lake. High dunes rise along stretches of the Gold Coast, including **Sleeping Bear Dunes National Lakeshore,** west of Traverse City.

The eastern side of the Lower Peninsula, bordered by Lake Huron, also has fine sand beaches curving along the "Sunrise Shore." **Tawas Point State Park,** near Tawas City, is noted for its pure white sand, while **Port Crescent State Park,** near the tip of the Thumb, offers three miles of sandy beach and dunes. The Huron shore is also famous for its many lighthouses, which were needed to signal mariners traveling near this low-lying shore.

The beaches of the Upper Peninsula have a completely different mood—often wild and windswept, rocky and remote. Striped cliffs rise directly from Lake Superior at **Pictured Rocks National Lakeshore;** nearby, the **Grand Sable Dunes** provide enough sand to thrill even the most devoted beachcomber. You probably won't see many people here, but you may glimpse a deer, or even a black bear, headed to the water's edge for a drink. While these beaches are perfect for long, sandy walks, only a hardy few actually swim in Lake Superior—the water temperature rarely climbs out of the 40s.

The U.P. shares its southern shore with Lake Michigan, a winding border filled with bays and inlets. A favorite of anglers, it also has some good beaches—if you know where to look. Public access is a little more difficult here. The best spots are along US-2 from Naubinway to the Straits of Mackinac, where rest stops and county parks point you toward nice sandy beaches hidden behind the pines. You'll find another good stretch along Green Bay between Menominee and Escanaba, where **J. W. Wells State Park** and several county parks feature good swimming beaches.

WINTER ACTIVITIES

The Great Lakes churn out plentiful lake-effect snows, which drop onto some of the Midwest's hilliest terrain, making Michigan the top ski destination in the region. While you can't really call anything here mountainous, resorts do an admirable job of working with the terrain they've got, carving out 600-foot vertical drops and runs that wind through the pines or offer jaw-dropping views of the Great Lakes.

Though downhill ski areas can be found

SAFETY TIPS FOR UNDERWATER ENTHUSIASTS

Many residents and out-of-state visitors relish the chance to dive amid the numerous ship-wrecks that litter the chilly waters surrounding Michigan. Although scuba divers should take care not to remove or disturb any underwa-ter artifacts (which is, incidentally, a felony), human safety is also an important aspect of proper underwater etiquette. The Great Lakes are unpredictable; storms and heavy seas can arise without warning. Here are several precau-tions that all underwater enthusiasts should take:

- Check weather conditions before venturing out, as strong winds and rough seas can cre-ate unsafe conditions.

- If operating your own vessel, make sure that you stay at least 300 feet from diver-down flags in open water and at least 100 feet from flags in rivers and inlets; if you cannot maintain such distance, slow down to an idle speed when passing other divers.

- Make sure that you've had proper scuba-diving instruction.

- When in doubt about your abilities, don't hesitate to hire a dive charter operator.

- Always tell someone on land where you're planning to go and when you intend to return.

- If you plan to be in the water for a while, apply ample waterproof sunscreen and in-vest in a full wetsuit or drysuit.

- Make sure that your mask and flippers fit properly, and check that you have all nec-essary equipment, such as weights and air tanks.

- If you find it difficult to walk on the boat while wearing flippers, carry them into the water before putting them on.

- Never dive without displaying a proper red-and-white diver-down flag on your vessel, and always remove said flag when all divers have returned to the boat.

- Always dive with a buddy, and try to stay together.

- Plan your entry and exit points before jump-ing into the water.

- Swim into the current upon entering the water and then ride the current back to your exit point.

- Don't touch any tempting sea creatures, as they may hurt you.

- Look above the water every now and again to ensure that you haven't drifted too far away from the boat; try to stay within 300 feet of the diver-down flag when in open water and within 100 feet when in a river or inlet.

- If you have a diving emergency, dial 911 from your cell phone, or use a VHF radio to signal a "MAYDAY."

A helpful saying to remember is "Dive ALIVE," with the letters in "ALIVE" standing for:

- **Air:** Monitor your air supply, always surface with at least 500 PSI, and practice out-of-air procedures.

- **Lead Weights:** Wear only enough lead to achieve proper buoyancy, and know how to release your and your buddy's weight systems.

- **Inspection:** Inspect your gear before every dive trip, replace missing or worn gear, re-place batteries in any electronics, and have regulators serviced annually.

- **Verification:** Verify your dive skills, and re-view your dive plan, signals, and lost buddy procedures with your diving buddy.

- **Escape:** Always dive with surface signaling devices; if you become entangled, remain calm and do what you can to free yourself; and if you're lost on the surface, inflate your buoyancy compensation device (BCD), re-main calm, maintain your position if possible, and try to attract others' attention.

For more safety tips, consult area diving opera-tors or the **Michigan Underwater Preserve Council, Inc.** (MUPC, 800/970-8717, www. michiganpreserves.org). Additionally, if you have any information about the theft of any underwater artifacts, don't hesitate to report such violations to the **Michigan Department of Natural Resources** (800/292-7800, www. michigan.gov/dnr).

throughout the state, they're concentrated in two primary areas: in the western U.P. from Ironwood to the Porcupine Mountains, and in the northwest corner of the Lower Peninsula, from south of Traverse City to just north of Petoskey.

Cross-country skiers have even more options. Garland Lodge & Resort, near Lewiston, pampers guests with a beautiful log lodge hidden away in the northeastern Lower Peninsula, surrounded by miles and miles of groomed Nordic trails. In fact, Michigan has several privately run Nordic trail systems. Many of the downhill resorts, such as Crystal Mountain in Thompsonville and Shanty Creek in Bellaire, also have notable Nordic trails. The national lakeshores and many state parks groom trails for skiing, and the state and national forests offer virtually limitless opportunities for backcountry skiing.

Other popular wintertime activities include snowboarding, snowshoeing, snowmobiling, ice skating, ice fishing, and, of course, dogsledding. For more information about Michigan's winter sports, consult the **Michigan Snowsports Industries Association** (MSIA, 7164 Deer Lake Ct., Clarkston, 248/620-4448, www.goskimichigan.com) and **Travel Michigan** (888/784-7328, www.michigan.org).

Accommodations

Michigan has a wide range of accommodations, from luxurious resorts to primitive campgrounds. Of course, where you plan to stay depends on your interests, destination, and budget. Though spontaneity can be fun on a vacation, be aware that you might have to make reservations far in advance of your trip. Inns and campgrounds can fill up quickly, especially in the summer or during certain annual events.

While Michigan has plenty of unique lodges and inns, you'll find all the big hotel and motel chains, from Holiday Inn to Super 8, here, too. If you prefer staying in such a tried-and-true establishment, pick up a copy of the chain's national directory (or use its website) to find current locations, rates, and services. Just remember that all Michigan lodgings charge a 6 percent "use tax." For more information about Michigan's accommodations, consult **The Michigan Travel Companion** (www.yesmichigan.com) or the **Michigan Lodging and Tourism Association** (3815 W. St. Joseph Hwy., Ste. A200, Lansing, 517/267-8989, www.milodging.org).

INDEPENDENT HOTELS AND MOTELS

In the last few decades, the combination of interstate highways, corporate motel chains, and America's love of efficiency dealt a fatal blow to hundreds of independently owned motels. The pendulum seems to be swinging the other way these days—interesting inns and distinctive lodges seem to be cropping up in the most unlikely places. Nothing fancy—just those good old mom-and-pop motels, the kind of places now romanticized along Route 66.

The happy news is that they never went away in northern Michigan, including the Upper Peninsula. Perhaps too out-of-the-way to attract the big chains, many U.P. towns have several independent motels. Although some are kind of rundown, many mom-and-pop motels are clean, tidy, and inexpensive, and offer perks most chains don't—allowing pets, for example. Additionally, they're often pedestrian-friendly, situated in small towns or along the waterfront, rather than stranded out beside a highway. Just be advised that some don't take credit cards, but prefer cash or traveler''s checks.

BED-AND-BREAKFASTS

Michigan has hundreds of bed-and-breakfasts. Some are the traditional, old-fashioned variety—a spare room or two in someone's quaint old farmhouse—but those have become the exception rather than the rule. Today's B&Bs run the gamut from large inns with pools to renovated lighthouses. For a directory of Michigan's bed-and-breakfasts, contact the **Michigan Lake to Lake Bed and Breakfast Association** (6757 Cascade Rd. SE, #241, Grand Rapids, 888/575-1610, www.laketolake.com).

RESORTS AND LODGES

Many of Michigan's ski resorts double as golf resorts in the summer, ringed with lodging that ranges from motel-style rooms to condo units and townhouses with kitchens (which allow you to save considerable money on meals). Many also offer other amenities like pools, game rooms, and fitness centers, so they can be a particularly good choice for families with active kids. While golf resorts tend to be pricey, ski resorts that *don't* have the summer golf draw can be great bargains.

For those interested in other activities, like fishing and hunting, Michigan also has a number of seasonal lodges, such as Fish Point Lodge near Saginaw Bay. For information on ski/golf resorts and seasonal lodges, contact **Travel Michigan** (888/784-7328, www.michigan.org).

CABINS AND COTTAGES

A delightful way to experience the rustic beauty and down-home charm of Michigan's varied regions is by staying in a quaint cabin or cottage during your trip here. Several state parks offer inexpensive lodging in the great outdoors, from furnished cabins at Albert E. Sleeper State Park to tepee rentals at Baraga State Park. Besides cabins, Porcupine Mountains Wilderness State Park also provides basic yurts as well as a historic lodge overlooking Lake Superior. For more information, contact the **Michigan Department of Natural Resources** (517/284-7275, www.michigan.gov/dnr). To reserve a unit, call 800/447-2757 or visit www.midnrreservations.com; just be prepared to pay the nonrefundable $8 reservation fee.

Private cottages, often equipped with amenities like cable television and laundry facilities, are available in resort communities and small towns like Saugatuck, Cadillac, and Petoskey. Whether situated along the beach, beside a golf course, or in the woods, such dwellings can vary in price, size, and amenities, so do your research far in advance of your trip. Also bear in mind that reservations are often necessary. For more information about available cabins and cottages throughout the Great Lakes State, consult **The Michigan Travel Companion** (www.yesmichigan.com).

CAMPING

It's not easy to sum up camping in Michigan in a few paragraphs. Here, you can park an RV next to a pool with a waterslide, or you can pitch a tent in backcountry so remote that you might never see another soul. Most of us, of course, seek something in between. With tens of thousands of campsites in the state, you can probably find it, too.

While Michigan features a wide array of campgrounds, from primitive lots to highly developed RV properties, most travelers favor the state park campgrounds because they are almost universally good—usually the nicest campgrounds in a particular area. Some can get busy in the summer months, though. You can reserve a site ahead of time (though specific spots aren't guaranteed) by contacting the **Michigan Department of Natural Resources** (800/447-2757, www.midnrreservations.com) and paying the requisite, nonrefundable $8 reservation fee.

State and national forests also tend to have nice camping facilities, often more rustic but in appealing, out-of-the-way locations. Backcountry camping is permitted in many forests. To reserve a spot in a state forest campground, contact the **Michigan Department of Natural Resources** (800/447-2757, www.midnrreservations.com), and for information about camping in Michigan's national forests,

camping with a view

contact **Recreation.gov** (877/444-6777, www.recreation.gov) or the **U.S. Forest Service** (414/297-3600, www.fs.fed.us).

For a complete list of private campgrounds, request a free *Michigan Campground Directory* from the **Association of RV Parks and Campgrounds Michigan** (ARVC, 4696 Orchard Manor Blvd., #11, Bay City, 989/619-2608, www.michcampgrounds.com) or a free *RV & Campsite* magazine from the **Michigan Association of Recreation Vehicles and Campgrounds** (MARVAC, 2222 Association Dr., Okemos, 517/349-8881, www.marvac.org).

Food and Drink

REGIONAL CUISINE

Most of the "Indian" food featured in Michigan these days is the kind flavored with curry, not the wild fish and game enjoyed by the state's Native Americans. Short of the few annual powwows held around the state, there's no place to sample the staples of the region's original inhabitants. The ethnic heritage of Michigan's immigrants is well represented, however. From Hamtramck to Frankenmuth, Dearborn to Detroit, the state's diversity has found its way to the dinner plate.

In Detroit, you can feast on *saganaki* in **Greektown** (www.greektowndetroit.org) and soul food in **Bricktown.** In the waterfront area known as **Mexicantown** (www.mexicantown.com), busy restaurants stay open until 4am to serve the hungry mole and margarita fans who wait for up to two hours for a table. Not far away is **Hamtramck** (www.hamtramck.com), a Polish enclave within the Detroit city limits known for traditional Polish kielbasa and pierogies; on Fat Tuesday, Detroiters of all nationalities jam the glass-fronted bakeries to buy up *paczki,* fresh

PASTIES

Pasties (PASS-tees) have long been a Michigan delicacy, especially in the Upper Peninsula. While folks fill these tasty pies with a variety of ingredients, from blackberries to broccoli to mackerel, the traditional recipe is a Cornish concoction of meat and vegetables. To begin, prepare your favorite pastry dough, enough for four nine-inch pies. Then prepare the following ingredients:

- 2 pounds cooked pork and/or beef, cut into half-inch cubes
- 2 cups onions, diced
- 1 cup turnips, diced
- 1 cup potatoes, diced
- 4 tablespoons butter
- Salt, pepper, and parsley to taste

Divide the dough into four equal pieces and roll each one out to the size of a nine-inch plate. For each pie, layer one-fourth of the potatoes, turnips, onions, and meat on one half of the dough. Season each layer as desired, and top the pile with a tablespoon of butter. Fold the dough over the filling, then roll and crimp the edges so that the pasty is a sealed half-moon. Using a fork, poke several holes in the top of the dough, then bake on a greased cookie sheet for one hour at 400°F. Yields four large pasties.

jelly doughnuts. A little farther west, **Dearborn** is home to one of the largest groups of Arab peoples in the United States; here, eateries sport signs in English and Arabic and serve up lentil soup, tabbouleh, and *fattoush*.

In **Frankenmuth** (www.frankenmuth.org), a village near Saginaw settled by Germans in the mid-1800s, buses and cars come from miles around for all-you-can-eat chicken and strudel in two cavernous restaurants owned by the Zehnder clan. Made popular by traveling salesmen and Detroit families "out for a drive" in the 1950s, the Bavarian-inspired town has become one of the state's top tourist attractions. In Holland, Dutch food naturally reigns, and flaky pastries are the specialty at the popular Queen's Inn Restaurant at **Dutch Village** (www.dutchvillage.com).

Throughout the Upper Peninsula, many main street cafés and bakeries serve up the **pasty** (PASS-tee), a pot-pie creation of beef, potatoes, onions, turnips, and other vegetables. Brought to the U.P. by Cornish miners, the pasty made for a hearty and filling meal, one that was easy to transport deep into the mine and warm up later with their candles. The same concept works well today if you're headed from town to your campfire.

Another Michigan food well worth tasting is the state's abundant fresh fish, from brook trout to walleye. In Great Lakes ports, you'll often be able to find a commercial fishery operating a small retail store, usually down by the docks. They often sell both fresh catch and smoked fish. The latter is absolutely superb with a bottle of wine and a Great Lakes sunset.

WINERIES

With temperature extremes moderated by prevailing western winds across Lake Michigan, two areas of the Lower Peninsula have developed into bona fide wine-producing regions. Both in the southwestern corner and around Grand Traverse Bay, local wineries have won international acclaim by producing wines from Michigan grapes. White wines like rieslings and chardonnays tend to be their best offerings, but some vintners have had success with reds, too.

Many Michigan wineries offer free tours and tastings. A few worth trying include **Warner Vineyards** (Paw Paw, 800/756-5357, www.warnerwines.com), **Tabor Hill Winery & Restaurant** (Buchanan, 800/283-3363, www.taborhill.com), **L. Mawby Vineyards** (Suttons Bay, 231/271-3522, www.lmawby.

com), and **Chateau Grand Traverse** (Traverse City, 231/223-7355 or 800/283-0247, www.cgtwines.com). For more information, contact the **Michigan Grape & Wine Industry Council** (517/284-5733, www.michiganwines.com).

BREWERIES

Wine isn't all that Michigan has to offer the connoisseur; the state ranks fifth in the nation for the total number of breweries. Each of its eight regions has at least three—if not several—breweries, microbreweries, and brewpubs. From the Quay Street Brewing Company, a brewpub in Port Huron, to the Keweenaw Brewing Company, a microbrewery in Houghton, Michigan hosts more than 100 independent establishments for beer lovers. Be sure to sample a few varieties on your tour of the Great Lakes State—just remember not to drink and drive. For more information, consult the **Michigan Brewers Guild** (225 W. Washtenaw, Ste. C, Lansing, www.mibeer.com).

GROCERIES AND MARKETS

Whether you're traveling via RV or staying in a place with a kitchen, you'll be pleased to know that, despite its acres of rugged countryside and numerous out-of-the-way villages, Michigan has plenty of supermarkets, independent groceries, specialty stores, and farmers markets. So, no matter how long you plan to stay, you'll surely be able to purchase the produce and products to which you're accustomed.

You'll find major supermarket chains throughout the Lower Peninsula, including **Meijer** (877/363-4537, www.meijer.com), which is prevalent throughout the southern half and offers everything from fresh produce and pet products to electronics and furniture. Another helpful chain is **Glen's Markets** (800/451-8500, http://glens.spartanstores.com), which you'll find mainly in the northern L.P. Meanwhile, mom-and-pop groceries are pretty much everywhere, even on remote country roads.

But, if you're hoping to experience Michigan's regional treats and ethnic cuisine, you should visit some of the state's many farmers markets, U-pick farms, and specialty stores—from cheese and sausage shops in Frankenmuth to Traverse City's cherry-related emporiums. For a statewide list of farmers markets, consult the **Michigan Farmers Market Association** (MIFMA, 480 Wilson Rd., Rm. 172, East Lansing, 517/432-3381, www.mifma.org).

Tips for Travelers

CONDUCT AND CUSTOMS

Michigan is similar to other Midwestern states in temperament and traditions. While major cities like Detroit and Flint might not follow the general rule, most areas of Michigan, especially smaller towns in the U.P. and the northern half of the Lower Peninsula, have a down-to-earth, wholesome vibe. Most residents seem to embrace the values of good education, hard work, and close family ties. As in other U.S. states, more and more women are working outside the home (whether in the auto plants of southeastern Michigan or the corporations of the Heartland), and yet traditional gender roles still do exist in many families, where men typically work while women tend to the children.

Given the state's multiethnic history, reliance on tourism, and proximity to Canada, foreigners and tourists are generally welcome here. Overall, the residents are helpful, hospitable, and forthright. They might use strange terms like "pop" and have unique accents, especially in ethnic enclaves and throughout the U.P., but politeness and good manners are prevalent. You'll often hear "please," "thank you," "yes, ma'am," and "no, sir." So, while in Michigan, do as the natives do. Be kind and considerate, ask for help when you need it, thank others for

FUDGE AND CHERRIES

cherries galore at the National Cherry Festival

Since the 19th century, the regional cuisine of Michigan has been largely influenced by two factors: immigrant cultures and seasonal crops. Visitors interested in ethnic dishes can sample Polish pierogies in Hamtramck, Bavarian bratwursts in Frankenmuth, and Cornish pasties throughout the Upper Peninsula. Depending on the season, gourmands can enjoy a wide assortment of homegrown products, from maple syrup to blueberry jam, in various stores throughout the state. In addition, U-pick farms and orchards are abundant in the northern and southwestern portions of the Lower Peninsula; oftentimes, motorists need only watch for the hand-painted signs alongside country roads.

Fudge and cherries are two of the state's most popular treats, especially in summer. "Fudgies," as tourists are often called by Michiganders, flock to the fudge emporiums that dot the northern half of the Lower Peninsula, from Petoskey to Mackinac Island. In July and August, visitors can even watch the fudge-making process in shops like **Murdick's Fudge** (800/238-3432, www.murdicksfudge.com), which offers locations in Acme and downtown Traverse City and specializes in 14 different flavors, including black cherry and maple walnut.

As for cherries, Traverse City's **National Cherry Festival** (231/947-4230 or 800/968-3380, www.cherryfestival.org) is one of the state's most well-attended summertime events, where connoisseurs can, among other activities, compete in pie-eating and pit-spitting contests. Of course, no visit to the world's largest tart cherry-growing region would be complete without stopping by the headquarters of **Cherry Republic** (6026 Lake St., 800/206-6949, www.cherryrepublic.com) in Glen Arbor, west of Traverse City. Not far from Sleeping Bear Dunes, Cherry Republic boasts everything from cherry wines to cherry-flavored condiments to chocolate-covered cherries.

Needless to say, you won't go hungry while touring the Great Lakes State.

their time, and as a courtesy, ask permission before taking a photo.

OPPORTUNITIES FOR STUDY AND EMPLOYMENT

With several notable universities and thriving industries in the Heartland, Michigan offers plenty of educational and work-related opportunities for residents and travelers. If you're interested in such a long-term stay, your best bet would be to research the schools and companies that interest you, consider details like transportation and accommodations, and, for foreign travelers, look into U.S. visa policies *before* making travel or relocation plans.

VOLUNTEER VACATIONS

Sometimes, being a tourist isn't enough. If you want to get to know Michigan *and* lend a helping hand, then perhaps a volunteer vacation is right up your alley. National and state parks can especially use some extra assistance, and working in such diverse environments can be a truly rewarding experience. Isle Royale National Park, for instance, is almost always on the lookout for campground hosts, museum assistants, wilderness rangers, and the like. Meanwhile, many of Michigan's state parks and recreation areas need volunteer guides for their summertime State Park Explorer Program.

For more information about volunteering in Michigan's national parks and lakeshores, contact the **National Park Service** (www.nps. gov/volunteer). For more information about Michigan's State Park Explorer Program, contact the **Michigan Department of Natural Resources** (517/284-7275, www.michigan. gov/dnr).

TRAVELERS WITH DISABILITIES

Michigan is a very accessible state for those with disabilities. Most welcome centers and rest areas are equipped with features that can accommodate wheelchairs, such as convenient parking spaces, entrance ramps, wide passages, automatic doors, and spacious restrooms. The same can be said for major store chains, such as Walmart and Meijer; major hotel chains like Days Inn; and key attractions, including the football stadium at the University of Michigan, the Michigan's Adventure amusement park in Muskegon, and the visitors centers at Pictured Rocks National Lakeshore. When in doubt, though, about the possibility of access, simply call the establishment in question.

TRAVELING WITH CHILDREN

With its multitude of beaches, state parks, museums, train rides, boat tours, ice-skating facilities, and other amusements, Michigan is clearly a kid-friendly place. If you're traveling here with children, you'll surely find something for them to do. Even better, many restaurants and hotels go out of their way to accommodate young travelers. In Frankenmuth, for instance, **Zehnder's Splash Village Hotel & Waterpark** offers a video arcade, several waterslides, a 24-hour fitness center, and shuttle service to the restaurant.

© DANIEL MARTONE

Zehnder's Splash Village Hotel & Waterpark

When traveling with children, just remember to supervise them at all times, both to keep them safe from harm and to minimize the possibility of disturbing others. If you decide to venture into Canada, be sure to have proper identification for them as well as for yourself.

TRAVELING WITH PETS

Although pets aren't allowed in much of Michigan's national parkland and in many of the state's hotels, restaurants, and stores, plenty of places do welcome them, including highway rest areas. In locations where dogs, cats, and other pets are allowed, it's crucial that you understand and follow any relevant rules. Typically, you are asked to keep your pets on a leash at all times, walk them in designated areas, control their behavior so as not to disturb or endanger others, and always pick up after them. Barking or aggressive dogs are usually forbidden everywhere. When in doubt, call ahead to verify the pet policies of a particular park, attraction, or establishment.

WOMEN TRAVELING ALONE

While it's admirable for an independent woman to explore the world on her own, it's important to take precautions, especially in urban centers like Detroit and Flint. Although Michigan is a relatively safe place, there are still too many things that can go wrong—on the road, in a campground, even in a crowd.

If you must venture out alone, tell someone back home about your intended travel plans, stick to daytime driving, and stay close to busy attractions, streets, and campgrounds. Try to stow your money, credit cards, and identification close to your person; big purses make easy targets. If you feel that someone is stalking you, find a public place (such as a store, tourism bureau, police station, etc.) and don't hesitate to alert the police. Keep the doors to your lodging and vehicle locked at all times.

Before heading out on your trip, you should invest in a cell phone, which can be useful in an emergency. Just remember that cellular reception is limited in the state's more remote areas.

SENIOR TRAVELERS

Michigan is an exceptionally helpful place, so senior travelers should have little trouble getting assistance here. For help with directions, there are several welcome centers and tourism bureaus throughout the state, not to mention plenty of locals able to point you in the right direction. In addition, many establishments, especially restaurants, offer discounts to senior travelers. The National Park Service (www.nps.gov/findapark/passes.htm) even offers a special lifetime pass ($10) for U.S. citizens and permanent residents aged 62 or over, allowing them and all passengers in their vehicles (or up to four adults at places that charge per-person fees) free access to any national park or federal recreational land that charges an entrance fee, including the parks and lakeshores in Michigan.

GAY AND LESBIAN TRAVELERS

Although Michigan, like many Midwestern states, isn't openly friendly to gay and lesbian travelers, some towns and establishments can make you feel more welcome than others, such as Ann Arbor, home to the gay-friendly University of Michigan, and the nearby towns of Chelsea and Ypsilanti. Along the Southwest Coast, towns like Benton Harbor have a large number of gay-owned vacation homes, and the neighboring villages of Saugatuck and Douglas (www.gaysaugatuckdouglas.com) offer more than 120 gay-friendly shops, art galleries, restaurants, and lodging options. For more information about related issues, events, and establishments in Michigan, contact the **Pride Source Media Group** (20222 Farmington Rd., Livonia, 734/293-7200, www.pridesource. com), which produces an annual business directory for the state's lesbian/gay/bisexual/ transgender (LGBT) community.

Health and Safety

Despite the best-laid plans, trouble can occur at any time. Before hitting the road, it's critical that you pack a well-stocked first-aid kit and prepare yourself for the common pitfalls of travel in Michigan.

HEALTH RISKS
Contaminated Water
Although the state's crystal-clear streams may look inviting for a drink, don't take a chance. Many of Michigan's most pristine lakes and streams may be tainted with *Giardia lamblia,* a nasty little organism that is most commonly transmitted in the feces of beavers, moose, and other mammals. Giardiasis can result in severe stomach cramps, vomiting, and diarrhea. As one Isle Royale ranger once said, "It won't kill you, but it may make you wish you were dead." Neither chemical treatment with Halizone nor a water filter will make water safe from giardia. You need a water purifier filtering down to 0.4 micron or less. Boiling is also effective, but make sure to get your water to a full, rolling boil for five minutes. In addition, Isle Royale waters may be infected with the hydatid tapeworm, which can also be eradicated by first purifying or boiling the water in question.

Insects
Wood ticks and deer ticks are found in Michigan woods and grasslands. The larger wood tick, about a quarter inch long, attaches itself to your skin and gorges on your blood—gross, yes, but relatively harmless. If you find a wood tick on yourself, your companion, or your pet, grasp it as close to the head as possible and yank. Don't leave a piece of the animal imbedded, or it might cause an infection. Though not super particular, ticks prefer warm areas—such as the scalp, neck, armpits, and genitals. Ditto for your dog; check under the collar and all around the ears, too.

Deer ticks are the more dangerous beast. They may be transmitters of Lyme disease, a potentially debilitating condition. Lyme disease shows up as a temporary red rash that often resembles a ring, slowly expanding outward. As the disease progresses, other symptoms include sore joints, fatigue, and nausea; if left untreated, it can lead to arthritis and severe neurological and cardiac problems. Caught early, it can be treated effectively with antibiotics.

To complicate matters, deer ticks are tiny—hardly larger than the head of a pin. Like wood ticks, they burrow into the skin, especially in warm places. After hiking, check yourself and your hiking partners carefully. If it's large enough, grasp the tick and pull it off, or use tweezers. If you've been in a tick-infested area, watch for a developing rash within the next week and have anything suspicious looked at by a doctor promptly. Your best defense against ticks is to wear long pants and long sleeves, and spray yourself liberally with a hard-core repellent like those containing deet.

Dogs are also highly susceptible to Lyme disease. Check your dog carefully and thoroughly for deer ticks by slowly running your fingers or a comb through his coat to get a look at the skin—a task that requires a lot of patience on the part of you and your dog. Again, ears, necks, bellies, and genitals are favorite hiding places. Signs that your dog may have acquired Lyme disease include nausea, fatigue, and lameness that may come and go from different joints. If you see potential symptoms, get to a vet right away. Like humans, dogs respond well to antibiotics if the disease is caught early enough.

There is a canine vaccine for Lyme disease, but veterinarians are divided on how effective it is. At the very least, you should be aware of the various tick repellent sprays on the market—and be sure to use them before venturing into the deep woods.

Plants
While hiking amid Michigan's forests, marshes,

AVOIDING ANIMAL ATTACKS

Porcupines, black bears, moose, gray wolves, and other wild animals roam freely throughout Michigan, so it's quite possible that you might spot them during your travels, especially while exploring the state's vast forests. Although many of these creatures are wary of people, some may be all too curious. At such times, it might be easy to forget how to handle an encounter with a wild animal. So, whether you spot a grazing elk, a scurrying raccoon, a prowling bobcat, or something else entirely, you should always adhere to the following rules:

- Observe wildlife from a distance; do not follow or approach the animals.

- Never feed wildlife; feeding wild animals can damage their health, alter their natural behavior, and expose them to predators.

- Never taunt or disturb wildlife.

- Protect wildlife by storing your food and trash securely.

- Control pets at all times, or leave them at home.

- Avoid wildlife during sensitive phases, such as mating or nesting.

For more information about respecting wildlife, consult the **Michigan Department of Natural Resources** (517/284-9453, www.michigan.gov/dnr) or contact the Colorado-based **Leave No Trace Center for Outdoor Ethics** (303/442-8222 or 800/332-4100, www.lnt.org).

and beaches, be careful where you step. It's easier than you think to trip on a root or other obstruction. In addition, unless you're certain that you've found a patch of wild blueberries or other recognizable fruit, you should refrain from digesting any tempting berries, flowers, plants, and the like without first consulting local residents or expert field guides.

Wild Animals

As for large animals, deer are by far your biggest danger—they cause thousands of collisions a year on Michigan roads. But black bears certainly seem more frightening, especially when you're deep in the woods. Black bears are found throughout northern Michigan; the Upper Peninsula has an especially large population. They usually live in areas of heavy forest, but will routinely wander into open areas in search of food. They're beautiful animals, and you should consider yourself lucky to observe one.

Black bears are generally shy creatures that would prefer to have nothing to do with you. If they hear you coming down the trail, they'll likely run the other way. If you happen to see

one before it sees you, leave it an "escape route," then clap, yell, or bang pans. Give especially wide berth to a mother and cubs. There are very few documented cases of black bear aggression against humans, and theories vary on what to do if you should ever find yourself in such a situation. Most behaviorists believe that, unlike grizzlies, black bears will be intimidated by dominance behavior like shouting and waving your arms.

The biggest problems come when bears are lured into populated areas by human carelessness. It's always sad to see a bear relocated from its home territory, but it happens frequently in campgrounds where humans don't properly store food or dispose of garbage. If you're car camping, keep all food in your car—with doors and windows closed! If you're tent camping, keep everything in airtight storage containers, and suspend the containers on a line between two trees, high enough off the ground and far enough apart to be out of a bear's reach. Latched coolers shoved under a picnic table are not sufficient to keep out bears.

Clean pans and utensils right away, dumping the water well away from camp, and store them with the food. Never keep any food (even gum) in your tent. Bears have an extremely good sense of smell and may be tempted to join you. Some say cosmetics also can attract them, so play it safe and store your soap and toothpaste with the food. You might want to leave your tent unzipped during the day while you're gone. Bears are curious; if they want to check out your tent, they'll make their own entrance if they can't find one.

If you're at a campground, deposit garbage in the animal-proof refuse containers provided. If you're backcountry camping, pack out all trash. Needless to say, never attempt to feed a bear, no matter how "tame" it may seem.

Heatstroke

Despite Michigan's mild summers (especially in the northern regions), hot, sunny days are common, and it's crucial that you prepare for them. Although sunscreen will help to prevent sunburn (which, if experienced often, can cause long-term problems for your skin), you must apply it often (and liberally). Prolonged sun exposure, high temperatures, and little water consumption can also cause dehydration, which can lead to heat exhaustion—a harmful condition whereby your internal cooling system begins to shut down. Symptoms may include clammy skin, weakness, vomiting, and abnormal body temperature. In such instances, you should lie down in the shade, remove restrictive clothing, and drink some water.

If you do not treat heat exhaustion promptly, your condition can worsen quickly, leading to heatstroke (or sunstroke)—a dangerous condition whereby your internal body temperature starts to rise to a potentially fatal level. Symptoms can include dizziness, vomiting, diarrhea, abnormal breathing and blood pressure, headache, cessation of sweating, and confusion. If any of these occur, you must be taken to a hospital as soon as possible; in the meantime, your companions should move you into the shade; remove your clothing; lower your body temperature with cool water, damp sheets, or fans; and try to give you some water to drink, if you're able.

Extreme Cold

While winter can be a beautiful time to visit the Great Lakes State, there's no doubt that Michigan winters can be long, hard, and cruel, especially for those unaccustomed to such cold, snowy conditions. If you plan to travel here November-March, be sure to pack plenty of warm clothes, including sweaters, mittens, hats, and waterproof boots. Be prepared to dress in layers (including your feet), as it's always better to remove clothing than to not have enough, especially if you plan to be outside for a while.

One condition to avoid is hypothermia, whereby the body temperature begins to decline to a dangerous level. Being cold and wet for an extended period of time, such as during a snowstorm, can be fatal. Try to keep warm and dry at all times. If you start to shiver, slur your speech, stumble, or feel drowsy, do not fall asleep. Instead, find some shelter, change into dry clothes, try to move around, and eat a quick-energy snack.

You should also watch out for frostbite, which can occur when blood vessels near the skin constrict, sending more blood to your vital organs and allowing outer tissues to freeze. The body parts most susceptible are your nose, cheeks, ears, and extremities. Initially, affected areas might tingle, itch, burn, whiten, go numb, or turn cold. Prolonged frostbite could cause swelling, blisters, and, ultimately, blackened skin. Diabetes, alcohol consumption, tobacco use, fatigue, dehydration, high altitude, and improper clothing can make the situation worse. To avoid long-term damage (and possible amputation), you should find shelter immediately and warm the affected areas. If your condition is severe, a doctor will need to oversee the rewarming process, in order to determine the extent of the damage.

Getting Lost

Part of Michigan's charm is its plethora of untamed backcountry and the possibility of exploring it in any season. Losing oneself in such wilderness might sound romantic, but it can be downright deadly, especially during extreme weather. To protect yourself from harmful, long-term exposure to the elements, it's crucial that you plan your route ahead of time, consult local residents before heading into an isolated area, and inform someone else of your intentions—in case you don't return as scheduled. When venturing into the wilderness, it's also advisable to travel in a group of at least four; in an emergency situation, one of you can stay with the afflicted person while the other two seek help.

If you stick to the main highways, you might need little more than a reliable map to navigate Michigan. But, if you have any intention of exploring the state's more remote areas, it's imperative that you bring a compass and GPS (global positioning system) with you. Be advised that, despite improved coverage over the past decade, cell phones still have a tendency to lose signal in the Lower Peninsula's northern forests and throughout the Upper Peninsula.

MEDICAL SERVICES
Emergency Care
All of Michigan is tied into the **911** emergency system. Dial 911 free from any telephone (including pay phones) to reach an operator who can quickly dispatch local police, fire, or ambulance services. This service also works from cell phones. Be aware, however, that cellular towers can be few and far between in rural areas. Much of the Upper Peninsula, including Pictured Rocks National Lakeshore, remains without reliable cellular and digital wireless service.

Hospitals and Pharmacies
If you experience an illness or injury while traveling in the Great Lakes State, rest assured that, as with other U.S. states, hospitals and pharmacies abound here, especially in major cities like Detroit, Flint, Grand Rapids, and Marquette. Just be advised that most medical facilities will require you to have insurance or make a partial payment before admitting you for treatment or dispensing medication.

Insurance
Although you might be the sort of traveler who likes to live dangerously, insurance is highly recommended while traveling in Michigan. Whether you're a U.S. citizen driving your own car or an international traveler in a rented RV, you should invest in medical, travel, and automotive insurance before embarking upon your trip—in order to protect yourself as well as your assets. Research your insurance options and choose the policies that best suit your needs and budget.

CRIME
Despite the crime-ridden reputations of places like Detroit and Flint, Michigan is a relatively safe place. It might be hard to believe in modern-day America, but residents of the northern rural parts rarely lock their doors at night—of course, that could be partially due to the fact that most northern Michigan residents own firearms. People here are, for the most part, friendly and helpful. Still, whether you're visiting the Motor City or a small town on the Leelanau Peninsula, it's important to take precautions.

Never leave valuables in plain view on a car seat; secure them in the trunk, where they're less tempting to thieves. Similarly, in case of an accident on the highway, do not abandon your vehicle, as this might also invite thieves. When sightseeing, keep your money, credit cards, identification, and other important items hidden on your person; purses and backpacks are much easier to steal. Do not walk alone at night, even in a small town, and try not to travel on the highways after dark. Even if you have AAA roadside assistance, help can be slow to come if you break down on a country road in the wee hours of morning. Just to be on the safe side, lock your hotel and car doors at night.

If you're traveling via RV, do not dry-dock alone in an isolated place. Try to stay in an RV park, a campground, or, at the very least, a well-lit parking lot. When venturing into the wilderness, try to camp with others. If you do find yourself in trouble, don't hesitate to find a phone and dial **911**. Of course, the time that it takes police and emergency vehicles to reach you will depend upon your location, especially in the U.P.'s more remote areas.

Information and Services

MAPS AND TOURIST INFORMATION

For general information on traveling in Michigan, your best source is the state-run **Travel Michigan** (888/784-7328, www.michigan.org, 9am-5pm Mon.-Fri.). Your call will be answered by a live person who can send you brochures and field your questions about festivals, activities, lodgings, and more. You may find it even more convenient to surf the website, which offers a comprehensive database of communities, accommodations, activities, golf courses, parks, attractions, shops, events, restaurants, and other aspects of the state. Just be aware that some of the information can be outdated, so always call ahead when making travel plans.

Suggested Maps

Michigan's official state road map is a rarity: Unlike most maps, it doesn't relegate the U.P. to the opposite side. Pick one up at a **Welcome Center** or request one from **Travel Michigan** (888/784-7328, www.michigan.org). **AAA** (800/222-6424, www.aaa.com) also offers a helpful Michigan map ($4.95 nonmembers, free for members).

For more detail, **DeLorme** (207/847-1165 or 800/642-0970, www.delorme.com) produces the *Michigan Atlas & Gazetteer,* with the state portrayed in 102 large-scale maps. Though the 15-inch-long format is unwieldy for hikers, it's a great resource for planning your trip; it even identifies campgrounds, golf courses, wineries, historic sites, bicycle routes, and other points of interest. You can find it at many Midwestern bookstores and gas stations for $19.95.

If you'll be exploring the backcountry, you should invest in an official topographical (topo) map produced by the **U.S. Geological Survey** (888/275-8747, www.usgs.gov). Michigan's national parks and forests have topo maps for sale at their visitors centers or ranger stations. Outside federal lands, you may find them (or other detailed maps) in local outfitter shops, but don't count on it. If the shop you visit doesn't have the map you need, you may be a hundred miles from a store that does. If you can, buy or order one ahead of time through an outfitter or travel store.

Welcome Centers

The **Michigan Department of Transportation** (MDOT, 517/373-2090, www.michigan.gov/mdot) operates 14 year-round welcome centers throughout the state. Stocked with maps and brochures, these facilities are staffed with "travel counselors" who are knowledgeable about the state in general and their region in particular. The centers are marked on the state map and by signs on the nearest highway. Hours vary.

WELCOME CENTERS IN THE LOWER PENINSULA

- Clare: US-10/127, north of town

- Coldwater: I-69, six miles north of the Indiana-Michigan state line

- Detroit: Off I-75 at 2835 Bagley Street

- Dundee: US-23, six miles north of the Ohio-Michigan state line

- Mackinaw City: I-75 at Nicolet Street

- Monroe: I-75, 10 miles north of the Ohio-Michigan state line

- New Buffalo: I-94 at the Indiana-Michigan state line

- Port Huron: I-69/94, west of the Blue Water Bridge

WELCOME CENTERS IN THE UPPER PENINSULA

• Iron Mountain: US-2/141 in the downtown district

• Ironwood: US-2 at the Wisconsin-Michigan state line

• Marquette: US-41/M-28, two miles south of town

• Menominee: US-41 at the Wisconsin-Michigan state line

• Sault Ste. Marie: I-75, south of the International Bridge

• St. Ignace: I-75, north of the Mackinac Bridge

Regional Tourism Bureaus

All of Michigan's major cities and many of its small towns offer tourism services through area convention and visitors bureaus (CVBs) or chambers of commerce. The state also has several regional tourism offices, which cover larger areas.

In the Lower Peninsula, you can contact the **Thumb Area Tourism Council, Inc.** (TATC, 810/569-6856, www.thumbtourism.org), the **Southwestern Michigan Tourist Council** (269/925-6301, www.swmichigan.org), the **Michigan Beachtowns Association** (www.beachtowns.org), and the **West Michigan Tourist Association** (WMTA, 616/245-2217, www.wmta.org). In the Upper Peninsula, contact the **Northern Michigan Tourist Association** (www.travelnorth.org), the **Western U.P. Convention & Visitor Bureau** (906/932-4850 or 800/522-5657, www.explorewesternup.com), and the **Upper Peninsula Travel & Recreation Association** (UPTRA, 906/774-5480 or 800/562-7134, www.up-travel.com). To reach local tourism offices, consult the **Michigan Association of Convention and Visitor Bureaus** (MACVB, 231/823-0015, www.visitmichigan.org).

COMMUNICATIONS AND MEDIA

Postal and Shipping Services

In Michigan, a post office is never very far away via car, so it's fairly easy to purchase stamps, receive mail (via "General Delivery" for temporary visitors), and send letters and packages all around the world. While major cities and towns, such as Detroit and Lansing, have numerous post offices, even small U.P. towns like Skandia have at least one. To locate a post office in your area, consult the **United States Postal Service** (800/275-8777, www.usps.com).

If you need to send a package quickly (and cost isn't an issue), you'll find plenty of shipping stores throughout Michigan, especially in major towns. For more information about shipping locations and services, contact **FedEx** (800/463-3339, www.fedex.com) or **UPS** (800/742-5877, www.ups.com).

Phones and Internet

Public pay phones can be found throughout Michigan—at airports, gas stations, stores, bars, restaurants, hotels, etc. To place a call, listen for a dial tone, deposit the necessary coins, and dial the desired number (including "1" and the area code, if you're making a long-distance call). In the case of an emergency, you can dial **911** at no charge. For international calls, it's probably best to use a prepaid phone card, which you can often purchase in gas stations or convenience stores. To figure out the correct international calling code, visit www.countrycodes.com.

Nowadays, a cell phone is a necessary tool for travelers. It can make it easier to get roadside assistance, call an establishment for directions, and seek help in an emergency situation. Just be advised that cellular reception is still unreliable in many rural areas, especially in northern Michigan.

As for the Internet, it's hard to imagine the days when travel was possible without it. With the help of a computer and a modem, you can research Michigan's native flora, book a fishing charter, monitor the day's weather, view the menu of a Traverse City restaurant, and perform a host of other duties. Access to your own laptop can make such tasks even more convenient, especially since several of Michigan's hotels and other establishments offer wireless Internet access. Internet cafés also make it difficult to stay out of touch for long—even in remote areas of the Upper Peninsula. Just remember that not all websites are updated regularly. Consult local residents or contact businesses directly before making any firm travel plans.

Media

Most of Michigan's major towns have at least one daily newspaper, from the *Detroit News* (www.detnews.com) to Escanaba's *Daily Press* (www.dailypress.net). Some places, such as Traverse City, even have their own magazine. Such periodicals are terrific sources of information for festivals, restaurants, sporting events, outdoor activities, and other diversions.

Local television and radio stations, such as Detroit's ABC affiliate WXYZ (www.wxyz.com), are also excellent sources for regional information. Pick up a newspaper in your area for a list of channels.

MONEY
Currency and Credit Cards

Bank debit cards and major credit cards (like Visa and MasterCard) are accepted statewide, even in the smallest towns. In addition, automated teller machines (ATMs) have become more prevalent, allowing travelers to withdraw cash whenever they need it. If you're uncomfortable using ATMs, you're sure to find a bank open during business hours (and sometimes on the weekend). That said, you'll need cash at self-registration campgrounds, and many independent motels, eateries, and stores will accept only cash, traveler's checks, or personal checks (sometimes even out-of-state ones). As any wise traveler knows, never count on getting by with only plastic.

If you're traveling to or from Canada, you'll find currency exchanges at the border and at nearby banks in both countries. Since the exchange rate between Canadian and U.S. dollars can change at any time, you should plan to exchange currencies whenever coming or going. For up-to-date exchange rates, consult www.xe.com.

If you're a U.S. resident with Canadian money "left over" at the end of a trip, try to end up with bills, not coins. Many banks (especially away from border towns) will exchange only paper money, so you can easily find yourself with $10 or $20 worth of heavy souvenirs.

Sales Tax

In Michigan, you'll find that most goods and services, save for perhaps movie tickets, often cost more than their listed price. That's due, of course, to state taxes—specifically, the 6 percent sales tax on taxable retail items such as clothing and the 6 percent use tax imposed on accommodations.

Tipping

Although the amount of a gratuity depends on the level of service received, general tipping guidelines exist in Michigan (and throughout the United States). Typically, restaurant servers, delivery drivers, and bartenders should receive 15-20 percent of the pretax bill; taxi, limousine, and shuttle drivers should receive at least 15 percent of the entire fare; valets, porters, and skycaps should receive $2 per vehicle or piece of luggage; and hotel housekeepers should receive at least $1-2 per day. Be advised, though, that while on your travels you might also need to tip restaurant hosts, hotel concierges, restroom and coat-check attendants, spa and salon personnel, musicians and street performers, adult entertainers, tattoo artists, and other service providers, so be prepared.

It's also worth noting that tour guides, fishing guides, boat captains, and other excursion operators should be tipped as well. In fact, no matter how much such tours or trips cost, the gratuity is never included in the quoted price. Of course, how much you choose to tip is entirely up to you. While the exact amount of a tip will depend on the cost, length, and nature of the trip in question—not to mention your satisfaction with the services received—it's generally accepted to tip between 10 and 20 percent of the overall cost of the trip. If a guide or operator makes an exceptional effort, such as unexpectedly extending the length of a trip, then it's highly recommended that you increase the size of your tip accordingly. Tipping badly could harm your reputation among other guides and operators, while tipping well could ensure even better service the next time.

WEIGHTS AND MEASURES
Electricity
In Michigan, most standard electrical outlets operate at 120 volts. So, if you're coming from Europe, Asia, or a country that operates at 220-240 volts, you'll need to bring an adapter in order to use your hair dryer, laptop, or other small appliance. Outlets here vary between the two-pronged and three-pronged variety, for which you might also need an adapter (easily purchased in any decent hardware or electronics store).

Time Zone
Most of Michigan is located in the Eastern Time Zone (ET), with the exception of the four Upper Peninsula counties that border Wisconsin. Gogebic, Iron, Dickinson, and Menominee Counties are in the Central Time Zone (CT). Be advised, too, that Michiganders observe Daylight Saving Time between mid-March and early November, so adjust your clocks and watches accordingly.

RESOURCES

Glossary

The following regional terms and abbreviations will help you navigate your way across the state of Michigan, and perhaps better understand its unique people and culture:

The Big Lake: a reference to whichever Great Lake is nearest to one's current position in Michigan

Big Mac: a nickname for the Mackinac Bridge, the link between Michigan's Upper and Lower Peninsulas; also called simply "The Bridge" by many residents, especially those who don't live close to any of the bridges that cross the United States-Canada border

The Cottage: a term often used to describe a vacation home in the northern parts of Michigan, whether a cabin in the Upper Peninsula or a beach house near Traverse City; also called "Da Camp" in the Upper Peninsula

dethaw: a commonly, if incorrectly, used term to signify the act of thawing or defrosting an object

doorwall: a euphemism for a sliding-glass door

downriver: a reference to the Wayne County suburbs south of Detroit, along the Detroit River

downstate: a reference to Michigan's Lower Peninsula

D-Town: a nickname for the city of Detroit

eh: a spoken interjection commonly used by Upper Peninsula natives to solicit a response or add emphasis to a statement (e.g., "There's no place like Michigan, eh?")

Eight Mile: the boundary between Detroit and its wealthier northern suburbs

euchre: a trick-taking card game popular throughout the Midwest, especially in Michigan

fudgies: a nickname for tourists, especially in the northern part of Michigan's Lower Peninsula, which is known for its ubiquitous fudge shops

glovebox: an alternate term for a glove compartment

Hockeytown: since the mid-1990s, a nickname for the city of Detroit, in celebration of its NHL team, the Detroit Red Wings

hourlies: a nickname for factory workers paid by the hour, especially those in the automotive industry

The Joe: a popular nickname for the Joe Louis Arena, home to the Detroit Red Wings hockey team

"Kripes Almighty!": a regional expletive for polite company

The L.P.: a seldom-used abbreviation for Michigan's Lower Peninsula

Michigan bankroll: a term used to describe a large roll of money in small denominations, often covered by one larger bill to give the appearance of a lot of money

Michigander: a nickname for a Michigan resident, occasionally used to specify a male resident

Michiganian: a longtime nickname for a Michigan resident

Michigoose: a less-common nickname for a Michigan resident, occasionally used to specify a female resident

Mighty Mac: a reference to the Mackinac

Bridge, the link between Michigan's two peninsulas; also called "Da Crossing" or "Troll Turnpike" by residents of the Upper Peninsula

The Mitten: a commonly used nickname for Michigan's Lower Peninsula; also called "Troll Land" by residents of the Upper Peninsula

Motor City: a nickname for Detroit that honors the town's rich automotive history

Motown: a record label and musical style that originated in Detroit; also used as a nickname for the city itself

parking deck: an alternate term for a parking garage; also known as a "parking ramp"

party store: a common euphemism for a liquor store

pasty: a hand-held pastry filled with meat and vegetables, popular in Michigan's Upper Peninsula

The Plant: a term often used for a factory, though normally relating to the automotive industry

pop: a common euphemism for soda or soft drinks

The Ren Cen: a nickname for the Renaissance Center, a General Motors-owned skyscraper in downtown Detroit

The Soo: a commonly used nickname for Sault Ste. Marie, a city in the eastern half of the Upper Peninsula

Spartan: the mascot of Michigan State University in East Lansing

The Thumb: a generally accepted term for the region of Michigan's Lower Peninsula that lies between Saginaw Bay, Lake Huron, and I-75 and oddly resembles the thumb of a mitten

tip of the Mitten: a reference to the Straits of Mackinac

tip of the Thumb: a reference to the town of Port Austin

townies: a derogatory nickname for residents of small northern Michigan tourist towns, sometimes uttered by wealthy summer vacationers from cities like Detroit or Chicago

Trolls: a nickname for residents of Michigan's Lower Peninsula, who live "below" the Mackinac Bridge

Trooper: a nickname for a Troll who has relocated to the Upper Peninsula, essentially a combination of the terms "Troll" and "Yooper"

trunk slammers: a scornful nickname for visitors to the Upper Peninsula; also known by the more derogatory term "citiots"

The Union: a commonly used nickname for the International Union, United Automobile, Aerospace and Agricultural Implement Workers of America, better known as the "United Auto Workers"

The U.P.: a frequently used abbreviation for Michigan's Upper Peninsula

up north: a reference to a place north of wherever one is in Michigan, typically used to refer to the Upper Peninsula or the northern part of the Lower Peninsula

The Windsor Ballet: a facetious term utilized by Detroiters to refer to the strip clubs of nearby Windsor, a city in Ontario, Canada

Wolverine: the mascot of the University of Michigan in Ann Arbor

Yooperland: a nickname for Michigan's Upper Peninsula; also called "Da Yoop" or "Yoopsconsin" by U.P. residents

Yoopers: a nickname for residents of Michigan's Upper Peninsula

Suggested Reading

While by no means an exhaustive list of Michigan-related titles, the following books will shed some light on the state's singular geography, history, culture, and diversions. Peruse some of them before your trip, and bring them along for the ride.

CUISINE

Beeler, Jaye. *Tasting and Touring Michigan's Homegrown Food: A Culinary Roadtrip.* Traverse City, MI: Arbutus Press, 2012. Written by a former food editor of the *Grand Rapids Press,* this book celebrates the state's popular trend of relying on local food, from the cranberry bogs of the Upper Peninsula to the inner-city gardens of Detroit.

Breckenridge, Suzanne, and Marjorie Snyder. *Michigan Herb Cookbook.* Ann Arbor, MI: University of Michigan Press, 2001. Written by two Midwest natives, this cookbook offers growing tips, a detailed history about herbs, and, of course, regional recipes made from homegrown Michigan herbs and produce, such as dill, pumpkins, and cherries.

Eustice, Sally. *History from the Hearth: A Colonial Michilimackinac Cookbook.* Mackinaw City, MI: Mackinac State Historic Parks, 1997. This collection of traditional 18th-century recipes is complemented by snippets of letters and journals from inhabitants of the original fur-trading village.

Johnson, Chuck, Blanche Johnson, and Matt Sutherland. *Savor Michigan Cookbook: Michigan's Finest Restaurants, Their Recipes & Their Histories.* Belgrade, MT: Wilderness Adventures Press, Inc., 2007. Part cookbook, part travel guide, this selection enables epicureans to plan their route across Michigan and bring their favorite dishes home with them.

Michigan Lake to Lake Bed and Breakfast Association. *Celebrate Breakfast!: A Cookbook & Travel Guide.* Woodruff, WI: The Guest Cottage, Inc., 2005. The innkeepers of several bed-and-breakfasts throughout Michigan provide recipes for their favorite foods, from prune muffins to asparagus pepper quiche.

Michigan Lake to Lake Bed and Breakfast Association. *Michigan Bed & Breakfast Cookbook.* Boulder, CO: 3D Press, 2013. This compilation includes more than 300 breakfast, lunch, dinner, and dessert recipes from over 70 unique inns across the state.

Williams, Angela, ed. *With a Cherry on Top: Stories, Poems, Recipes & Fun Facts from Michigan Cherry Country.* Bay City, MI: Mayapple Press, 2006. Besides offering recipes that celebrate northern Michigan's cherry industry, this collection also features memoirs and stories by Michigan writers.

FICTION AND PROSE

Catton, Bruce. *Waiting for the Morning Train: An American Boyhood.* Detroit: Wayne State University Press, 1987. Reflecting on his childhood in Benzonia, southwest of Traverse City, a Pulitzer Prize-winning journalist and historian offers a beguiling look at boyhood memories, which segues into more serious discussions about the impact of technology on our society. Catton (1899-1978) originally published this memoir in 1972.

Emerick, Lon L. *The Superior Peninsula: Seasons in the Upper Peninsula of Michigan.* Skandia, MI: North Country Publishing, 1996. A collection of essays and "love letters" about the big lake, categorized by seasons.

Gruley, Bryan. *The Hanging Tree.* New York: Simon & Schuster, Inc., 2010. In this follow-up mystery to *Starvation Lake,* small-town newspaper editor Gus Carpenter must struggle, with the help of his old flame, to understand what really happened to Gracie McBride, an apparent suicide victim found dead shortly after returning to her hometown.

Gruley, Bryan. *The Skeleton Box.* New York: Simon & Schuster, Inc., 2012. The last of a trilogy that includes *Starvation Lake* (2009) and *The Hanging Tree* (2010), this mystery features small-town newspaper editor Gus Carpenter as he investigates the most difficult story of his life: the murder of his ex-girlfriend's mother, whose body was found in his own mother's house.

Gruley, Bryan. *Starvation Lake.* New York: Simon & Schuster, Inc., 2009. Set within a small northern Michigan town, this debut mystery follows Gus Carpenter, a failed *Detroit Times* reporter who has recently returned to his hometown and must, as editor of the local newspaper, uncover the truth about his former hockey coach's disappearance a decade earlier.

Hamper, Ben. *Rivethead: Tales from the Assembly Line.* New York: Warner Books, Inc., 1992. Originally published in 1986, this compelling collection includes first-hand experiences from a former General Motors factory worker.

Harrison, Jim. *Wolf: A False Memoir.* New York: Dell Publishing, 1971. A native of Grayling, Michigan, Harrison is the award-winning author of countless poems, reviews, essays, short stories, novellas, and novels, not the least of which is this tale of a Manhattanite who heads into northern Michigan, hoping to glimpse a rare wolf in the wild.

Hemingway, Ernest. *The Complete Short Stories of Ernest Hemingway.* New York: Simon & Schuster, Inc., 1987. Hemingway's works have been packaged and repackaged, of course, but this volume includes his finest Michigan-based short stories: "Up in Michigan," set in Horton's Bay, and numerous Nick Adams tales, including "Big Two-Hearted River," about fishing in the Upper Peninsula.

Leonard, Elmore. *Out of Sight.* New York: Delacorte Press, 1996. Famous for his crime novels, several of which have been turned into films, Leonard tells the story of a career thief and his unlikely relationship with a U.S. marshal, which takes them both to the gritty streets and posh suburbs of Detroit.

Shiel, Walt. *Devil in the North Woods.* Lake Linden, MI: Slipdown Mountain Publications, LLC, 2004. Based on contemporary reports and recorded oral histories about the 1908 wildfire that ravaged northeastern Michigan, obliterated the town of Metz, and killed several people, this novel traces the real-life story of an adolescent boy who survived the ordeal.

Steinberg, Michael, ed. *Peninsula: Essays and Memoirs from Michigan.* East Lansing, MI: Michigan State University Press, 2000. An eclectic regional anthology of nearly 40 contemporary, evocative essays and memoirs, written by current and former Michiganders, from Jim Harrison to Jack Driscoll, and focused on the state's great outdoors and metropolitan areas.

Stocking, Kathleen. *Lake Country: A Series of Journeys.* Ann Arbor, MI: University of Michigan Press, 1994. A series of essays from a talented local writer, who expands her observations beyond her native Leelanau Peninsula to other areas of Michigan.

Stocking, Kathleen. *Letters from the Leelanau: Essays of People and Place.* Ann Arbor, MI: University of Michigan Press, 1990. Poignant personal essays about the inhabitants and features of Stocking's native Leelanau Peninsula.

Traver, Robert. *Anatomy of a Murder.* New York: St. Martin's Press, 1983. Originally published in 1958, this popular novel-turned-movie was penned by former Michigan Supreme Court justice and U.P. resident John D. Voelker (a.k.a. Robert Traver), about a lover's-triangle murder that took place in nearby Big Bay.

Traver, Robert. *Trout Madness*. New York: Simon & Schuster, Inc., 1989. Originally published in the 1960s, this collection of fishing tales serves as "a dissertation on the symptoms and pathology of this incurable disease by one of its victims."

Traver, Robert. *Trout Magic*. New York: Simon & Schuster, Inc., 1989. Filled with tall tales and amusing opinions, this collection of essays, originally published in 1974, offers a joyous look at trout fishing by the prolific Michigan author and judge.

GEOGRAPHY AND ECOLOGY

Barnes, Burton V., and Warren H. Wagner Jr. *Michigan Trees: A Guide to the Trees of Michigan and the Great Lakes Region*. Ann Arbor, MI: University of Michigan Press, 2004. Originally published in 1913 by different authors, this updated field guide was written by two University of Michigan professors of forestry and botany, respectively.

Blacklock, Craig. *The Lake Superior Images*. Moose Lake, MN: Blacklock Nature Photography, 1998. Blacklock, son of famous nature photographer Les Blacklock, circumnavigated Lake Superior by kayak to capture images for this award-winning book, which surely belongs on every northern coffee table.

Dickmann, Donald I., and Larry A. Leefers. *The Forests of Michigan*. Ann Arbor, MI: University of Michigan Press, 2003. Two forestry professors from Michigan State University examine the natural history, ecology, management, and economic importance of the varied forests that cover roughly half of the state.

Huber, N. King. *The Geologic Story of Isle Royale National Park*. Washington, D.C.: U.S. Department of the Interior Geological Survey, 1983. For a government publication, this is a rather colorfully written study of Isle Royale's distinctive topography. Understanding even a little makes an Isle Royale backpacking trip all the more memorable.

Mueller, Bruce, and Kevin Gauthier. *Lake Huron Rock Picker's Guide*. Ann Arbor, MI: University of Michigan Press, 2010. Featuring both color and black-and-white images, this identification guide assists rockhounds along the eastern side of Michigan's Lower Peninsula.

Mueller, Bruce, and Kevin Gauthier. *Lake Michigan Rock Picker's Guide*. Ann Arbor, MI: University of Michigan Press, 2006. Filled with several helpful photographs, this rock identification guide appeals to beachcombers of all skill levels.

Mueller, Bruce, and Kevin Gauthier. *Lake Superior Rock Picker's Guide*. Ann Arbor, MI: University of Michigan Press, 2007. Besides identifying numerous rocks found along the shores of Lake Superior, this guide also offers helpful advice on where to locate each stone and how to polish what you find.

Peterson, Rolf O. *The Wolves of Isle Royale: A Broken Balance*. Ann Arbor, MI: University of Michigan Press, 2007. In this firsthand study, a wildlife biologist and professor of wildlife ecology scrutinizes the ancient predator-prey relationship between the mysterious Isle Royale wolf and the native moose.

Smith, Gerald R. *Guide to Great Lakes Fishes*. Ann Arbor, MI: University of Michigan Press, 2010. Written by a former University of Michigan professor of ecology and evolutionary biology, this comprehensive guide features informative essays, illustrations, and photographs about more than 60 of the region's most commonly found fish species.

Tekiela, Stan. *Birds of Michigan Field Guide*. Cambridge, MN: Adventure Publications, Inc., 2004. With color photographs and an easy-to-use format, the second edition of Tekiela's indispensable field guide can help even amateur bird-watchers observe Michigan's native species.

Tekiela, Stan. *Wildflowers of Michigan Field Guide*. Cambridge, MN: Adventure Publications, Inc., 2000. As with all of Tekiela's colorful field guides, this one is ideal for both beginners and those familiar with Michigan's varied wildflowers.

Voss, Edward G., and Anton A. Reznicek. *Field Manual of Michigan Flora*. Ann Arbor, MI: University of Michigan Press, 2012. Written by two world-renowned plant curators at the University of Michigan, this incredibly comprehensive, thoroughly updated field guide offers everything that naturalists might want to know about more than 2,700 of Michigan's native and nonnative seed plants.

HISTORY AND CULTURE

Alexander, Jeff. *The Muskegon: The Majesty and Tragedy of Michigan's Rarest River*. East Lansing, MI: Michigan State University Press, 2006. An examination of the creation, history, uses, devastation, and restoration of Michigan's second-longest river.

Ashlee, Laura Rose, ed. *Traveling Through Time: A Guide to Michigan's Historical Markers*. Ann Arbor, MI: University of Michigan Press, 2005. This revised edition is the definitive, illustrated guide to nearly 1,500 of Michigan's historic sites, found along various highways and within assorted neighborhoods and city centers.

Ballard, Charles L. *Michigan's Economic Future: A New Look*. East Lansing, MI: Michigan State University Press, 2010. Authored by an award-winning economics professor at Michigan State University, this book examines the structure of Michigan's economy, including its agricultural roots, up-and-down automotive industry, and manufacturing downturn, and proposes several solutions to stimulate the state's economic growth.

Bjorn, Lars, and Jim Gallert. *Before Motown: A History of Jazz in Detroit, 1920-1960*. Ann Arbor, MI: University of Michigan Press, 2001. Written by a sociology professor and a veteran jazz broadcaster, this book explores the history of Detroit jazz within its social, often racially charged context.

Bohnak, Karl. *So Cold a Sky: Upper Michigan Weather Stories*. Negaunee, MI: Cold Sky Publishing, 2006. Using eyewitness accounts, this book chronicles weather-related events in the Upper Peninsula from the 1600s to the late 1990s.

Carson, David A. *Grit, Noise, and Revolution: The Birth of Detroit Rock 'n' Roll*. Ann Arbor, MI: University of Michigan Press, 2006. A narrative history of the long-haired, hard-rocking musicians who helped to change the face of rock 'n' roll.

Clifton, James, James McClurken, and George Cornell. *People of the Three Fires: The Ottawa, Potawatomi, and Ojibway of Michigan*. Grand Rapids, MI: Grand Rapids Inner-Tribal Council, 1986. An excellent introduction to these three cultures, not only with an emphasis on history and traditions, but also a solid discussion of modern Native American issues.

Darden, Joe T., Curtis Stokes, and Richard W. Thomas. *The State of Black Michigan, 1967-2007*. East Lansing, MI: Michigan State University Press, 2007. An investigation of how Michigan's black population and its interactions with the white community have changed since the terrible race riots that swept through Detroit during the summer of 1967.

Dempsey, Dave, and Jack Dempsey. *Ink Trails: Michigan's Famous and Forgotten Authors.* East Lansing, MI: Michigan State University Press, 2012. This engaging book explores the secrets and legends surrounding some of Michigan's poets, novelists, and other writers, including those that were born here or found inspiration in the state's varied towns, cities, and landscapes.

Dodge, R. L. *Michigan Ghost Towns of the Lower Peninsula.* Berkeley, CA: Thunder Bay Press, 2002. A compilation of the settlements and communities that have faded into Michigan's history.

Dorson, Richard. *Bloodstoppers & Bearwalkers: Folk Traditions of Michigan's Upper Peninsula.* Madison, WI: University of Wisconsin Press, 2008. Originally published in 1972 and since revised by James P. Leary, this collection of folk tales sheds light on the loggers, miners, sailors, trappers, and villagers that founded and sustained the U.P.'s communities.

Dunbar, Willis F., and George S. May. *Michigan: A History of the Wolverine State.* Grand Rapids, MI: William B. Eerdmans Publishing Co., 1995. First published in 1965 and since revised, this widely praised, comprehensive work covers the rich history of Michigan, from the early days of the first Native American settlers to the political developments of the mid-1990s.

Gile, Marie A., and Marion T. Marzolf. *Fascination with Fiber: Michigan's Handweaving Heritage.* Ann Arbor, MI: University of Michigan Press, 2006. Based on oral histories, interviews, and artifact research, this is surely the first comprehensive history of Michigan's rich tradition of handweaving, from pioneer days to the contemporary era of computer-aided looms.

Glazer, Lawrence M. *Wounded Warrior: The Rise and Fall of Michigan Governor John Swainson.* East Lansing, MI: Michigan State University Press, 2010. A former assistant Michigan Attorney General and State Circuit Court judge examines the FBI investigation, 1975 trial, and ensuing aftermath of Swainson, a little-known public figure who, after being wounded in World War II and returning home to Michigan, rose from state senator to governor to Michigan Supreme Court justice, only to be indicted in 1975 on federal charges of bribery and perjury.

Gustin, Lawrence R. *Billy Durant: Creator of General Motors.* Ann Arbor, MI: University of Michigan Press, 2008. Initially published in 1973, this well-researched biography explores the man who cofounded General Motors and made Flint one of America's greatest industrial centers.

James, Sheryl. *Michigan Legends: Folktales and Lore from the Great Lakes State.* Ann Arbor, MI: University of Michigan Press, 2013. Compiled by a Pulitzer Prize-winning journalist, this collection celebrates the state's most legendary people, events, and places, from the mythical lumberjack Paul Bunyan to *Le Griffon*, a ghost ship that allegedly still haunts the Great Lakes.

Jolly, Ron, and Karl Bohnak. *Michigan's Upper Peninsula Almanac.* Ann Arbor, MI: University of Michigan Press, 2009. Authored, respectively, by a veteran radio broadcaster and a respected meteorologist, this comprehensive almanac offers a ton of information about the Upper Peninsula, including longtime businesses, popular tourist spots, record snowfalls, curious myths, and so much more.

Maki, Craig, and Keith Cady. *Detroit Country Music: Mountaineers, Cowboys, and Rockabillies.* Ann Arbor, MI: University of Michigan Press, 2013. Written by two dedicated musicians, researchers, and radio broadcasters, this groundbreaking book uncovers the musicians, labels, radio programs, and performance venues that nurtured Detroit's little-known but vibrant country and blue-grass music scene.

Michigan Department of Natural Resources. *A Most Superior Land: Life in the Upper Peninsula of Michigan.* Lansing, MI: Two Peninsula Press, 1983. Loaded with historical photos, this wonderful series of short essays and anecdotal tales illustrates the history of the Upper Peninsula.

Rosentreter, Roger L. *Michigan: A History of Explorers, Entrepreneurs, and Everyday People.* Ann Arbor, MI: University of Michigan Press, 2013. This well-researched book chronicles the multifaceted history of the Great Lakes State, from the early days of pioneering fur traders and missionaries to the contemporary struggles between employers and labor unions.

Stonehouse, Frederick. *The Wreck of the Edmund Fitzgerald.* Gwinn, MI: Avery Color Studios, 2006. Though one of several related books about this famous shipwreck, this particular title is considered by many historians to be the definitive work on the subject, scrutinizing the events leading up to the tragedy and offering various theories about the cause of the ship's demise. Originally published in the mid-1970s, this is in fact the 30th anniversary edition.

Taylor, Sprague. *Tahquamenon Country: A Look at Its Past.* East Lansing, MI: Michigan State University Press, 2008. The history of the people who depended on Michigan's mighty Tahquamenon River, as told by a lifelong resident of the eastern Upper Peninsula.

Thurner, Arthur W. *Strangers and Sojourners: A History of Michigan's Keweenaw Peninsula.* Detroit: Wayne State University Press, 1994. The socioeconomic history of the diverse immigrants who established and sustained the communities that comprise the U.P.'s Keweenaw, Houghton, Baraga, and Ontonagon counties.

PARKS AND RECREATION

DuFresne, Jim. *Backpacking in Michigan.* Ann Arbor, MI: University of Michigan Press, 2007. Written by a Michigan native and author of more than 20 wilderness and travel guides, this book features 50 backpacking trails across both peninsulas, plus photographs and detailed maps.

DuFresne, Jim. *The Complete Guide to Michigan Sand Dunes.* Ann Arbor, MI: University of Michigan Press, 2005. In addition to providing a comprehensive explanation of dune formation, this guide offers all the necessary information—including more than 40 detailed maps—for swimmers, picnickers, hikers, skiers, and campers to explore nearly 50 duneland areas, from the remote to the well known.

DuFresne, Jim. *Isle Royale National Park: Foot Trails & Water Routes.* Clarkston, MI: MichiganTrailMaps.com, 2011. Now in its fourth edition, this is the definitive guide to Isle Royale, filled with practical information about campsites, portages, fishing spots, and more.

DuFresne, Jim. *Michigan's Best Campgrounds: A Guide to the Best 150 Public Campgrounds in the Great Lakes State.* Berkeley, CA: Thunder Bay Press, 2011. In his updated fourth edition, this expert outdoorsman and writer suggests the best campsites for anglers, canoeists, hikers, bikers, and bird-watchers during the state's most popular season, May-October.

Funke, Tom. *50 Hikes in Michigan's Upper Peninsula: Walks, Hikes, and Backpacks from Ironwood to St. Ignace.* Woodstock, VT: The Countryman Press, 2008. This guide features daylong and overnight trips for hikers, backpackers, and other recreationists throughout the Upper Peninsula. Each hike description is accompanied by a detailed topographical map, a difficulty rating, directions to the trailhead, and commentary about any related natural and cultural history.

Hillstrom, Kevin, and Laurie Hillstrom. *Paddling Michigan.* Guilford, CT: The Globe Pequot Press, Inc., 2001. An invaluable survey of 70 of Michigan's finest lakes, streams, and coastal waterways, whether known for amazing scenery, historical significance, or marine wildlife and activities. Ideal for canoeists and kayakers of all skill levels, this admittedly outdated guide contains detailed maps, preparation advice, seasonal tips, and lists of local paddling organizations.

Powers, Tom. *Michigan State and National Parks: A Complete Guide.* Berkeley, CA: Thunder Bay Press, 2007. Compiled by a former Flint librarian, this handy guide, now in its fourth edition, offers an overview of the layout, facilities, fees, and camping options for each of Michigan's state and national parks.

Sharp, Eric. *Fishing Michigan: Tales and Tips from an Avid Angler.* Detroit: Detroit Free Press, 2002. Written by a veteran reporter and outdoors writer for the *Detroit Free Press,* this guide describes the state's major game fish, their frequent hangouts, and the best ways to snag them.

REGIONAL TRAVEL

Burcar, Colleen. *Michigan Curiosities: Quirky Characters, Roadside Oddities & Other Offbeat Stuff.* Guilford, CT: The Globe Pequot Press, Inc., 2012. Popular among residents and tourists alike, this amusing guide and almanac, now in its third edition, offers a panoply of Michigan's wildest aspects, including wacky residents, bizarre destinations, and chuckle-worthy state facts.

Cantor, George. *Explore Michigan: Detroit.* Ann Arbor, MI: University of Michigan Press, 2005. Cantor, a former media personality and writer for the *Detroit News,* who died in 2010, prepared a series of travel and activity guides for key Michigan destinations, including the Motor City itself.

Cantor, George. *Explore Michigan: Leelanau.* Ann Arbor, MI: University of Michigan Press, 2005. Though brief, this guide can definitely assist visitors on their tour of the Leelanau Peninsula, northwest of Traverse City.

Cantor, George. *Explore Michigan: Little Traverse Bay.* Ann Arbor, MI: University of Michigan Press, 2005. This compact guide explores the restaurants, historic hotels, beaches, and other recreational diversions in and around Petoskey.

Cantor, George. *Explore Michigan: Mackinac.* Ann Arbor, MI: University of Michigan Press, 2005. As with all of Cantor's compact travel guides, this one offers enough history, photographs, and practical information for any first-time visitor to experience Mackinac Island.

Cantor, George. *Explore Michigan: Traverse City.* Ann Arbor, MI: University of Michigan Press, 2005. Cantor's comprehensive take on the Traverse City area.

DuFresne, Jim. *Lonely Planet Road Trip: Lake Michigan.* Footscray, Victoria, Australia: Lonely Planet Publications, 2005. Longtime Michigan travel writer DuFresne guides readers along the "Michigan Riviera."

DuFresne, Jim. *Michigan Off the Beaten Path: A Guide to Unique Places.* Guilford, CT: The Globe Pequot Press, Inc., 2013. Now in its 11th edition, this guide presents a quirky take on the Great Lakes State, complete with the less-traversed routes and little-known attractions of both peninsulas.

Franklin, Dixie. *Compass American Guides: Michigan.* New York: Fodor's Travel Publications, Inc., 2005. Filled with photos and full-color illustrations, and now in its second edition, this guide focuses more on the cultural, historical, and geographical aspects of each region, and less on practical travel details.

Godfrey, Linda S. *Weird Michigan: Your Travel Guide to Michigan's Local Legends and Best Kept Secrets.* New York: Sterling Publishing Co., 2006. Part of a series of state-by-state guides focused on odd places, this is an ideal guide for those who prefer visiting sights off the beaten path.

Hutchins, Brian. *Michigan's West Coast: Explore the Shore Guide.* Roscommon, MI: Abri-Press, 2005. This book invites visitors to explore 500 public parks and points of access along the Lake Michigan shoreline of the Lower Peninsula.

Newhof, Susan. *Michigan's Town & Country Inns.* Ann Arbor, MI: University of Michigan Press, 2013. Now in its fifth edition, this guide offers travelers helpful information about more than 50 inns, bed-and-breakfasts, and other historic lodging options throughout the Upper and Lower Peninsulas.

Roach, Jerry, and Barb Roach. *The Ultimate Guide to East Michigan Lighthouses.* Durand, MI: Bugs Publishing, LLC, 2006. Rife with stunning images, this guide offers descriptions, directions, historical notes, contact numbers, and area travel information for more than 30 lighthouses along the eastern side of the Lower Peninsula, stretching from the Detroit River Light to the Old Mackinac Point Lighthouse.

Roach, Jerry, and Barb Roach. *The Ultimate Guide to West Michigan Lighthouses.* Durand, MI: Bugs Publishing, LLC, 2005. Filled with winning photographs, this guide (the first in a series of three) offers descriptions, directions, historical notes, contact numbers, and area travel information for more than 30 lighthouses along the western side of the Lower Peninsula, extending from the St. Joseph Pier Lights to McGulpin's Point Light.

Roach, Jerry, and Barb Roach. *The Ultimate Guide to Upper Michigan Lighthouses.* Durand, MI: Bugs Publishing, LLC, 2007. This handy guide explores more than 50 of the Upper Peninsula's lighthouses, from the St. Helena Lighthouse to the Wawatam Light. As with their previous lighthouse guides, the authors have included helpful descriptions and directions, historical background notes, colorful photographs, and plenty of travel details, such as contact numbers and information about area events and attractions.

Royce, Julie Albrecht. *Traveling Michigan's Sunset Coast: Exploring Michigan's West Coast Beach Towns.* Berkeley, CA: Thunder Bay Press, 2007. This comprehensive guide gives visitors all the practical information needed to explore the Lake Michigan coast, from New Buffalo near the Indiana border to Mackinac City at the tip of the Lower Peninsula.

Royce, Julie Albrecht. *Traveling Michigan's Thumb: Exploring a Shoreline of Small Pleasures and Unexpected Treasures.* Berkeley, CA: Thunder Bay Press, 2008. This helpful book invites visitors to leave behind day-to-day stresses and explore Michigan's undiscovered jewel, a region of quiet harbors, quaint villages, less-crowded beaches and inns, and small-town festivals.

Vachon, Paul. *Moon Michigan's Upper Peninsula.* Berkeley, CA: Avalon Travel, 2012. Updated by a Michigan native, this insider's view of the Upper Peninsula invites visitors to explore the forests, waterfalls, former mining towns, and isolated islands that define this one-of-a-kind place.

Westervelt, Amy. *Michigan's Upper Peninsula: A Great Destination.* Woodstock, VT: The Countryman Press, 2012. A comprehensive guide to the U.P., with regional maps, historical tidbits, and practical details about area hotels, restaurants, and the like.

Suggested Viewing

Michigan has long been a favorite spot for film-makers and television producers. While gritty Detroit has received most of the screen time, as in television shows like *Hung* (2009-2011), *Detroit 1-8-7* (2010-2011), and *Low Winter Sun* (2013-present), the wilds of the Upper Peninsula have served as a unique cinematic backdrop, too.

Anatomy of a Murder (1959)

Written by Wendell Mayes. Directed by Otto Preminger. Starring James Stewart, Ben Gazzara, Lee Remick, and George C. Scott. Based on the famous novel by a former Michigan Supreme Court justice, this engaging courtroom drama focuses on a small-town lawyer struggling to defend his client, a hot-headed army lieutenant arrested for the murder of a bartender who allegedly assaulted his wife. Set in the Upper Peninsula, the film features historic locations like the Marquette County Courthouse, the Ishpeming Carnegie Public Library, and Big Bay's Thunder Bay Inn.

8 Mile (2002)

Written by Scott Silver. Directed by Curtis Hanson. Starring Eminem, Kim Basinger, Mekhi Phifer, and Brittany Murphy. During the course of one critical week, a young, angry rapper from the wrong side of Detroit's Eight Mile tries to achieve his musical goals while contending with various problems in his life.

Escanaba in da Moonlight (2001)

Written and directed by Jeff Daniels, based on the eponymous play. Starring Jeff Daniels and Harve Presnell. In this whimsical comedy about deer-hunting season amid the wilds of the Upper Peninsula, a macho man must deal with his eldest son's curse of never having killed a buck of his own.

Gran Torino (2008)

Written by Nick Schenk. Directed by Clint Eastwood. Starring Clint Eastwood and Bee Vang. When a young immigrant tries to steal a prized automobile from his prejudiced neighbor—a retired Polish American automobile factory worker, Korean War veteran, and recent widower—the older man attempts to reform the teenager and protect his family from the gang members that infest their Highland Park neighborhood.

Grosse Pointe Blank (1997)

Written by Tom Jankiewicz, D. V. DeVincentis, Steve Pink, and John Cusack. Directed by George Armitage. Starring John Cusack, Minnie Driver, Joan Cusack, Dan Aykroyd, and Alan Arkin. In this dark comedy, a professional assassin is compelled to reevaluate his life when he returns home to Grosse Pointe, Michigan, for a contract hit and, coincidentally, his 10-year high school reunion.

Hoffa (1992)

Written by David Mamet. Directed by Danny DeVito. Starring Jack Nicholson, Danny DeVito, Armand Assante, and J. T. Walsh. Inspired by legendary labor union leader Jimmy Hoffa, this controversial film follows Hoffa's tumultuous career, from his numerous battles with the RTA and President Roosevelt to his supposed 1975 disappearance.

Out of Sight (1998)

Written by Scott Frank. Directed by Steven Soderbergh. Starring George Clooney, Jennifer Lopez, Ving Rhames, Steve Zahn, and Don Cheadle. Based on the eponymous Elmore Leonard novel, this humorous crime thriller follows the unlikely relationship between a career thief and a female U.S. marshal, from the sweltering heat of Miami to the bitter cold of Detroit.

The Road to Wellville (1994)

Written and directed by Alan Parker. Starring

Anthony Hopkins, Matthew Broderick, Bridget Fonda, and John Cusack. Based on the eponymous novel by T. Coraghessan Boyle, this madcap comedy explores the inner workings of the Battle Creek Sanitarium, an unusual health facility run by cereal king Dr. John Harvey Kellogg during the early 20th century.

RoboCop (1987)
Written by Edward Neumeier and Michael Miner. Directed by Paul Verhoeven. Starring Peter Weller, Nancy Allen, Ronny Cox, Kurtwood Smith, and Miguel Ferrer. In a futuristic, crime-ridden Detroit, a fatally wounded cop returns to the city's overrun police force as a powerful cyborg, determined to clean up the streets. The remake, released in 2014 and directed by José Padilha, takes place in 2028 Detroit and stars Joel Kinnaman in the title role.

Roger & Me (1989)
Written and directed by Michael Moore. In the first of several films that have defined Moore's "docuganda" style, the filmmaker tries to confront General Motors CEO Roger Smith about the massive downsizing that contributed to Flint's decline.

Somewhere in Time (1980)
Written by Richard Matheson, based on his novel *Bid Time Return*. Directed by Jeannot Szwarc. Starring Christopher Reeve, Jane Seymour, and Christopher Plummer. After meeting an elderly actress who seems to know him from the past, a young Chicago playwright uses self-hypnosis to travel back to the early 1900s, where he embarks upon an ill-fated love affair inside Mackinac Island's Grand Hotel.

The Upside of Anger (2005)
Written and directed by Mike Binder. Starring Joan Allen, Kevin Costner, Erika Christensen, Keri Russell, Alicia Witt, Evan Rachel Wood, and Mike Binder. When her husband unexpectedly vanishes from their wealthy Detroit suburb, a sharp-tongued wife and mother of four daughters turns to alcohol, anger, and an unlikely romance with her boozy neighbor to help her cope with her husband's abandonment.

Internet Resources

CUISINE AND TRAVEL

Michigan Association of Fairs & Exhibitions
www.michiganfairs.org
You can use this website's "fair/festival locator" feature to learn more about Michigan's numerous county fairs.

Michigan Back Roads
www.michiganbackroads.com
If you enjoy exploring less-traveled destinations, then you'll appreciate this website, which offers suggestions on short getaways along Michigan's back roads, where you'll encounter small towns, local inns and shops, historic sites, and other unique locales.

Michigan Cuisine
www.micuisine.com
Ostensibly, the company that runs this website is a graphics design firm for Michigan-based restaurants, but you'll also find regional recipes and cookbook suggestions, plus links to many of the state's eateries, festivals, culinary schools, and food associations.

Michigan Festivals & Events Association
www.mfea.org
Search this website for information about many of Michigan's cultural and community events, from art fairs to corn mazes.

The Michigan Travel Companion
www.yesmichigan.com
Use this comprehensive website to research

Michigan's accommodations, from motels to resorts. You can browse options by region, city, or type of lodging.

Michigan's Upper Peninsula
www.uptravel.com
Operated by the Upper Peninsula Travel & Recreation Association (UPTRA), this portal offers complete travel and lodging information for the U.P., including details about events, activities, restaurants, campgrounds, waterfalls, lighthouses, and other attractions, plus up-to-date weather reports.

MyNorth.com
www.mynorth.com
The online home of *Traverse* magazine serves as a useful repository for those eager to explore the northern part of the Lower Peninsula, from Manistee to Mackinac Island. Listed here are recipes as well as details about lodging, dining, events, wineries, outdoor activities, and the arts.

Pure Michigan
www.michigan.org
Michigan's official travel and tourism website offers just about everything you need to know about the state's cities, accommodations, restaurants, casinos, attractions, shops, parks, events, recreational activities, and entertainment venues. Just be aware that some of the information can be out of date, so always call ahead when making travel plans.

Southwestern Michigan Tourist Council
www.swmichigan.org
Travelers hoping to explore the varied beaches, wineries, golf courses, museums, antiques shops, U-pick farms, and other attractions in the southwestern corner of Michigan's Lower Peninsula will find plenty of useful information on this website, including details about the area's dining and lodging options.

Thumb Area Tourism Council, Inc.
www.thumbtourism.org
The TATC website is a helpful resource for those planning a trip to the Thumb. Here, you'll find information about area attractions, parks, beaches, marinas, events, accommodations, historic sites, and more.

TravelNorth.org
www.travelnorth.org
The official portal for the Northern Michigan Tourist Association offers visitors helpful information about the northern part of Michigan's Lower Peninsula and the eastern half of the Upper Peninsula. Besides special deals, you'll find details about shops, restaurants, accommodations, seasonal sports, festivals, outdoor diversions, and cultural attractions.

West Michigan Tourist Association
www.wmta.org
Based in Grand Rapids, the WMTA has been promoting West Michigan—the western half of the Lower Peninsula, from the Indiana border to the Straits of Mackinac—since 1917. The group's website provides a wealth of travel information, from events to attractions to accommodations. Here, you can also make reservations, find travel deals and coupons, and peruse maps and suggested itineraries.

GENERAL INFORMATION
Absolute Michigan
www.absolutemichigan.com
As its slogan states, this comprehensive website offers both visitors and residents "all Michigan, all the time"—a collection of links, features, news, and information about everything from wineries and art galleries to historic events and vacation cottages.

Country Codes
www.countrycodes.com
If you decide to phone someone in a foreign country while visiting Michigan, you'll need this handy website, an easy-to-use directory of international dialing codes for long-distance calls.

MDtravelhealth.com
www.mdtravelhealth.com
Updated daily, this medical website is an excellent resource for travelers. Here, you'll find information about specific destinations, available clinics, infectious diseases, and illness prevention, as well as tailored advice for those with special needs, such as diabetics and pregnant women.

OnlineConversion.com
www.onlineconversion.com
This website will help you make any U.S.-metric conversion, for everything from temperatures and distances to clothing sizes and cooking measurements.

State of Michigan
www.michigan.gov
Michigan's official website offers a wide array of information about the state's economic growth, educational issues, health and safety considerations, environmental resources, and governmental departments. Here, you can check road closures, purchase fishing and hunting licenses, and even learn more about the state's symbols, landmarks, and little-known historical facts.

Travel.State.Gov
www.travel.state.gov
Whether or not you're a U.S. citizen, this website, operated by the U.S. Department of State's Bureau of Consular Affairs, will help you travel safely across the United States-Canada border near Detroit, Port Huron, and Sault Ste. Marie. International travelers will also find guidelines for flying into and out of Michigan.

HISTORY AND CULTURE
Historical Society of Michigan
www.hsmichigan.org
This website features a wealth of information related to the preservation of Michigan's history, including comprehensive lists of historic events, local historical organizations, and libraries, plus links to publications like *Michigan History* magazine—the ownership of which was transferred from Michigan's now-defunct Department of History, Arts and Libraries to the Historical Society of Michigan in October 2009.

Michigan State University Press
http://msupress.msu.edu
Here, you'll find a number of titles by Michigan-based writers, from statewide economic studies to personal essays about the Great Lakes to historical accounts of Michigan's immigrants, colleges, railroads, and shipwrecks.

University of Michigan Press
www.press.umich.edu
Peruse this website for a wealth of Michigan-related books that shed light on the state's history and culture. Included here are historical accounts, personal memoirs, biographies, and even field guides.

PARKS AND RECREATION
Boating Safety Resource Center
www.uscgboating.org
Use this comprehensive website, operated by the U.S. Coast Guard's Boating Safety Division, to prevent accidents and fatalities while boating in Michigan.

GORP
www.gorp.com
An in-depth portal for adventure travel and outdoor recreation in the United States, this website is an invaluable resource for information about campgrounds, national parks, recreational activities, and outdoor gear. There are even pages devoted to Michigan activities, such as articles on fly-fishing near Traverse City and a whole section about exploring Sleeping Bear Dunes National Lakeshore.

League of Michigan Bicyclists
www.lmb.org
Road and mountain bikers can explore this website for biking routes, clubs, events, and shops throughout the state.

Mackinac State Historic Parks
www.mackinacparks.com

Visitors to Mackinaw City and Mackinac Island should stop here first for information about the area's various historic sites, including details about admission rates, hours of operation, and special events.

Michigan Charter Boat Association
www.michigancharterboats.com

In addition to fish species descriptions and current fishing reports, this website offers access to hundreds of charter fishing boats, river fishing guides, sailing excursions, and diving trips that service the coastal areas and open waters of the Great Lakes and Lake St. Clair.

Michigan Department of Natural Resources
www.michigan.gov/dnr

From this recreation portal, you'll learn most of what you need to know about fishing, hunting, camping, boating, hiking, biking, and snowmobiling in the Great Lakes State. Also included here are maps, publications, and information about law enforcement, forest management, state parks, historic sites, trails, and wildlife.

Michigan Interactive
www.fishweb.com

Besides offering numerous maps and lodging options, this website provides tons of advice for anglers, boaters, paddlers, hikers, golfers, snowmobilers, off-road enthusiasts, and even mushroom hunters.

Michigan Snowsports Industries Association
www.goskimichigan.com

Skiers and snowboarders should peruse this website for details about Michigan's downhill ski slopes, outfitters, and snow conditions.

Michigan Underwater Preserves
www.michiganpreserves.org

For divers, this website offers advice and information about all of Michigan's underwater preserves, from Isle Royale to Sanilac Shores.

National Park Service
www.nps.gov

The National Park Service provides detailed maps, brochures, and contact information for each of its roughly 400 parks, monuments, recreation areas, and other natural and cultural sites throughout the United States. Use the state-by-state search function to learn more about Michigan's protected places, including Isle Royale National Park, Keweenaw National Historical Park, Pictured Rocks National Lakeshore, Sleeping Bear Dunes National Lakeshore, and Motor Cities National Heritage Area.

National Wild & Scenic Rivers System
www.rivers.gov

Learn more about Michigan's federally designated wild and scenic rivers, from the Au Sable to the Sturgeon.

Sam Crowe's MichiganBirding.com
www.michiganbirding.com

Peruse this website for information about bird-watching hot spots, tours, and festivals throughout Michigan.

U.S. Fish & Wildlife Service
www.fws.gov

Here, you can find useful information about Michigan's endangered species, including the gray wolf and Kirtland's warbler, as well as details regarding the state's wildlife refuges, such as Shiawassee National Wildlife Refuge and Detroit River International Wildlife Refuge.

U.S. Forest Service
www.fs.fed.us

Through this website, you can learn more about Michigan's national forests, from the Upper Peninsula's Hiawatha National Forest to the Lower Peninsula's Huron-Manistee National Forests.

Index

List of Maps

Acknowledgments

Although it seems impossible to thank all of the people who have contributed to this guide, I'll certainly give it a try.

Since the summer of 2000, my husband and I have often traveled to the Great Lakes State—ostensibly to visit his parents, who live here during the summer months. While on such trips, we've always taken the time to explore the nooks and crannies of this fascinating state, from the quiet shores of Pictured Rocks National Lakeshore to the art galleries of Saugatuck. In recent years, we've also joined the ranks of Michigan's seasonal residents. While we dwell for much of the year in New Orleans, we spend the summer months near Big Bear Lake in the northeastern part of the Lower Peninsula. Now, we have even more time to explore one of our favorite places.

During every stay, we've encountered plenty of friendly, helpful residents, usually willing to point us in the right direction—for the best blueberry patch, the least crowded beach, the most innovative winery, the wackiest event, or whatever else we sought at the time. So, thanks to everyone who's made each of our trips through Michigan a rejuvenating experience.

Of course, there are a few folks to whom I'm particularly grateful. First, I offer a special thanks to the many innkeepers, restaurant owners, park rangers, adventure outfitters, and tourism officials who made the job of compiling this guide a little easier. Thanks, too, to those who provided photographs for this book, and to the patient editors of Avalon Travel who offered valuable assistance during the preparation of this guide. Thanks also to Tina Lassen who wrote the first two editions of this book—and helped me in ways she'll never know.

In addition, I'd like to thank my friends and relatives, all of whom have supported me during each of my frenzied writing projects. Most of all, I'm grateful to my beloved kitty, Ruby Azazel, who encouraged me to take breaks whenever possible, and to my husband, who supported me at each and every turn, even providing many of the images in this guide. As I often say, they're the best traveling companions a girl could ask for.

Lastly, I thank you, the reader. May your next trip to Michigan be as memorable as ours have been.

MAP SYMBOLS

▬▬▬	Expressway	◖	Highlight	✗	Airfield	⚓ Golf Course
▬▬▬	Primary Road	○	City/Town	✈	Airport	🅿 Parking Area
▬▬▬	Secondary Road	◉	State Capital	▲	Mountain	▀ Archaeological Site
▬ ▬ ▬	Unpaved Road	⊛	National Capital	✚	Unique Natural Feature	
- - - - -	Trail	★	Point of Interest			🛉 Church
⋯⋯⋯	Ferry	•	Accommodation	🐾	Waterfall	⛽ Gas Station
▬-▬-▬	Railroad	▾	Restaurant/Bar	▲	Park	〰 Glacier
▓▓▓	Pedestrian Walkway	▪	Other Location	⏚	Trailhead	Mangrove
�🜓	Stairs	Λ	Campground	⛷	Skiing Area	Reef
						Swamp

CONVERSION TABLES

°C = (°F − 32) / 1.8

°F = (°C x 1.8) + 32

1 inch = 2.54 centimeters (cm)

1 foot = 0.304 meters (m)

1 yard = 0.914 meters

1 mile = 1.6093 kilometers (km)

1 km = 0.6214 miles

1 fathom = 1.8288 m

1 chain = 20.1168 m

1 furlong = 201.168 m

1 acre = 0.4047 hectares

1 sq km = 100 hectares

1 sq mile = 2.59 square km

1 ounce = 28.35 grams

1 pound = 0.4536 kilograms

1 short ton = 0.90718 metric ton

1 short ton = 2,000 pounds

1 long ton = 1.016 metric tons

1 long ton = 2,240 pounds

1 metric ton = 1,000 kilograms

1 quart = 0.94635 liters

1 US gallon = 3.7854 liters

1 Imperial gallon = 4.5459 liters

1 nautical mile = 1.852 km

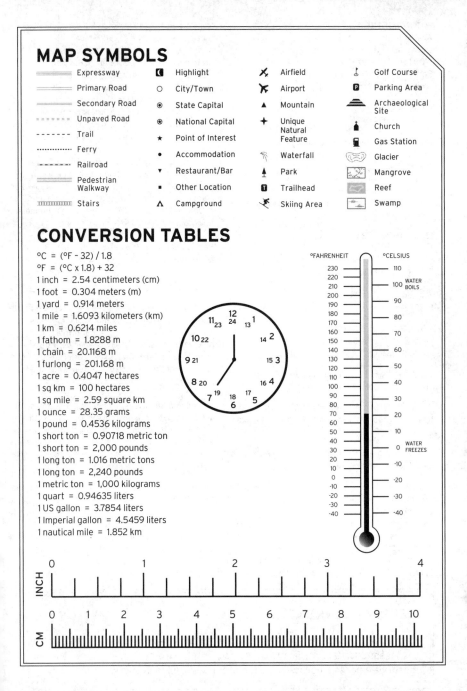

MOON MICHIGAN

Avalon Travel
a member of the Perseus Books Group
1700 Fourth Street
Berkeley, CA 94710, USA
www.moon.com

Editor: Erin Raber
Series Manager: Kathryn Ettinger
Copy Editor: Ann Seifert
Graphics Coordinator: Elizabeth Jang
Production Coordinator: Elizabeth Jang
Cover Design: Faceout Studios, Charles Brock
Moon Logo: Tim McGrath
Map Editor: Kat Bennett
Cartographers: Kat Bennett, Stephanie Poulain
Indexer: Greg Jewett

ISBN-13: 978-1-61238-749-9
ISSN: 1099-8780

Printing History
1st Edition – 1999
5th Edition – June 2014
5 4 3 2 1

Front cover photo: Mason County farm © Todd Reed of Todd & Brad Reed Photography/www.ToddandBradReed.com

Title page photo: the North Bar Lake overlook at Sleeping Bear Dunes, Kerry Kelly/NPS Photo

Interior color photos: p. 4 freshly picked apples © Jeff Greenberg; p. 5 Grandpa Tiny's Farm in Frankenmuth © Frankenmuth Chamber of Commerce/CVB; p. 6 (top left) a snow-covered church in southeastern Michigan © L. Diggs of Picture This..., (top right) Sparty the Spartan, MSU's official mascot © Greater Lansing CVB, (bottom) fireworks celebration in Detroit © Ivan Cholakov/123rf.com; p. 7 (top) competing sailboats in the Port Huron to Mackinac Race © Cindy Lindow, (bottom left) © Rick Zepp/123rf.com, (bottom right) moose taxidermy display at Tahquamenon Falls State Park © ehrlif/123rf.com; p. 8 a view of Big Mac from the Lower Peninsula © Daniel Martone; p. 9 (top) Holland's iconic De Zwaan windmill at Windmill Island Gardens © Daniel Martone, (bottom left) fresh produce at the Ann Arbor Farmers Market © VisitAnnArbor.org, (bottom right) the Fort Gratiot Lighthouse in Port Huron © Cindy Lindow; p. 11 photo provided by the National Park Service; p. 12 © Bonita Cheshier/123rf.com; p. 13 © Mark Herreid/123rf.com; p. 14 Dan Johnson, National Park Service; p. 15 © Henryk Sadura/123rf.com; p. 17 © Darren Brode/123rf.com; p. 18 © Maciej Maksymowicz/123rf.com; p. 20 © Donnie Shackleford/123rf.com; p. 21 © alexandragl/123rf.com; pp. 23 - 24 © Daniel Martone

Back cover photo: Charlevoix South Pier Light © Kenneth Keifer/123rf.com

Printed in Canada by Friesens

All recommendations, including those for sights, activities, hotels, restaurants, and shops, are based on each author's individual judgment. We do not accept payment for inclusion in our travel guides, and our authors don't accept free goods or services in exchange for positive coverage.

KEEPING CURRENT

If you have a favorite gem you'd like to see included in the next edition, or see anything that needs updating, clarification, or correction, please drop us a line. Send your comments via email to feedback@moon.com, or use the address above.